# Corps Commanders

STUDIES IN CANADIAN MILITARY HISTORY
*Series editor: Dean F. Oliver, Canadian War Museum*

The Canadian War Museum, Canada's national museum of military history, has a three-fold mandate: to remember, to preserve, and to educate. Studies in Canadian Military History, published by UBC Press in association with the Museum, extends this mandate by presenting the best of contemporary scholarship to provide new insights into all aspects of Canadian military history, from earliest times to recent events. The work of a new generation of scholars is especially encouraged, and the books employ a variety of approaches – cultural, social, intellectual, economic, political, and comparative – to investigate gaps in the existing historiography. The books in the series feed immediately into future exhibitions, programs, and outreach efforts by the Canadian War Museum. A list of the titles in the series appears at the end of the book.

Canadian War Museum      Musée canadien de la guerre

# Corps Commanders
# Five British and Canadian Generals at War, 1939-45

*Douglas E. Delaney*

**UBC**Press · Vancouver · Toronto

21 20 19 18 17 16 15 14 13 12    5 4 3 2

Printed in Canada on FSC-certified ancient-forest-free paper (100% post-consumer recycled) that is processed chlorine- and acid-free.

**Library and Archives Canada Cataloguing in Publication**

Delaney, Douglas E. (Douglas Edward), 1964-
    Corps commanders : five British and Canadian generals at war, 1939-1945 / Douglas E. Delaney.

(Studies in Canadian military history, 1499-6251)
Includes bibliographical references and index.
ISBN 978-0-7748-2089-9 (bound)
ISBN 978-0-7748-2090-5 (pbk.)

    1. Generals – Canada – Biography. 2. Generals – Great Britain – Biography. 3. Canada. Canadian Army – Officers – Biography. 4. Great Britain. Army – Officers – Biography. 5. World War, 1939-1945 – Canada – Biography. 6. World War, 1939-1945 – Great Britain – Biography. I. Title. II. Series: Studies in Canadian military history

| D768.15.D44 2011 | 940.53'71 | C2010-908003-3 |

e-book ISBNs: 978-0-7748-2091-2 (pdf); 978-0-7748-2092-9 (e-pub)

Canadä

UBC Press gratefully acknowledges the financial support for our publishing program of the Government of Canada (through the Canada Book Fund), the Canada Council for the Arts, and the British Columbia Arts Council.

This book has been published with the help of a grant from the Canadian Federation for the Humanities and Social Sciences, through the Aid to Scholarly Publications Program, using funds provided by the Social Sciences and Humanities Research Council of Canada.

Publication of this book has been financially supported by the Canadian War Museum.

Printed and bound in Canada by Friesens
Set in Helvetica Condensed and Minion by Artegraphica Design Co. Ltd.
Copy editor: Frank Chow
Proofreader: Jenna Newman
Indexer: Patricia Buchanan

UBC Press
The University of British Columbia
2029 West Mall
Vancouver, BC V6T 1Z2
**www.ubcpress.ca**

FOR CHRISTINE

# Contents

# Illustrations

# Acknowledgments

I SHOULD HAVE KEPT a list. I have many people and organizations to thank and I'm worried that one or more might slip my memory. I'll do my best.

To start, I could not have conducted the research for this book if it were not for the financial support of the Social Sciences and Humanities Research Council (SSHRC) and the Academic Research Programme (ARP) at the Royal Military College of Canada. Funds from these two granting agencies allowed me to spend many months in archives and many weeks walking far-away battlefields. Once the research and the writing were done, the Aid to Scholarly Publications Program (ASPP) supported the production and publication of my manuscript. I am grateful for the support of all three organizations. I am also grateful that they exist.

Many friends and colleagues have guided me in my research and helped shape the final product. I'm in their debt. Jack Granatstein has been a tremendous friend and mentor – passing on research material, reading the entire manuscript, providing well considered criticism where necessary, and offering encouragement when needed. David French, who very kindly wrote the foreword to this book, also reviewed the manuscript and saved me from several embarrassing gaffes. I have gained much as well from Terry Copp and Jim Finan, who both read portions of the manuscript and provided useful insight. At UBC Press, Emily Andrew, Ann Macklem, and their team have been magnificent – kind, conscientious, and consummately professional. I have great help close to home too. Jane Boulden, Rebecca Tiessen, Cathy St-Georges, Chemagne Faux, and Danielle Tardif-Smith make life in War Studies fun and rewarding. They save me less from gaffes than from myself. I can't believe I'm writing this, but I'll say it anyway: I'm happy that they've accepted me as "one of the girls." It all helped. Any faults or deficiencies that remain in these pages are there in spite of all their best efforts. The errors are mine alone.

I've had help with sources as well. The staffs at the Library and Archives Canada (LAC), The National Archives (UK), the Imperial War Museum (IWM), the Liddell Hart Centre for Military Archives (LHCMA), the Tank Museum (Bovington), Churchill College, Cambridge, and the Royal Military College of Canada have all provided much needed assistance at one time or other. Mike Boire, Greg Liedtke, and Jason Ridler also mined many of these sources and shared their findings with me. Sir John Crocker's grandson, John Bingham, very kindly provided me with wonderful material from his grandfather's files. So did Colonel (retired) Charles Simonds when it came to his father's papers. I appreciate every bit of assistance that I received.

My greatest debt though is to my family. Dad drove me from battlefield to battlefield in northern France over a period of two very enjoyable weeks during the summer of 2006 and Mum was good enough to go without him for that time. Christine, Allison, and Connor are my rock. I don't know how else to put it. They make everything possible and I'd be absolutely useless without them. By the time this book appears in print, Allison will have settled into the University of Waterloo and I'll have been taken into the care of some kind therapist to figure out how I'll deal with missing her. That won't be easy. I expect that I'll have recovered just in time to repeat the same sad exercise when Connor heads off on his post-secondary experience in two years' time. I love my kids. I love their mother too and I have for a long time. I don't know how many fifteen-year-olds are fortunate enough to find the love of their life *and* have enough good sense to understand what they've found, but I'm glad I was one of them.

# Foreword

CORPS COMMANDERS ARE SOME of the forgotten soldiers of the Commonwealth wartime army. There are a plethora of biographies of the top generals, often focusing on their sometimes fraught relations with each other and with their political masters, and just as many studies of life in the front line. But we know little about the men who stood between them. Doug Delaney has already written a fine biography of one Canadian divisional commander, Bert Hoffmeister,[1] and now he looks at five men who commanded one step up.

In the course of the Second World War, the British and Canadian armies underwent the same experience of massive expansion on the basis of a small – or, in the case of the Canadian Permanent Force, tiny – cadre of regular officers and men. This is a book that explains how these armies went about finding a key group of men who could organize and lead them, and the job that these commanders did on the battlefield. Not the least of its merits is that it has shown me one of the shortcomings of my own work. Nearly a decade ago, I published a study of the British Army during the Second World War that made no mention of the Canadian Army. For that omission I now apologize, for Dr. Delaney has demonstrated how wrong I was. The army that landed in Sicily and Italy in 1943 and in Normandy in 1944 was not a *British* army; it was a *British Commonwealth* army in which Canadian divisions and corps fought alongside their British counterparts. That they were able to do so with only a moderate amount of friction owed everything to two things: the Canadian Permanent Force and the militia it trained were organized, trained, and equipped on British lines, and a handful of the very best Canadian regular officers had passed through, and been taught alongside, the best of the British regular officer corps at either the British Army Staff College at Camberley or the Indian Army Staff College at Quetta.

In 1939, the tasks facing the likes of Simonds, Horrocks, and their contemporaries were formidable. Not only was the enemy in front of them, the Germans, intent on causing them problems, but they were surrounded by almost equally intractable difficulties in their own armies. Between 1939 and 1942, the British Commonwealth forces underwent a period of massive expansion that had been largely unplanned before 1939. What was surprising is not that the men at the top made mistakes, and that their armies suffered defeats. That was likely to happen to any army expanding more than tenfold in the midst of a war. The small cadre of British and Canadian staff-trained officers were one of the keys to explaining how and why the Commonwealth armies eventually overcame these difficulties and went on, not without some further mistakes, to create a force that could defeat the best that the *Wehrmacht* could throw against them. They had gone to Camberley or Quetta as captains and majors when their practical experience was limited to commanding companies and batteries, and some Canadian officers lacked even that command experience. But the Staff College had at least given them the opportunity to think hard about how they might manage and command corps and armies. It was knowledge and understanding that they would put to good use in the war. And, as Delaney points out, by 1944 the system had bedded down sufficiently that even a commander of Foulkes's modest tactical competence could survive.

But *Corps Commanders* does more than just show how the British and Canadian armies shared a common doctrine and forms of organization. Dr. Delaney has also provided answers to one of the most fundamental questions that military historians ought to ask about any army, which is not just who commanded them but how they did so. What were the mechanics that permitted a single man to guide, animate, and control the activities of a corps of one hundred thousand men on a battlefield? They did not do it by sitting in a chateau, content to run their battles from the end of a telephone line. They liked to get well forward to see for themselves. A successful corps commander needed to be clever enough to read the tactical problems in front of him and to devise workable solutions to them. If he was sensible, he left the job of working out the details to his staff, while he personally worked to inspire his subordinates, encouraged those who needed encouragement, and sacked those who could not or would not do the job. The five commanders examined here were men of very different personalities. Horrocks was wonderful with people. Simonds was too cold to win any soldier's heart. Horrocks encouraged his subordinates. Simonds drove his. Both were successful battlefield commanders. Burns neither encouraged nor intimidated people, and ultimately got sacked because of it. But what they, together with Foulkes and Crocker, did have in common were professional and technical skills and intelligence. There was not a Colonel Blimp among them. This is one of the most enlightening books about how generals actually fought battles that you are likely to read.

David French
Professor Emeritus
University College London

# Abbreviations

| | |
|---|---|
| AA & QMG | Assistant Adjutant and Quartermaster General |
| AAI | Allied Armies in Italy |
| ADC | aide-de-camp |
| AEAF | Allied Expeditionary Air Forces |
| AG & QMG | Adjutant General and Quartermaster General |
| AGRA | Army Group Royal Artillery |
| armd | armoured |
| BAOR | British Army of the Rhine |
| BCD | British Columbia Dragoons |
| bde | brigade |
| BGS | Brigadier General Staff |
| BL | British Library |
| CCRA | Commander, Corps Royal Artillery |
| CE | Chief Engineer |
| CGS | Chief of the General Staff |
| CIGS | Chief of the Imperial General Staff |
| C-in-C | Commander-in-Chief |
| CJWSC | Canadian Junior War Staff Course |
| CMHQ | Canadian Military Headquarters (London) |
| CO | commanding officer |
| Comd | commander |
| COS | Chief of Staff |
| coy | company |
| CRA | Commander Royal Artillery |
| CRE | Commander Royal Engineers |
| CSO | Chief Signals Officer |
| DA & QMG | Deputy Adjutant and Quartermaster General |
| DHH | Directorate of History and Heritage (National Defence Headquarters) |
| Div | Division |
| DMO & I | Director Military Operations and Intelligence |
| DSO | Distinguished Service Order |

| | |
|---|---|
| dvr | driver |
| FOO | Forward Observation Officer (artillery) |
| GOC | General Officer Commanding |
| GS | General Staff |
| GSO | General Staff Officer |
| H & PER | Hastings and Prince Edward Regiment |
| HE | High Explosive |
| IDC | Imperial Defence College |
| instr | instruction |
| IOR | India Office Records |
| LAA | Light Anti-Aircraft |
| LAC | Library and Archives Canada |
| LHCMA | Liddell Hart Centre for Military Archives |
| mov | move/movement |
| NCO | non-commissioned officer |
| NDHQ | National Defence Headquarters (Ottawa) |
| NPAM | Non-Permanent Active Militia |
| OO | Operation Order |
| OP | observation post |
| ops | operations |
| PF | Permanent Force |
| PIAT | Projector, Infantry, Anti-tank |
| PLDG | 4th Princess Louise Dragoon Guards |
| PPCLI | Princess Patricia's Canadian Light Infantry |
| psc | Passed Staff College |
| RAF | Royal Air Force |
| recce | reconnaissance |
| REME | Royal Electrical and Mechanical Engineering |
| RMC | Royal Military College (of Canada) |
| SHAEF | Supreme Headquarters Allied Expeditionary Force |
| SP | self-propelled |
| sqn | squadron |
| ST | supply and transport |
| Tac | Tactical Headquarters |
| TEWT | Tactical Exercise without Troops |
| tk | tank |
| TNA | The National Archives (Kew) |
| USAAF | United States Army Air Forces |
| WD | War Diary |
| WO | War Office |

# Corps Commanders

# Introduction:
# Who, How, and the Common Ground

> *The great test of an officer who aspires to high command will be his ability to grasp quickly the essentials of a military problem, to decide rapidly what he will do, to make it clear to all concerned what he intends to achieve and how he will do it, and then to see that his subordinate commanders get on with the job ...*
>
> *He must [also] possess a high morale ... Without high morale, and in this will be included confidence, resolution and enthusiasm, he will not be able to stand the strain of battle for long nor will he radiate that confidence so necessary for the inspiration of subordinates.*
>
> – WAR OFFICE, CONDUCT OF WAR

WHO WERE THEY AND how did they fight their battles? These questions are central to this collective biography of five generals who commanded corps in the British and Canadian armies during the Second World War. E.L.M. Burns, Guy Simonds, Charles Foulkes, Sir Brian Horrocks, and Sir John Crocker all moved easily between the national armies of the British Empire, even though the first three were products of the Canadian Permanent Active Militia, or Permanent Force, while the last two had learned their trade in the British and Indian armies. Burns commanded 1st Canadian Corps as part of the British Eighth Army in Italy from March to October 1944, and his replacement, Charles Foulkes, also fought several actions under British command before taking the corps to Northwest Europe, where he spent the remainder of the war with General H.D.G. Crerar's First Canadian Army. Simonds fought his 2nd Canadian Corps in that army, even commanding it in an acting capacity during the battles of the Scheldt Estuary, but not before he had cut his corps' teeth with Miles Dempsey's British Second Army in Normandy. The two Britons, Horrocks and Crocker, each commanded their British corps for a while under First Canadian Army command, Crocker from July 1944 to March 1945, Horrocks during the Rhineland battles of February and March 1945. Both came to the Canadians with battle experience gained in other British armies. Crocker had commanded the 9th Corps with the British First Army in North Africa, and he too had fought the first phases of the Normandy campaign under Dempsey. Before being wounded and returning to action at the head of 30th Corps in the British Second

Army during the summer of 1944, Horrocks had commanded two different corps in Sir Bernard Law Montgomery's Eighth Army during the Western Desert battles of 1942-43. That these five generals could move so easily between the armies of the British Empire suggests that it might also be a good idea to ask *how they learned* their business. Surely, their portability owed much to common training, doctrine, and experience.

We know a little bit about their lives, their learning, and what they did during the war thanks to a few memoirs, operational histories, and biographical studies. Burns and Horrocks both left memoirs and have been the subject of some historical study.[1] Simonds never finished his memoirs, but several scholars have taken to writing biographical works and analyses about him.[2] Very little has been written on either Crocker or Foulkes, although their names pop up here and there in various official histories and operational studies.[3] Generally, however, our knowledge of *who* they were is uneven and we have no in-depth analysis of *how* any of these men exercised command, which Martin Van Crevald defines as "a *function* that has to be exercised, more or less continuously, if the army is to exist and to operate."[4] Neither do we have a comparative analysis of how a group of British Commonwealth generals learned to organize, train, and direct the personnel and arms in their charge. This book will be the first to connect the *who* and the *how* for a group of British and Canadian corps commanders who had the common experience of serving under Canadian command.

The command *function* of which Van Crevald writes depends largely on the technical and human skills of the commander.[5] He must know his stuff – no great revelation there. Tactical analysis, making timely decisions, conveying clear direction, supervising subordinates: a commander must do these things well if he is to stand a chance of winning battles. A general must also know how to exploit the staff, subordinate commanders, and communications infrastructure that are the apparatus of command. At the same time, he must be able to tap the intangible – to inspire subordinates and staff, to motivate them, or to drive them to work extra hours or to walk extra miles, often in the face of great personal danger. Superlative plans executed by insipid subordinates rarely succeed, so he must enliven them himself or provide them with subordinate commanders who can. For a general, the accumulation of technical skill takes place over decades of staff training, army courses, schemes, and practical experience. Human skills he acquires over a lifetime of dealing with people and learning what makes them tick. Both sets of skills warrant inquiry, and a balance of biography and battle will be necessary to elucidate and explain them. To this end, I have tried to track the development of each corps commander as closely as the available sources would allow, and I have been selective in the battle actions analyzed. Sufficient resolution of the commander's action in battle is necessary for a reasonable determination of how he got things done; there is not the space, however, for a definitive account of each action. Even so, the following analysis of how five generals acquired and used their skills will offer some useful contrasts in the exercise of command, and it will also reveal something of the armies, and the imperial system, that trained them.[6]

They were a surprisingly eclectic bunch. Brian Horrocks was the lone extrovert of the lot, a skilled operator with acting skills to rival Sir Laurence Olivier's, and capable of winning the hearts of the most hard-bitten soldiers. "Tommy" Burns was the other extreme. Academic and introverted, he wrote widely and brilliantly on military and political affairs, even tried his hand at a romance novel, but he had an uncanny knack for making everyone around him uncomfortable. John Crocker was just as quiet and just as skilled as Burns, but less theoretically minded, and he could relate to people, both in words, when he used them, and in deed. He was also a gentleman of great bravery, honesty, and example. Guy Simonds was equally reticent, relying more on his formidable technical skill, singular focus, and ruthless determination to drive people and get things done. He did not slap many backs. Charles Foulkes had the weakest skills of the group – a man of marginal tactical ability who was hated by most who worked with him – but he was a cutthroat army bureaucrat who, despite handling his division poorly in battle, clawed his way to corps command and made few mistakes once he got there. For a group of white, Anglican forty-somethings, they probably could not have been more different.[7]

And yet they all fit quite readily into the British Commonwealth armies and fought their corps in similar fashion. All three Canadians commanded British formations and served under British army commanders at one time or other, and the two Britons worked for and commanded Canadians as well. That they spoke the same "language" – a common method for solving military problems and for communicating solutions – made such inter-army adjustments relatively simple. All senior army officers of the British Empire learned that "language" at either the British Army Staff College at Camberley or the Indian Army Staff College at Quetta. Their curricula, as Richard Preston pointed out years ago, "permeated" thoroughly the senior ranks of the British, Indian, and Dominion armies.[8] This was done quite deliberately. Common entrance examinations, similar curricula, continuous exchanges of Directing Staff and students, and reserved vacancies for Dominion officers ensured uniformity for the staff colleges and all who passed through their gates.[9] The dividend, as Canadian general A.G.L. McNaughton stated, was that "we have gained the priceless advantage of knowing each other so well, of organizing our forces in the same way, of writing our orders in identical manner."[10] British generals like Eric Dorman-Smith agreed: "The 'common doctrine' survived ... [w]hich is what we all went to the Staff Colleges to ensure."[11] No officer in either British or Canadian armies could have expected advancement to senior rank without first qualifying "psc" (Passed Staff College). Canada, for example, sent seventy-five of its army officers to either Camberley or Quetta between 1905 and 1939, and forty-eight of them were still serving at the start of the Second World War.[12] This remaining core of staff-trained officers, which included Burns, Simonds, and Foulkes, all went on to senior rank and were the embryo of the First Canadian Army. They built the brigades, divisions, and corps of the army, and they played a large part in training the staff officers to run them, based largely on what they had learned at Camberley and Quetta.

The comprehensive two-year curriculum that they had studied at the staff colleges was demanding. During the first year, or Junior Division, students mostly mastered "Staff Duties within a Division," but that was a bit more complex than it sounds.[13] They studied tactics for the attack, the defence, withdrawal, and pursuit.[14] They learned how to conduct appreciations, prepare orders, and communicate those orders in fixed formats that everyone could understand. They learned the proper separation of staff functions within a headquarters: to assist the commander of any formation, "G" staffs tracked operations and intelligence, "A" staffs supervised personnel reinforcements and replacements, and "Q" staffs looked after logistics and administration, including transport.[15] Candidates learned how to complete the full gamut of these staff tasks – everything from writing intelligence assessments to planning road moves. Sometimes they did the work themselves; most of the time, however, students worked in syndicates of four or five students under the tutelage of a lieutenant-colonel on the Directing Staff. Frequently, they conducted map exercises indoors, during which a student could play any part from "an Army Commander to Staff Captain."[16] Just as frequently, they would go outside to plan attacks, defences, withdrawals, and other operations of war on representative pieces of terrain. These Tactical Exercises without Troops (TEWTs), as they were called, forced the candidates to apply lecture-learning in a more realistic setting, one in which they gained a greater appreciation for the factors of time and space in military operations. Students also engaged in a fair amount of historical study, analyzing past campaigns such as the battle of Waterloo and British operations in Palestine during the First World War.

The Senior Division, or second year of Staff College, focused at a higher level – corps, army, and combined operations.[17] Whereas students in the Junior Division had confined their study mostly to army matters and army branches (infantry, artillery, cavalry, and service corps), Senior Division students learned a lot more about the Royal Air Force, the Royal Navy, and how these services fit into combined operations. Staff learning in the Senior Division remained practical, however. Students could one day find themselves developing a corps casualty evacuation plan and, on another, preparing a written operation order as a General Staff Officer First Grade (GSO 1) of a division. The Senior Division student also learned how to conduct training – run ranges, plan TEWTs, and organize field exercises. Overall, Camberley and Quetta were less about telling the students how to do things than they were about conveying the method and the structures that could be reasonably applied in any military situation. In other words, students did not learn a one-size-fits-all method for artillery fire planning; they learned instead what British artillery was capable of doing, factors that should be considered when making a fire plan, and the ways in which a fire plan could be conveyed, supervised, and altered. For imperial armies oceans apart, this was critical. Even when wartime exigencies demanded abbreviated staff training, the basic "language" and method stayed the same. The condensed seventeen- to eighteen-week curricula of 1940-45 War Staff Courses were shorn of historical studies and pitched almost entirely to the GSO 3 (captain) level of staff training, but they conveyed much the same material and the efforts to ensure commonality endured, even when staff training became decentralized at a number of different schools.[18] For any given Canadian War Staff Course conducted at Kingston, Ontario, for example, roughly one-third of the Directing Staff came from the British Army.[19]

Canada's willingness to follow the British lead on training, doctrine, and equipment helped. At the 1926 Imperial Conference in London, Canadian Prime Minister William Lyon Mackenzie King had reaffirmed Canada's policy of maintaining conformity with Britain on matters of defence. Not that it meant Canada was willing to defer to Britain on all aspects of defence policy; far from it. In 1937, for example, King insisted that the long-standing periodic exchange of letters between the Canadian Chief of the General Staff (CGS) and the Chief of the Imperial General Staff (CIGS) be revised so that the letters were routed through the Canadian Department of External Affairs.[20] King was happy enough to have his CGS and even his Minister of National Defence discussing rifles, battalion orders of battle, or staff training with their British counterparts, but he did not want them making any commitments or giving tacit approval to war plans that originated in Britain. Canadian generals were just as conscious of national sovereignty concerning the use of Canadian troops in training and in war. As General Officer Commanding (GOC) 1st Canadian Corps, "Andy" McNaughton hit the roof when he heard that elements of the 1st Canadian

Infantry Division had been detached to British formations during a January 1941 exercise.[21] No division of Canadian formations, he insisted, would take place without his consent as the military representative of the Canadian government, a line that his successor as Senior Combatant Officer Overseas maintained, and a line with which British military authorities complied, if somewhat grudgingly at times.

Common doctrine, training, and equipment yielded common organizations, something that applied much more to corps staffs than it did to the composition of the corps themselves. In fact, a corps was not a fixed organization at all. As Brian Horrocks described it, "a corps consist[ed] only of a permanent H.Q. staff, certain administrative echelons and usually some corps artillery regiments."[22] Corps were organized based on their tasks. To break into the formidable Siegfried Line during Operation Veritable, Horrocks had seven divisions and some 200,000 troops in 30th Corps. A little over two years earlier, however, his 13th Corps had commanded little more than its own headquarters and a salvage unit because there was nothing for it to do after the battle of El Alamein. Typically, though, a corps consisted of the headquarters, two to four divisions,[23] some corps troops,[24] and an Army Group Royal Artillery (AGRA), consisting of one field and three medium regiments to supplement the fire of the divisional artillery organizations. If needed, a corps could count on the fire support of additional AGsRA. Simonds had three of them supporting Operation Totalize in August 1944, and Horrocks had a whopping five for Veritable five months later.[25] The organization and strength of corps really depended on the priorities and roles assigned them by army commanders.

The apparatus for controlling these task-tailored organizations was fairly fixed, however (see Figure 1). The Corps headquarters consisted of two essential parts: a General Staff (GS) branch and an Adjutant General and Quartermaster General (AG & QMG) branch. The GS branch assisted the commander with planning, current operations, and intelligence.[26] To do this, it had functional sub-branches dedicated to operations and staff duties,[27] air support, intelligence, and liaison. The Commander Corps Royal Artillery (CCRA), the Chief Engineer (CE), the Chief Signals Officer (CSO), and their staffs rounded out the GS branch, which consisted of some thirty to thirty-five staff officers in total.

Early in the war, the GS branch functioned under the supervision of the Brigadier General Staff (BGS); by 1943-44, however, most British and Canadian headquarters had adopted the chief-of-staff system, in which one senior staff officer coordinated the work of both the GS and AG & QMG branches. When that happened, the BGS became the Chief of Staff and the GSO 1 assumed the hands-on responsibility of coordinating GS branch activities.[28] As far as matters of personnel, logistics, and administration were concerned, they remained the

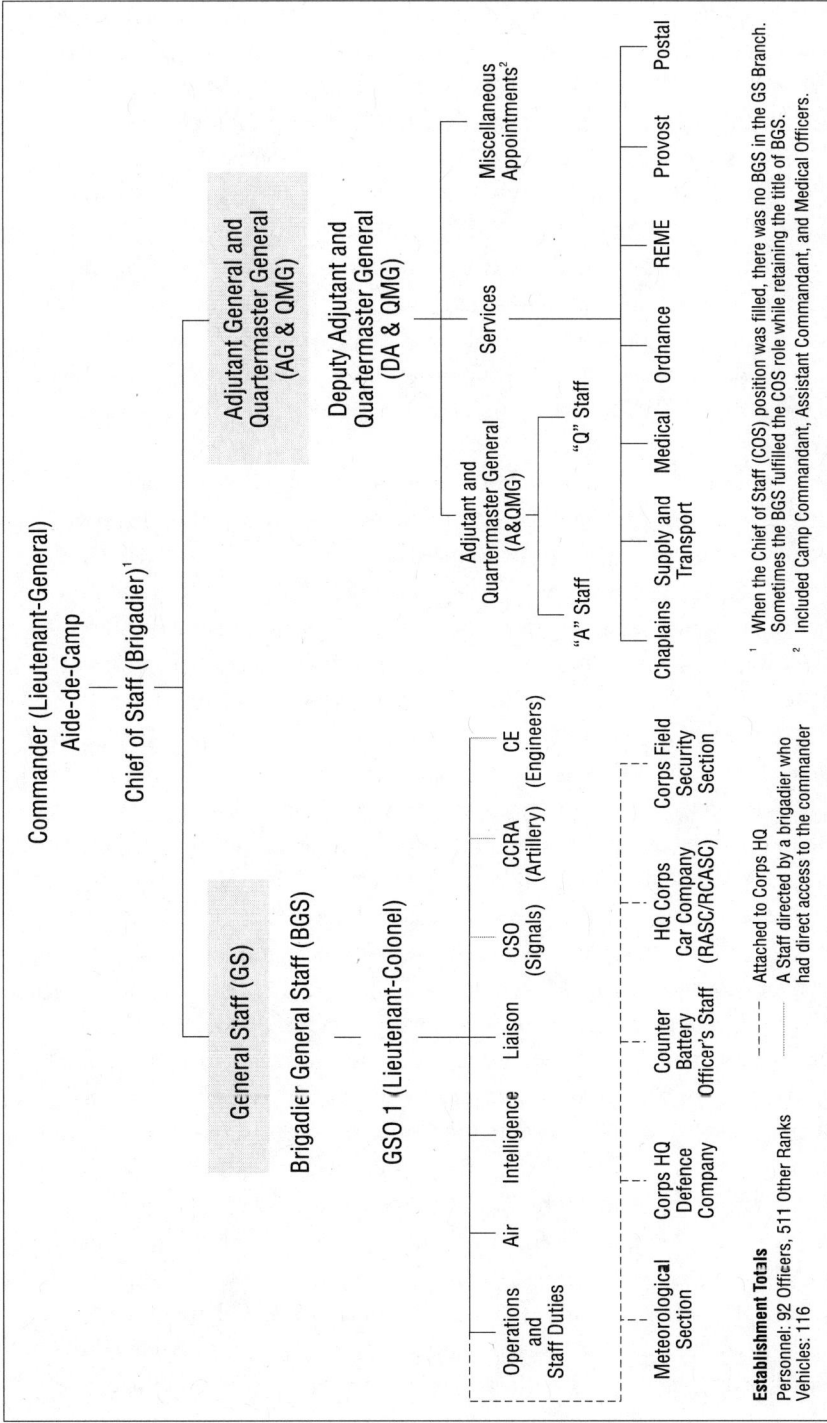

Commander (Lieutenant-General)
Aide-de-Camp

Chief of Staff (Brigadier)[1]

**General Staff (GS)**

Brigadier General Staff (BGS)

GSO 1 (Lieutenant-Colonel)

Operations and Staff Duties
Air
Intelligence
Liaison
CSO (Signals)
CCRA (Artillery)
CE (Engineers)

Meteorological Section
Corps HQ Defence Company
Counter Battery Officer's Staff
HQ Corps Car Company (RASC/RCASC)
Corps Field Security Section

----- Attached to Corps HQ
——— A Staff directed by a brigadier who had direct access to the commander

**Establishment Totals**
Personnel: 92 Officers, 511 Other Ranks
Vehicles: 116

**Adjutant General and Quartermaster General (AG & QMG)**

Deputy Adjutant and Quartermaster General (DA & QMG)

Services

Miscellaneous Appointments[2]

Adjutant and Quartermaster General (A&QMG)

"A" Staff
"Q" Staff

Chaplains
Supply and Transport
Medical
Ordnance
REME
Provost
Postal

[1] When the Chief of Staff (COS) position was filled, there was no BGS in the GS Branch. Sometimes the BGS fulfilled the COS role while retaining the title of BGS.
[2] Included Camp Commandant, Assistant Commandant, and Medical Officers.

FIGURE 1 British and Canadian corps headquarters, 1943-45. Based on Joint Services Command and Staff College (JSCSC), Staff College War Courses 1539-45, Senior Officers War Course: SD/INT/A/Q Precis, S.D. 4, SD in a Corps, Appendix A.

primary responsibility of the Deputy Adjutant and Quartermaster General (DA & QMG), a staff-trained brigadier who directly supervised AG & QMG branch activities. He had an "A" staff to plan and administer personnel issues and a "Q" staff to look after logistics and other administrative matters. For planning purposes, the DA & QMG also had at his disposal the heads of the various service branches, including those for the medical services, the ordnance corps, supply and transport (ST), the Royal Electrical and Mechanical Engineering (REME) branch, the Provost Corps, the chaplaincy, and postal services. Finally, corps headquarters had on their establishment a headquarters defence company, which included infantry and anti-aircraft personnel, to provide location protection. British and Canadian corps headquarters were not small. Fully manned establishments called for a total of 92 officers, 511 other ranks, and some 116 vehicles.[29]

Organizations that large could not possibly be moved quickly or easily, which is why they were broken down for mobile operations. The terminology was inconsistent, but there were essentially three elements to all British and Canadian corps headquarters: a Main Headquarters, "concerned chiefly with the actual fighting"; a Rear Headquarters, "concerned with administration"; and a Tactical Headquarters, or "Tac," which enabled the commander to place himself well forward or visit formations, while still exercising control.[30] The composition of the various elements, naturally enough, suited their primary purposes. Main Headquarters contained the "G" staff, the CCRA, the CE, the CSO, and, sometimes the DA & QMG.[31] Very often, corps Main Headquarters were as close, or closer, to the forward troops than divisional headquarters, which were normally within six to seven kilometres of the frontline fighting. The operations room, which was the focal point of command and staff activity at the Main Headquarters, had a fairly standard layout: an Armoured Command Vehicle, the BGS caravan, and the Intelligence Office truck "formed three sides of the operations room, the intervening space covered by a tarpaulin."[32] Artillery, engineer, air, and counter-battery staffs were nearby, as was the commander's small caravan, if he had one. Rear Headquarters moved less frequently and typically consisted of the "A" and "Q" staffs complete, plus a representative or two from the "G" staff. The distance between Main and Rear varied greatly, depending on the situation. In the fluid operations in North Africa, Horrocks's 10th Corps Headquarters had a Main-Rear separation of 100 kilometres on a few occasions, but on the congested Normandy battlefield, he found the two headquarters components only a few kilometres apart.[33] The headquarters element that differed most from commander to commander was the "Tac." Sometimes these were semi-permanent control stations – complete with radios, antennae, and map boards – sited where the commander could see the fighting, and which operated without interruption for the duration of an operation. More often than not, however, "Tacs" were just a tiny group of key staff and vehicles that moved around with the commander by day and returned to Main Headquarters at night. They were small enough in composition that the commander could visit forward headquarters without causing a fuss, yet complete enough that he had the advisors and communications apparatus he needed to exercise control. A typical "Tac" contained the commander, the CCRA, the CE, a "G" staff officer, perhaps an aide-de-camp, and no more than a handful of vehicles, but how Tactical Headquarters were used depended very much on the commander. Headquarters, after all, were meant to aid their commanders, so there had to be some allowance for the individual preferences and needs of the man orchestrating the battle.

That sort of accommodation speaks to the primary finding of this inquiry, which is how five men so different in personality, point of view, and upbringing could fit so well into the imperial armies they served. Neither of those armies was in good shape when the war started, by the way. The Canadian Army, in particular, was on life support, so it took some time – years, in fact – to nurse it back to life, allow it to mature, and prepare it for its primary function – fighting and winning the nation's wars. Long though that rebuilding process may have been, it would not have happened without the hard work of a cadre of trained professionals and the British staff system that helped them put things right. By 1944, the First Canadian Army – what historian John Allan English has called "the last great British imperial army" – had corps that could fight, and fight well, and it could also count on the help of British corps that had been cast in the same mould.[34] The five corps commanders of this study may not have been successful 100 percent of the time, and they may not always have liked the people around them, but the imperial system that trained them and provided them with both the staffs to organize their thoughts and the formations to fight their battles also implanted a connectivity that cut across oceans, ensuring that, when the time came, they could do what was asked of them in war.

# 1

## The Actor: Lieutenant-General Sir Brian Horrocks

> *The troops have a saying that if you want to get on in the Army you must be in the right place at the right time and your face must fit. I can think of no one to whom this applies more than to myself.*
>
> – SIR BRIAN HORROCKS

THERE IS A WONDERFUL scene in the 1977 film *A Bridge Too Far,* based on Cornelius Ryan's book about Operation Market Garden.[1] As the troops of the Guards Armoured Division are lined up nose-to-tail on a winding road, ready to launch on one of the riskiest Allied operations of the war, their corps commander, Lieutenant-General Brian Horrocks, driving his own jeep, weaves past them. While doling out directions to his passenger, who happens to be the commanding officer of the armoured regiment that will lead the ground advance in Market Garden, he waves at the waiting soldiers, cracks the odd joke, and addresses many of them by their first names: "Morning, Derek. I'm glad to see someone knows where we're going!" The troops laugh and wave back. Edward Fox, the English actor who portrayed Horrocks in the film, played the part brilliantly. Horrocks really was that likeable. Every soldier or officer who served under him, it seems, has a story of how the general tapped them on the shoulder during a battle, knelt beside a wounded soldier in hospital, or emerged out of the dust to tell frontline soldiers how the battle was going.[2] Horrocks made leadership look easy and Fox captured that beautifully – the down-to-earth general with a natural ability to inspire, the general who rarely fussed over the details, the general untroubled by self-doubt. This is the image of Horrocks that has endured.[3] In a way, it is a lens through which we view the historical evidence, but it is also a lens that can distort our interpretation of the man and his actions.

This is not to say that the *Bridge Too Far* image of Horrocks is false, but rather that it does not do justice to the complexity of his character. There is no doubt that Horrocks understood completely the human dimension of war and how well British and Commonwealth soldiers responded to the carefree and casual professionalism he projected, but they saw only what Horrocks wanted them to see. Montgomery's Chief of Staff, Major-General Sir Francis de Guingand, said that he always thought of Horrocks as "a Marshal Ney," one of Napoleon Bonaparte's most colourful and daring generals.[4] What they perhaps did not realize was how deliberate he was about planning operations, how at times he exuded a confidence that was not always there. Horrocks would have admitted to that – and he did, in his memoir, *A Full Life*. Take, for example, the passage dealing with how he conducted himself during the first morning of the battle for Alam Halfa in August 1942: "It was difficult ... to shave, dress calmly then *walk* over to the operations room. I would have liked to have leapt out of my valise and run over, but the appearance of an unshaven, out-of-breath corps commander would not have created a favourable impression."[5]

This was a man hiding his anxiety. In a way, Horrocks was an actor – for all the right reasons. In fact, he used the acting metaphor several times in *A Full Life*.[6] True, cheeriness and confidence were part of his character, but no one is cheerful and confident all the time. At tense times, particularly at the start of major operations such as Market Garden, like a good character actor, Horrocks hid his doubts, slipping into the persona of the unflappable gentleman general. No one, neither soldier nor staff officer, needed to see their general fretting or brooding over upcoming operations, so Horrocks lived the maxim of his mentor, Field Marshal Viscount Montgomery: "However bad the situation may be, *the commander must always radiate confidence*."[7] This is the key to understanding how Horrocks exercised command. He had sound technical skills, but he was also a masterful performer who consistently managed to tap the full capacity of the people who worked for him.

HE MAY HAVE LIVED through some of the grimmest events in modern times, but Brian Horrocks was a genuinely happy person. He was happy in the sense that he enjoyed, without guilt, life's good moments and he accepted, without self-pity, that he could gain from the bad ones. This was the case from the very beginning. Born at Ranniket, India, to a Royal Army Medical Corps surgeon from Lancashire and an Irish Presbyterian mother, Horrocks, who adored his parents, had "an extremely happy childhood."[8] Whereas some may have found "the usual wandering service life" difficult, Horrocks found it an adventure. His preteen years in Gibraltar were packed full of fun – "bathing, hunting with the Calpe hounds, cricket matches, race meetings and children's parties." He loved the boat rides between his home in Gibraltar and his preparatory school at Durham. Later, when his father had been posted to the War Office in 1909, he moved on to Uppingham School in Leicestershire and found it fulfilling as well. Not that Horrocks enjoyed the academic curriculum. Far from it; he loved games: "My entire life was devoted to sport." Mathematics and history took a back seat to rugby and cricket. Not surprisingly, his school reports noted "impetuosity – too prone to answer without thinking – inclined to rush things without making sure of what he is doing." Life was simply too entertaining for serious study, so Horrocks naturally drifted into the army class, because it seemed so much more compatible with his propensity for fun.

The experience of the Royal Military College, Sandhurst, did little to shape him up though. In January 1913, his army career commenced inauspiciously when he passed into Sandhurst, 173rd in order of merit, second from the bottom in his class.[9] He was, by his own admission, "idle," "scruffy," and "careless."[10] Consequently, he "achieved nothing at all and remained a gentleman cadet (the equivalent of a private soldier) throughout [his] entire time at the college." To cap off an undistinguished college career, he ended his time at Sandhurst with three months on restrictions, which meant confinement to barracks, menial duties, and show parades.[11] He and a few friends had gone to the races at Gatwick, confident that they had a "certainty" for the third race, only to find that the certainty was distinctly and disappointingly uncertain. It had also drained all their funds for the return journey. Horrocks did not worry about much in those days, but he felt lucky to have passed out of college in July 1914, again near the bottom of his class. Within a month of leaving Sandhurst, he was off to war.

He did not last long in battle, but he learned a lot. Like most Britons, he was swept up in the romance that preceded the disillusion of the Great War, feeling "like a king among men" as he marched past cheering crowds at the Chatham railway station on 11 August 1914 with a ninety-five-man reinforcement draft for the 1st Battalion Middlesex Regiment.[12] In France and Belgium, he grew to admire the average soldier's ability to scrounge and make himself comfortable; and he loved the "priceless Cockney sense of humour," which he thought the perfect tonic in times of stress. Wisecracks like "Why don't you give your face a holiday, chum? Try a smile," can bring a little lift of spirits, even during the most draining of days.[13] He also learned from his company commander, a Captain Gibbons, who stressed the importance of knowing one's subordinates and sharing their misery. When the battalion officers were offered billets in a comfortable farmhouse away from a manure-packed paddock in which the soldiers were bedding down, Gibbons fumed: "If the men sleep out, we sleep out."[14] Horrocks recognized the importance of the gesture: "My heart sank but I knew instinctively that he was right." The willingness of soldiers to follow was constructed on gestures like this. It is interesting how some events, though seemingly insignificant in the bigger scheme of things, become embedded in memory, making lifelong lessons of themselves. Forty-five years later, Horrocks wrote a lesson that Gibbons had left him into his memoirs.

On 21 October 1914, Horrocks became a prisoner of war, something he described in hindsight as "probably the best apprenticeship for the difficult business of command in war."[15] At the town of Maisnil, during the First Battle of Ypres, he received a bullet wound through the lower abdomen and upper thigh while defending the town against a German attack.[16] Not long after he was wounded, the German attackers surrounded Horrocks's platoon: "The stretcher bearers could not possibly get any of the wounded away at all and, as our men were pressed back, I was taken prisoner."[17] A miserable month of pain and infection in a filthy German field hospital followed. When Horrocks began to mend, he was moved back to prisoner-of-war camps, where, away from "C.O., adjutant, company commander, or kindly platoon sergeant," the first life lesson was one of self-sufficiency.[18] It was an internal battle against what Horrocks called the "deadly monotony" of prison camp life, a monotony feeding a despondency that could cause one to deteriorate, mentally and physically, as many did. Horrocks kept himself mentally and physically alert trying to escape. He never succeeded, however. He made it outside the wire on several occasions, once even making it to the Dutch border, but he was always apprehended and always sent to solitary confinement.

But even solitary confinement had its upside – more time to think about and plan the next escape attempt. Simply having something to scheme about kept him sane. He had probably never been this methodical about anything in his life: "Escaping was a profession in itself and like all professions the more one worked at it the more proficient one became ... My first efforts at escaping were very clumsy ... But I built up experience, and was quite confident that if the war went on long enough I would eventually succeed."[19] That meant gathering whatever information could be gained on sentries, perimeter barriers, and even the terrain and routes to be traversed, then thinking through, in detail, the preparations for each stage of the escape – getting civilian clothes or something that looked like them, finding a compass, or acquiring some German currency. Despite his lack of success, Horrocks believed that the experience had been a useful period of mental conditioning: "I had learned at an early age and in a hard school to stand on my own feet and make my own decisions, often in a split second. I had also acquired the useful habit of thinking things out from the enemy point of view so that I might always be one jump ahead. These were lessons which served me well later on."[20] He also had plenty of time to study human behaviour, something that became a lifelong interest. Why did some people crack, while others endured difficult times with a smile? How important was routine, or humour, or leadership to morale? Horrocks came to despise the infectious defeatism of some senior officers in captivity, many of whom warned Horrocks and his fellow escape enthusiasts against trying to break out.

To Horrocks they were cowards. Their fear and their pessimism dragged down soldiers who looked to them for example.[21] These observations would inform his method of command in the years to come. Horrocks happily left captivity in 1918, aged only twenty-two years but a fairly confident subaltern who did not need to be told what to do in order to act.

Useful though the experience of captivity may have been, Horrocks did not wish for more of it; sadly, however, that is what he got. After spending a month or two – and all of his back pay – "beating it up in London," in January 1919 Horrocks volunteered for service in the British contingent that was to assist the White Russian armies in their fight against the Bolsheviks. It proved a most depressing experience. He arrived at Vladivostok in April, travelled inland to join a ragtag brigade of the 1st Siberian Army in May, retreated in front of Bolshevik advances in the final weeks of 1919, and wound up, once again, a prisoner of war in January 1920.[22] This time, Horrocks did not put his escape skills to good use, mostly because he thought the Bolsheviks would surely send him home, and partly because Siberia on foot was a certain death sentence. Much to his disappointment, however, the Red Army's promises of repatriation to the United Kingdom buckled under organizational incompetence, and a nearly fatal bout with typhus kept Horrocks bedridden in a squalid hospital for several weeks. Not until October 1920, after miles of train travel and weeks in various prisoner-of-war camps, did Horrocks and his fellow Britons cross the border into Finland. In his memoirs, Horrocks had little to say about the lessons of his Siberian experience except that near-starvation, bitter cold, and filth had taught him "to live life rough."[23] Future stresses and strains would surely pale in comparison.

In late November 1920, Horrocks returned to an army life that was, for him, disappointingly dull. Since passing into Sandhurst, Captain Horrocks had spent eight years in the army doing little that would have prepared him for higher command, and the next ten years did little to change that trend. As the British government struggled with post-war retrenchment, the British Army in turn struggled with miserly budgets that curtailed field training and equipment acquisitions. Promotion was also painfully slow and field exercises featured soldiers wearing placards that read "this represents a section."[24] Horrocks could get only so excited about that sort of thing. A year of occupation duty during 1920-21 with the British Army of the Rhine was uneventful, as was a deployment in aid of the civil power during a coal miners' strike immediately after the 1st Battalion Middlesex Regiment returned to the United Kingdom. A year in Ireland during 1921-22 did little to raise his morale.[25] Horrocks, who was half-Irish, hated the whole business of "search[ing] for hidden arms, patrols, keeping a lookout for road-blocks and dealing with ambushes by the Sinn Feiners."[26]

Security duties during the 1923 Silesian plebiscite only compounded the hum-drum.[27] Horrocks needed more challenge and excitement than the army of the 1920s was offering, so it is not surprising that, when his battalion settled into Aldershot in late 1923, he returned to one of his passions: games. The self-confessed "games addict" found the modern pentathlon much to his liking because it combined riding, swimming, running, fencing, and shooting. He took to it with great enthusiasm, training like a demon, eventually winning the national championships and representing Great Britain in the 1924 Olympic Games in Paris. This was a significant personal achievement, but, as Horrocks reflected some thirty-five years later, "I was now unquestionably in danger of ruining any chances of success which I may have had by allowing sport to fill my life to the exclusion of everything else."[28]

That began to change in 1927. About that time, Horrocks's father gently en-couraged his "work-shy, sport-loving son" to settle down and sit the entrance examination for the Staff College, Camberley. Without the designation of "psc" (Passed Staff College), no officer could expect to achieve senior rank in the army, so the junior Horrocks, who by this time was a fairly long-in-the-tooth captain with an undistinguished career, listened: "I at last started to work at my profession."[29] The timing was also right. In 1928, he married Nancy Kitchin, and within a year they had a daughter. Horrocks also had to consider that he was not a wealthy man. His father made a decent living as a colonel in the Royal Army Medical Corps, but there was certainly no family fortune to fall back on. As he later wrote: "I am one of those impecunious people who has always lived on his pay."[30] If he wanted to provide a comfortable living for his family, he would have to progress in rank. Family responsibility forced him to focus on his career; getting into staff college was an important first step.

During the course of his preparations for the entrance examinations, he spent nearly four years working with the Territorials as Adjutant of the 9th Battalion Middlesex Regiment.[31] Having turned down a posting to China to concentrate on the Camberley and Quetta examinations, Horrocks had not expected much to come of his time with "Saturday night soldiers," but he found it "a most in-vigorating experience and a vital step in my military education because, after all, these are the people who in the final analysis win or lose our wars."[32] Mo-tivating volunteers, who gave of their free time and who were even more budget-restricted and kit-deprived than regular army troops, was challenging work, but it honed Horrocks's human skills for the citizen army that would fight the Second World War. Iron discipline, he found, did not work; better to make the citizen soldier feel guilty about missing a parade and make him want to train harder, for the good of his mates.[33] His unorthodox approach to training stemmed from this period: "In training I am a great believer in running before you can walk, because, by finding out how difficult it is to run, men take greater interest in the problem of learning to walk. All training must be done through the brain; the bored man absorbs nothing."[34] The lifelong student of human behaviour was becoming a masterful practitioner of the art of leadership. He still needed the technical training of Staff College, however, if he hoped to advance any further.

In 1931, after sitting the exam five times and at the age of thirty-five, Horrocks happily passed into Staff College, Camberley. A few years later, he would have been three years too old even to sit the examinations.[35] For someone who had never been given to academic study of any kind, Horrocks took amazingly well to the program at Camberley. As it had been for so many other officers, Staff College was the "turning point" in his life.[36] He found the curriculum engaging, and the syndicate method of instruction, he thought, "could not have been better." The Commandant at the time was Major-General Sir John Dill, whom Horrocks admired for his "integrity, great charm and ... first-class brain," and the Directing Staff (DS) – which included Lieutenant-Colonels Henry Maitland Wilson and Robert Forbes Adam as well as Wing Commanders John Slessor and Trafford Leigh-Mallory – exuded professional competence.[37] There was also a comforting familiarity about the curriculum for Horrocks.[38] The process for conducting appreciations was not unlike the one he had developed informally while trying to escape German captivity – gathering the factors, weighing courses of action, assessing possible enemy actions, and so on. Now, instead of doing that for one or two people at a time, he was learning how to do it for brigades, divisions, and corps, and he liked it. He did well at it too.[39] Horrocks was becoming a professional.

He applied himself fully in a series of appointments between the time that he completed Staff College in 1932 and the outbreak of war in 1939. Following a brief ten-month return to his regiment in Egypt, Horrocks accepted a posting to the War Office in London.[40] Although initially unenthusiastic about life as a staff captain to the Military Secretary's Branch of the War Office in 1934, he soon found working on personnel issues quite interesting. In his particular sub-branch, which handled officer promotions between the ranks of second-lieutenant and lieutenant-colonel, he found that "few secrets were hidden."[41] It also gave Horrocks a window on who was a rising star and who was not. After two years at Whitehall, he received the plum appointment of Brigade Major for the 5th Brigade at Aldershot.[42] As the chief staff officer for a brigade earmarked as part of a proposed expeditionary force for the continent, Horrocks had opportunity to use what he had learned at the Staff College – planning contingency operations, coordinating collective training for three infantry battalions, and honing the skills of his own headquarters.

Aside from the opportunity the two years at Aldershot gave Horrocks to fine-tune his staff skills, it also afforded him a lesson in how not to command. The 5th Brigade was one of three in Sir Archibald Wavell's 2nd Infantry Division.[43] For Horrocks, Wavell was a prime example of how intellectual brilliance and technical competence were not enough for command: "[Wavell's] brilliant, imaginative brain lay behind the most expressionless, poker face I have ever come across ... We who knew Wavell admired him immensely, but owing to his almost pathological taciturnity he was completely unknown to the bulk of officers and men under his command. He was quite incapable of going round inspiring the troops."[44] Horrocks would not make that mistake. From the 5th Brigade, he went back to Camberley as a member of the Directing Staff in the summer of 1938, a posting that would not have happened had he not proven himself an adroit staff officer. By the time the Germans invaded France in May 1940, he had been promoted to lieutenant-colonel and risen to the position of College GSO 1 (General Staff Office First Grade). In fact, he was holding this position when, on 10 May 1940, he received orders to assume command of the 2nd Battalion Middlesex Regiment, which was then deploying to Belgium with the rest of the British Expeditionary Force to meet the German advance.

The 1940 campaign in France and Flanders lasted less than a month for Horrocks, but it was a critical period for two reasons: he impressed the right people and the right people impressed him. The 2nd Battalion Middlesex Regiment was a machine gun unit in Major-General B.L. Montgomery's 3rd Division and, as the commanding officer of a divisional unit, Horrocks reported directly to Montgomery. No other infantry battalion commander in the division had such a direct line to the boss. This was a make-or-break situation with a general who was "known to be ruthlessly efficient, but somewhat of a showman," and Horrocks knew it: "I was told sympathetically that I wouldn't last long under his command, and, to be honest, I would rather have served under any other divisional commander."[45] But Horrocks held up well in very demanding circumstances. As Montgomery conducted one of the most difficult operations in war – a withdrawal in contact with the enemy – Horrocks's machine-gunners efficiently supported the infantry brigades while they disengaged from the enemy and made their way back to the Channel coast. On 18-19 May, Montgomery had Horrocks commanding a rearguard of two machine gun battalions and two anti-tank batteries to cover the division's withdrawal across the Escaut Canal.[46] This was a tricky operation and Horrocks handled what was practically a brigade with ease, increasing his currency with Montgomery such that two weeks later, Montgomery nominated Horrocks as acting brigade commander for the 11th Brigade in the 4th Division.

Horrocks, too, was impressed. Montgomery he found to be supremely competent. On the night of 27-28 May, he managed to disengage his division from a position on the frontier near Roubaix and reposition it some thirty miles north to Noordschote to fill a hole in the line left by the surrendering Belgians, and cover the withdrawal to Dunkirk.[47] In an operation conducted largely at night and over refugee-clogged roads, the first unit to move was the 2nd Battalion Middlesex. Horrocks conducted his own reconnaissance of the new defensive area on the morning of 27 May, met the company commanders at a designated rendezvous point at 1400 hours to give orders, then had the companies move directly into their positions at 1600 hours. For an anxious evening, Horrocks and his machine-gunners barely straddled the thirteen-mile-wide gap in the front until the arrival of the rest of the division on the morning of 28 May.[48] Montgomery never doubted that he could execute the manoeuvres of 27-28 May. Indeed, as far as Horrocks could tell, Monty never doubted anything he did. But it was more than Montgomery's competence that Horrocks admired; it was his calm. He remembered Montgomery's air of normalcy in a time of crisis: "During the whole of the withdrawal, he insisted on having meals at regular hours and he never missed his normal night's sleep."[49] Horrocks appreciated that sort of composure.

Another senior commander who Horrocks thought played a critical role in the preservation of order and morale was his corps commander, and a future Chief of the Imperial General Staff (CIGS), Lieutenant-General Sir Alan Brooke: "I felt vaguely at the time that this alert, seemingly iron, man without a nerve in his body, whom I met from time to time at 3rd Division Headquarters and who gave out his orders in short clipped sentences, was a great soldier ... We regarded him as a highly efficient military machine."[50] Years later, after having read excerpts of the Alanbrooke diaries in Arthur Bryant's *Turn of the Tide,* and after having acquired his own lens of command experience, Horrocks came to "appreciate what a consummate actor he must have been ... he never gave us any indication of those moments of utter despair when it seemed to him almost impossible that any of us would ever escape."[51] Confidence and calm, even if they had to be affected, had to radiate from the top, especially at times when catastrophe seemed so near and rumours were rampant. They percolated down the chain of command and preserved the discipline and morale of the soldiers, who carried on "seemingly indifferent to the chaos around them."[52] It also preserved the sense of humour that Horrocks loved so much. After a very close call with the enemy during a rearguard action, one of Horrocks's company commanders quipped: "Don't look round, sir, I think we're being followed."[53] For the British soldier, it was the unruffled composure of the Montgomerys and

Brookes that worked best, not the hell-raising speeches of the Pattons or the melodrama of the MacArthurs.[54]

After Dunkirk, the two years that Horrocks spent in the United Kingdom, doing his part to rebuild a shattered army, offered him plenty of opportunity to watch Montgomery – and learn. Taking command of the 3rd Division's 9th Brigade, Horrocks was quite happy to be "back in the fold with Monty again."[55] He commanded the 9th Brigade from June 1940 to January 1941, after which he went to Eastern Command as Brigadier General Staff. Six months later, he went back to Montgomery when he was promoted to major-general and appointed to command the 44th (Home Counties) Division, a formation in Monty's Southeastern Army. This, Horrocks believed, was another critical period in his development as a commander: "I always reckon that I learned most of my practical soldiering first of all as a brigade-major at Aldershot under Wavell and secondly during the nine months which I spent in south-east England under Monty."[56] Montgomery was an excellent trainer and a first-rate people picker, but there was also a good deal of "stage management" with him. He talked of stage-managing his battles – getting all the arms properly synchronized and supplied such that each element could play to his plan – but he also had knack for simply putting across clear messages to subordinates. Horrocks marvelled at how Monty could fill a film theatre full of officers and keep them spellbound for an hour, sometimes more, while he explained an operation, dissected an exercise for salient lessons, whatever. He spoke plainly and utterly without ambiguity. In fact, the topics of Monty's talks mattered little. Horrocks took in that Monty was really selling himself, and the message was quite simple: "I know what I'm doing. I'm completely confident we'll succeed. You should be too." Montgomery understood that soldiers at all levels have doubts, so whatever he could do to expunge, or at least mitigate, those doubts by radiating confidence or keeping troops informed would only make them perform better.

Horrocks grasped the lessons thoroughly and put them into practice. He copied Montgomery's method of addressing groups: "I have held many similar conferences and have always tried to follow the Monty technique."[57] He also copied Montgomery's habit of getting out of his headquarters and visiting the units under his command. The war diary for the 44th Division shows that, in his first full month as GOC, Horrocks addressed all the officers under his command once, supervised two exercises, conducted a cloth model exercise with senior divisional officers, and made no less than eight inspections of, or visits to, brigades or units, including service support troops.[58] All ranks in the 44th Division knew their white-haired GOC, and they liked him. As one trooper recalled: "He was known as a man's man. Whilst he had the [rank], he seemed to think and talk, particularly to us, as if he was one of us."[59] Of course, Horrocks was not really one of them at all. With his English public school background and having spent much of his life abroad, he had little in common with the common soldier. But he was approachable and he was genuinely interested in the many people who worked for him. He conducted himself the same way when he left the Southeastern Army to command the 9th Armoured Division in March 1942. Not that he was easy on his troops. Shortly after arriving at the 9th Armoured Division, Horrocks "came to the conclusion that they had been too long in Northamptonshire. The wives and families had of course arrived and they were all living too soft."[60] He moved them out of their current billets to the Newmarket area, where most of the units lived under canvas but where they were also close to good training areas for armoured manoeuvre: "I worked them very hard indeed; exercise after exercise, and the harder they worked the more they seemed to enjoy it." The exercises progressed very rapidly in complexity and difficulty, starting first with harbour drills in April, then advancing to road movement in May, and culminating with opposed river crossings in June and July.[61] This was an extremely quick progression in training, but Horrocks believed that troops, and their commanders, had to be challenged, especially at a time when he had ripped them from their cozy Northamptonshire lives. He also believed in "working hard, then playing hard," so, after a particularly tough set of exercises, he gave the entire division four days leave to attend the derby in Newmarket.[62] The troops loved it. In August 1942, he was making good progress with his armoured division when his time in command was cut short. Montgomery, who had just assumed command of the Eighth Army in North Africa, needed him again. Horrocks was now going to command a corps, in battle, in the desert.

IT MADE HIM NERVOUS. British fortunes in the Western Desert had not been good in the preceding eighteen months, and many a British general had paid a price. As Horrocks recounted: "Command in the desert was regarded as an almost certain prelude to a bowler hat."[63] But shortly after his arrival, Montgomery put him at ease somewhat with "one of the most remarkable military appreciations I ever heard."[64] Monty explained that, after weeks of recoiling in front of Field Marshal Erwin Rommel's advances, the Eighth Army had established a defensive position along the El Alamein Line, a thirty-five-mile front at the bottleneck between the sea on the northern flank and the Qattara Depression to the south (see Map 1). The army commander envisioned a campaign in which he would first defend against an attack by Rommel's German-Italian forces, then, after he had assembled and trained a mobile armoured corps, launch

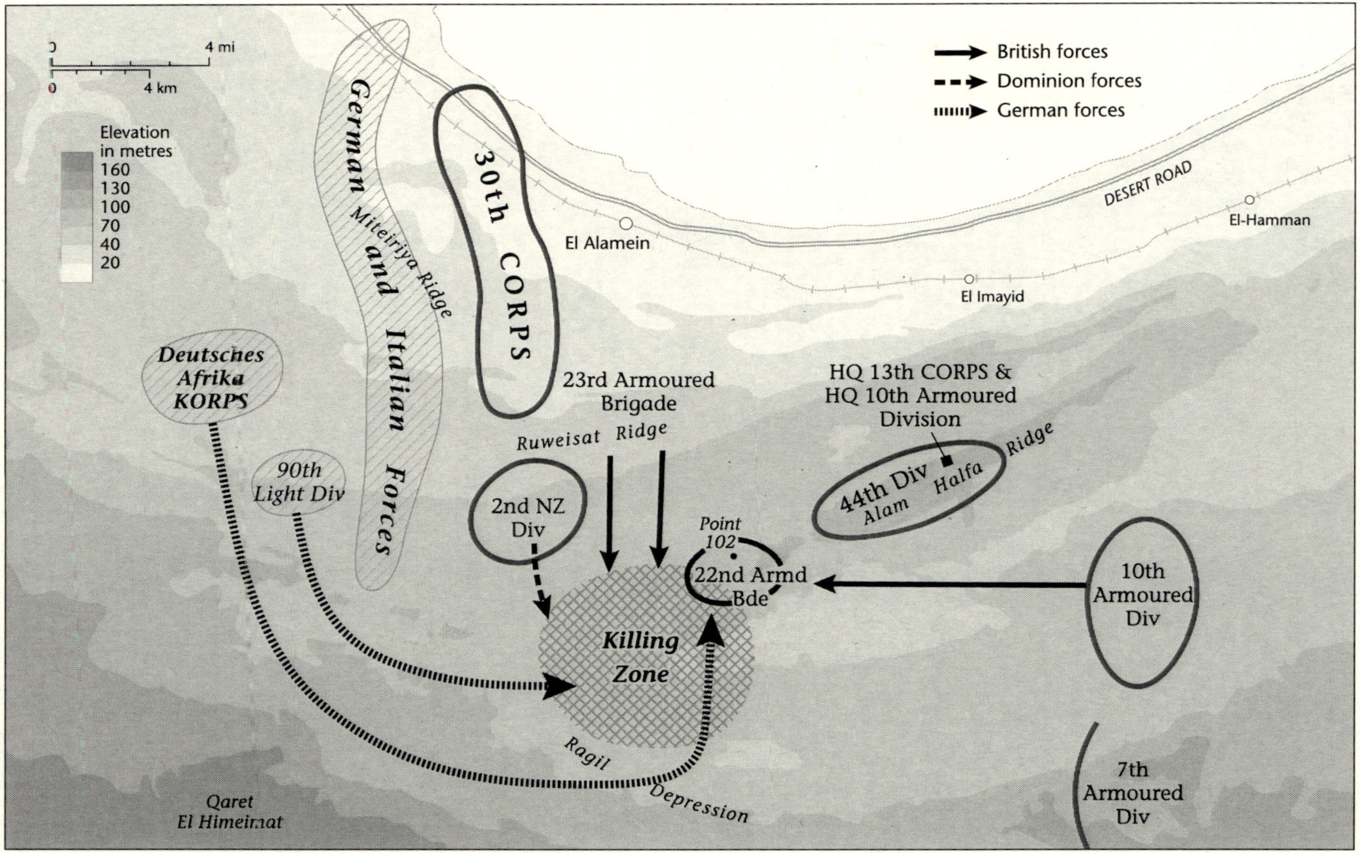

MAP 1   The battle of Alam Halfa. Adapted from Sir Brian Horrocks, *A Full Life* (London: Collins, 1960), 117.

an offensive to drive Rommel out of Africa. Horrocks was to play a crucial role in the first stage of Montgomery's plan. His 13th Corps – consisting of the 2nd New Zealand, 44th (Home Counties), and 7th Armoured Divisions, plus an incomplete 10th Armoured Division – defended the southern half of the line in front of Rommel. Whereas William Ramsden's 30th Corps in the north had a deep defensive position behind a deep minefield, Horrocks's corps was actually "rather thin on the ground," having eighteen miles of frontage and the task of holding the key terrain features of the Ruweisat and Alam Halfa Ridges against German attack. Most Eighth Army commanders and staffs, including Horrocks's predecessor, "Strafer" Gott, anticipated that Rommel would attack in the south, "with ALAM EL HALFA as his first objective ... subsequently cutting the road in the HAMMAN area and thrusting straight for Alexandria."[65] Horrocks had to hold the vital ground of Alam Halfa Ridge, which dominated both the northern axis along the desert road to Alexandria and the open approach along the barrel track to the south. And he had to do it "without getting unduly mauled in the process."[66] That was how Montgomery put it. By that he meant that Horrocks was not to lose too many tanks, because they would be needed for the October offensive.

Montgomery had given his newly arrived subordinate a difficult task, tactically and psychologically. He had to stop Rommel and he had to convince his troops that he, and they, could do it. Intelligence reports anticipated that Rommel would almost certainly attack with his Deutsches Afrika Korps (DAK) and 90th Light Division through the lightly held gap between Alam Nayil to the left of the 2nd New Zealand Division and the Qattara Depression. Once through the gap, Rommel would either swing long and left to envelop the key terrain at the Alam Halfa Ridge, or turn sharply left and drive directly at the ridge, which would be a threat to his left flank if he wanted to drive on to Alexandria. Because of Rommel's critical fuel shortage, Horrocks and the intelligence analysts believed the second course of action to be the more likely. In very simple terms, Horrocks planned to draw Rommel into a big bowl then shoot him up with tanks, anti-tank guns, artillery, and the Desert Air Force.

Some controversy surrounds who deserves credit for the Alam Halfa battle plan. In *The Desert Generals,* Corelli Barnett argues that Horrocks and Montgomery simply "adopted" the plan developed by Gott and Auchinleck.[67] This is simply not true.[68] Having the same battle positions did not equate to fighting in the same manner. Horrocks and Montgomery fought a very different battle from the one envisioned by Gott and Auchinleck. It is true that Gott had previously identified that his best course of action in the short term was to "lure the enemy out in front of the minefields to fight on ground disadvantageous to him."[69] Gott had also designated the Alam Halfa Ridge as vital both to holding the current position and to preventing any enemy advance towards Alexandria. After Gott's death in a plane crash on 7 August, the 13th Corps staff, and Gott's temporary successor, Lieutenant-General Bernard Freyberg, refined this concept of operations over the course of two weeks. By the time Horrocks arrived, the plan had been developed such that the 7th Armoured Division (less the 22nd Armoured Brigade) would fight a delay battle, drawing the enemy into the killing zone south of Alam Halfa, then take up positions backstopping the eastern end of the bowl, while the 2nd New Zealand Division held the Alam Nayil position in force. The 22nd Armoured Brigade and a battery of anti-tank guns would occupy a defensive position at Point 102, the southwestern extremity of the Alam Halfa position, "from which to fight and manoeuvre as directed by the Corps Commander."[70] This was merely a framework – nothing more – for the battle that Montgomery and Horrocks eventually fought.[71]

Montgomery and Horrocks both committed themselves to holding the vital ground, but they were far less willing to risk losing tanks. One day after his arrival in the desert, Montgomery ordered the 44th (Home Counties) Division out of Cairo to occupy the Alam Halfa Ridge with two brigades, while the third brigade would bolster the 2nd New Zealand Division defences. Auchinleck had been reluctant to commit the newly arrived 44th Division to battle before it had undergone more training; oddly, neither he nor Gott had planned to occupy the vital ground at Alam Halfa in force. Montgomery did – immediately. Horrocks also changed the role of the 22nd Armoured Brigade. An order dated 14 August had tasked the brigade to "be prepared to seize any favourable opportunity to destroy any enemy main forces or their maintenance which penetrate East of the minefield."[72] When Horrocks arrived at 13th Corps, the 22nd Armoured Brigade "was practising these attacks."[73] As Brigadier Pip Roberts, the brigade commander, described it: "On code word 'so and so' we would move to a certain area with a specific task; on another code word we would move somewhere else, etc, etc ... the multiplicity of tasks as far as 22nd Armoured Brigade was concerned did not inspire the greatest confidence."[74] Horrocks would have none of it. The 22nd Armoured Brigade had, at that time, sixty Grant tanks – dubbed the E.L.H. (Egypt's Last Hope) by Eighth Army troops because they were the only thing nearly equal to the German Mark IIIs and Mark IVs – and Horrocks "hated the idea of committing them head-on against a superior number of German tanks estimated to be about 234."[75] He decided instead to fight a "purely defensive battle" and ordered Roberts to dig in his tanks on Point 102. This came as a relief to Roberts and his staff: "Gone were all the other plans and we gladly destroyed the mass of traces with different code names ... There was one firm plan and one position to occupy and we all felt better."[76] Horrocks would use the fire of the Grants to grind Rommel down during the defensive battle and save them for another day. To complete the plan, Horrocks also had the 10th Armoured Division, when it became available, take up the backstop position at the eastern end of the killing zone, and he arranged with Montgomery to have the 23rd Armoured Brigade move into the gap between the 2nd New Zealand Division and 22nd Armoured Brigade, should that become necessary.[77] With the bowl sealed, Horrocks could shoot up Rommel's troops with direct fire, indirect fire, and air attack. This was significantly different from the previous plan.

Now all Horrocks had to do was convince his soldiers they could win, and this was perhaps the more difficult undertaking. Rommel had driven them out of two successive defensive lines since June, forcing them to recoil some 250 miles to their current position at El Alamein. And a series of offensive moves in July had failed to recapture the initiative.[78] Putting those defeats out of their minds would be difficult, especially for a newcomer to the desert. Simplifying the plan helped. Montgomery's "no further withdrawal" set the right tone, but it was not so much the order itself as it was the accompanying actions that made an impact. It may be true that Auchinleck had intended to hold on to the El Alamein Line with a view to taking the offensive in several weeks' time, and it may be true that withdrawal plans to save the Eighth Army for the defence of the Middle Eastern Command east of the Nile were only prudent contingencies,[79] but it would take more than mere orders and discussions among generals to convince an army that had been on its heels for weeks that it could win. Montgomery was a great communicator, something that Auchinleck was not. In his first meeting with the Eighth Army Staff on 13 August, Monty directed that any orders for withdrawal be burned: "We would fight on the ground we now held, and if we couldn't stay there alive, we would stay there dead."[80] This, of course, was pure drama, but dramatic measures were necessary. He also backed up the drama with action. His decision to commit the yet-untested 44th Division to the Alam Halfa Ridge sent an even stronger message, which was this: we will hold here because we have to hold here; there is nothing left in Cairo.

Montgomery also visited all his units, wearing an Australian slouch hat on which he had pinned the cap badges of the Eighth Army's regiments, exuding confidence, explaining how he "would hit Rommel for six out of Africa," and making sure that as many people as possible set eyes on their new army commander. Auchinleck's troops had seen him standing on the side of the road as they retreated from Mersa Matruh to El Alamein.[81] The two images speak volumes – one of confidence and vigour, the other of exhaustion and impending defeat. Impressions mattered and Horrocks understood completely what Monty was trying to do:

There had grown up [in the Eighth Army] a Rommel myth. He was regarded by our troops as a sort of ubiquitous and invincible figure. Nobody realised better than Monty that almost the first and most important thing which he had to do was replace this feeling with a Montgomery fable ... Very soon the soldiers were discussing their strange new commander, who wore curious hats and, while buzzing about all over the place, constantly stopped and talked to them.[82]

Some veteran desert officers "were not particularly impressed with [the] self-assured, white-kneed export from Britain," but, by and large, the soldiers' re-action to Montgomery was favourable.[83] From the bottom up, Montgomery repaired the Eighth Army's confidence.

Horrocks worked at it too. On 19 August, he held a conference at which "he explained his plans for meeting any enemy offensive" to all lieutenant-colonels and above in his corps.[84] Explaining the alterations he had made to existing plans was important, but Horrocks's main aim was to make an impression on his subordinates – to project confidence. Succeeding the popular and competent Gott was a tough act, and Horrocks understandably sensed a "speculative look in people's eyes."[85] In some cases, it was more than speculation. The GOC 2nd New Zealand Division, Bernard Freyberg, senior even to Montgomery on the Army Lists, was peeved at being passed over by a brand new lieutenant-general for command of 13th Corps.[86] He had also been through several disastrous battles – in Greece, on Crete, and at Mersa Matruh, so his skepticism was understandable. Horrocks recalled that Freyberg questioned "every order I issued."[87] It may not have been clear to Horrocks at the time, but Freyberg was also exercising his right as the commander of a national contingent to question most orders issued him by the corps.[88] In addition, Freyberg and his New Zealanders were not alone in their "most intense distrust, almost hatred" of British armour, which they believed had left them stranded too many times in the past, and the chain of command that had allowed it to happen.[89] The GOC 7th Armoured Division, Major-General J.M.L. Renton, also openly questioned both Horrocks and Montgomery about their plan to dig in the tanks of the 22nd Armoured Brigade and fight a static battle.[90] Montgomery responded by detaching the 22nd Armoured Brigade from Renton's division and placing it under Headquarters 13th Corps, where he could ensure that the tanks would be used as he intended.[91] Horrocks later placed the brigade under the control of the very experienced Major-General Alec Gatehouse, GOC 10th Armoured Division, whose headquarters was immediately adjacent to his own. Naturally, this arrangement led to some "annoyance" in the 7th Armoured Division.[92]

The conference of 19 August was a first step in redressing the mistrust. Horrocks strode onto the Alam Halfa stage without speaking notes and beaming confidence. He smiled. He spoke clearly. He gestured deliberately. And he explained a simple plan in simple terms. As one 13th Corps staff officer testified: "He gave us a taste of what became the famous Horrocks oratory. Enormous confidence, dynamic and forceful delivery and great charm and manner ... We lapped it up and I for one went away feeling a lot better."[93] Brigadier Howard Kippenberger of the 5th New Zealand Brigade felt much the same way: "The whole plan for the battle was thoroughly explained to us and I liked it more than that for any action I had taken part in. More pleasing than the plan was the ready, balanced feeling that we all had." Even Freyberg, whose resentment never fully dissipated, liked what he heard. He particularly appreciated that his division would fight as a division – and not in isolated brigade groups as it had done under the previous regime – but he also described Horrocks as being "full of optimism."[94] At the very least, Freyberg was confident in this battle plan.

Indeed, confidence was one of the first points Horrocks emphasized in his "Personal Memorandum From Com[man]d[er] 13 Corps," which he sent to his divisional commanders on 23 August: "The importance of this battle and the way we propose to fight it should be explained to all ranks throughout the corps. This is vital. We have a good plan with every chance of success and provided the men realize this they will fight with confidence and intelligence ... We are one corps with complete confidence in each other."[95] Getting this message out to every soldier in the corps would require the full effort of the chain of command, which Horrocks enlisted: "Inspiration comes from officers and officers must assemble their men and talk to them." To underline his own assuredness that the coming battle would go the Eighth Army way, he reminded his divisional commanders "that there is no withdrawal from this area – we fight it out here. So no plans will be prepared for the destruction of water points or dumps of material."[96] It was one thing to say that the corps would fight "to the last man and the last round";[97] it was another to back it up with action that left little choice but to do exactly that. Horrocks also understood that training and repetition underpinned confidence, so he arranged for two exercises, one on 22 August and one on 28 August, to rehearse the defensive battle and fine-tune the plan.[98] He did everything he could to expunge doubt.

This was when he needed his acting skills most, to cloak his insecurities and convey confidence. Who would not have been nervous? A new corps commander, fighting his first formation-level battle, fighting it with a corps that had been in combat for nearly three years, fighting it with senior commanders who resented him as an inexperienced newcomer from England, and fighting against an enemy many believed unbeatable: this was an incredible test of fortitude and skill. But he did manage to veil his anxiety, even after the start of the battle. When Rommel finally attacked in force after dark on 30 August, Horrocks entered his headquarters to discover that the battle was shaping up very much as anticipated:

> For me this was the most exciting period of my life, my first corps battle, and I would have given anything to have stayed there and watched the battle develop on the operations map. But I had already learned one lesson, the value of sleep. The plans were all made. There was nothing I could possibly do that night, and it wouldn't be a very good example to my staff if the corps commander kept fussing round all night ... So assuming a nonchalant air which I certainly didn't feel I said good night and walked over to the small hole in the sand where my valise awaited me. I didn't expect to sleep very much, but I had quite a good night's rest.[99]

It was precisely the performance his audience at the headquarters required.

When Horrocks walked back into his headquarters the next morning, as nonchalantly as he had left it, he found, much to his relief, that it was "one of the few battles from my point of view that went according to plan."[100] Horrocks's nerves betrayed him briefly when he got into a bit of "an acrimonious conversation" with Renton about the amount of delay his brigades had imposed.[101] Renton believed that he had sufficiently slowed the advancing enemy and worried that his 7th Motor Brigade would be cut off as Rommel pushed back 4th Light Armoured Brigade in the south. Without asking Horrocks, he ordered both his brigades back to their fallback position at the eastern end of the Ragil Depression. Horrocks thought that the withdrawal had happened too quickly. He wanted more delay. So did Freyberg, who believed that the southeastern corner of his position was now vulnerable as a result of the rapid withdrawal of the 7th Motor Brigade.[102] A longer delay would have forced the enemy to burn even more fuel and exposed his administrative echelon vehicles to air attack when they came forward to refuel and replenish. Annoyed, Horrocks ordered Renton to send a squadron of Crusader tanks back to the area just south of the 2nd New Zealand Division position. Whether Horrocks was right in this particular dispute matters less, for this discussion, than the fact that the new corps commander momentarily lost his composure, something he surely regretted.

That slip-up aside, the battle still unfolded as predicted. By 1100 hours, Horrocks's staff had identified the vehicles of the 15th Panzer Division and 21st Panzer Division of the Deutsches Afrika Korps, which had breached the minefields and were now approximately eight to ten miles south and southwest of Point 102. Getting there had not been easy for the Germans either. While they were delayed west of the minefields, the 7th Armoured Division and the Desert Air Force had pounded the DAK, wounding the corps commander,

Major-General Walther Nehring, and killing the commander of the 21st Panzer Division, Major-General George von Bismarck.[103] With 200-plus enemy tanks south of the gap between the 2nd New Zealand Division and the 22nd Armoured Brigade, Horrocks "telephoned General Montgomery and asked him to release the 23rd Arm[oure]d B[riga]de."[104] Monty kept three squadrons of tanks in the 30th Corps sector, but he released the remainder of the brigade to Horrocks, who in turn sent 100 Valentine tanks to pre-dug tank run-up positions between the 2nd New Zealand Division and the ninety-two Grants of the 22nd Armoured Brigade. He now "felt reasonably confident of the outcome of the battle as all my armour was well positioned to defend the ground vital to the defence – Alam el Halfa."[105]

With the enemy thus contained in the bowl, it remained only to keep him there and to kill as many Germans as possible. At midday on 31 August, the DAK had halted to refuel, but Rommel's intentions were still unclear. Would he continue to the east and try to take the Alam Halfa position from behind? Or would he turn left and drive north, straight at the Alam Halfa position? An afternoon dust storm prevented the Desert Air Force from engaging Rommel's tanks. It also obscured the enemy from view and prevented Horrocks and the rest of 13th Corps from divining his intentions, so Roberts deployed two of his light squadrons "up to five miles south and south-west" of Point 102 to regain contact with the advancing enemy. At 1530, the squadrons reported a "strong force of enemy tanks" moving northeast.[106] For a while, it looked as though Rommel might be executing the long envelopment, and Roberts relayed the reports to Gatehouse and Horrocks, who were sitting next to each other. Concerned that the enemy would bypass Point 102 and possibly encircle Alam Halfa Ridge from the east, Gatehouse warned Roberts: "I don't want you to think we are in a blue funk here or anything like that, but if these fellows [the DAK] continue on as they are doing you will have to come out and hit them in the flank."[107] Roberts issued warning orders to two of his regiments to execute such a flank attack, but it proved unnecessary, as Horrocks recalled: "The critical point in the battle came at about [1745] on the 31st August when they delivered their initial attack on the 22nd Arm[oure]d B[riga]de."[108] By then, the DAK tanks had halted their eastern advance, turned north, and started advancing slowly on Point 102 and the Alam Halfa Ridge. Sometime around 1900, they collided with Roberts's tanks and anti-tank guns, all of which had held their fire until the enemy was well within 1,000 yards. The Germans managed one breach in the brigade's defences, but Roberts held them off by calling in the artillery fire of all available guns and repositioning his depth regiment to plug the gap. Before last light, his troops had destroyed a total of twenty-four German tanks while sustaining seventeen tank casualties of their own.[109] With darkness blanketing the battlefield, the DAK limped its way to the Ragil Depression, where the Desert Air Force bombarded tanks and motor transport. These incessant attacks also had the added benefit of subjecting DAK soldiers to their second sleepless night in a row. All British arms were doing their part and Horrocks was pleased – and relieved: "This fateful day, 31st August, had gone well for us and the crisis was over."[110]

That did not mean he could relax, however. Horrocks knew Rommel would not give up that easily and he still had to hold his position "without getting unduly mauled." He ordered Gatehouse to bring the 8th Armoured Brigade forward from the east so that it would make contact with the 22nd Armoured Brigade's left flank, close the bowl further, and "block the wide encircling movement, the other alternative Rommel might adopt."[111] The 4th Light Armoured Brigade in the south continued to harass the enemy. Its Stuart and Crusader tanks may not have been capable of killing the German Mark IIIs or Mark IVs, but they were "excellent for shooting up German soft vehicles" and fuel trucks, which they did.[112] The morning after the initial assault of 31 August, Horrocks visited Roberts at Point 102, to get a better appreciation for the battle at the main point of enemy attack and also to assure Roberts that, despite his seventeen tank casualties from the previous day's fighting, all was well. While enduring the insult of a shelling by British 25-pounders that the Germans had captured earlier in the summer, he advised Roberts of all the latest friendly moves to seal the bowl, assuring the young brigadier that "Monty [had] the whole thing in hand."[113] Neither the shelling nor the gravity of this decisive battle put the actor off his game. Commenting on the effect of the visit, Roberts remembered that Horrocks had "that wonderful knack of inspiring confidence and enthusiasm, wherever he [went], and the raised morale he [left] behind quickly [spread] to those he [had] not even seen." Roberts still had a fight on his hands though. Because the 8th Armoured Brigade had slammed into a German anti-armour screen before it could reach the left flank of his brigade, the 15th Panzer Division was able to mount an attack against his easternmost positions. This was the most Rommel could muster due to critical fuel shortages. The attack failed. With an uncertain supply of fuel, with no hope of breaking through the enemy defences before Montgomery or Horrocks could counter him, and with the moral and physical effects of aerial bombardment taking their toll on his troops, Rommel decided late on 1 September to break off offensive operations.[114] The following day, he gave orders for a phased withdrawal back to positions west of the minefields. Roberts had done the job expected of him.

Other subordinates proved more like Renton, questioning and less cordial. On 1 September, Montgomery ordered Horrocks to attack southward with the 2nd New Zealand Division, from Alam Nayil, to the depression at Deir el

Munassib, and then to Qaret el Himeimat. This would cut Rommel's lines of communication, but arranging the manoeuvre was not as simple as passing an order to Freyberg, who was not one to remain reticent when he harboured objections.[115] Freyberg believed that removing troops from his intricately connected defensive position would surely affect the ability of the New Zealanders to defend against the enemy now poised to the west and east of his position. When Freyberg suggested that all he could spare for the attack was a battalion group, Horrocks asked him to consider that the advance should be conducted by at least one of the two New Zealand brigades. To allay Freyberg's concerns, he promised another infantry brigade – the 5th Indian Brigade – and some armoured support. Loath to remove his troops from their current task – in fact, loath to conduct the attack at all because he had been caught in the open against Rommel's tanks only a month earlier[116] – Freyberg proposed that the 5th Indian Brigade be used for the attack. This was definitely not what either Montgomery or Horrocks had intended, however. They had agreed to give Freyberg the 5th Indian Brigade so that he might free up one of his experienced New Zealand Brigades for the assault. Freyberg knew this, and it is difficult to escape the conclusion that he was simply playing dumb at this stage, which must have been trying for Horrocks. The corps commander maintained his composure, however, and continued to work through the problem. After conferring with his brigadiers on 2 September, Freyberg suggested that the assault be conducted by at least two brigades – a sensible suggestion given that a single brigade advance would have produced a narrow three-mile salient, vulnerable to counterattack by German armour. Horrocks agreed with the rationale, although he originally objected to the use of the 132nd Brigade, newly arrived and detached from the 44th (Home Counties) Division, because he was uneasy about the untested formation's ability to conduct offensive operations. After some discussion, Horrocks acceded to Freyberg's proposal on the grounds that leaving the 132nd out of the attack would have complicated greatly the number of reliefs-in-place that had to be conducted.[117]

Unfortunately, the corps commander's original misgivings about the 132nd Brigade proved justified. While the 5th New Zealand Brigade managed to capture its first-phase objectives on the night of 3-4 September, the 132nd Brigade crossed the start line an hour late, failed to reach its first objectives some two miles south of Alam Nayil, and suffered a staggering 697 casualties.[118] The attacks having failed in the face of vicious German resistance and counterattacks, Freyberg recommended the withdrawal of both brigades, lest the 5th New Zealand Brigade remain isolated and stranded. His much-irritated corps commander agreed. Horrocks made no mention of his difficulties with Freyberg in his memoir – he was too much of a gentleman for that – but, to an official historian, he did express some personal regret that he had given in on the 132nd Brigade attack:

> My only regret about this battle was the comparatively severe losses incurred by the 132nd Inf Bde when they carried out their attack under the orders of the 2nd New Zealand Division. I feel now, looking back, that this was rather an ambitious attack for a brigade which had just arrived in the desert ... I would much rather have been able to give them an easier battle as their first experience of war in the desert.[119]

The attack may have been costly and it may not have closed the gap behind Rommel, but it did harry him. Spooked at the prospect of having his fighting echelon severed from its administrative tail, Rommel quickened his withdrawal and repositioned his forces more or less to where they had been before he had started his assault. The "Six Days' Race," as the Germans called it, was over by 5 September.

Alam Halfa had been a good battle – for the Eighth Army, for the new army commander, and for Horrocks too. The army that had fought in the bits and pieces it called brigade group "boxes" only to be trounced by Rommel had finally stopped the unstoppable general. It was not that Montgomery had a material advantage on the battlefield; it was more a matter of using all of his arms intelligently and to their best advantage in a well-orchestrated army defensive battle. Montgomery certainly did not have an advantage in tanks. He may have had over 400 tanks of various models and makes, but only the 152 Grants, with their 75-millimetre guns, were a match for Rommel's 203 Panzer Mark IIIs and Mark IVs; and the Grants were handicapped by their high silhouette and limited ability to traverse their main armament, which was mounted in the hull of the tank, not in the turret. Letting Rommel impale himself on the fire of the Grants and their supporting anti-tank guns was the right thing to do. Of the 18 Grants destroyed in the battle, only 5 were lost on the 22nd Armoured Brigade position where they were dug in, while 13 were lost in the open with the 8th Armoured Brigade.[120] Montgomery took a longer view of the campaign, so saving the Grants was important. He also needed time to build up his formations and train them for offensive operations, especially since he would be integrating reinforcements and new equipment. The shipping situation also favoured the Allies and a cautious approach in the short term. In August and September, the Middle East Command received 1,027 tanks from the United Kingdom and North America, many of which were the new Shermans.[121] In the meantime, the Stuarts and Crusaders, even though they could not kill Rommel's panzers, were not useless. The 7th Armoured Division in the south, augmented with anti-tank guns, forced

Rommel to burn precious fuel (even idling tanks consume petrol), and they exacted a toll on the administrative "tail" of Rommel's formations once the "teeth" had gone past. Stringing Rommel's fighting formations out over twenty-five miles not only exposed static or slow-moving German administrative vehicles to ground attack, it also set them up for air-to-ground attack by the Desert Air Force as they slinked along the limited roads and barrel tracks.[122] Montgomery's decision to co-locate his headquarters with that of the Desert Air Force meant closer coordination of target air reconnaissance, target acquisitions, and engagements. Using all the resources at his disposal, Montgomery held the El Alamein Line, inflicted 2,910 personnel casualties on the German-Italian forces, and destroyed or damaged 55 guns, 49 tanks, and 385 other vehicles.[123] His casualties, by comparison, amounted to 18 tanks destroyed and 1,750 troops killed, wounded, or captured, the key difference being that his numbers were increasing while Rommel's were not.

In all of this, Horrocks supported his army commander completely and successfully. He stopped Rommel as he said he would do, despite some difficulties with subordinate commanders, and without getting "unduly mauled" in the process. The win at Alam Halfa also helped Horrocks shake the stigma of the pale-faced "new boy" with the desert veterans. One of his corps staff officers recalled that Horrocks had proven himself to be "wonderful ... first-class. We were all very fond of him and thought he was doing a great job."[124] Some of the old desert sweats would take longer to convince. The future general Sir John Hackett was one of them. He remembered how, after the battle, Horrocks travelled around the corps to explain what had happened: "Horrocks came up, out of the blue in a staff car, out of the dust, with an ADC in front with a blackboard ... He explained how *he* won the battle of Alam Halfa!"[125] Horrocks must have sensed some of this lingering resentment, but, with a significant victory under his belt, he did not let it bother him. One of his first moves after the battle was to fire Renton and replace him with the very competent John Harding.[126]

In the next three months, though, he and his corps played only a minor role in the Eighth Army battles, a fate he owed to an earlier decision. When he arrived in the desert on 15 August, Montgomery had offered him command of his *corps de chasse,* which was just beginning to form at that time. Designed for the pursuit phase of the campaign and modelled on Rommel's DAK, it was to consist of two armoured divisions and the motorized 2nd New Zealand Division. Horrocks thought the armoured *corps de chasse* a good idea, but he also thought himself all wrong as its commander, and he told Montgomery so. Horrocks explained his objection: "It was most unlikely that an infantryman straight from home would be welcomed by the cavalry and tank corps formations which formed the hard core of his mobile force. It would take some time to break down their prejudices."[127] He was right about the cavalry and the tank corps – he had experienced something similar as an infantryman walking into the 9th Armoured Division – and he had probably sensed that the same cool response would be forthcoming from Freyberg, although he did not mention it specifically. At any rate, in the days before Alam Halfa, he was not yet confident enough to command an armoured corps. Montgomery accepted his rationale for not wanting the appointment and nominated instead Lieutenant-General Herbert Lumsden to command 10th Corps.[128] This meant Horrocks played only a minor role during Montgomery's Battle of El Alamein in October and November and no role in the pursuit battle that followed the breakthrough of Operation Supercharge. As Oliver Leese's 30th Corps and Lumsden's 10th Corps advanced on Tripoli, "poor old 13 Corps became the 8th Army's Mrs. Mopp, left behind with the unpleasant task of cleaning up the battlefield of Alamein."[129] Horrocks considered this period his "lowest ebb as a corps commander."[130]

His personal fortunes changed early in December when Montgomery asked him, again, to take command of 10th Corps in replacement of Lumsden. Montgomery had formed the opinion that "command of a corps in a major battle was above Lumsden's ceiling."[131] He also found Lumsden too much one of the old regime generals who "had their own ideas about operations in the desert, and had not liked a firm grip from above."[132] Horrocks, on the other hand, could be counted on to work within the army commander's intent, as he had done at Alam Halfa. This time Horrocks leapt at the chance to command 10th Corps. The victory of Alam Halfa and more than a month of boredom following the Battle of El Alamein had submerged whatever insecurities he had harboured in August, and Horrocks took command of 10th Corps on 9 December.[133]

He fought that formation well, but not without difficulties, not least of which was having to deal with an aggrieved Bernard Freyberg. During the battle of the Mareth Line, Horrocks's 10th Corps was the reserve formation for an attack in which Oliver Leese's 30th Corps would execute the main assault through the enemy defences while Freyberg's New Zealand Corps threatened to envelop the southern flank of the defences. But when the 50th (Northumbrian) Division's attack in Leese's northern sector failed on 23 March, Montgomery decided to switch the main effort to the south, where Horrocks was to take the entire New Zealand corps *under his command*. After months of "Mrs. Mopp" and second fiddle, Horrocks was exhilarated by the enterprise – Montgomery's Chief of Staff, Freddie de Guingand, less so, as he explained to a visibly energized Horrocks: "It's all right you going off like a dog with six tails, but I am a little worried about your reception. The New Zealand corps has done all the hard fighting, now you are going to arrive at the last moment, take over the whole show and carry out a spectacular victory. I cannot see you receiving a very warm welcome, and we don't want the attack messed up by friction."[134] Given pause, and thinking back to the cool reception he had received from Freyberg in August, Horrocks realized that de Guingand was right. He suggested that any direction from the Eighth Army should be addressed jointly to the two corps commanders, as though they were co-commanders, despite the fact that the "N[ew] Z[ealand] Corps came under com[man]d 10 Corps at 1830 hrs on 25 March."[135] De Guingand followed Horrocks's tack by playfully addressing the "co-commanders" as Hindenberg and Ludendorff. Still, as anticipated, when Horrocks and his small Tactical Headquarters pulled into the Main Headquarters of the New Zealand Corps, "it was quite obvious that General Freiberg [sic] was not at all pleased" to see him.[136] More tact was required. Horrocks "explained that there was no question of my being sent around to run the New Zealand attack; the main reason was that the number of troops now involved in this left hook was more than one divisional headquarters could handle. It was my corps H.Q. rather than me that was required there."[137] This was not an empty attempt to patronize. There was much truth in what Horrocks said. The New Zealand Corps, although it had under command its own two brigades, Philippe Leclerc's "L" Force (a division-sized organization) and the 8th Armoured Brigade, was a corps in name only because its headquarters was still division-sized and it had none of the supporting corps troops. Horrocks's 10th Corps Headquarters had a full staff complement, enough to man fully the Main, Rear, and Tactical Headquarters.

In spite of the friction that Freddie de Guingand had predicted, Horrocks and Freyberg planned the breakthrough based on a sensible division of responsibilities. Freyberg looked after the infantry break-in battle, while Horrocks focused on dashing through whatever hole Freyberg managed to make. Because it was better equipped and better staffed, 10th Corps Headquarters coordinated the air and artillery support for the operation. Freyberg still had his doubts about British armour, however: "If we punch a hole will the tanks really go through?" Horrocks, despite the normal apprehensions and what turned out to be "the most worrying night of [his] life," had the perfect answer: "Yes they will, and I am going with them myself."[138] Freyberg, who had won a Victoria Cross on the Somme in 1916, had to have appreciated that. It was not the clearest chain of command in the history of warfare, but it suited the situation. At 1600 hours on 26 March, following low-level attacks by the Desert Air Force, Freyberg's troops advanced behind an artillery barrage, took their objectives, and made a hole.[139] By 1800 hours, the tanks of the 2nd Armoured Brigade, followed by Horrocks in his little Tactical Headquarters sped through the opening that Freyberg had drilled in the German defences. With British and New Zealand forces breaking through behind them, the defenders had little choice but to withdraw hastily from the Mareth Line, which they did. Horrocks had handled a sticky interpersonal situation with grace.

He showed some ingenuity and technical know-how as well. Three days after his arrival at 10th Corps, he announced his intention to reorganize the headquarters.[140] With the assistance of his Brigadier General Staff (BGS), Brigadier R. Peake, and his Deputy Adjutant and Quartermaster General (DA & QMG), Brigadier George Webb, he subdivided Main and Rear Headquarters such that they moved only the minimum necessary components when managing a mobile battle. In the new structure, the Main Headquarters would be capable of "throwing off" a Commander's Reconnaissance Group (Commander's Recce) and a Main Echelon. Horrocks rejected the idea of a semi-permanent Tactical Headquarters as essentially "unsound and dangerous" because it was too remote from the Main Headquarters, where the bulk of the staff action took place, and vulnerable due to its isolation.[141] He instituted instead the Commander's Recce, which was "intended only to enable the Com[man]d[er] to move [for]w[ar]d to gain personal contact with lower formations, to see things for himself or to take hold on the spot at a critical time." The Commander's Recce (Horrocks would later revert to calling it a Tactical Headquarters, or "Tac") usually consisted of the Commander; the Commander, Corps Royal Artillery (CCRA); a General Staff Officer Second Grade (GSO 2); and an aide-de-camp; plus a few drivers, gunners, and batmen, who were ferried around in either three tanks or two armoured cars and a station wagon.[142] On occasion, Horrocks even went forward of battalion headquarters to "smell the battlefield," something that would have been impossible with a full-blown Tactical Headquarters of ten vehicles or so. These forays forward "up with the leading troops" gave him a greater appreciation for the battle and helped him to make decisions faster; and fast command decisions were critical to a higher tempo of operations. His appearances near the forward edge of the battle area also "had a tremendous effect" on the troops who were "quite surprised to see a corps commander actually up at the front with us."[143] Still, the hub for control of 10th Corps formations was Main Headquarters, so the Commander's Recce, as a rule, returned every evening. Not that Horrocks's Main Headquarters would be far behind the fighting; by shedding itself of a Main Echelon, those vehicles and personnel "not immediately necessary for the conduct of operations," it could venture "right forward." At times, a Main Headquarters consisting of only the BGS, the "G" (operations and intelligence) staff, the corps artillery and engineers staffs, and the necessary signals personnel could be "just outside enemy MMG [medium machine gun] fire." Rear Headquarters consisted of "A" and "Q" staffs (personnel, administration, and logistics staffs), plus supporting signals troops, and remained well behind Main Headquarters, preferably close to road hubs.

If need be, it could detach an Administration Post of staff and services "not immediately required at Rear HQ," but it was still well behind Main Headquarters.

Good standard operating procedures (SOPs) enabled the headquarters to move quickly and function effectively. Brigadier Guy Simonds observed two moves by 10th Corps Main Headquarters during a two-day visit in April 1943. In the course of one particular move, he noted with some surprise how the headquarters was able to tear down with as little as 40 minutes' notice then be "ready to operate with inter-office communications and messes ... within 30 min[ute]s of reaching the new site."[144] This would not have been possible without standard layouts for the various components of the headquarters and well-practised drills. "The general impression," as Simonds noted, "was that every officer and man knew what to do in each situation, and went about his business quickly and efficiently."[145] Horrocks also stuck to the Eighth Army convention of issuing verbal orders, when possible, to speed up battle procedure. Again, however, verbal orders and short bits of direction "on the fly" would have amounted to nothing had it not been for well-established operating procedures, something that Montgomery preached and Horrocks reinforced.

There were still some tense times with subordinate commanders and even Montgomery. Before departing for a three-day Allied planning conference for the invasion of Sicily, on 22 April Montgomery directed Horrocks to develop a plan for breaking through to Tunis "by a strong attack up the coastal plain."[146] Horrocks, whose corps had just engaged in very tough hill fighting at Enfidaville, did not relish the prospect. Neither did two of his divisional commanders, Bernard Freyberg and Francis Tuker, who commanded the 4th Indian Division. Freyberg had been difficult in the past, as we have seen, and was so again north of Enfidaville. Tuker, an Indian Army officer who had been commanding his division since December 1941, had no time for the new crowd under Montgomery, including Horrocks. He thought Montgomery's tactics pedestrian, and blamed him "and his colleagues – the Horrockses and Leeses" – for not properly training the troops and formations that had been sent to the desert during the first two years of the campaign.[147] Neither Freyberg nor Tuker had any difficulty telling Horrocks that they "hated the idea of attacking up the coastal funnel" against strong enemy opposition. Considering that the end of the campaign was so near and the fact that the main push on Tunis was supposed to come from the First Army front in the west, they felt they could not justify the very high casualties that were certain to result.[148] The trouble was that Horrocks agreed with them. He "hated the idea of blunting" those divisions in what he imagined would be a costly attack. Too vivid an image of what could go wrong wore on his nerves at times like these. But planning had to continue, despite the misgivings he shared with his subordinates, and he determined that "on no account must I show anyone what I felt." The exception to that rule was Montgomery. When the army commander returned from Cairo a few days later, Horrocks raised the concerns he shared with his two divisional commanders. Montgomery was annoyed that 10th Corps had not made much progress and accused Horrocks of "belly-aching, a favourite Montgomery expression when a subordinate disagreed."[149] Horrocks retorted, "Of course we can break through, but there won't be much left of your fine 8th Army when we have done it. Why can't we make an attack on the 1st Army Front where the terrain is more suitable for a break through than it is here?" Montgomery gave no immediate answer, but a few days later the plan changed. The main thrust into Tunis would take place on the First Army front and Horrocks would lead it in temporary command of 9th Corps, where he replaced a wounded John Crocker.[150] For the attack, he brought with him from the Eighth Army the 7th Armoured Division, the 201st Guards Motor Brigade, and Tuker's 4th Indian Division. Tunis fell on 6 May.

But Horrocks's days in the Mediterranean were numbered. When he returned to 10th Corps, he occupied himself with preparations for an amphibious assault on beaches at Salerno. For this operation, he was to be under the command of the American General Mark Clark, Commander Fifth (US) Army. Horrocks immersed himself in the intricate planning for the assault, which he found excruciating – the sequencing of the assault, the cross-loading of troops and stores, and the timings. In *A Full Life,* he hinted at how closely he supervised the preparations when he described the loading tables for troops and stores as his "undoing."[151] He never did get to see the execution of Operation Avalanche in September 1943. On 17 August, while he was watching an amphibious assault rehearsal by the 46th Infantry Division at Bizerta, a lone German fighter strafed the beaches below.[152] Horrocks was hit, the only one hit, and wounded for the second time in his career. The wounds were serious, the round drilling through the top of his chest, smashing through his abdomen, and leaving an exit hole near the bottom of his spine. He required emergency surgery to patch the worst of the wounds, and he would need no less than five more abdominal surgeries, later in England, to repair the extensive damage. In all, Horrocks was invalided for nearly fourteen months, a period in which he became, as he described it, a "sort of tame parrot," with whom nurses and a succession of other visitors came to chat and joke around.[153] In the spring of 1944, Horrocks visited Montgomery at his billet near St. Paul's School in London, in the hope that he could convince his mentor that he was ready for a return to active duty, but Montgomery took one look at the gaunt Horrocks and said, "You haven't recovered yet ... Go away and get fit. Then we shall see."[154]

The next time Horrocks saw Montgomery, it was early August 1944 and he was taking over 30th Corps, replacing Lieutenant-General "Jerry" Bucknall, whom Monty had sacked following the disappointment of Operation Bluecoat four days earlier. This was the fourth time Horrocks would go through the painful process of taking over a corps, and he wondered if it would be as challenging as when he had taken command of 13th Corps in the desert. Montgomery looked Horrocks up and down, checking for signs of frailty or weakness, but he could see no obvious sign that "Jorrocks," as Montgomery called him, was anything but fit for battle.[155] He briefed Horrocks on the situation in the Allied bridgehead – how the American breakout in the west was well underway and how the British Second Army and the First Canadian Army would assist that breakout with offensive operations designed to pin German armoured formations to the eastern bridgehead. Montgomery's "grip" of the situation reassured Horrocks, as it had done some two years earlier in North Africa. So did Monty's steadiness in the face of mounting criticism, both in the press and in some quarters of the Allied Expeditionary Force.[156]

Horrocks was understandably apprehensive, however: "Fourteen months was a long time to be out of action and many things would have changed. I felt rather out of touch. Moreover, all my friends must surely still be in the Middle East or Italy and I would be very much a stranger."[157] He was relieved to find that his Brigadier General Staff, Harold "Pete" Pyman, and his Brigadier Q (Quartermaster), George Webb, were both veterans of the campaign in the Western Desert; he knew them fairly well and, more importantly, they knew him. Pyman, known for his "preciseness and tidiness," had previously commanded the 3rd Battalion Royal Tank Regiment in the 7th Armoured Division and he had earlier been GSO 1 to the same division.[158] A very able officer, Pyman would rise to the rank of general and hold the appointments of Deputy Chief of the General Staff (1958-61) and Commander-in-Chief Allied Forces Northern Europe (1961-64). Webb had been DA & QMG under Horrocks in 10th Corps.[159] They knew their stuff. Horrocks considered himself "lucky" to have inherited probably "the most experienced H.Q. in the British Isles," and he later wrote Bucknall a very kind letter in which he gave his undoubtedly disappointed predecessor credit for creating such an efficient team: "There is no doubt that you handed me over a first-class show. I have never had such a staff in my life."[160] Because the corps was still clawing its way towards its Bluecoat objective of Mont Pinçon, Horrocks quickly got to know his staff and how it worked.

He also set about making his mark on the fighting units under him. Spending the first few days of his new command "rather like an American presidential candidate on a whistle-stop tour of the Corps," Horrocks spoke to his troops, gathering groups wherever he could find them and explaining, with the aid of a large map, how the battle was going and how it would go in the next few days. His audiences on the "whistle-stop tour" had been fighting in the miserable *bocage,* which gave all the advantages to the defender and made progress depressingly slow. They were tired and no doubt wondering whether there was any point to what they were doing. Horrocks understood the psychology of soldiers and what made them fight: "I have always made a practice of this ... because the modern soldier is much more intelligent than his grandfather, and probably than his father, who fought the First World War. In battle he is risking his most precious possession – his life – and he will only give of his best if he has confidence in his leaders and, above all, knows what is going on."[161]

He was absolutely right. One trooper in the 4th/7th Royal Dragoon Guards recalled that the "pep talk" was "great." The new corps commander gave them "an overall picture of what was happening ... [Horrocks] was known as a man's man."[162] These "pep talks" had a positive effect, especially with soldiers who knew him from the desert: "The lift of morale at seeing Horrocks again was absolutely terrific ... He congratulated us on what we had done during the Normandy Campaign ... [and] said he was glad he hadn't been there himself."[163] As one of the 43rd (Wessex) Division brigadiers noted, "his vivid and amusing description of General George Patton motoring through Brittany stirred the imagination of the troops."[164] His whistle-stops might not have had their intended effect if Mont Pinçon had not fallen to the 43rd (Wessex) Division, which it did on 6 August. Horrocks had no delusions that his presence had turned the battle – that was the result of some extremely difficult fighting that had been initiated before his arrival – but he did capitalize on his good fortune to be at the right place at the right time.

His reputation as a "motoring general" grew as a result of the actions he fought in the next few weeks.[165] After the defeat in Normandy, the enemy was disorganized and on his heels, a perfect time for taking risks and pressing the pursuit. Horrocks crossed the Seine with 43rd (Wessex) Division on 25 August and broke out of that bridgehead on 29 August with two armoured divisions and an armoured brigade, and dashed towards Brussels and Antwerp. Horrocks's corps would advance 400 kilometres in six days, a remarkable feat that would not have been possible without good drills and quick verbal orders. This did not mean *no* written orders, however. When on the move, Horrocks usually issued direction while he was forward visiting his divisional commanders. One of his staff officers, usually a GSO 2, would keep notes and later relate what was said to Pyman, who would send out confirmatory written orders, mostly for the benefit of staffs who had to initiate action in support of the various operations. This system kept command decisions and staff actions synchronized. For Operation Supercharge II (the advance from the Seine to Amiens on the Somme River), Pyman sent out a 5½-page confirmatory order; he later issued a concise 4-page order for Operation Sabot, the capture of Brussels and Antwerp.[166] With that guidance, the two advancing divisional commanders and their staffs drove ahead with their tasks, which they completed with considerable dash. Brussels fell to Major-General Allan Adair's Guards Armoured Division on 3 September, and the 11th Armoured Division, under Major-General Pip Roberts, captured the port of Antwerp intact on 4 September. The 30th Corps machine functioned well. Thus, two weeks later, when Montgomery planned a narrow thrust into Holland and over the Rhine to encircle the German industrial region of the Ruhr, Horrocks's 30th Corps seemed the logical choice to spearhead the advance.

The story of Operation Market Garden has been told many times elsewhere, so there is no need to repeat the details of the operation here.[167] A brief sketch will do. The plan was for Horrocks's 30th Corps to make an all-out 100-kilometre run into Holland to seize a bridgehead over the lower Rhine. This was the first step of encircling the strategic Ruhr valley. Getting there would not be easy. Horrocks would have to cross five rivers or canals, and he would have to do it using only one major road to keep the whole thing moving. To assist him in this unenviable task, an "airborne carpet" of three divisions – the 1st British, 101st US and 82nd US – would be dropped ahead of 30th Corps to seize key bridges intact. Ultimately, Market Garden failed. There were too many flaws in the plan for it to have worked: the airborne drops were spread over too long a period to achieve complete operational surprise; the 1st Airborne Division's drop zone was too far from its objective of Arnhem bridge; and moving an entire corps along one road proved almost impossible. On top of these difficulties, the German opposition, having recovered somewhat since the end of August, was not nearly so dispirited and disorganized as had been anticipated. Despite everything, Horrocks still managed to push his corps some 95 kilometres in nine days, no small accomplishment given the restrictions of his one road, one blown bridge, heavy opposition at every river or canal line, and continuous German counterattacks on his extended flanks. Not everyone thought so. Major-General Robert E. Urquhart, the GOC 1st Airborne Division, who was ultimately stranded at Arnhem, felt that "30 Corps were doing it in a relaxed way ... [they] never really picked it up. I don't think Horrocks was well ... I don't think he had the drive he had early on."[168] Urquhart's view is understandable; from his besieged position near Arnhem, everyone else and everything else would have looked "relaxed."

But Montgomery, who thought Market Garden a "partial success," believed that Horrocks had done well given the circumstances, and still held his subordinate in high esteem. In November 1944, he sought Horrocks's advice on how many divisions would be required to clear the Rhine's west bank to the River Meuse, from Nijmegen to Wesel.[169] This was the first that Horrocks had heard of Operation Veritable, and the evidence suggests that Montgomery intended that Horrocks would play a key part in the action that would set the stage for a full-blown crossing of the Rhine and a march into the heart of Germany. When the 21st Army Group staff studies precluded Dempsey's Second Army from executing the operation because it was too far south along the Meuse, and also too far from the intended start line near Groesbeek, Montgomery decided to place 30th Corps under General H.D.G. "Harry" Crerar's command for the operation.[170] This was a measure of Montgomery's confidence in Horrocks. He had to augment Crerar's army for the operation, but he could have chosen either Lieutenant-General Neil Ritchie's 12th Corps or Lieutenant-General Sir Richard O'Connor's 8th Corps. He chose neither. Instead, he went back to Horrocks, even though the 30th Corps commander had taken ill and had been ordered on bed rest by Montgomery himself for four days in August.

What neither Horrocks nor anyone else knew at the time was that the source of Horrocks's recurring illness was an "elongated stone ... [that had] formed round a piece of cloth which was evidently shot into his liver" when he was wounded at Bizerta.[171] The offending object, which would not be discovered until a seventh abdominal surgery in 1947, continued to plague Horrocks for the remainder of the campaign. His acting skills managed to mask his frail condition from just about everyone – except Montgomery, who saw through it. On 27 December, he wrote Brooke that Horrocks had become "nervy and difficult with his staff."[172] Before the start of Veritable, he even ordered Horrocks back to England for a week's rest: "I want you to go home and have a rest before the big battle I have in store for you."[173] Veritable was to be the biggest and arguably the most complex battle Horrocks ever fought.

It would also be the first time that Horrocks worked closely with the Canadians. If he had any apprehensions about working again with Dominion divisions under command, he never mentioned them. The situation was also different from when he had worked with the New Zealanders in the desert. Although he would have two Canadian divisions under command, Major-Generals Dan Spry and Bruce Matthews (commanding the 3rd Canadian and 2nd Canadian Infantry Divisions, respectively) really had no need to object to orders in the same way that Freyberg had done. Their army commander, General Crerar, was giving orders to Horrocks, and Horrocks got along well with Crerar, who he believed had "always been much underrated, largely because he was the exact opposite to Montgomery. [Crerar] hated publicity, but was full of common sense and always prepared to listen to the views of subordinate commanders."[174]

Horrocks also found that the administrative preparations between his head-quarters and the headquarters of the First Canadian Army "went very smoothly," which was a good thing because there was much to prepare.[175]

A number of factors complicated this operation, starting with the terrain (see Map 2). The Rhine on the left and the Meuse on the right forced the attackers into a funnel – sixteen kilometres wide at the start line near Groesbeek and widening to forty-eight kilometres near the end of the First Canadian Army objective area, between Wesel and Venlo. The German decision to flood the polder land of the west bank of the Rhine exacerbated matters by placing a third of the available manoeuvre space under water. Most of the towns and villages had been turned into strongpoints. The very large and elevated Reichswald forest sat squarely in the centre of Horrocks's battlefield, further hampering a high-speed advance. South of the Reichswald was more low-lying ground, with marshes, streams, and the occasional copse of trees. When Horrocks first surveyed the battlefield from a 2nd Canadian Infantry Division observation post near Groesbeek, he immediately identified the high ground at the Materborn gap, between the town of Cleve and the Reichswald, as the vital ground for this battle. If he could get there before the Germans could rush up reserves, he could break out into the plain beyond Cleve and use his tanks. If not, the Germans would "stuff" his advance and a costly slogging match would ensue.

The enemy would not make the race for Materborn easy. The Siegfried Line stretched across the Rhineland battlefield in three defensive belts, which First Canadian Army intelligence had well "taped," largely as a result of extensive aerial reconnaissance and patrols.[176] Immediately across the start line, an outpost line ran from Wyler to Gennep. The main defences, with minefields and an anti-tank ditch, extended from east of Kranenburg in the north, through the Reichswald to Hekkens, then it branched to both Gennep and Goch. These defences also extended in depth along the Nijmegen-Cleve road to Cleve then south to Goch. The depth or "layback" position was anchored on the Hochwald forest. Troops of the German 84th Division and the 2nd Parachute Regiment manned these positions with a total of eight battalions between them, while the 180th Division occupied positions along the Meuse, facing west. The First Canadian Army had a very good picture of where and how they were deployed, so Horrocks did not expect many surprises there. The greater concern was what the 86th Corps and the First Parachute Army could throw at the Reichswald, and how quickly. Although Anglo-Canadian intelligence sources had not detected elements of any other division in the immediate Reichswald area, they estimated that, in response to a crisis, the First Parachute Army and even the 25th Army could shift forces such that they could reinforce the Reichswald sector with one infantry division in a day, a panzergrenadier and a panzer division in two days, another panzergrenadier and panzer division in four days, and two extra infantry divisions in seven days.[177] Thus, within a week, the First Canadian Army could be facing nine enemy divisions in the constricted Rhineland battlefield. The 30th Corps battle would have to develop quickly.

There would also have to be a larger plan to fix German forces that might be redeployed to the Veritable area, and indeed there was. Veritable was just one prong in a two-pronged pincer operation by the 21st Army Group. Montgomery planned the enterprise such that two days after the First Canadian Army had initiated its attack to the southeast from Groesbeek, the US Ninth Army, under 21st Army Group command for this operation, would attack northeast from the area of the Roer River in the south. The two armies would meet in the area of Wesel, thereby offering the German defenders two options: fight an attrition battle in two directions on the west bank of the Rhine, or withdraw across the river. Montgomery hoped for the former. His directive of 21 January 1945 stated his intention "to destroy all enemy in the area west of the Rhine from the present forward positions south of Nijmegen as far south as the general line Julich-Dusseldorf, as a preliminary to crossing the Rhine and engaging the enemy in mobile war to the north of the Ruhr."[178] Four days later, he passed his plan for the operation to his army commanders.

Crerar intended to smash the Siegfried Line in three phases, based on the layout of the German defences and the terrain. In the first phase, 30th Corps, consisting of one armoured and six infantry divisions, would clear the Reichswald to a line that ran from Gennep to Cleve. The second phase would see the breaching of the enemy defences to roughly the line from Weeze to Emmerich. In this phase, 2nd Canadian Corps would be brought up on the left of 30th Corps to add more weight to the attack. The third and final phase would be the breaching of the Hochwald layback position, the main blow being delivered by 2nd Canadian Corps. Throughout the operation, John Crocker's 1st Corps, deployed along the Waal River north and west of Nijmegen, would do its best with raids and minor attacks to keep the enemy deceived as to army intentions.

In planning his portion, Horrocks recalled that, although it seemed a "perfectly straightforward plan," orchestrating the whole business was "not quite so easy as it looked."[179] Very early in the planning process, in mid-December, before the German Ardennes Offensive put Veritable planning on hold, Horrocks decided on a basic course of action: "The main principle of 'VERITABLE' is that 30 Corps will start with a heavy strike and will go on striking night and day until there is nothing left to strike."[180] That was the easy part. Coordinating fire support from artillery and air resources, allocating objectives, assembling the attacking divisions, dumping ammunition and stores, arranging for traffic

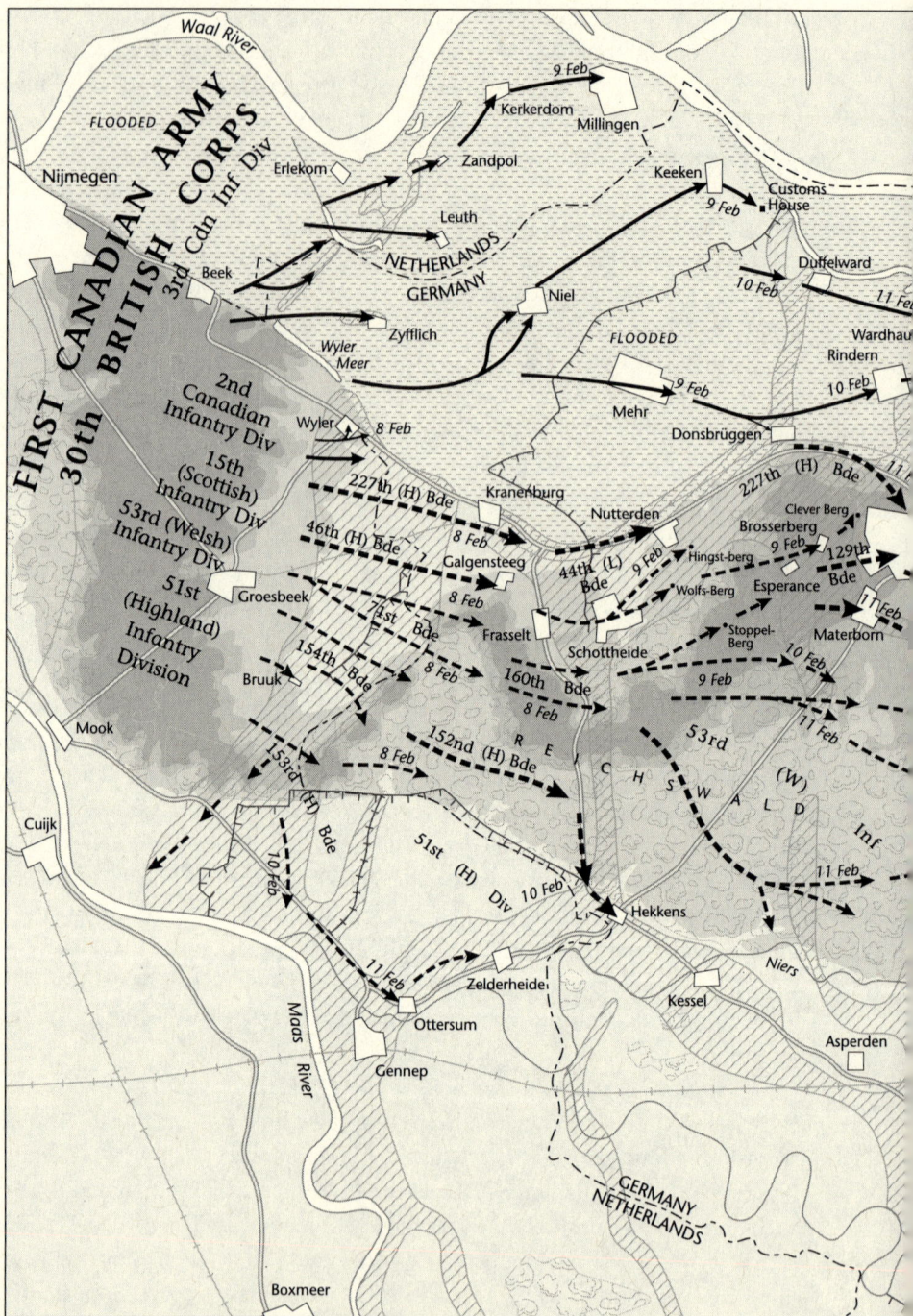

MAP 2   Operation Veritable, 8-14 February 1945.

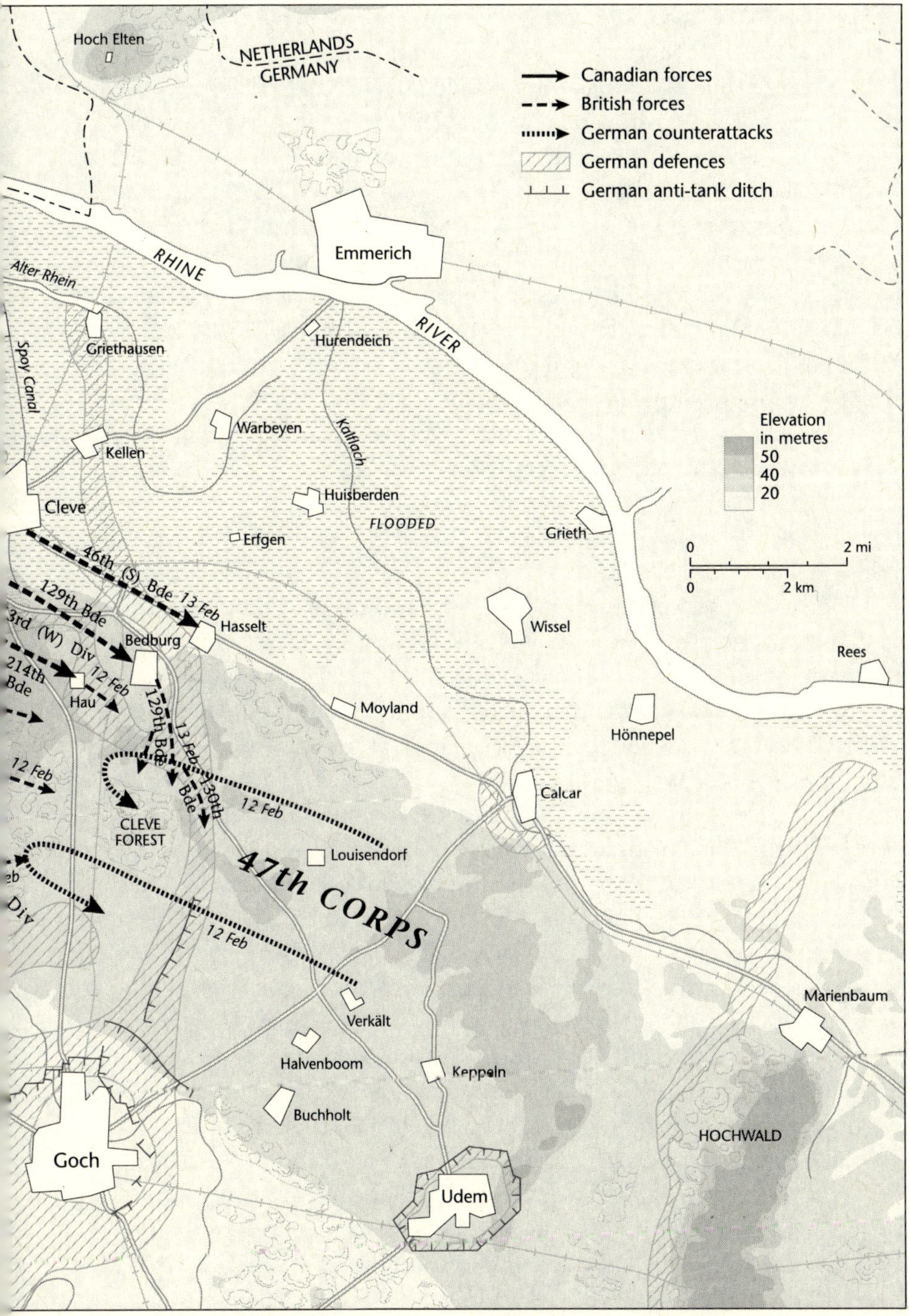
Hoch Elten
NETHERLANDS
GERMANY
Canadian forces
British forces
German counterattacks
German defences
German anti-tank ditch
Emmerich
RHINE
RIVER
Alter Rhein
Griethausen
Spoy Canal
Hurendeich
Warbeyen
Kalflach
Kellen
Elevation in metres
50
40
20
Cleve
Huisberden
FLOODED
Grieth
Erfgen
0
2 mi
0
2 km
46th (S) Bde 13 Feb
129th Bde
Hasselt
Wissel
3rd (W) Div
Bedburg
12 Feb
214th Bde
Hau
Rees
Moyland
129th Bde
13 Feb
Hönnepel
130th Bde
12 Feb
12 Feb
Calcar
CLEVE FOREST
Louisendorf
47th CORPS
12 Feb
Marienbaum
Verkält
Halvenboom
Keppeln
Buchholt
HOCHWALD
Goch
Udem

Adapted from Colonel C.P. Stacey, *The Victory Campaign: The Operations in Northwest Europe, 1944-1945* (Ottawa: Queen's Printer, 1966), map 10.

control: these were the tricky parts. How would he assemble five attacking divisions and their supporting artillery in the cramped forming-up place between Nijmegen and Groesbeek? How would he do it without the Germans detecting the action and firing on the troop-dense area with their supporting artillery? He had some first-rate help to work these issues: "I used to work out my battle plans for the Corps in consultation with my B[rigadier] G[eneral] S[taff], my Brigadier Q[uartermaster] as well as with the Corps Commanders Royal Artillery and Engineers and with a liaison officer from the R.A.F."[181] In early January, Pyman left 30th Corps to become Dempsey's Chief of Staff at the Second Army, so the bulk of the intricate Veritable staff effort fell on his replacement, the capable and affable Brigadier C.B. "Splosh" Jones. Between 12 December and 3 February, when Horrocks issued his orders for Veritable, 30th Corps promulgated thirty-four separate planning notes on everything from artillery manoeuvre areas, air support, deception planning, and forward reconnaissance.[182] Most of these notes were the results of planning conferences, the majority of which were presided over by Jones, and Horrocks attended a good number of them.

Of course, Horrocks consulted his divisional commanders as well, less for input on the basic plan than for points of coordination. For example, on 26 January he called a conference, attended by his divisional commanders, his BGS, his CCRA, other key staff from 30th Corps, and representatives from both the First Canadian Army and the 21st Army Group. They reached decisions on a variety of important issues, including the exploitation phase of the battle, the artillery fire plan, the deception plan, movement to forward assembly areas, use of the Wyler-Cleve road, air support, and timings.[183] If a 1946 re-enactment with most of the principle players is to be believed, the coordination conference took the form of a guided discussion.[184] Horrocks started with the issue of the fire plan and its relation to H-hour: "Once the C[ounter] B[attery] and preliminary bombardment start, surprise is lost. I therefore want them done in the shortest time that will do the job thoroughly. (To CCRA). How long do you want for them and is daylight necessary? This governs H-hour to some extent."[185] The CCRA responded that it would "take four hours altogether; they can of course start before first light, but for several reasons I should like as much daylight as possible." He added that three hours of daylight should allow his gunners to observe and adjust the fire such that they could accurately subdue the enemy defensive positions. Horrocks agreed and suggested 0930 as an H-hour, which would give the gunners 3½ hours after first light to see their targets. He then asked the divisional commanders if they could live with an H-hour of 0930. All responded "yes," except the GOC of the 15th (Scottish) Division, who expressed his concern that an H-hour after last light meant less time for him to reach his first objective at Kranenburg, but he could manage a 0930 start, "provided nothing [went] wrong." Other planning issues were sorted in a similar manner. Many such conferences took place in the two months leading up to Veritable. This was not a commander or a staff running a battle off the back of a cigarette pack.

Horrocks still worried. He "found it difficult to sleep towards the end of preparations for that battle."[186] As the ground began to thaw in early February, it did not take a military genius to imagine that Veritable would look more like Passchendaele than it would any battle from the current war. The cross of his command weighed upon his imagination: "If I made a mistake, it wasn't only this deal that was going to be lost. It was lives, and this gets to you ... if you've got any imagination ... I think perhaps I had a bit too much imagination ... to be ... in high command [in] war."[187] He was also troubled by his decision to destroy the picturesque town of Cleve with heavy bombers. Initially, he demurred when Crerar asked him whether he wanted Cleve "taken out," but when he considered that any Germans reinforcing the sector would have to pass through Cleve, he agreed to its destruction: "If I could delay them by bombing, it could make all the difference in the battle. And after all, the lives of my own troops came first."[188] Still, he "felt a murderer." On top of it all, his abdominal pain had begun to come back and this affected his mood.

Few people noticed, however. On 4 February, he visited the 8th Canadian Infantry Brigade and its commander, James Alan Roberts, who described Horrocks as "his usual bubbling self."[189] Roberts took Horrocks on a tour of his forward positions, right up to a Queen's Own Rifles of Canada standing patrol. Horrocks chatted with the patrol commander for a bit about enemy activity in the area and asked the corporal's advice on where to get the best view of the enemy forward positions. Before setting off on foot to the recommended vantage point, an "ebullient" Horrocks asked the corporal whether he might borrow his rifle green beret (to avoid arousing enemy suspicion if spotted). The young soldier naturally obliged, then Horrocks "took off his scarlet cap with general's rank badges and plopped it on the corporal's head," leaving the entire patrol "with open mouths." Worry, guilt, and abdominal pain – and yet he could not have appeared more confident. After Horrocks had left, Roberts "sat a few moments, thinking of the impact of [Horrocks's] personality ... Here was a man who really led, a general who talked to everyone, down to the simplest private soldier ... By his personal qualities of leadership he brought out a respect and an affection which made better soldiers of his officers and men." That was the point. The actor showed his audiences only what he wanted them to see – a cheerful and confident commander, not a general who was worried and unwell.

In the end, Horrocks stayed with a fairly conservative plan to blast his way through the enemy defences to Materborn using as much firepower as possible. He would attack with five divisions up, each on a two- to three-kilometre front, and two divisions in reserve to exploit the breakthrough.[190] From north to south, the five attacking divisions would be the 3rd Canadian, 2nd Canadian, 15th (Scottish), 53rd (Welsh), and 51st (Highland) Divisions. In reserve, Horrocks had the 43rd (Wessex) Division and the Guards Armoured Division. In concept, as soon as the 15th (Scottish) had secured as far as the Goch-Cleve railway line, the GOC, Major-General Colin Barber, was to "pass through without further delay the whole of 2 H[ousehold]C[avalry]R[egiment], which at that time will be under his command."[191] With armoured reconnaissance fanning out to the south, Barber was then to follow with "mobile columns [of tanks and infantry] direct on UDEM, CALCAR ... and EMMERICH ... Immediately behind these mobile columns of 15 (S) Div, 43 Div will be passed through the MATERBORN feature and will be directed on GOCH which it will capture without delay."

Interestingly, Horrocks proved more conservative in his planning than even Crerar, who was not known for a willingness to take risks.[192] On 22 January, Crerar had suggested doing without an extended preliminary bombardment in favour of a simultaneous combination of counter-battery and barrage fire to avoid telegraphing the coming assault. Crerar hoped to repeat the surprise that he had helped achieve as Staff Officer Royal Artillery at Amiens in August 1918.[193] In that battle, the lead battalions had started their assault "immediately," just as the barrage and counter-battery fire both commenced at H-hour, with the result that they were on their initial objectives within minutes, much to the surprise of the German defenders.[194] Horrocks must have found Crerar's proposal too risky. What if the counter-battery fire did not neutralize all the enemy's batteries? What if the enemy opened fire on the crowded assembly areas between Nijmegen and Groesbeek? Unwilling to court these possibilities, Horrocks opted instead for a cleaner separation between the preparatory fire, which would take more than five hours, and the barrage. So his CCRA, Brigadier Stewart Rawlins, planned destructive fire for the preliminary bombardment – as opposed to neutralizing fire – that delivered an average of 8.8 tons of shell on each of 159 headquarters and defensive position targets, 11.5 tons of shell on each of thirty enemy mortar and gun positions, and 8.9 tons of shell on identified targets in depth.[195] To ensure that they also hit yet-undetected batteries, after two hours and thirty minutes of destructive fire, Rawlins built in a pause, between 0730 and 0750 hours on 8 February, during which 30th Corps' supporting guns fired a smokescreen. This would deceive the enemy defenders into thinking that an assault was imminent, convincing them to fire on their defensive targets, or just behind the smoke barrage, as had been their custom. Once the enemy gun batteries and mortars opened up, 30th Corps' counter-battery organization could pinpoint them and hit them with a storm of counter-battery fire, which would last until the barrage started. The barrage would be heavy as well, and thick – 500 metres deep and advancing at a rate of 300 yards every twelve minutes.[196] Further supplementing the artillery fire were divisional "pepperpots," in which the fire of all unengaged weapons systems such as tanks, anti-tank guns, mortars, and machine guns were grouped to engage targets once the barrage had lifted and moved on. To isolate the battle space from German counterattacks, Horrocks and Crerar also called on the 9th US Bomber Division and Bomber Command to attack bridges and railways before D-day, and to "obliterate" Cleve, Goch, and Emmerich the evening before D-day. Fighter bombers from 84th Group RAF would be available to support ground operations and strike enemy reserve concentrations throughout the operation, weather permitting.[197] In a nutshell, Horrocks's plan depended on drenching the enemy with fire. He did not believe he could risk doing otherwise.

The administrative preparations for a firepower-intensive attack along these lines, and on such a narrow front, were enormous. Placing the medium and heavy guns of the five Army Groups Royal Artillery – and their ammunition dumps – within range of Cleve meant placing them fairly close to the front line of assaulting troops in the crowded space around Groesbeek. The field regiments also had to be close if they were to fire to the initial objectives. Adequate rail lines and a traffic control organization of 1,600 men assisted in assembling 200,000 troops and the supplies they needed to fight the battle. Crerar estimated that "if the ammunition allotment for the operation, which consisted of 350 types, were stacked side by side and five feet high, it would line a road for 30 miles."[198] Horrocks remembered that "it would have been almost impossible to drop a pea into the area without hitting something."[199] The vulnerability of such a precarious pre-H-hour concentration was obvious. Horrocks described himself as "terrified" that the Germans would detect the enormous administrative build-up and open up with their supporting guns. Luckily for the troops assembled near Groesbeek on 7 February, tactical intelligence was not a German strong point. In spite of all the Anglo-Canadian movement and all their preparation, a German intelligence report of 6 February still had 30th Corps marked as "whereabouts unknown."[200]

Horrocks might have felt reasonably assured of his plan and its prospects of success were it not for two worrying developments just as Veritable was getting started – an early thaw and the German decision to jam open the floodgates of the Roer dams. Had the ground remained frozen, tracked vehicle movement, including that of tanks, would have been relatively easy. Horrocks understood that the thaw would make the going difficult and slow, although, "fortunately for [his] peace of mind" on 8 February, he did not realize "just how bad."[201] And as H-hour approached, he knew that the US First Army in the south still had not seized the Roer dams. The worst-case scenario was that the Germans would flood the Roer valley, thereby delaying any crossing of the river indefinitely. That is what happened. When the Americans captured several of the dams intact on 9 February, they found that the Germans had jammed open one dam, which caused the river to overflow its banks. Operation Grenade, scheduled to start on 10 February, would be postponed nearly two weeks, until 23 February. Again, it was perhaps fortunate for Horrocks and his nerves that he did not receive confirmation of Grenade's delay until four days into Operation Veritable. With little happening on the US Ninth Army front, the Germans would be free to fling whatever reserves they had at the First Canadian Army. And they would.

Despite the thaw, the first part of the battle went fairly well. In the early hours of 8 February, heavy bombers struck Cleve and Goch, reducing the two cities to rubble as planned, while smaller concentrations attacked Weeze, Udem, and Calcar. The massive artillery fire plan, which would see the 30th Corps supporting guns fire 500,000 rounds on the first day alone, commenced at 0500. The planned pause and smokescreen between 0730 and 0750 had the desired effect of bringing enemy guns and mortars to life, which in turn enabled 30th Corps gunners to target them for counter-battery and counter-mortar fire. This was very effective and "prevented any large scale retaliatory enemy shelling during the attack."[202] The 30th Corps fire plan, with its "prolonged strain on the nerves," affected the enemy's frontline defenders as well. Interrogations of prisoners from the German 84th Division and 2nd Parachute Regiment afterwards revealed that they had "the impression of overwhelming force opposed to them, which in their isolated state, with no communications, it was useless to resist."[203] The assaulting infantry of 2nd Canadian, 15th (Scottish), 53rd (Welsh), and 51st (Highland) Divisions exploited the demoralizing effects of the bombardment, following quickly behind the barrage to "surprise the enemy very much." So far, so good.

Horrocks monitored these early developments closely through a combination of well-placed observation posts and visits to subordinate headquarters. He spent most of his daylight hours away from his Main Headquarters, normally returning only after last light.[204] His actions on 8 February set the pattern for how he controlled the battle. He started from the unusual position of "a platform half-way up a large tree" on the high ground near Groesbeek. From this perch, which Horrocks ascended at 1045, he could see most of the battlefield below, and he "was connected by line with a group of small scout cars below [him] at the bottom of the tree, each of which was tuned in on the same wireless link

with a similar vehicle at the advance H.Q. of each of the divisions taking part."[205]
It was fairly easy to follow the progress of the battle. He could see the shells of
the barrage exploding and the yellow smoke indicating when the barrage was
about to lift. He could also see "small scattered groups of men and tanks all
moving slowly forward."[206] In the early stages of the battle, the stiffest enemy
resistance came from the 2nd Parachute Regiment in front of the 51st (Highland)
Division. The other three divisions seemed to be progressing well enough, with
only a few tanks or flails bogged in the soggy ground. Horrocks observed at
1235 that all the tanks of the 34th Brigade supporting the 53rd (Welsh) Division
were "up with [the] inf[antry]."[207] He must have been somewhat relieved when
he descended his lookout post at 1305 to meet with Crerar at 1345 hours.[208]

His feeling of relief did not last long, however. By the time he reached the 3rd
Canadian Infantry Division headquarters at 1620, reports from the other attacking divisions indicated that most tanks and flails travelling cross-country
had become bogged in the mud. After conferring with Dan Spry about his
division's upcoming "island-hopping" operation from town to town in the
flooded Rhine flats using amphibious Buffaloes, Horrocks returned to his Main
Headquarters, sometime around last light. He slept after conferring with his
own staff, and rose early to receive a situation report at 0405 hours.

The first day had been satisfactory. In the north, the 3rd Canadian Infantry
Division had conducted its amphibious assaults and captured Zyfflich and
Zanpol against light opposition. The 2nd Canadian Infantry Division had subdued an enemy strongpoint at Wyler and established a bridge across the anti-
tank ditch a half-mile south of the town. On the main Nijmegen-Cleve road,
the 15th (Scottish) Division, completely mounted in armoured personnel carriers and supported by the 6th Guards Tank Brigade, had cracked through
Kranenburg and reached the intersection with the Fresselt-Hekkens road. In
the Reichswald, the 53rd (Welsh) Division had managed to reach the same
Fresselt-Hekkens road despite having had all their flails and crocodile flamethrowers immediately bogged. The stiffest fight of the first day happened in
the south, where the 51st (Highland) Division fought the troops of the 2nd
Parachute Regiment to cut the Mook-Gennep road. Horrocks was also encouraged to hear that, except for some elements of the 7th Parachute Division that
had been committed from Geldern to the southern Reichswald, there was yet
no evidence that the Germans had taken any major action to reinforce their
positions in the Veritable area. The 7th Parachute Division was all that General
Alfred Schlemm, Commander 1st Parachute Army, had to commit in the short
term. This was largely because Colonel-General Johannes Blaskowitz, Commander Army Group H, still believed that the Allied main effort would be

further south, in the Roermond sector, where Dempsey's Second Army had fought Operation Blackcock in January. That is where Blaskowitz kept his 47th Panzer Corps in reserve near Dulken and Dusseldorf, nearly forty miles away.[209] Horrocks had achieved operational surprise, but how long would it be before the Germans figured out that the main blow had been landed in the western Reichswald area? The battle was still a race, and reports of rapidly deteriorating roads did not bode well for getting the 43rd (Wessex) Division, now assembled in Nijmegen, through the Materborn gap and into the open ground around Goch. Anticipating that it would take some time to bring forward his reserves, Horrocks put this division on one hour's notice to move from 1200 hours on 9 February; the Guards Armoured Division was placed at the same state of readiness from midnight the same day.[210]

The main effort of the corps battle was still in the 15th (Scottish) Division sector, along the Nijmegen-Cleve road then south of Cleve through the Materborn gap. Horrocks joined Major-General Barber at his Main Headquarters at 0825 hours. There he would have been briefed that the 15th (Scottish) attack across the anti-tank ditch east of Nutterden had only just begun, after several delays as a result of "very bad going" and "great difficulty in opening routes f[or] w[ar]d."[211] Secondary routes all over the area had become impassable to tracked-vehicle movement, and even the Nijmegen-Cleve road was under a foot of water. The 44th (Lowland) Brigade attempted to breach the minefield and anti-tank ditch in five locations, but accomplished only one gap because the flail tanks in the other four lanes got stuck in the mud.[212] Since he was behind schedule, and because the road network was worsening by the minute, Barber changed his plan of passing the 46th (Highland) and 227th (Highland) Brigades through the gap to Materborn, and instead ordered the exhausted 44th (Lowland) Brigade to carry on and capture the vital ground south and southeast of Cleve.[213] In spite of all the difficulties, the 44th (Lowland) Brigade persevered, forcing three battalions through the single gap, capturing Nutterden, reaching the western outskirts of Cleve by 1545.[214] Barber ordered his reconnaissance regiment forward to find and secure routes beyond Cleve and Materborn for the 43rd (Wessex) Division, but the movement forward was slow because the one route that was usable by tracked vehicles, the Nijmegen-Cleve road, was now "choked with traffic."[215] Anxious to get through the Materborn gap, Horrocks ordered this division forward at 1900 hours. This, as he admitted later, "was one of the worst mistakes I made in the war."[216] He was right. It exacerbated the problems of an inadequate road network and caused a colossal and unnecessary traffic jam.

Why would Horrocks have made such an ill-advised move? His rationale is not easy to discern. Early in the day, he had been at 15th (Scottish) Division headquarters and he was no doubt aware of the difficult going for vehicles of any sort, the near total collapse of every track in the area, and the traffic problems that had forced Barber to send the 44th (Lowland) Brigade after the objectives of 46th (Highland) and 227th (Highland) Brigades. The main route between Smorenhook and Kranenburg was under "17 in[che]s of water," the water levels were rising, it was raining, and the weather forecast called for more rain. The Market Garden experience of running a corps on a single road had not been good, and that operation had been launched in good weather. Hubert Essame, who commanded the 214th Brigade during Operation Veritable, thought future historians would fault Horrocks for his "optimism."[217] But Horrocks's own words speak to a less sanguine mood: "My only excuse is that all too often during the war I had witnessed a pause in the battle, when one division was ordered to pass through another, which had allowed the enemy time to recover. In this case speed was absolutely vital and I was determined that our attack should flow on."[218] He cannot have been thinking clearly. Vehicles lined the Nijmegen-Cleve road "nose to tail" because they simply could not pull off the road without sinking in mud or submerging in water. So when the 43rd Brigade started to move forward with the 214th Infantry Brigade Group, the 43rd (Wessex) Division Tactical Headquarters, the 8th Armoured Brigade, and the 129th Infantry Brigade Group, it jammed an extra 1,060 vehicles into the problem, all of them trying to skirt past 15th (Scottish) vehicles half-pulled off the road.[219] And the total of 1,060 did not include any of the 43rd (Wessex) Division's artillery or ammunition carriers (430 vehicles), the administrative echelons of the brigades (400 vehicles), or the 130th Brigade Group (390 vehicles). It is difficult to imagine how Horrocks – or his key staff, for that matter – could have thought that this might work. One wonders why Horrocks did not simply let Barber keep fighting with perhaps a brigade group from the 43rd (Wessex) added to his command. Barber was fighting very well to that point, and placing an extra brigade group at his disposal would have obviated the need for stuffing one division through another, at least in the short term, and he still would have had substantial combat power to face a German counterattack. As it was, Horrocks had to intervene personally shortly after noon on 10 February. From the headquarters of the 3rd Canadian Infantry Division, where he had gone to check on the state of the Nijmegen-Cleve road, Horrocks set the following order of priority for road movement: 43rd Reconnaissance Regiment, 214th Infantry Brigade Group, 43rd (Wessex) Division artillery, a two-hour resupply block for the 15th (Scottish), 43rd (Wessex), and 53rd (Welsh) Divisions, then the balance of the 43rd (Wessex) Division.[220] He also ordered that the road be closed for two hours after darkness for maintenance by engineers. In the next twenty-four hours, the 15th (Scottish) and 43rd (Wessex) Divisions untangled themselves, while the 3rd Canadian Infantry Division in the north and the 53rd (Welsh) and 51st (Highland) Divisions in the south pressed forward against increasing German resistance.

The Germans were reinforcing fast. On 9 February, 30th Corps had identified prisoners from one battalion of the reserve 7th Parachute Division. By 10 February, "seven b[attalion]s from three different reserve div[ision]s 6 Para[chute], 7 Para[chute] and 180 Inf[antry] had yielded prisoners."[221] That these elements had been committed piecemeal across the front testifies to how seriously Schlemm viewed the crisis across the Reichswald front. There were still more reinforcements to come. On 10 February, Field Marshal Gerd von Rundstedt, Commander-in-Chief West, who had been monitoring the battle closely, warned Blaskowitz of "incalculable consequences of a breakthrough to the Rhine" and directed the army group commander to release the 15th Panzergrenadier and 116th Panzer Divisions, under the headquarters 47th Panzer Corps, to Schlemm.[222] With the Roer now flooding and any serious action in the south postponed by two weeks, von Rundstedt felt comfortable reinforcing his northeastern flank. To stop the hemorrhage, Schlemm ordered General von Luttwitz, commander of 47th Panzer Corps, to counterattack in force and recapture Cleve. Luttwitz moved his troops to Udem on the night of 11-12 February in preparation for that task.

British actions in the meantime forced him to rethink his attack. While Luttwitz was moving into Udem, the 15th (Scottish) and 43rd (Wessex) managed to separate themselves and continue their advance, as Horrocks confessed, "in spite of me."[223] The Scottish division took over the clearing of Cleve, and pushed to its western outskirts, while the Wessex division, in a series of daring and gruelling attacks, pushed to the southeast, through Materborn to Hau and the western outskirts of Bedberg, where they established themselves sometime after daybreak on 12 February. Further south, the 53rd (Welsh) had reached the eastern outskirts of the Reichswald and were only hours from linking up with the right flank of the 43rd (Wessex). This was the climax of the Reichswald battle. When Luttwitz saw that British forces had established themselves in strength at Cleve, Bedberg, and Hau, he decided to direct his attack south of Cleve, through the Reichswald, to cut the Cleve-Hekkens road.[224] His attack, which started only at 0930 hours on 12 February, crashed on the rocks of British tank, anti-tank, and artillery fire. His losses were so severe that he broke off the attack and ordered the remnants of his corps to establish itself on the defensive line that ran from Ertgen to Goch. Horrocks's corps, in spite of its difficulties, had won the critical race.

In his memoirs, Horrocks described the rest of the Reichswald battle as a "slogging match, under the worst possible weather conditions."[225] It certainly was that. On 12 February, Montgomery handed him the depressing news that the Roer flooding would postpone Operation Grenade for at least ten days. This meant that the Germans were relatively free to throw their reserves at the First Canadian Army, which they did. By 16 February, the Germans had committed to the Veritable battlefield one panzer division, one panzergrenadier division, three infantry divisions, and four parachute divisions.[226] It began to look, sound, and feel more and more like Passchendaele as the Germans piled up what they could on the mushy ground between the Rhine and the Meuse to meet the attack.[227] Montgomery gave Crerar two more divisions – the 52nd (Lowland) and 11th Armoured – to pound through the German defences. Crerar, in turn, handed Horrocks the 52nd (Lowland), which the latter placed on his far right along the Meuse, and the army commander also brought Guy Simonds's 2nd Canadian Corps up on the left.[228] It took five days of ceaseless fighting, from 17 to 21 February, for Horrocks to capture Goch with a converging attack – 15th (Scottish) from the northeast over tank ditch crossings seized by the 43rd (Wessex), 51st (Highland) from the northwest, and 53rd (Welsh) from the north. At the same time, Simonds was slugging forward his two infantry divisions to cut the Goch-Calcar road. With these two objectives secure, Crerar took a quick two-day pause before switching the main effort to 2nd Canadian Corps in a renewed offensive codenamed Blockbuster (23 February to 10 March 1945).

When Horrocks reflected on what he regarded as "unquestionably the grimmest battle" he had ever fought, he was quite candid about his limitations as a commander. We have already seen how he bore the blame for the traffic snarls of 9-10 February, but Horrocks understood, better than most generals, what he could and could not do. Especially after the capture and defence of the Materborn gap, when the Germans rushed in reinforcements and cloud cover kept Allied aircraft on the ground, the contest turned into a "soldier's battle."[229] Horrocks understood how battles like Veritable assailed the nerves of the average soldier. It is worth quoting at some length from *A Full Life*:

> The strain to which the soldier of today is subjected is far, far greater than anything experienced by his grandfather or great-grandfather ... The 53rd Welsh Division and, further south, the 51st Highland Division were fighting their way through that sinister black Reichswald Forest. Their forward troops would very often consist of two young men, crouching together in a fox-hole ... they were quite alone for they might not be able to see even the other members of their own section and all around them was the menace of hidden mines ... It is this sinister emptiness that depresses them most – no living thing in sight ... Then the seemingly empty battlefield will erupt into sudden and violent life. When that moment arrives, they must force themselves forward with a sickening feeling in the pit of

their stomachs, fighting an almost uncontrollable urge to fling themselves down as close to the earth as they can get. Even then they are alone amidst all the fury; carrying their loneliness with them.[230]

It takes a general with very acute human skills to understand that, even on a crowded battlefield like the Reichswald, the soldier's greatest enemy was loneliness. They needed a connection, to each other, to their chain of command, to the plan, to their cause. Horrocks understood the psychology, but he also understood that even his "whistle-stop" tours could not possibly influence each soldier directly. For the most part, he made his connection with his soldiers through their commanding officers: "The men who really influenced [the battle] were the Battalion Commanders who ... never gave up the struggle which continued by day and night against some of the best and most experienced German Panzer and Parachute troops ... so I spent my days 'smelling the battlefield.' I always made a point of visiting Brigade and Battalion H.Q. which had been having a particularly gruelling time."[231] Hubert Essame remembered that Horrocks was a "familiar figure in the forward areas," bringing with him an "infectious enthusiasm."[232] A soldier of the 51st (Highland) Division remembered Horrocks driving his own jeep near the front and giving a "marvellous" wave: "It made my day."[233] Horrocks knew what he was doing. Generals who commanded the loyalty and affection of their troops could make a Materborn-type mistake and get away with it. He just couldn't make too many. And he didn't.

Not that the rest of his war was easy; it was tough on him for a variety of reasons. His abdominal ailments continued to flare up with annoying regularity, and that made most chores difficult. Two weeks after Veritable, his corps crossed the Rhine, then advanced steadily into Northern Germany, ending the war in the Cuxhaven peninsula on the north coast. None of it was easy. The Germans were fighting for their homeland, so the opposition, even in the face of certain defeat, was always strong. Near Bremen, the Guards Armoured Division liberated a Nazi concentration camp. As Horrocks remembered, "Up to now I had been fighting this war without any particular hatred for the enemy." That changed after Bremen. The sight of the camp's emaciated and dying occupants shocked Horrocks, as it would have shocked any civilized person:

Many of them were too weak to walk but they managed to heave themselves up and give us a pathetic cheer. Most of them had some form of chronic dysentery and the stench was so frightful that I disgraced myself by being sick in a corner ... I was so angry that I ordered the burgomasters of all the surrounding towns and villages each to supply a quota of German women to clean up the camp and look after these unfortunate prisoners, who were dying at an alarming rate.[234]

When the time came to accept the surrender of German forces in his sector, Horrocks was in no humour for posturing or playing games. He told the German generals that the terms of the surrender were non-negotiable and that he would have no mercy if they were not obeyed: "Having seen one of your horror camps my whole attitude towards Germany has changed." When one of the German officers stood up to protest that the German Army had nothing to do with those camps, Horrocks told him bluntly to sit down: "There were German soldiers on sentry duty outside those and you cannot escape responsibility. The world will never forgive Germany for those camps."[235] It had been a long war.

Horrocks did not last long in the army after it ended. In February 1946, he left Germany to take up the post of General Officer Commanding (GOC) Western Command in England, but, unfortunately, his fevers, pain, and sickness persisted. A seventh abdominal surgery, which finally removed from his hepatic duct the obstruction that was at the root of all the trouble, took place in December 1947, just as Horrocks was appointed Commander of the British Army of the Rhine (BAOR). Having had no previous success with Royal Army Medical Corps surgeons, Horrocks had the procedure performed by a civilian specialist in Manchester, only to find that the army would not cover his expenses.[236] In March 1948, he attempted to take the helm of the BAOR, but he had not fully recovered and soon had to go on sick leave. Unfortunately, that sojourn lasted until he retired from the Army for good in January 1949[237] – an anti-climactic end to a magnificent career. Horrocks did not fade away altogether, however. He wrote pieces on military issues for the *Sunday Times* and he put his acting skills to good use in a series of Huw Wheldon–produced television programs, *Men in Battle* and *Epic Battles*. With the same clarity and enthusiasm that had characterized his wartime conferences, Horrocks explained the great battles and great men of history to television audiences, and both series proved popular. When he was not performing for cameras in the BBC studios, Horrocks carried out the duties of the Gentlemen Usher of the Black Rod in the House of Lords, a post he held from 1949 to 1963. He also served on the board of a building company, wrote two memoirs, and edited a series of regimental histories. He died in 1985 at the age of 89 – after having lived a very full life indeed.

BRIAN HORROCKS WAS A late bloomer. Only in his thirties did staff work and soldiering supplant sports and fun in his order of priorities, but once they did his command skills truly flourished. They built upon a rock-solid foundation of first-rate human skills. Horrocks had always been a personable man, quick to make friends and influence people, and nearly five years in enemy prison camps offered him every opportunity to study what made men tick. Such a long period in such depressing circumstances might have forced many to submit to their pessimism. Not Horrocks. While he learned how to be self-sufficient in the dreary and occasionally painful circumstances of captivity, he also studied the morale and motivation of his fellow prisoners. What kept them going? What brought them down? When was humour the best tonic? When was it inappropriate? When was a stern approach best? What kind of routine fostered mental alertness? Horrocks watched, practised, and learned. Of course, he built upon what he had learned in *stalags* – while he trained with the Territorial Army, struggled to maintain order during the Fall of France, prepared Home Forces for battle, and commanded corps in North Africa and Northwest Europe. He became an absolute master of the human dimension of command. When he added solid technical skills to his repertoire, a process that began with his attendance at Staff College, he became a very potent commander. Horrocks did his best to look breezy about his business, but that belied how seriously he took his responsibilities. He planned deliberately, he arranged his apparatus of command carefully, and he executed the majority of his missions well and with precision. It helped that the people around Horrocks liked him and wanted to serve him, nearly everywhere he went. He got the most out of his men. Montgomery wrote of Horrocks (with characteristic curtness), "I knew I could not have a better man and so it turned out."[238] Horrocks admired Montgomery tremendously, but, unlike his mentor, he was not confident all the time. At times he had to act – even when he was painfully ill – to give the appearance of complete confidence when in fact there was doubt, to preserve calm when panic was at the gates of men's minds, and to keep his soldiers fighting.

# Wit in Want of Will: Lieutenant-General E.L.M. Burns

*Staff Officer: Lovely day, General.*
*Burns: Have you been out?*
*Staff Officer: No.*
*Burns: Oh.*

– H.O. Moran, staff officer under
Major-General E.L.M. Burns, 1944-45

IT MUST HAVE BEEN awkward – a young staff officer trying to make light conversation with his general, and the general making him feel stupid for trying. Another general, a Horrocks for example, might have played along and said something like, "Every day in the army is like a day on leave," or "If it were any better, we'd be in Britain." Not Burns. He was never one for pointless prattle and his meticulous mind demanded accurate information. He was a thinker, whose taciturnity only occasionally gave way to sarcastic commentary. Few people shared either his quick wit or his caustic sense of humour, so he did not have many friends in either the Canadian or British armies. But that alone does not explain why, after fighting two successful corps battles in 1944, Burns lost his job. Guy Simonds also had few friends and was similarly deficient in human skills – he even had a few battlefield failures – but very few people questioned his ability to command, then or since. What was it about Burns that so alienated him from his superiors, subordinates, even peers? Jack Granatstein pointed to "problems of personality" as an explanation, and there is more than a little truth in this assertion.[1] It was also a problem of will. Burns had difficulty imposing his will on subordinates, even when he recognized that they were doing wrong.[2] One of his two army commanders in Italy described him as lacking "personality, initiative, tactical sense and power of command,"[3] while the other described his manner as "depressing, diffident and unenthusiastic."[4] Simonds could never have been accused of those faults. Most important, though, Burns was unlike Simonds in that he had trouble confronting people in person. His sharp mind easily found fault, but he lacked the will to excise the defaulters. He rarely fired people; by the end of his tenure as corps commander, his divisional commanders regularly questioned or ignored his direction, and Burns did little to stop it.[5] No one who confronted Simonds lasted long in their job. That ruthless streak was necessary for a commander who could not engender affection, and Burns simply did not have it. He was a tragic figure – one with plenty of brains and technical skill, but painfully adrift in the human dimension of command. In spite of his ability to think through problems, develop sound tactical plans, design balanced military organizations, and implement effective training regimens, he could neither inspire nor intimidate, and that left him vulnerable to enemies from above and below.

FROM A VERY EARLY age, Eedson Louis Millard Burns demonstrated academic ability. Born on 17 June 1897 to George Eedson Burns and Louise Mills, "Tommy," as he was nicknamed, grew up in the affluent Montreal borough of Westmount and attended St. John the Evangelist School, which became Lower Canada College in 1909.[6] His file of report cards reveals an aggregate average around 80 percent for most years between 1906 and 1913, comments such as "very good" and "excellent" only occasionally blemished with the rare bit of tepid praise such as "fair" in singing, or "tries hard, but has not made very great progress," which accompanied his earliest marks in French.[7] His headmasters consistently praised his punctuality, his propensity for hard work, and his self-discipline. His early education served him well. When he sat the entrance examination for the Royal Military College of Canada (RMC) in May 1914, he scored top marks, or very near top marks, in geometry, trigonometry, English grammar and composition, and history. He passed into RMC in the autumn of 1914 with the second highest aggregate marks of all applicants who sat the examinations for that year.[8] During his first and only year at RMC, Burns had the highest overall academic average among his classmates, finishing best or second-best in the subjects of English, artillery tactics, military history, mathematics, field sketching, and administration.[9] At first unenthused about the idea of going to battle in France or Flanders, his "attitude about the war changed without [his] perceiving it."[10] In June 1915, having just turned eighteen years of age, Burns put his formal schooling on hold, accepted a "Certificate of Discharge of a Gentleman Cadet," and took a commission into the Royal Canadian Engineers. Like most of his classmates, and without much thrill or thought, he chose the battlefield over books and joined the Canadian Expeditionary Force (CEF) overseas.[11]

After very little military training, Lieutenant Burns spent his first two years of the Great War as a signals officer with the 4th Canadian Infantry Division. Besides his time at RMC, his only military training had been with the 17th Hussars, a Montreal militia unit in which he had served as a private soldier between June 1913 and August 1914.[12] Shortly after arriving in England in the spring of 1916, Burns proceeded to Newark for six weeks of engineer training.

It was very basic and very brief, but on returning from Newark in May 1916, he went back to the 4th Canadian Infantry Division Signals Company. He crossed the English Channel to France in August 1916 as a signals officer with the 11th Canadian Infantry Brigade, and remained in that post for eighteen months. In this appointment, Burns considered that he had secured "a bomb-proof job,"[13] at least as far as Great War standards of bomb-proofing were concerned: "The signal officer lived at brigade headquarters, which was usually a mile or so behind the front line and nearly always exempt from shellfire; nevertheless close enough for us to have constantly in mind the conditions under which the infantry lived. Brigadiers and their staffs toured the forward areas day by day, and the record shows that not a few of them were killed or wounded."[14] Despite his "bomb-proof" employment, Burns was awarded the Military Cross in January 1917 for conspicuous gallantry: "In addition to organizing and running the signals lines, he personally laid and repaired ... cables under very heavy fire. He displayed great courage and coolness throughout."[15] He was also wounded twice, once when he sustained a very minor wound during the attack on Vimy Ridge in April 1917, and a second time when he caught a piece of shrapnel in his left hand in September 1917. He made light of the second wound, which he sustained near the town of Lens: "I was slightly wounded in the hand by a shell splinter travelling in a parabola from a burst more than 1000 yards away ... It ... earned me (pretty cheaply) the right to wear the little gold braid wound stripe, and another leave to England."[16] Burns confessed to a certain humility when he compared his lot with that of the "poor bloody infantry," nearly a fifth of whom could be killed in large attacks.[17] He had followed behind the infantry waves at Vimy, stumbled past their crumpled corpses, watched the life ebb away from a soldier shot through the chest, had a bullet pass through his own respirator and crease his helmet, and had another bullet strike so close to him on the ground that it sent "a shower of tiny stones and splinters into my face."[18] And Vimy was a "good" battle. From Vimy, Burns went with his brigade to Lens in the summer and then to Passchendaele in October, where, although his brigade did not attack, he saw several seemingly futile and costly actions across the cratered and mud soaked fields.

In early 1918, Burns transferred to the 3rd Canadian Infantry Division. He sought and received a posting as a "staff learner" to the 9th Canadian Infantry Brigade because he "concluded (perhaps conceitedly) that he could do as well as some of [the other staff learners]" he had observed in the 11th Brigade Headquarters.[19] There he worked as an understudy to the Staff Captain A & Q (Adjutant and Quartermaster), the staff officer in charge of personnel and logistics. Shortly after the battle of Amiens in August 1918, which he missed because he was on leave, Burns moved to the 3rd Canadian Infantry Division Headquarters as a general staff learner. In this capacity, his job was "to be reconnaissance during operations," relaying information back to the Main Headquarters on how far the lead troops had advanced, and so on. This was the period of Canada's Hundred Days, the high point of Canadian arms in the Great War, perhaps any war, and Burns had a front-row seat. He watched well-planned, deliberate attacks succeed and ad hoc attacks fail, all of which left him with a disdain for what he called "quickie attacks": "An attack without enough time for reconnaissance and preparation will usually fail."[20] This lesson stayed with him. By the last month of the war, Burns was back at the 9th Canadian Infantry Brigade as the Staff Captain A & Q.

Like most Canadian and British officers who survived the Great War, Captain Burns was deeply affected by the experience, but, perhaps surprisingly, not bitter. He did not enjoy the war, but he coolly took from it what lessons he could. In a 1927 piece that he published in H.L. Mencken's *The American Mercury,* he reflected that the experience of war had actually been good, that it had made him "a more complete being, better able to face life, and to extract from it whatever satisfaction it may contain."[21] And he was positively caustic in his condemnation of "sentimentalists" who dwelled on the empty theme of disillusion:

> As for those who can be rightfully said to be disillusioned (and not merely jealous) I observe that a man who goes to war, deluding himself that he is fighting for any abstract thing like the salvation of the world or the suppression of militarism, must be a singularly infantile idealist, and as everyone knows, idealists spend their lives being disillusioned, and no doubt come to take a masochistic delight in it.[22]

In his writing, Burns rarely resisted the temptation to use his biting wit for biting.

With the experience of the Great War behind him, in April 1920 Burns joined a Canadian Permanent Force in which promotion was slow and the work less than lively. When he left the CEF for the Permanent Force, his brigadier recommended him for a "full course" at the School of Military Engineering at Chatham, England, which he attended between June 1920 and December 1921.[23] He did well, his course report noting that he was "very good at survey and at construction" and that he was an "exceptionally hard worker."[24] From Chatham, Burns went to Halifax, Nova Scotia, where he briefly worked in the Military District Headquarters before being detached to the Topographical Survey Section at what was then the Department of Militia and Defence. For nearly two years, he mapped parts of rural Quebec and earned high marks on his confidential reports, which noted that he was "a superior topographer" and "energetic."[25] He taught military engineering at RMC from 1924 to 1926, during which time he attended the Staff College Preparatory Course. While at RMC, he met and married Eleanor Phelan, who accompanied Burns to the Indian Army Staff College at Quetta in 1927. The young couple enjoyed life in northern India and Burns did well on his course, his Directing Staff praising his "strong and imperturbable" character, his mental quickness, and his "ability to express himself well on paper."[26] Interestingly, although the report also recommended him as a staff college instructor for the future, it added the caveat that "his elocution is not easily understandable." Burns was much better with written words than spoken ones.

Staff training led naturally to a series of staff appointments in which he excelled. From Quetta, he returned to Military District Number 5 in Quebec City as a General Staff Officer Second Grade (GSO 2) before returning to the survey business in May 1932. Working in the Surveys Branch of the General Staff at National Defence Headquarters, Burns served much of that time under Colonel H.D.G. Crerar, future Chief of the General Staff and Commander First Canadian Army. His pioneering work in aerial photography and mapping yielded the Modified British Grid system for military maps, an achievement that earned Burns admittance as an Officer to the Order of the British Empire in 1935. Shortly after his promotion to brevet lieutenant-colonel in 1935, Burns moved to Montreal, where he was GSO 1 of Military District Number 4 for three years before attending the Imperial Defence College (IDC) in 1938-39. Burns was a star in the Permanent Force. Invariably, his confidential reports for the interwar period were impeccable in the areas of professional ability, initiative, judgment, and intellectual qualifications.[27] His only middle or average marks came in the areas of sociability and tact. One of his supervisors noted that he was "somewhat shy and reticent" and possessed of "a tendency to be sarcastic and cynical."[28] The same supervisor echoed the comments of the Directing Staff at Quetta: "His written work is better than his oral."

It was, and writing became an important occupation for Burns's restless mind. His work in the Permanent Force was steady, and he genuinely liked the people around him, but Burns needed more. As he wrote to a friend in 1924, "I feel now that I would like a little change of society. The fellows with me are excellent eggs, in their way, but there's little food for the soul in their conversation."[29] That statement spoke volumes about how he felt about himself and his subordinates. He had a high opinion of his own intellect, and, although he was fond of his fellow soldiers, he never doubted that they were lesser intellectual beings. In 1924, under the pen name of Arlington B. Conway, he published the first of the eight articles on military affairs that he wrote for *The American Mercury,* a literary magazine whose contributors included the likes of William Faulkner, F. Scott Fitzgerald, and Eugene O'Neill. Six other essays on subjects such as mechanization, military organizations, and tactics appeared in the *Canadian Defence Quarterly* between 1924 and 1938. He also co-authored a romance novel on life in rural Quebec, and, throughout the 1920s and 1930s, he kept up a fairly high-brow literary correspondence with his co-author, Madge Macbeth.[30] He won the Bertram Stewart Prize Essay Competition for 1932, a competition open to all officers of the British Empire, an accomplishment that prompted the Chief of the General Staff, Major-General A.G.L. McNaughton, to place a memorandum in his file noting "the outstanding ability of this officer."[31] Burns also won the *Canadian Defence Quarterly* essay competition for the same year.

In his writing, Burns wrestled with the most serious problems of modern warfare. War had become a difficult and dramatically dangerous business in the early twentieth century, and this presented innumerable challenges for military professionals such as Burns. How did one restore manoeuvre to a battlefield so dominated by firepower? Was there an alternative to attrition? How could the infantry soldier move across a battlefield on which anyone with a rifle, let alone a machine gun, could kill him stone dead at any range under 400 metres? What was the proper role, or roles, for the new air arm? How could field officers and staff officers be trained to face the challenges of modern warfare? Burns thought hard about these things. He wrote a lot about them as well.[32] Understanding the potential of new technology and the new tank arm to restore mobility to the modern battlefield, Burns theorized about ways, means, and organizations to make it happen.[33] He read widely and was heavily influenced by the British officer and tank theorist J.F.C. Fuller.[34] He also drew on what he had heard and read about battles like Cambrai in November 1917, an action that had featured "the massed use of tanks on firm ground which had not been turned into a waste of craters by prolonged bombardment."[35] He analyzed actions like the battle of Amiens in August 1918, and he dissected what he had experienced during the Hundred Days, when the Canadian Corps combined all arms to break through a series of German defences between Arras and Mons.[36] He saw the potential of tanks: "Before Cambrai, artillery bombardment had to be relied on to make gaps in the enemy's barbed wire entanglements ... But at Cambrai, it was the massed tanks that broke down the wire in wide avenues, through which the infantry could rush ... Taken all together, the tactics first employed at Cambrai were those which brought victory in the battle of Amiens on August 8 1918."[37]

Neither battle succeeded completely in rupturing the German line or causing the hoped-for paralysis of the German command and control networks, but Burns saw that tanks, or armoured vehicles, could succeed where horses had fallen short. The animals and their riders were simply "too vulnerable" to automatic weapons fire to be of any real use on a modern battlefield. If, however, cavalry were to be mechanized, armoured for protection against small-arms fire, and perhaps fitted with automatic weapons of its own, the promise of horse-mounted actions at Cambrai and Amiens might be realized.

Reorganizing armies and re-equipping them for the conditions of modern war were the major themes of Burns's interwar writing. In 1924, he published "The Mechanization of Cavalry" in the *Canadian Defence Quarterly,* the first piece in the new journal to make a case for replacing horses with machines: "The cavalry machine would be for reconnaissance, rapid transport of the fire-power of its crew, [and] the more open varieties of offensive action – encounters when neither side would be organized for attack or defence, and speed essential for success."[38] The cavalry machine, as he proposed it, was not a tank. It was something altogether separate, yet a necessary complement to the new tank arm: "A cavalry mounted on machines would be able to reconnoitre, pursue, escape easily in rear guard actions, co-operate with and protect the movements of fast tanks, and most important of all, attack unshaken infantry in lightly wired positions."[39] Of course, mounting cavalry on machines meant overcoming institutional resistance from a cavalry branch still wedded to horses, so Burns did his biting best to discredit opposition to change: "Whenever one reads or hears a cavalryman's pronouncement on the work of cavalry in the late war ... one at once perceives an undertone of timorous apology; one feels that his arguments and pleadings amount to 'We did pretty well in this unsporting and unusual war – considering – and you really will find us most probably quite useful, given certain conditions, in the future.'"[40] Cavalry-conducive conditions were gone, not likely ever to return, so the remedy was simple. Cavalry had to "follow the trend [towards mechanization] or be lost."[41]

So did the infantry. In 1935, Burns picked up on Fuller's notion of "motor guerrillas" as a viable principle on which to reorganize the Canadian militia – "a fast moving swarm which will not only search the area of advance, picket bridges and tactical points, block roads etc., but will fight off the enemy swarm, and so clear the area of advance."[42] Motorized infantry was a reasonable role for the Canadian militia, given the conditions of Canadian geography, fiscal limitations, and the country's role within the framework of imperial defence. Britain would likely field a tank corps but, "unless we are resigned to Canadian land defence forces being merely lines of communication, or third line troops ... we must remedy this defect in our training and equipment." As he so plainly put it: "A 2½ mile an hour soldier in a 60 mile an hour age is an anachronism."[43] The Canadian Army had to reorganize to keep pace.

The realistic Burns may not have seen a central role for Canada in the tank-heavy armies he envisioned for the British Empire, but that did not stop him from writing about tanks, how they should be organized, and how they should be used. In 1938, he attacked the recent reorganization of the British Army's divisions.[44] Although he confessed, somewhat tongue-in-cheek, that it might be "presumptuous for an officer of a Dominion ... to propose reorganizing the British Divisional system," he recognized that, because "the British regular division [was] the prototype of all the divisions of all the forces of the Empire," he had to address this central issue if there was to be any change at all.[45] The recent reorganization of the British Army had established two divisional structures – the Mobile Division and the 1938 model infantry division. The Mobile Division consisted of two mechanized cavalry brigades of light tanks, one tank brigade of medium tanks, two motorized infantry battalions, and two artillery regiments. Its purpose was to exploit through any breach in the enemy's line and deep into his defences. The hard breaching of the enemy line – the dogfight, as Montgomery called it – would be fought mostly by the infantry divisions, which, in 1938, had been organized with three infantry brigades and three regiments of supporting artillery – but no tanks. Tank support for the assaulting infantry divisions would be provided by the heavy infantry tanks of the Army Tank Brigade. For Burns, this was insufficient. On the mobile battlefield that he and others envisioned for the next war, all divisions had to move quickly – and attack. This meant tanks for the assault on short notice, something unlikely considering the 1938 model infantry divisions had no organic tanks of their own. The idea of separate infantry tanks, held in an army tank brigade, was "a retrogression in tactical ideas" and sure to reduce both the mobility and the tempo of battle. He asked: "In gearing the tank to the pace of infantry – 100 yards in three minutes – are we not going backward instead of forward?"[46] As far as Burns could foretell, organizing divisions in terms of arms designations was a waste of time anyway; better to organize them based on a balance of arms that afforded every division the ability to attack, pursue, defend, or withdraw. He suggested that a division capable of attacking would consist of one tank brigade (of medium tanks), two infantry brigades (with motorized transportation), three artillery regiments, and a light tank (cavalry) regiment for reconnaissance. Putting these arms together in one formation would do more than simply combine their capabilities; it would foster all-arms cooperation: "Tanks, infantry and artillery can only co-operate if they are trained to it ... Co-operation sounds very simple, but in fact it runs counter to the ordinary human tendency to think of oneself and those nearest to one first ... Units of different arms need much practice together, and this can only be effectively organized if the co-operating units are permanently under the same command, and that means, in the British Army, in the same division."[47]

Not everyone agreed. Criticism of Burns's proposed reorganization came from the young Captain Guy Granville Simonds, who defended the 1938 model

infantry division on the principle that the offensive striking power of an army
– the tanks – should remain under the control of the army commander "to allot
in accordance with his plan and in proportion to the importance he attaches to
the various phases of his attack or attacks."[48] Because "only a proportion of
divisions will need the additional strength to make them divisions that can
attack," there was no point in giving every division tanks and dissipating the
hitting power of the army commander. As Simonds saw it, the primary function
of an infantry division was to defend or hold, not to attack. Perhaps in response
to the caustic tone of Burns's piece, Simonds also defended the War Office "de-
signers" of the 1938 model infantry division, stating that they had not taken their
decisions out of "obtuseness or stupidity," but rather in careful consideration of
the likely tasks of infantry divisions in the next war.[49] True to form, Burns's
response was savagely sarcastic: "I must confess that Capt Simonds' tribute to
the grave and silent geniuses who sit in Whitehall, preparing 'specifications'
and 'designing' divisions affected me greatly. If I seemed unappreciative of their
scientific method, it was only through ignorance."[50] He then went on to re-
emphasize, in very clear terms, his point that in "rapidly moving warfare ... a
division may have to advance, attack, retire, defend and guard in various directions in the space of a few days ... [and] it will be extremely difficult for a higher
commander to distribute and redistribute his 'offensive' weapons in time to
meet the needs of the changing situations." Grouping tanks within the infantry
divisions would mean both that divisional commanders would have tanks *when*
they needed them and that tanks and infantry would know *how* to work together
when that time came. Looking back on this eve-of-war debate, it is hard not to
conclude that Burns was the more reasoned and prescient of the two. Infantry
divisions attacked all the time during the 1939-45 war, and, as David French has
noted, "by placing the tanks outside the divisional organization, the General
Staff made achieving [tank-infantry-artillery] co-operation difficult because
they deprived the three arms of the opportunity to live and work together."[51]
Indeed, after a series of British defeats linked to poor all-arms cooperation in
North Africa, in 1942 General Sir Claude Auchinleck, Commander-in-Chief
Middle East and Acting Commander Eighth Army, suggested the abolition of
armoured and infantry divisional organizations in favour of single "mobile"
divisional structure – based on one armoured and two infantry brigades.[52]
Auchinleck lost his job before he had a chance to reorganize the Eighth Army's
divisions, but it is interesting to note that Burns had predicted the difficulties
that arms-based divisional structures would present for all-arms cooperation.[53]
   Burns also had some interesting ideas about the men who would man these
new organizations and the officers who would command them, ideas that he
packaged into some of his most mordant pieces and published in *The American*

*Mercury.* On morale, he wrote: "Good morale, in brief, is simply a feeling in the mind of the soldier that, on even terms, he can trounce his enemy. He may have had the worst of it battle after battle, but if he is still able to make excuses for himself, and is willing to have another go, his morale is all right for practical purposes."[54] For Burns, the soldier best equipped to survive modern battle with his morale intact "is a primitive honest fellow, uncomplicated by elaborate thought machinery or superfluous ideas. He makes a simple reliable tool which, though perhaps limited in its applications by its simplicity, will not get out of order at critical moments or commence to function erratically."[55] Patriotism or the righteousness of one's cause was not enough to sustain a soldier's morale in modern war, as Burns expressed with Sassoonesque contempt: "Let him spend five minutes in a trench listening to the blurred wailing of a comrade shot through the belly, and if he thinks of patriotism at all it will only be to curse it."[56] In preparing men to endure battle, Burns granted that a dose of paternalism was necessary, but he was adamant that officers had to be clinical in their approach as well: the best way to prepare a soldier for war, to inoculate him for war, was "to train him to respond as automatically as possible ... to reduce his necessity for thought to a minimum, and to refrain from stuffing him with ideas except the idea that he had better kill the enemy quickly and ruthlessly, lest he be killed himself."[57] Burns's ideal soldier was a simple one, not a creative one.

Creativity was more the purview of officers, particularly general officers. In "The Mind of the General," Burns argued that an officer with aspirations of generalship should, first and foremost, train his brain such that it could "evolve original conceptions and combinations, and penetrate the enemy's designs."[58] Burns believed in military genius, but where was an apprentice genius to learn his craft? Not in the peacetime army. There, too much of an officer's life was occupied with doing humdrum administration and teaching others. "He must discipline his men, see that they wash their necks and shine their shoes, and make sure that their equipment is complete and serviceable and that they are properly housed, fed and have suitable recreation."[59] Such things were "little suited for the development of military genius."[60] Even instructing subordinates at a staff college had a "blighting effect" on an officer's development: "If he is kept at it too long, these doctrines will be so ground into him that he will be incapable of regarding them critically, that is to say, incapable of military thought." So what should the army do to prevent "promising military brains from decaying or ossifying"?[61] Send them away: "Let promising officers of about ten years' service, who have shown themselves capable in their military duties and who have original and active minds, be kicked out of the army on half-pay. Jobs might be found for them with patriotic bankers, bond houses and industrial corporations ... If they found they could not succeed, they could be taken back into the army."[62] It was a very modest proposal, in a Jonathan Swift kind of way, and of course Burns was not serious about banishing the best officers from the army, but he made a powerful point – to whomever may have been reading – that officer training, particularly in Canada, did little in the 1920s and 1930s to prepare officers for higher command. It did even less to encourage creative thought. A serious officer had to seek out opportunities for learning and forging acute mental faculties, and Burns had no time for officers who were disinclined or incapable of challenging themselves with the few military training opportunities available: "An officer today who finds it impossible to qualify [for staff college] is either too stupid or too lazy to be entrusted with high command in the future."[63] Burns sought and found what he believed the best opportunities available to prepare his mind for high command – staff training, self-study, writing, experimental survey work, and so on. It is also interesting to note, however, that Burns was almost exclusively concerned with developing the mind and the technical skills of senior officers. He wrote almost nothing on leadership, officer/soldier relations, or commander/staff relations. "The Mind of the General" had no companion article on the personality of the general. That spoke volumes.

Burns never adequately developed his human skills. He was quick-minded, but he always seemed to rub people the wrong way. The same sardonic wit that appealed to readers of *The American Mercury* always seemed a put-down to those who worked for him. They undoubtedly sensed that they were not offering him sufficient "food for the soul" or that he regarded them as "simple reliable tools." That might have been an unfair impression, but Burns's reticence, his disdain for sentimentalism, and his inability to communicate as well in speech as he did in writing definitely prevented him from winning many hearts or minds. Burns acknowledged the shortcoming too. In his memoirs, he expressed his admiration of Montgomery's ability to communicate with groups large and small, to make himself known to soldiers. He regretted that he had none of that ability: "Being a poor public speaker, and thus averse to talking to larger groups than could fill a medium-sized room, I never tried the Montgomery technique. Looking back, I regret that I never had any instruction in public speaking – or thought that I needed it, until with seniority in rank I appreciated its importance."[64]

It was more than just lacklustre oratory. Burns lacked command experience, plain and simple. He missed the opportunity to use more than his smarts to get things done. From the time that he commanded a handful of signallers during the Great War, he did not have another command appointment until he took over the 4th Canadian Armoured Brigade in February 1942.[65] None of his Permanent Force appointments – or indeed any of his appointments during the first thirty months of the Second World War – required him to influence a group larger than a few fellow surveyors or a small circle of staff officers. This was hardly enough man-management training for someone destined for high command. Unfortunately, Burns's experience in this regard was not unique among his Permanent Force colleagues. Crerar, Simonds, and Foulkes, for example, all suffered to some degree from a lack of face time with soldiers and too much time on staff. Although Burns himself acknowledged that "too much continuous staff duty is bad,"[66] it does not seem to have occurred to him that influencing soldiers was not the same as impressing H.L. Mencken, Madge Macbeth, or Andy McNaughton.

He did, however, make a positive impression on Harry Crerar, the man most responsible for his rise in the Canadian Army. As the General Staff Officer Surveys in 1933, Burns worked directly for Crerar, who was acting Director of Military Operations and Intelligence (DMO & I) at National Defence Headquarters in Ottawa. Crerar found Burns to be "most efficient and thoroughly reliable," an assessment with which McNaughton, as Chief of the General Staff, concurred.[67] In 1935, Crerar recommended Brevet Lieutenant-Colonel Burns for the Imperial Defence College course and for employment in "any branch of the General Staff at higher rank and grade," and, in 1936, he added "any command" appointment to the list of future job options for the "exceptionally able" Burns.[68]

Intelligent and productive, Burns was perfect for Crerar's needs when war came. Not long after becoming Senior Officer Canadian Military Headquarters (CMHQ) in London, he called on Burns, who was at the Imperial Defence College at the time. In the autumn of 1939, Burns found himself working alongside his former boss as the GSO 1 CMHQ. Burns admired Crerar, whom he described as "a man of determination, of will ... and drive."[69] He also remembered that Crerar "liked his subordinates to get things done quickly, with not too much chat about it" – a modus operandi not unlike his own. There was much for both of them to do in establishing the "overseas military portion of the Department of National Defence," an entity that would handle matters of administration on behalf of the field force in the United Kingdom, deal with the War Office on issues of policy and training, and advise the Canadian High Commissioner in London on military issues.[70] In 1939 and 1940, Burns saw to the reception of the 1st Canadian Infantry Division and its subsequent accommodation in Aldershot, and he helped coordinate both the acquisition of armaments and the use of various training facilities in Britain. In July 1940, he returned to Canada with Crerar, who had just been appointed Chief of the General Staff (CGS) and promoted to the rank of major-general.[71] As Crerar's Assistant Deputy Chief of the General Staff (ADCGS), Burns took on numerous special projects. He analyzed the organization of the Canadian Army and the

Canadian Army Headquarters. He made recommendations on the size and composition of the field force Canada should raise. He sat as the General Staff representative on the Tank Production Committee, a body that oversaw the production of tanks in Canada. He briefed the Cabinet War Committee on army matters. And perhaps most importantly, he did much of the staff planning that led to a Canadian field force of three infantry divisions, two armoured divisions, and two independent armoured brigades.[72] Crerar trusted Burns's judgment and Burns benefited from Crerar's confidence and friendship. In April 1941, Crerar had Burns promoted to brigadier and assigned as Brigadier General Staff (BGS) to the Canadian Corps in England, where he replaced Brigadier Miles C. Dempsey, future commander of the British Second Army.

Unfortunately, Burns did not last long as McNaughton's BGS – only four months, to be exact. In July, the civilian censorship authorities intercepted an indiscreet letter that Burns had written to his mistress, a married woman in Montreal. The letter is intriguing, not simply because it contains flagrant "indiscretions" concerning certain political and military authorities but also because it is flagrantly sappy, which seems strange for someone so taciturn and reserved. But Burns was a shameless womanizer, something that came as a surprise to most of his contemporaries, who thought him too bookish for such things. They would have been even more surprised to read a letter that began: "My Darling: – A sad disaster has befallen – I've lost your beautiful sweater, and I'm really heartbroken ... I've been feeling gloomy all day, on account of this – you've no idea how much it depressed me."[73] He clearly enjoyed the correspondence and it was clearly welcome distraction from his normal duties: "You say you feel guilty, that I write to you often when I must be tired. I am tired sometimes, but I only write when I want to! Because I love to, and because it brings you close to me and comforts me." They playfully discussed finding her some employment in England so that they could be together: "I wish you were here, so I could test your shorthand – dictating some notes on these lofty [strategic] subjects ... But if you *were* here, the uncharitable might say it would be for another use to which stenographers are often put! ... So often you said you were wearing a nightie, or pyjamas – that is liable to give me ideas!" These frisky comments may have caused a hearty laugh or two among the censors, and maybe even the Vice Chief of the Imperial General Staff (VCIGS), who forwarded the censors' report to McNaughton, but they were not enough to get him fired. There was nothing truly exceptional about a senior officer having an extramarital affair, and, in fact, none of his lovey-dovey comments made it into the censors' report.[74] But they do say something about Burns's personality and how he compartmentalized it. The women in his life presumably saw a much more lively and vulnerable person than the men, who simply saw a lack of personality. His letters to his mistress, even his letters to Madge Macbeth, struck a completely different tone from the cold and occasionally sarcastic one he used in writing to his male contemporaries.

What did make it into the censors' report, and what did get Burns fired, were numerous comments on the Allied war effort, and a few less than compliment-ary remarks on key political and military figures, both in Canada and in Britain. He told his lover that he did not favour Canadian participation in the raiding operations currently under consideration: "I have urged McN[aughton] not to have anything to do with operations which don't serve a really promising stra-tegic conception."[75] He told her that he thought Canadian materiel production was outpacing the output of trained soldiers: "In Canada now the bren gun production is in excess of our needs, and it will soon be the same with other items. But we won't have enough trained men to use the weapons." He conveyed his low opinion of the Royal Air Force: "The Germans have gained much of their military success from air superiority ... [But] our R.A.F. is designed for fighting an independent air war. They begrudge every aeroplane that is detailed for army co-operation ... We are now bombing the wretched French – because our airmen won't think of moving where the fighters and day bombers might get at the Hun." He suggested that British military leadership was lacking: "No one knows definitely [the situation on the Russian Front], certainly not the British W.O. [War Office]." He mentioned that he had seen C.G. "Chubby" Power, Minister of National Defence for Air, drunk and "in a disgusting state." He intimated that McNaughton thought little of the new Commander-in-Chief Middle East, General Sir Claude Auchinleck: "McN[aughton] ... apparently did not like him, or have much opinion of his capacity."

It was all very embarrassing, and it was all very hard to explain how someone so smart could have done something so stupid. He posted the letter from Du-noon, Scotland, so he probably thought the chances of it ending up in the hands of military censors was low. It is obvious, however, that his intellectual conceit had gotten the best of him on this occasion: "I have some ideas for a strategy that could win this war for us, I think. But no one has asked me to do it yet ... The imbeciles still can't see we shall soon be needing men in hundreds of thou-sands."[76] Crerar, who apparently did not consider himself one of the imbeciles, thought that the contents of the letter had their roots in "an excess of professional vanity."[77] Whatever the reasons for Burns's indiscretions, the action taken on the part of the Canadian chain of command was swift. The day after receiving the censors' report from the VCIGS, McNaughton responded that Burns had been "removed from his appointment as B.G.S. ... for return to Canada by the first available sailing."[78] Burns managed to avoid court martial, but he did revert in rank to colonel and he assumed the duties of Officer Administering Canadian Armoured Corps under Brigadier F.F. Worthington at Camp Borden, Ontario.

The wounds from the incident lasted well beyond the five months that he spent in the backwater of Camp Borden. When Minister of National Defence J.L. Ralston interviewed Burns, he expressed his "grave displeasure" at the transgression, but added "that abilities like [Burns's] were needed," and he assured Burns that "he could [redeem] himself and regain the confidence of his associates which was bound to be severely shaken by his action, and that he would have every chance to do this."[79] And Burns did indeed regain the confidence of those closest to him. Crerar had never really wavered. He had even recommended to Ralston that Burns retain the rank of brigadier.[80] But people who were not close to him, or who were never likely to get close to him, would not be so willing to look past the incident. News of what had happened to Burns travelled quickly on the "rumour telegraph" to officers in the Canadian army.[81] It could hardly have happened otherwise. Brigadiers do not disappear without anyone wondering why or speculating about it. And then there were the British. The same "rumour telegraph" would almost certainly have carried news of Burns's dismissal through their senior ranks, where the Canadian's low opinion of the War Office and the RAF would not have been well received.[82] General Sir Alan Brooke, the Commander-in-Chief Home Forces at the time, had to have known the reason for Burns's dismissal. It can only have soured his opinion of the Canadian Army's senior leadership, particularly at a time when the Canadian Corps was still experiencing difficulties in training and he had begun to doubt McNaughton's ability as a commander.[83] McNaughton had a well-developed superiority complex; that his BGS should have had one too, especially in view of the problems the Canadian Corps had recently experienced during Exercise Waterloo, must have been particularly galling. Suffice it to say that Burns's indiscreet correspondence with his mistress damaged his credibility in a way that might not have been so severe for a man with better human skills. His credibility had always rested on his brains and technical skill, but it was an unbalanced base that could not take many hits. Officers like Burns did not get to make many mistakes, then or now. He did not have the ability to win followers who would support him, peers who would stand by him, or British bosses who would tolerate him. It is impossible to say how much this incident affected Burns for the rest of the war, but it certainly did him no good.

Still, in spite of his inability to connect with subordinates and his propensity for annoying the British, Burns managed a resurrection of sorts. After a five-month period of contrition at Camp Borden, he ascended to the rank of brigadier once more and took command of the 4th Canadian Armoured Brigade in

Debert, Nova Scotia. McNaughton welcomed him back with open arms: "I would like Burns to know that Crerar, Montague, Sansom and Worthington, as well as myself are all happy in the new opportunity which is being given him."[84] They were his only real base of support. Collectively, they ensured that Burns got his career back on track, and they were not entirely unjustified in their actions. As the Officer Administering Canadian Armoured Corps, Burns had demonstrated a level of knowledge in tank technology, tactics, and training that far outstripped that of any of his peers. The armoured arm was new in Canada, so there were significant challenges to training all the "drivers, gunners, radio operators, and of course the commanders of the tank, officers and sergeants."[85] They needed equipment to train on, syllabi for standardized training courses, and instructors to teach them.[86] Then they needed to be assigned either to the units of the armoured corps or to reinforcement units that would feed the rest of the corps with trained troops. Eventually, Borden produced and sustained two divisions and two brigades of armoured-trained troops and officers. In tending to these issues, and in turning Borden into "more or less a mechanical, mass production" training facility for the armoured corps, Burns convinced enough of his Canadian superiors that he should be given another chance. Not many Canadians knew more about armour, so Burns seemed the obvious choice to convert an infantry brigade into an armoured one.

Burns assembled the brigade at Debert then took it to England in October 1942. He could only assemble the brigade because he could not at this stage accomplish any meaningful collective training. Officers, non-commissioned officers (NCOs), and soldiers were constantly rotating in and out of Borden to qualify for their new armoured trades, and this made even squadron-level training difficult. But Burns did manage to conduct what training he could, given the constant rotation of personnel and equipment shortages. He ran a number of Tactical Exercises without Troops (TEWTs), such as Exercise Gopher, in which he conveyed to brigade officers how an armoured brigade should attack a dug-in infantry formation.[87] Exercise Shock in August 1942 practised road and convoy movement for all the brigade's echelon vehicles.[88] Later that month, the wireless exercise Belcher tested brigade communication and reporting procedures, and it was followed by Exercises Ringer and Roll, more road movement exercises using whatever vehicles Burns could scrounge up – Ram tanks without armament, trucks, armoured cars – to simulate a brigade administrative move.[89]

Collective training did not take place until after the brigade reached England in the autumn of 1942. Teaching armoured drills or even tank-infantry standard operating procedures was not easy either because, as Burns recalled, "at this time there was no clear and established tactical doctrine for the employment of armoured troops in the British Army."[90] So Burns, who kept up-to-date on the lessons of the Desert War in North Africa, issued his own guidance on tactics and training. One such piece or direction, "Principles of Tank vs Tank Fighting," distributed in August 1942 after some discussion among the senior officers of his brigade, was intended "as a guide for officers and non-commissioned commanders in solving tactical problems, until we have something more authoritative."[91] The sensible seven-page document reflected Burns's approach to training and his keen ability to boil down a series of factors into sensible conclusions – without the smug flair that characterized his *American Mercury* pieces: "In war, it is nearly always an advantage to act quickly; but to act *effectively as well as quickly*, we must, at some time, have reasoned out what action should be taken on certain situations arising ... This [we] should do in the training period." Burns believed in drills, but he also believed that, before practising them, officers and NCOs should think about what drill was appropriate for which circumstances. Thus "Principles of Tank vs Tank Fighting" considered factors such as ground and offered guidance on what troop or squadron formations should be adopted for open terrain, for successive ridges, or for defiles between tanks obstacles. It acknowledged that in some instances – defiles, for example – infantry or other arms may have to be brought forward to clear the area before tanks could proceed. It considered typical enemy and friendly tank formations and gave direction on how to engage enemy tanks and in what priority. With the exception of some guidance on engagement ranges (500-700 yards), which were based on the Canadian Ram tank and the German Panzer Mark III, it could pass for guidance today. It was good counsel before the start of collective training in which officers and NCOs, it was hoped, would practise and repractise their ability to apply the guidance, and the drills that went with them, on field training exercises. Burns remembered that training in England "advanced fairly well," reaching a reasonable level of proficiency at the squadron level by February 1943, but a survey of the brigade war diary shows that field training exercises, even road movement exercises, were far less frequent than wireless exercises and indoor exercises.[92] Equipment shortages and access to training areas made it difficult to advance to regimental or brigade manoeuvre. In fact, the 4th Canadian Armoured Brigade and its parent division had to sit out Exercise Spartan in March 1943 because their training had not advanced sufficiently to allow meaningful participation.[93] But brigades were not made overnight and Burns had done well with the 4th Canadian Armoured Brigade, especially for an officer who had never fought a tank battle or even participated in a mock battle during a field training exercise.

By the spring of 1943, less than two years after he had been unceremoniously reduced in rank and relieved as BGS Canadian Corps, Burns was a major-general and General Officer Commanding (GOC) of the 2nd Canadian Infantry Division. On 4 May 1943, he succeeded Guy Simonds, who had commanded the division for only three weeks before he left to command the 1st Canadian Infantry Division, replacing Major-General H.L.N. Salmon, who had just been killed in a plane crash. The 2nd Canadian Infantry Division was not in good shape. Since suffering 3,367 casualties in its disastrous one-day raid on the French port of Dieppe in August 1942, the division had just replaced its manpower losses and had barely resumed the process of collective training. The Dieppe episode obviously angered Burns. In his memoir, the discussion of his time in command of the division deals almost exclusively with the conduct of the raid.[94] He was too intelligent not to have been bothered by it. A passage that compares the raid on Dieppe to raids conducted by the Canadian Corps in the summer of 1917 warrants quoting at length because it reveals a complex combination of his own tactical insight, his anger at the loss of life, and his complete contempt for the leaders – McNaughton and Crerar first among them – who let Dieppe happen:

> 1917 – the attack was over a relatively flat plain, which afforded little advantage to the enemy; in 1942, the attack was over beaches commanded by enemy-held cliffs or high ground.
>
> 1917 – there was precise information about enemy defences, because of the preceding close contact; in 1942, knowledge of defences was limited to what could be learned from air photographs.
>
> 1917 – there was strong artillery support by barrages fired by field artillery established in positions and registered; in 1942, fire support was given only by air strikes and naval gunfire.
>
> 1917 – raiding battalions had previously fought in several major battles; in 1942, troops went into action for the first time.
>
> 1917 – attacks were launched from behind firmly held positions on land, behind which troops could form up in the exact way required by the operational plan; in 1942, attacking troops came on shore from landing craft, under fire from some distance before touching down.[95]

Having lost none of his intellectual arrogance, Burns also expressed his disdain for the "planning staffs in the Canadian formations and in Combined Operations H.Q., and those commanders who authorized the Dieppe operation in its final form."[96]

Determined to rebuild the 2nd Canadian Infantry Division, Burns found himself in the familiar role of trainer, and he was troubled by what he found to help him do the job. Neither the NCOs nor the officers of the division impressed him. In his preferred manner of communicating, Burns put his thoughts in writing for distribution down the chain of command. In a memorandum entitled "Tr[ainin]g of the NCO," he outlined measures "to raise the standard of leadership of NCOs, and their status generally."[97] It included ways in which NCOs could "learn the habit of com[man]d in simple things first" – like inspections of troops and their weapons. He told their commanders that "it must be impressed on the NCO that his duties do not end when parades are dismissed, but that *at all times* he must check infractions of discipline and disorder." The division was still feeling the effects of its near-destruction at Dieppe, and Burns sensed that NCO lethargy was a symptom of resentment and anger against the chain of command that had sent them into an inferno. He understood their contempt. He felt it too, but it could not continue if the division was ever to rebuild and ready itself for battle, so he set out to identify the problems and eliminate them. The day after his memorandum on NCO training, he published a memorandum to redress the problem of men "wearing torn or dirty battle dress."[98] A piffling issue maybe, but Burns saw it as a collective nose-thumbing at the chain of command. He had reason to think so. Why did NCOs allow soldiers to appear slovenly in garrison? Two weeks later, he again felt the need to intervene in the province of NCOs when he wrote a directive to correct "many faults in the org[anization] and carrying out of weapon tr[ainin]g" that had led to a "waste of time and am[munitio]n."[99] This problem, too, he linked to the soldiers' immediate leaders, the NCOs who failed to inspire them: "*It is essential to arouse [their] interest and engage [their] enthusiasm.*" That was the job of section commanders and the results of recent range practices suggested to Burns that they were not doing it.

Officers were not blameless either. After watching his brigades on Exercise Outburst in July, he waded in on them as well: "Com[man]d[er]s have been told many times that the tr[ainin]g of their off[ice]rs is one of their chief responsibilities ... The experience of Outburst ... shows that results are not satisfactory."[100] Junior officers, he believed, should never carry out an exercise with troops until their commanding officers were satisfied that they had demonstrated sufficient tactical knowledge on sand-table exercises and TEWTs, which he thought senior NCOs might attend as well. This had clearly not been the norm: "For the last month there have been very few such exercises shown on the tr[ainin]g programmes." War was too serious for officers to keep banker's hours: "Off[ice]rs must be prepared to work most nights of the week studying and preparing tr[ainin]g." This was not a man blind or out of touch with the problems of his division. The 2nd Canadian Infantry Division experience in Normandy suggests that Burns's concerns about regimental leadership were not unfounded. In two separate incidents, the Essex Scottish and the Queen's Own Cameron

Highlanders of Canada withdrew in disorder, a very definite indication of leadership difficulties at the lowest levels.[101] In addition, the division's count of deserters between September 1944 and January 1945 (135) was double that of the 3rd Canadian Infantry Division (72) for the same period, with two units in particular – Les Fusiliers de Mont-Royal and Le Régiment de Maisonneuve – accounting for half the divisional total.[102] Burns rightly identified leadership problems in some of his battalions, but writing memoranda was not going to change much. It was an altogether uninspiring way to address a division in desperate need of inspiration, but Burns was an introvert by nature and absolutely allergic to putting on a show of any kind. As one wartime subordinate remarked, it "would have been psychologically impossible for [Burns] to have stood on a jeep and address troops."[103] He also refrained from firing anyone. No battalion or brigade commander lost his job while Burns commanded the 2nd Canadian Infantry Division.

In his quiet and clinical way, Burns did his level best to prepare the 2nd Canadian Infantry Division for its likely tasks in the breakout phase of Operation Overlord. He arranged a number of officer study sessions and TEWTs on attacks, advances, and pursuits, and he led a number of them himself.[104] His battalions and brigades practised tank-infantry attacks in June and July, but the results were not encouraging.[105] One of his brigades produced a ridiculously complicated seven-phase operation order for a simple brigade attack.[106] In preparation for Exercise Harlequin, a 1st Canadian Corps exercise in late August and early September, he put his divisional headquarters through its paces on several wireless exercises and he took his division on its own manoeuvres during Exercise Pickaxe in August. From Pickaxe, Burns wrung three pages of lessons on such disparate issues as the supervision of minefield breaching operations, the method of advance in the 4th Canadian Infantry Brigade, poor handling of small arms, and poor positioning of machine guns in defence – lessons he personally passed to every officer down to company during a 14 August debriefing.[107] After Harlequin, the autumn training session included a return to individual, platoon, and company training to correct identified deficiencies, while Burns and his headquarters conducted a number of skeleton and wireless exercises.[108] The culminating event of the autumn training session was a brigade-on-brigade exercise named Prodder in late October, and, thankfully, there were no seven-phase attack orders during that scheme. It was a sensible training regimen, Burns executed it to the best of his ability, and he made some headway in rebuilding the badly damaged 2nd Canadian Infantry Division and honing the skills of its headquarters. The subsequent performance of the division confirms, however, that he did not expunge all of its problems.

His poor human skills prevented him from leveraging the effect of his sensible training program. The division was depressed and it needed someone who could make its officers and men believe in themselves again. There was more than one way of achieving that. Someone like a Horrocks could have made men smile, made them think they shared a common bond and purpose. Someone like a Simonds might have excised the deadweight early and scared the rest out of their lassitude. But Burns possessed neither the charisma to inspire nor the ruthlessness to instill fear. He criticized without decapitating, and that left subordinates annoyed and unafraid at the same time. Leaving too many incompetents in place, even a scattering of them between the ranks of corporal and brigadier, while at the same time "nitpicking," was not the best formula for rebuilding a broken division. Still, Burns did do many things right, and that was good enough for Crerar, who recommended him to the Minister of National Defence as a future corps commander in November 1943.[109] Two months later, Burns handed over his division to Charles Foulkes, who, incidentally, also failed to inspire the division or fire inadequate commanders. (See pages 265-74.)

But before Burns could take the next step in the command climb – barely two years since he had been busted to colonel – his superiors deemed that he should gain some battle experience, so he deployed to Italy to take command of the 5th Canadian Armoured Division. For the second time, he succeeded Guy Simonds, who was leaving the Mediterranean to become GOC 2nd Canadian Corps in England. Burns's command time with 5th Canadian Armoured Division did not amount to much. He assumed command on 23 January and left to take acting command of 1st Canadian Corps on 1 March, and those thirty-seven days were, as the official historian of the Italian campaign put it, "almost totally devoid of major action."[110] The entire British Eighth Army had adopted a defensive posture to wait out the winter months, build up supplies, integrate reinforcements, and prepare for a spring offensive. So Burns's two brigades – 5th Canadian Armoured and 11th Canadian Infantry – took their turn defending the Ortona salient, conducting patrols, repairing obstacles, and fine-tuning fire plans. Burns made the normal series of visits to familiarize himself with what was going on to the corps headquarters, to the flanking divisions, to his brigades, and to his units.[111] He did not win many people over, however. His quick brain focused reflexively on finding faults and figuring out ways to remedy them. At one early conference with subordinate commanders and senior staff, he explained the division's present tasks in the line, how they were going to accomplish them, and how they would also train for the spring offensive – all fairly reasonable stuff. But he also felt compelled to mention "the importance of insisting upon a high standard of cleanliness in the billets, and of all ranks generally ... Saluting and other details of discipline [were] impressed on com[man]d[er]s."[112] George Kitching, who was a brigadier commanding the 11th Canadian Infantry Brigade at the time, remembered Burns lecturing the soldiers of the Irish Regiment of Canada in the rain about the importance of proper dress.[113] That might have been appropriate for 2nd Canadian Infantry Division soldiers on garrison duty in England, but not for troops straight out of the line in Italy. Combined with a dour demeanour and a humourless delivery, it was poison for a new commander trying to make an impression. It was not that Burns did not care for his troops. He did, which is why he worked so hard to put things right. On 16 February, he visited the Westminster Regiment to find that their machine guns had been poorly sited – "with short fields of fire and directly to the front."[114] He made the Westminsters dig them up and resite them, which of course was the right thing to do, but Burns lacked the cold-bloodedness to hold people accountable or to put one or two "heads on sticks" as examples to others. So he sounded rather like an old lady unhappy with how a picture had been hung than a general smart enough to know the right thing to do and strong-willed enough to do it. He always thought about *what* he would say or write, never *how* he would say it.

His poor human skills did not keep him from corps command, however. Crerar was satisfied that Burns had "act[ed] up to expectations" and confirmed that the new Commander Eighth Army, Lieutenant-General Sir Oliver Leese, was "satisfied to accept Burns" as the Commander 1st Canadian Corps.[115] Crerar also arranged for Burns to take acting command of the corps on 3 March, a handover period that blended into official change of command, which took place on 12 March. That day, Leese arrived at 1st Canadian Corps Headquarters to discuss current operations and "various possibilities" of future operations for the Canadians now under Burns.[116] Leese was not at all thrilled to have had a Canadian corps headquarters shoved into his command, but he got on with integrating the untested headquarters into upcoming operations, even if he did so somewhat grudgingly.[117] The various possibilities all involved offensive operations of some sort in May and June, so Burns set out to prepare the corps accordingly.

He started with a staff study. Having conferred several times with Leese, Burns learned that 1st Canadian Corps would likely be the army reserve for Operation Diadem, the spring offensive to capture Rome. In that capacity, his corps would likely be committed after a break-in operation by 13th British Corps. To prepare himself, his staff, and his subordinate commanders for their impending tasks, on 22 March Burns put out an instruction for a staff study on "The Break-through Operation."[118] It was a good idea. It started the corps staff thinking about issues such as terrain management, obstacle crossings, the movement and possible dumping of artillery ammunition, route control, and training priorities for the upcoming operation. Burns thought hard about it. His personal war diary shows that he spent all day on 21 March at his headquarters "studying [the] problems of future op[eration]s," and he took the entire morning of 22nd to produce the instruction. Acknowledging that it was impossible to study very definite tasks for the corps at that early stage of the planning, Burns presented a scenario wherein 13th Corps had drilled a hole in the Hitler Line, through which 1st Canadian Corps would drive up the Liri Valley towards Frosinone (see Map 3). He gave his staff until 27 March to study the problems before presenting their deductions at a conference he would chair. Some of what had to be practised was obvious. Even before the staff presented their findings, Burns had his BGS issue a training instruction to the two divisions on tank-infantry cooperation, "to lay down a drill to be followed in the sq[uadro]n-co[mpan]y g[rou]p."[119] Major-General Bert Hoffmeister's 5th Canadian Armoured Division had already begun infantry-tank training with the Sluggem series of exercises in March, and it continued along the lines laid down by Burns with Exercise Thruster in April.[120] Major-General Chris Vokes's 1st Canadian Infantry Division was in the line during most of the month of April, but its units did manage to conduct tank-infantry training with the 25th Army Tank Brigade during the first week of May. Battle preparations proceeded along logical lines.

As a result of an 11 April conference with Leese, Burns prepared a solid skeleton appreciation for the upcoming operation.[121] Leese told him that he should be prepared to "attack and break through the HITLER Line in conjunction with 13 Corps" if German defences proved to be very strong. Based on that, Burns saw the operation unfolding in five phases:

I – Adv[ance] to contact with the HITLER line
II – Break through [the] HITLER Line
III – Adv[ance] from HITLER line to seize br[idge]heads over R[iver] MELFA
IV – Adv[ance] from R[iver] MELFA to the line Arce ... Ceprano ...
V – Exploitation to FROSINONE and beyond.[122]

To make it work, Burns decided that he would have to determine forming-up places for his two divisions, how they would move forward from their assembly areas, how he would pass them through 13th Corps, where he would place his artillery to support the break-in battle if there was one, how he would move his artillery to support the breakthrough and pursuit, how he would move or dump artillery ammunition, how he would bridge the Melfa River when he came to it, and where he was likely to find the best going for tanks in the constricted Liri Valley.

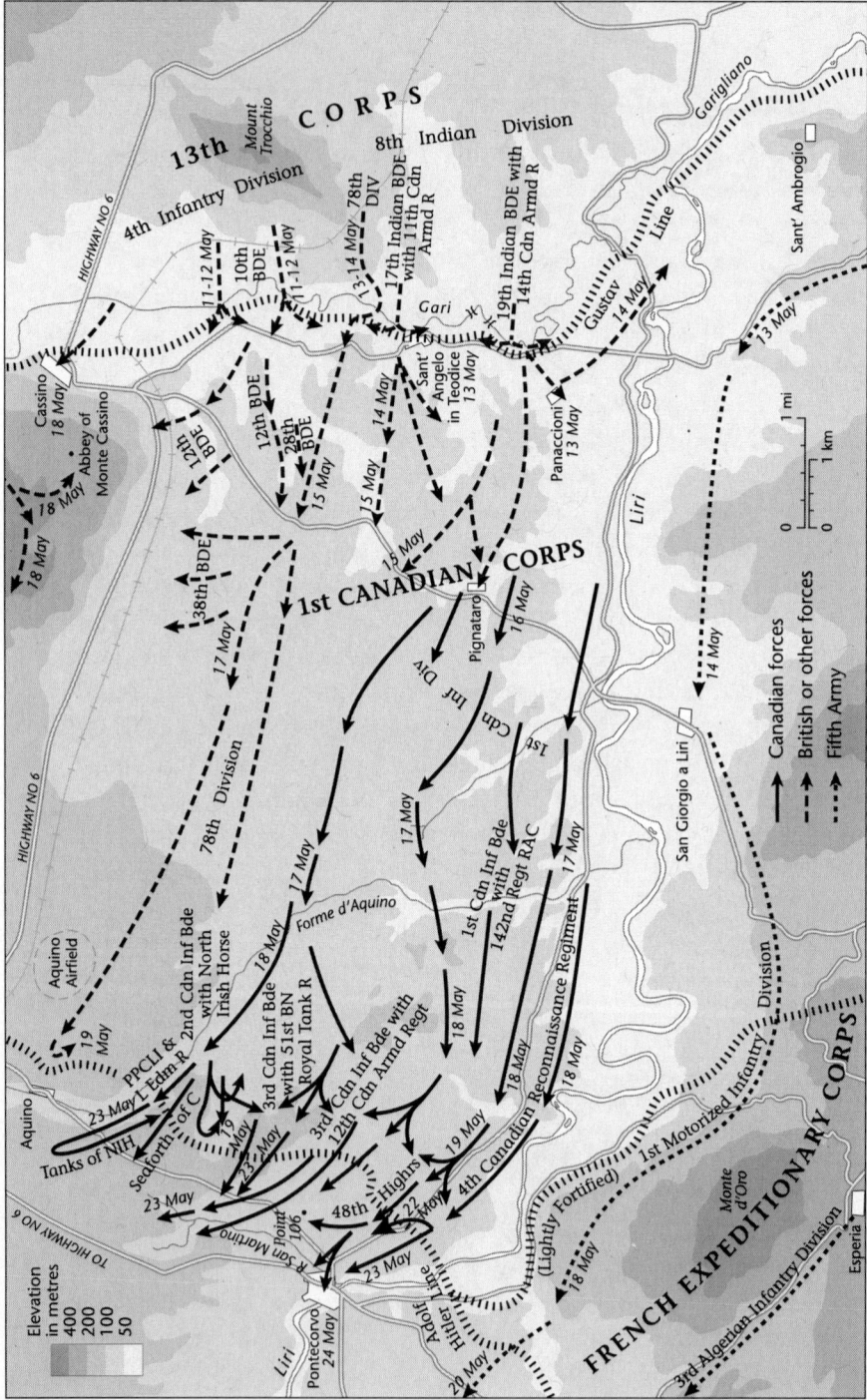

MAP 3   Breaking the Gustav and Hitler Lines. *Source*: Lieutenant-Colonel G.W.L. Nicholson, *The Canadians in Italy, 1943-1945* (Ottawa: Queen's Printer, 1966).

CORPS

13th

Mount Trocchio

4th Infantry Division

8th   Indian   Division

11-12 May

10th BDE

13-14 May   78th DIV

17th Indian BDE with 11th Cdn Armd R

19th Indian BDE with 14th Cdn Armd R

HIGHWAY NO 6

Cassino 18 May

Abbey of Monte Cassino

12th BDE

12th BDE

28th BDE

Gari

Sant' Angelo in Teodice 13 May

Gustav   Line

14 May

13 May

Garigliano

Sant' Ambrogio

18 May

18 May

18 May

38th BDE

15 May

15 May

14 May

Panaccioni 13 May

1 mi

1 km

17 May

15 May

78th Division

1st CANADIAN   CORPS

Pignataro

16 May

Liri

0

HIGHWAY NO 6

17 May

1st Cdn Inf Div

14 May

San Giorgio a Liri

Canadian forces

British or other forces

Fifth Army

Aquino Airfield

19 May

17 May

17 May

1st Cdn Inf Bde with 142nd Regt RAC

17 May

Forme d'Aquino

18 May

18 May

18 May

Division

PPCLI & 2nd Cdn Inf Bde with North Irish Horse

L Edm R

3rd Cdn Inf Bde with 51st BN Royal Tank R

1st Cdn Inf Bde with

18 May

1st Motorized Infantry Division

TO HIGHWAY NO 6

23 May

Aquino

Tanks of NIH

Seaforth of C

19 May

23 May

3rd Cdn Inf Bde with 12th Cdn Armd Regt

18 May

19 May

4th Canadian Reconnaissance Regiment

18 May

FRENCH EXPEDITIONARY CORPS

Monte d'Oro

23 May

San Martino

R

106

48th

Highrs

22 May

19 May

(Lightly Fortified)

18 May

Esperia

Pontecorvo 24 May

Adolf Line

Hitler Line

20 May

20 May

18 May

3rd Algerian Infantry Division

Liri

Elevation in metres
400
200
100
50

The process was sensible, but the follow-through actions of the green corps staff left something to be desired. Burns identified both movement and traffic control as priority tasks that should be studied and practised, both in his 11 April appreciation and in his staff study notes of 22 March, but his staff did not give them sufficient consideration. As D-day for the offensive drew near, his key staff became entirely preoccupied with the break-in battle, to the virtual exclusion of issues such as road movement, traffic control, and the pursuit battle. In preparation for a staff study period, for example, his BGS, G.A. McCarter, issued an instruction containing a list of eleven "Suggested Points for Study."[123] It included items such as enemy defences, approaches, frontages for the attack, and minefield reconnaissance, but not a thing on road movement or traffic control as Burns had directed earlier. After the war, McCarter commented that there had been "some informal discussion of, and comment on" the possibility of having a single corps control all traffic movement in the Liri Valley,"[124] and this was probably true, but informal discussions between staff officers did not solve problems unless they led to action, and here they clearly did not. Burns had to have been aware of the staff activity, just as he most certainly read the staff reports, but he did not correct McCarter, probably because he knew the brigadier too well. They had been classmates at RMC, they had both taken their commissions in 1915, they had both served in the Permanent Force during the interwar period, and McCarter had briefly commanded the 6th Canadian Infantry Brigade under Burns in the 2nd Canadian Infantry Division, a post he left in October 1943 to become BGS 1st Canadian Corps.[125] Burns let his personal feelings get in the way of confronting McCarter. It should not have been so.

But Burns did a lot of things right, such as conducting his own reconnaissance and liaison. On three occasions, he went forward to areas just behind Cassino to look at the terrain over which he would attack, once by himself, once with Hoffmeister, and once with Vokes.[126] This gave the senior commanders a much better appreciation for the terrain and the tasks that lay ahead. Before being committed to action on 16 May, he also met no less than twelve times with the army commander or the army chief of staff to discuss his plans for the upcoming operation. He also had at least four face-to-face meetings with Lieutenant-General Sydney Kirkman, GOC 13th Corps, to coordinate the forward passage of 1st Canadian Corps through Kirkman's divisions. The planning and preparation for battle made sense, and at this time, Burns made a very positive impression on Leese, who reported to the War Office: "The Canadians under Burns are developing into a very fine Corps. He is an excellent commander and will, I feel sure, do well in battle ... I like Crerar very much as a man but I am sure that Burns is a better soldier."[127]

His subordinate commanders were harder to impress. The same fussiness without force afflicted his dealings with them. While watching one of the infantry-tank exercises in early May, Burns sat stoically on a hill with Vokes and the battalion commander of the participating infantry battalion. In his diary, Burns noted that "very good progress was being made," but all he could manage to say at the time was, "Why do they have no entrenching tools?"[128] Vokes reportedly reassured the battalion commander with a wink, an indication that Burns's subordinates understood each other but not him. Bert Hoffmeister captured the contradictions in Burns when he said that "no senior officer tried harder, but he had the unfortunate knack of doing stupid things."[129] The corps commander was also drawn irresistibly to minutiae. After observing the training conducted by the 2nd Canadian Armoured Regiment, much of his commentary to the armoured brigade commander dealt with why "the M55 telescope was not being used ... as I understand the later model of Sherman t[an]ks are to be equipped with improved telescope[s] of this pattern which give the g[un]n[e]rs a better definition and a better opportunity to pick up distant targets."[130] Surely a new corps commander preparing for a major battle against a first-class enemy had more important issues to occupy him.

He did, and the preservation of manpower was one of them. On the eve of battle, Burns briefed division and brigade commanders on the limited pool of infantry reinforcements, which had the potential to run dry by July. He also emphasized the necessity of reducing wastage due to "malaria, dysentery, V[enereal] D[isease]" and battle exhaustion, all of which he considered "a direct indication of the efficiency of the unit and its com[man]d[er]."[131] It was a serious problem that required serious action, but Burns was typically flaccid in his direction to his divisional commanders and his brigadiers: he asked them to relay the "gist" of his remarks to the unit commanding officers, and he suggested that the "remedy" for units continuing to show a high rate of wastage was "obvious." Indirect and insufficiently ruthless – too much of Burns's direction came out that way. He suggested that his subordinate commanders excise inefficient underlings, but at the same time did not hold them accountable if they failed to do so. And everyone knew that Burns had a reputation for finding fault but firing no one. Actions like his manpower address, and the letter that went with it, only undermined his credibility, reinforcing the perception that he was weak-willed.[132]

The first operation to test Burns's ability as a battlefield commander was part of an army group offensive that commenced on 11 May (see Map 4). General Sir Harold Alexander, commander of the Allied Armies in Italy (AAI), wanted "to destroy the right wing of the German Tenth Army; to drive what remains of it and the German Fourteenth Army north of Rome; and to pursue the enemy to the Rimini-Pisa line, inflicting maximum losses on him in the process."[133] To do this, Alexander had shifted the weight of the AAI west of the Apennines – the US Fifth Army along the Tyrrhenian coast and facing the Aurunci Mountains and the British Eighth Army poised to strike into the Liri Valley. Believing that only a concentrated thrust could break the German positions on the Gustav and Hitler Lines, Alexander planned to drive simultaneously with the Fifth Army towards Gaeta and Terracina, and with the Eighth Army through the Liri Valley towards Anagni. Several days after the start of these operations, he wanted the US 6th Corps to attack out of the Anzio bridgehead, where it had been since the end of January, towards Valmontone. For the Eighth Army portion of the battle, Leese lined up the bulk of his forces in the crowded Cassino sector, turning over everything from the area north of Cassino to the Adriatic to Lieutenant-General Charles Allfrey's 5th Corps. In the main assault area, he stacked up his corps north to south – 10th Corps in a holding task north of Cassino, 2nd Polish Corps at Cassino, 13th Corps in the Liri Valley, and 1st Canadian Corps in reserve, poised for employment in the Liri corridor. After five days of hard fighting to break the Gustav Line, and after 13th Corps had suffered heavy casualties in two of its three divisions, Leese committed the Canadians to the battle.

However, he did not have the Canadians pass completely through 13th Corps and assume full control of the cramped Liri corridor. Instead of placing the fresh 78th Division under Burns and giving him control of all movement in the Liri Valley, Leese decided to cram two corps into a four-mile-wide space with only one major route, Highway No. 6. In the north, 13th Corps would lead with the 78th Division along the axis of Highway No. 6, while in the south, where there were no major routes, 1st Canadian Corps would relieve the 8th Indian Division and squeeze its two divisions into the bottom portion of the valley. Leese's decision defies any rational explanation. Forcing two corps into a limited battle space meant that they would have to compete for route access, a process that would have to have been meticulously managed by his army headquarters. It did a very poor job of that. The fact that 13th Corps and 1st Canadian Corps each had different code names for major routes indicates clearly that the army headquarters had failed to manage route control.[134] As the battle had developed, Burns had made various arrangements with 13th Corps and the Eighth Army to bring forward his two divisions in brigade groups, because that was all he could fit on the restricted frontage. If he had serious concerns about traffic and route control, he did not record them in his war diary, although there were delays bringing forward the 1st Canadian Infantry Brigade Group on 14 May. This difficulty notwithstanding, on 15 May Burns issued confirmatory orders

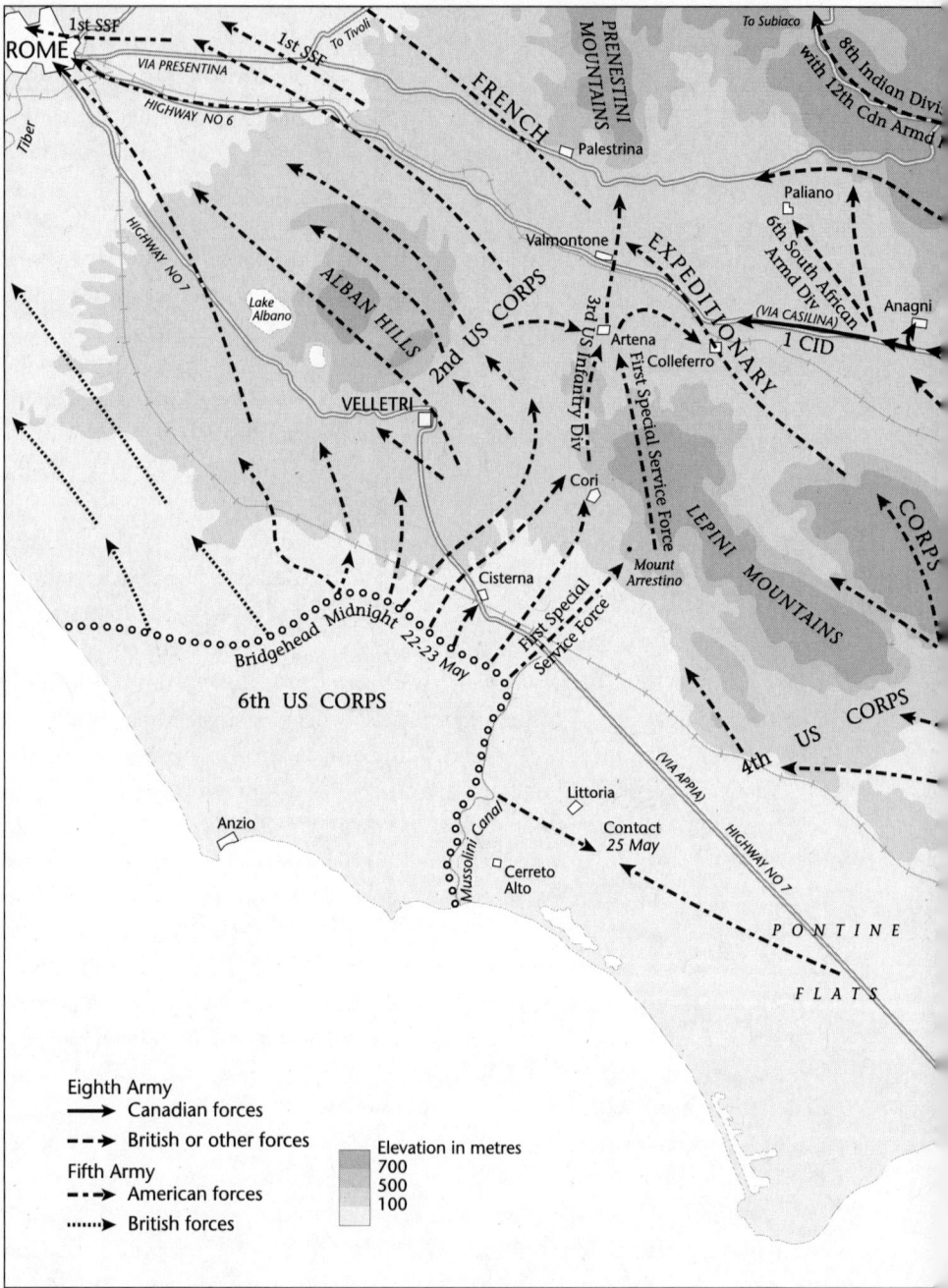

ROME

1st SSF

1st SSF

VIA PRESENTINA

HIGHWAY NO 6

To Tivoli

Tiber

PRENESTINI MOUNTAINS

FRENCH

Palestrina

To Subiaco

8th Indian Divi.
with 12th Cdn Armd

Paliano

6th South African
Armd Div
(VIA CASILINA)

Anagni

Valmontone

EXPEDITIONARY

1 CID

HIGHWAY NO 7

ALBAN HILLS

Lake
Albano

2nd US CORPS

VELLETRI

3rd US Infantry Div

Artena

Colleferro

First Special Service Force

Cori

LEPINI MOUNTAINS

CORPS

Cisterna

Mount
Arrestino

First Special
Service Force

Bridgehead Midnight

22-23 May

6th US CORPS

4th US CORPS

Anzio

Mussolini Canal

Littoria

Contact
25 May

Cerreto
Alto

(VIA APPIA)

HIGHWAY NO 7

P O N T I N E

F L A T S

Eighth Army
Canadian forces
British or other forces
Fifth Army
American forces
British forces

Elevation in metres
700
500
100

MAP 4   The battle for Rome.

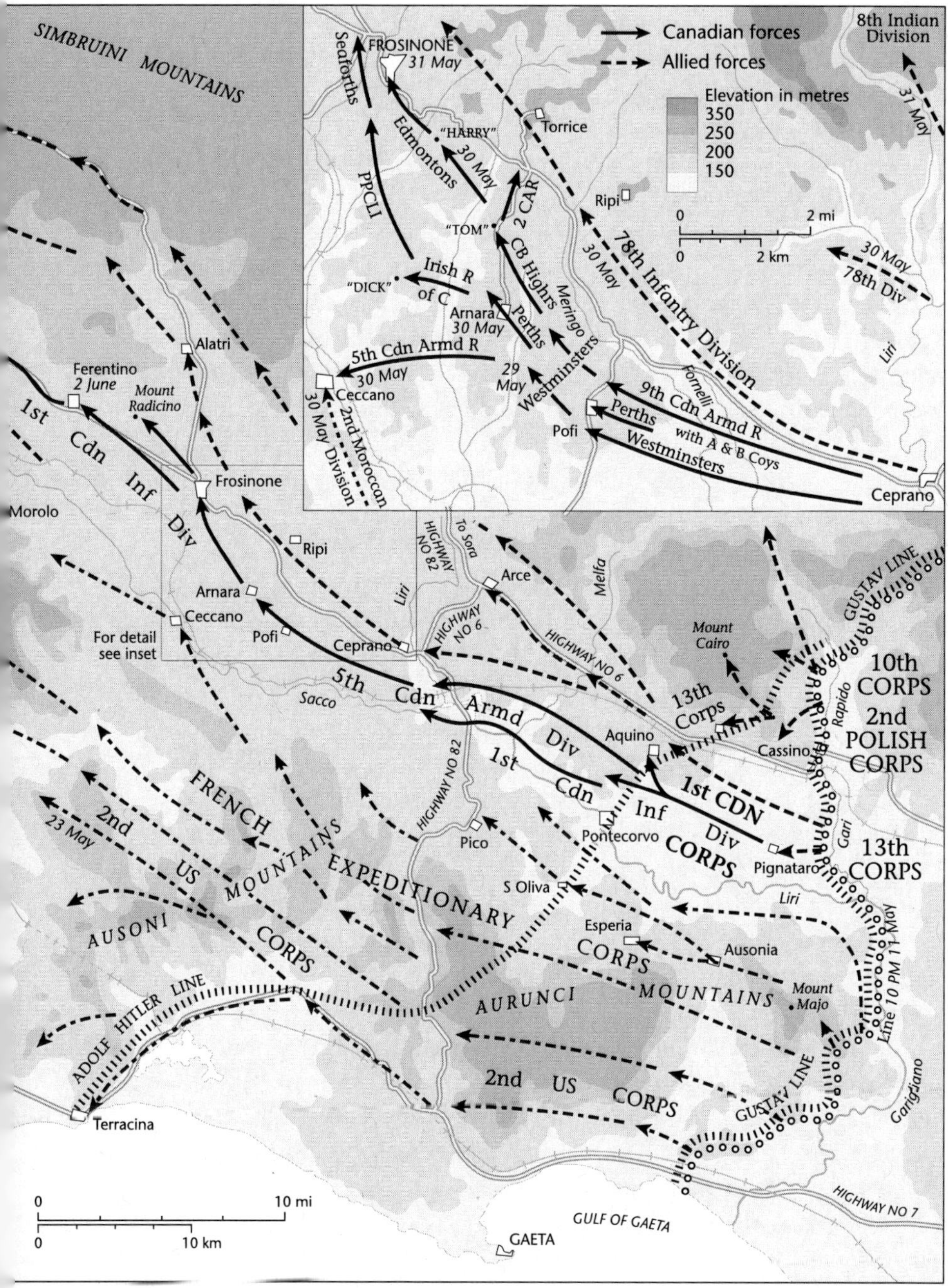


*Source:* Douglas E. Delaney, *The Soldiers' General: Bert Hoffmeister at War* (Vancouver: UBC Press, 2005), 134-35.

for the 1st Canadian Infantry Division to "relieve 8th Ind[ian] Div[ision] and adv[ance] to contact with the ADOLPH HITLER Line."[135] As Burns had anticipated more than a month earlier, the 1st Canadian Infantry Division would have to break into the Hitler Line.

The Canadian advance was slow to start and Burns had to intervene to speed things up. By the end of 16 May, the 1st Canadian Infantry Brigade Group had advanced barely a kilometre, and Leese was "disappointed that no greater progress was made in the face of quite light opposition."[136] The brigade was in contact with the enemy the whole time, and it had managed to take 60 prisoners, but it was an undeniably slow start.[137] Vokes needed stern encouragement to press his brigades more aggressively, and Burns did send him a note, but it was not stern and the corps commander did not take ownership of the rebuke. It began: "I have just been to see the Army Com[man]d[er] and gave him an outline of progress ... today."[138] The letter also conveyed that it was Leese who was "disappointed" and that it was Leese who thought it "very urgent that a determined advance should be made tomorrow." Burns did close with "it is most important that you send your b[riga]des f[or]w[ar]d with great determination," but the tone of the letter definitely implied that the impetus for its contents came from someone else, and this did not leave a good impression. The rough-edged Vokes already thought Burns a bit of a schoolmarm, so the corps commander's unwillingness to take responsibility for the admonition only added to the impression of impotence. Vokes pressed ahead with his task on 17 May, advancing another 1.5 kilometres on a two-brigade front to the Forme d'Aquino and taking 200 prisoners in the process.[139]

The slow pace of the advance owed much to a combination of enemy delaying actions and the difficulties of bringing forward fighting forces and supplies on the few congested routes available. The enemy belonging to the 361st Grenadier Regiment and the 190th Panzer Reconnaissance Battalion fought skillful delaying battles, which impeded the 1st Canadian Infantry Division's advance. Traffic also confounded the advancing forces. At one point, the Three Rivers Regiment received a last-minute task to support the 3rd Canadian Infantry Brigade advance because the assigned regiment from the 25th Army Tank Brigade could not thread its way through the traffic jams to reach the battle area in time to start the advance.[140] After much difficulty, on 19 May, the 1st and 3rd Canadian Infantry Brigade Groups finally pounded past the last enemy covering forces, "made contact with the defences of the ADOLPH HITLER Line and began to tap them out."[141]

The "tapping out" of the enemy defences, on both the 1st Canadian and 13th Corps fronts, revealed the enemy to be extremely well posted in fixed defences and supported by substantial obstacles, so planning proceeded for a set-piece attack. On the other side of the Hitler Line defences were two battalions of the 3rd Parachute Regiment in the area of Aquino, four battalions of the 90th Panzergrenadier Division between Pontecorvo and Aquino, the 44th Ersatz Battalion to the immediate southeast of Pontecorvo, the 334th Engineer Battalion in the town of Pontecorvo itself, and the 190th Engineer Battalion south of the town.[142] These units were well under strength, the strengths of the battalions ranging from 150 to 220 troops, for a total of approximately 1,000 troops across the 1st Canadian Infantry Division front. But the 90th Panzergrenadier Division still had forty to forty-five assault guns and tanks,[143] and the defensive works of the Hitler Line were formidable. They included tank turrets mounted "on concrete foundations with elaborate chambers below," which had been sited to enfilade tank approaches, "steel portable pillboxes" for machine guns, concrete gun emplacements, fully revetted trenches, wire, and mines.[144] If the defences had a weakness at all, it was that they were shallow, most of the positions being only 500 to 700 yards deep. Still, it would be no simple task to breach the line.

Cracking through it would require an infantry-heavy attack to break in, followed by a tank-heavy assault to break out (see Map 3). Leese gave formal orders to Burns and Kirkman on the morning of 20 May. The main attack would be executed by 1st Canadian Corps between Aquino and Pontecorvo during the night of 21-22 May, while 13th Corps would "maintain pressure" on Aquino, whatever that meant. Burns gave the task of breaching the Hitler Line to Vokes, and he ordered Hoffmeister to have a brigade group poised for a breakthrough once a hole in the line had been made.[145]

On the afternoon of 20 May, Burns held a conference attended by the divisional commanders, his key staff, commanders of the corps supporting arms, and the Eighth Army Chief of Staff, Major-General George Walsh.[146] All the key players briefed on their plans and raised whatever coordination issues they wanted addressed. Vokes, who had spent three hours stuck in traffic en route back to corps headquarters, which was three kilometres east of the Gari River, could not contain his contempt at having been dragged back, and he told Burns how he felt before the briefing started.[147] He also asked the corps commander if "any son of a bitch on his staff was aware that the only road forward [Highway No. 6] was jammed with trucks nose to arse."[148] Burns did not respond and the two men made their way in silence to the briefing room. Once there, Vokes announced that he would attack on a narrow 2,000-yard front with the 2nd Canadian Infantry Brigade Group, supported by the Churchill tanks of the North Irish Horse and a heavy barrage.

No one at the conference raised any concerns about this course of action, but when Walsh returned to Eighth Army headquarters and explained the plan of attack to Leese, the army commander was not happy. In fact, Leese travelled back to 1st Canadian Corps Headquarters early that evening to tell Burns that an attack on so narrow a front would not succeed because it would permit the enemy to concentrate his firepower on the attacking forces. He suggested that the attack should be executed instead with "two b[riga]des up" and with more tanks, a regiment supporting each brigade. An attack with three or four battalions in the line would stand a much better chance of breaking apart the enemy's defences. It was a sound alteration and Burns agreed to the proposed changes, but in a note to Vokes, he again attributed the change to the army commander: "The Army Com[man]d[er] has just been with me and has made the following comments on the plan as we have developed it."[149] Burns went on to explain the concerns raised by Leese, the remarks all being preceded with "he says" or "he feels" or "the Army Com[man]d[er]." He also apologized: "I am sorry not to have raised this point before as your planning and preparation may have gone ahead on the other idea, but on thinking it over and hearing the Army Com[man]d[er]'s reason (and he has great experience in this type of battle), I am sure he is right." Leese was right, but the letter did little to raise Vokes's estimation of Burns's strength of will. Right or wrong, Vokes's contempt was understandable given the circumstances. Burns had already failed to put him in his place following the tirade earlier that day. And ascribing the attack plan changes almost entirely to Leese only reinforced the perception that Burns was weak. A simple face-to-face meeting with a clear statement of intended changes would have been better: "*I've* thought about your plan. *I* don't think it will work because of *x, y,* and *z*. Here's what I'd like to see changed." But that was not Burns.

Vokes implemented the changes, but a combination of factors led him to explore a possible end run on the Hitler Line defences from the south. First, the French Expeditionary Corps under General Alphonse Juin had made excellent progress, in fact penetrating just beyond Pontecorvo on the west side of the Liri River. It was worth exploring whether an attack might be arranged from the French sector to encircle Pontecorvo. Second, the 4th Princess Louise Dragoon Guards (PLDG), in "tapping" the enemy defences just north of Pontecorvo, had taken twenty-two prisoners of the 44th Ersatz Battalion, a reinforcement unit assessed to be "very poor" and with "little stomach for fighting an aggressive enemy."[150] Burns and Leese agreed to the development of attack options in the area of Pontecorvo – provided they did not detract from the main blow to be delivered in the area just south of Aquino, Operation Chesterfield. Vokes sent Brigadier Dan Spry to the French sector to explore the possibility of putting one battalion across the Liri River from the south and west, but this proved impractical. The enemy's defences on the north side of the Liri River near Pontecorvo were simply too strong, and coordinating an attack across corps boundaries would take too long. Vokes opted instead to attack the section of the line believed to be held by the 44th Ersatz Battalion on 22 May with one battalion, reinforced with tanks and supported by an artillery barrage.

It failed. From a mountaintop in the French sector, Burns watched the 48th Highlanders of Canada and supporting tanks from the 142nd Royal Tank Regiment move through a minefield breach that had been made by the PLDG the night before and inch towards Pontecorvo. But the assault, which had been hurriedly arranged over the protests of both the brigade commander and the assaulting battalion commander, soon slowed southeast of Point 106 as enemy resistance stiffened steadily in response to the isolated attack. At 1100 hours, Burns conferred with Vokes, who insisted that the attack had made better progress than had appeared from Burns's vantage point, and the attack limped on. Burns had been right about the stalled attack, but it was not until 1600 that Vokes ordered the 48th Highlanders to "consolidate on the high ground running southeast from Point 106."[151] Burn passed on the news to Leese, who, according to Burns, said that the operation had been a valuable one in that it was a diversion from the main point of the impending attack near Aquino, and it had made an initial breach that might be expanded for the breakthrough and exploitation of the 5th Canadian Armoured Division.

This was a glass-half-full assessment. The Pontecorvo attack was a dangerous distraction from the main effort for Operation Chesterfield. Putting together the hurried operation against a strongly defended enemy position badly delayed preparations for the main attack on a strongly defended position. That was how Burns saw it – at least, that was how he saw it after the event. Although he recorded none of his misgivings about the Pontecorvo prodding operations in his war diary at the time, Burns later wrote that he was "not very happy about it," even before the start of the operation. The Pontecorvo attack seriously complicated the task of the Commander Royal Artillery (CRA), 1st Canadian Infantry Division, Brigadier William Ziegler, who already had the responsibility for planning the fire of some 810 guns in support of Operation Chesterfield.[152] Ziegler had received his tasks from the Commander, Corps Royal Artillery (CCRA), Brigadier Edward C. Plow, at an afternoon conference on 20 May.[153] Within seventy-two hours, Ziegler would have to coordinate a counter-battery plan, a preparatory fire plan, and a barrage using the guns of 1st Canadian Corps, plus those in range from 13th Corps, 2nd Polish Corps, and the French Expeditionary Corps – a monumental task. Having to prepare *another* fire plan and *another* barrage for the Pontecorvo operation stretched Ziegler and his staff very near their breaking point. As it was, the gun regiments did not receive the fire plan or their tasks for Operation Chesterfield until late on the evening of 22 May, with amendments still arriving two hours before H-hour.[154] Worse still, Vokes held back the 2nd Canadian Infantry Brigade until 1700 hours on 22 May – a mere thirteen hours before H-hour – hoping he could use it to exploit any break-in that may have been achieved by the 1st Canadian Infantry Brigade at Pontecorvo. Burns apparently had no knowledge that Vokes had taken this action, which left very little time for the assaulting battalions to reconnoitre their objectives or marry up with their assaulting tanks.[155] The whole Pontecorvo business was a largely wasted effort, but Vokes was confident both that he knew better than the corps commander and that the corps commander would not have the nerve to confront him.

He was right in the latter assumption. Vokes badly needed to be gripped, told to abandon his flighty plans for Pontecorvo, and get on with the preparations for the main attack, but Burns simply could not do it. He understood the problems. Where were the attacking troops and tanks going to go once they got into the rubbled and well-defended town? Ortona had swallowed the same brigade for nearly a week only five months earlier.[156] Had there been sufficient time for detailed reconnaissance near Aquino, the 2nd Canadian Infantry Brigade's attacking battalions – the Princess Patricia's Canadian Light Infantry (PPCLI) and the Seaforth Highlanders of Canada – might have found the most dangerous enemy positions on the Forme d'Aquino and refined plans to deal with them, provided there was enough time to implement the changes. A cursory look at the ground and a quick map study certainly convinced the two battalion commanders that the 13th Corps' task "NOT to attack the HITLER Line but ... to deceive the enemy into thinking that the main attack will be directed along Highway 6" would not be sufficient to silence the defiladed machine guns and the anti-tank weapons covering the Canadian axis of advance. A little past midnight on 24 May, Lieutenant-Colonels Cameron Ware of the PPCLI and Rowan Coleman of the Loyal Edmonton Regiment went to their brigadier, Graeme Gibson, to see whether some sort of artillery support – high explosive or smoke – might be arranged on the north bank of the Forme d'Aquino to neutralize the German defenders in the event that the feint attack by the 78th Division did not amount to much. That kind of amendment to the fire plan would have meant some nettled negotiation of artillery targets across the boundary with 13th Corps, and the target lists were already late getting out. Ware and Coleman were informed that "no further changes could be made."[157] They would have to attack into an area they had not adequately reconnoitred and without full assurance that their right flank was secure. These were the knock-on effects of Burns's unwillingness to confront Vokes.

The results of the attack on the corps right flank were predictable. Vokes's division attacked with the 2nd Canadian Infantry Brigade on the right and the 3rd Canadian Infantry Brigade on the left, while, furthest west, the 1st Canadian Infantry Brigade prodded towards Point 106. At 0600 hours on 23 May, the lead battalions and their supporting tanks made their way towards their objectives supported by a barrage and selected concentration fire.[158] Almost immediately, the attack in the 2nd Canadian Infantry Brigade area ran into trouble. The German defenders, who had registered their defensive fire targets and who had good observation on the 2nd Canadian Infantry Brigade attack from Aquino and Mount Cairo, caught the attackers with mortar and artillery fire between the start line and the enemy wire. Then, as the 3,200-yard-wide barrage moved beyond the German forward positions, defiladed enemy machine guns in the Aquino area began to take a terrible toll on the PPCLI, closest to the Forme d'Aquino. Elements of two Patricia companies made it into the wire, but the casualties were heavy and the commanding officer, despite moving his Tactical Headquarters dangerously forward, lost contact with the pinned-down survivors of those two lead companies within two hours and was forced to rely on the reports of the walking wounded who straggled back. It got worse as the day wore on. Seventy-seven Patricias were all that remained of Ware's battalion by last light.[159] The supporting tanks of the North Irish Horse bumped into a hitherto undetected minefield, which set them up for destruction by anti-tank gun fire from the other side of the Forme d'Aquino. It was so bad that mines or German anti-tank gunners knocked out forty-one of the fifty-eight tanks supporting the 2nd Canadian Infantry Brigade attack.[160] The Seaforth Highlanders attack managed to penetrate the wire, fight through a maze of defensive positions, and reach the intermediate objective of the Aquino-Pontecorvo road, but not without heavy losses. By the time they got there, Lieutenant-Colonel Syd Thomson had only a hundred men left. In all, the 2nd Canadian Infantry Brigade suffered 543 killed, wounded, or captured, the heaviest brigade casualty toll for any single day of fighting during the Italian Campaign.[161] Most of the killing came as a result of direct and indirect fire from the right flank. The 78th Division feint, which had started with a brief artillery concentration before 0600 hours, and which was over by 0800, had done next to nothing to neutralize enemy positions in and around Aquino.

How could the 2nd Canadian Infantry Brigade attack have been such a disaster? Part of the problem was largely a function of how someone had drawn a line on a map. Aquino itself was in the 13th Corps sector, outside of Burns's control. The notion that the 78th Division, while still under command of another corps, would put in a "feint" attack in support of the main assault was foolish.

The only way the 78th Division attack could have helped was if it had been a full-scale assault, fully supported by artillery. The 4th Parachute Regiment and the two battalions of the 3rd Parachute Regiment were too well posted and too determined to be subdued by anything less. More extensive reconnaissance of the objective area might have revealed the strength of the Aquino positions, but Vokes had kept the attacking battalions away from their objective area while he diddled around Pontecorvo. Because the boundary between 1st Canadian Corps and 13th Corps ran along the Forme d'Aquino, Burns could not fire artillery concentrations on the Aquino positions without 13th Corps' say-so. Just before 1000 hours, as German anti-tank gunners were picking off North Irish tanks at will, Burns "asked" his CCRA if he could "neutralize" enemy anti-tank guns in the Aquino area.[162] Not knowing the exact locations of the anti-tank guns, Burns referred only to the map grid square (1,000 metres × 1,000 metres) in which the town of Aquino was located. Plow passed on the task to Ziegler and contacted 13th Corps about engaging targets in its sector. But when Ziegler found that specific targets could not be identified, at 1227 he requested permission to fire a "William" target on Aquino – meaning that the town would be engaged by every Eighth Army gun within range.[163] Initially reluctant, Kirkman and the commander of the 78th Division relented and allowed an army artillery shoot on a position from which the German defenders were killing Canadians and their supporting British tank troops. At 1300, 668 guns fired a total of 3,509 rounds at Aquino, and in fairly quick succession.[164] Thirty-three minutes was quite a quick time frame in which to arrange a cross-boundary shoot with that many guns, and it was an impressive display of firepower. But it was too late. The grain fields on the south side of the Forme d'Aquino had already been littered with burning British tanks and bleeding Canadian infantry. And, as Burns observed after the battle, the shoot did not destroy the defensive positions around Aquino; it only neutralized them for a short period: "It does not appear that we took adequate measure to screen [the 2nd Canadian Infantry Brigade attack area] by smoking the line of the Forme, or by blinding the enemy O[bservation] P[ost]s on MONTE CAIRO."[165] Clearly, the boundary was a huge part of the problem.

If Burns did ask to have the inter-corps boundary moved north, making the town of Aquino an objective within his sector, he did not record it. McCarter could not recall "that any C[ana]d[ia]n officer in authority suggested to 8 Army ... that one corps H.Q. should control all formations taking part in the battle of the Liri Valley."[166] But this was an obvious remedy for the coordination difficulties on the right flank of the 1st Canadian Corps attack. Leese's headquarters had drawn the inter-corps boundary in the worst possible place, to say nothing of the fecklessness of establishing *any* inter-corps boundary in an area only wide enough for a single corps. Aquino, and the high ground to the west and south of it, dominated everything south of the Forme d'Aquino – precisely the area across which 2nd Canadian Infantry Brigade attacked – and the salient of the German defences had its apex along the little river, ensuring that the defenders of 4th Parachute Regiment would have flanking fire on anyone moving along the south side. And Burns had to trust that the 78th Division feint would be enough to keep them quiet – with an attack that everyone knew would end sixty minutes after H-hour and without any real plan for neutralizing artillery fire. Six hours before the attack was to start, a 78th Division message described the plan for the feeble feint: the 11th British Brigade on the Canadian right would "put down a fire program" of artillery and mortars "from H to H+60," while the 14th Canadian Armoured Regiment, under British command for the operation, would pop out of the 78th Division lines at H+30, then pop back in at H+60.[167] That was it. In fact, after the "feint," the 78th Division planned no other attacks until "after [the] success [of] 1 Cdn Corps attack." How could anyone, least of all Burns, have figured that this would be enough to neutralize the German paratroopers in and around Aquino? Given his reticence with Vokes, and his general unwillingness to confront subordinates, it seems highly unlikely that Burns would have challenged Leese on the boundary, even if he had fully anticipated its consequences, and it is difficult to imagine that he did not. He was new to the Eighth Army "club," and he was well aware that neither Leese nor Alexander wanted a Canadian corps headquarters. He must also have wondered how many of the senior British commanders and their staff knew why he had been relieved as BGS in the summer of 1941, and what he had said about the senior British leadership in the indiscreet letter to his mistress. Maybe he thought it best to defer to the experience of an Eighth Army that had been piling up victories since El Alamein in the autumn of 1942. Whatever the reason for his reticence, avoidance of confrontation was a well-established pattern in Burns's behaviour by this point.

In spite of the right flank difficulties, the 3rd Canadian Infantry Brigade broke through the German defences in the centre of the 1st Canadian Infantry Division attack. There, the situation had been different. The brigade had been in front of its objectives since 19 May, when it had attacked with the Carleton and York Regiment, the Royal 22e Régiment, and the 51st Royal Tank Regiment to probe the enemy defences and test it for weak spots. In the four days that followed, the units of the brigade had patrolled extensively, gathered information on enemy defences, and figured out how they would fight their way through the position in detail. The Carleton and York Regiment had even conducted a diversionary attack in support of the 48th Highlanders assault on Pontecorvo during the morning of 22 May, managing to slip two platoons through the wire and into the main defensive area.[168] They knew how to get through the wire and mines in a way that the battalions of the 2nd Canadian Infantry Brigade could not have known, given that they moved into their attack areas only hours before H-hour. Because the 3rd Canadian Infantry Brigade attackers knew where they were going, they avoided most of the mine and wire obstacles, they kept close to the barrage, and they pushed quickly to the intermediate objective of the Aquino-Pontecorvo road, before the enemy's defensive fire could cut them up in the same way it was doing with the PPCLI and the Seaforth Highlanders. The Carleton and York Regiment, which spearheaded the 3rd Brigade assault, also did not have to deal with direct fire from its right flank because it was not attacking a bend in the defences and the 2nd Canadian Infantry Brigade was attacking all-out beside it.

Conditions were definitely more favourable on the 3rd Canadian Infantry Brigade front. It took less than two hours for the Carleton and Yorks to reach the Aquino-Pontecorvo road. Less than two hours after that, they were joined by twenty supporting tanks, some anti-tank guns, and the lead elements of the West Nova Scotia Regiment. Vokes did not reinforce this success immediately. He wanted to wait until the 2nd Canadian Infantry Brigade caught up before proceeding with the next phase of the assault, an advance on a two-brigade front. By 1230 hours, however, it was clear that the 2nd Canadian Infantry Brigade attack had failed, so Burns advised Vokes to "take the bold course of exploiting the success on the left."[169] Vokes agreed and he committed his division reserve – the Royal 22e Régiment and two squadrons of the Three Rivers Regiment – to expand the Carleton and York bridgehead. After some delay, the attack was launched at 1650 hours, driving rapidly through the crumbling defences, rolling up the enemy positions, and seizing what would have been second-phase Seaforth objectives between the Aquino-Pontecorvo road and Highway No. 6. It was so quick that forty minutes later, Bert Hoffmeister, who had been monitoring the battle from Vokes's headquarters, called Burns and advised him that the conditions were set for a 5th Canadian Armoured Division breakout.[170] Burns agreed. He told Hoffmeister to attack immediately, and he advised Leese that the breakout was on.

Unfortunately, it was not on just yet. There were delays as traffic control problems conspired to set the operation back. Burns had wanted elements of the breakout force well forward, ready to smash through any opening offered by the 1st Canadian Infantry Division, but the terrain close to the forward battle area was jampacked with troops, vehicles, and guns. Hoffmeister managed to squeeze a tank-infantry battle group, based on the British Columbia Dragoons (BCD) and the Irish Regiment of Canada, behind the 2nd Canadian Infantry

Brigade, but that was all he could fit close to the front given the crammed conditions and the road congestion.[171] Repositioning that Dragoon-Irish battle group barely two kilometres westward to the 3rd Canadian Infantry Brigade bridgehead should not have been overly difficult, but in the chaotic traffic conditions of the Liri Valley it was a painful and protracted undertaking. Burns's headquarters did not help matters by allowing the surviving tanks of the 25th Army Tank Brigade to move rearward on the main Canadian route to refuel – hardly a priority activity for tanks not involved in the breakout battle.[172] With difficulty, Hoffmeister managed to position Brigadier J.D.B. Smith's 5th Canadian Armoured Brigade in and behind the 3rd Canadian Infantry Brigade hole in the Hitler Line, but the breakout did not occur until the morning of 24 May.

Once it got going, a little after 0800 hours on 24 May, Smith fought his combined-arms battle groups aggressively and well.[173] His tasks were to advance out of the Hitler Line bridgehead, bounce across the Melfa River, and establish a bridgehead through which the 11th Canadian Infantry Brigade would pass to take up the advance on Ceprano. That was a lot for a single brigade, so Hoffmeister had added the following to Smith's three armoured regiments and his motorized infantry battalion: an extra infantry battalion mounted in carriers (the Irish Regiment of Canada), a regiment of self-propelled artillery for immediate indirect fire support, two batteries of anti-tank guns to harden the Melfa bridgehead against counterattack, a field squadron of engineers to clear any obstacles, and two squadrons from the divisional reconnaissance regiment to guard the right flank.[174] The Dragoon-Irish battle group dashed ahead to Mancini by 1030 hours, killing three enemy tanks and eighty-nine infantrymen in the process. Smith kept up the tempo. Even before the Dragoons and Irish had consolidated at Mancini, he ordered the follow-on battle group, based on the Lord Strathcona's Horse (Royal Canadians) and a company from the lorry-mounted Westminster Regiment, to pass through and seize a crossing over the Melfa River, which it did by 1530 hours. It was a tiny and tenuous bridgehead, held at first by only a Strathcona reconnaissance troop, which had managed to skirt past a delaying screen of German tanks in the close country between Mancini and the Melfa River. Major Jack Mahony's "A" Company of the Westminsters reached the reconaissance troop at 1700, just in time to help fend off jarring German counterattacks, as Smith fed two more companies of Westminsters into the bridgehead. The heroic actions at the Melfa capped a heroic first day of the breakout.[175]

The problem was that neither Burns nor his headquarters were clear about the situation at the Melfa River. Burns noted in his diary that "only very fragmentary news was received from 5 Cdn Armd Div."[176] Hoffmeister's headquarters, also fighting its first battle, was experiencing problems of its own. From about 1645 hours, the corps "G" staff pressed the 5th Canadian Armoured Division for confirmation that it had troops and tanks across the Melfa River, but even by 2100 Hoffmeister's headquarters could report only that the location of the Strathconas was "unknown."[177] They also incorrectly reported that their GOC's Tactical Headquarters was with the British Columbia Dragoons "astride" the Melfa River, when in fact the Tac had harboured north of Mancini for the evening. This frustrated McCarter, who needed reasonably accurate and timely information so that his corps commander could plan for the next twenty-four to seventy-two hours. On 25 May, he vented in his diary: "It is a hopeless task to try and get any information out of HQ 5 Cdn Armd Div. They are behaving like complete amateurs. We have to badger them continually about sending back information and even that seldom produces results."[178] The 5th Canadian Armoured Division was fighting extremely well, but its staff work and its communications were wanting. To his credit, Burns went to the division's headquarters and, finding that Hoffmeister was still out in his Tactical Headquarters, "asked [the GSO 1] to get his com[man]d[er] to make better arrangements for getting back information."[179] This very proper intervention on Burns's part had the desired result. Hoffmeister immediately sent a handwritten synopsis of the situation via dispatch rider. It included his intentions for the next twenty-four hours, which were to expand the bridgehead then drive on to Ceprano with the 11th Canadian Infantry Brigade. Burns was satisfied.[180] It looked as though the pursuit battle would continue at its current rapid pace.

Unfortunately, decisions made by the army commander hobbled operations badly. Leese still insisted on advancing with two corps up in the Liri Valley,[181] and a little after noon on 24 May, he had visited Burns, with Kirkman and the GOC 6th British Armoured Division, Major-General Vyvyan Evelegh, in tow. They wanted the 5th Canadian Armoured Division to clear 1st Canadian Corps' main route, which ran between Pontecorvo and Aquino, so that they might bring forward the 6th British Armoured Division to "mop up the enemy in the CASTROCIELO and ROCASECCA area, thus securing the right flank of 5 Cdn Armd Div."[182] This ill-conceived manoeuvre, designed as it was to skirt the enemy still resisting in the Aquino area, could not have come at a worse time. Hoffmeister had barely broken through the Hitler Line, his armoured brigade was about to establish a toehold on the Melfa River line, he was trying to bring forward his infantry brigade for the next breakout to Ceprano, and his staff had to figure out how to move the supporting artillery and its ammunition carriers on limited roads that were now drenched by rain. Did Burns not anticipate the problems that passing forward a British armoured division would pose? Perhaps he was thrown off balance by the presence of three Desert War veterans.[183] Perhaps he actually thought it was possible to execute the manoeuvre without too much disruption to ongoing operations. Whatever the reason, he did not protest. Neither did McCarter. They ordered the 5th Canadian Armoured Division to clear the route as soon as possible. Hoffmeister's headquarters estimated that their troops and vehicles could be off the route by 1430 hours, but finding off-road waiting areas where hundreds of vehicles would not bog down proved difficult, as did moving on tracks that were already jammed bumper to bumper. Not until late in the evening, sometime after 2100, was the 6th British Armoured Division able to start inching forward.

All of this slowed the advance, of course. A first-light attack by the Irish Regiment to expand the Melfa bridgehead on the morning of 25 May had to be delayed several hours because the supporting artillery was snarled in traffic.[184] The advance to Ceprano by the 11th Canadian Infantry Brigade was similarly delayed by traffic until the morning of 26 May.[185] This was unfortunate because the German 51st Mountain Corps had been badly mauled at the Hitler Line. The infantry of 90th Panzergrenadier Division, for example, had been reduced to the 300 troops of the 200th Grenadier Regiment and 100 men of the 361st Grenadier Regiment.[186] The German 1st Parachute Division by this time fielded less than 1,000 fighting troops.[187] On 25 May, the 51st Mountain Corps received orders that "the Melfa Line must be held for several days," but the rapid actions of the 5th Canadian Armoured Brigade on 24 May had already rendered that order an impossibility.[188] Instead, the Germans would put their effort into establishing a strong delay position along the Liri River, from the intersection of the Liri and Sacco Rivers to roughly the town of Arce. As a result of the slow breakout from the Melfa River, the enemy got back to the Liri in time to develop the defences around Ceprano, where his depleted forces could take maximum advantage of the natural obstacles and the close terrain. And they did. While the two Anglo-Canadian corps tied themselves in knots, the Germans moved back to the Liri River, where they blew up the bridges and established a formidable set of delaying positions along the western slopes of the river valley.

A series of other factors also affected the pace of the pursuit. First among them was the painfully deliberate movements of the 11th Canadian Infantry Brigade commander, Brigadier T.E.D'O. Snow. It took him from 0700 hours on 26 May until nearly last light to advance only four miles against very light opposition; even at that, Hoffmeister had to prod him to continue advancing and at least patrol the last mile into Ceprano. It took most of 27 May for the 11th Canadian Infantry Brigade to cross the Liri, clear the far bank of observation and direct fire, and hastily build a tank bridge, which collapsed at 0730 hours the next morning. Hoffmeister briefed Burns on his plan to expand the bridgehead with the 11th Canadian Infantry Brigade on 28 May, make room for Smith's

5th Canadian Armoured Brigade, then have that formation break out from Ceprano to Frosinone. While Smith's brigade was snaking its way forward, another army-level decision had the unintended effect of putting the brakes on the pursuit. Sometime around midday, the Eighth Army Chief of Staff called on Burns to see whether the 78th Division could outflank stubborn German paratroopers in the town of Arce by dipping down into the Canadian sector, again using the main Canadian route, and crossing at Ceprano. This made no sense. A failed bridge, a bridgehead still in the process of being formed, limited roads, an armoured brigade moving forward for a breakout – and Burns agreed to the proposal? A blind man could have seen the traffic troubles this manoeuvre would cause and Burns was not blind. His unquestioning compliance is difficult to explain. As the reconstruction of the tank bridge dragged into the late afternoon, and as the hours of available daylight dwindled, Leese assigned priority on the Ceprano tank bridge to the 78th Division; so Burns decided to send at least part of Hoffmeister's division to the south, where the 1st Canadian Infantry Division had established bridges over the Sacco and Liri Rivers. At this time, Leese, quite incredibly, sent a sharp admonition to Burns because of the "slowness of the advance."[189] In his memoir, Burns wrote that he felt he deserved the rebuke because he was "not quick enough to appreciate ... there was a crossing on the left." Perhaps. But that was only a part of a bigger mess. If Burns deserved a dressing-down for anything, it was for not playing his hand as a national commander and telling Leese that he had no intention of executing such a foolish plan.

The ground got worse as the advance limped along. As Burns had directed, Hoffmeister had Smith send a battle group, based on the British Columbia Dragoons and the Westminster Regiment, around the Isoletta Reservoir in the south, over the 1st Canadian Infantry Division bridges on the Liri and Sacco Rivers, then northward to the 11th Canadian Infantry Brigade bridgehead southwest of Ceprano. This manoeuvre took four hours to execute. The terrain between Ceprano and Frosinone was also terrible going for tanks. Once the advance resumed on 29 May, the Dragoon-Westminster battle group crawled through very close and rocky ground to the town of Pofi, reaching this point only by last light. Because the going was so unsuited to armoured manoeuvre, Hoffmeister pushed the battalions of the 11th Canadian Infantry Brigade, and the Strathconas, three miles northwest of Pofi on 30 May, and Burns, who had gone forward on 29 May and seen the same difficult going for tanks, decided to pass the 1st Canadian Infantry Division through Hoffmeister's armour on 31 May. Once that forward passage had taken place, the 5th Canadian Armoured Division battle for the Liri Valley ended.

The final stages of the Liri Valley battle were anti-climactic for 1st Canadian Corps. After taking the lead from the 5th Canadian Armoured Division on 31 May, the 2nd Canadian Infantry Brigade advanced to Frosinone, encircled the town, and cleared it of the enemy rearguard therein. Vokes continued the advance the following day with the 1st Canadian Infantry Brigade pushing on to Ferentino, which it captured against light opposition, and the 2nd Canadian Infantry Brigade clearing a difficult enemy delay position in a convent at Mount Radicino.[190] With the 1st Canadian Infantry Brigade and the 12th South African Motor Brigade (temporarily under command from the 6th South African Armoured Division), Vokes pushed on to Anagni, which the Royal Canadian Regiment soldiers found to have been abandoned by the Germans. By this time, the right wing of the German 10th Army was in trouble. With the American Fifth Army driving hard towards Valmontone from the south, and the Canadians closing in from the east, part of the German 14th Corps, which was now facing the Canadian advance, was in danger of being destroyed. So Field Marshal Albert Kesselring, Commander-in-Chief Army Group C, ordered Colonel-General Heinrich von Vietinghoff to withdraw the 14th Corps and the 51st Mountain Corps north towards Subiaco.[191] This was about the time that General Mark Clark decided to turn his army sharply left and head straight into Rome, instead of continuing the drive north and closing the trap on a substantial portion of Vietinghoff's army. On 4 June, the Canadian part in the Liri Valley action ended as the 1st Canadian Infantry Division handed control of its sector to the 6th South African Armoured Division and joined the remainder of the corps in army reserve to rest, refit, digest the lessons learned, and correct what had to be corrected.

There was a lot of work to do, much of it tied to key personnel changes. Burns had a "long discussion" with Leese in which they talked about the recent operations and thrashed out points that needed to be addressed before the Canadian corps was committed to action in a month or two.[192] First among the dissatisfactions Leese mentioned was the performance of the 1st Canadian Corps Headquarters. In response to the criticism, Burns asked the army commander "whether he was satisfied to have me continue as corps commander."[193] Leese did not answer directly. Instead, he asked Burns whether he felt he was up to the task. When Burns said yes, they moved on to other issues. Later, Burns wrote that his "impression, perhaps naive, was that General Leese was prepared to have me carry on." With that issue seemingly out of the way, they went on to discuss staff work, engineering organization and control, and "technique of command."[194] In Leese's opinion, part of addressing the first two issues meant firing people. Accordingly, he suggested strongly that Burns axe both McCarter, who as BGS was primarily responsible for staff work in the corps, and his chief engineer, Brigadier A.B. Connelly. Burns agreed. (He could hardly have done otherwise, given his own precarious situation.) He made arrangements to replace Connelly before the end of July. In the case of McCarter, he immediately brought in Desmond Smith from the 5th Canadian Armoured Brigade, but he was clearly uncomfortable letting McCarter go: "I had to proceed with the distasteful task of telling several senior officers that I was obliged to replace them. It happened that they had been officers in the Permanent Force, whom I had known well, and [McCarter] was a friend of long standing."[195] It was probably painful, but it was the right thing to do. McCarter did have difficulty keeping the headquarters in working order, and he had a very tough time keeping the 5th Canadian Armoured Division headquarters in check. As Burns wrote to Crerar on 7 June: "From the beginning, I felt that the G side [operations staff] did not have a grip on operations ... It soon became apparent that [McCarter's] juniors did not understand their responsibilities about obtaining and disseminating information in a systematic way."[196] When Burns was out visiting his divisions during the day, as he had done almost daily during the battle, McCarter had difficulty making decisions or passing direction in accordance with his commander's intent. This made it difficult for McCarter to be a true chief of staff, one who ensures "that the battle keeps going according to intention when the Com[man]der has not got his finger on it."[197] Burns concluded: "I felt that Nick [McCarter] had not shown the requisite grasp of the business to operate under this system." All of this raises the question of why Burns had to be pushed into firing McCarter. McCarter protested that Burns had given no indication of dissatisfaction with his performance as BGS until the corps commander replaced him. Burns had talked around the issue with McCarter: "I did point out omissions and errors of the G S[taff] to him during operations, and he gave me the impression that he was more concerned to excuse his juniors than to correct their faults."[198] It is hard to escape the conclusion that Burns could not bring himself to confront an old friend directly. He needed Leese's encouragement to do it, but, to his credit, at least he did what was necessary. And with McCarter and Connelly out, or on their way out, Burns believed he could turn his full attention to redressing other shortfalls in the performance of the 1st Canadian Corps.

Dissecting the corps' performance, identifying areas for improvement, and implementing remedies was an undertaking more suited to Burns's analytical mind. This was where he shone. The process of his after-action review, and the training regimen that stemmed from it, made efficient use of the personnel he had working for him and the limited time he had available to make the necessary changes. On 7 June, he met with his two divisional commanders and his new BGS. Burns understood that some training did not have to wait for the fully fleshed out lessons of an after-action review, so he told Hoffmeister and Vokes that they needed first to integrate reinforcements and work on methods for improving their ability to pursue a retiring enemy and to break into another prepared defensive position like the Hitler Line.[199] More specifically, he emphasized that the divisions should practise company quick attacks on hastily prepared delay positions and work on drills for breaching minefields. These subunit activities could take place while senior officers and staffs collated lessons on recent operations, lessons that they presented orally at a conference attended by all officers in the corps above the rank of major on 16 June. Participants raised numerous sensible points – the importance of always attempting at least two crossing sites per division in case one fails (as had happened at Ceprano), the necessity of clearing or neutralizing enemy artillery observers before commencing obstacle-crossing operations, the need for additional infantry in the armoured division, ways of dealing quickly with an isolated enemy delaying position, and the need for better traffic control and convoy discipline.[200] Over the next few days, the written after-action reports from the divisions and the CCRA arrived at corps headquarters, confirming most of the points raised at the 16 June conference.

Burns also had his Deputy Adjutant and Quartermaster General (DA & QMG), Brigadier J.F.A. Lister, chair a conference specifically to address the problems of traffic control. Representatives of the divisions, corps troops, and the corps Main and Rear Headquarters gathered on 5 June to tackle the problem.[201] They emphasized the obvious point that the Liri Valley floor had only enough serviceable roads and tracks for one corps, and that the two occasions during which the Eighth Army allowed divisions from 13th Corps to use 1st Canadian Corps routes had resulted in unnecessary delays. There was nothing new in this, but eventually Lister and a few selected officers developed a system "that resembled the block system used by railways."[202] The routes would be divided into blocks, with traffic control posts and assigned waiting areas between each block. If a situation arose in which a unit or formation had to clear a route, the corps traffic control centre could relay a message to the posts concerned, and they could in turn shunt the low-priority traffic into waiting areas while high-priority traffic used the route. It was a well-conceived solution, but it needed an enhanced traffic control organization to make it work. The corps and division Provost Corps companies lacked both the radios and the personnel to function in this new system, so Burns converted the 35th Light Anti-Aircraft Battery to a traffic control unit.[203] This would pay dividends in the battle for the Gothic Line.

In July, Burns also produced two important documents of his own that gave guidance to the summer training – "The Pursuit from the Melfa to Anagni" and "The Set-Piece Attack: Lessons from the HITLER Line."[204] Among other things, the pursuit piece emphasized the need for "bold action" to chase down a disorganized enemy, and advised that "firm bases will only be necessary when resistance is stiff and counter attack possible." The set-piece memorandum stressed the need to attack on a wider front, and laid down methods with which to effect better reconnaissance of prepared enemy defences and deliver better counter-battery and counter-mortar fire. Significantly, both pieces highlighted the problem of overcrowding of limited routes during the May battles. This was the closest Burns came to criticizing Leese directly:

> On two occasions it was attempted to pass divs [divisions] of the adjoining fmn [formation] through gaps or passages over obstacles which had been made by the [1st] Cdn Corps, using routes that were within our boundaries ... There were very sound tactical reasons for this manoeuvre in each case, but the actual result was that excessive confusion developed through [an] inability to get the change of orders and plans down to units and individual dvrs [drivers] and TC [Traffic Control] pointsmen. Great delay was caused in the fwd [forward] move of 5 Cdn Armd Div, with an adverse effect on subsequent ops [operations].[205]

As another means of avoiding traffic control problems, Burns suggested that the army retain at least one armoured division in reserve with a view to using it for exploitation. And when that armoured division was committed, it should be placed under the command of the corps commander in whose sector the exploitation was occurring. That way, the corps could manage the movement forward of the newly committed armoured division, obviating the cumbersome tasks of passing one corps through another, or cramming two corps into a constricted space. Sound points all, but, given the wide circulation of after-action reports, both in 1st Canadian Corps and in the Eighth Army, they did not sit well with Leese.

Burns was already in a vulnerable position with the Eighth Army commander. Leese was not nearly so willing to leave Burns in command as he had let on during their 5 June meeting. Three days after their meeting, he wrote to the War Office about his "difficult problem with Burns."[206] He lamented that "neither Burns nor his staff are up to Eighth Army standards," highlighting that Burns "finds it difficult to put [his point] across to Vokes and Hoffmeister." He explained that he had discussed the problems with Burns and hoped that "with encouragement, teaching and training, they will improve." Long before Burns had a chance to show any improvement, however – less than three weeks later, in fact – Leese had a "long conversation" with Alexander during which he was less sanguine about the future of Burns and 1st Canadian Corps. Again, he emphasized that Burns was "intelligent and easy to work with" but "sadly lacking in tactical sense and has very little personality and power of command."[207] This left Leese in a "very difficult position regarding the employment of the Canadian corps," or so Leese said. He explained that he "must either give them a task beyond the powers of their commander or below the capacity of the troops." Leese was also "loath to put a British or Indian Division under a Commander in whom he has so little confidence." Alexander concluded that there were essentially two options – the replacement of Burns by a "first class" Canadian corps commander, or "the disbandment of the Canadian Corps in Italy" and the assignment of its divisions to other British formations – and he relayed this point of view to the Chief of the Imperial General Staff (CIGS), Field Marshal Sir Alan Brooke. From Brooke, the concerns made their way to Canadian Military Headquarters in London and then to Crerar, Commander First Canadian Army. An annoyed Crerar, who ordered Lieutenant-General Ken Stuart to conduct an investigation into the allegations, suspected that Leese's complaints had their roots in "the Englishmen's traditional belief in the superiority of Englishmen" and the "military inconvenience" of having an indivisible Canadian corps under command.[208] Crerar threw cold water on the idea of disbanding 1st Canadian Corps, which was "not a prospect even worth discussing," but he did relay to Stuart the importance of determining whether or not Burns's divisional commanders shared Leese's opinions, and "how Leese's abilities as a higher Com[man]d[er] impressed themselves on 1 Cdn Corps."

On this last point Crerar's instincts were right. Leese had badly fumbled the pursuit battle. That was what all the after-action reports implied. Even an Eighth Army inquiry that Leese had ordered to determine why the pursuit had slowed down so badly said as much: "Movement of formations across the inter-Corps boundary lost nearly a day in each case."[209] His actions and his quick change of opinion about Burns suggest strongly that he felt the pointing of fingers at him. On 23 May, in a letter to his wife, his opinion of Burns was still high: "The Canadian Corps here have broken through the Adolf Hitler Line ... I am very glad that Burns and his Corps staff have had a success in their first battle. It will give them poise and confidence."[210] On 26 May, the day after the first traffic kerfuffle, it had not diminished to any great extent, despite what Leese saw as novice growing pains with "staff work, inter-communication and traffic control." He assessed that "Burns is learning and will, I think, be good."[211] By early June, however, as commanders and staff officers pored over the problems of the pursuit battle, he was telling the War Office, Alexander, and even his wife that Burns "was a man of no personality and little power of command."[212] Burns had problems to be sure, but just as certain was Leese's attempt to deflect blame. A number of Burns's contemporaries sensed it too. One staff officer under Burns described Leese as "one of the great assholes of all time. On any list of assholes, he'd rank 3rd or 4th."[213]

Ken Stuart, who investigated the allegations against Burns during the week of 10-16 July, seemed to agree. Stuart began on 11 July, when he had a three-hour interview with Leese during which the army commander reiterated the same points he had made to Alexander. Following the meeting with Leese, Stuart spent the next few days with 1st Canadian Corps, interviewing Burns, his divisional commanders, and his key staff. With Burns, he took in the corps commander's version of events and emphasized that both he and Crerar "had great confidence in him." He also took the opportunity to counsel Burns that he should "keep away from detail and so give himself time to think about essential matters," and "to exercise his power of command" because his "Div Comds and his principal staff officers would welcome more specific and definite direction from him." This was exactly the type of talking-to and advice the corps commander needed. Before leaving Burns, Stuart also advised him that he would be interviewing Vokes, Hoffmeister, Lister, and Smith, to see whether, as Leese had suggested, they had lost confidence in Burns's abilities. A bit perplexed by the suggestion that subordinates and staff had doubts, Burns inquired where the accusation might have originated. Stuart suspected that it had come from a disgruntled McCarter, who had been interviewed by the Eighth Army Chief of Staff after his removal as BGS 1st Canadian Corps.[214]

Whatever the source, Stuart found no evidence of any crumbling confidence on the part of Burns's subordinates. Both divisional commanders stated that "they respected his tremendous fairness in all his dealings with them ... and found no fault whatever in any tactical decision he had made during the operation."[215] According to Stuart, they professed themselves to be "quite happy to go into the next operation under Burns and his present staff," although they hoped Stuart would "speak to Burns about his manner and his personality." Smith and Lister were even "more emphatic" in expressing their confidence in the corps commander, as were all the majors and lieutenant-colonels of the corps and division staffs. Stuart could only conclude that there was nothing to Leese's accusations, and he told Alexander so on 13 June. In fact, over the course of his investigation, he came to suspect that "something had happened since the operation to make General Leese change his mind [about Burns]," although he could not say what the catalyst had been.[216]

Burns should be given another chance – that was the overarching recommendation that Stuart passed on to Alexander, to Leese, and to Crerar. Stuart also recommended that, in the interest of preserving morale, 1st Canadian Corps should be inserted into operations as soon as possible, and that the Canadians should fight the next battle as a formed corps, with all its parts. Alexander accepted the recommendations graciously. Not so with Leese, "who lost his temper and accused [Stuart] of criticizing many of the decisions he had made." After the meeting, Leese stressed that, although he would accept the decision of Stuart and the Canadian government, having to continue with Burns at the helm of 1st Canadian Corps would make his army "inflexible."[217] "Through my lack of faith in their commander," Leese complained, "I may be prevented from employing my best troops on the most critical task." Leese's tantrum did not stop there. In a letter to the War Office eleven days later, he launched an ad hominem attack on Stuart: "Stewart [sic] understands nothing of modern battle and appeared to me only to be interested in Canadian politics. He seemed to take little interest in the main war effort or the success of Eighth Army."[218] Despite Leese's protestations, Crerar happily accepted Stuart's recommendations and advised Brooke that Burns would stay on as the commander of 1st Canadian Corps. Brooke had served eighteen months with the Canadian Corps during the Great War, so he understood the Canadian "national feeling," believing that it was "quite useless going against it." He accepted the decisions, both on Burns and on the integrity of 1st Canadian Corps, without reservation, adding also that there was no point at all in discussing a British general as a replacement for Burns. In a letter to Alexander, Brooke also suggested that Leese was not blameless in the whole affair: "He is not a thruster and I feel that he requires the application of considerable stimulus from behind."[219] By the end of July, the issue of Burns's command had settled down, at least for the short term.

While the hubbub surrounding corps command was in full swing, Burns and his key subordinate commanders and staff continued to refine the organizational and procedural changes they had implemented. Subunit training in June continued with quick attacks, minefield breaching, and tank-infantry cooperation, all progressing to brigade-level schemes for crossing obstacles by the end of July.[220] Smith shook the corps G Staff into shape, making completely clear "the standard of efficiency he wanted from all ranks."[221] This included the "paying of compliments by all ranks and smartness of turnout." He conducted several command post exercises to give his staff practice in "intercom[munications], signal procedure and office administration,"[222] and he "test[ed] the resourcefulness and also the temper" of his liaison officers during the appropriately named Exercise Guess What?[223] Exercise Vital, another command post exercise that took place on 23-24 July, addressed the flow of information between the G staffs, the engineers, and the artillery in corps and divisional headquarters, and Exercise Timeout, a corps road movement exercise, was the first trial run of the new railway block system for traffic control.[224] The Corps General Staff war diary noted that the new system worked well and identified minor points for remedy: "35 Cdn LAA [Light Anti-Aircraft] Bty (TC) did an excellent job of traffic control but their report of units' progress was not as complete as it might have been." The divisions also conducted similar exercises of their own.[225] Burns participated fully in the corps exercises; when he was not doing this or visiting Canadian casualties in hospitals, his days were full observing the training of his battalions, brigades, and divisions. He seemed to be gaining confidence and his divisional commanders "were convinced that the time now being spent in training would be very profitable and were confident that the mistakes of the past would not be repeated in the future."[226] This was progress.

Burns also had another major organizational change to effect. He had to create a second infantry brigade for the 5th Canadian Armoured Division. Leese had already reorganized both the 6th British Armoured and the 6th South African Divisions such that they each had one armoured brigade and two infantry brigades because "the armoured division with one infantry brigade is no good in this type of fighting." He asked Burns "to signal Harry Crerar to ask if he could send him out another Canadian Infantry Brigade," and he also pursued the issue through Alexander, who, to Leese's disappointment, found that there was no support in the War Office for any "diversions from Overlord."[227] Burns got much the same response from CMHQ, so Leese asked him whether a second infantry brigade might be assembled from within the current 1st Canadian Corps establishment.[228] Burns studied the problem and submitted to CMHQ a proposal to form the 12th Canadian Infantry Brigade by taking the Westminster Regiment out of the 5th Canadian Armoured Brigade, and converting both the 4th Canadian Reconnaissance Regiment (4th Princess Louise Dragoon Guards) and the 1st Light Anti-Aircraft Regiment (Lanark and Renfrew Scottish) to infantry. Stuart approved the proposal on 12 July, after which the organization of the brigade proceeded very rapidly. Burns appointed the experienced Brigadier Dan Spry from the 1st Canadian Infantry Brigade as the commander and scraped together enough staff officers from within the corps to man the headquarters. Spry oversaw the assembly of the establishments and the field training to battalion level before he left Italy on 13 August to take command of the 3rd Canadian Infantry Division in Northwest Europe. Brigadier J.S. Lind then took the brigade to the field for Exercise Canyon on 16-17 August, to give the new formation practice in attacking across an obstacle and consolidating on a bridgehead line.[229] Considering how new the formation was, how new most of its troops were to the infantry role, and how unhappy the troops were about their new lot in life, the exercise went quite well. Of course, the effectiveness of this hasty training program would not be truly tested until the brigade's first battle, but for now Burns was pleased.

He had every reason to be pleased, not only with the remarkable progress that the 12th Canadian Infantry Brigade had made but with the fine-tuning that had taken place in the rest of the corps. He had guided commanders and staffs through an extensive review of their collective performance during the Liri Valley battles, and he had implemented sensible changes in the most expeditious manner possible. The corps was as ready as it could be before its next action.

As early as 20 July, Burns had to start thinking about the next battle and how he would employ his corps, even though plans were far from fixed. At this early stage in the planning, Leese advised Burns that 1st Canadian Corps could expect "to continue the offensive against the enemy and break through the GOTHIC Line."[230] As the plan was then conceived, Alexander would advance with the Eighth Army through the Apeninne Mountains from Florence to Bologna, while the US Fifth Army would advance on the left between Florence and the coast. Burns wanted his subordinate commanders and staff to start thinking about how to crack through the Gothic Line in the mountainous terrain north of Florence, so on 23 July he issued a planning directive asking them to look at possible enemy dispositions, how to deploy tanks in such close country, and how to make use of the very limited road space. He also wanted them to estimate the scale of the engineering problem likely to be encountered.[231]

However, as events progressed in the summer of 1944, Burns had cause for concern. By the beginning of August, the 1st Canadian Infantry Division had been placed under the command of the British 10th Corps. Worse, Burns also learned that 1st Canadian Corps would be employed in a static role for the Eighth Army advance, with both its divisions detached to other corps. As he recalled, "it would not be the 1st Canadian Corps that would be holding the front; it would be the headquarters of the Canadian Corps commanding an assortment of formations which at the time were not judged fit for offensive operations."[232] This was neither in accord with government policy nor in line with what Brooke had agreed and passed to Alexander on 22 July. So, on 1 August, Burns went to see Leese about "re-uniting the Cdn Corps at an early date."[233] The next day, he went to Alexander and made the same case. This was a milestone for Burns – confronting his superiors in the chain of command. He got what he wanted too. Although he conceded that it was "operationally desirable" to keep the 1st Canadian Infantry Division detached for the time being, he wrested from each of them a promise to reassemble 1st Canadian Corps as soon as possible. As it turned out, the plan to detach the 1st Canadian Infantry Division and leave the rest of the corps in a static position changed. The whole plan for the offensive changed, so it was a combination of factors that led to a new role for a unified

1st Canadian Corps. But Burns's intervention did help secure a significant role for the Canadians in Operation Olive. Leese and Alexander needed the Canadian divisions. Once Burns asserted that they could not be detached, a new and more important 1st Canadian Corps mission was virtually certain, no matter where the Allied Armies in Italy attacked.

The new plan for the army group offensive was largely the result of a meeting between Leese and Alexander on 4 August.[234] Leese hated the idea of an advance in the Apennines. His concern was that the Germans appeared to be arranged in depth to block an advance on Bologna; more importantly, the mountainous terrain of that sector did not suit the strengths of the Eighth Army: "It was obviously advisable to fight this major battle in country where we could best exploit our great advantages in tanks, guns and aircraft, and the most suitable country appeared to be along the Adriatic coast."[235] Alexander, whose plans had already been upset by the loss of four French and three American divisions to Operation Anvil in Southern France, was receptive to Leese's argument. He settled instead on what he called a "two-handed punch" – threatening Rimini and Ravenna with the Eighth Army in order to draw German reserves to the Adriatic front, then attacking along the Florence-Bologna line with the Fifth Army. In the new plan, 1st Canadian Corps would attack towards Rimini with the British 5th Corps on its left and 2nd Polish Corps on its right, along the Adriatic coast.

Leese's argument for employing the Eighth Army in the open Adriatic sector was well considered – it was better ground for the use of tanks, artillery, and the Desert Air Force – but the manner in which he deployed his forces left much to be desired. He placed the exploitation force, the British 1st Armoured Division, under the command of Lieutenant-General Charles Keightley's 5th Corps, which was to advance not in the open ground of the Adriatic Plain but in the tank-unfriendly foothills of the Apennine Mountains. Further complicating matters in that constricted terrain, Keightley also had to find room to manoeuvre an additional four infantry divisions and two armoured brigades, whereas in the more open and rolling ground of the centre, Burns had only his two divisions and the British 21st Tank Brigade. Again, Leese's decision to arrange his attacking corps in that way defied any explanation. True, he did not have enough faith in Burns to place either British or Indian divisions under Canadian command, but that does not explain why he assigned his heaviest corps to the most mountainous sector, where tanks would have the most difficulty.[236] Burns must have had doubts about the plan, even though he did not record them.

In the meantime, Burns, delighted that 1st Canadian Corps would be united and employed in a key offensive role, settled down to study the tactical problems of his task. His diary records that, after receiving the change of plans on 4 August, he spent the better part of the next three days at his headquarters "planning for future op[eration]s."[237] Several visitors called during that time – Keightley (twice), Hoffmeister, and Brigadier D. Dawnay, the commander of the 21st Tank Brigade – and Burns discussed the upcoming operations with them and his staff. He received confirmatory orders from Leese on 11 August, the army commander emphasizing the importance of speed, getting through to deep objectives, and surprise for the attack on the Gothic Line.[238] Acknowledging that an opportunity for effective pursuit had been missed in the Liri Valley, Leese also emphasized the need for good traffic control and a willingness to "gate-crash" if the attacking corps found the Gothic Line defences either ill prepared or lightly manned. Burns took that guidance and began building a plan that was simple yet flexible in concept.

After careful consideration, he sketched out a four-phase operation to carry 1st Canadian Corps through the Gothic Line and on to Rimini (see Maps 5 and 6). In the first two phases, the 1st Canadian Infantry Division would cross the Metauro River then dash to the defences of the Gothic Line proper at the Foglia River. These two phases were fixed. The third phase, however, provided for flexibility of action, depending on what the attackers found at the Foglia River. If the battalions of the 1st Canadian Infantry Division found the Gothic Line defences disorganized or lightly held, they were to "push [forward] with all speed and break through the GOTHIC LINE without waiting for the arrival of 5th Cdn Armd Div."[239] If, on the other hand, the enemy managed to man his positions in strength, then Burns would bring up the 5th Canadian Armoured Division on the left, prepare for a set-piece attack, then smash into the Gothic Line with two divisions up, heavily supported by air and artillery attack. The fourth and final phase of the operation would be a pursuit to Rimini. It was a simple plan, but it still required a great deal of coordination. Routes had to be selected, waiting areas for low-priority traffic had to be picked, boundaries had to be adjusted, assembly areas had to be chosen, fire plans had to be designed, close air support had to be coordinated, and so on.

That meant meeting with a lot of key players. Burns confirmed this concept of operations with both Vokes and Hoffmeister on 12 August, and he met with each of them almost every other day after that to discuss how their plans fit in the framework of his, and to ensure that the necessary administrative arrangements had been made. He met as frequently with the army commander and the corps commanders on his left and right, and he conducted several reconnaissance flights over the battle area.[240] Everything and everyone in the chain of command was working as it should. Burns really had done a good job of anticipating the requirements of the coming battle and getting his commanders and staffs working on them.

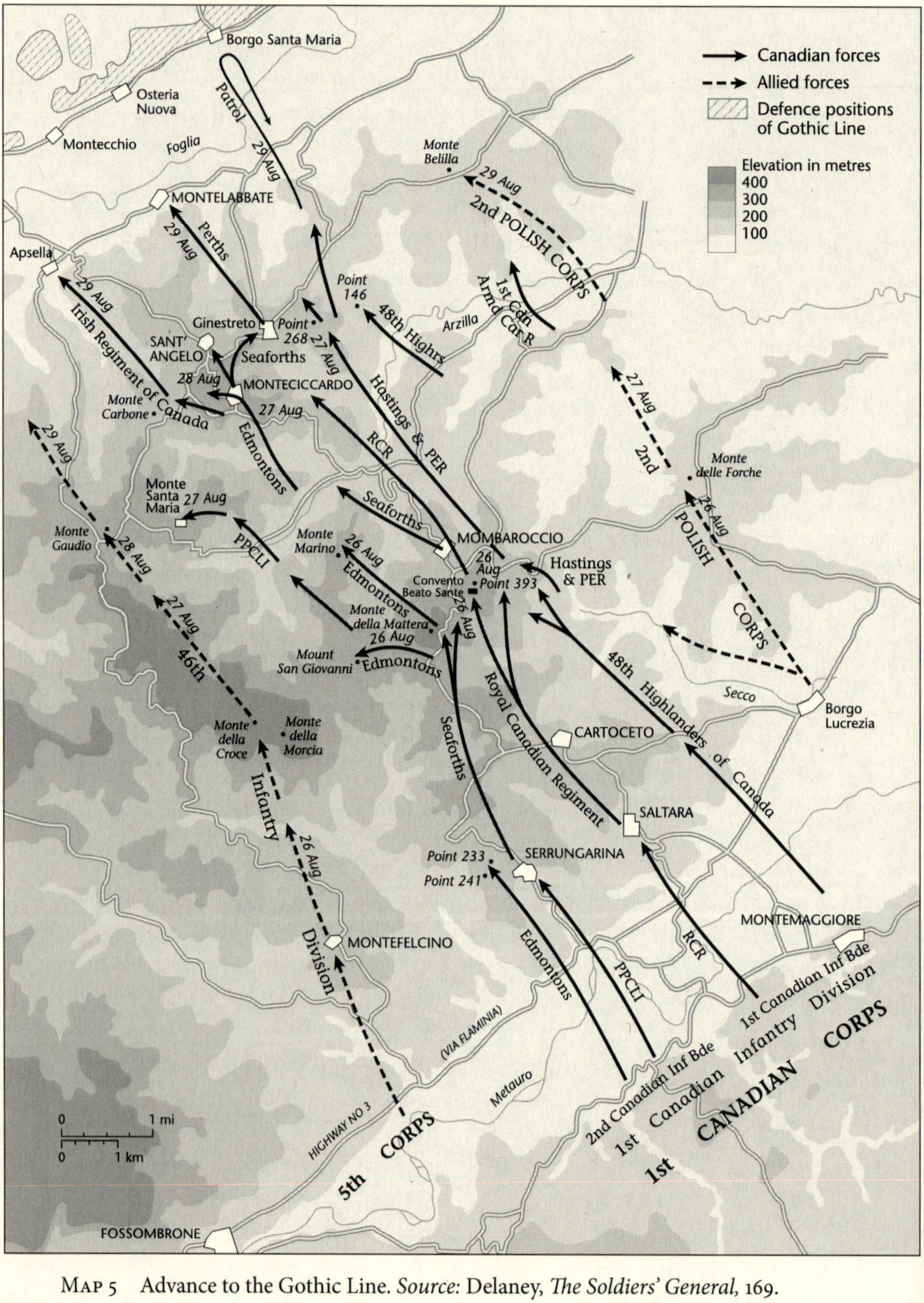

MAP 5  Advance to the Gothic Line. *Source:* Delaney, *The Soldiers' General*, 169.

He still lacked the ability to fire them up, though. There was something sad about that. As Hoffmeister once told historian Jack Granatstein, "no senior officer tried harder."[241] Burns had turned his formidable faculties to improving the corps and preparing it for a landmark battle – with excellent results. And yet he still lacked the ability to inspire. It was not because he refused to go forward and share the risks of his soldiers. He did that often. It was not that he could not come up with sensible programs for training or workable plans for battle. He did all of that too. What he lacked was the "poise and charisma" to make people believe in him. Hoffmeister's recollection was that he "moved slowly, gave orders in a monotone [manner] and lacked [the] enthusiasm to 'sell' the plan."[242] Burns had long understood his inability to connect with a crowd or anything more than a handful of staff officers; it appears that in August 1944 he did not even try. He issued a crisp eight-page operation order on 21 August,[243] but there was no associated conference, no verbal orders, no forum for making an impression, no attempt to mine the emotions of his subordinates. Not once during August did he bring together all his subordinate commanders and staff to impart his thoughts to them. Very nearly all of his guidance was issued one-on-one. On 22 August, the day after he had disseminated his written orders, Burns brought in Leese to address all 1st Canadian Corps officers down to the rank of lieutenant-colonel on the upcoming operation, and to explain the "important part" that the Canadians would play in it.[244] Burns had held conferences before the Liri Valley battles, but they had fallen flat with his audiences. Neither actor nor orator, he chose instead to surrender the stage. He probably figured that doing so would cause less harm. Leese, for all his bad judgment, was still able to rivet a crowd with his "racy informality" and his "abounding confidence" (however ill-founded that confidence may have been).[245] Hoffmeister sold a plan as well as anyone and Vokes's blood-and-guts bluntness appealed to a good portion of the soldiery. Better to let them tap the human element of battle. They were better at it anyway. That may have been so, but, in the end, Burns's inability – unwillingness, even – to address the human dimension of command only compounded the perception that he was weak of will and a one-dimensional commander. In choosing not to call a conference of his own, Burns missed an opportunity to capitalize on the good work he had done with the corps since the Liri Valley battles and demonstrate that he really was in charge.

That was a shame because he made good tactical decisions during the Gothic Line battle. The day after an easy crossing of the Metauro on 26 August, the 1st Canadian Infantry Division met some stiff opposition from the German 71st Division just west of the Arzilla River. The enemy was fighting for time to deploy two reserve divisions – the 26th Panzer and 29th Panzer Grenadier – from the

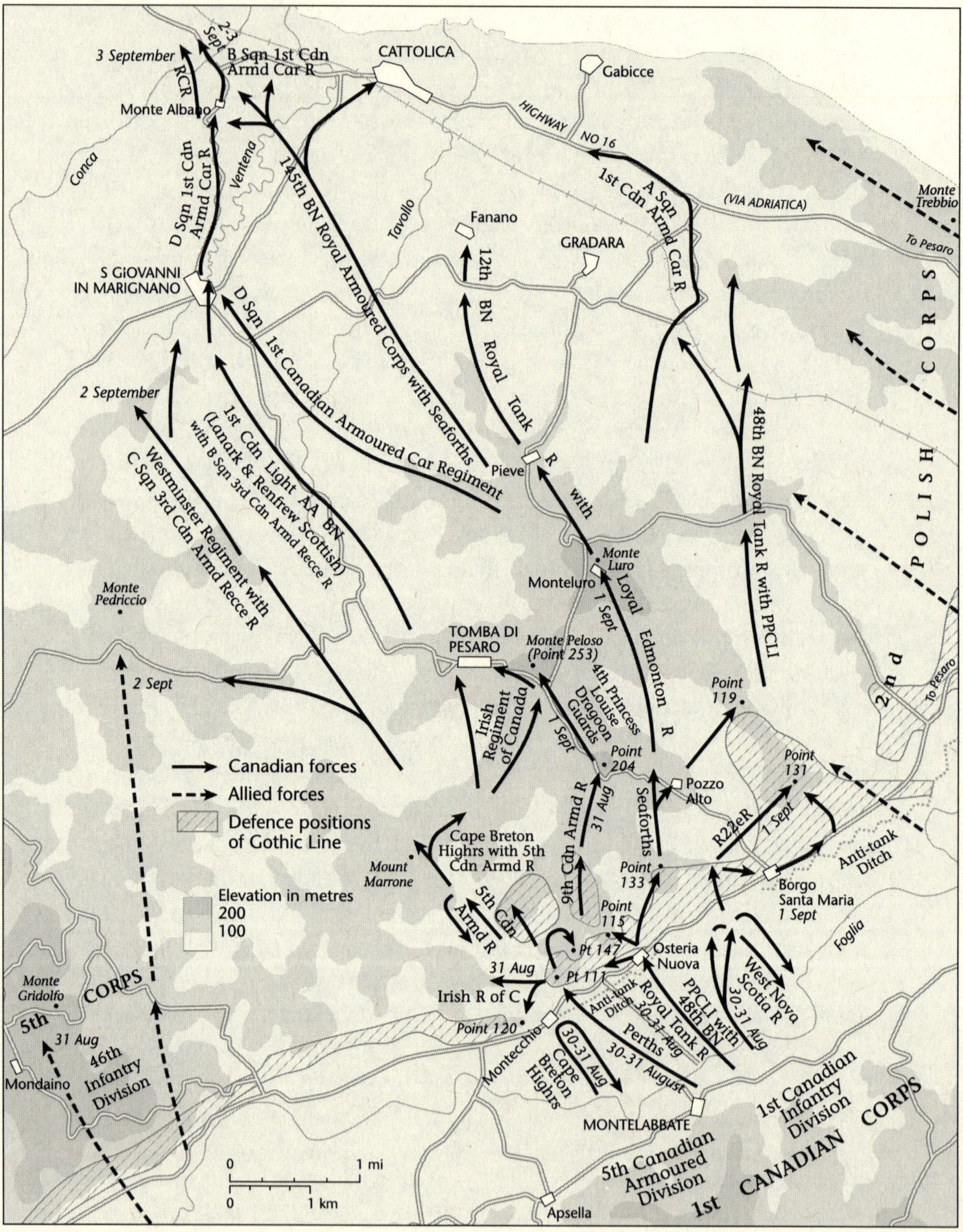

MAP 6   Breaking the Gothic Line. *Source:* Delaney, *The Soldiers' General,* 171.

Bologna sector to meet what they now assessed to be the main Allied thrust in the Adriatic area.[246] Having watched the battle from a forward observation post on 26 August, and having flown over the Foglia River on 27 August and noting "no activity visible" to the west of the river, Burns asked Vokes if he thought it might be a possible to reach the Foglia by the morning of 28 August and "gate-crash" the German defences.[247] When Vokes, who was in the middle of a nasty battle with the 71st Division's delaying elements on 27 August, responded that it was "unlikely," Burns went ahead with plans to bring up Hoffmeister's formation for a two-division set-piece attack.[248] Given what he knew of the ongoing battle and the high casualties that the 1st Canadian Infantry Division had incurred in breaking the Hitler Line, this prudent action was understandable. Leese agreed, and Burns spent the next two days adjusting the boundaries so that his corps could concentrate on a narrower frontage, arranging for twelve field regiments of artillery to deliver the necessary indirect fire support, and coordinating air attacks on the main defensive positions between Borgo Santa Maria and Montecchio. That the preparations and preliminary movements went so smoothly owed much to the changes he had made to his traffic control organization earlier in the summer. The railway block system and the communications infrastructure that supported it enabled the corps staff to move low-priority traffic off the main routes and into waiting areas so that the 5th Canadian Armoured Division and the supporting artillery (with its ammunition carriers) could move into position for the set-piece assault.

The deliberate attack did not take place as planned, but the arrangements proved useful for the gate-crashing exercise that did. Remembering what had happened at the Hitler Line, when the 2nd Canadian Infantry Brigade had not been afforded sufficient time in which to patrol, define its objective, identify routes, and designate on-call artillery targets, Burns ordered both divisions to reconnoitre aggressively to the Foglia River, and beyond it if possible. Accordingly, the lead brigades of the two Canadian divisions dispatched patrols shortly after they reached the line Sant' Angelo–Monte Belilla on 29 August. In the 5th Canadian Armoured Division sector, Hoffmeister moved forward to have a look for himself. From atop Monte Santa Maria, he had an excellent view of the Gothic Line positions, and what he saw, or did not see, led him to believe that the Germans were not ready to fight: "We could by careful examination pick out the odd concrete gun emplacement, and we could see the barbed wire, and we saw the minefields; but there was no life around the place at all ... the whole thing looked terribly quiet."[249] It was terribly quiet because the 71st Division and the 1st Parachute Division were in the final stages of withdrawing behind the Gothic Line position, but they were doing so before the 26th Panzer Division – still rushing forward from the Bologna sector – had properly taken their place in the line and the 98th Division had relieved the 71st Division. The 10th Army did not believe that these manoeuvres would be complete until the night of 30-31 August at the earliest.²⁵⁰ Sure enough, shortly after noon on 30 August, patrol reports confirmed that the forward defences of the Gothic Line position were not manned, and, based on that welcome news, Burns directed both his divisional commanders to "push forward ... to effect a lodgement in the line while it was still unmanned."²⁵¹ He need not have done so. Hoffmeister had already ordered Brigadier Ian Johnston to shove his 11th Canadian Infantry Brigade battalions through the Montecchio position. In doing so, Johnston fought essentially the same plan he had been refining for two weeks – a night attack on the Montecchio positions with two battalions up, each supported by a squadron of tanks. He had hoped to slip into the enemy positions on Point 120 and Point 111 before having to bring down the on-call artillery fire, but the troops of the 26th Panzer Division arrived just as the Canadian attack began, so he needed the fire support once his troops had made it across the anti-tank ditch. Still, Johnston's battalions got the jump on a disorganized enemy and the artillery support was there when they needed it – not stuck in traffic. The traffic control arrangements that had been settled beforehand also made it easy for Hoffmeister to bring forward an armoured battle group from the 5th Canadian Armoured Brigade and park it in a waiting area near Montelabbate, from which point it would be ready for rapid exploitation of any breakthrough.

Much to the satisfaction of both Burns and Leese, the Canadians cracked the crust of the Gothic Line defences within twenty-four hours on both divisional fronts. Burns acknowledged that "the battle to get through the GOTHIC Line and to seize the commanding high ground about two and a half miles beyond it ... was mainly a battalion and regimental commander's battle."²⁵² He was right. Low-level leadership was a determining factor in the success of the assaulting battalions. The Perth Regiment would not have succeeded at Point 111 had it not been for the actions of a very gallant company commander who got his pinned-down troops moving when he stood up and led them across the last fifty bullet-swept metres into the enemy positions.²⁵³ On the 1st Canadian Infantry Division front, the PPCLI would not have made it through Osteria Nuova had it not been for the actions of Major Colin McDougall and Lieutenant Chambers, who decided to lead their men, single-file, through a 600-yard-deep minefield, "accepting casualties as they went."²⁵⁴ There were many other acts of bravery in the Gothic Line battle, just as there had been many in the Hitler Line battle; this time, however, the Canadian formations were able to capitalize quickly and avoid the horrendous casualty count of 23 May. With justifiable satisfaction, on the morning of 31 August, Burns watched Hoffmeister feed successive battle groups into the 11th Canadian Infantry Brigade breaches, before the enemy could effectively counter these moves.[255] Vokes did much the same on the 1st Canadian Infantry Division front. That both divisional commanders could execute these moves with such efficiency owed much to the changes Burns had made in the corps traffic control system and the training that he had demanded take place at the company-squadron level.

Unfortunately, Leese's earlier decision to place the pursuit force with 5th Corps in the mountains precluded the full exploitation of the opportunity that Burns and his troops had created. The Gothic Line was much deeper than the Hitler Line, and by the time the Canadians had fought through to Tomba di Pesaro and Monteluro on 1 September, they were all but spent. They had very little with which to pursue the enemy or cut off the remnants of the 1st Parachute Division, now withdrawing in front of the 2nd Polish Corps along the coast. Burns had Vokes hastily assemble a pursuit force based on the 21st Tank Brigade, the battalions of the 2nd Canadian Infantry Brigade, and the Royal Canadian Dragoons. It fought well on short notice, but it was not powerful enough to smash through to the coast and intercept the withdrawing German paratroopers before they made it across the Conca River on 2 September. That was the day that Leese's exploitation force, the British 1st Armoured Division, finally reached the Metauro River, more than forty kilometres and two river lines away.[256] Not only had Leese failed to group his forces effectively for their tasks, he had also failed miserably to read the battle and make adjustments to capitalize on the Canadian breakthrough.

In spite of the missed opportunity, Burns had done well. On 2 September, Alexander advised him that he would receive a Distinguished Service Order (DSO) for the Gothic Line battle, probably the minimum a corps commander could have expected for such a feat. Nevertheless, Leese had to acknowledge the accomplishment:

> The dash and gallantry of the troops was beyond praise and the Divisions and Brigades were very well handled indeed.
>
> Under yourself, the B.G.S. and the Staff at your Corps Headquarters controlled the battle well at every stage. I shall rely on their capacity to handle any larger operation entrusted to the Corps in the future.
>
> Indeed, in our next operation the Canadian Corps has the decisive role ... There are no troops in whom I place greater reliance than the Canadians for such an important task.[257]

By the time Leese wrote this note, the advance had stalled because 5th Corps and 1st Canadian Corps had banged into a very strong German position at Coriano Ridge. There the 29th Panzer Grenadier Division had established its

71st Regiment in strong reverse slope positions that were well supported by artillery. There would be no getting past them without a well-coordinated attack. Overcoming his earlier reservations about Burns and the Canadian corps, Leese placed the British 4th Division, the 2nd New Zealand Division, a Greek mountain brigade, and the British 25th Tank Brigade under Burns to blast past the Coriano Ridge position, drill through the Rimini Line, and break into the open ground that extended into the Po River Valley. Leese even shifted the boundary between 1st Canadian Corps and the British 5th Corps to the west, so that the Canadians could take Coriano Ridge, an objective that had originally been in the 5th Corps sector. Burns was pleased: "I also took it as a sign that the generals had decided that I could handle my command and that confidence had replaced the doubts which had formerly existed."[258] His subordinates must have felt buoyed by the corps success as well. This was a high point for Burns.

The Canadians captured Coriano Ridge on 13 September and crossed the Marano River a day later; unfortunately, however, the speedy successes of early September gave way to slow grinding as the enemy recovered and rain ruined any plans for rapid advances. Even with the slowed advance, Burns might have built on the Gothic Line successes had it not been for his habit of doing what Hoffmeister called "stupid things." Burns liked to go forward and discuss ongoing operations and battle plans with the commanders on the ground, but he had an annoying tendency of speaking with brigade and battalion commanders – without advising his divisional commanders that he was doing so. His war diary for September and October 1944 shows that he met no less than ten times with brigade or battalion commanders, without the respective divisional commanders being present.[259] This was poor practice, especially considering how much influence the divisional commanders had on Burns's future. The real outcome of Stuart's July consultations with the divisional commanders and staff was that it left Burns's fate in their hands. All they had to do was withdraw their support and Burns was all but gone. His actions from mid-September had the effect of ensuring just that. Hoffmeister recalled that, during a visit to the 11th Canadian Infantry Brigade, he was surprised to find Burns in conference with Johnston. Burns stated matter-of-factly that he "was just going over the operation" with Johnston, but Hoffmeister was furious that the corps commander would speak with one of his subordinates without first advising him, and rightly so.[260] Hoffmeister even demanded to be paraded in front of the army commander. Here was the nub of the problem. Burns's subordinates could "pull the trigger" on him at any time, and they knew it. On 8 October, both Hoffmeister and Major-General Weir, GOC 2nd New Zealand Division, objected to Burns's plan for their divisions to attack across the Fiumicino River because weeks of rain had left the ground waterlogged and nearly impassable to tanks.[261] The following day, during the first formal orders group that Burns had held since the Liri Valley, the corps commander pressed the point, attempting to explain "that the gen[eral strategic] situation required the offensive action of this corps and that other troops in Italy and on the Western front were attacking despite bad weather conditions and mud."[262] But he did so in classic Burns fashion, with plenty of off-putting sarcasm that "lack[ed] dignity" and embarrassed those concerned.[263] With subordinates and staff, this rubbed salt into still-open wounds. Hoffmeister, Vokes, and Weir all balked at his direction, and Hoffmeister again asked to see the army commander, Lieutenant-General Sir Richard McCreery, who had replaced Leese on 1 October, and who was just as unsympathetic towards Burns. Burns was all but finished. No corps commander could have carried on with divisional commanders refusing direction and two army commanders after his head.

Another investigation into his competence for command ensued. This time, the investigator was Brigadier E.G. Weeks, the Officer-in-Charge Canadian Section 1st Echelon Allied Armies Italy. Someone in the Canadian chain of command, or staff, had apparently aired their concerns about Burns to the Eighth Army. Hoffmeister emphatically denied doing so,[264] and so did just about every other senior Canadian commander and staff officer in Italy.[265] The Eighth Army Chief of Staff later intimated, however, that one or more Canadian officers had aired their concerns at Eighth Army Headquarters, and it is hard to believe that McCreery, who had been commanding the army for only three weeks, could have written so round a condemnation without some encouragement:

> I am strongly of the opinion that a change of command is necessary in 1st Canadian Corps. Lieutenant-general Burns has not the attributes of a Higher Commander. I find that he is indecisive, and appears to lack that grasp of the whole situation which is essential in battle, in fact he does not lead ... His manner is depressing, diffident and unenthusiastic and he must completely fail to inspire his subordinate commanders.[266]

McCreery had briefed Burns on the contents of the letter twelve days before he sent it to Alexander, right about the time the divisional commanders were objecting to the Fiumicino crossing.[267] Vokes had some pretty strong feelings about Burns that he shared with a friend on the CMHQ staff in London as well:

> Things have reached a crisis here regarding the subject of Nick's [McCarter] conversation with you. The matter is on hand at the highest levels, but whether any action is taken by the parties responsible at your end is impossible to predict. If nothing is done and done quickly Bert [Hoffmeister] and I, plus Pres [Gilbride],

Des [Smith], Johnny [Plow], Collie [Campbell] are prepared to adopt the only course possible. Personally I am absolutely browned off ... we have continued to bear the cross for an individual who lacks one iota of personality, appreciation of effort or the first goddamn thing in the application of book learning to what is practical in war & what isn't. I have done my best to be loyal but goddammit the strain has been too bloody great ... Thank God [the army commander] took action before our hands were forced.[268]

However the players disseminated their opinions, they were remarkably consistent: Burns lacked personality, failed to inspire, and, more often than not, annoyed subordinate commanders. After a series of interviews, Weeks reported that the situation between Burns, his two divisional commanders, and his Chief of Staff was "intolerable."[269] After the earlier inquiry into his competence for command, probably the worst-kept secret in the 1st Canadian Corps or Eighth Army, it could hardly have been otherwise, even if Burns had changed his approach to leading. As Burns stated in a letter to Crerar, his subordinate commanders "would have been more than human, if in moments of stress, when their opinions did not coincide with mine, they had not remembered that the Army Commander had doubts of my fitness for command. Their confidence was sapped."[270] He was right. Everyone had doubts. There was no way he could have carried on. On 10 November, Charles Foulkes took command of 1st Canadian Corps, and Burns went to Northwest Europe as a major-general, where he looked after Canadian rear echelon units in the 21st Army Group.

AFTER THE WAR, BURNS put his intellectual powers to good use. After nine years with the Department of Veterans Affairs, the last four as Deputy Minister, he accepted the post of Chief of Staff for the United Nations Truce Supervisory Organization (UNTSO), a military observer force for the supervision of a truce between Israel and the Arab states. In 1956, he became the first commander of the United Nations Emergency Force in Egypt, an appointment he held for three years, and he was promoted to lieutenant-general in 1958. He wrote a lot too. He published an astute analysis of the manpower problems that had plagued the Canadian Army during the Second World War,[271] he criticized the manner of UN intervention in the Middle East in his 1962 book *Between Arab and Israeli*,[272] he commented on what he perceived as the folly of the nuclear arms race in *Megamurder*,[273] he wrote about disarmament,[274] he attempted to explain Canadian defence policy in a nuclear age to Canadians,[275] and, of course, he produced a first-class memoir, *General Mud*. Some recognition for his life's work and expertise came his way as well. In 1960, with the rank of ambassador, he became an advisor to the Canadian government on disarmament, continuing in this role until he became Chair of Strategic Studies at the Norman Paterson School of International Affairs, Carleton University, in 1967. He was admitted as one of the first Companions to the Order of Canada that same year, and he received the Pearson Medal of Peace from the United Nations Association in Canada in 1981. Burns had accomplished much and contributed much before he passed away in 1985.

And yet, for all his intellect and all his accomplishments, his record as corps commander confirms the adage that, for a battlefield commander, it is not enough simply to be smart. Human skills matter. Corps, like any army organization, are composed of people and it takes more than technical skill to carry them through the confusion and terror of combat. Successful commanders prepare their people for their task, but they also convey confidence and attract affection. Those who cannot manage this easily had better have the ruthlessness and the strength of will to coerce their underlings into completing their tasks. The sad thing about Burns was that he could do neither.

# 3

# The Quiet Gentleman: General Sir John Crocker

*I am sure a humble attitude towards life and one's fellow man is best – even for a general, so long as he knows his stuff and does it to the best of his ability.*

– LIEUTENANT-GENERAL JOHN CROCKER

JOHN CROCKER WAS NOT much of a talker and he was a lousy self-promoter because of it. Yet he was one of the most important British soldiers of the Second World War, commanding a corps in North Africa and subsequently being assigned "the most ambitious, the most difficult and the most important task" of any Allied corps commander during Operation Overlord.[1] His influence was not limited to the period of the war either. He was intimately involved with the development of British armoured forces during the 1920s and 1930s, and after the war he oversaw the production of the doctrine and training publications that would guide the British Army for much of the Cold War. He also served as Commander-in-Chief Middle East Land Forces, and he finished his career as Adjutant-General to the Forces. Field Marshal Montgomery would have preferred it if Crocker had retired as Chief of the Imperial General Staff (CIGS), but in 1949 Prime Minister Clement Atlee chose Sir William Slim for the post instead.[2] By almost any standard, Crocker had a very successful army career. So, how did someone so quiet achieve so much?

Crocker's influence, and his rise in the British Army, rested squarely on a foundation of technical competence and unimpeachable integrity. These were also the qualities that underpinned his method of command. A keenly intelligent man, Crocker found himself in high demand whenever there were problems to be solved, whether they concerned testing the abilities of tanks, building an armoured formation, or sequencing an amphibious assault. He had excelled at staff college and at just about everything else he had tackled during the interwar period, so it is no wonder that he attracted the attention of people like Alan Brooke and Percy Hobart. They trusted him, and not just for his technical ability. His Great War record had shown him to be completely composed under fire, and his reputation for being straight with everyone, whether they wanted to hear what he had to say or not, had earned him the nickname "Honest John."[3] In 1935, Hobart wrote that Crocker was "trusted by me and by all ranks of the

Tank Brigade ... his patience, tact and integrity have won him affection."[4] There was also an understated determination about Crocker. During tough times like the battles for Caen, he could grit his teeth and drive on to his objectives, even when the fighting was tough and the casualty count high. That steely resolve faded for a while when he suffered the agonizing loss of his only son, Wilfrid, in October 1944, but his skills and his quiet nobility never left him.

JOHN CROCKER WAS EVERY bit the gentleman officer of his period, even if his upbringing was anything but typical. The son of Mary (Tredinnick) and Isaac Crocker, a secretary with the Champion Reef Gold Mining Company, John Crocker was born on 3 January 1896, one of five siblings who lived in a modest Exbury Road dwelling in Catford, Lewisham.[5] Owing to a respiratory ailment, young John was too sickly to attend public school, so his mother, who had been widowed with five children since John was only four years old, somehow managed to send him instead to a retired parson for instruction.[6] The parson was a voracious reader whose disciplined self-study and rectitude rubbed off on his pupil, as did a certain piety. Crocker remained a deeply religious man his entire life. Under the tutelage of his parson instructor, he also learned to think before speaking, to choose his words carefully, and never to lie. His tutor liked things done properly, something Crocker would always demand of his own charges. One future subordinate would later comment that he possessed "a most penetrating insight into character and behaviour. Anyone who tried to hoodwink him was on a forlorn and dangerous path."[7] Odd as it may have been, his unorthodox education served him well in his military career.

From the time he entered military service in November 1915, Crocker distinguished himself as a soldier to watch. At that time, the gangly nineteen-year-old, who stood nearly six feet tall and weighed only 154 pounds, volunteered as a private soldier in the Artists Rifles.[8] An elite Territorial Army regiment whose enlistees included the likes of Wilfrid Owen and Noel Coward, the London-based unit was really a selection-ground for potential officers. Once a soldier had been sufficiently assessed and deemed worthy of a King's commission, he would be sent for officer training, which is precisely what happened to Crocker in 1917. In January of that year, he accepted a provisional commission in the Machine Gun Corps and, after some training at the Machine Gun School at Grantham, he joined the 174th Machine Gun Company of the 59th Division in France. During the Third Battle of Ypres in September, Second-Lieutenant Crocker saved two guns from his nearly destroyed section, brought them forward under fire, and provided critical fire support for an infantry battalion that was under heavy counterattack. For these actions, he received the Military Cross (MC). Six months later, during the German offensive of March 1918,

Lieutenant Crocker again showed the same unflappable calm that was to distinguish his entire military career. This time he received the Distinguished Service Order (DSO), which, as the citation indicates, probably should have been a Victoria Cross:

> When in charge of four machine guns he broke down two strong enemy attacks, holding on from 10 a.m. till dusk, when infantry and reinforcements arrived. The following day he maintained his position till outflanked when he stood up between two of his guns and directed their fire on the enemy, who were within 30 yards, then covered the withdrawal with bombs and rifle fire, killing many himself at close range. [He t]ook up a fresh position until almost surrounded again, when he again went out with bombs. His example throughout was magnificent.[9]

Indeed it was, and not just for those who witnessed the event. Everyone in his unit would have known of his DSO and what he had done to earn it. A lieutenant with a DSO and an MC to his credit was someone to be respected.

After the war, Crocker tried life as a civilian, but he soon found his way back to the army, where the challenges were many and more to his liking.[10] Shortly after marrying Hilda Mitchell in 1920, he accepted a commission in the Middlesex Regiment, but he did not last long in the infantry. Intrigued by the potential of the new tank arm, Crocker transferred to the Royal Tank Corps (RTC) on a probationary basis in October 1921 and accepted a permanent reassignment in June 1923, after completing his tank training.[11] Working in a new corps with new technology suited Crocker's studious nature, and he enjoyed himself immensely.

In December 1924, he led an arduous trial of two Vickers medium tanks in India and produced "Tanks in India," an article that appeared in the *Royal Tank Corps Journal* in July 1925.[12] A largely technical piece, the article chronicled the conduct of the trials over all types of terrain, made note of strengths and weaknesses in tank design, and also drew conclusions concerning the capabilities of the tanks. Crocker observed, for example, that tanks could reasonably expect to move "fifty miles per day ... at an average speed of eight to ten miles per hour ... without damage to the tank or exhaustion of the personnel."[13] He also determined that tanks could be maintained away from workshops for short periods, requiring only a "normal daily maintenance" of approximately two hours to do so. Perhaps most importantly, the trials had clearly demonstrated the versatility of the new weapon system in very rugged terrain: "The performance over rough ground ha[d] hardly been sacrificed for the enormously increased speed and mobility." These were useful and grounded observations for anyone thinking more broadly about armour and the mechanization of the army, and it established Crocker as a knowledgeable and practical operator, a role he much preferred to theorist.

There was no denying his command of the new technology. It led to employment with the 10th Armoured Car Company in Delhi, after which came a tour as an instructor at the RTC School in Ahmednagar.[14] His confidential report for 1927-28 stated that he was an "officer of exceptional ability ... his clear brain, and knowledge of his trade have been of great value to the school. He plays games [sports] with the men and has taken considerable trouble with organization of their sports. He has a marked influence with those under him."[15] In 1927, the Chief of the General Staff India endorsed a recommendation for accelerated promotion to captain. Promotion did not come until July 1929, but the recommendation was clear confirmation that Crocker's abilities were being recognized. Crocker attended the Staff College at Quetta from 1928 to 1929, still a lieutenant, and again achieved outstanding results, his course report making note of his "strong and independent character."[16] It noted in particular that he had "decided views on mechanization which he expresses in a sound and reasonable way both verbally and in writing." The rare A-grade that he earned in the course also marked him as an "officer of exceptional merit and outstanding ability."

From the end of 1929, his career progression accelerated. In January 1930, he joined the 2nd Battalion Royal Tank Regiment at Aldershot, and served there until he was selected for a third-grade staff appointment with the 2nd Division in March 1931. He proved himself to be a "first class administrative staff officer" in that role, and within fifteen months found himself with the brevet rank of major and in the staff billet of Brigade Major at the RTC Centre at Bovington. There, he caught the eye of Brigadier Percy Hobart,[17] who brought Crocker to his newly formed 1st Tank Brigade in April 1934.

The new post suited Crocker completely. It also suited his dynamic new boss. Hobart, whose capacity for innovation was matched only by his unfortunate irascibility, knew that he needed someone who could offer sober second thought to his ideas, someone patient enough to make practical the principles he dreamt up. Crocker quickly picked up that "Hobo" had a bad "tendency to exhaust his nervous energy by overstrain" and occasionally needed someone to save him from himself.[18] Once, during a large exercise, Crocker found Hobart "asleep in a tank, too exhausted to respond."[19] Crocker, who genuinely admired Hobart, was every bit as intelligent as his mentor, only his mind had the harness of a more stable disposition. This enabled him to operate on a much more even keel – calmly identifying the essence of a problem, developing solutions, working through the details, and seeing the selected solution through to completion.

For example, Hobart believed deeply in the potential of tank formations to drive deep into enemy defences and he had thought broadly about reducing the brigade's logistic echelon in an effort to achieve greater freedom of manoeuvre. Crocker took the idea, analyzed what vehicles and equipment could be eliminated from the echelon, issued direction for organizational changes, then supervised a trial run of the new operating procedures to see whether the revised order of battle actually worked.[20] It did. Quietly and efficiently, Crocker made the organization run, and reticent though he may have been, Hobart recognized in his brigade major an officer of considerable ability: "He is a man of very strong character, great determination and complete self-control. A tendency to taciturnity masks a quick brain and a sound and well balanced intelligence. His personality inspires confidence. He is accurate and absolutely reliable."[21]

Crocker was a problem solver, not a theorist, and Hobart would have had a hard time turning ideas into reality without him. At no time did he seem offended or put out by Crocker's willingness to state simply, "I do not agree," then explain the point in well-considered and reasonable terms. In fact, Hobart even arranged a one-year extension for Crocker as brigade major, and wrote such glowing confidential reports that accelerated promotions soon came Crocker's way, first to brevet major in January 1935 then to brevet lieutenant-colonel in July 1936.

Stellar confidential reports also led to command. Crocker assumed command of a tank company in the spring of 1936. In his own way, he gripped and trained his tank company with great skill and efficiency. He taught tactics, he practised drills and standard operating procedures, and he participated in battalion sports. The results were good, his commanding officer remarking that "he trained and commanded his company with considerable success during the ... collective training season."[22] He also recognized that Crocker had a "quiet determined manner with force of character that create[d] a feeling of confidence" and was "a commander who [got] the very best out of those under him." One of those underlings was the future Field Marshal Lord Carver, who would have agreed wholeheartedly with that assessment: "[John Crocker] had an excellent, clear brain and was a man of outstanding ability and absolute integrity, setting and demanding the highest standards in every respect. He spoke quietly, even when angry, and was always calm and cool-headed ... I learnt more from him about how to command soldiers than from any other man."[23] The army chain of command must have seen the same ability because, in April 1937, it posted Crocker to the Senior Officers' School at Sheerness, where he instructed future commanding officers until February 1938.[24] He made the same impression on the Commandant of the Senior Officers' School that he had made on previous bosses: "He is one of the clearest thinkers I have ever had the pleasure of working with."[25]

Like Hobart, the Commandant at Sheerness also picked up on Crocker's reticence. So did most of his other interwar supervisors. Reviewing Crocker's confidential reports for the period, one is immediately struck by the regularity with which the words "quiet" and "taciturnity" appear in the narratives; such references to his quiet demeanour are always accompanied, however, by qualifiers such as "strong personality," "conscientious," "most determined," "strength of character," "exceptionally efficient," "unselfish," or "likeable."[26] No one saw Crocker's reticent manner as a weakness. Most agreed with Hobart, who wrote that "[Crocker's] taciturnity does not cover up a slow mind. Far from it. But he always thinks before he speaks. He is popular with officers and men; is quite imperturbed by responsibility or crisis; has unruffled serenity and a cool judgement under all circumstances." One commander, who had known Crocker for only "a few weeks," had the initial impression that his new subordinate did not "suffer fools (or foolishness) gladly and may possibly allow his enthusiasm to lead him to show this too plainly," but a year later wrote that his subordinate was "outstanding ... in the highest class of staff officer," and having "all the essential qualities of a commander."[27]

Crocker's sterling reputation in the Royal Tank Corps also led to his being handpicked as the General Staff Officer First Class (GSO 1) for the 1st Armoured Division (then called the Mobile Division) under Major-General Alan Brooke in 1938. Brooke, who would become CIGS in 1941, could not have been more unlike Hobart, both in his temperament and in his ideas about the place of armour in the British Army. Both men had brilliant minds, but whereas Hobart was fiery and headstrong, Brooke was deliberate, confident, and calm in crisis. Hobart favoured all-tank formations that were not tied to the range of guns or the footpace of infantry, and he hated cavalrymen for their resistance to change.[28] Brooke, a gunner by trade, opposed Hobart's proposal for a tank army, was determined to work out methods for *all-arms* cooperation, and did his best to smooth out tank-cavalry relations. Looking back on his tenure as General Officer Commanding (GOC) Mobile Division, Brooke wrote:

> There was on the one hand the necessity to evolve correct doctrines for the employment of armoured forces in the field of battle, and on the other hand some bridge must be found to span the large gap that existed between the extremists of the Tank Corps and of the Cavalry ... The work of that year was intensely interesting, there was so much to be worked out. There were no precedents to work on as regards the handling of either light or heavy tanks in open warfare. The role of the close support Rifle Battalions had to be worked out from bedrock, the question of Artillery support for armoured forces on the move presented many new problems.[29]

Unhappy with the GSO 1 he had inherited on taking over the Mobile Division in 1937, Brooke sought Crocker out. In a January 1938 letter to General Sir Archibald Wavell, he wrote: "[I] am hoping to get Crocker who should be first class."[30] Crocker was an obvious choice. Not many people knew more about armoured formations – their capabilities, quirks, and limitations – and he did not have the handicap of Hobart's volatile disposition. Brooke never regretted his decision:

> For my own personal staff, I had John Crocker as my G.S.O. 1. I cannot speak too highly, and it would have been impossible to have been better served than I was by him. Having been Brigade Major to Hobart when he commanded the Armoured Brigade, he already had an intimate knowledge of the handling of armour. I thought at first that he might be so much imbued with Hobart's doctrine that I might have difficulty in getting him to agree with my views, which were not always in tune with those of Hobart. On the contrary, I found him the most loyal supporter of the views and doctrine I wished adopted.[31]

Crocker's close association with a future CIGS on the rise helped his career immensely, as Brooke would later be instrumental in arranging appointments to higher command.[32] But it also says something of Crocker's character that he worked well with, and won the admiration of, men as far apart as Hobart and Brooke; making things work meant more to him than any particular corps allegiance or dogma. His knowledge and his unshakeable calm continued to impress people.

He needed these qualities in spades as an armoured brigade commander during the Fall of France in the spring of 1940. Soon after Brooke had been promoted to corps command, Crocker took the helm of the 3rd Armoured Brigade in April 1940. His was one of two armoured brigades in the 1st Armoured Division, which deployed to France via Cherbourg late in May as part of the Second British Expeditionary Force. Major-General Roger Evans, who had taken over from Brooke, had his division hastily flung into battle on 27 May to dislodge the enemy from its bridgeheads over the River Somme. It did not go well. Having received sparse and confusing information on the enemy dispositions, Evans could do little more than delineate brigade boundaries for the fifteen-mile advance to the river, where he hoped a collision would knock the Germans from their positions.[33] But because the enemy was well established, British brigades, including Crocker's,[34] did little but lose tanks. To make matters worse, the French 5th Division's infantry, which was supposed to "follow up the advance," seemed unwilling or unable to help.[35] The situation deteriorated further in the days and weeks that followed. In mid-June, after having withdrawn to Rouen to refit and repair following the dismal attacks on the Somme, Crocker had to race the remnants of his brigade 200 miles to Cherbourg to avoid being cut off by Rommel's 7th Panzer Division, which had broken through British and French defences on the Seine River. Crocker got there first and evacuated out of Cherbourg, but the race had been so close that he had to leave thirteen of his remaining twenty-six tanks behind.[36] It was a frenetic situation, but Crocker maintained a firm grip on things throughout. For his cool-headed handling of an impossible situation in France, Crocker was rewarded with promotion to major-general and command of the newly formed 6th Armoured Division, shortly after his return to England.

France had taught him much, and confirmed much. Having watched the French collapse, and having been on the receiving end of deep armoured manoeuvre, Crocker was more convinced than ever of the ability of armoured formations to cause havoc, present the enemy with a multitude of tactical problems in rapid succession, and short-circuit the adversary's ability to make decisions. And the disappointing Somme counterattacks drove home the lesson that tanks should not be squandered in hasty frontal assaults against prepared enemy positions – especially if there is little or no infantry for the break-in battle. Armoured formations were best suited for deep and rapid manoeuvre – beyond the crust of enemy forward defences – as the Germans had used them in 1940. To do that well, however, everyone in an armoured organization had to be thoroughly trained and there had to be well-established and well-understood operating procedures. This had been a key to German success. Thus, when taking over the 6th Armoured Division, one of Crocker's earliest bits of written direction was on individual training.[37] It was a brand-new division with brand-new soldiers, so there was no point in leaping to divisional exercises until soldiers knew their weapons drills, tank crews could drive and shoot, NCOs and officers could read maps and make tactical decisions, and everyone could talk on a wireless set. Individual training was a necessary building block; collective training was pointless without it.

Having to prepare for counter-invasion tasks slowed the process of collective training somewhat in late 1940 and early 1941, but the 6th Armoured Division did get started in that direction. Concurrent with the individual training for soldiers and NCOs, commanding officers held "informal discussions," the purposes of which were "to get officers to study the various training manuals, pamphlets, etc., and through the medium of discussion to clear up any difficulties they may have encountered in their studies."[38] Officers had to have a common understanding of how troops, squadrons, and regiments would fight and move.[39]

Crocker more or less accepted War Office doctrine concerning the organization and roles of an armoured division and its regiments, but he did have his staff draft and disseminate standard operating procedures for such common yet critical things as road movement, the conduct of reconnaissance, and the composition of reconnaissance parties.[40] Having been a brigade major, a GSO 1, and a brigade commander, he was well equipped to promulgate the standard operating procedures on such matters. He knew what worked and he knew how to present it in a comprehensible manner. What followed was plenty of training and practice to ensure that the drills and operating procedures became second nature.[41] This was all part of preparing his division for a war of rapid manoeuvre, and the rationale was relatively simple: if everyone understands how we do things, we need not slow down to explain every move and procedure. That was Crocker's way.

The same necessity for common operating procedures applied to headquarters as well. A headquarters organization of 50 to 100 people would have had an awfully tough time taking a commander's concept, calculating what it takes to make the formation move, shoot, and keep shooting, if it was not proficient at setting up its own shop and communicating. When Crocker succeeded Lieutenant-General F.P. Nosworthy in command of 9th Corps in September 1942, he had his staff hammer out thirty pages (plus annexes) of standing orders, which outlined the general organization of the headquarters, movement organizations, procedures for tank harbours, and drills for signals traffic.[42] Exercise Robin, which included the headquarters of the 11th Armoured Division and the 1st Division, took place on 2-5 November 1942. It confirmed the validity of the standing orders and resulted in some minor amendments, with the final product being issued in December 1942. These seemingly banal chores were worth the effort because a smooth-functioning headquarters was absolutely critical to Crocker's method of command. He preferred being forward in battle, in his small Tactical Headquarters and in a position to view things for himself. He did not spend a lot of time in the Main Headquarters, so it had to be capable of operating on its own.

Well-established and well-understood procedures paid other dividends as well – brief and simple-to-produce orders. During Exercise Robin, and later during the Tunisian Campaign in April 1943, Crocker's headquarters never issued a written order longer than four typed pages.[43] Occasionally, the orders contained overlay graphics as attachments, or even a matrix for road movements, but the orders themselves were generally simple pieces of direction based on the commander's intentions. Complicated orders that explained every intention, manoeuvre, and supporting action would simply have taken too long to produce and pass on. After having run the gauntlet with Rommel in 1940, Crocker understood that fast decision cycles, good drills, and the rapid translation of orders into action were the keys to both increased operational tempo and the success of armoured formations in battle.

Crocker was known for his command of these issues, which is why so many people sought his opinion on them. The armoured theorist and journalist Sir Basil Liddell Hart was one person who used Crocker as a sounding board. In December 1942, for example, he sought Crocker's comments on a paper entitled "The Problem of Quickening Manoeuvre."[44] Liddell Hart was always seeking an influential outlet for his ideas and he corresponded with a dizzying array of people, Crocker being just one of hundreds with whom he exchanged letters. Liddell Hart understood that, by this time, Crocker was a man of considerable influence in both the Royal Tank Corps and the army. He was also a member of Prime Minister Winston Churchill's "Tank Parliament," and had been since its inception in May 1941.[45] For someone looking to spread his ideas, Crocker was the right person to contact. In "The Problem of Quickening Manoeuvre," Liddell Hart had proposed a "shortening of the chain of command" as a means of "quickening the tempo of operations" in Britain's land formations, which seemed, at that point, incapable of keeping pace with the German adversary in the Western Desert.[46] Specifically, the paper argued that the British Army should adopt a system of "fives" for subunits instead of "threes" – five companies in a battalion, five battalions in a brigade, five brigades in a division, and so on. This reorganization, its author hoped, would lead to savings in the number of head-quarters across the army; the fewer the number of headquarters, the less often an order would have to be interpreted, transmitted, and acted on, and, therefore, the quicker the operational tempo. In fact, Liddell Hart went so far as to argue that the corps, as a formation, could be eliminated altogether.[47] It all seemed logical enough.

But Crocker was too practical a man with too much headquarters experience to be swayed. Still, in responding to "The Problem of Quickening Manoeuvre," Crocker, true to form, was gracious, polite, and yet straightforward with his opinion. While he acknowledged that there was "still something clogging the works and tending to perpetrate the old slowness and inflexibility," he balked at Liddell Hart's remedy: "For too long we have sought the answers to all our problems in changes in organization."[48] He emphasized instead his belief that well-understood drills, combined with "training, practice and experience" in current organizations, would pay greater dividends in quickening tempo than "expend[ing] more time in attempting to forge new [organizations]." Far from wanting to eliminate the corps as an organization, Crocker favoured bigger ones, although he did add the humorous disclaimer "not for personal reasons." Having just spent the better part of the past fifteen months building corps – first

11th Corps, then 9th Corps – he explained the real reason why: "Our corps HQ (and commanders I hope) are designed now for mobile conditions. Our Army HQ, being first a development from the old peace time Command HQ are physically [in terms of communications and mobility] and mentally unsuited for direct command in the field." Crocker was even more direct in his opposition to Liddell Hart's proposed changes lower in the chain of command. A brigade of five battalions, with all its usual attachments, was, he explained, "beyond the capacity of the Brigade Commander and [his] staff ... I am [also] thoroughly opposed to the application of 'fives' to the B[attalio]n and lower, particularly as regards the inf[antry] sec[tion]. An estab[lished] sec[tion] of 5 would be reduced to ineffectiveness by normal wastage to say nothing of battle casualties."

Crocker had credibility and Liddell Hart listened. Within a week of receiving Crocker's comments on "The Problem of Quickening Manoeuvre," he produced a scaled-down article entitled "Too Much Top Hamper?" in which he still advocated the elimination of corps (albeit only in armies with less than ten divisions) but no longer proposed the binning of brigades or the pruning of infantry sections to five men each.[49] The newer version appeared in the *Daily Mail* on 11 February 1943, under the title "Is Our Soldiery Carrying Too Much Top Hamper?"[50]

Crocker had designed his corps headquarters for speed. He divided it in a fairly doctrinal fashion – Main Headquarters, Rear Headquarters, and Tactical Headquarters – although he used the terms Advanced Headquarters, Rear Headquarters, and Command Post.[51] Unlike Horrocks's small and very temporary Tactical Headquarters (see pages 35-36 above), Crocker preferred a more traditional and permanent set-up for his command post, which he established at the start of the operations and kept open until the end of the action. Crocker used it as a sort of commander's forward operating base, from which he visited brigades and divisions during daylight hours, returning to the Advanced Headquarters by last light every evening. He definitely controlled the battle from his "Tac." That was where he made most of his decisions, or at least he relayed them to his Main Headquarters from there, with the assistance of several staff officers, his Chief Engineer (CE), and his Commander, Corps Royal Artillery (CCRA). In general, this system functioned well for him, and Crocker was well served by a talented Brigadier General Staff (BGS), Brigadier G.H.A. MacMillan. An Argyll and Sutherland Highlander who had won an MC during the Great War and who served in the Experimental Brigade in 1927-28, MacMillan had earned a reputation as a superbly skilled soldier. In fact, he would go on to command the 15th (Scottish) Division in Normandy until he was wounded in July 1944. He would also command twice under Crocker – once as GOC 49th (West

Riding) Division in 1st Corps (November 1944 to March 1945), then later as GOC Palestine while Crocker was Commander-in-Chief Middle East Land Forces (1947-48).[52] He understood what Crocker wanted and he designed a set of standing orders that established clearly how the headquarters would set up, tear down, harbour, move, and communicate.[53] As Crocker related to Liddell Hart, the system worked well in mobile battle: "[9th Corps Headquarters] had 17 operational moves (i.e., moves in battle) during a period of 42 days over 450 miles – never went into a building ... and was really mobile in every sense."[54]

Well though the headquarters may have functioned, the manoeuvre battle he had hoped to achieve in Tunisia never really took place. The closest opportunity Crocker had for scoring a major manoeuvre victory came in early April 1943 (see Map 7). As the enemy was withdrawing in front of Montgomery's Eighth Army in the south, the First Army, which included Crocker's 9th Corps, had a chance to slice across the line of withdrawal and close the trap – if Crocker could break through the Fondouk Pass from the west. To do this, Crocker planned first to seize the high ground north and south of the 2.5-mile-wide pass on 7-8 April, then send Major-General Charles Keightley's 6th Armoured Division through the gap and across the German lines of communication.[55] His reconnaissance of the terrain, which he conducted with MacMillan in tow, led him to believe that the key to controlling the gap was grabbing quickly the dominating high ground on either side of the pass. Before hurling the 6th Armoured Division through the defile, Crocker planned to have the 128th Brigade seize Djebel Houfia in the north while the 34th US Division captured Djebel Haouareb in the south.[56] At a 6 April conference, Major-General Charles Ryder, who commanded the American division, expressed some concern about the Djebel Rhorab feature, which would be on his left flank as he advanced towards Djebel Haouareb. Crocker assured him that the feature was lightly held, but allowed that Ryder's artillery could fire smoke to blind whatever enemy might be there, but no high explosive as it might endanger British forces advancing on Djebel Rhorab from the north. After the war, Ryder would suggest that he had objected strenuously to the plan, but MacMillan, who made notes on the meeting, was convinced that Ryder was "satisfied with the plan as given out" and that there "was no question of 'objections' by Gen Ryder being 'overruled.'"[57] In fact, after the conference, when Ryder asked for a two-and-a-half-hour advance in H-hour so that he might conduct the first phase of the attack in darkness, Crocker approved.

The attack faltered nearly from the start. Early on 8 April, the 128th Brigade knocked the enemy off the high ground east of Pichon and, by noon, was making its way south towards Djebel Rhorab. South of the gap, however, where the

34th US Division attacked, the Americans were more than two hours late in getting started, lost their barrage, made a very tenuous advance in daylight, and failed to make a dent in the enemy position at Djebel Haouareb. Frustrated with the slowness of the American attack, which he believed was not being pressed with sufficient determination, and, sensing a fleeting opportunity, an impatient Crocker ordered Keightley to launch a strong reconnaissance in force towards Fondouk, to determine the nature of the enemy defences and to assist the 34th US Division.[58] A regimental group based on the 17th/21st Lancers, which Crocker visited "under considerable mortar and observed shell fire" on 9 April,[59] prodded into the pass near Fondouk, only to be stopped abruptly by well-placed anti-tank guns covering the defile. With the chances of cutting off an enemy withdrawal fast fading, the army group commander, General Sir Harold Alexander, convinced Crocker to ignore the situation on the 34th US Division front and smash through the pass. Crocker, who could see that the battle had reached a critical stage, agreed and ordered the 6th Armoured Division "to find or make a gap, as the success of the operations ... was being jeopardized by the delay." Meantime, the 128th Brigade would continue its advance on Djebel Rhorab from the north, while the 3rd Welsh Guards would attack the same objective from the west. These were costly moves because the enemy, "realising the danger of this threat to his flank, rushed troops into area North and North West of the Gap, which had previously been reported clear – in particular the RHORAB feature."[60] This was unfortunate. If Crocker had made Djebel Rhorab an objective for the first phase of the attack, the enemy would not have been able to reinforce and the failure of the 34th US Division attack would not have mattered as much. Crocker was going for speed, but he was fast learning that an attack on a well-posted enemy with well-sited weapons and carefully placed minefields could not be rushed without paying the price of high casualties. As it was, the 26th Armoured Brigade of the 6th Armoured Division did manage to penetrate beyond Fondouk, but only at the cost of thirty-four tanks, and 108 Welsh guardsmen fell in their successful assault on Djebel Rhorab.[61] It might have been different if the American attack had succeeded in the first phase. The Germans might not have reinforced a position that was all but lost, and the breakthrough might have occurred sooner. But that did not happen. The 6th Armoured Division secured its own flanks *and* forced its way through the gap, and that took time. The end result was that, by the time the 6th Armoured Division finally barged its way through and got reorganized for the pursuit on 10 April, most of the enemy had slipped away to the north.

Disappointment set in as Crocker pondered what had happened at Fondouk, but his criticism of the 34th US Division's performance has been exaggerated by a succession of authors, starting with the Commander-in-Chief Allied Forces North Africa, General Dwight D. Eisenhower.[62] First, Crocker did not indiscreetly blurt out a scathing appraisal of American battle performance at a press conference, as Eisenhower suggested in his memoir. There was no press conference. As an aggrieved Crocker acknowledged in a January 1949 letter to Eisenhower, "it is true that some newspaper men came to my C[ommand]. P[ost]."[63] They came during the second phase of the attack, while the 6th Armoured Division "was making its successful break through," and they were openly "critical of the slowness of the advance." In response to their queries and their comments, Crocker was characteristically direct in explaining why he thought his corps seemed to be crawling, not running, through the pass. The 34th US Division "had failed and nothing could conceal the fact." This was true, even if it ignored the failure to take Djebel Rhorab in the first phase. Ryder complained that the enemy from that feature had interfered with his attack, yet the 26th Armoured Brigade had forced its way past the position, and Crocker had been right up near the front during the fighting. Crocker thought he was "guarded" in his comments to his press visitors, but the result of this brief encounter was a *Time* magazine article, which stated that the American effort at Fondouk was "downright embarrassing ... All day the British worked their way efficiently along the ridges; all day U.S. troops tentatively approached but never stormed the first of their heights."[64] Eisenhower was livid.

His concern was keeping the peace in a "family squabble." Even before the release of the *Time* article, piqued national sensitivities had worn at Anglo-American coalition relations in North Africa. Fondouk made matters worse. The day after the battle, a delegation of American staff officers under Major-General Clarence Huebner called on Crocker. As they were compiling a report on Eisenhower's behalf, they asked Crocker "to tell [them] frankly what had happened," and seemed somewhat taken aback when the British corps commander took them at their word.[65] Crocker walked Huebner to his caravan and, "with no others present," offered his frank assessment that there was a "lack of leadership" in the 34th US Division, mostly because the divisional headquarters was "too far back and largely out of control," which was fair criticism. Although Crocker had gone into the very mouth of the pass to get an idea of the fighting in front of the 17th/21st Lancers, Ryder had done no such thing, and so his impression of the battle was much the poorer. Crocker also found that in the "forward [US] troops, which [he] had visited during the battle, leadership in all aspects was conspicuously absent" and that there was an unwillingness to close resolutely with the enemy. Troops were reluctant to advance due to a "lack of coordination of the action of the various components of the attack." By this

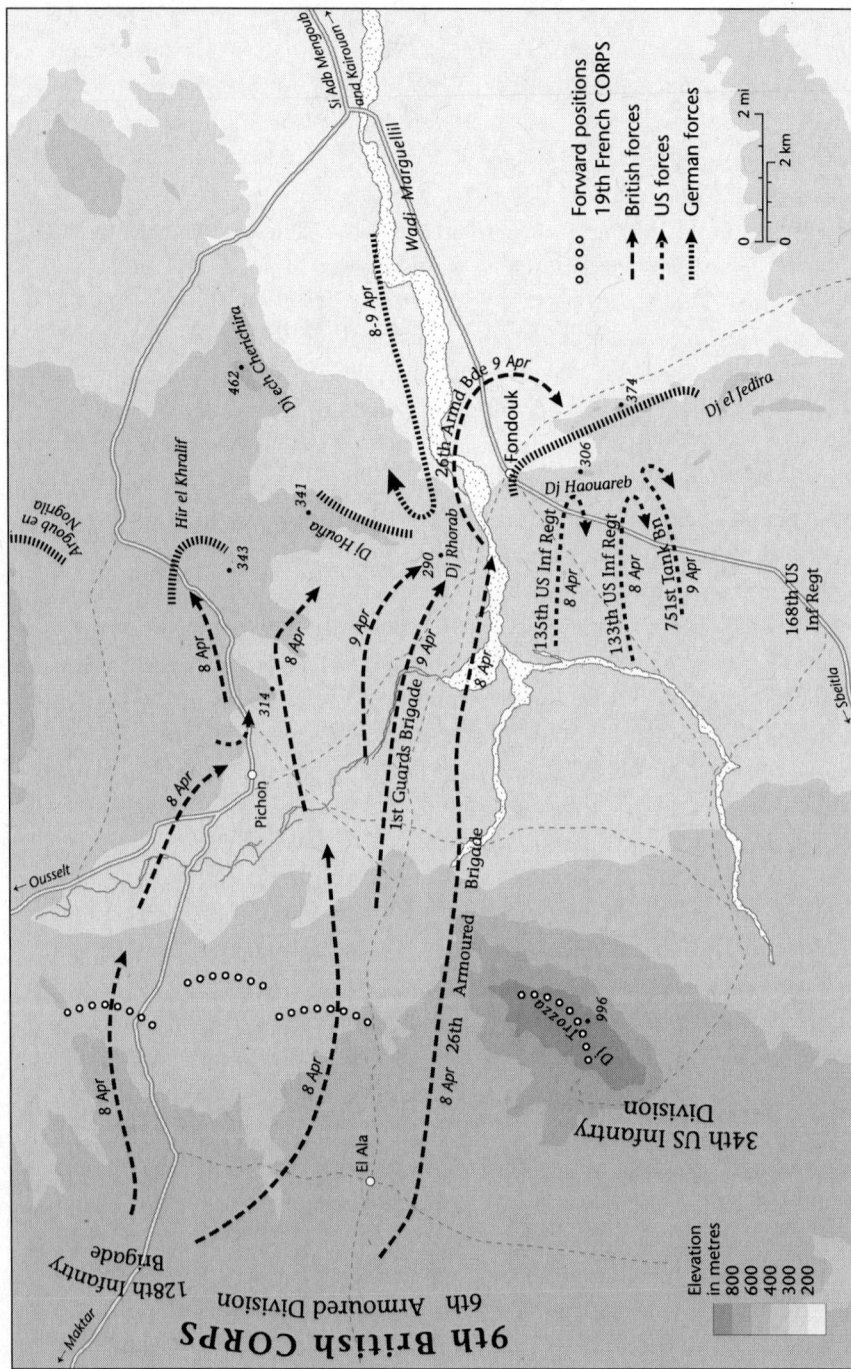

MAP 7  The 9th Corps attack on Fondouk. Adapted from Major-General I.S.O. Playfair, *The Mediterranean and the Middle East*, vol. 4 (London: Her Majesty's Stationery Office, 1960), map 36.

Crocker meant that armour, infantry, artillery, and even air attacks in the 34th US Division sector were not properly synchronized, which was also fair comment. When Ryder advanced his H-hour by two and a half hours to 0300 hours on the morning of 8 April, he lost the preparatory air bombardment of enemy positions because the air forces would not attack that close to friendly troops in the dark. Then, to compound the problems, his attack started more than two hours late, long after the supporting artillery fire had passed, leaving the infantry of the two attacking regiments to advance in daylight, without the benefit of any neutralizing fire. Ryder and his regimental commanders seemed incapable of rectifying the problems. They did not use smoke to blind the enemy, as had been discussed on 6 April. They sent tanks forward without infantry or artillery support. Nothing worked. This was hard for Huebner to hear, especially considering that it came within two months of the bad American setback at Kasserine Pass. Huebner may not have appeared "in the least resentful" to Crocker, but, by the time the officers got back to Eisenhower, he had formed the impression that the British general had been "severe and caustic" in his comments, and this upset his chief. Eisenhower's half-page account of the incident in his memoir painted an unflattering portrait of Crocker, leaving the impression that the latter was "the garrulous commander of a futile and abortive operation who not only failed in his task but who was the one officer in the whole of the North African campaign who deliberately, through his irresponsible and unjustified criticism, caused serious friction between the Allies."[66]

This was unfair and Crocker said so in his postwar letter to Eisenhower. He pointed out his surprise at the allegation that he had "severely criticized to press representatives the failure of the American division" and caused "Anglo-American recrimination" for "almost the only time during the African operations."[67] Highlighting that "neither [Eisenhower], nor Field Marshal Alexander, nor [his] then immediate commander General Anderson ever mentioned this matter to me at the time or since," Crocker explained what had happened from his point of view.[68] He did not believe that he deserved to be remembered to history only as a "wrecker" of Anglo-American relations: "I would like to reinstate myself in the opinion of a Chief for whom I give way to none in my admiration and I should like to learn that you, on reflection, feel that your too pointed comments have done me some injustice." Crocker never went public with his objections. Eisenhower never responded.

Crocker missed the climax of the campaign, which only deepened his disappointment. On 27 April, just before his corps was to play a leading role in the final assault on Tunis, he was wounded while watching a demonstration of the

PIAT handheld anti-tank weapon. A piece of shrapnel entered his upper chest wall and ended his war in North Africa. In Crocker's place, Lieutenant-General Brian Horrocks, then commander of the Eighth Army's 10th Corps, temporarily took the reins of 9th Corps and fought it through the finale in Tunisia. After watching stoically from the sidelines, Crocker returned to England in May. The reason, as he explained to Liddell Hart in June 1943, was "not because of my injury, but because my Corps H.Q. was disbanded." He added the brave and self-deprecating quip "a circumstance which you will approve of thoroughly,"[69] but it did little to hide his melancholy mood: "It is hard to applaud when you see an instrument, which you have built up with much difficulty and which has developed into a really well run-in machine broken up."[70] Frustration followed by unemployment; this was not the happiest time in Crocker's career.

But because his currency was still good in the British Army establishment, especially with Brooke, who was now CIGS, he did not want for work long. Although Crocker did not know it at the time of his June letter to Liddell Hart, Alexander had already recommended to Brooke that Crocker return to England and take command of a corps for the upcoming campaign in Northwest Europe.[71] The CIGS, who had long thought highly of Crocker, agreed.[72] On 1 August, Crocker assumed command of 1st Corps, the formation with which he would fight his biggest battles. An infantry-heavy formation, it had been earmarked as one of the assaulting corps for Operation Roundup/Overlord, and now, to lead it through a frontal assault on a defended beach, it had a Royal Tank Corps officer who had spent his career thinking about how to effect deep armoured manoeuvre.

Crocker's reputation as a competent and flexible officer had not diminished at all. Montgomery, who assumed command of the 21st Army Group in January 1944, appears to have accepted Crocker's appointment without question. The new army group commander was well known for fiddling with senior appointments and placing his own people in key positions,[73] but he did nothing to change Crocker's appointment before D-day. On the contrary, he assigned Crocker the most complex task of any corps commander for Overlord: the capture of Caen after a combined assault against a defended beach.

This was a dramatic, and ironic, departure for Crocker. Four-page operation orders simply would not cut it in this instance, as Crocker quickly discerned: "The complexity of its staging can hardly be realised except by those intricately concerned and when all is said and done there remain many imponderables which cannot be resolved."[74] The interesting thing is not so much that Crocker had to fight somewhat out of his element but rather that he adapted so easily to the change. After some preliminary analysis of the tactical problem, he placed his finger squarely on the paradox of amphibious operations against defended localities: "The very complexity [of the operation] breeds a rigidity where flexibility is so desirable to meet the unknown."[75]

He relied on the same propensity for practical analysis that had served him so well in Hobart's experimental Tank Brigade to think about, test, refine, and develop solutions to the tactical problems he faced. This was just a new set of problems. One of his first activities was to exercise his new headquarters on the basics – "Office org[anization] and Movement and harbouring."[76] With the help of his BGS, Brigadier P.M. Balfour, a set of standing orders came less than a month later, followed by a number of Corps Headquarters exercises to practise road movement, convoy discipline, and the setting up and tearing down of the Main Headquarters complex.[77] Then, to refine headquarters procedures and to think about how to breach the Atlantic Wall, 1st Corps conducted Exercise Euclid, which was really more of a corps officer study period than anything else. The exercise scenario involved the establishment of a bridgehead in the Pas-de-Calais, and was divided into three main parts: a corps planning period (16-21 August), a division and brigade planning period (29 August-13 September), and demonstrations and lectures with landing craft (27-28 August). Its objects were very practical:

(a) To give 49 Inf Div practice in planning an assault on a heavily defended beach.
(b) To ascertain if it is possible to land a follow-up div on the second tide of D-Day
(c) To study the problems connected with the landing and concentration of a follow-up division in the bridgehead ...
(d) Consideration of when Corps HQ should take over operational and administrative control and the means to do so.[78]

These issues were not examined in isolation; naval liaison officers, the commanders of beach groups, the assaulting engineer company commanders, and representatives of the 27th Armoured Brigade, 33rd Tank Brigade, and 6th Airborne Division took part as well. Everyone contributed and Crocker managed to wring eight pages of lessons and recommendations from this first crack at the combined assault.[79] There were conclusions on the amount and type of fire support required prior to landing, the use of smoke such that it did not interfere with the fire support, suitable objectives for airborne forces, and assault frontages for companies (250 yards) and battalions (750 yards), just to cite a few. Drawing on the lessons of previous combined assaults such as the ones conducted at Dieppe, Sicily, and Salerno, planners also gained a greater appreciation for how the assault should be sequenced: Duplex Drive (DD) tanks landing at H-hour for direct fire on beach defences, followed by Armoured

Vehicles Royal Engineers (AVsRE) to breach the obstacles at H+5, followed by the infantry companies at H+15 to H+25, to pour through the gaps, clear the enemy from the defences, and establish a bridgehead. Later, a brigade of the 3rd Canadian Infantry Division validated most of these tactical conclusions during Exercise Pirate, a trial run of an assault on a defended beach held on 16-19 October.[80]

Timings mattered immensely in operations of this magnitude, mostly because of the follow-on forces. The assaulting troops had to gain a bridgehead – quickly – otherwise the forces necessary to hold and expand the bridgehead against a determined enemy could not be landed. Here was the crux of Crocker's paradox: the operation was so complex, and the timings so rigid, that the assaulting troops had to be willing to improvise in order to achieve their objectives on time. Crocker and his staff recognized this from the start: "Things may well go wrong ... It is most important that no-one get the impression that he can rely on the AVREs and need do nothing himself. Both inf[antry] and R[oyal] E[ngineers] must be taught that they must be prepared to gain their objectives without them."[81] Considering that 1st Corps had not, to that point, conducted anything larger than a battalion-level combined exercise, these were remarkably prescient points, and a very sound start for further training. The two-day Exercise Bridgehead in October, for example, looked at how to avoid the congestion that could be caused as follow-on brigades were fed into the bridgehead.[82] Amphibious training to fine-tune all the actions of the assault continued as brigade groups from Crocker's corps passed through the Combined Training Centres at Inverary and Castle Toward, Scotland. And divisional exercises took place between February and April 1944.[83] This was the sort of "training, practice, and experience" that he had mentioned to Liddell Hart a year earlier.

A full account of the D-day assaults need not be made here; in any case, they have been well told elsewhere.[84] Suffice it to say that no assaulting Allied corps commander had a bigger task. Not only did Crocker have the most ambitious D-day objective – the capture of Caen – he also had more formations to control than any other Allied corps commander: the 3rd Division, 3rd Canadian Infantry Division, 6th Airborne Division, and 4th Special Service Brigade in the assault, plus the 51st (Highland) Division in the follow-up phase. This was a complex combined affair; Crocker's orders for Overlord amounted to fifteen pages plus an additional twenty-two appendices – long, but not exceedingly so given the task.[85] That the assaults went so well, in spite of some things going wrong, owed much to the detailed planning of Crocker and his staff and how they trained for the imponderables. To cite just one example of how the preparations paid off, during the 3rd Canadian Infantry Division assaults, only one assaulting battalion had its DD tanks land before the infantry as planned,[86] yet the assaulting troops managed to improvise and seize their initial objectives, pushing further inland than any Allied division on D-day.

Crocker did not capture Caen on D-day, and for another thirty-three days neither would anyone else. The city was simply too good a hub for operations against the Allied bridgehead for the Germans to give it up without a tremendous fight. From the Caen area, elements of the 12th SS Panzer Division had checked the 3rd Canadian Infantry Division advance on Carpiquet on 7-8 June, while the 21st Panzer Division had done the same to the 3rd Division's attempt to grab Lebisey and the high ground north of Caen.[87] Indeed, by 10 June, Field Marshal Erwin Rommel, Commander of Army Group B, had committed the equivalent of four panzer and three infantry divisions to the eastern Allied bridgehead.[88] In fact, he had hoped to use his panzer forces to destroy the Allied bridgehead and tried to do so, albeit in a somewhat piecemeal fashion.[89]

Although the Germans had not been able to deliver a concentrated blow to drive the Allied troops back into the English Channel, the Second Army had still not been able to expand the bridgehead significantly and take Caen. Major-General Richard Gale's 6th Airborne Division, with its badly depleted numbers, had done well simply to consolidate and hold its bridgehead east of the Orne against several enemy counterattacks. An attempt to encircle Caen from both the west and the east had failed on 11-12 June when Lieutenant-General Gerald Bucknall's 30th Corps had proved incapable of driving the 7th Armoured Division from Bayeux to Villers-Bocage, and Crocker had likewise been unable to drill the newly-arrived 51st (Highland) Division through Gale's bridgehead to Cagny.[90] Operation Epsom, an offensive from the west to capture the high ground south of Caen with Sir Richard O'Connor's recently activated 8th Corps, had also ground out in the face of determined German counterattacks just two miles east of the Odon river, 26-29 June. Although the Allies had failed to capture the city of Caen, they had managed to maintain the initiative, and operations like Epsom had forced Field Marshal Gerd von Runstedt, Commander-in-Chief West and Rommel's immediate superior, to feed divisions piecemeal into the eastern bridgehead, something he had hoped to avoid because, as he had predicted, it depleted his tanks and manpower.[91] By the end of June, von Runstedt had committed fourteen of his twenty-one divisions in Normandy to the Caen-Bayeux sector, and eight of them were panzer divisions.[92] The Germans never did muster a concentrated offensive blow, mostly because they had frittered away their infantry. On 2 July, Army Group B reported that its panzer divisions had lost a total of 5,000 panzergrenadiers, and were continuing to lose them at a rate of 100 men a day.[93] Still, they could defend, and defend well, so, by the beginning of July, Allied commanders had begun to think that Caen might have to be taken head on.

The prospect of breaking into well-prepared defences that were supported by armoured reserves and an extensive road and rail network, and then conducting a street-by-street city fight, led Allied planners to look for a little help. As Montgomery wrote: "The plan involved an assault against well organized and mutually supporting positions based on a number of small villages which lay in an arc north and northwest of the city, and, in view of the strength of these defences, I decided to seek the assistance of RAF [Royal Air Force] Bomber Command in a close support role on the battlefield."[94] The idea of using Bomber Command was not entirely Montgomery's, though. It had emanated from the headquarters of Air Chief Marshal Sir Trafford Leigh-Mallory, Commander-in-Chief Allied Expeditionary Air Forces (C-in-C AEAF).[95] The first recorded interservice discussion on the use of heavy bombers in tactical support of a ground assault on Caen took place at 21st Army Group Headquarters at 1700 hours on 14 June. There, Leigh-Mallory, who was anxious to break the deadlock and secure airfields west and south of Caen, offered the Commander Second British Army, Lieutenant-General Sir Miles Dempsey, "Bomber Command, 8 USAAF [US Army Air Forces] and all the mediums [bombers] for tactical support of an infantry attack ... at first light on 17 June."[96] With this promise of support, Dempsey agreed to "attack with the LEFT of 1 Corps and take Caen."

Planning time was short, however. Ninety minutes later, Dempsey met with Crocker and "gave him the plan for the taking of Caen," adding that "RAF representatives would fly over from the UK tomorrow to settle details."[97] Crocker was caught a little flat-footed and, with equal haste, called a meeting of his key staff and representatives from the 3rd Canadian, 3rd British, 6th Airborne, and 51st (Highland) Divisions at midnight.[98] After a very quick analysis of the tactical problem, the two assaulting divisions – 3rd Canadian and 3rd British – submitted their target lists to 1st Corps Headquarters at 0600 hours on 15 June. There was only time enough for one more conference of key commanders and staff at 0745 before Crocker headed off to Dempsey's headquarters to coordinate with RAF and USAAF representatives at 1030. He remembered:

> On arrival Dempsey said in effect, "we've got Bomber Com[man]d reps here and I'll leave you to make a plan with them." He then left. There followed a discussion examining the possibilities and we reached a stage when we agreed that what would be required would be a "carpet" laid by heavy and medium bombers to help us cross the open ground in front of the 3rd Cdn Div sector, plus certain other selected localities.[99]

In the middle of these discussions, a puzzled and somewhat amused Crocker watched as a "much disturbed" Air Chief Marshal Sir Arthur W. Tedder,

Eisenhower's deputy at Supreme Headquarters Allied Expeditionary Force (SHAEF), barged into the room and demanded to huddle separately with the air force representatives in attendance. When they emerged a half-hour later, they announced that the project was off.[100] Crocker and the others were dumbfounded. Later, he speculated that the "still widely uneducated" group of air force officers, who clung to the notion that Bomber Command could still win the war, had objected to wasting heavy bomber missions on tactical targets, and had "won the day." He also considered, quite rightly, that personalities played a part too, as there were many "anti Leigh-Mallory" senior air force officers, like Tedder, who worried that the C-in-C AEAF's willingness to support ground operations would detract from what they deemed to be higher-priority objectives, such as the strategic bombing campaign against Germany.[101] These were reasonable speculations as to why the operation had been nixed.

To the list of reasons for the project's cancellation, Crocker should also have added the unfamiliarity of his staff – and the rest of the army, for that matter – with the capabilities of heavy bombers. Although bombers had very recently been used to break up the assembly of German armoured forces near Villers-Bocage, this would be the first real task in close support of attacking ground formations. It was new to everyone, as the target selection by 1st Corps suggested. The "carpet" they proposed to lay on German positions in front of the 3rd Canadian Infantry Division was too close to the assaulting troops to be conducted safely by heavy bombers.[102] Owing to the inaccuracy of heavy bombers at the time, air force planners believed that a bombline could not be closer to forward troops than 6,000 yards.[103] In most cases, the targets that 1st Corps and 3rd Canadian Infantry Division picked were within 1,000 to 1,500 yards of their own positions. Moreover, the army representatives "had to admit the tasks appeared to be within the scope of Tactical Air Forces."[104] This was the reason for Major-General Freddie de Guingand's assessment that "the corps had not prepared its case sufficiently."[105] In any case, the project died – for a couple of weeks anyway.[106] In the meantime, Crocker continued his "active defence" of the eastern bridgehead and dealt with personnel problems.

First among the latter was the GOC of the 3rd Canadian Infantry Division, Major-General Rod Keller. On 5 July, Crocker wrote to Dempsey: "I am afraid the opinion that I had previously formed is now confirmed. Keller is not really fit temperamentally and perhaps physically (he is a man who has the appearance of having lived well) for such a responsible command."[107] The action that prompted the letter was Operation Windsor, the 3rd Canadian Infantry Division's 4 July attack on the airfield and the village at Carpiquet. This is worth a brief digression because of the lessons it carried and for the deleterious effect it had on Crocker's relationship with Keller. Carpiquet had been a D-day objective for the 3rd Canadian Infantry Division, but strong counterattacks by the 12th SS Panzer Division had prevented the Canadians from seizing it on 7-8 June. A month later, German troops at Carpiquet could observe the troops of 8th Corps south of the Odon river valley, making life for the 8th Corps soldiers unpleasant with indirect fire. O'Connor appealed to Dempsey, who agreed that Carpiquet should be captured and handed the task to Crocker.[108] Instead of incorporating Windsor into Charnwood, the corps operation to capture Caen, Crocker figured that the operation could be executed in advance of Charnwood by the 3rd Canadian Infantry Division, and he assigned the job to Keller.

The operation did not go well. Keller decided to use Ken Blackader's 8th Canadian Infantry Brigade, reinforced with an extra battalion (the Royal Winnipeg Rifles), a regiment of tanks (10th Canadian Armoured Regiment), flails (mine-clearing tanks), and crocodiles (flamethrowers).[109] Blackader also had a tremendous amount of fire support to neutralize enemy machine guns, mortars, and artillery: twenty-one artillery regiments, a battleship, and two squadrons of typhoons.[110] In spite of all the extra fire support and diversionary attacks on both flanks, the 8th Canadian Infantry Brigade advanced into a hailstorm of direct and indirect fire on the morning of 4 July. The plan had been to advance in the first phase with three battalions up – the North Shore Regiment and a squadron of tanks on Carpiquet village, Le Régiment de la Chaudière with a squadron of tanks in the centre, and the Royal Winnipeg Rifles (with no tanks) in the south. In the second phase, the Queen's Own Rifles of Canada were to pass through the Chaudières to capture the control buildings in depth. In the north, the diversionary attack by the Sherbrooke Fusiliers on Chateau St. Louet and Gruchy, impressive though this daring little action may have been, did not suppress enemy fire from Franqueville, which poured down on the North Shores as they struggled towards their objective at Carpiquet village. The Chaudières in the centre had less of a problem from direct fire and managed to make it into Carpiquet village, but the Royal Winnipeg Rifles in the south suffered terribly. Without tanks, the Winnipegs, who had to advance nearly 1.5 kilometres across open ground, did not have weapons with sufficient range to suppress the enemy fire from the high ground just south of the control buildings. Worse still, the enemy, who had monitored radio traffic and observed movement west of Carpiquet in the two days preceding the attack,[111] simply waited for the barrage to start, then dropped mortars behind it to catch the Winnipegs advancing in the open. Not until nearly four hours after the 0500 H-hour, and after sustaining horrendous casualties, did the Winnipegs reach the first of the Carpiquet hangars, which they were unable to clear. Instead, they withdrew to their start line, from which they recommenced their attack at 1600 hours, this time with tanks, but it too failed. As a result of the failure to capture the objective of the hangars, Blackader cancelled the second-phase assault by the Queen's Own Rifles on the control buildings, formed a defensive fortress on the village, and braced for the inevitable German counterattacks.

Within hours of the attack on Carpiquet, commanders from company to corps began asking what had gone wrong. The operation had cost the 8th Canadian Infantry Brigade Group a total of 377 casualties, including 117 killed.[112] The 8th Canadian Infantry Brigade concluded that the narrow-front attack in Operation Windsor had permitted the enemy to "fire in enfilade from localities not being attacked" and to concentrate the indirect fire of his mortars and artillery.[113] Neither of the flanking feints worked because their objectives were poorly chosen. The Sherbrooke attack on Chateau St. Louet accomplished little in the way of neutralizing the enemy ensconced in the Franqueville area. The same situation played out in the south, where the 43rd (Wessex) Division attack on Verson, through the low ground of the Odon river valley, did nothing to suppress enemy observation and fire from the high ground south of the control buildings or the southern heights of the re-entrant one kilometre south of the hangars. The fire plan did not help either. The orders for Operation Windsor allocated a medium artillery regiment "for the protection of each flank," but the accurate fire from both flanks indicates quite clearly that they were not used to best effect.[114] In addition, the counter-battery plan did not do enough to keep enemy batteries quiet after the initial stonks, and the neutralizing fire of barrages was transitory at best.[115] At Carpiquet, too many rounds were expended in creeping barrages that won firefights only briefly then passed over the heads of enemy defenders, falling harmlessly on unoccupied ground beyond. One enemy defender from 1/26th Panzergrenadier Regiment recalled the short-lived effect of barrage fire: "The explosions were of such violence that bits of concrete inside the bunker burst from its walls. Once the artillery fire had moved on to the rear, I leaped ahead some ten metres to the front squad ... to repel the expected attack ... There was no problem repelling the infantry attack. We concentrated our fire at the massed groups of attacking infantrymen until they retreated."[116]

The after-action report recommended assigning a much lower percentage of gun ammunition to barrages and a far greater proportion of rounds to neutralizing known or suspected enemy positions of fire and observation – not just with brief concentrations that came and went quickly but with steady, less-dense fire that simply prevented the enemy from comfortably raising his head above a parapet.[117] The enemy at Carpiquet would not have been able drop mortar rounds on advancing troops if the enemy's observers had not been able to see both the barrage line and the troops advancing behind it.

Trusting too much in barrages and predicted fire was not a peculiarly Canadian proclivity; most formations in the Anglo-Canadian armies clung too long to this doctrine.[118]

Crocker believed that a good divisional commander would have recognized at least some of the shortcomings in the 8th Canadian Infantry Brigade plan and given firm guidance on how to proceed. But not only did Keller fail to find the flaws, he barely bothered to look. Prior to the attack, his GSO 1, Lieutenant-Colonel Don Mingay, the attacking brigade commander, and the Commander Royal Artillery (CRA), Brigadier P.A.S. Todd, went on a reconnaissance of the battle area, but Keller refused to attend.[119] Crocker saw through Keller's problem and gave his opinion to Dempsey, "in case Gen. Crerar requires information on this subject." Keller lacked the calm and confidence that Crocker valued:

The Div as a whole carried out its D-Day tasks with great enthusiasm and considerable success ... Once the excitement of the initial phase passed, however, the Div lapsed into a very nervy state ... Exaggerated reports of enemy activity and of their own difficulties were rife; everyone was far too quick on the trigger and a general attitude of despondency prevailed ... It was just here and now that the steadying hand of the Commander was required. It was totally lacking, indeed the state of the Div was a reflection of the state of its commander. He was obviously not standing up to the strain and showed signs of fatigue and nervousness (one might almost say fright) which were patent for all to see.[120]

Crocker's assessment of "a general attitude of despondency" across the division was a little off the mark,[121] but there is plenty of corroborating evidence that he was spot-on as far as Keller was concerned. Despite his tough talk before the invasion, Keller was indeed jumpy and nervous in battle. After D-day, his staff and subordinate commanders formed the opinion that Keller was "yellow," but it was more than his nerviness in battle.[122] Even before D-day, all three brigadiers had expressed their concerns to both Mingay and Todd about Keller's excessive drinking and his flouting of security procedures to visit his mistress in London. In fact, they often avoided Keller and dealt directly with Mingay, Todd, or the Assistant Adjutant and Quartermaster General (AA & QMG), Lieutenant-Colonel Ernest Coté.[123] Crocker's observations of "despondency" probably owed much to his dealings with the 3rd Canadian Infantry Division's brigadiers and staff, who could not have been happy. Keller was no rock of a divisional commander and his removal was definitely long overdue. Dempsey agreed, as did Montgomery, who referred the matter to the Commander First Canadian Army, General H.D.G. Crerar: "I consider that he is not good enough to command a

Canadian division; the Canadian soldier is such a magnificent chap that he deserves, and should be given, really good generals."[124]

Dragging his feet somewhat, Crerar asked the commander of 2nd Canadian Corps, Lieutenant-General Guy Simonds, to investigate the issue and make a recommendation. When interviewed by Simonds, Keller seemed to confirm the accusation of his being "yellow," stating that "he did not feel that his health was good enough to stand the heavy strain and asked that he be medically boarded."[125] On further investigation, Simonds also found "that unit commanders and brigadiers [were] apprehensive about operations not through fear of becoming casualties themselves or of having casualties, but because they feel their units are unfitted in their present state of training to put up a good show."[126] A combination of casualties, newly integrated reinforcements, and insufficient time out of the line to train new teams, Simonds believed, was the root cause. After weighing the issues, Simonds decided that Keller should stay on for the time being. Sacking him now would have sent a message that the division had failed, and Simonds considered that the divisional commander's shortcomings were "unimportant at the moment in comparison with the bigger problem of maintaining the morale of 3 Canadian Division."[127] This was a very questionable call, and Simonds would later reconsider his recommendation, but errant USAAF bombers would remove Keller from command before Simonds had a chance to act.

What are we to make of Crocker's actions in this case? He really had nothing to gain by them. When he wrote his letter on 5 July, Operation Charnwood was only two days away and he cannot have expected that Keller would be gone before the battle had begun. He also knew that soon enough, with the activation of 2nd Canadian Corps on 11 July, Keller would be an exclusively Canadian problem. Why not wait and simply pass the problem on to someone else, Simonds in this instance? That would have been completely out of character. Conscience and uncompromising honesty had compelled him to do what he thought right in the past, and they were doing it again now. Crocker was simply taking action on something the Canadian chain of command had either missed or, what is more likely, simply chosen to ignore, and it says something of his character that he was willing to do so. Soldiers' lives were at stake, and his moral compass told him that the weight of that consideration trumped any national or personal sensitivities. As he wrote to Dempsey: "I am very sorry to have to write in this way because I have appreciated very much the great privilege it has been to have a Canadian Div. under my command, but I feel it is my duty to let you have this personal opinion."[128] He was not picking on the Canadians; a week later, he also recommended and got the removal of Major-General Charles

Bullen-Smith from command of the 51st (Highland) Division.[129] But all of this happened after the capture of Caen. In the meantime, Crocker still had to fight Operation Charnwood with Keller at the helm of one of his assaulting divisions.

The failure of Operation Epsom to encircle Caen from the east and air force anxiety at the delay in obtaining airfields west and south of Caen soon resurrected the plan for using heavy bombers to support an attack on Caen (see Map 8). The area that Bomber Command eventually blasted on the evening of 7 July was actually two circular target areas based on two specific aiming points, one in northern Caen and its suburbs, which was struck by 300 bombers, the other in open fields northwest of the city, hit by 160 bombers.[130] This was not exactly what Crocker wanted. In planning the operation, he had originally asked that the bombers target Colombelles just before H-hour, to rubble the town and make it impenetrable to counterattack by the 21st Panzer Division, which was then situated south of the river Orne. To Crocker's annoyance, however, at 1815 hours on 7 July, he received late confirmation that the heavy bombers would actually strike the northern outskirts of Caen at 2150, nearly seven hours before the 0420 H-hour.[131]

For all the angst and excitement about heavy bombers in close support, Crocker's concept of operations revealed a definite unwillingness to trust still-untested tactics.[132] The corps commander presented his plan for Operation Charnwood at 2100 hours on 4 July. Crocker and his key staff had designed Charnwood as a "steamroller" of firepower and mass. By this point, they had endured enough limited narrow-front attacks that had been blunted by concentrated enemy firepower and counterattacks[133]; so, to start Charnwood, the three assaulting divisions would attack on a broad eleven-kilometre front from the northeast, north, and northwest, respectively, each with a well-balanced complement of tanks, anti-tank weapons, and engineers. The wide attack frontage would make it more difficult for the German defenders to mass their counterattack forces and their artillery at decisive points, much as they had managed to do during Epsom, or even during the Canadian attack at Carpiquet.[134] In addition, the attack would be phased, so as to keep the Germans guessing as to the area of the corps main effort.[135] In the first phase, only the 3rd Division (with one regiment from the 27th Armoured Brigade) and the 59th (Staffordshire) Division (supported by the other two regiments of the 27th Armoured Brigade) would attack to capture Galmanche, La Bijude, and Lebisey. In the second phase, the weight of the fight would shift as the 3rd Canadian Infantry Division (supported by the 2nd Canadian Armoured Brigade) pushed

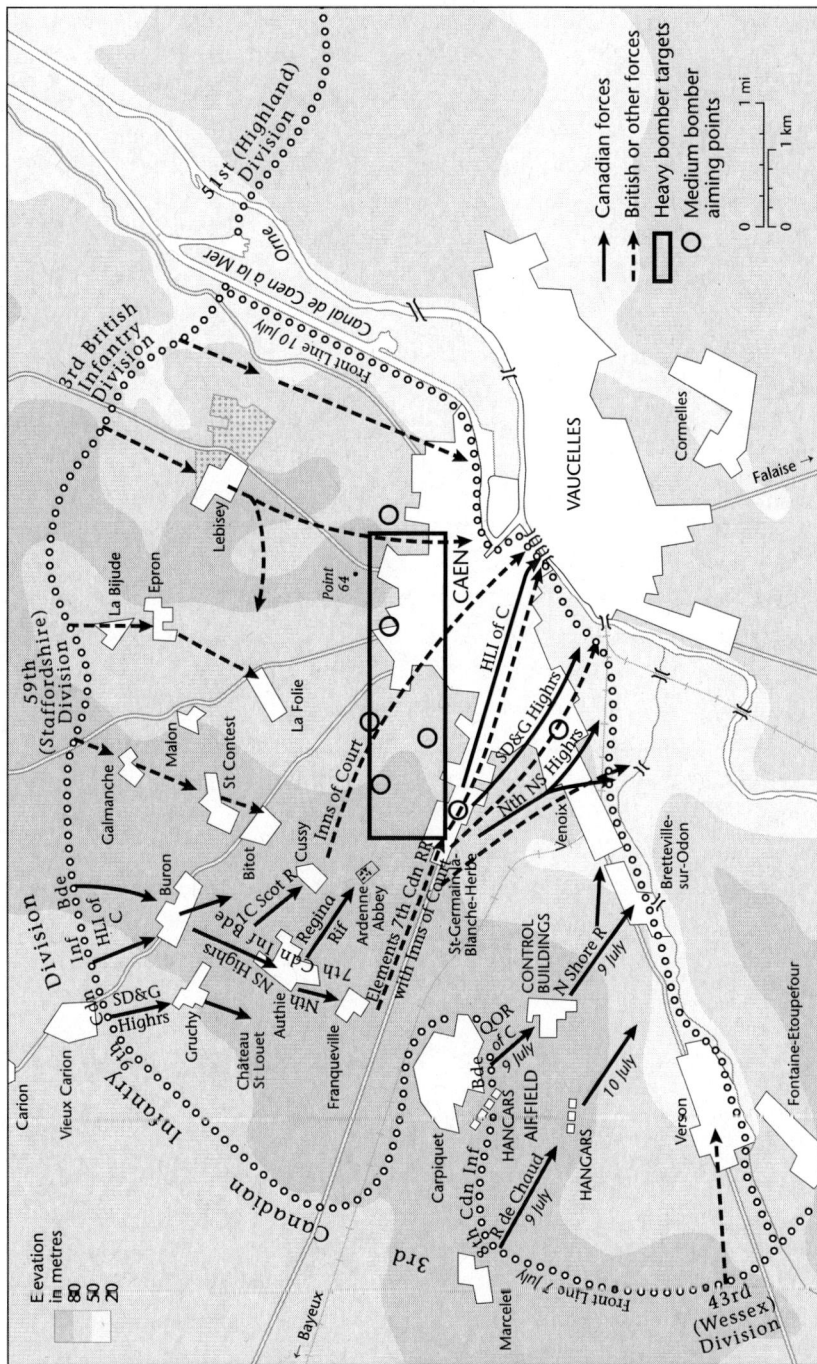

MAP 8  The capture of Caen, 8-9 July 1944. Adapted from Colonel C.P. Stacey, *The Victory Campaign: The Operations in Northwest Europe, 1944-1945* (Ottawa: Queen's Printer, 1966), sketch 11.

to the line Buron-Authie-Chateau St. Louet and the 59th (Staffordshire) Division slugged forward to take St. Contest and Epron. This would be followed by a broad push with all three divisions to the line Carpiquet-Ardennes-Point 64 in the third phase. In phase 4, the intention was to move into Caen and close with the Orne and Odon rivers. A planned fifth phase would have seen the 59th and 3rd Divisions seize crossing points on the Orne, while the 3rd Canadian Infantry Division cleared south from Carpiquet to the Odon. Because the bombers could not be safely employed to lay down a "carpet" on the German forward positions, and because there would be a pause of six hours from the time the bombers did their work on the evening of 7 July to the time when the assault troops crossed the start line on 8 July, Crocker decided to rely heavily on the extra firepower of artillery, naval gunfire, and tactical air forces – lots of it – to keep the heads of German defenders down, silence enemy guns, and disrupt the inevitable counterattacks.[136] For artillery, he had two Army Groups Royal Artillery (AGsRA) and the divisional artillery from the three attacking divisions, plus that of the Guards Armoured Division and the 51st (Highland) Division – a total of 632 guns for barrages and counter-battery work.[137] A battleship, a monitor, and two cruisers added their firepower to subdue strongpoints, soften key objectives like Point 64, strike enemy gun batteries, and break up counter-attacking formations. And if this was not enough, the typhoons of the Second Tactical Air Force (2 TAF) and the medium bombers of the American Ninth Air Force could be brought into the fight as well, with spotter planes directing fire on targets of opportunity. As a reserve, Crocker had the 33rd Armoured Brigade to exploit any breakthrough or destroy an enemy counterattack. Crocker, quite evidently, did not expect that Bomber Command could do it all for him.

This was a wise assumption for two reasons: Second Army intelligence on the disposition of enemy forces in depth was not good, and the air bombardment was only partially successful. They had a pretty good idea of who was immediately in front of them and how they were deployed.[138] In the northeast, two battalions from the 16th Luftwaffe Field Division defended Libesey and Hérouville. In the centre, La Bijude and Epron were held by 1/25th Panzergrenadier Battalion, while 11/25th Panzergrenadier and nine panzers defended Galmanche, Malon, and St. Contest. 111/25th Panzergrenadier occupied the defences anchored on Buron. Defending to the west, from Authie to Verson, was a hodgepodge of reconnaissance, engineer, and flak units (with 88-millimetre guns), a handful of panzers, and a very weak 11/26th Panzergrenadier Battalion. By 5 July, Second Army intelligence had the enemy defences in the fortified villages well mapped out – including trenches, mortar pits, dug-in tanks, machine guns, and anti-tank weapons.[139] Beyond that, though, the picture was very sketchy. Pinpointing counterattack forces proved much more difficult. In fact, British and Canadian intelligence officers did not realize how few mobile forces there were north of the Orne and Odon rivers. The 12th SS Panzer Division had only three such combat teams that could influence the battle quickly: seventeen tanks from I/12th SS Panzer near the Abbaye Ardennes, twenty-three tanks of II/12th SS Panzer just west of Caen, and III/26th SS Panzergrenadier on the northwestern outskirts of the city. Everything else, including the 21st Panzer Division, 1st SS Panzer Division, and the remaining elements of the 12th SS Panzer Division had been withdrawn south of the river line. In an effort to preserve his armoured forces, Rommel concluded that "we must try to get out of the bridgehead with as little damage as possible."[140] That meant saving his mobile panzer and panzergrenadier forces by replacing them with second-tier troops, putting up a good fight for northern Caen, then withdrawing south of the Orne.[141] This had already begun when the 16th Luftwaffe Division relieved the 21st Panzer Division on 1-2 July, but there had not been enough time to pull the 12th SS Panzer Division out of their forward positions and replace them with the 271st Infantry Division, which was still in transit.[142]

To isolate the battlefield, soften these enemy defences, and silence enemy guns and mortars, the enormous weight of firepower assigned to Operation Charnwood went to work in the forty-eight hours preceding the assault. On 6 July, fighter-bombers attacked enemy mortars, and tank concentrations south of Caen, near St. André-sur-Orne.[143] They also attacked the Caen bridges, the air staff at army headquarters claiming that they had destroyed one and damaged three of the critical crossings.[144] Naval gunfire pounded the vital ground at Point 64 during the afternoon of 7 July, and typhoons struck at the enemy's forward defences near Buron at 2100 hours. The aerial bombing that had been discussed off and on for over three weeks rained down on Caen between 2150 and 2230 later the same day. A magnificent show of sound, light, and fire, the attack shook the earth for miles, and lifted the spirits of Crocker's troops as they waited to commence their assault, but the bombing did not help them nearly as much as they had hoped. Operational research in the aftermath of Operation Charnwood concluded that "the material effects produced by this bombing attack do not appear to be sufficient to account for the marked success of the operation it preceded."[145] It will be remembered that the bombing area, because it had to be well forward of friendly troops, was also well behind the arc of mutually supporting and fortified villages four to five kilometres north of Caen. That disposition, combined with the German decision to deploy the bulk of their forces south of the Orne, is the reason researchers found only one 88-millimetre gun and a handful of damaged vehicles in the fields northwest of Caen. In terms of denying the enemy counterattack routes or forming-up areas, however, the researchers did note that, in the built-up areas of northern Caen, "blocking resulted from quite a small density of bombs (less than 5 per acre) and was very much more difficult to clear because of huge masses of fallen masonry."[146] In the curiously long pause between the air bombing and the start of the assault, artillery and aircraft attacked selected targets, including the fortified villages. At 0420 on 8 July, the designated H-hour for Charnwood, a metal-curtain barrage dropped in front of the 59th (Staffordshire) and 3rd Canadian Infantry Divisions as they stepped out of their trenches to commence the assault.

Charnwood was a tough operation and Crocker directed the many moving parts with the same quiet determination that characterized everything he did. Relentless forward movement across the entire front of attack was the key to success in this operation. The brief five-page operation order twice emphasized the need to minimize the pause between phases, the authority for progressing from one phase to the next resting with the corps commander himself.[147] To know when to make those calls, just before H-hour, Crocker propped his Tactical Headquarters on a high feature only 2.5 kilometres behind the assaulting troops.[148] From that location, about two kilometres north of Villons-les-Buissons, he could see (after first light) good stretches of the 3rd Canadian Infantry and 59th (Staffordshire) Division battlefields, and even a small portion of 3rd Division's fight. Combined with situation reports sent over wireless, the ability to view the battlefield afforded Crocker a near-complete grasp of the situation that helped him decide when to initiate each successive phase. Most importantly, it helped him decide where and when to commit his reserve.

As the early reports came in and as he surveyed what he could of the battlefield, Crocker surmised that phase 1 was progressing well. Within twenty-five minutes of H-hour, he learned that the 185th Brigade of the 3rd Division and all its supporting tanks had crossed a major ditch and were fighting in the Lebisey Wood, while the 9th Brigade was in the process of taking Hérouville.[149] In the 59th (Staffordshire) Division battle, the 176th Brigade reported pushing well into La Bijude at 0530, while the 197th Brigade had just begun a very bitter fight for Galmanche.[150] At 0620, shortly after receiving word that the fighting at Galmanche had moved into the streets of the village itself, and that all but the southeastern corner of Lebisey Wood had been cleared, Crocker gave the order to initiate phase 2 at 0730. This was a bold call on the corps commander's part, considering that none of the phase 1 objectives had yet been fully secured, but the move did have much to recommend it. First, the attacking brigades still had another seventy minutes to mop up their objectives before the start of phase 2, and the initial reports indicated that good progress was being made. The seventy-minute warning also gave the 59th (Staffordshire) Division enough "battle procedure" time to push a battalion from its right forward brigade, the 197th Brigade, past the very difficult strongpoint at Galmanche to assault St.

Contest.[151] Had Crocker waited until all his phase 1 objectives had been captured before launching the next phase, the resultant pause might have given the enemy time to recover and perhaps coordinate effective counterattacks.

He wanted to keep the Charnwood wave moving, and bringing the 3rd Canadian Infantry Division into the battle at Buron and Gruchy would force another set of crises on the enemy, and therefore another set of potential counterattack points to be considered. Would it be best to attack in mass at one decisive point, or divide mobile reserves and indirect fire to plug holes across the eleven-kilometre front? Should mobile forces already south of the Orne be brought into the fight, even though the goal was to preserve them? These were the sorts of questions enemy commanders had to ask themselves.

Crocker did what he could to compound their difficulties. With the 3rd Division in firm control of Lebisey Wood and Hérouville, he ordered Major-General L.G. Whistler to "push some armour f[or]w[ar]d" to the high ground north of Point 64, "as he feels this flank may become very important if the centre becomes sticky."[152] The centre did indeed become sticky, particularly at Galmanche and Malon, where the 2nd Battalion of the 25th Panzergrenadier Regiment resisted fiercely. The uninterrupted attacks of the 59th (Staffordshire) Division in phases 1 and 2, combined with the weight of air and artillery attack, convinced the enemy divisional commander that "the *schwerpunkt* of the attack seemed to lie with the 59th Infantry Division," so Kurt Meyer, commander of the 12th SS Panzer Division, committed the III/12th SS Panzer Regiment to a counterattack at Buron and St. Contest.[153] With the enemy committing to the centre, Crocker decided to force the flanks. Reinforcing the 3rd Division's success against the 16th Luftwaffe Division on the left, Crocker placed his reserve, the 33rd Armoured Brigade (less one regiment) under Whistler's command at 1130. This would ensure that the high ground north of Point 64 could be used to bring direct fire to bear on the enemy line of withdrawal from the area of Galmanche-Malon-Epron.[154] On the right, in the 3rd Canadian Infantry Division sector, Crocker wanted to push in just as quickly.

Unfortunately, the troops of the III/25th Panzergrenadier Regiment, who moved to Buron, proved to be just as tenacious as their brethren in front of the 59th (Staffordshire) Division. The Stormont, Dundas, and Glengarry Highlanders, with the support of a substantial artillery barrage, had driven the enemy from Gruchy by 0938, but on their left, the Highland Light Infantry (HLI) of Canada faced a much tougher and much bloodier battle. Although the battalion and some of its supporting tanks managed to reach a large anti-tank ditch north of the town without too much difficulty, the infantry had to press the assault into Buron without the support of their tanks, which could not immediately negotiate the obstacle. The German defenders, reinforced by survivors of Gruchy, fought on in the ruins of Buron, forcing the HLI to fight a gut-wrenching battle to ferret them out of all the buildings and cellars. Only after suffering 262 casualties and defeating a tank counterattack by the III/12th SS with well-placed seventeen-pounder anti-tank guns could the HLI safely say that the town was theirs.[155] By that time, it was early afternoon.

Crocker, who at 0840 had received an overly optimistic report from his Armoured Car Regiment, the Inns of Court, that "Gruchy and Buron have been taken and mopping up in progress,"[156] was anxious to initiate phase 3 and grew impatient with the delay in the capture of the 3rd Canadian Infantry Division's phase 2 objectives – Authie and Chateau St. Louet. At 1000, he ordered Major-General Keller to attack Authie,[157] despite the hold-up at Buron, but the attack did not get underway until later in the afternoon, when the start line for the North Nova Scotia Highlanders – in Buron – had been completely secured. Keller had already ordered Brigadier D.G. Cunningham to move with the North Nova Scotians on Authie, but why he did not force Cunningham to launch the attack from Gruchy is unclear. The delay did not do anyone any good. As it was, the Stormont, Dundas, and Glengarry Highlanders spent the better part of the day taking casualties from mortar fire while it waited to assault the Chateau St. Louet. An annoyed Crocker announced a "new plan" at 1130. The 3rd Division would take the high ground at Point 64 – its phase 2 objective – "without waiting for 3rd Canadian Division."[158] Whistler's division would "press on ST CONTEST EPRON GALMANCHE" from the spur north of Point 64 to threaten the rear of the 25th Panzergrenadier Regiment defenders, and capture Point 64 itself.

Crocker's actions had the desired effect. Enemy commanders squabbled over where and when to counterattack. The crises in the 16th Luftwaffe Division sector forced General Eberbach, the commander of Panzer Group West, to move forward and determine for himself whether anything could be done to restore the line in front of the 3rd Division.[159] When he reached the headquarters of the 12th SS Panzer Division in Caen, however, he found Meyer fully engaged in his own crisis at Buron and St. Contest. Meyer made the case that he could not counterattack in the 16th Luftwaffe Division sector, despite the fact that the loss of Point 64 would render his own defences untenable. This short-sighted decision left Eberbach with the unenviable alternative of trying to bring a battle group from the 21st Panzer Division across the damaged bridges of the Orne, through the rubble of northern Caen, to run the gauntlet of naval gunfire at Point 64 and counterattack towards Lebisey. He tried, but the 21st Panzer battle group, although it did cross the Orne, never made it through to influence the battle in any significant way. Meyer drove the III/12th SS Panzer Regiment on Buron, but it ran headlong into the fire of the seventeen-pounder anti-tank guns that the HLI had deployed there to block any counterattack from the south.[160] The German defenders, faced with a number of concurrent tactical problems, were fast running out of options.

Crocker continued to force their decision cycles and wear down their forces. By 1500 hours in the afternoon of 8 July, the 3rd Division was both fighting for its phase 3 objective at Point 64 and pressing the rear of the enemy defences at Couvre-Chef, the 59th (Staffordshire) Division was holding the line at St. Contest-Galmanche-Epron, and the 3rd Canadian Infantry Division had just begun its simultaneous attacks on Authie and Chateau St. Louet to complete its phase 2 tasks. An opportunity to trap the remnants of the 12th SS Panzer Division beckoned and Crocker decided to seize it. The 1st Corps operations log entry for 1545 recorded his direction to the divisional commanders: "Corps Comd has told the Cdns to press on with 7 Bde [to Cussy and Ardennes] and to be prepared for 8 Bde to become active in their task [advancing south to Bretteville-sur-Odon]. He has impressed on 3 Br Div the need for speed. He has agreed with Comd 59 Div to form his firm base before pushing on."[161] To hasten the move into Caen, Crocker also ordered the Inns of Court Regiment, to "proceed at once along rd LA VILLENEUVE to Caen."[162] He must also have taken heart from a report that the 3rd Canadian Infantry Division was preparing to have the 7th Canadian Infantry Brigade exploit beyond their objectives of Cussy and Ardennes to St.-Germain-la-Blanche-Herbe "between 1730 and 1830."[163]

Unfortunately, operations did not unfold that quickly. Although the Inns of Court managed to slip past enemy defenders to reach St.-Germain-la-Blanche-Herbe at 2010 hours,[164] behind them the 7th Canadian Infantry Brigade fight for Cussy and Ardennes had only just begun.[165] The Canadian Scottish Regiment, which was slowed by enemy fire in Bitot and Ardennes, had just entered Cussy, while the Regina Rifles were still 600 to 700 metres shy of the Abbaye Ardennes. After a very tough battle, which required the reinforcement of two Winnipeg companies just to hang on, the Canadian Scottish managed to capture and hold Cussy by last light. The fight for Ardennes proved even more difficult. Fighting desperately to keep withdrawal routes open, Meyer personally directed a counterattack by a company of tanks and an under-strength battalion from the 1st SS Panzergrenadier Regiment.[166] The German defenders held, but shortly after midnight, Meyer returned to Caen and arranged a withdrawal during the hours of darkness, lest the 12th SS Panzer Division, already badly mauled, be completely destroyed.[167]

Crocker, who undoubtedly sensed the enemy's desperation, had grown increasingly frustrated with the slow rate of the Canadian advance. It had taken an inordinately long time to tee up the unopposed attack on Authie earlier in the day, and the next series of attacks were also slow in getting started. The corps commander had hoped, based on earlier reports, to be beyond Cussy and Ardennes and well into Caen itself by last light, a push that Meyer thought would have resulted in his division being "completely annihilated."[168] Crocker's direction to Keller reflected his dissatisfaction: "Understand that Inns of Court with ... 7 Cdn Recce Regt is astride BAYEUX-CAEN immediately WEST of ST GERMAINE LA HERBE BLANCHE. Corps Comd directs that this force remains in present posn in observation until first light when they will push into ST GERMAINE and as far possible into CAEN. Arrangements should be made by you NOT to hold them up."[169]

Early the next day, when the 3rd Canadian Infantry Division advance into Caen seemed to be suffering yet another delay, Crocker went forward to the Abbaye Ardenne to assess the situation for himself. Instead of finding the 7th Canadian Infantry Brigade ready to advance on Caen as had been forecast the previous afternoon, Crocker learned that the task had been handed off to the 9th Canadian Infantry Brigade, which again was painfully slow to initiate action. In fairness to the 9th Canadian Infantry Brigade, though, the 3rd Canadian Infantry Division's operation order had set the tone for a slow advance. Despite corps direction that there would be "as short a pause as possible between PHASES," Keller's operation order stated that the advance beyond Ardennes "would only be carried out in the event that it becomes evident that [enemy] defences are crumbling and then only on orders of the Div Comd."[170] Clearly, this was not within the corps commander's intent. Given his concerns about Keller before Charnwood, Crocker should have scrutinized the Canadian preparations for battle more closely.

With all enemy fighting forces, save for a small rearguard, now south of the Orne, Operation Charnwood played out its sad denouement on 9 July. With much of Caen in ruins, and many of its bewildered residents emerging from cellars and shot-up buildings, 1st Corps converged on the city. On the left, the 3rd Division fired on Couvre-Chef and Folie, while the 9th Brigade struggled through the rubble to reach the city centre at 1100. In the centre, the 59th (Staffordshire) Division conducted limited attacks to hold what was left of the enemy. And on the right, the 8th Canadian Infantry Brigade advanced south to capture the hangars at Carpiquet airfield and exploit to Bretteville-sur-Odon. The 9th Canadian Infantry Brigade pushed from the Abbaye Ardenne, cleared the last enemy resister from St.-Germain-la-Blanche-Herbe, and entered Caen at 1335. Finally, more than a month after D-day, Caen, the northern part of it anyway, was in Allied hands.

Crocker fought a solid but very tough battle in Charnwood. Everyone from Montgomery on down had expected a difficult fight and that was exactly how it had turned out. The operation had cost 1st Corps 3,500 casualties – a grim tally indeed – but it had accomplished all of its goals, except for the capture of crossing sites on the Orne.[171] True, Crocker did have at his disposal tremendous resources, but he used them to best effect, despite some criticism that the heavy bombing of Caen had been brought in as a "frill to a ground plan that was already made."[172] This was a valid point, but as far as Crocker was concerned, he had little choice but to plan the operation on the assumption that there would *not* be any bomber support. Most of the coordination with Bomber Command had been done at army group level in any case. Montgomery, under enormous political pressure to capture Caen, more or less foisted the heavy bomber support on Crocker, and confirmation of the bombing targets came late anyway. It only made sense to ensure that artillery, tactical air support, and naval gunfire could do the job without the assistance of heavy bombers. The broad-front attack also prevented the enemy from concentrating counterattacks and indirect fire to stop him. Perhaps Crocker's biggest accomplishment in Charnwood, however, was his ability to maintain the momentum of the attack. It may not have been lightning-fast momentum, but it was steady and it had the desired effect. In his memoirs, the 12th SS Panzer Division commander made mocking reference to the slowness of the Anglo-Canadian assault, but even he had to admit that his options for action dwindled steadily as, in his words, "the steamroller trundled on."[173] To keep it trundling, Crocker had to push divisional commanders, as he did Keller, even in the face of mounting casualties. Sometimes this meant venturing well forward to assess the situation for himself, as he did at the Abbaye Ardenne on 9 July. It also helped that he was flexible enough in abandoning the steady three-up advance of Charnwood in favour of holding in the centre with the 59th (Staffordshire) Division, and pinching in on the flanks with the 3rd Division and the 3rd Canadian Infantry Division. All in all, Crocker fought a fine battle.

Within two weeks of Charnwood, his corps, which was still on the far left flank of the Allied bridgehead, came under the command of the First Canadian Army, but his relationship with Crerar got off to a rocky start.[174] On 22 July, in line with the verbal direction he had received from Montgomery to expand the First Canadian Army bridgehead eastward to the River Dives, Crerar sent Crocker written instructions before he assumed responsibility for 1st Corps.[175] In a relatively brief one-page note, he directed that Crocker make plans "to advance [the] left flank Eastwards so that OUISTREHAM will cease to be under close enemy observation and fire and so that use can be made of the port of CAEN."[176] With that in mind, he went on to tell Crocker that, in addition to consolidating the high ground around Troarn, the 1st Corps' immediate task was to attack eastward and secure the line of the road that ran from Breville, through the hamlet of Le Marais, to Le Petit Homme on the sea. When he visited

Crocker at 1st Corps Headquarters on 24 July, however, he was taken aback by Crocker's objections to the direction. It was not so much that Crocker found Crerar's instructions "overly detailed,"[177] it was that he thought no good would come of the operations Crerar was proposing: "Such an operation would involve an attack on narrow front through close and difficult country where the enemy is well posted in some strength and would, in its latter stages, involve clearing an extensive built up area."[178] In Crocker's opinion, even if the corps succeeded in capturing Breville–Le Petit Homme, "it would still be impossible to operate the CAEN Canal which would [still] remain dominated by the observation and guns from the high ground East of the R[iver] DIVES." It could result in "purposeless losses." Instead, Crocker proposed an operation by the 3rd Division to capture the high ground between Troarn and Bures-sur-Dives and, potentially, a heavily supported broad-front attack to clear up to the River Dives, even if the best that could be hoped for the latter was an "economy in t[roo]ps required" to hold the front along the river obstacle. Crocker was right. He had not forgotten the experiences of the fights for Carpiquet and Caen: "Limited attacks on narrow fronts in this area will get nowhere." His actions were completely consistent with his behaviour in the past. This was the same thoughtful "I do not agree" approach that people like Hobart and Brooke had appreciated. Crerar was a different story.

Crocker's actions triggered all of Crerar's insecurities. The Canadian general's situation was a difficult one, from both a personal and a national perspective. Above him and below him were commanders who had something he had yet to acquire: experience in command of major formations in combat.[179] He was anxious to prove himself and win credibility as a fighting soldier. Montgomery, however, who harboured doubts about Crerar's command abilities, had delayed the establishment of the First Canadian Army in Normandy, and Crerar had undoubtedly sensed it. Already sensitive to anything that hinted at old colonial attitudes, Crerar also resented British queries about the suitability of Canadian commanders, such as those dealing with Keller in Normandy or E.L.M. Burns, the GOC 1st Canadian Corps, in Italy. (See pages 101-7 above.) His feeling was that his British counterparts clung to the conviction "that no Canadian, or American, or other 'national' Comd, unless possessing phenomenal qualities, is ever rated as high as the equivalent Britisher."[180] Crocker's part in the Keller episode only picked the scab of Crerar's sensitivity and prejudiced Crerar against the British corps commander. Keller had, after all, been Crerar's choice as the next corps commander.[181] He questioned Crocker's motivation: "I have something more than the impression that Crocker has not been beyond reproach, from the Canadian point of view."[182] Crerar was wrong in thinking that Crocker held an anti-Canadian bias. Four months later, when Crocker had to leave his command for seven days, he would hand over his formation to Major-General H.W. Foster, GOC 4th Canadian Armoured Division, giving the Canadian the nod over the commanders of the 49th (West Riding) Division and the 52nd (Lowland) Division.[183] Crerar did not know this in July, however, and given his attitude, to say nothing of the stress he was under, it is not surprising that his indignant response to Crocker's objections was immediate. He asked Crocker to put his opinion in writing, which he did, then Crerar took the matter to Montgomery.

Fortunately, Montgomery defused the situation. Crerar's letter of 24 July reveals how personally he took Crocker's position: "Crocker gave me the impression, at the commencement of the interview, that he resented being placed under my command and receiving directions from me ... I do not know whether this attitude is personal, or because of the fact that I am a Canadian – but it certainly showed itself. There was no tact, nor any desire to understand my views, shown on his part."[184] Crerar then went on to make the bizarre suggestion that Crocker be swapped for either Lieutenant-General Neil Ritchie or Lieutenant-General Jerry Bucknall, then commanding 12th Corps and 30th Corps, respectively. The quarrel, which Montgomery found quite unnecessary, did nothing to improve the army group commander's opinion of Crerar: "I fear [Crerar] thinks he is a great soldier and he was determined to show it the very moment he took command at 1200 hrs on 23 July. He made his first mistake at 1205 hrs; and his second after lunch."[185] Montgomery did not move Crocker to another corps, but he did speak with him about his relationship with Crerar and the First Canadian Army. Crocker kept no notes of the conversation, but, in a letter to Crerar, Montgomery claimed to have told Crocker that he had to be a "loyal subordinate," that he had to "lead the way" to prevent "bickering" between his corps and the First Canadian Army, and said that he had reminded the corps commander that "we [were] all trying to win this war – and he [would] not contribute to winning it by 'sticking his toes in' when it does not really matter."[186] Montgomery also took the opportunity to remind Crerar that he should stick to telling his subordinates what to do, not how to do it, especially when dealing with a "very experienced fighting commander" like John Crocker, who "knows his stuff."

The intervention certainly did not make friends of Crocker and Crerar, but at least it forced them to meet each other halfway and work things out. Crocker and his staff drew up plans to meet Crerar's intent of expanding the bridgehead eastward. Operations Byng and Rawlinson, significantly named by Crocker for the British commander of the Canadian Corps (1916-17) and the Fourth Army Commander under whom the Canadian Corps fought many battles, called for an attack by the 3rd and 49th (West Riding) Divisions, supported by aerial bombardment "on a GOODWOOD scale" and naval gunfire for counter-battery tasks east of the River Dives.[187] Crerar, for his part, had his staff line up a significant package of fire support and special equipment to support an eastward drive by 1st Corps, but higher-priority operations in the southward thrust from Caen to Falaise soon precluded the execution of Rawlinson and Byng.[188] The planning process showed at least a grudging willingness on the part of both men to try and work amicably, but for the rest of their time together, they worked best when they had a little distance between them.

Operation Astonia, the siege of Le Havre in early September, was exactly the sort of semi-independent operation that suited their uneasy relationship. Crerar and his Plans Section had been studying the problem of capturing France's second-largest shipping port since 1 March 1944.[189] Anticipated to take place some ninety days after D-day, the capture of Le Havre was to be the fourth and final phase of Operation Axehead, which in the pre-invasion period also included the crossing of the Seine, the capture of Rouen, and a rapid advance to the Channel coast. Axehead was never executed as one all-encompassing operation, but by 2 September, eighty-eight days after D-day, Crerar's army had crossed the Seine, captured Rouen, and reached the coast between St. Valery-sur-Somme and St. Valery-en-Caux. While Guy Simonds's 2nd Canadian Corps headed east along the coast to reduce the ports of Boulogne and Calais, Crocker, having received direction on 1 September to take Le Havre, turned left and closed on the largest Channel port.[190]

With the benefit of the detailed studies conducted by the First Canadian Army, Crocker and his staff analyzed the problem (see Map 9). Water obstacles protected Le Havre on three sides – the English Channel in the west, the Lezarde River in the east, and the Seine Estuary in the south. An extensive system of mutually supporting concrete strongpoints, supplemented with anti-tank ditches and minefields, stood in the way of the only obvious landward approach from the north, while to the east the German defenders bolstered the flooded Lezarde River with another chain of concreted strongpoints along the Northern and Southern Plateaus, as well as a series of outposts around Harfleur. Fortunately, the corps had an exceptionally good picture of enemy defences; the air photographic coverage was excellent, so most of the enemy strongpoints, anti-tank ditches, and gun troops of all sorts had been found and plotted on maps or printed on the air photographs themselves.[191] Reconnaissance patrols from the 49th (West Riding) Division confirmed much of the information on the forward enemy defences, as did the interrogation of prisoners and deserters. In one

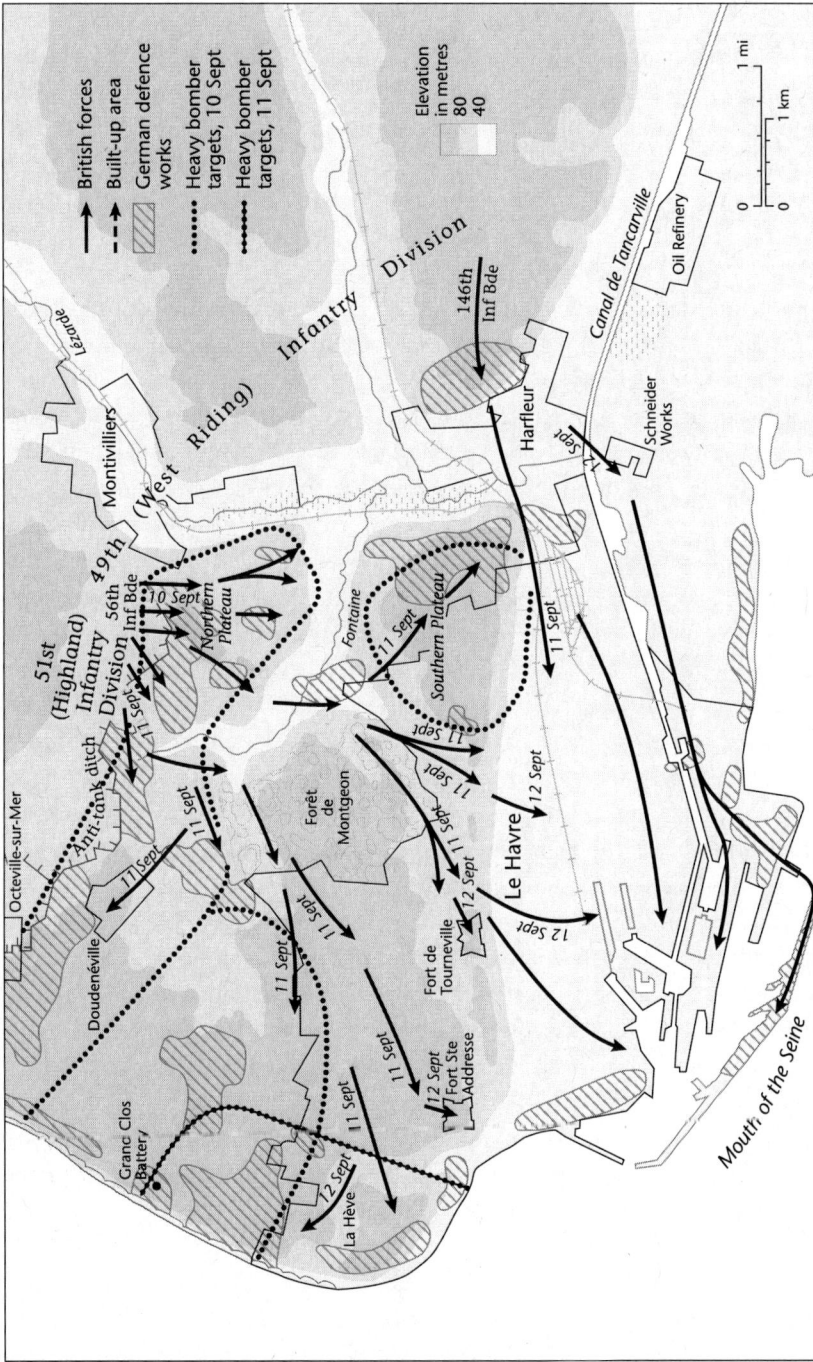

Legend:

- → British forces
- - - → Built-up area
- ▨ German defence works
- ⋯⋯ Heavy bomber targets, 10 Sept
- ⋯•⋯ Heavy bomber targets, 11 Sept

Elevation
in metres
80
40

0 ___ 1 mi
0 ___ 1 km

Labels on map:

Lézarde

49th (West Riding) Infantry Division

Montivilliers

51st (Highland) Infantry Division

56th Inf Bde

10 Sept

11 Sept

Northern Plateau

Anti-tank ditch

Octeville-sur-Mer

11 Sept

Doudeneville

11 Sept

Forêt de Montgeon

Fontaine

Southern Plateau

11 Sept

146th Inf Bde

Harfleur

12 Sept

Schneider Works

Canal de Tancarville

Oil Refinery

11 Sept

11 Sept

Le Havre

12 Sept

12 Sept

11 Sept

11 Sept

Fort de Tourneville

Fort Ste Addresse

12 Sept

11 Sept

11 Sept

Granc Clos Battery

La Hève

12 Sept

Mouth of the Seine

MAP 9  Le Havre: Operation Astonia, 10-12 September 1944. Adapted from Stacey, *The Victory Campaign*, sketch 26.

fortunate instance, "an ALSATIAN deserter brought back with him a set of plans showing in detail the defences of FONTAINE-LE-MALLET."[192] This uncommonly clear resolution of the battlefield made the business of targeting the enemy and planning friendly manoeuvres much easier. The only thing that Crocker did not have a good fix on was the number of enemy defenders at Le Havre. At first, he thought there were only "3000 to 5000 fighting men"[193] defending the port, a figure that was soon raised to 8,700,[194] and which, as it would turn out, was still 2,300 Germans too few.

On 3 September, after two days of study and consultations with key staff, Crocker held a coordination conference at his Tactical Headquarters to reveal his concept of operations. In addition to his principal staff, the meeting was also attended by representatives from the First Canadian Army, 84th Group RAF, the Royal Navy, and his old friend and former boss Major-General Hobart, now GOC 79th Armoured Division. Brigadier Churchill Mann, Chief of Staff First Canadian Army, took notes that reveal much about Crocker's thought process for the operation.[195] Crocker commenced with a short synopsis of the enemy situation. As mentioned, the intelligence estimates on enemy strengths were too low, but based on the 49th (West Riding) Division's easy encounters with enemy outposts, he reasonably determined that "their morale was believed NOT to be good." Based on that assessment, Crocker "believed it should NOT be necessary actually to deliver a full scale attack." This is a key point. The sheer weight of firepower assigned to this operation can distract the historian from seeing how much emphasis Crocker placed on the psychological dimension of the battle. First of all, to place the seeds of doubt in the enemy commander's head, he intended to offer an opportunity for surrender. In support of this initiative, pamphlet drops and amplifier announcements emphasized that refusal to surrender would result in the full weight of army, navy, and air forces being unleashed on the garrison. A series of heavy aerial bombings, designed to wear away the enemy's will to resist, were accordingly arranged in the event that the enemy commander chose the hard course. True, the bombing would target enemy defences to soften them up before an assault, but Crocker saw that they would have a strong effect on morale as well: "The corps com[man]d[er] considered that the best moral[e] effect would be obtained if the bombing was spread over a considerable period."[196] In spite of his hopes that the enemy might crack early, Crocker prudently proceeded with plans for a full-scale assault, which would require the intricately coordinated efforts of all three services. Drawing on his experience with Charnwood, he requested "direct comm[unication] between Bomber Com[man]d and 1 Brit Corps" and confirmation of each bombing attack at least twenty-four hours before the first bombs were due to fall. Both conditions were met and preparations continued for a full-scale assault. However, because he was still in the process of moving the 51st (High-land) Division from St. Valery to Le Havre, and because there were significant logistical preparations yet to be made, particularly in terms of moving forward artillery and ammunition, Crocker did not believe that the assault could com-mence before 8 September.

He confirmed his plan of attack during an orders group held at 1600 hours on 5 September.[197] With the enemy having refused the surrender offer of 4 September, Operation Astonia, the full-scale assault on Le Havre, was on. Crocker planned a four-phase ground offensive from the north and the east.[198] In the first phase, the 49th (West Riding) Division, with the 34th Tank Brigade as well as some flail and crocodile tanks from the 79th Armoured Division under command, would capture the Northern Plateau. With that high ground secure, the 51st (Highland) Division, with the 33rd Armoured Brigade under command, could drill through enemy defences to the west and capture the ground between the Forêt de Montgeon and Doudenéville. At the same time, the 49th (West Riding) Division would press southward onto the Southern Plateau and assault enemy defences there in tandem with an attack on Harfleur from east of the Lezarde River. Phase 3 would see the 51st (Highland) Division splitting its attack – driving northwest to clear the enemy from the Octeville-sur-Mer area and heading south to destroy the enemy gun and flak positions west of the Forêt de Montgeon. In the fourth and final phase, both divisions would "exploit relentlessly into the town and crush any resistance." For fire sup-port, Crocker had the guns of two AGsRA and those of the two assaulting divisions, for a total of some 310 guns and howitzers, plus the monitor HMS *Erebus* and the battleship HMS *Warspite* to help with counter-battery tasks. He also used four separate Bomber Command attacks to smooth the way for his assaulting divisions – one consisting of 348 aircraft to soften perimeter defences and reduce gun emplacements on 5 September, another of 109 aircraft to do the same on 6-7 September, a third of 932 aircraft to initiate the ground assault on 10 September, and a final attack of 146 aircraft to subdue final enemy resistance on the western edge of the city.[199] Needless to say, this was to be another fire-power-intensive battle, the most unfortunate aspect of which was French civilian casualties. In all, some 1,500 non-combatants would lose their lives as a result of the bombardment.[200]

In pure military terms, the synchronization of army, air, and naval assets had improved since Charnwood, with the 49th (West Riding) Division's capture of the Northern Plateau providing an excellent example of just how much so. The aerial bombing that took place between 1615 and 1745 hours on 10 September had a "considerable" impact on the defenders. German prisoners subsequently reported that, although their concrete defences prevented Bomber Command from inflicting a significant number of casualties on the German garrison, "the most important result was a breakdown in communications, which, for example, prevented the German Artillery Commander from controlling his resources and precluded centralized direction of the defences as a whole."[201] The ground assault followed quickly to take full advantage of the confusion. Past experience in operations and operational research had revealed that the effect on morale of heavy bombing was "temporary" and "almost useless if it [was] not followed up rapidly."[202] At Le Havre, the assaulting troops, having been drawn back before the bombing, commenced their move forward at precisely 1745 hours, the moment the last bombs fell, with flail tanks reaching the edge of the minefield at the Montivilliers-Octeville road between 1825 and 1837 hours. While artillery went to work on the German positions, the flails churned their way through the minefield, attempting to establish eight safe lanes for the assaulting troops. Soft ground and mines that had been buried to a depth of one foot reduced the effectiveness of flailing operations, but the breaching teams did manage to put in three lanes by 1950 hours and a fourth, with some difficulty, by 2055 hours.[203] This was perhaps the most difficult part of the entire operation. The meticulously synchronized fire plan ensured that only three assaulting vehicles were knocked out by anti-tank fire, but mines put out of action twenty-six flails, two command tanks, and six engineer vehicles.[204]

The lanes were tenuous, but they were good enough to support the 56th Brigade assault on the Northern Plateau. The brigade plan called for the 2nd Battalion South Wales Borderers to assault right forward and capture the strongpoints on the western half of the plateau, while the 2nd Battalion Gloucestershire Regiment did the same on the left, or the eastern half of the plateau.[205] Once those objectives had been secured, the 2nd Battalion Essex Regiment, mounted in Kangaroo armoured personnel carriers and supported by a squadron of tanks, would pass rapidly through to seize a bridgehead onto the Southern Plateau. Through the four "safe" lanes, the tanks of the 7th Royal Regiment passed shortly after 1930 hours. Once on the enemy side of the obstacle, they took up fire positions to cover the move forward of the flame-throwing crocodiles, which "soaked" the strongpoints. This was not easy due to fire from a strongpoint on the brigade's western flank – a strongpoint in the 51st (Highland) Division area, in fact. A planned artillery concentration between 1745 and 1915 hours, plus 2,200 rounds of high explosive and smoke from supporting mortars, helped, but it took nearly two hours to winkle crocodiles to within their 150-metre range.[206] The effect of flame on the morale of defenders cannot be overstated. Once a strongpoint had been doused in flame, resistance rarely lasted more than a few minutes. By 2240 hours, the South Wales Borderers had captured their objective, snagged fifty prisoners, and destroyed an 88-millimetre anti-tank gun. To the east, 2nd Battalion Gloucestershire Regiment, because they did not have to deal with flanking fire, had an easier time of it. Using the same combination of tank and crocodile support, they drove through the gaps at 1922 hours and secured all four of their strongpoint objectives by 2115 hours. Having witnessed the progress of the "Glosters," the brigade commander, Brigadier M.S. Ekins, had ordered the 2nd Battalion Essex Regiment to move forward in their Kangaroos at 2045 hours, such that they were ready to launch on their depth objectives at 2130 hours. Due to the chewed-up state of the sodden ground, the battalion had to proceed on foot through the minefield, but even with this delay, they captured two depth strongpoints, seized two bridges across the River Fontaine, and established a toehold on the Southern Plateau by 0400 hours on 11 September.[207]

With the Northern Plateau secure, Crocker could proceed with the second phase of his plan, the break-in by the 51st (Highland) Division and the capture of objectives between Doudenéville and the Forêt de Montgeon. In fact, he had actually initiated this action while the 56th Brigade was still in the process of consolidating its objectives. At 2345 hours, the 5th Battalion Seaforth Highlanders of the 152nd Brigade passed through the gaps made by the 56th brigade, fumbled their way forward in the dark, and conducted a left-hook attack to take out the strongpoint that had so menaced the South Wales Borderers.[208] This action was completed against minimal opposition by 0245 hours. At the same time, three obstacle-breaching teams rumbled towards the anti-tank ditch and minefield in pitch-darkness. Lights and directional tracer fire helped, but the handicap of thirty-yard visibility inevitably caused some confusion in both bridging and flailing operations.[209] By 0400 hours, however, one lane was complete and the rest of the 152nd Brigade passed through to march on their objectives, which they secured by 0810 hours. In fact, the steady progress of operations encouraged the GOC 51st (Highland) Division, Major-General T.G. Rennie, "to embark forthwith on the first part of Phase III of the Corps plan, the capture of the gun areas WEST of the FORET DE MONTGEON."[210] Rennie, who had commanded the 3rd Division under Crocker during Overlord, did not need to be prodded here. He sent the 153rd Brigade through the Forêt de Montgeon and on to the enemy batteries, which fell with 400 prisoners to the 1st Battalion Gordon Highlanders by 1545 hours.[211] Further north, the 152nd Brigade drove westward, through Doudenéville and onto Octeville, where the 2nd Battalion Seaforth Highlanders captured 634 prisoners at a cost of only 4 killed and 10 wounded.[212]

With their northern defences shattered and the bulk of their guns now in British hands, the German defenders crumbled quickly. East of the Lezarde River, the 146th Brigade had a stiff first-light fight for two strongpoints that guarded the main approach to Harfleur, one requiring a second attack with crocodiles to terrorize the defenders into surrendering. Once those two strong-points fell at 1335 hours on 11 September, however, the remaining defenders east of the Lezarde surrendered within two hours.[213] The subsequent exploitation into Le Havre proper benefited from the final Bomber Command attack on the western defences shortly after first light, as well as typhoon attacks on selected defensive localities throughout the day.[214] Meeting minimal resistance, the 51st (Highland) Division pushed to the Octeville-La Hève-Fort Ste. Addresse line on 11 September, while the 49th (West Riding) Division reached Fort de Tourneville and the bottom of the Southern Plateau. With British troops closing in quickly, the German garrison commander surrendered at noon on 12 September, joining the 11,301 other defenders who marched into captivity. The port facility, despite enemy demolitions, was functioning less than a month later.

Operation Astonia, with very few difficulties, had rolled along according to plan and the evidence suggests that Crocker was well pleased with how events unfolded. At one-tenth of Charnwood's cost in casualties, Astonia had taken less than forty-eight hours to complete, and it had been fought against at least twice as many defenders.[215] Undoubtedly, the quality of German defender made a huge difference; the fortress defenders at Le Havre had only a fraction of the will to fight displayed by the troops of 12th SS Panzer Division. The 1st Corps after-action report expands on how the Astonia plan chipped away at a lesser enemy's will to resist:

> There is no doubt that the speed and comparative ease with which the operation was accomplished were largely due to the absence of a determined will to resist on the part of the garrison, and that this condition was created by a sense of complete isolation by land, sea and air, culminating in the concentrated and undisturbed bombardment of the defences by the Royal Artillery, the Royal Navy, and above all, The Royal Air Force. The corps plan, both in its conception and execution, made full use of this condition; all available arms were employed to their best advantage; the momentum of the attack was never allowed to relax.[216]

As if to emphasize that the battle was as much about psychology as it was about physical destruction, the after-action report closed with the statement that "before it had time to recover, the garrison was overwhelmed" – not destroyed, not crushed, but overwhelmed. This was what Crocker had tried to do, but not nearly so successfully, in Charnwood. But, things had been different at Caen. There, the enemy had been far more resilient. The synchronization of army, navy, and air assets had not been nearly so well developed. And, perhaps most of all, the commanders in Charnwood, especially Keller, had required much more supervision. The battle for Le Havre, on the other hand, was well fought at all levels. That 1st Corps captured a key port and more than 11,000 prisoners in forty-eight hours, and at a cost of only 388 casualties, was a major accomplishment – especially at a time when Allied logistics were strained for want of port facilities and the British Army was disbanding divisions for want of infantry reinforcements.[217]

In spite of his solid fighting record, for a variety of reasons, Crocker fought the rest of the campaign in Northwest Europe somewhat out of the limelight. During Operation Suitcase (20 October to 8 November), a push from Antwerp to the Maas River, he commanded four divisions from four different nations – the 4th Canadian Armoured Division, the US 104th Infantry (Timberwolf) Division, the 1st Polish Armoured Division, and the 49th (West Riding) Division.[218] Large and successful though the operation may have been, it was still only a supporting action to protect the right flank of the First Canadian Army as it struggled to clear the Scheldt Estuary. Later, as the First Canadian Army liberated Holland and the Second Army drove into Germany, he mostly watched while his formations were fed into other corps and armies. Why did a general of such competence drift into the shadows of the campaign?

There were two principal reasons. One was his poor relationship with Harry Crerar. In an October 1944 letter to O'Connor, Crocker alluded to how his enmity with Crerar had affected his employment: "We have had quite an interesting war since we left you [in Second Army] – not quite the sort I'd have chosen for myself, but it has had the merit of being an almost independent role all the way. Too close or intimate supervision by my particular authorities would have been irksome indeed. As it was, flashpoint was nearly reached once or twice."[219]

There was also the issue of geography. When 1st Corps had finished Operation Suitcase, it was positioned east of the Scheldt Estuary and on the south side of the Maas River – facing the German 25th Army, which was still on the north bank and would remain there until the final German surrender in May 1945. Someone still had to defend against enemy action from the north and Crocker's corps was in position; incidentally, it was also further away than any other corps in the 21st Army Group from upcoming operations in the Rhineland. With the passing of the German Ardennes Offensive in December 1944, and with the success of Allied operations on the Rhine in February and March of 1945, defending the Maas against enemy attack from the north became more and more an economy-of-force operation, and Crocker's force strength was reduced accordingly. Thus, his position after the Scheldt operations, combined with his touchy relationship with Crerar, resulted in Crocker's assumption of a secondary role from October 1944 to the end of the war. It had nothing to do with anyone, Montgomery in particular, losing faith in Crocker's abilities as a corps commander.

It was probably just as well that Crocker had only a secondary role after October 1944. On the 20th of that month, his son, Wilfrid, an armoured officer like his father, was killed while fighting with the 5th Inniskilling Dragoon Guards in Holland. Crocker took the news very hard, but he had just launched Operation Suitcase and felt compelled to continue in command of his corps for another three weeks, until his tasks in support of the Scheldt operations had been completed and his Tactical Headquarters closed down. Only then did he take some time, one week in November, to grieve.[220] Crerar, who was on sick leave in England when he heard of Crocker's loss, immediately sent a message of condolence to Crocker: "Have just received painful message from [Lieutenant-General Guy] Simonds that your son whom I remember has been killed in action. While I realize that no words of mine can really help you at this time, I offer my deepest sympathy."[221] Despite their differences, Crerar's sympathy was genuine and he understood how Crocker had been shaken. He did not need the burden of a centre-stage task added to his grief. A letter to his brother George, written six weeks after Wilfrid's death, reveals something of Crocker's state of mind:

> I was glad to be able to get home for a few days, for I felt it would help Hilda if she could share the burden. It is hard to see clearly and think clearly. The awful finality of the physical separation keeps returning like a cloud. It isn't that one doesn't believe, if somewhat blindly and inarticulately, in the love and wisdom with which these things are ordered. It is just the pain of having a great chunk of oneself cut away, and the pain of seeing those dear to one hurt. Still we must go on. We have so much to be thankful for, and there are so many others who have harder things to bear.[222]

In February 1945, Montgomery asked Crocker "if he would like to have a change"[223] – promotion and posting to an army command back in England. It would have been uncharacteristically altruistic of Montgomery simply to offer Crocker a break, and, sure enough, Montgomery did have other motives – namely, making room for one of his inner-circle protégés, Lieutenant-General Sidney Kirkman, who was then in search of a corps to command.[224] Crocker correctly caught on to the fact that he was being "kicked upstairs" and declined the offer.[225] Even so, the fact that Montgomery asked Crocker what he wanted – a courtesy that the army group commander did not extend to either Jerry

Bucknall or Richard O'Connor when he got rid of them[226] – suggests that Montgomery still respected the ability of a man whose wind had been knocked out by a family tragedy.

Montgomery's faith in Crocker extended into the postwar period, when, as the successor to Brooke as CIGS, he tapped Crocker for a number of key tasks and appointments. From June 1945 to June 1947, Crocker served as GOC Southern Command, an army-level appointment. Then, during the height of the crisis in Palestine, Montgomery had the cool-headed Crocker appointed as Commander-in-Chief Middle East Land Forces, a post the latter held until 1950. And when the rewriting of British Army training and doctrine manuals began to go awry, he turned to Crocker: "D.G.M.T [Director General Military Training] has been working away for some considerable time on various training publications. It is obvious that new ones are necessary since most of the existing ones are completely out of date. I have glanced through the drafts and am not at all satisfied with them ... I have accordingly decided that the whole matter will be dealt with ... by a small committee, of which you will be the Chairman."[227]

Crocker's committee submitted a crisp four-page report, recommending three categories of publication – a "Conduct of War" pamphlet on higher command, operations, and training for lieutenant-colonels and above; a series of army training manuals on a variety of subjects such as the armoured and infantry divisions in battle, civil defence, imperial policing, administration, and staff duties; and finally a series of more specialized arms training manuals for NCOs and officers in the various arms and services.[228] Production for the pamphlets proceeded more or less on these lines, and Montgomery was well pleased with the clarity and direction Crocker had brought to the project – so pleased, in fact, that he did not hesitate to tap Crocker for yet another favour: "I have come to the conclusion [that] the 'Armoured Division' part of the 'Armoured and Infantry Divisions in Battle' should be written by you, and that you should use Pat [Percy] Hobart to do it under your direction. What do you think?"[229]

In response to this latest bit of direction from the CIGS, Crocker wrote dryly: "I am sure that you do not expect me to thank you for it! But I will do my best."[230] He did complete the task, although *The Armoured Division in Battle* appeared in 1952 as a separate but complementary volume to *The Conduct of War* (1950) and *The Infantry Division in Battle* (1950).[231] These three volumes did not represent a dramatic departure from the 21st Army Group manner of doing business.[232] The basic organization of an armoured division – one armoured brigade and one infantry brigade – remained unchanged, and the armoured division was still an organization to be used en masse. One commentator has even remarked that "the hallowed battle drills of the Twenty-First Army Group were brought out, polished lovingly and put to work again."[233] This is a bit unfair. The 21st Army Group publication *The Armoured Division in Battle* was a short thirty-two-page pamphlet that outlined broad principles for employing an armoured division in battle. The 1952 *Armoured Division in Battle* honoured those doctrinal principles, but, at twice the length, it was far more prescriptive. It expanded on the various operations of war – advance to contact, the attack, the pursuit, the defence, the counterattack, and the withdrawal – and it gave more guidance on command and control. It was classic Crocker – bringing practicality to a broader doctrine. At any rate, these keystone documents guided conventional British Army doctrine for much of the Cold War and Crocker was the man most responsible for their production.[234]

Montgomery also felt strongly that Crocker should inherit the CIGS appointment. Having a like-minded successor in the CIGS chair would ensure both his legacy and his own influence as he moved on to Western Union Defence Organization and, later, NATO appointments. Quite probably, however, Crocker would not have been Montgomery's first choice if General Sir Miles Dempsey had not just retired, or if Lieutenant-General Sir Brian Horrocks had not been ill and on his way to retirement.[235] Such speculations aside, the evidence is clear that Montgomery tried very hard to convince Clement Atlee's Labour government of Crocker's suitability for the position.[236] In the end, however, Atlee chose Sir William Slim, and Montgomery had to break the news to Crocker:

> For some days the Prime Minister has been considering the question of who is to succeed me as CIGS. I have all along strongly advised him that you are the man and so has the Secretary of State. The Prime Minister has however always been of the opinion that he wants SLIM and he has now finally decided that he will recommend SLIM to the King as my successor. I am personally very sorry indeed but we will have to accept this decision. The appointment is of course entirely in the hands of the Prime Minister ... I was most anxious to let you know this before any announcement in the press.[237]

Crocker took it all in stride. He was grateful for Montgomery's recommendation, adding that he was "very happy" to continue serving in the Middle East,[238] which he did for another year, until he assumed his final appointment as Adjutant General for the Forces in 1950.

John Crocker retired from the military in 1953 after a long and distinguished career. It began with exemplary service as a subaltern in the Great War. It continued into the interwar period when his first-rate technical skills helped hone the new tank arm of the British Army. And it flourished during the Second World War, despite setbacks like the disappointment at Fondouk. He made mistakes, as any general who fights does, but he fought his formations with skill. He conducted an enormous combined assault on a defended beach, and he integrated the firepower of army, naval, and air forces in two successful corps operations. "Honest John" Crocker, as Lord Carver wrote, was "a man of outstanding ability and absolute integrity,"[239] a man on whom peers and superiors relied to solve problems, a man subordinates trusted for his competence. Hobart told him that "there is no officer in the [Royal Tank] Regiment, nor ever has been, who has acquired the absolute confidence and trust of all ranks to a greater degree."[240] Crocker led by gallant example, but he was not a talker, so even for people who admired him, words did not come easily while they were in his presence. His aide-de-camp, Captain John Cross, finally found the words over a month after Crocker had left 1st Corps for Southern Command:

> Twice in these last 6 weeks I have found myself completely inarticulate ... I consoled myself by saying that on the day you would leave the corps I could say it all then. But now you have gone and the last time was even worse than the first! There is so much for which I wanted to thank you. An ADC's job is so dependent on the general he serves and I know how very fortunate I was; you even made it possible for me to marry before D-day. That is something for which I shall ever be grateful ... I know that I have been privileged to be a year, and more, with you – to have the opportunity to learn from you more of life than I ever could absorb ... and especially to be with you during those great days a year ago when this last campaign was won.
>
> All this I should have said – and meant to – before you went, but I failed miserably to rise to the occasion. I only hope that you may have realised that the gratitude was there.[241]

Crocker needed that. He refolded the letter, placed it back in its envelope, and saved it in his files.

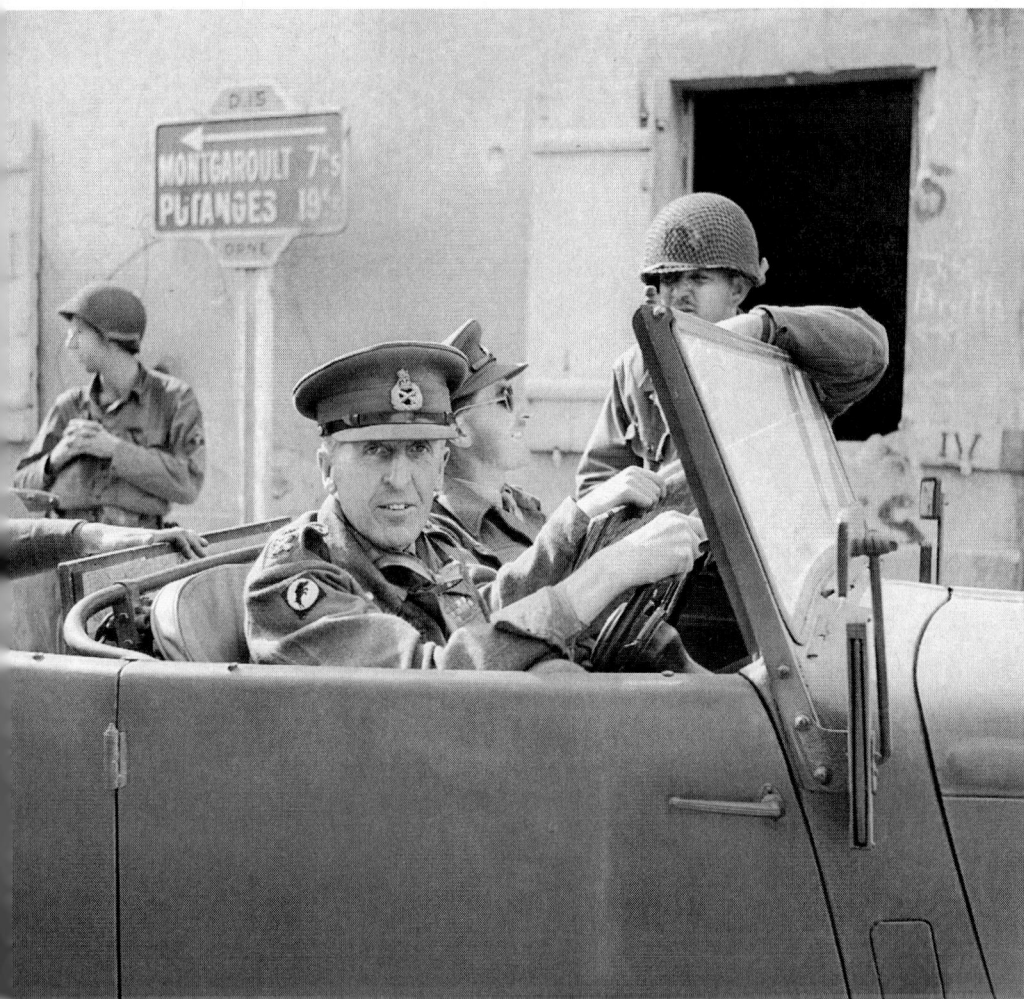

General Brian Horrocks returns to duty. After spending a year recovering from wounds sustained in North Africa, Horrocks assumed command of 30th Corps in August 1944. Imperial War Museum, B9532.

Lieutenant-General Charles Foulkes, Commander 1st Canadian Corps, speaks with Lieutenant-Colonel Logan Vencta, Senior Protestant Padre. LAC, e010770494.

The Operation Veritable team. *Front row:* Brigadier M. Elrington, Major-General Ivor Thomas, Lieutenant-General Brian Horrocks, General H.D.G. Crerar, Lieutenant-General Guy Simonds, Major-General A. Bruce Matthews. *Back row:* Major-General C.M. Barber, Major-General Dan Spry. LAC, e010770496.

King George VI and "Tommy" Burns during the King's visit to Italy, July 1944. LAC, PA113008.

*Facing page, top to bottom:*

Brigadier John Rockingham, Commander 9th Canadian Infantry Brigade, and Lieutenant-General Brian Horrocks share a light moment before Operation Plunder (the Rhine River crossing), March 1944. LAC, e010770497.

Eighth Army Commander, Lieutenant-General Sir Oliver Leese speaking with Regimental Sergeant Major G.D. Gilpin, 1st Field Regiment, Royal Canadian Horse Artillery, Italy, 8 September 1944. LAC, PA131420.

Foulkes and his
aide-de-camp,
Lieutenant E.C.
Argue, Falaise, August
1944. LAC, PA132732.

Burns and his
Brigadier General
Staff, Nick McCarter,
1st Canadian Corps
Headquarters, March
1944. LAC, PA134175.

Burns in his planning van, March 1944. LAC, PA134176.

The senior leadership of the First Canadian Army, May 1945. *Seated:* H.S. Maczek, RAF Air Vice Marshal E.C. Hudleston, Guy Simonds, Harry Crerar, Charles Foulkes, Bert Hoffmeister, S.B. Rawlins. *Standing:* W.P. "Pres" Gilbride, Churchill Mann, J.F.A. Lister, George Kitching, R.H. Keefler, A. Bruce Matthews, E.L.M. "Tommy" Burns, Harry Foster, Robert Moncel, N. Elliot Rodger, H.V.D. Laing. LAC, PA138509.

Lieutenant-General John Crocker with members of a visiting Soviet delegation, 28 July 1944. LAC, PA162340.

Charles Foulkes (hand on windshield) stands with his patron and protector, Harry Crerar, outside the Mairie in Dieppe, 3 September 1944. LAC, PA167574.

Corps Headquarters from the outside. This photograph shows the G (Operations) Section of 2nd Canadian Corps Main Headquarters in the Reichswald Forest, March 1945. Note that the caravans, including one for the supporting air element, are backed up to a tented briefing area. LAC, e010791456.

General Sir John Crocker. Tank Museum, Bovington. 1573/B5.

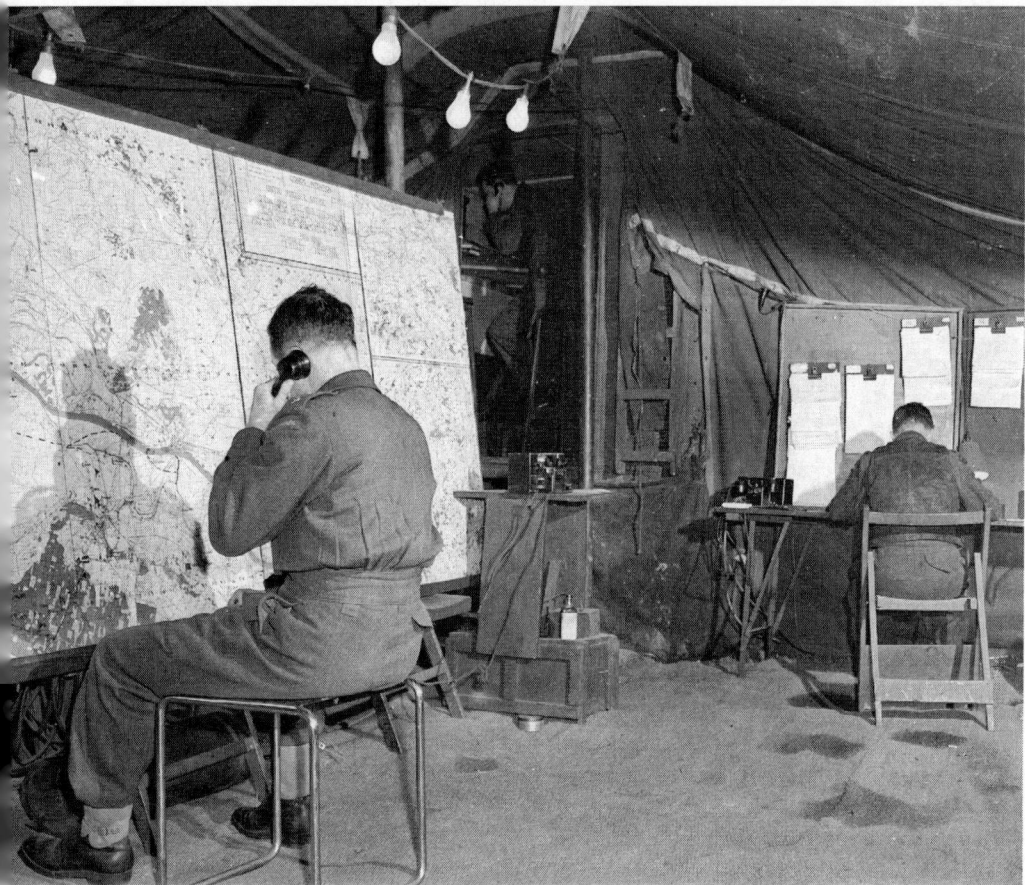

Corps Headquarters from the inside. A duty officer updates the briefing map at 2nd Canadian Corps Main Headquarters. LAC, e010791457.

This photograph captures the essence of the three-way relationship between Guy Simonds, Field Marshal Montgomery, and Harry Crerar. Here Simonds confers closely with the army group commander, while Crerar strolls along the edge of the walking path – and the conversation. LAC, e010796910.

Guy Simonds (right) speaking with one of his battalion commanders, Lieutenant-Colonel Pat Bogert of the West Nova Scotia Regiment, in Sicily, July 1943. LAC, PA193388.

John Crocker (right) speaking with the troubled commander of the 3rd Canadian Infantry Division, Rod Keller, 25 June 1944. Ten days after this photo was taken, Crocker recommended that Keller be relieved of his command. LAC, PA129170.

# 4
# Wit with Will to Spare:
# Lieutenant-General Guy Granville Simonds

*The generation of good ideas and intentions becomes useless theorizing unless they show results in the form of high morale, battle discipline and fighting efficiency of a formation or unit. A man who originates good ideas and intentions but who is unable to get them into practice may be useful in pure research or in an advisory capacity, but is quite useless in any executive command. A man who has the character, determination and drive to get things done, even if barren of original ideas, may draw inspiration elsewhere and will be useful as an executive even if his lack of original imagination limits the field of his usefulness.*

– LIEUTENANT-GENERAL GUY GRANVILLE SIMONDS

GUY SIMONDS LACKED FOR neither original ideas nor determination. Historians and contemporaries alike have acknowledged the originality of his operational plans and his strength of will to force them through to completion.[1] No one could deny the ingenuity of an operation like Totalize. Neither could anyone question the conviction of a corps commander who fired his closest friend for falling short in battle. But no man is perfect, and there were plenty of people, then and since, who have found flaws in Simonds's character and in his capabilities as a commander. He was too cold to win the hearts of his soldiers, too my-way-or-the-highway in his dealings with subordinate commanders, too inclined to mimic Montgomery.[2] Chris Vokes, a Royal Military College (RMC) classmate who commanded a brigade and a division under Simonds, has often been quoted as saying that, although Simonds was "the finest Canadian general we ever had," he was not worth "a pinch of coonshit" when it came to leading men.[3] Vokes was wrong. Simonds may not have had the warmth and charm of a Horrocks, but he more than compensated with a combination of first-class technical skill, which impressed nearly everyone who worked with him, and a ruthlessness that put subordinates on notice that they had better do their jobs, and well, or they would be working elsewhere. He also had the good sense to choose a chief of staff like N. Elliot Rodger, who was outgoing and affable, qualities that did not come easily to Simonds. His battle record shows that he had little problem getting subordinates to do his bidding, even in very trying circumstances. He proved this as a divisional commander in Sicily and Italy, as corps commander in Normandy and Northwest Europe, and as acting army commander in the Scheldt Estuary. Some senior Canadian staff officers thought that Simonds was "unquestionably the ablest senior officer in the [Canadian] army," or "the only innovative mind we had."[4] Others found him "brusque and demanding, but reasonable."[5] All found him impressive. If Simonds had a weakness, it was not his aloofness – that really did not affect his performance – it was his pride. Supremely confident, driven to succeed, and fiercely competitive, he hated being anything but the best, and his desire to prove himself and his troops got the best of him now and then. These occasions were the exception, however. His battlefield performance was strong. From July 1943 to May 1945, Simonds used his well-honed technical skills, his will, and his ruthlessness to command effectively at division, corps, and army level. Not without reason did Montgomery say that "Canada produced only one general fit to hold high command in war, and that was Guy Simonds."[6]

WHO WAS GUY SIMONDS? Born on 24 April 1903 at Ixworth, England, he was the son of a Royal Artillery officer, the grandson of a major-general in the Indian Army, and the great-grandson of an officer in the army of the Honourable East India Company. From the earliest age, Simonds wanted to continue the same line of service to the British Empire, and he had every confidence he could do it.[7] At the age of nine, a year after the family had emigrated to British Columbia, the precocious youngster won a short-essay competition with a piece on the benefits of military training for boys and men:

> If a boy learns to box and uses his fists properly, knowing how to defend himself, he may when he goes to school or other places be attacked by a bully or have to defend a weaker boy against one; although he may be smaller and younger ... he may, if he knows how to fight, thrash the bully splendidly. Of course, he may never be obliged to fight at all, but if he does, he must know how to do it. It is the same with nations as with boys. With proper training and courage, they can defend themselves and protect weaker nations against the larger and unfair ones. This is better for everything and everyone, and keeps a nation strong.[8]

He had most likely benefited from some parental assistance in crafting the little piece, but the authoritative tone is interesting because it indicates that Simonds had learned to express himself with conviction and confidence from a very early age – not a bad trait for a young man with the career aspirations of an army officer.

Despite the lineage of male military service in his family, the person who probably exerted the greatest influence on his development, for better and for worse, was his mother. An American émigré to Britain, Eleanor (or Nellie) was the daughter of a wealthy Virginia horse breeder. Nellie lived lavishly, assuming, as Dominick Graham has stated, "that country house living, nannies to look after the children, good food, and a host of inside and outside servants were her birthright."[9] This would have been fine if she had married an army officer of independent means, or if her inheritance had lasted, but Cecil Simonds had only his army salary and he spent long periods in places like Kenya and Nigeria while Nellie burned through her share of the family inheritance in short order. In fact, making money was the real reason that Cecil Simonds had left the army in 1911 and emigrated to Canada with his wife, three sons, and daughter. There he hoped to make a small fortune as a surveyor and land speculator, but the opportunity for making money was not what he had expected, as Canada was in a major economic recession, and Nellie never sufficiently curbed her spending. Their four-bedroom home in Victoria was a far cry from the family estates of Suffolk and County Meath, so she had to make some adjustments; living within her means, however, was not one of them. Thus, one of her lasting legacies to her son was that of perpetually cash-strapped circumstances. She and Cecil did manage to send Guy and his brother Peter to Ashbury Collegiate Boarding School in Ottawa in 1919, but even then a chronic lack of funds forced Guy to drop out for a year and accept work as a clerk in a law office. Money would be a persistent problem for Simonds, mostly because of his mother. This was a "pride stinger" that never really went away.

The other trait that his mother passed on was a notion that he was a cut above the rest. A born socialite, Nellie loved cavorting with the "great and good" of British society, something that had been a normal part of her life in England and Ireland, and she continued to seek out and charm high-placed people in British Columbia after the move to Canada. Some of this rubbed off on Guy, who grew to enjoy the company of talented and influential people as well. It meant keeping up expensive pretences, however, and there simply was not the money to do so, not on the income of a struggling half-pay officer. Even after Cecil had been recalled to the British Army in 1914, promoted to lieutenant-colonel, and sent overseas, Nellie still had to sell a number of "pictures and other family treasures" to supplement the allowance that her husband sent back to his family.[10] Guy even took jobs during the war years to augment the family's finances. The money from these combined measures was enough, just enough, for Nellie to send her children to school and keep up their English pastimes, such as riding, shooting, and rugby. This was important to her. Guy excelled in all of these activities and at school too, where he always did well on his exams. Indeed, he was almost conditioned for success. It was expected of him and he himself expected it. He differed from his mother, however, in that he understood that his success, and his ability to be at the forefront of any group that he be-longed to, was the result of hard work, not birthright.

Simonds took this work ethic and self-confidence to the Royal Military College in 1921. That year, he sat the Canada-wide entrance examinations and passed into RMC with the second-highest marks overall. Other notable classmates, such as Churchill Mann, Chris Vokes, and E.C. "Johnny" Plow, placed well below him in order of merit.[11] Soon identified as a budding leader of some promise, Simonds became the senior cadet for his class, an appointment he held until the end of his third year. He excelled academically, maintaining excellent grades in all his subjects throughout his four-year program and graduating with the second-highest grades overall in 1925.[12] Nicknamed "the Count," the five-foot-ten-inch youngster with the jet-black hair and the pale blue eyes was quiet and distant – some even said shy[13] – but everyone recognized his talent.[14] Not least among his admirers was the Commandant, Major-General Sir Archibald Cameron Macdonnell, who described Simonds as a "winner" and a "brilliant student."[15] Macdonnell so believed in Simonds that he intervened directly when Cecil and Nellie Simonds could not muster the funds to pay for his tuition, a sad state of affairs that persisted from 1922 to 1925. Macdonnell found young Simonds employment with the Canadian Pacific Railway in the summer of 1922; he arranged for the youngster to work on a survey crew during the summer of 1924; and he garnered three separate loans or grants from the Leonard Foundation. This was embarrassing for Simonds – being regularly called into the Staff Adjutant's office, told that his account was in arrears, and asked whether he knew when, or if, his parents would put things right by paying up. Simonds was understandably grateful to Macdonnell, whom he described as "a great gentleman and a soldier with an outstanding war record," and he was determined to prove that Macdonnell's efforts were not in vain.[16] Despite the constant threat of suspension due to non-payment of tuition, he persevered, remained focused on his studies, and excelled. He was thankful for the experience of RMC, which he thought a "magnificent institution ... to which I owe a great deal."[17] The curriculum gave him a solid education and the demands of military training and college life forced him to organize his time efficiently. It also taught him the "very important lesson that there are things in life that matter a great deal more than self – the College, one's class, one's company, one's platoon ... all come before self."[18]

Simonds had a strong sense of the right thing to do and how to do it. During his third year, some of his classmates – he did not know who – had taken to "the systematic stealing of examination papers" from the unlocked offices of careless professors, and passing them around for profit. Needless to say, this practice contravened any number of RMC regulations and orders. It was also an affront to someone with so certain a sense of right and wrong and who did not have it in him to ignore a fault. In many ways, confronting peers was more difficult than confronting subordinates, even superiors. In a place like RMC, where the support of one's peers was so crucial to ultimate success, one had to be wary about alienating them. But Simonds managed to do the right thing without disaffecting the majority of his mates: "As senior of the class, I was held responsible for giving leadership in conduct and discipline. When the [exam-stealing situation] came to light, I was determined to stamp out this dishonest practice. I was in no easy position ... [but w]hen I put the issue clearly to my classmates, I immediately received the backing of the vast majority."[19] With most of his classmates behind him, Simonds then "detailed all night guards on each flat" to ensure that no would-be exam thieves could leave the dormitories at night, and he arranged for cadets to patrol the administrative and academic buildings to deter anyone from pinching exams on their way back from town leave. He used a bit of a carrot-and-stick approach:

> I ... made it plain that if any members of the class were caught trying to steal examination papers, I would charge him before the Commandant with "Conduct Unbecoming," which could lead to his dismissal from the Royal Military College with disgrace. Further, I reiterated ... that those of us who had high academic standing would always make ourselves available to give extra coaching and tutoring to those who experienced difficulties.[20]

Lest he be accused of addressing the cheating issue to further his own career and position in the college, Simonds took all of these actions without informing the military staff or the chain of command. It worked. The stealing of examination papers soon stopped, and Simonds's stock with his classmates, far from being devalued by the experience, remained high. He had acted for all the right reasons and his peers respected him for it. Upon graduation, they voted him the winner of the Victor Van der Smissen Award as the best all-round cadet, "mentally, morally and physically."[21] Simonds also took the Sword of Honour for Conduct and Discipline and the Governor General's Silver Medal for having the second-highest aggregate marks upon graduation.[22]

From RMC, Simonds went into the Permanent Force, receiving a commission in the Royal Canadian Horse Artillery (RCHA) in June 1925. He joined B Battery RCHA at Kingston, Ontario, which was one of only three Permanent Force batteries in the country. Its primary function during the interwar years was to furnish instructors for militia training, so Simonds spent a lot of time acquiring the technical knowledge of his trade then passing it on to militia officers and soldiers on weekends and at summer camps. He took his duties seriously. His confidential reports for the period 1926-29 contained comments like " a promis-ing young officer," "should make a first-class staff officer," and "a very good section commander and instructor."[23] By 1927, he had passed the first of his promotion exams to captain and, by the summer of 1929, he had aced the second set, which permitted his promotion to brevet captain. In 1932, after three years of service with C Battery RCHA in Winnipeg, he attended the Gunnery Staff Course at Woolwich, England, where he attained the rare and coveted Instructor Gunner qualification. During these first ten years of his military career, Simonds set the foundation of his reputation as a skilled gunner and officer.

It was also during this time that Simonds married and started a family. In 1932, after a two-year courtship, he married Katherine Taylor, the daughter of a prominent Winnipeg businessman. A bit of a tomboy, Katherine was an "adventurous spirit" who taught herself to drive an automobile and took flying lessons.[24] She was in many ways the opposite of Simonds, who was serious and reserved, but they determined to marry and they had their first child, Ruth, while Simonds was on course in England during 1933. A son, Charles, was born the following year after the couple had returned to Canada. Simonds was not a doting father by any stretch of the imagination. The army came first. He was away when Ruth was born and was absent for much of her childhood, but, to place this behaviour in context, he was not unlike most military men of that period. Women raised the children while men worked to provide food, shelter, and other necessities. Simonds himself had lived without any paternal guidance for the four years that his own father served in France and Flanders, and even before that, Cecil Simonds had been away for long periods at various posts throughout the Empire. The idea of building dollhouses or escorting children to piano lessons would therefore have been completely foreign to someone like Simonds. He cared for his family; he simply did not see the need to spend all his time with them, especially when service to King and country demanded so much of him. While away from them during the war, he would have an affair with a married woman in England.[25] This hardly placed him in exclusive com-pany, but it did play a large part in wrecking his marriage to Katherine after the war.

Throughout the remainder of the 1930s, Simonds remained focused on his career, which continued its upward trajectory. As one subordinate from the period put it, Simonds was a "'super snap,' he'd been singled out and everyone knew it."[26] The same subordinate also recalled joining B Battery RCHA in the late 1930s to find senior non-commissioned officers (NCOs) who remembered Simonds from the 1920s and "sang his praises." Not everyone liked him, however. For every person who found "the Count" amusingly noble, there was another who did not see the charm in the persona, regarding Simonds instead as "snooty" or "snobbish."[27] Still, there was no denying his technical ability. His confidential reports, already very strong in the 1920s, were even stronger in the 1930s. He consistently attained top marks in the assessment areas of imagination, tactical knowledge, technical ability and perception, judgment, and leadership.[28] Interestingly, he scored only average marks for sociability.

Key to his development as an officer and to his reputation was his attendance at the British Army Staff College at Camberley, where he studied for two years during 1936 and 1937. Managing to make it into the college on his first attempt, Simonds thoroughly enjoyed the experience, taking very well to the Camberley method of instruction: "The essence of teaching at the Staff College was not to indoctrinate officers with preconceived theories, but to make them think and come up with their own solutions to the problems of modern war."[29] He loved it. He excelled in fact, as his course report reflected:

> A very capable and well rounded officer with breadth of vision and strength of character. A very hard worker and highly reliable ... He has an infinite capacity for detail but does not allow that to fog his grasp of the major issues. His capabilities are fully recognized by his fellow students with whom he is popular ... Would undoubtedly make a good commander but he has even more the qualities of the high grade staff officer in an appointment ... An officer of considerable promise who should go far.[30]

The report also commented that Simonds "would make a really good instructor at the Camberley Staff College." This was a very rare recommendation, one reserved for only the best Camberley graduates, and Simonds, a Dominion officer, had done extraordinarily well to get it.

Already known as an officer of substantial technical ability, Simonds returned to Canada as an officer to watch. In April 1938, he was promoted to brevet major and appointed as an associate professor of Tactics at RMC, where he worked for Brigadier Harry Crerar, then Commandant of the college. This was not the first time Simonds had worked for Crerar. He had been one of Crerar's officers in B Battery RCHA in 1927. Crerar had been impressed with Simonds then, and his latest dealings with the razor-sharp major only reinforced his positive assessment. On Simonds's 1938 confidential report, the future army commander wrote: "A keen, enthusiastic type of officer, hard-working and with marked ability. A pleasant, and at the same time, a forceful personality. A good instructor ... In short, an excellent officer from all points of view ... Recommended for higher rank or grade in Command or Staff."[31] His students would not have agreed that he was a "pleasant" personality. From their point of view, he was too distant and too serious to be considered pleasant, and his level of knowledge intimidated most. Still, with the admiration of Crerar, a brigadier whose own star was on the rise, Simonds's speedy progression up the rank ladder was all but certain. Naturally enough, this annoyed certain peers and superiors, some of whom thought Simonds acted a bit too much like he knew his rise was a foregone conclusion. As a captain, he did after all challenge Lieutenant-Colonel E.L.M. Burns's views on the use of tanks in *Canadian Defence Quarterly*.[32] (See pages 66-67 above.) This sort of temerity on top of his normal taciturnity was bound to put some people off. Some would have agreed with the comment of future Chief of the General Staff Kenneth Stuart that Simonds "has a strong self-confident personality which at times inclines him to be intolerant of views that run counter to his own."[33] That was a fair comment.

As might have been predicted, Simonds found himself in key jobs following the Canadian declaration of war against Germany on 10 September 1939. At the end of October, he assumed the duties of General Staff Officer Second Grade (GSO 2) in the 1st Canadian Infantry Division Headquarters. At that time, the 1st Canadian Infantry Division was to be Canada's land force contribution to the war effort, but it had yet to be fully manned and staffed.[34] Major-General A.G.L. McNaughton, former Chief of the General Staff, was called back to uniform from the National Research Council to lead it, and he quickly went to work pulling in the people he needed to begin the process of making the formation battle-ready. Simonds was a natural choice. For one thing, there were not many staff-trained officers from which to choose. Canada had managed to send only 63 officers to either Camberley or Quetta during the interwar period, and only 48 of them were still serving in 1939[35] – not enough to do everything the Canadian army needed to do. A division alone required 20 to 25 staff officers to function, and there were still staff officer billets to be filled at National Defence Headquarters (NDHQ), the Canadian Military Headquarters (CMHQ) in London, and the division's three brigades. None of the 17 staff-trained majors had a reputation that came close to rivalling that of Simonds, who was also the second youngest of the lot.[36]

He took to his duties as GSO 2 with alacrity. In fact, he took the lead on most training issues. Shortly after the arrival of the divisional headquarters at Aldershot in December 1939, Simonds wrote and disseminated a key training instruction that set the division on a two-month period of individual training.[37] Drivers had to learn to drive, gunners had to learn to shoot, leaders had to learn how to navigate, and all ranks had to be proficient in marksmanship as well as first aid and gas drills, before unit and formation training could take place. This required the procurement of maps, training areas, ranges, ammunition, training pamphlets, and vacancies at British Army training schools, none of which was easy to come by in 1940 as the British army was ramping up its own training.

But Simonds did a good job of it and he got on well with British military authorities, many of whom he knew well after having spent a total of three years training in the United Kingdom.

To train officers, battalion and brigade commanders in particular, Simonds's training instruction called for divisional Tactical Exercises without Troops (TEWTs) in the same training period. The TEWTs were to cover twelve separate topics or operations, including the approach march, the defence, relief in a defensive position, an attack against an organized defence, night operations, and the crossing of obstacles, each one being conducted in two stages, first on sand tables or cloth models indoors, then "on the ground" outdoors. The division staff would "run through it and discuss it with the Brigadiers of the Inf[antry] B[riga]des, C[ommander].R[oyal].A[rtillery], C[ommander].R[oyal].E[ngineers] ... who will act as directing staff for their own subordinate com[ma]nd[er]s."[38] This was a good idea in theory, but by the end of May 1940, the division and the brigades had completed only about half of the TEWTs they had intended to do.[39]

There were mitigating factors. There were, as we have seen, few fully trained staff officers in the divisional headquarters and they were completely occupied with addressing equipment shortages, planning for counter-invasion tasks, arranging visits for a multitude of dignitaries, and supervising the individual training that was taking place.[40] Moreover, the level of training at this early stage was so low that even the brigadiers needed guidance. Brigadier Armand Smith in the 1st Brigade had seen active service during the First World War and earned a Military Cross, but he had spent most of the interwar period running a jam-making company. The 2nd Brigade's George Pearkes was the most charismatic and experienced of the brigade commanders – he had won a Victoria Cross as a major during the battle of Passchendaele and then served in the Permanent Force throughout the interwar period – but his thinking was firmly entrenched 1918.[41] Basil Price of the 3rd Brigade had really not commanded anything since 1929, when he had retired from the militia to run his dairy business. He admitted that "in that very early stage we were all learning so much."[42] There was a lot of teaching to do and very few teachers like Simonds. Matters only got worse after May 1940, when the Canadian government decided to field a corps for overseas service, a decision that increased fivefold the requirement for staff officers and senior commanders.

Simonds believed, then and later, that McNaughton was part of the problem. In 1969, he wrote: "From the very beginning, I had a running argument with Andy [McNaughton] ... to make 1 Div, then 1 Cdn Corps, then Cdn Army, *fighting* headquarters, and to do his other roles through CMHQ, which was established for that purpose. He simply would not listen."[43] McNaughton, as

Simonds remembered, "tended to be so absorbed in the technical and equipment and organization problems" that he simply could not concentrate on the training of subordinate commanders and staffs.[44] This frustrated Simonds, who thought the business of training areas, equipment acquisition, liaison with the War Office, and VIP visits – essentially anything not directly related to training the units, brigades, and headquarters of the 1st Canadian Infantry Division – should not have detained the commander or the division staff. Their main concerns were fighting and training to fight, but McNaughton had no sense of urgency about such matters. He believed that if the division had modern equipment and reasonably intelligent staff officers and commanders, it could overcome any challenges it might encounter as it encountered them. He saw no need for practising battle procedure, or regularly putting the headquarters through its paces to ensure that drills for the production and dissemination of orders were sharp, and he never took a personal hand in TEWTs or officer training. He occupied his time with technology and defending Canada's national position – but little in between. McNaughton did not arrange or participate in a single divisional headquarters exercise during the first six months that the Canadians were in England.

He was not helped by his GSO 1, Lieutenant-Colonel G.R. Turner, who was also Simonds's immediate boss. Turner had served with distinction in the Canadian Expeditionary Force during the First World War and was a McNaughton favourite. An engineer by trade, he had passed through Staff College at Quetta in 1926, but he had very little aptitude for higher command or staff. Few who worked on his staff had anything good to say about him.[45] Most of them thought that Simonds, whose knowledge of staff procedures and tactics was very thorough, made Turner "look ridiculous" during divisional TEWTs.[46] He also had a warped sense of what was important. The minutes of one particular staff meeting in January 1940 show who really ran the division staff. Simonds spoke about machine gun course vacancies, anti-tank gun training, the distribution of training pamphlets, and the future conduct of divisional TEWTs. Turner gave a vague statement about the "importance of all units, headquarters and staffs being properly trained in their duties," then went on to discuss how to address envelopes and how to answer the phone "stating name and appointment" and not using the word "hello."[47] In that sort of command climate, it is no wonder that junior staff officers looked to Simonds for guidance. As one of them reflected: "If he hadn't been there, I don't know what we would have done."[48]

Simonds solved problems. In July 1940, he was promoted to lieutenant-colonel and appointed Commanding Officer (CO) of 1 Royal Canadian Horse Artillery. The unit had just been through the aborted attempt to field a second British

Expeditionary Force (BEF) 1940 after the evacuation of the first BEF from Dunkirk. It had deployed with the 1st Canadian Infantry Brigade to Brittany on 13 June, only to be hurriedly evacuated four days later, leaving everything except its guns in France. Its morale was sagging and Simonds was determined to rebuild it through tough training and personal example. As one regimental officer described it, Simonds gave the unit a "great electric jolt."[49] He may not have been the most personable commanding officer, but he understood the value of good morale and how to go about constructing it. He planned purposeful training, and he arranged inter-battery competitions to foster a competitive spirit. He also taught people. His reputation for being dismissive of those who underperformed preceded him and he terrified most of his junior officers, but he could be patient with someone who had the potential and the willingness to learn. His adjutant at 1 RCHA, Captain R.P. Rothschild, had never attended staff college and was at a loss for how to produce a regimental training plan. He admitted as much to Simonds, who then spent a morning explaining to Rothschild what had to be done and how to do it.[50] Simonds could mentor and mend morale; he just wouldn't throw his arm around shoulders to do it.

By November 1940 he had another problem to solve. The new Canadian corps[51] was short of staff officers, and the British staff colleges, already over-tasked with producing enough staff officers for the British Army, could not provide enough vacancies to meet Canadian needs. Both Camberley and Quetta had suspended their year-long courses in September 1939, implementing instead seventeen- to eighteen-week courses designed to give officers the minimum knowledge they needed "for the appointments of Brigade Major, G.S.O. 3 and staff captain whilst giving them general knowledge ... to enable them to fill 2nd grade [GSO 2] appointments after practical experience in those of a lower grade."[52] Ten percent of the 100 or so vacancies were reserved for Dominion officers, five of them for Canadians. It was not enough for either army. The British eventually had to establish Junior War Staff Courses at Sandhurst, Sarafand, and Quetta, while Senior Division courses for second-grade appointments were offered at Camberley, Haifa, and Quetta. And the Canadians would have to run their own courses as well.

To do this, McNaughton tasked Simonds with designing a curriculum and running it. Simonds was ideal for the role, not just because he had achieved such high grades at Camberley and proven his mettle in the first year of the war but also because he got on well with his British counterparts. They respected him too. In January 1940, they requested him by name as an instructor at Camberley, but CMHQ had to decline because Simonds was too critical to the training and operations of the 1st Canadian Infantry Division to be spared.[53] This mutual respect was critical to ensuring commonality between British and

Canadian curricula. There was no point in designing a uniquely Canadian staff program. Canadian divisions, corps, and army had to fight and function as part of a larger British Army. If that was to work at all, Canadian staff officers needed to speak the same language as British staff officers – that is, they needed to learn the same terminology, procedures, and doctrine as their British counterparts. The system simply could not have functioned otherwise. Simonds understood this and he ensured that the curriculum and method of the Canadian Junior War Staff Course (CJWSC) largely mirrored that which was offered at Camberley. With singular focus he zipped through all of the curriculum and administrative preparations in a matter of weeks, starting the job on 4 November 1940, issuing his first order on 6 December, and commencing the course on 2 January 1941. One subordinate claimed that Simonds concocted it all "in a room, with just a table and chair."[54] This was an exaggeration, but Simonds did knock down a small mountain's worth of work in very short order, "set[ting] a stamp on Canadian Staff Training that ... remained for fifty years."[55] The first Canadian Junior War Staff Course, which ran at Ford Manor in Surrey from 2 January 1941 to 12 April 1941, went well and produced fifty-two graduates who were trained in elemental staff duties – thanks mostly to the efforts of Guy Simonds.

The rapidly expanding Canadian army of 1941 could not have done without someone like him. Indeed, it probably needed numerous men like Simonds, but Canadian officers with his level of intellect, drive, and knowledge were rare, so Simonds again found himself assigned to a series of nascent organizations still struggling to their feet. Immediately after completing the first run of the CJWSC, Simonds assumed the responsibilities of GSO 1, 2nd Canadian Infantry Division. The division had not been in Britain long – its deployment had been completed only in December 1940 – so it was experiencing many of the same growing pains that had plagued the 1st Canadian Infantry Division a year earlier – equipment shortages, a lack of trained staff officers for the headquarters, inexperienced commanding officers, and so on. It also had a sixty-one-year-old divisional commander, Victor Odlum, who had seen service in both the Boer War and the First World War, but who was also a militiaman who had been retired from the service between 1925 and 1940 and therefore was not nearly *au fait* with the modern battlefield.[56] Simonds helped him organize the divisional headquarters and place the division on a fairly rigorous training regimen. He drafted and issued operational guidance.[57] Odlum was receptive to all of it. Of course, he *had* to be receptive, given how unfamiliar he was with any military developments since 1919. Unfortunately for him, Simonds remained with the division for only four months. In August 1941, he left to assume the duties of Brigadier General Staff (BGS) 1st Canadian Corps, but his work with the division had done much to help the formation progress, all of which Odlum acknowledged in a letter to McNaughton:

> He came to us facing certain very definite obstacles. However, by characteristic ability and tact he quickly overcame them and in a very short time established himself in the confidence and esteem of the Div.
>
> I cannot speak too highly of him as a staff officer. He has, in outstanding degree, all the required qualities ... I will miss him in the days to come. Had it not been for the fact that he was going to join you and to assume even greater responsibilities, I could not have spared him.[58]

But spare him Odlum did and Simonds moved on to yet another challenge.

What awaited him at 1st Canadian Corps was not encouraging. McNaughton was no more inclined to take a direct hand in the training of his headquarters or his commanders than he had been at the 1st Canadian Infantry Division a year earlier.[59] If anything, he had gotten worse, and people in high places were beginning to notice. After observing 1st Canadian Corps' performance on Exercise Waterloo (14-16 June 1941), General Sir Alan Brooke, the Commander-in-Chief Home Forces, noted in his diary that he was "not happy with some of their senior officers." Some years later he added:

> The more I saw of the Canadian Corps at that time the more convinced I became that Andy McNaughton had not got the required qualities to make a success of commanding the corps. A man of exceptional ability where scientific matters were concerned, but lacking the required qualities of command. He did not know his subordinate commanders properly and was lacking in tactical outlook. It stood out clearly that he would have to be relieved of his command.[60]

In that leadership void, Simonds took the reins in training the headquarters. He tried to bring rigour to staff procedures in the field, and he established a routine that commenced with "morning prayers" at 0830 daily.[61] In an effort to correct the road movement deficiencies that umpires had noted for Waterloo, he drafted and issued "Canadian Corps Operation Instruction No. 24: Road Moves,"[62] which led to some improvement. He steered McNaughton through Exercise Bumper, a counter-invasion exercise that took place from 29 September to 3 October, and umpires did not single out the Canadians for poor road movement and staff procedures, as they had for Exercise Fox in February. Simonds also took it upon himself to produce a training directive that included a reinvigoration of physical fitness training, increased emphasis on officer training, and progressive collective training from platoon to corps level. McNaughton, in the meantime, crashed. His preoccupation with national issues and technology had so sapped his energy that he had to take a period of sick leave beginning in November 1941.

McNaughton's departure coincided with two other important appointments – Montgomery's appointment to command of the Southeastern Army and Harry Crerar's assumption of temporary command of the Canadian Corps. The former was determined to raise the level of training and leadership in all the formations of his army, including the Canadians; the latter was willing to fall in line with that direction. Officer training and teaching officers *how* to train were high priorities. Montgomery and Simonds were like-minded in this regard. Initially, however, Montgomery proposed to send a large number of Canadian officers away on courses, and this concerned Simonds. Who would train platoon commanders if the company commanders and commanding officers were away? True to form, Simonds brought the issue to the attention of Montgomery's Chief of Staff. He made the point that although most platoon commanders were "capable of training platoons," and although most company commanders in the 1st and 2nd Canadian Infantry Divisions had the capacity to supervise platoon training, the 3rd Canadian Infantry Division's company commanders were "much weaker" and in need of "further training and, above all, practice in the handling of a company."[63] Worse, as Simonds explained, the picture got bleaker the higher one looked up the chain of command: "very few" battalion commanders were "up to handling a battalion." And only "4 out of 9" brigadiers were "capable of training their C.O.s." Instead of sending most of its field officers on course, the corps needed to make best use of its capable officers to supervise training, which would be conducted from the bottom up. Simonds proposed that a period of platoon training be scheduled from mid-December to mid-January, and recommended that "the minimum number of Platoon and Company Commanders should go on courses" during this time. For the second half of January, he also recommended that battalion commanders "be left free to supervise [company] training and themselves be trained in T.E.W.Ts." February would be devoted to battalion training, a period during which "potential company commanders and weak but trainable ... company commanders" could be spared to attend courses at the Canadian Company Commanders' School. Finally, Simonds suggested that the month of March be devoted to brigade and division training; however, since Montgomery's plan to hold army-level manoeuvres on 8 March would preclude this, Simonds requested that the army exercises be cancelled. He emphasized that what the officers of 1st Canadian Corps needed was "to be made to train their own show and to get down to it." They wanted "to be left alone as far as possible to carry out a steady training programme." Astonishingly, Montgomery agreed. Simonds had presented a well-considered and progressive approach to training, one very much in accord with Montgomery's own principles, and the army commander decided to support it. This was also one of the army commander's first encounters with Simonds, who had the audacity to question his training direction, and yet the impression he formed of the thirty-eight-year-old brigadier was favourable.

He saw a lot of Simonds over the course of the next eight months, and his opinion of the young Canadian grew steadily. Each evening, Montgomery's Chief of Staff met with the two corps Chiefs of Staff at his headquarters to co-ordinate matters of operations and training, so Simonds and the army commander chatted regularly.[64] Montgomery soon formed the opinion that Simonds was the real brains behind 1st Canadian Corps. The army commander may have worked with Harry Crerar, who willingly accepted all of his recommendations on command appointments and training, and he was genuinely pleased with the progress that 1st Canadian Corps made during the period it was under his command, but he became convinced that Crerar could not have done it without Simonds.[65] After the army Exercise Tiger in May 1942, Montgomery told Crerar that he had done "splendidly" during the manoeuvres, but he also added, "You have a 1st class B.G.S. in Simmonds [sic]; I would like you to tell him I thought he was very good."[66] The implication, of course, was that Simonds had been responsible for a large share of the corps' success.

It helped that Crerar took the business of training more seriously than McNaughton had ever done, and was receptive to what Montgomery (and Simonds) were proposing. Improving the training regimen, and replacing the old and the unfit with the young and the keen, raised the proficiency of the corps. Road movement improved. Brigades and divisions were more responsive to direction because their headquarters were well practised. And the units and formations of the corps could execute all manner of operations – advances, attacks, defences, withdrawals – fairly efficiently. In March 1943, Brooke commented that Crerar had "improved that [1st Canadian] Corps beyond all recognition."[67] Indeed, he had, and Simonds had been a big part of it.

Simonds soon found himself working for McNaughton again. In July 1942, British Prime Minister Winston Churchill asked McNaughton, now Commander First Canadian Army, to look at the feasibility of capturing airfields in northern Norway in December. The British Chiefs of Staff Committee had already assessed Operation Jupiter as impracticable, but Churchill wanted a second opinion. McNaughton called upon Simonds, who calmly dove into the details of the appreciation. After weeks of careful study, Simonds concluded that Operation Jupiter was "extremely hazardous." Its success depended too much on achieving tactical surprise, which was unlikely, and good weather, which was equally unlikely for northern Norway in December: "With good fortune and quick and decisive action success might be gained – on the contrary, the result might be a military disaster of the first magnitude."[68] The British Chiefs of Staff Committee agreed, of course. Its members thought that the Jupiter appreciation "one of the clearest and most ably worked out appreciations which they ever had before them."[69] Their delight was somewhat predictable; it gave them the leverage they needed to get Churchill to drop the whole silly undertaking. Interestingly, Simonds was working on Jupiter at precisely the same time that renewed plans for a raid on Dieppe (Operation Jubilee) were being studied by Crerar and the commanders and staffs of the 2nd Canadian Infantry Division. One wonders what might have been had Simonds not been tasked to look at Jupiter but had been involved instead in the planning for Jubilee, another operation in which the expectation of good luck thoroughly trumped tactical reality.

The Jupiter assignment complete, Simonds packed up his things and moved to the 1st Canadian Infantry Brigade, where he assumed command on 11 September 1942. His tenure there was not long – just long enough to set a routine for the headquarters, visit his units and formations, and make a few training changes. The emphasis during the summer and autumn was on correcting low-level deficiencies that had been identified during Exercise Tiger and the exercises that had preceded it.[70] In December, Simonds brought his brigade to Inverary for combined operations training, which proved challenging and worthwhile. The period of brigade command was all too brief for him. By January 1943, McNaughton needed him again, this time as BGS, or chief of staff, for the First Canadian Army.

Working for McNaughton was not going to be any easier than it had been a year or so earlier. He was still disinclined to exercise his headquarters and turn it into a fighting one. At best, he only "played along" during skeleton exercises for the headquarters; in truth, he "hated" them.[71] As a result, he had very little appreciation for either staff work or the coordination necessary to manoeuvre formations in the field. This was painfully obvious during Exercise Spartan in March 1943.[72] McNaughton was advancing with three corps forward – the British 12th Corps on the right, 1st Canadian Corps under Harry Crerar in the centre, and the newly formed 2nd Canadian Corps commanded by Major-General Ernest Sansom on the left. When the enemy seemed to be holding firm in the centre, McNaughton decided to move Sansom's corps to that area and stuff it between the other two corps to "break the hinge" of the enemy defences. This caused all manner of problems. To begin with, McNaughton showed very little appreciation for how long this manoeuvre would take to execute. It would take at least twenty-four hours for orders to percolate down to the troops in the units, who would then need to be organized into road movement serials for the redeployment. Worse, the decision to move the entire 2nd Canadian Corps and its two armoured divisions essentially layered one corps traffic control organization on top of another. If McNaughton really thought it necessary to commit armour to the centre, why did he not consider detaching one armoured division, or even both, to Crerar? This at least would have alleviated the traffic control issue because Crerar would have controlled the movement forward of the reinforcing tanks. Brooke, now Chief of the Imperial General Staff (CIGS), was visiting on the morning of 7 March while McNaughton was going through these gyrations, and he was not impressed: "[McNaughton] is quite incompetent to command an army! He does not know how to begin the job and was tying up his forces into the most awful muddle."[73] Within twenty-four hours, McNaughton had rethought his decision and countermanded his order, cancelling the concentration of 2nd Canadian Corps in the centre and ordering Sansom to advance, more or less as originally planned, on the left. What did Simonds think of this dog's breakfast? Surely, he saw the folly of the decision to move 2nd Canadian Corps into the centre, but what advice did he give McNaughton at the time? We do not know for sure what counsel he proffered during Spartan, but, based on his record of confronting superiors, it would have been in character for him to have advised McNaughton against the move. Perhaps McNaughton simply dismissed his advice. We also know that Spartan was the final straw for Simonds as far as working for McNaughton was concerned:

> He simply would not listen and matters finally came to a head after "Spartan" ... and the fiasco which resulted was clearly *all* his own doing ... Following "Spartan," I went to see Andy privately. I told him I would continue to serve him in any capacity he wished, except that I would not remain as chief of staff at Army HQ unless he would accept my advice on the matter of organizing Army headquarters to fight a battle and concentrating on the training of operational aspects ... He kicked me out of his office and within 48 hours I left on attachment to 8th Army.[74]

Simonds vacated his appointment as Chief of Staff First Canadian Army on 3 April 1943, and departed on an Eighth Army staff visit to North Africa shortly thereafter.[75]

His assignment as an observer with the Eighth Army in North Africa is significant here, mostly for the report he wrote and what he had to say about his views on command in the field. On 6-7 April, he was in the company of Lieutenant-General Brian Horrocks, Commander 10th Corps, during the battle of the Wadi Akarit.[76] What he saw and experienced influenced his view of modern battle and how to manage it. Like everyone else in England, Simonds had heard much about the freewheeling manoeuvre battles of the desert and of the *blitzkrieg* that had ripped through France in barely a month, but the fight at Wadi Akarit looked nothing like that. Simonds watched as Lieutenant-General Sir Oliver Leese's 30th Corps attacked with three divisions up to make holes in the enemy line, through which the tanks of Horrocks's 10th Corps were supposed to pass. What began as a silent attack by 30th Corps wound up requiring fifteen field and four medium regiments firing a total of 82,000 rounds, plus 160 Desert Air Force sorties just to crack the crust of the defences.[77] And when Horrocks attempted to send his tanks through the holes, they ran smack into the fire of German 88-millimetre anti-tank guns that had been sited in depth. When the enemy withdrew the following day, it was not because he was in danger of being outflanked or outmanoeuvred but because he had been mauled by tremendous firepower and infantry attacks. Simonds stayed with Horrocks during the pursuit to Sousse, but he believed that the spectacular manoeuvres of the 1940-42 period would now be unlikely. Anti-armour weapons, minefields, and concentrated fire from guns and mortars had greatly enhanced the ability of the defender to hold ground and stymie manoeuvre. Even if manoeuvre could be achieved, it would be only after a series of break-in battles by infantry, supported by artillery and tanks – meaning many closely coordinated infantry attacks. This was a definite departure from his thinking in his 1938 *Canadian Defence Quarterly* article, "An Army that Can Attack – A Division that Can Defend," in which he argued that infantry divisions would not need tanks because they would be used mostly for defence.[78]

Simonds also gleaned some lessons on how a corps headquarters should function. He liked the way in which Brian Horrocks's 10th Corps' Main and Rear Headquarters had standard layouts and standard drills for moving. He also admired the ability of Horrocks and his commanders to issue quick verbal orders, or short written ones, because they already had well-established and well-understood drills: "The battle procedure of the formations is excellent and manoeuvres have been carried out by formations on timings that could be ruled as impossible by many exercise umpires."[79] To make his point, he cited the example of how Horrocks received orders to move the 1st Armoured Division around the Mareth Line in an afternoon, then moved the formation sixty miles in the dark such that it was deployed by first light the following day. Simonds also liked Horrocks's practice of using a very small and non-permanent Tactical Headquarters. Tactical Headquarters that remained operational for an entire operation, like the one used by Montgomery at Eighth Army Headquarters, contained several staff officers, an aide-de-camp, and representatives from the artillery and the engineers, yet it still required principal staff officers to spend too "much time travelling between TAC and MAIN HQ" to ensure that they were in effective communication with the commander. Horrocks's Commander's Reconnaissance Group (Commander's Recce) was much smaller, usually consisting of only himself, a GSO 2, and an aide-de-camp, plus a few drivers, gunners, and a batman in a handful of vehicles. He used it "to visit forward divisions" during the day, but he did not control the battle from it, and he almost always returned to the Main Headquarters at night.[80] This arrangement enabled Horrocks to visit his divisional commanders and sniff the battlefield without degrading the locus of control, the Main Headquarters. That was the place from which he could get the most complete view of the battle at any one time – what was happening with all the divisions, the artillery, the engineers, and air forces – and influence the fight most directly. Main Headquarters was the hub. This is how Simonds would exercise control of his own headquarters in a little over a year's time.

In the meantime, he gained valuable experience as a divisional commander. At the end of April 1943, Simonds took command of the formation with which he would fight the first of his many battles – the 1st Canadian Infantry Division. Taking over from Major-General H.L.N. Salmon, who had been killed in a plane crash earlier that day, Simonds leapt into his new responsibilities with distinctive vigour.[81] He was the obvious choice to succeed Salmon on short notice. McNaughton realized that and put aside past differences to give Simonds the leading role for Canada's part in the invasion of Sicily. He arrived at the divisional headquarters in Norfolk House, London, on 29 April, familiarized himself with the limited planning that had been done for the operation to that point, and departed for Cairo on 1 May to work out the 1st Canadian Infantry Division's part in Operation Husky.[82] In Cairo, he met on 5 May with Oliver Leese, who was still commanding 30th Corps, the formation under which the Canadians would fight as part of Montgomery's Eighth Army. His GSO 1, Lieutenant-Colonel George Kitching, was amazed at how quickly Simonds determined what had to be done: "After writing out his intention, he told me to start writing as he dictated his plan."[83] This was typical of how Simonds operated. As one staff officer recalled, Simonds "was always working to a plan with a clear objective, which he took care to let us know in simple and direct terms ... he reduced problems in a flash to basic facts and variables, picked out those that mattered, ignored those that were side issues and made up his mind and got on with it."[84] He made his own plans and he tended towards one-option planning, weighing the factors and doing most of the computations in his head. If he compared various courses of action, he did not talk about them or write them down. What his staff got was *the* plan.

The plan set, Simonds turned his attention to training his troops for their tasks. A series of brigade and division exercises at the Combined Training

Centre, Inverary, Scotland, during May and June did much to raise the proficiency of the division.[85] To make certain that all units would train and fight the Simonds way, he issued direction to all commanding officers on 15 May. Without divulging the location of the upcoming operation, Simonds emphasized that it must be "thoroughly impressed on all troops that their objectives lie *inland* and that the capture of the beaches is only a means to an end."[86] He also wanted to be sure that order was established early and maintained for the advance to inland objectives: "The drift inland of disorganized groups of two or three men will offer the enemy an easy dispersed target for counter attack ... Platoon and company commanders must take hold ... *Quick reorganization, Proper organization of command and control, Determination of the commander to be master of the situation* are the secrets to success in the early stages of an assault landing." Consolidating captured objectives into firm bases was important too, because "the enemy is quick and skilful in counter-attack, and every operation must be launched from a firm base," where troops had deployed in a defensive posture, dug into shell scrapes, sited anti-tank guns and patrolled beyond the objective. He closed his message with this revealing thought on discipline: "There is ample scope for individual initiative in modern battle, but initiative must be directed towards the attainment of a common end in accordance with a common plan. Individual initiative which results in dispersion of effort on divergent plans, pulling in different directions, will not contribute to success." Simonds did not like disorganized battlefields.

He fought his division well in Sicily. They mounted a complicated combined operation from considerable distance, landed successfully at Pachino, marched nearly 200 kilometres in the heat of the Sicilian summer, much of it against German opposition, most of it over ragged mountains, and achieved all their objectives, including the critical task of unhinging the enemy's Etna positions. Of course, not everything was perfect. Simonds got into a shouting match with a brigadier who he did not believe was fighting his formation with sufficient drive, prompting the subordinate to resign.[87] Montgomery had to intervene to calm things down. Historian William J. McAndrew fairly criticized Simonds for failing to exploit the infiltration of an enemy delay position at Nissoria when he chose to relaunch a deliberate attack, heavily supported by artillery and air bombardment.[88] But Simonds learned too. A week after Nissoria, he quickly assembled a tank-infantry battle group to drive through a disorganized enemy position in the Salso River Valley.[89] The enemy was impressed. The 15th Panzergrenadier Division, which had encountered Canadians for the first time, noted: "Good soldier material ... English and Canadians harder in the attack than Americans. In general fair ways of fighting. In fieldcraft ... superior to our own troops. Very mobile at night."[90] Montgomery had a similarly favourable impression, and wrote to Crerar, "Your Canadians have done magnificently," noting also that "Simmonds [sic] handles his division well and their 'Q' side [logistics and administration] is first class."[91] With the confidence of Montgomery and a set of successful battles under his belt, Simonds's self-assuredness, already substantial, grew.

So did his knack for challenging superiors. Following the unopposed landing at Reggio Calabria on 3 September, Simonds used a number of combined-arms battle groups to advance quickly up the "foot" of Italy, against an enemy that was in the process of withdrawing to the area between Foggia and Salerno. On 20 September, he received orders from the Commander 13th British Corps, Lieutenant-General Miles Dempsey, to advance on two axes towards Foggia. But the two proposed axes were "separated by 70 miles" at the start. Simonds objected:

> I consider advancing a single division on such widely separate axes objectionable from both a tactical and an administrative point of view. The alternative is to split the division and place the right flanking brigade under command of another formation. This I believe to be contrary to the Army Commander's fixed policy and I certainly consider it unsound because the problem of dissipating the support arms and administrative effort remains.[92]

As an alternative, Simonds asked: "Would it not be better to place [on the far left flank] an independent brigade which has all its own allotment of supporting arms without cutting those of a division[?] ... Would it not be possible to pass 231 B[riga]de across to the Gravina area?" Simonds was right. It made no sense for one division to control a front so wide that the elements would be out of wireless range, but not much came of his protest. Shortly after writing the note, he came down with jaundice and had to be temporarily replaced in command by Brigadier Chris Vokes from the 2nd Canadian Infantry Brigade. The advance proceeded more or less as Dempsey had conceived it, but the corps commander did not seem to take excessive offence at Simonds's suggestions: "My dear Guy, I am so sorry indeed that you have had to fall out for a short time ... I will see that your Div. does not get into any trouble in your absence! If there is anything that you want, please let me know."[93] It was more than just etiquette. Dempsey harboured no ill feelings towards Simonds. Less than a year later, they would be working well together when Simonds commanded a corps in Dempsey's British Second Army.[94]

Simonds had no such collegial relationship with Crerar, mostly because of Crerar's insecurities. By December 1943, Simonds had recovered from jaundice and moved on to command the 5th Canadian Armoured Division, which had recently deployed to the Mediterranean as part of Crerar's two-division 1st Canadian Corps. The months of November and December were particularly frustrating for Simonds. He had left command of a highly successful division to take over a formation with commanders and staff he barely knew (and a few he did not like), and which was supposed to inherit the beat-up tanks and equipment of the 7th Armoured Division, a British formation that had re-deployed to England in preparation for Operation Overlord. It only annoyed Simonds further that he knew nothing of the decision to deploy the 1st Canadian Corps Headquarters and the 5th Canadian Armoured Division to the Mediter-ranean, let alone the attendant command changes that would affect him, until it happened. For some reason, he took his move to the 5th Canadian Armoured Division to be a sign that he had lost the confidence of the chain of command.[95] So he was probably in bad temper when he returned to his headquarters on 2 December to find one of Crerar's staff captains in his caravan, mucking about with muddy boots and taking measurements so that Crerar could build some-thing similar for himself.[96] Simonds blasted the young captain for not having obtained proper permission to enter the caravan and sent him on his way. Crerar, inordinately sensitive to slights of any kind, took the gesture to be a "personal discourtesy" from a subordinate whose recent experiences and accolades had made him too big for his britches.[97] He was envious of the battle experience Simonds had gained and personally piqued when people such as Montgomery made remarks like, "You have no one else with his experience."[98] Simonds's deci-sion to fire a number of "useless" commanders and staff, all of whom had trained under Crerar, only added fuel to the fire.[99] In particular, the 5th Canadian Ar-moured Division Commander Royal Artillery (CRA) and a few artillery unit commanders were on the chopping block, and Simonds was typically direct in explaining his rationale: "It is a very clear duty and responsibility to see that our troops have the *best* – not just the 'good enough' – leadership." What pre-vented commanders from doing the right thing when they found incompetent leaders was "outworn prejudices ... [of] seniority, positions on 'lists,' the fact that so and so has done such and such a job for a certain time and hasn't done anything wrong (probably because he hasn't done anything at all!) and lastly a failure to face up to the unpleasantness of coming face to face with an officer ... and telling him that he has shot his bolt."[100] Crerar took the tone and the content to be a personal indictment for having let this lethargy continue under his nose. It irked him.

But Crerar could be devious too. He accused Simonds of having "over-stretched nerves" and he sent letters to both Montgomery and the Canadian Chief of the General Staff, Lieutenant-General Ken Stuart, explaining that he "had serious cause to doubt [Simmonds's] suitability for higher command."[101] Montgomery, for one, was unmoved:

> I have the highest opinion of Simonds. He tried to go off the rails once or twice when he first went into action with his division; but I pulled him back again and taught him his stuff. Briefly, my views are that Simonds is a first class soldier. After a period with an armoured division he will be suitable for a corps. He will be valuable in the Canadian Forces as you have no one else with his experience ... I do not, of course, know what has taken place between you and Simonds. He is directly under my command for training and so on, but of course would deal with you on purely Canadian matters. If you have been sending him any instructions or directions on training he might possibly ignore them!! He gets that from me – verbally.[102]

This response might have helped Simonds in the short term, but it did nothing to ease Crerar's insecurities or his vindictiveness over the long term. The incident did not catch either Crerar or Simonds at their best. The uncompromising Simonds insisted on "absolute" control over officer appointments under his command and the nitpicking Crerar wanted to retain the final word on all senior officer appointments.[103] There was bound to be trouble, then and in the future.

Simonds still got his corps, though. On 30 January, he formally assumed command of 2nd Canadian Corps, then training in England for Overlord. He took over from Lieutenant-General Ernest W. Sansom, a now-corpulent First World War veteran, thirteen years Simonds's senior and widely regarded as a talentless nonentity by everyone except McNaughton.[104] Given that sort of stewardship over the preceding months, Simonds suspected that the corps would have a considerable amount of deadwood in the division's senior ranks. His instincts were good. A cursory review of the staff list for the 2nd Canadian Corps Headquarters revealed a few names that Simonds recognized as less-than-adequate talents who had to go. He also had to send a message that life for everyone in the headquarters was about to get much more serious – and he did. At his first meeting with the assembled headquarters staff officers, he walked into the room, announced to everyone that there were a number of them in whom he had "not much confidence," and advised them that he would let everyone know the following day who was staying and who was going.[105] Many went. One staff officer who stayed remembered that "each morning at breakfast another staff officer was gone," most being replaced by people whom Simonds knew and trusted from Italy.[106] To name just two, Lieutenant-Colonel Geoffrey

Walsh, Simonds's Commander Royal Engineers (CRE) at the 1st Canadian Infantry Division, came to 2nd Canadian Corps as Chief Engineer, and his old CRA, Brigadier A.B. Matthews, became Commander, Corps Royal Artillery (CCRA). His Brigadier General Staff, however, had not served with him in Italy. Brigadier N. Elliot Rodger had recently been commanding the 10th Canadian Infantry Brigade in the 4th Canadian Armoured Division, but he had caught Simonds's eye earlier when Rodger had worked as a personal assistant to McNaughton while Simonds was BGS 1st Canadian Corps. Rodger was a "young officer (36 years) with a keen brain."[107] No doubt, Simonds liked that, but it was probably more that Rodger was also described as having a "nice personality, most co-operative. Knows his own mind and impresses [sic] it in a nice manner." His Junior War Staff Course report also noted his "quick and methodical" brain, his capacity for "tackling details of problems," and his "pleasant personality."[108] That sort of affability was the perfect foil to Simonds's sometimes intolerant and abrupt manner, a failing that Simonds himself acknowledged: "I know I have a hot and quick temper ... It is a fault I know, but it has always been with me and I am afraid it always will be ... I am impatient of stupidity, dullness and indifference – or gaucheness, and I know I sometimes lose my temper when I shouldn't."[109] Rodger was the perfect buffer for these proclivities. Simonds chose him well.

Simonds took a scythe to the leadership of the divisions in the corps as well. He inspected the brigades in early February and quickly decided who was fit for command and who was not. This was entirely reminiscent of Montgomery's 1942 inspections of 1st Canadian Corps, and the result was a similar number of rolling heads. The 2nd Canadian Infantry Division seemed to be worst off. There Simonds prodded the newly appointed GOC, Major-General Charles Foulkes, to replace all three brigade commanders and his GSO 1. In the 4th Canadian Armoured Division, Simonds recalled Kitching from Italy, where he had been commanding the 11th Canadian Infantry Brigade, to replace the fifty-seven-year-old Major-General Frank Worthington.[110] He also replaced the CRA and the CRE, and he brought back from Italy Brigadier J.C. Jefferson to command the 10th Canadian Infantry Brigade and Brigadier B.L. Booth to assume command of the 4th Canadian Armoured Brigade.

In a 19 February directive entitled "Efficiency of Command," Simonds made it clear to all commanders in 2nd Canadian Corps that he expected them to do the same when they found subordinate commanders who were not "competent, fit and energetic."[111] The annex to the directive provided Simonds's criteria for determining whether or not an officer was fit for his job. Was he of good character, meaning did he have the "resolution, determination, and drive to get things done"? Was he loyal? Could his superiors, peers, and subordinates count on him? Was he confident? For without confidence no officer could expect to inspire others. Did the officer have a strong sense of duty? Did he know his job thoroughly as a commander? In other words, did he know "how to command – how to delegate to his subordinates and his staff, how to control, how to position himself on the battlefield and make use of his communications, and, most importantly ... [did he] have an understanding of human nature and how to 'get at' men"? Was he capable of sound judgment? Could he be counted upon to use his initiative? Was he both physically fit and mentally alert? Interestingly, Simonds wanted his formation commanders to ask whether each of their subordinate officers was young enough for the job: "A man is never too young for a job, but he may well be too old, for age reduces speed of mental and physical reaction." Nearly all the officers Simonds sacked were replaced with younger men. The Sansom era in 2nd Canadian Corps was over. That much was clear.

Although Simonds earned a reputation as a cold and callous fish for excising so many key command and staff officers, he was not entirely heartless. As he explained in a letter to Crerar, his mental exercise for determining whether an officer stayed or went ran something like this:

> I have before me an individual into whose record I have gone as thoroughly as I am able. I have reached the conclusion that he is really not up to his job and I realize that when I make an adverse report, it must seriously affect his future and the welfare of his family. But this officer is responsible for the training, efficiency and morale of a group of Canadian soldiers who also have families, whom they have left to do their duty in the service of their country. Am I justified in giving sympathetic consideration to this individual if, by doing so, all these others may suffer and their efforts and sacrifices perhaps be nullified through indifferent leadership or direction?[112]

Most people would have agreed with that sort of reasoning, but Simonds was one of the few Canadian general officers who could put personal feelings and relationships aside and do what he believed to be the right thing. Of his superiors in the Canadian Army, McNaughton had none of that quality, and Crerar did not have enough of it. That's why Simonds looked on Montgomery as a role model.

He continued Montgomery's progressive approach to training as well. It began with laying down an operational policy – how he intended his corps to fight. As his corps was not involved in the first wave of the Overlord assault, Simonds determined that his probable role would be "to pass through a beach-head which has been secured by assaulting forces and attack, wear down and destroy German troops."[113] He anticipated that German troops in opposition would do one of two things: delay and retire, or stand and fight a deliberate defence. Against a retiring enemy, "determined infiltration, with quick artillery support controlled by forward observation officers will usually dislodge these rear parties." But "when the Germans decide to stand and fight a defensive battle, attack without adequate reconnaissance and preparation will not succeed." Having seen how the Germans fought their defensive battles, Simonds also understood that the "success of the offensive battle hinges on the defeat of the German counter-attacks, with sufficient of our own reserves in hand to launch a new phase as soon as the enemy strength has spent itself. The defeat of these counter attacks must form part of the original plan of attack, which must include arrangements for artillery support and the forward moves of infantry supporting weapons – including tanks – on the objective." Simonds also stressed the importance of the initial attacks' penetrating to a depth of approximately 4,000 yards in order to overrun the enemy's mortars, which could cause so much damage from their reverse-slope positions. He also emphasized moving the artillery (and its ammunition) forward to support subsequent phases of the attack, and he prescribed three methods for using tanks, anti-tank guns, and artillery concentrations to defeat enemy armour and self-propelled guns in the counterattack: "Anti-tank guns well up with the leading infantry ... tanks following close behind the leading infantry ... [and m]edium artillery concentrations directed by a forward observing officer [FOO]." These were sensible suggestions, although they rested on the assumption that there would be sufficient time to implement any of the prescriptions *before* German tanks and anti-tank guns could counterattack. Indeed, this was to prove a problem in Normandy when tanks were not *with*, or *in front of*, the assaulting infantry. Still, in spite of this oversight, his superiors agreed with his policies. Montgomery was in "complete agreement" and Dempsey wrote, "I agree with everything you say."[114]

With a clear understanding of how the corps would fight, it remained only to pass on the operational policy and practise it. To do this, Simonds began with a corps study week, which took place during 13-18 March 1944, attended by "all commanders and commanding officers ... all staff officers and head of services down to grade II level" as well representatives from the 21st Army Group, First Canadian Army, Second Army, 12th Corps, CMHQ, the Canadian Reinforcement Unit (CRU), and the School of Artillery.[115] The only 2nd Canadian Corps formation that did not participate was the 3rd Canadian Infantry Division, which was by this time under the command of Lieutenant-General John Crocker's 1st Corps for the Overlord training and assault. The program that Simonds designed reflected his operational policy directive to a tee. There were sessions on the infantry and armoured divisions in the advance "following retiring German Forces" and "in the attack" against a deliberate German defence, and the respective General Officers Commanding from the 2nd Canadian Infantry Division and the 4th Canadian Armoured Division chaired the appropriate sessions, although Simonds insisted that "the officer responsible for each study ... discuss his subject with me as soon as he has had time to prepare an outline."[116] Other subjects were similarly parcelled out to the appropriate subject matter experts. The Chief Engineer led the session on the engineers in the advance and the attack, the CCRA did the same for the artillery, Rodger (as Chief of Staff) gave a lecture-demonstration on the organization of headquarters and its communications, the corps air advisor handled "Co-operation with Air Forces," and the Deputy Adjutant and Quartermaster General (DA & QMG) laid down procedures for administration in the field. There were also periods on obstacle crossings, road movement, passage through defiles, clearing towns and villages, and night attacks. In the delivery of the material, Simonds insisted that "each subject will be presented as a model demonstration or playlet. Lecturing will be reduced to a minimum ... Following each main subject, the audience will be encouraged to express views on points raised. I wish the discussion to be on strictly practical lines." Montgomery sat in on the final sessions during 18 March and he addressed the assembled officers at the close of the training, visibly pleased that the proceedings had been so much in line with his philosophy for training and fighting.[117]

To build on the groundwork of corps study week, Simonds planned a series of exercises. His intention was to start with several headquarters and signals exercises then build up to a full-scale corps field exercise.[118] During the first week of April, his headquarters began with the basics of staff procedures in the field and movement, conducting no less than six moves of the Main Headquarters in seven days.[119] As Chief of Staff, Rodger took the lead on most of the corps headquarters training, but Simonds participated too. He gave guidance on modifying the Main Headquarters layout to allow for greater dispersion and he "visited all branches of [the] headquarters ... to outline functions of the staff in each branch."[120] Concurrent with the corps headquarters exercise, the 4th Canadian Armoured Division conducted its own signals exercise down to brigade headquarters level, while the 2nd Canadian Infantry Division, which was further along in its training, carried out field training for an advance and an assault across a water obstacle during Exercise Step. A corps signals exercise (Last) took place on 13-19 April to train headquarters down to brigade level.[121] The scenario required the elements of the corps to advance against a delaying German enemy and to conduct a set-piece attack on a well-prepared enemy position. Simonds took the opportunity to exercise himself as well. The 2nd Canadian Corps war diary entry for 15 April records: "GOC spent the early part of the morning planning the corps attack on main enemy defensive position on Exercise 'LAST.'"

Later in the morning GOC went forward to 2 Canadian Infantry Division and 4 Canadian Armoured Division and outlined his plan for the attack."[122] This was the sort of thing that McNaughton had rarely done on exercise. Whereas McNaughton figured he could think his way through a tactical problem when the time came, and Foulkes never wanted to be caught making a mistake, Simonds wanted to keep his skills sharp. Unfortunately, Simonds never did get to have his full-scale corps exercise. A number of factors conspired against it – training area restrictions, equipment shortages, and the requirement to water-proof operational vehicles for Overlord among them. The 4th Canadian Armoured Division, for example, had to content itself with limited tank-infantry training in early April, some assault boat training for the battalions of the 10th Canadian Infantry Brigade in the middle of the month, and live-fire training for the infantry battalions in mid-May.[123] Kitching's division never had a full-scale exercise – and this mattered later on.

The 2nd Canadian Infantry Division had already had one full-scale exercise to its credit (Step) by the time it took part in Exercise Kate, which began on 26 April and lasted until 5 May. Kate had its origins in the First Canadian Army planning for the crossing of the Seine and the capture of Le Havre. Simonds had received orders on 11 April to conduct an exercise to practise the 2nd Canadian Infantry Division in the crossing of a tidal estuary, so he arranged an exercise on the Trent River in Yorkshire. Equipment and training area restrictions precluded assaults above battalion level, but the headquarters of the division and its brigades would participate fully in what was, in essence, a re-hearsal for the Seine river crossing. Simonds took a keen interest in Kate. He drafted the outline plan for the assault himself, he spent most of 20 April working on a TEWT entitled "The Assault Crossing of a Tidal Estuary,"[124] his Tactical Headquarters participated in the exercise, and he watched all the river crossing operations. Some of what he saw did not please him. On 29 April, after observing the 5th Canadian Infantry Brigade assault, Simonds "met all officers of 1 Canadian Army Troop Engineers and gave them a short talk on the necessity of maintaining strict discipline and also criticism of their work."[125] After seeing both the 4th and 5th Canadian Infantry Brigades conduct their assaults, he met on 4 May with the Chief Engineers from the 21st Army Group and First Canadian Army, his own Chief Engineer, his Chief of Staff, and Foulkes. He was not happy. He decided that the engineers as well as the 4th and 5th Canadian Infantry Brigades "would remain on the River Trent until 20 May 44 to carry out storm boat and rafting tr[ainin]g."[126] He also deemed that "any eq[ui]p[men]t required for the tr[ainin]g will be provided ... even if operational stocks had to be used." Kate continued until late May. The conduct of the manoeuvres did not reflect particularly well on Charles Foulkes, whom Simonds did not like in the first place.[127] No evidence exists that he considered relieving Foulkes at this stage, so any explanation of why he resisted the temptation to fire Foulkes remains a matter of speculation. Perhaps he thought it too late in the training before a major operation for a switch. Given his past difficulties with Crerar, and knowing that Crerar favoured Foulkes, Simonds probably thought that it would have been impossible to dump the divisional commander in the days before Overlord. Whatever the reason, in spite of Foulkes's lacklustre performance during the training period, Simonds kept him in command.

Simonds arrived in Normandy with his Tactical Headquarters on 25 June, but he did not enter battle for three weeks. Once in the bridgehead area, he made the normal round of visits to update himself on what was happening in the Anglo-Canadian sector. In the first few days, he met with Crerar at the First Canadian Army, Dempsey at the British Second Army, and Montgomery at the 21st Army Group. He watched as the 8th Corps' attempt to encircle the German-defended city of Caen from the west and south, Operation Epsom, faltered in the face of furious German counterattacks from 26 to 30 June. From John Crocker's Tactical Headquarters, he observed as 1st Corps, with the 3rd Canadian Infantry Division under command and bomber command aircraft in support, ground its way to the capture of northern Caen during Operation Charnwood, from 7 to 9 July.[128] (See pages 148-57 above.) These observations confirmed a conclusion he had reached at Wadi Akarit – "adv[ancing] in the face of the enemy is still only possible with properly combined fire and mov[ement]."[129] Simonds passed this message back to his "G" staff and his divisions, then still in England and awaiting imminent embarkation for France. He added: "Attacking t[roop]s MUST keep up with their supporting fire." Simonds would build his attacks around fire plans. His headquarters became operational on 11 July, assuming control of the Caen sector, which essentially ran along the river Orne in the city of Caen itself. At that time, he had the 2nd Canadian Infantry Division in western Caen, the 3rd Canadian Infantry Division in eastern Caen, and the 2nd Canadian Armoured Brigade and an Army Group Royal Artillery (AGRA) under command. On 13 July, Dempsey dropped by 2nd Canadian Corps Headquarters to advise Simonds of the part he would play in the upcoming operation, called Goodwood.[130]

An ambitious plan, Goodwood, like Charnwood, had its roots in the broader operational plan for the Normandy Campaign. On 10 July, Montgomery had sent his thoughts on the campaign to his four army commanders: "My broad policy remains unchanged. It is to draw the main enemy forces into the battle on our eastern flank ... so that our affairs on the western flank may proceed easier."[131] With that premise, Dempsey's Second Army operations would have to be "so staged that they will have a direct influence on the operations of [US

General Omar Bradley's] First Army." The outgrowth of this direction was Dempsey's plan to launch a three-armoured division thrust south of Caen from the shallow bridgehead east of the river Orne. Operations Epsom and Charnwood had cost the Second Army dearly in infantry casualties, but, as Dempsey later related, "our strength in tanks was increasing all the time ... So we could well afford, and it was desirable, to plan an operation in which we could utilize that surplus of tanks and economize in infantry."[132] Aided by the dropping of "7,700 U.S. tons" of bombs by Allied air forces in advance of the attack, Montgomery hoped that Lieutenant-General Sir Richard O'Connor's tank-heavy 8th Corps would be able to drive to the Vimont-Bourguébus area and even as far south as Bretteville-sur-Laize. While O'Connor's tanks were punching south, Dempsey wanted 2nd Canadian Corps to secure the right flank of 8th Corps. To that end, the Canadians would have to "capture VAUCELLES, get through communications and establish themselves in a very firm bridgehead on the general line FLEURY-CORMELLES-MONDEVILLE."[133] Only when that was secure could 8th Corps "crack about" to destroy any remaining enemy between their tank corridor and the Canadian bridgehead on the southern outskirts of Caen. Faced with an attack of such force, surely the Germans would be forced to throw armoured reserves into the eastern bridgehead battle, thereby making the American breakout in the west easier – or at least that was the rationale.

Simonds's plan, which he issued on 16 July, reflected both his predilection for firepower and his uneasiness with his two infantry divisional commanders.[134] We have already seen how the Overlord work-up training had alerted Simonds to Foulkes's shortcomings. Keller, on the other hand, was a lesser-known commodity. He had a reputation as a blood-and-guts infantry soldier, but Simonds had never served in the same formation with him. Crocker, though, had written Crerar on 5 July recommending Keller's removal, and it is hard to imagine that he and Simonds would not have discussed Keller in their many meetings before 16 July, especially since Crerar had asked Simonds to look into the matter on 10 July.[135] Simonds can only have been shocked and discouraged when Keller, on being interviewed concerning Crocker's observations, was "distinctly upset" and replied that he was not medically fit to withstand the strains of high command in battle.[136] How much planning latitude does a commander grant a subordinate like that?

Very little. Simonds more or less told both Foulkes and Keller how to deploy their brigades, and he set the fire plan through his CCRA, Matthews.[137] (See Map 10.) Keller's 3rd Canadian Infantry Division would advance with two brigades – the 8th and the 9th – from the area of Le Bas de Ranville, along the east bank of the Orne, through Colombelles, and into Faubourg de Vaucelles and Giberville. Given that the enemy was well posted, Simonds might have liked more time for patrols to gather "details of the minefields, wire obstacles, [and defensive] localities,"[138] but there was no time for detailed reconnaissance because the 8th and 9th Canadian Infantry Brigades would not arrive at their forming-up places on the other side of the river until a few hours before the attack. Without a clear picture of how the enemy was deployed, and in what strength, Simonds decided to blast Keller's brigades onto their objectives behind a barrage fired by four field regiments. He directed Keller to have the 7th Canadian Infantry Brigade standing by in Caen, prepared to patrol across the river into Faubourg de Vaucelles if the attacks of the 8th and 9th Canadian Infantry Brigades were delayed. In the 2nd Canadian Infantry Division sector, Simonds directed Foulkes to capture Louvigny in the west, bridge the river Orne in the city of Caen, and be prepared to exploit to the high ground from St. André-sur-Orne to Verrières if possible.

The attacks ran into trouble within three hours of the 0745 H-hour on 18 July. The 8th Canadian Infantry Brigade advance from Le Bas de Ranville met with stiff enemy opposition at Colombelles and the steelworks northwest of Giberville. On the right, Le Régiment de la Chaudière ran into sniper and machine gun fire from a very strong enemy position anchored on the chateau north of Colombelles. They wanted to deal with it, but the problem was that any neutralizing fire that the barrage may have provided had already disappeared when the curtain of shells passed harmlessly over the heads of the German defenders and out of sight. On-call fire might have been arranged, but Forward Observation Officers (FOOs) and Air Observation Posts (OPs) had a difficult time identifying targets through the combined dust and smoke of the barrage and the Goodwood air attacks.[139] At 1330 hours, with the follow-on battalions piling up behind the Chaudières, the brigade commander, Brigadier Ken Blackader, arranged for an air strike, which proved ineffective and disappointing. Not until 1440, four hours after the initial encounter, could a divisional artillery concentration be arranged to shell the chateau and pave a way for the Chaudières to enter and clear the position. On the left, the Queen's Own Rifles of Canada also lost the barrage, but at least they had the tank support of the 6th Canadian Armoured Regiment. They skirted the steelworks, which Blackader now assigned to his depth battalion, the North Shore Regiment, then moved into Giberville for a tough day of fighting against a combined half-battalion-sized force from the 16th Luftwaffe Field Division and the 21st Panzer Division, finally securing the town by late afternoon. About this time, Keller decided that 9th Canadian Infantry Brigade would bypass the steelworks and push into Faubourg de Vaucelles.

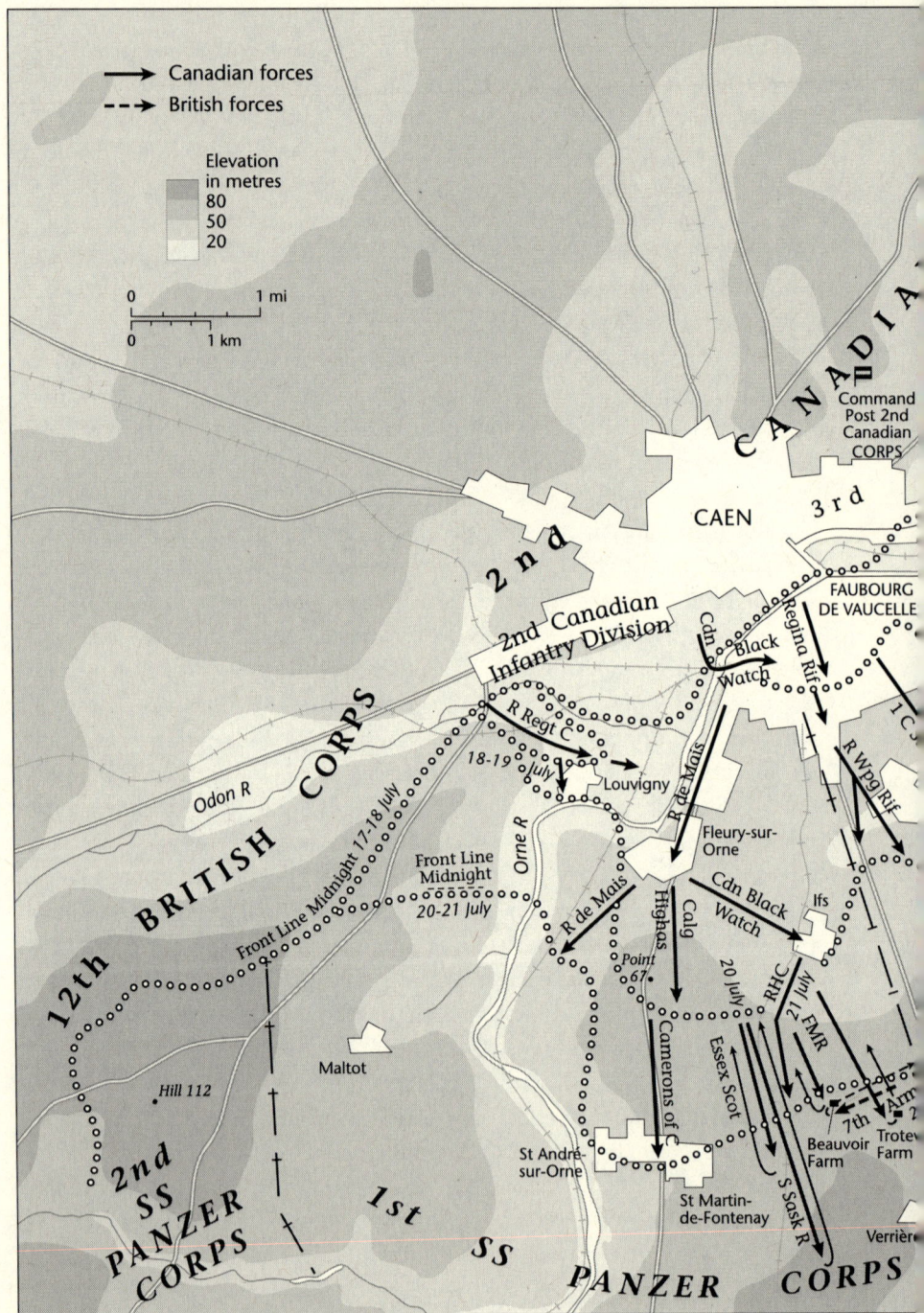

**MAP 10**   The battle of Bourguébus ridge, 18-21 July 1944.

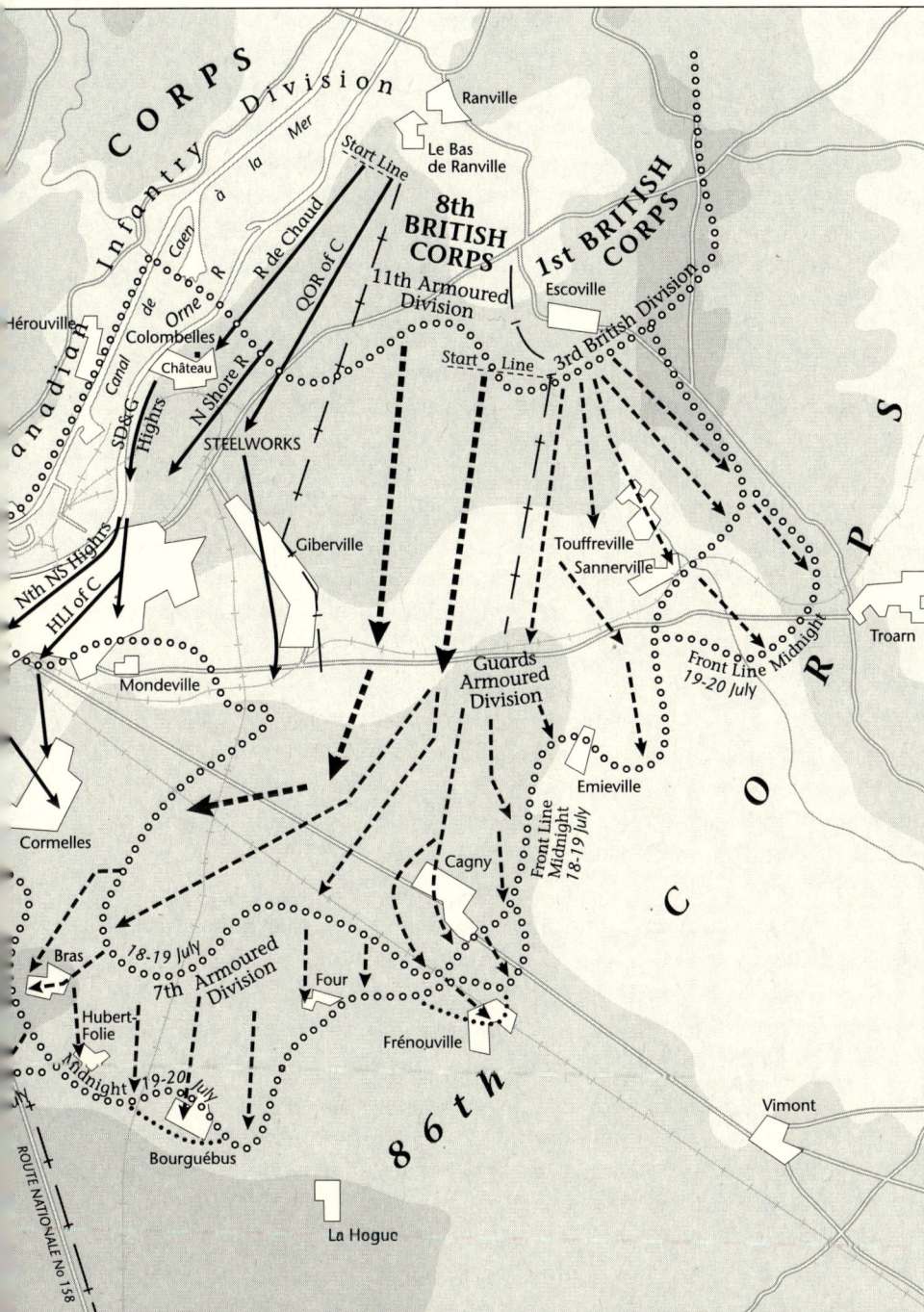

Adapted from Colonel C.P. Stacey, *The Victory Campaign: The Operations in Northwest Europe, 1944-1945* (Ottawa: Queen's Printer, 1966), map 3.

Simonds, however, had been observing the battle from the high ground immediately north of Caen and had long since determined not to wait for the 8th or 9th Canadian Infantry Brigades. Late in the morning, as it became clear that the chateau and the steelworks would be major problems, he ordered Brigadier Harry Foster's 7th Canadian Infantry Brigade to patrol across the Orne and reinforce any success that might be attained. Soon scouts from the Regina Rifles were across the river and, with the assistance of a few French resistance fighters, were making their way into Vaucelles and identifying both routes and enemy positions.[140] Before the main body crossed the river, Simonds dropped by the 7th Canadian Infantry Brigade location in Caen and "spoke to individuals congratulating them on the efforts of their f[or]m[atio]n during the day."[141] When the Reginas crossed the river a few hours later, the artillery had pinpointed targets to neutralize, and the assaulting infantry were led to their objectives by scouts who had reconnoitred routes earlier. This skillful action contrasted sharply with the blind-barraging exercise at Colombelles. Sometimes it paid to spend a few more hours on reconnaissance.

The second phase of Operation Atlantic saw the 2nd Canadian Infantry Division in action for the first time since its horrible baptism by fire at Dieppe two years earlier. Early in the evening of 18 July, the 4th Canadian Infantry Brigade advanced with the support of divisional artillery against Louvigny, west of the Orne. Simonds had hoped that Brigadier Sherwood Lett's brigade might move quickly through Louvigny and establish a crossing over the river for an advance on Fleury-sur-Orne and St. André-sur-Orne, but the advance was slow. Elements of the newly arrived German 272nd Infantry Division fought tenaciously and held the 4th Canadian Infantry Brigade's battalions out of Louvigny for the night. When there appeared to be little likelihood of going forward on the western flank, Simonds prodded Foulkes to cross the Orne in the centre of Caen with the 5th Canadian Infantry Brigade. Foulkes in turn passed the order on to Brigadier W.J. Megill, who crossed the Orne with the Black Watch of Canada at 2215 hours, against surprisingly light opposition. This enabled the engineers to begin work on a tank-bridge, which was complete by noon on 19 July.

Over the next two days, Simonds expanded his bridgehead over the Orne. At 1000 hours on 19 July, he met with Foulkes and Keller in Caen to discuss the attacks that were to begin shortly after noon that day.[142] Not long afterwards, the 3rd Canadian Infantry Division cleared Faubourg de Vaucelles and forced the remaining enemy out of Cormelles, while the 2nd Canadian Infantry Division pushed out to capture, in succession, Fleury-sur-Orne, Point 67, and the town of Ifs. These objectives were not obtained without some difficult fighting, and they were heavily supported by artillery fire, including several concentrations by medium regiments to subdue pockets of resistance and to break up counterattacks, but Simonds had reached the objective line that Dempsey had set out for him.

This is where the Canadian advances in Operation Atlantic should have ended. The armoured advance of Goodwood had lost all momentum, the tanks of O'Connor's 8th Corps having reached only the line Bras-Bourguébus-Frénouville, a full eight kilometres short of their objective at Bretteville-sur-Laize, and at a staggering cost of 322 tank casualties to well-sited German anti-tank guns and strong counterattacks from the 21st Panzer Division and 1st SS Panzer Division.[143] Given that situation, Dempsey prudently decided to discontinue the advance. O'Connor was only to complete the capture of Bourguébus with the 7th Armoured Division, and he was to hand Bras and Hubert-Folie over to Simonds, whose infantry would hold those positions. Simonds had already seized his Atlantic/Goodwood objectives, but he decided to "clear [St.] ANDRE-SUR-ORNE, and [the] high ground VERRIERES" and he confirmed the tasks during an orders group at 2nd Canadian Infantry Division Main Headquarters at 1000 on 20 July, well before the time he met with Dempsey later that afternoon.[144] Historian Terry Copp has rightly questioned Simonds's intentions here.[145] There was no need to push on to the ridge at this point. The Goodwood advance had stalled, so his flank protection operation was no longer necessary. Besides, Dempsey had no intention of being dragged into a costly infantry slugging match; the tank-heavy Goodwood operation had been designed in part to avoid that kind of attrition battle. Quite likely, Simonds's personal and national pride interfered with his judgment in this instance. Earlier, he had spoken of the need to "counterbalance [the] small numbers of [the] C[ana]d[ia]n Army by excellence of performance" when he addressed the newly arrived 4th Canadian Infantry Brigade.[146] That was no rationale, however, for launching an unnecessary attack.

The hastily arranged attacks of 20 July proved very costly. Simonds gave Foulkes the task of capturing the Verrières ridge with the yet-uncommitted 6th Canadian Infantry Brigade under Brigadier H.A. Young, and he had Matthews coordinate extensive artillery and air support for the task, something that took until midday on 20 July to arrange. On the right, three Army Groups Royal Artillery (AGsRA) and the divisional artillery of both the 2nd and 3rd Canadian Infantry Divisions fired at rapid rate for three minutes on St. André-sur-Orne at noon, a full three hours before the attack by the Queen's Own Cameron Highlanders of Canada.[147] When the Camerons stepped off shortly after 1500 hours, they did so behind smaller timed concentrations, and with the support of a tank squadron from the 27th Canadian Armoured Regiment, which preceded the infantry, engaging targets on the outskirts of St. André-sur-Orne. The

Camerons made it into the town and managed to hold on despite several counterattacks and indirect fire, which the enemy directed with great accuracy from the heights of Hill 112 on the west side of the Orne. On the left, where the 7th Armoured Division tanks had been withdrawn from the Troteval and Beauvoir Farms, Les Fusiliers de Mont-Royal, supported by two squadrons from the 27th Canadian Armoured Regiment, failed to capture their objective of Verrières. They only managed to reach the ground recently abandoned by the 7th Armoured Division, where they held on for barely a day before counterattacks drove them back to the area just north of Beauvoir Farm on 21 July. In the centre, the South Saskatchewan Regiment, moving behind a 300-metre-deep barrage – but without supporting tanks – made it onto the ridge. Once the neutralizing fire of the barrage had moved on, however, the assaulting companies found themselves dangerously exposed to enemy indirect fire and counterattacking tanks from the 2nd Panzer Division, which had emerged from the area of the Verrières village to intercept the anti-tank guns that the South Saskatchewans were trying desperately to bring forward. When the South Saskatchewans attempted a withdrawal from the ridge to more defensible ground, some of their understandably haggard troops passed through the Essex Scottish Regiment, which was in the process of pulling up behind them. Interpreting the Saskatchewans' haste as panic, two companies of Essex soldiers broke and fell into disorderly retreat, while the two remaining companies held their ground, barely, at the foot of the ridge overnight. Frantic calls for fire resulted in several concentrations on enemy counterattacks, but they were not enough to stave off the near-decimation of the remaining Essex troops, who had become ineffective by mid-afternoon on 21 July. It took an attack at 1800 hours by the Black Watch, supported by tanks from the 6th and 27th Canadian Armoured Regiments plus a barrage, to recapture the ground on which the Essex had been overrun and regain the salient the enemy had carved between the Camerons and the Fusiliers. The unsuccessful and unnecessary attempt to take Verrières ridge had cost the 2nd Canadian Infantry Division 1,149 casualties, 254 of them killed.[148]

Simonds was stubborn, though, and four days after Atlantic had stalled at the foot of Verrières ridge, he again tried to capture the terrain feature, with similar results (see Map 11). For Operation Spring, he had the added punch of the British 7th Armoured and Guards Armoured Divisions, in addition to his two Canadian infantry divisions.[149] His plan was reasonable enough in concept. He would use his two infantry divisions to break into the enemy defences on the ridge before first light on 25 July, then exploit to the area of Cramesnil and beyond with the armoured divisions.[150] The attacks would be supported by timed concentrations instead of the "standard barrage support," which placed most of its rounds on terrain not occupied by the enemy and always alerted defenders

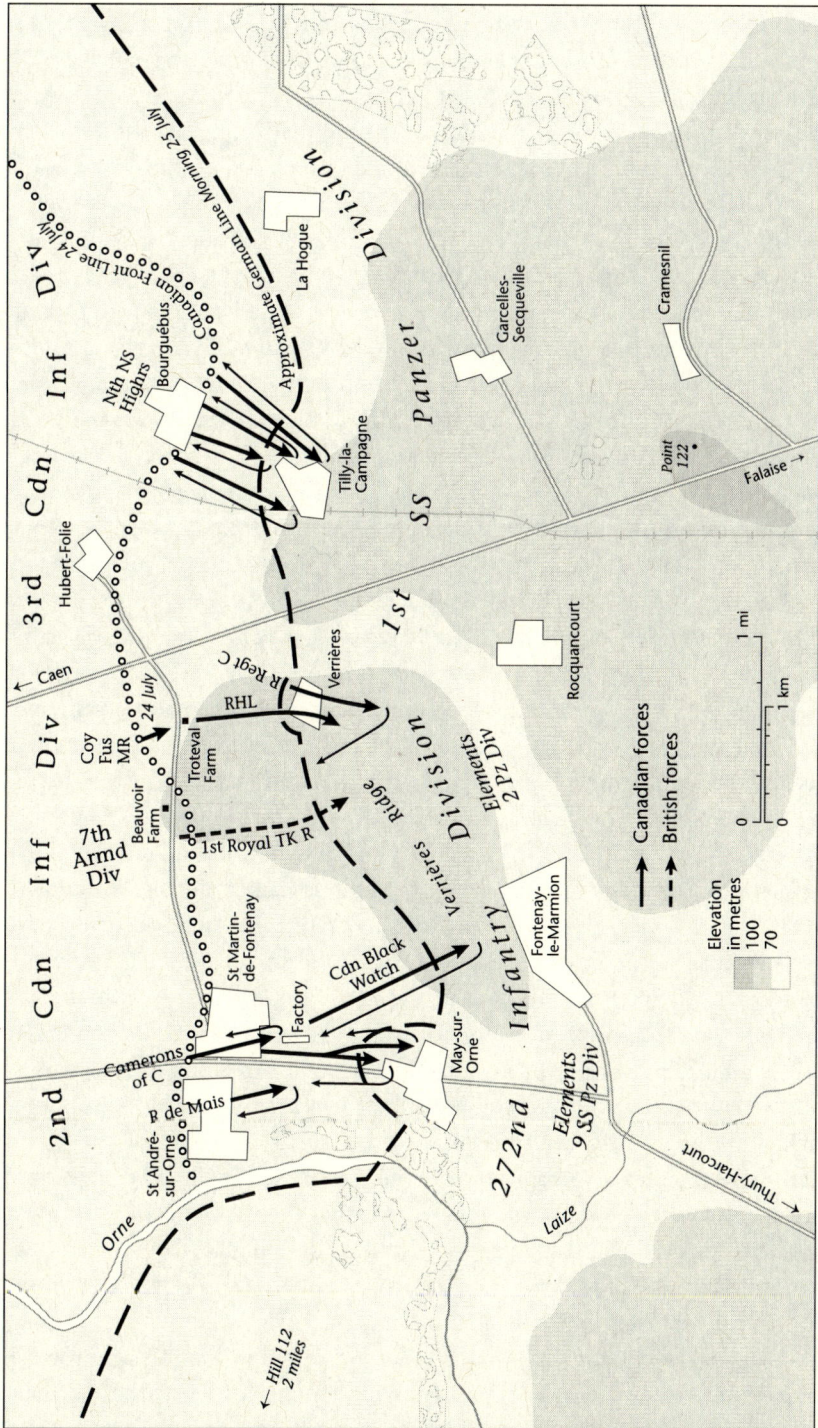

MAP 11 Verrières ridge–Tilly-la-Campagne, 25 July 1944. Adapted from Stacey, *The Victory Campaign*.

Map labels:

2nd Cdn Inf Div
7th Armd Div
3rd Cdn Inf Div
Nth NS Highrs
Bourguébus
La Hogue
Garcelles-Secqueville
Cramesnil
Tilly-la-Campagne
Hubert-Folie
Point 122
Falaise →
Canadian Front Line 24 July
Approximate German Line, Morning 25 July
← Caen
Coy Fus MR
24 July
Troteval Farm
Beauvoir Farm
St Martin-de-Fontenay
Verrières
RHL
R Regt C
1st SS Panzer Division
1st Royal TK R
Verrières Ridge
Elements 2 Pz Div
Rocquancourt
Factory
Cdn Black Watch
May-sur-Orne
Fontenay-le-Marmion
Verrières Infantry Division
Camerons of C
R de Mais
St André-sur-Orne
272nd Elements 9 SS Pz Div
Orne
Laize
← Thury-Harcourt
← Hill 112 2 miles

Legend:
— Canadian forces
--- British forces

Elevation in metres
100
70

1 mi
1 km
0

to the area of the start line for the attack. And to guard against enemy tanks and anti-tank guns in the counterattack, Simonds also gave two regiments of the 2nd Canadian Armoured Brigade to Foulkes and one to Keller.

The plan fell apart in the execution. One thing that should have been clear from Atlantic was that assaulting infantry stood a much better chance of capturing and *holding* their objectives if they were supported by tanks that were with, or in front of, them. This was a critical consideration because 2nd Canadian Corps faced, across its seven-kilometre front, "the most powerful German defence arrangement encountered by any of the Allied armies throughout the Normandy Campaign ... one infantry and one panzer division in the front-line, while two panzer divisions were in reserve" and two more panzer divisions were "within close proximity."[151] Against that sort of opposition, inadequate tank or anti-tank support left the infantry vulnerable, especially if the dismounted troops could not keep up with timed artillery fire. That was what had happened to the South Saskatchewan Regiment on 20 July. That was also what happened, most tragically, to the Black Watch five days later, when, during the second phase of Spring, the battalion attacked from an unsecure start line, up the open slope of Verrières ridge, in full view of the enemy from the west side of the Orne, with its right flank completely exposed, without the benefit of neutralizing artillery fire because the timed concentrations had passed, and without the support of its tank squadron, which had been held up by enemy tanks and anti-tank guns on the right flank at May-sur-Orne. (See also pages 268-71.) The North Nova Scotia Highlanders also suffered badly at Tilly-la-Campagne, when, as the only attacking battalion of the 3rd Canadian Infantry Division during the first phase of Spring, it initially assaulted an objective known to have "t[an]ks in close support" – without *any* of the 10th Canadian Armoured Regiment tanks assigned to the division.[152] Considering that intelligence summaries had confirmed the presence of the 1st SS Panzer Corps, with at least elements of the 1st SS Panzer and 9th SS Panzer Divisions in the area, the brigade and divisional commanders did an appallingly poor job of grouping their forces for tasks.[153] The passage of accurate information was erratic as well. Simonds launched the second phase of his plan – the disastrous attacks by the Black Watch on Fontenay-le-Marmion and the Royal Regiment of Canada on Rocquancourt – based on erroneous reports that the 6th Canadian Infantry Brigade had secured May-sur-Orne and that the 9th Canadian Infantry Brigade was in the process of capturing Tilly-la-Campagne.[154] It was difficult to make good tactical decisions with information that inaccurate.

Simonds was not blameless either. He had long emphasized the need for the timely deployment of tanks and anti-tank weapons to defeat the German counterattack. Why did he not insist that tanks accompany the infantry in the

Lieutenant-General Guy Granville Simonds 227

assault? If he felt it necessary to tell his divisional commanders how to deploy their brigades, could he not have asked, "What is your plan for defeating a tank-heavy counterattack?" He was with the 3rd Canadian Infantry Division Tactical Headquarters in Faubourg de Vaucelles between 0300 and 0630 and he spent from 0800 to 1200 with the 2nd Canadian Infantry Division Main Headquarters in Fleury-sur-Orne;[155] surely there was time to discuss the planned attacks. One wonders what Keller and Foulkes had to say. Both the Black Watch and the Royal Regiment of Canada advanced without the benefit of neutralizing artillery fire and withered under the combined effect of machine guns and mortars, the latter having been accurately directed by observers on the west side of the Orne. Clearly, the divisional artillery organizations failed to do enough to neutralize enemy machine guns and mortars. Just as clearly, Simonds and his corps staff should have done more to ensure that 12th Corps on the right did more to neutralize, or at least screen, the enemy west of the Orne. The losses for the single day of Operation Spring were 1,202 casualties, 362 of which were fatal – a terrible price for an operation designed to hold enemy armour formations in the eastern bridgehead.[156]

Simonds knew that he had issues to address within the corps, and the manner in which he addressed them revealed as much about his method of command as it did about the issues themselves. In analyzing what had happened and what had gone wrong, he did not seek the input of his subordinate commanders and staff. Time was short between the end of Spring and the start of the next major operation – thirteen days, to be exact – so it would have been difficult to hold an after-action conference and produce written reports, even if Simonds had been so inclined, which he most certainly was not. He met with subordinate commanders and he held orders groups in which "he discussed past and future op[eration]s in NORMANDY," but he did not ask for their input or their written submissions on lessons learned.[157] What could he have expected from Foulkes, whom he had very nearly fired during Operation Spring, or from Keller, whose removal he was willing to consider only "after a successful operation," for the sake of his division's morale?[158] He had a few people, such as his CCRA, Matthews, whom he trusted and with whom he discussed matters and exchanged ideas, but they were very few and he usually dealt with them one-on-one, never in a conference setting.[159] Conferences were for issuing direction, not for discussion.

First among the issues Simonds felt he had to fix were the morale and fighting spirit of his officers and troops. Not long after Operation Spring, he circulated the citation for the Victoria Cross that had recently been won by Major Jack Mahony at the Melfa River in Italy. He encouraged all officers to "read and think about how there was no question of 'giving in' because Major Mahony's company had 'lost touch' with the remainder of the battalion or was 'cut-off' or under 'overwhelmingly heavy fire.'"[160] Simonds was taking apart what he believed were the "excuses" that had been offered by units such as the South Saskatchewan Regiment, which had withdrawn from Verrières ridge on 21 July, or the Essex Scottish, which had fled the field in disorder during the same action. Mahony's company of Westminster Regiment, despite being as green in battle at the Melfa as the troops of 2nd Canadian Corps were in Normandy, had overcome similar adversity as a result of his "determined, courageous and skilled leadership." It is difficult to determine whether Simonds was trying to inspire or shame the officers under his command, but there can be little doubt that he apportioned to them a large share of blame for the failures of Atlantic and Spring. Immediately after the war, he ascribed the difficulties of Spring to four factors: failure to secure the start line, failure to follow closely the artillery supporting fire, failure to "mop up" captured objectives, and failure to consolidate objectives and establish firm bases that could withstand enemy counterattacks – all attributable to levels of command below his own.[161] Conspicuously absent from his comments was any mention of the poor employment of tanks, the danger of advancing while troops were exposed to observation (and directed mortar fire), and the failure of the artillery to neutralize anti-tank guns, machine guns, and mortars sited in reverse-slope positions.

But he understood them, as his appreciation and his plan for Operation Totalize demonstrated. Creative in concept and packed with promise, Totalize has captivated historians like no other Canadian operation of the Second World War, with the possible exceptions of D-day and Dieppe. It was a near-perfect reflection of its commander – the product of all his strengths and most of his weaknesses. Anyone wishing to learn more about Totalize would do well to consult Brian A. Reid's definitive work *No Holding Back,* the most in-depth analysis of the operation to date.[162] Here, we need only emphasize a few prominent points that illustrate how Simonds commanded his corps. To begin with, shortly after receiving direction from Crerar to plan "a thrust down [the] r[oa]d Caen-Falaise," Simonds locked himself in his caravan for several hours and developed – in isolation – his concept of operations for Totalize.[163] This was typical Simonds, producing a plan on his own, then announcing it to subordinate commanders and staff, who would coordinate and execute as Simonds had directed. Rodger remembered that "not I nor any of the Corps HQ Brig[adier]s knew of this plan" until Simonds presented it at an orders group on 30 July. Divisional commanders and staff sat in stunned silence as their corps commander described how "we will do this attack at night with armour."[164] When one of them finally spoke up to say that it had never been done before, Simonds replied curtly, "That's why I'm doing it."[165] His audience may have been gobsmacked by the sheer audacity of the plan, but Simonds had thought it through.

His one-page appreciation for the operation was a masterpiece of economy and common sense. (See Map 12.) Intelligence reports at the end of July informed Simonds that he faced "as good troops as the German Army possesses" – 1st SS Panzer Division east of the Caen-Falaise road, 9th SS Panzer west of it, and 12th SS Panzer somewhere "in close reserve."[166] The two forward divisions were deployed with one infantry regiment forward, "supported by all the tanks and S[elf]P[ropelled gun]s" along the line May-sur-Orne–La Hogue. The second infantry regiments in each division, according to intelligence sources, held a second defensive line that ran roughly from Hautmesnil to St. Sylvain. Given two defensive lines, Simonds determined that two break-in operations would be required. But how would this be done, considering that the ground so suited the enemy's defence? "It is open, giving little cover to either infantry or tanks and the long range of his anti-tank guns and mortars, firing from carefully concealed [reverse-slope] positions, provides a very strong defence in depth." Having experienced what German mortars, machine guns, and anti-tank guns could do when they could see their targets, Simonds decided it would be best to attack in "darkness when the advantage of long-range is minimized." Also to assist in the penetration of the two defensive lines, Simonds would enlist the support of heavy bombers to "obliterate" defiladed enemy positions tucked behind reverse slopes and therefore difficult to neutralize with artillery fire. These air attacks would take place on the flanks of his attack corridor astride the Caen-Falaise road – one round of bombings just before H-hour on 7 August, and another on the second-line defences the following day, when the forward troops would be nearly beyond the range of the their supporting guns.[167] This, he hoped, would "maintain a high tempo to the operations," enabling the forward troops to press on while most of their supporting guns (and ammunition) moved forward to support the next tactical bound in the attack.

The final plan for Totalize, as Simonds sketched it, was absolutely audacious in concept. The first phase break-in, which would carry the Canadians past the Verrières ridge, would be executed by two infantry divisions – 2nd Canadian right and 51st (Highland) left – each supported by a brigade of tanks. Simonds did not give his divisional commanders any latitude in how they used their tanks either. Tanks would lead. In fact, for the first break-in battle, they would be at the front of tightly packed columns, four tanks abreast, 16 metres wide. The infantry would not be far behind the tanks – and the moving barrage – because Simonds would mount them "in bullet and splinter-proof" armoured personnel carriers.[168] Once the heavy bombers had pounded targets left and

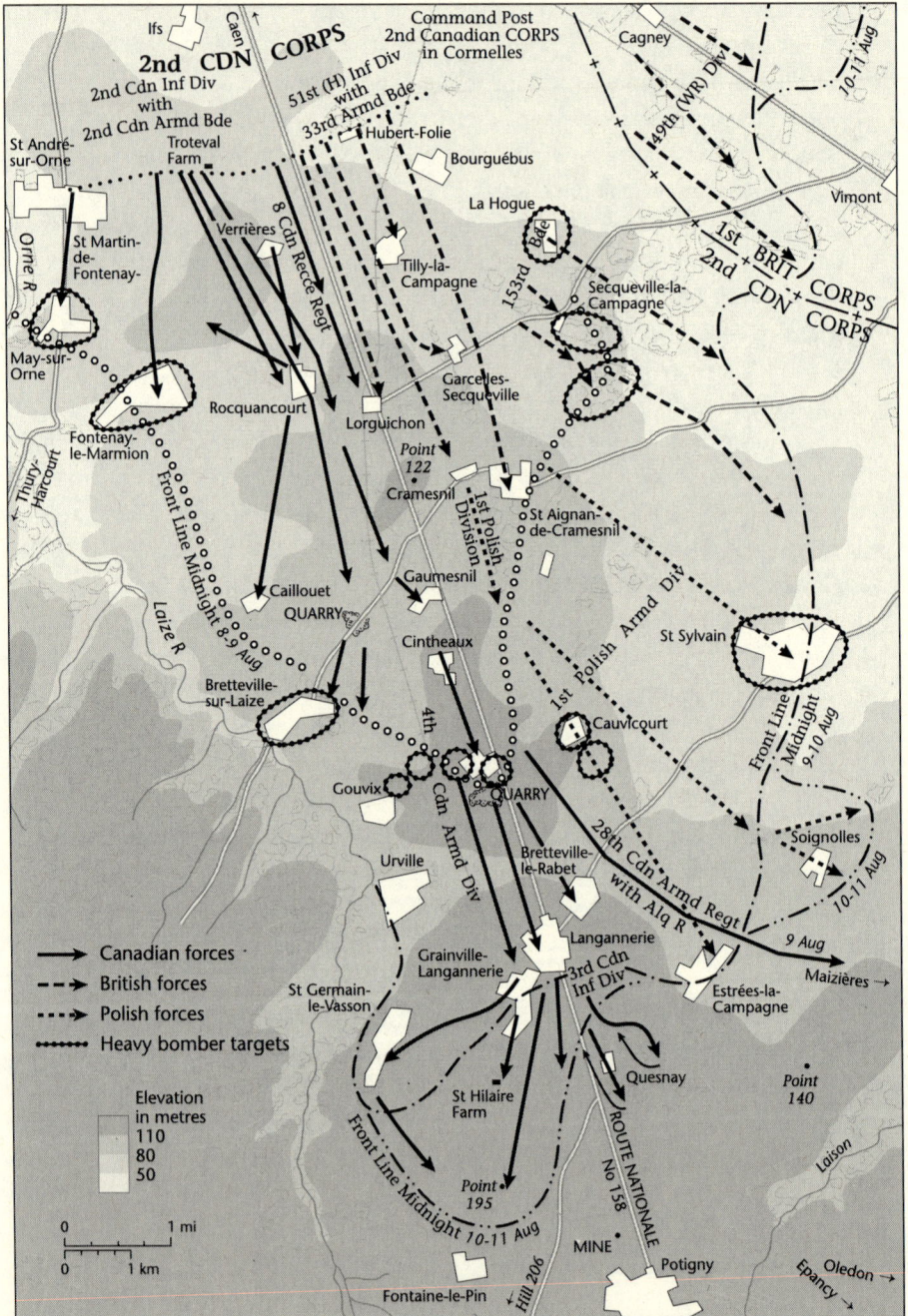

MAP 12   Operation Totalize, 7-10 August 1944. Adapted from Stacey, *The Victory Campaign*, map 4.

right of the Caen-Falaise road corridor, the two assaulting infantry divisions would advance, in the darkness, each with four battalion columns, each column led by two troops of flail tanks to clear lanes through minefields, a troop of the 79th Assault Squadron to mark the lanes, and two troops of Sherman tanks. The columns were to snake along at a pace of 200 metres every two minutes, behind a rolling barrage that was 4,050 yards wide and 6,000 yards deep, until they reached the dismount areas for the carrier-mounted infantry, some 5 to 8 kilometres deep into the enemy defences.[169] While those columns churned their way through the enemy's defences, dismounted infantry battalions would mop up bypassed towns on the left and right of the 4,000-metre-wide advance corridor. Thus, in phase 1, Simonds would be fighting simultaneous battles – one close to the forward defences and one deep in the enemy's defensive belt. In the second phase of the operation, heavy and medium bombers would start things off by attacking what was projected to be the enemy's very strong second-line defences, running roughly from Bretteville-sur-Laize through Hautmesnil to St. Sylvain.[170] Once that was done, the 4th Canadian Armoured Division and the 3rd Canadian Infantry Division would attack side by side in a cramped 3,000-metre-wide attack corridor, paving the way for a final exploitation by the 1st Polish Armoured Division to the high ground north of Falaise. That was the final plan.

With his plan, Simonds set in motion a fury of coordination and preparation. First, the fire plan had to be developed, so corps and divisional artillery staffs met between 4 and 6 August to work out the details of the counter-battery plan, which was supported by 312 guns, and the barrage, which was supported by 360 guns.[171] Coordination also included the dumping of 200,000 rounds of ammunition. The air program had to be tied down as well. Most of that was done through First Canadian Army Headquarters; the army chief of staff, Brigadier Churchill Mann, flew to England for meetings with Bomber Command, but Rodger still had to integrate, into the overall plan, what the air forces were willing to do.[172] The infantry battalions designated for the columns in phase 1 had to train with new armoured personnel carriers, but first these Kangaroos had to be made. An ad hoc organization called the Advanced Workshop Detachment worked feverishly to remove the main armament and mantlets from seventy-six Priest self-propelled guns, and bolt extra armour to their chassis between 3 and 5 August. This left only one day for the column-designated infantry to train with the new Kangaroos, a far cry from the week of special training that Simonds had originally projected would be necessary. And, of course, all the assaulting troops and their equipment had to move to their forming-up areas for the attack.

In its execution, Totalize achieved a tremendous success despite a number of difficulties. The air bombings that inaugurated the first phase went well. They did not "obliterate" their targets as Simonds had expected, but the bombs landed mostly in their target areas and caused some temporary confusion among the German defenders, even if the damage done to the German defences was "negligible."[173] The columns of both the 2nd Canadian Infantry and the 51st (Highland) Divisions moved steadily forward in the darkness, through the frontline defences of the German 89th Infantry Division, which had taken over the 1st and 9th SS Panzer Divisions' section of the line south of Caen on 6 August. The going was not easy, however. The bombings, the barrage, and the flails kicked up so much dust that crew-commanders and drivers could see only a few metres in any direction. Simonds had anticipated such difficulties and arranged for a number of control measures to keep the columns on course – homing beacons, Bofors tracers to point the way of the main axis, green marker shells on Point 122 to mark the interdivisional boundary – but the columns, understandably, still got mixed up. Even with the poor visibility and the confusion, however, they did reach their dismount areas five to eight kilometres inside the enemy's defences, making the first phase of Totalize the longest single-day advance in the 21st Army Group to that point in the campaign. On 8 August, the German Commander-in-Chief West, Field Marshal Gunther von Kluge commented that "there is an enemy penetration at Caen such as there has never been before."[174]

At this point, however, the attack began to stall. Waiting for the second round of bombers allowed the 89th Infantry Division to recover and place itself in a blocking position between Bretteville-sur-Laize and St. Sylvain, while the 12th SS Panzer Division, still strong with 76 to 113 tanks and assault guns,[175] redeployed to the area of the Quesnay Woods, from which they prepared to launch a series of counterattacks.[176] Alarmed at the gap Simonds had torn in his first-line defences, the 1st SS Panzer Corps commander, Sepp Dietrich, also rushed forward his 85th Infantry Division. The second series of bombings, far from assisting Simonds's ground forces, made matters worse. The US Eighth Air Force, which conducted the air attacks, dropped only a portion of its bombs on the intended targets, the rest landing in the southern outskirts of Caen, where they inflicted an estimated 315 casualties on Canadian and Polish troops. Major-General Keller was one of them. The attack quickly lost momentum. Despite repeated attempts to force his armoured divisions through the narrow gap at Cintheaux and on to Falaise, Simonds found his attack grinding to a halt in the area of the Quesnay Woods by 11 April.

He was furious. He believed that the tanks of his two armoured divisions had been too timid in pressing the attack. George Kitching, who was fighting his first major battle in command of an armoured division during Totalize, remembered how Simonds "blasted" all the armoured regimental commanding officers, brigadiers, and divisional commanders: "He quoted the heavy infantry casualties of the past month compared to armour. He demanded much greater initiative from arm[oure]d reg[imen]ts – drive on – get amongst the enemy etc. Forget about harbouring at night – keep driving on."[177] It is true that the 4th Canadian Armoured and 1st Polish Armoured Divisions managed to advance only another six kilometres in three days, and some units were definitely cautious,[178] but Simonds's comments were a bit unfair. Totalize was an attack built around a fire plan, not vice versa. The delay imposed by the timings of the aerial bombardment had given the enemy time to recover from the crisis caused by the phase 1 penetration of their first-line defences. By the time the second phase got going, Dietrich had flung the 12th SS Panzer Division into the battle and was in the process of bringing up the 85th Infantry Division to restore the situation, so the task of penetrating the second line became increasingly difficult. Once again, the enemy was able to take advantage of the open terrain and the long range of his weapons. Kitching did the operation no service by crowding an already-constricted three-kilometre-wide corridor with two brigades in the attack instead of one. Moving his attacking units forward and lining them near Gaumesnil took a long time, due to the resistance of enemy that had been bypassed during the initial assaults, and they were badly bunched up by the time they launched. One armoured-infantry battle group did press aggressively forward on the night of 8-9 August, but, owing to a navigational error, ended up six kilometres off its intended objective, where it was cut off, counterattacked, and destroyed with grievous losses.[179] It must also be considered that the highly centralized, highly controlled nature of the plan – which was consistent with the way Simonds had operated in previous battles – did not exactly foster a command climate that encouraged initiative. His blast to the armoured officers was tantamount to saying, "When I tell you to use your initiative, you will do so!" It also never seems to have occurred to Simonds that he might have been asking more of his formations – the two green armoured divisions, in particular – than they could deliver.

The rest of the Normandy campaign brought a mixture of success and the usual amount of frustration. Simonds finally reached the high ground north of Falaise in Operation Tractable (14-16 August), but a number of problems still hampered operations.[180] By this time, Hitler had given up his ill-considered and costly counterattack towards Avranches in the American sector, leaving the German 5th and 7th Armies trapped in a pocket between the 21st Army Group in the north and General George Patton's Third Army, which was approaching

Argentan in the south (see Map 13). Another massive set-piece effort, Tractable avoided the strong enemy defences at Quesnay Woods and Pontigny with a long left hook, two divisions up, each division preceded again by a brigade of tanks and flails, and again followed by carrier-mounted infantry. The ground leading into and out of the Laison River valley was open and undulating, and the Germans still knew how to use their anti-tank guns, mortars, and machine guns from behind reverse slopes, so Simonds again figured that he had to attack in "bad visibility," only this time he would use smoke instead of darkness. The 3rd Canadian Infantry and the 4th Canadian Armoured Divisions advanced behind a dense smokescreen, while heavy bombers attacked Quesnay Woods, Pontigny, and other German strongpoints on the corps' right flank. The attacks had the desired impact on their targets, despite the fact that 77 bombers of the 811 aircraft that took part in the mission dropped their bombs on friendly troops, causing 397 casualties.[181] An investigation into the incident later revealed that at least one cause of the difficulty lay in the use of yellow smoke, which Bomber Command used to indicate targets but ground forces employed to mark the location of friendly troops, a critical difference that tragically escaped the staff officers of the First Canadian Army, the Allied Expeditionary Air Forces, and Bomber Command who coordinated the air attack. As with Totalize, the smokescreen and the dust made it difficult to navigate through the grain fields, many of which were burning, and Simonds had badly underestimated how much of a tank obstacle the Laison River actually was, so there was a fair amount of confusion during the assault. In spite of all these difficulties, however, the Canadians smashed through the German defences along the Laison and made it to the high ground immediately south of the river on 14 August. By 16 August, after some very tough fighting against the remnants of the 12th SS Panzer and 85th Infantry Divisions, Simonds's troops were sitting on the low hills north of Falaise and poised to cross the River Dives, which the Poles did later that day. Simonds directed the Poles on Chambois to link up with the Americans in the south while the 4th Canadian Armoured Division moved to Trun and prepared to pursue the retreating enemy to the Seine. The last escape route for the withdrawing Germans – the Falaise Gap – was finally closed five days later, but only after some difficult and frantic fighting.

If the first month of 2nd Canadian Corps' fighting showed Simonds anything, it was the weakness of all his divisional commanders. He might very well have fired Keller after the final successes of the Normandy Campaign, as he had suggested to Dempsey he might do,[182] had US bombers not obviated the need for further consideration. Simonds was quite content to bring in the thirty-one-year-old Major-General Dan Spry, fresh from commanding a brigade in Italy, as Keller's successor.[183] Foulkes, in spite of his evident weaknesses and how lowly

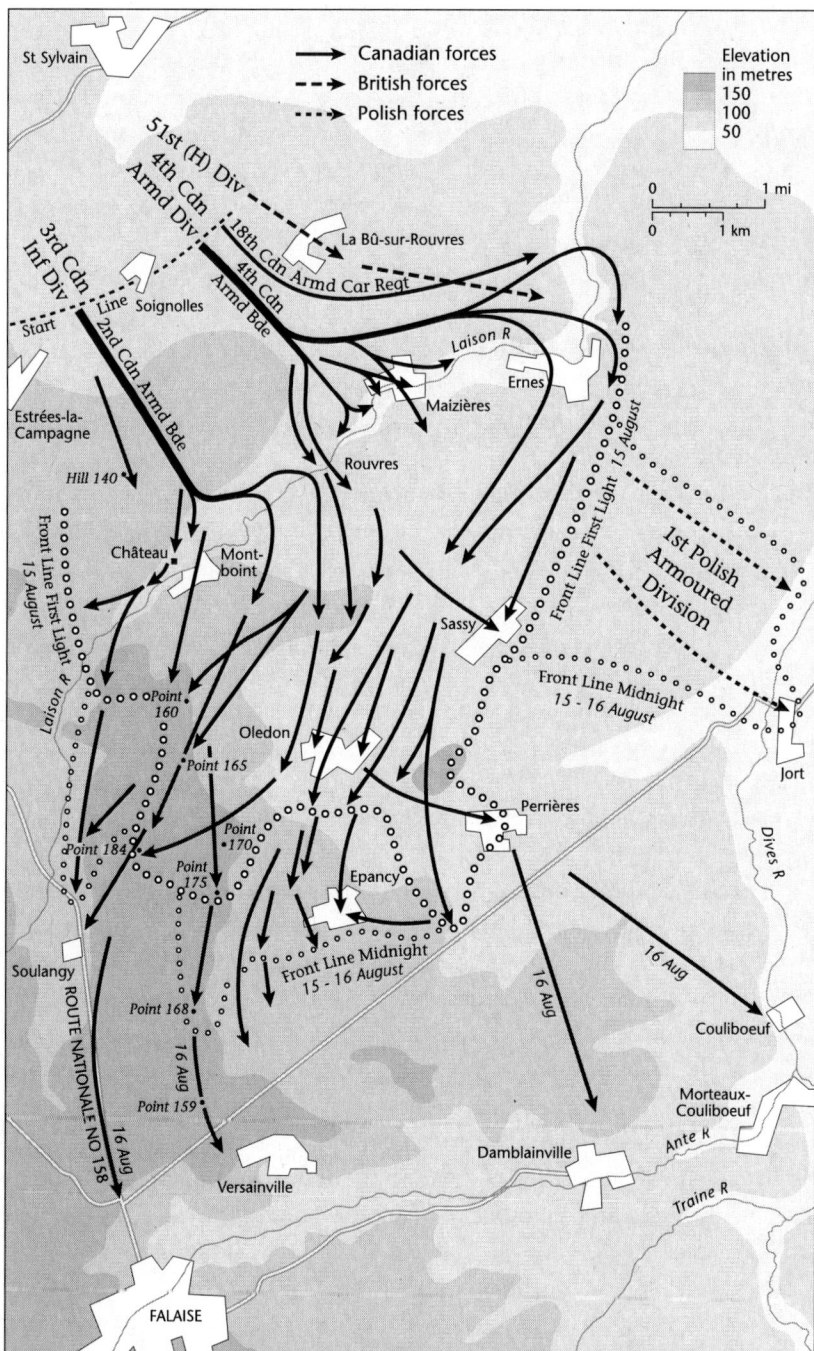

MAP 13  Operation Tractable, 14-16 August 1944. Adapted from Stacey, *The Victory Campaign*, sketch 18.

he rated with Simonds, hung on. The question is why. The most obvious explanation, although it can only be supported with circumstantial evidence, is that Simonds realized that Crerar, who was a strong supporter of Foulkes, would not have supported a change of command in the 2nd Canadian Infantry Division. There were no obvious successors either. Matthews, the current CCRA, might have been considered, but he had never commanded a brigade. Spry had to be plucked from 1st Canadian Corps in Italy. And the 7th Canadian Infantry Brigade's Harry Foster would be needed to replace Kitching in the 4th Canadian Armoured Division.

Kitching was by far the biggest disappointment for Simonds, both professionally and personally. As GSO 1 in the 1st Canadian Infantry Division, Kitching had proved himself a superb staff officer, and he would do so again as the BGS 1st Canadian Corps, but he was no commander. He was too nice. Unlike his corps commander, he tolerated substandard performance from his subordinates, the commander of the 4th Canadian Armoured Brigade, Brigadier Leslie Booth, being a case in point. Recalled from Italy, where he had commanded the 12th Canadian Armoured Regiment with distinction, Booth was "not the same keen and cheerful man" in Normandy that he had been in mid-1943,[184] to put it mildly. On the morning of 8 August, as the second phase of Totalize was beginning, Kitching found Booth dead-drunk in his command tank. Kitching was too much of a gentleman to relate the incident so plainly in his memoir – he wrote that he found Booth "fast asleep" – but years later, when pressed by inquisitive historians, he admitted the truth.[185] He gave Booth a "tongue-lashing," but why did he allow the pathetic spectacle of a brigadier to continue in command? Better still, why did he not relieve Booth before the Normandy Campaign? The brigadier's out-of-control drinking had revealed itself to Kitching on at least two occasions in England, and yet he kept it from Simonds, who almost certainly would have had Booth's head, even though he had been the one to place Booth in command of the 4th Canadian Armoured Brigade. When Booth was killed at the start of Operation Tractable on 14 August, it took nearly nine hours before an acting commander assumed control of the brigade, and then only upon Kitching's intervention. That there had been no clear succession of command spoke poorly of the operating procedures in the brigade – not surprising given the sad state of the man who had trained and commanded it until his tragic death.

There were other issues with Kitching. He lacked drive, for one. At the end of Tractable, as the last remnants of the German 5th and 7th Armies were scrambling through the Falaise Gap between Trun and Chambois, Kitching decided that this would be a good time to "abandon hard scale living from slit trenches" for the comfort of "caravans, messes and other vehicles."[186] Simonds ordered the 4th Canadian Armoured Division to Trun immediately, while the Poles moved on Chambois to close the gap. Kitching's plan in response to this direction, far from being a scheme for rapid manoeuvre, was almost certain to result in a low rate of advance at a high rate of losses. Simonds was furious to find that Kitching was planning a staged advance for the entire division on one axis, with little more than a tank squadron forward at any given time, on what was sure to be the most heavily defended route to Trun, the Falaise-Chambois road. He ordered Kitching to divert his armoured brigade north to a crossing site at Couliboeuf and from there to Trun on a separate northern axis. Kitching was proving himself untrustworthy as a commander. Three days later, when the Poles were cut off and besieged in their position at Hill 262, Simonds ordered Kitching to counterattack immediately with the 4th Canadian Armoured Brigade in order to relieve them. To ensure that Kitching was actually carrying out these orders, he also went to 4th Canadian Armoured Division Headquarters, where Kitching protested the order. This was not good. Kitching carped: "To hell with [the Poles]. They have run out of food and ammunition because of the inefficiency of their organization; our people have been fighting just as hard, but we have managed to keep up our supply system"[187] – as if keeping up the supply system was the most critical point of operations at this juncture. Simonds, quite rightly, cut Kitching off, told him to get his armoured brigade moving, and fired him the next day.

Firing a friend could not have been easy, but it had to be done. Kitching simply lacked the qualities of a commander. Most critically, he lacked tactical sense and what Simonds called the "determination and drive to get things done,"[188] and one wonders why Simonds did not see it earlier. In truth, however, this might have been hard for Simonds to discern, in part because of how he used his staff and did business. Kitching had served him extremely well as GSO 1, but it was not as though Kitching would have had much opportunity to display tactical acumen. He did not develop tactical options on his own then present them to his divisional commander. Simonds *never* operated that way. As we have seen, he developed a single plan on his own, handed it off to his staff to coordinate the details, and passed it on to his subordinates – taking no questions. As a chief of staff in this modus operandi, Kitching was fine. Indeed, Simonds found him an absolute staff stalwart, someone whom he came to trust implicitly. But left alone to lead operations, Kitching was out of his depth. He possessed neither the cold-bloodedness to fire people like Booth nor the cleverness to read tactical situations and devise suitable plans. Instead, he defaulted to fussing over administrative matters, which was his real talent, but it was not enough to drive an armoured division in operations. Having had enough of Kitching, Simonds sacked his friend on 21 August.

With a number of changes in key personnel and very little time to absorb reinforcements, 2nd Canadian Corps joined the other formations of the Allied armies in pursuing the defeated enemy across the Seine. Harry Crerar's First Canadian Army had the left flank along the Channel coast. As John Crocker's 1st Corps peeled off west to reduce the port of Le Havre, Simonds's 2nd Canadian Corps had the task of advancing along the coast and capturing the Channel ports. No easy set of chores, it involved two major siege operations – one at Boulogne (17-22 September), the other at Calais (25 September to 1 October) – plus a masking operation at Dunkirk.[189] While Simonds was advancing up the coast and closing in on these objectives, the Second Army, led by Brian Horrocks's 30th Corps, raced into Belgium, liberating Brussels on 3 September and capturing the port of Antwerp intact the following day.

Antwerp was an enormous strategic prize. In September, the Allied supply system still stretched back to the Normandy beaches and Cherbourg, some 550 kilometres away. Nearly one-third of the fuel the Allies brought into Northwest Europe was consumed by the 6,000 trucks needed to move supplies along the length of this logistic tether to the fighting troops, and Allied planners knew that Antwerp, in 1938, had taken in 60 million tons of cargo from 12,000 ships.[190] Even under wartime conditions, planners anticipated bringing in at least 43,000 tons per day.[191] They figured that the port, which was close to the fighting troops, had a discharge capacity of 100,000 tons a day, a tremendous amount considering that the combined daily output of Cherbourg, the Normandy ports, and the Normandy beaches was 26,800 tons.[192] But the capacity of the Antwerp port could not be tapped immediately because the Germans, with coastal defence batteries, controlled the Scheldt Estuary leading into the facilities. These defences had to be nullified.

The task of nullifying them was not helped by Montgomery's broader plans. On 13 September, he assigned the First Canadian Army the task of "setting in motion operations designed to allow us to use the port of Antwerp," but he also wanted Crerar to capture Boulogne, Dunkirk, and Calais at the same time.[193] This was too much for Crerar's army, which at this point was stretched 240 kilometres along the Channel coast, with Crocker's corps at Le Havre and Simonds's corps simultaneously preparing two major sieges and attempting to clear the West Scheldt. Montgomery's "real objective [was] the Ruhr,"[194] so he assigned the weight of his army group assets to Operation Market Garden, which was designed to capture it. Besides the promise of limited Bomber Command support and the possibility of two regiments from the US 17th Airborne

Division, he did not give Crerar any significant extra resources. After the war, Montgomery would admit that he "underestimated the difficulties of opening up the approaches to Antwerp," but he did it in a backhanded way that slighted Crerar and the First Canadian Army: "I reckoned that the Canadian Army could do it *while* we were going for the Ruhr. I was wrong."[195] Before the end of September, Crerar was able to bring 1st Corps Headquarters and the 49th (West Riding) Division to the Antwerp area, but the bulk of the enormous task of clearing the Scheldt would fall to 2nd Canadian Corps alone.

Crerar's Plans Section had been looking at the possibility of Scheldt operations since at least 8 September, but Simonds had by far the greatest influence on the final plan.[196] On 20 September, Crerar sent him the full appreciation that his planners had produced. This was fairly typical of Crerar, who liked a lot of feedback before deciding on a plan.[197] It was also fairly typical of Simonds to take the appreciation, examine it himself, and state bluntly what he did or did not like about it. To begin with, he took exception to the very object, or aim, of the operation. (See Map 14.) Whereas the Plans Section believed that the object was "to capture the islands of WALCHEREN and ZUID BEVELAND thus enabling the port of ANTWERP to be used," Simonds thought the object should be "to destroy, neutralize or capture enemy defences which deny us free passage through the WEST SCHELDT to the port of Antwerp."[198] This may seem like quibbling, but Simonds was right. The important thing was to gain the use of the port through the West Scheldt. If that could be done by destroying or neutralizing the enemy on parts of Walcheren or South Beveland, without capturing the whole of the island and the peninsula, then so be it. This was an important distinction for a formation with scarcely enough resources to complete its tasks. He also thought that the Plans Section had wished away the problem of clearing the south bank of the West Scheldt, by assuming that it would be complete before Operation Infatuate began. The 4th Canadian Armoured Division had just recently banged up against the defences of the 245th Infantry Division along the Leopold and Ghent canals and found them to be "strongly posted."[199] In addition, much of the ground had been saturated by the enemy, who also had the ability to inundate the area even more. As a result, Simonds surmised that the "clearing of this area may be a major operation," something that had to be fully considered and planned, not assumed away. Most of all, Simonds did not like the fact that none of the five proposed options for securing Walcheren Island involved an amphibious assault from the sea, an operation that Crerar's planners had deemed "reasonable to discard." Without that, Simonds believed that an assault onto Walcheren Island from South Beveland, even if supported by the landing of airborne troops on Walcheren Island, would be restricted to the

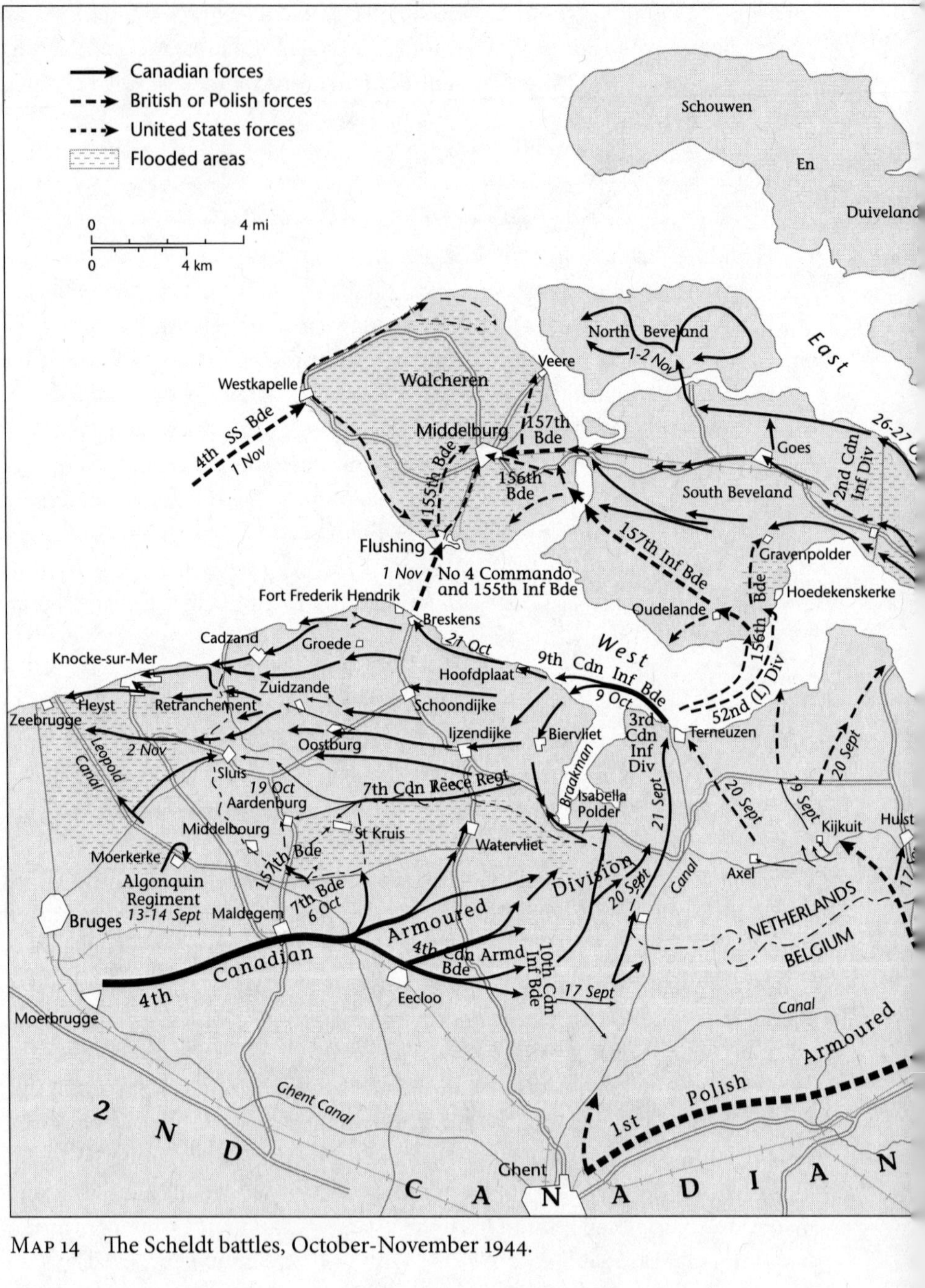

MAP 14   The Scheldt battles, October-November 1944.

Overflakkee

Hollandschdiep

Moerdijk

6 Nov

8 Nov

Maas R

29 Oct
Raams-
donk

Zijpe

4 Nov

First Canadian Army Boundary

Second British Army

7th Armd Div

Mark R

1st Polish

Steenbergen

4 Nov

Welberg

Tholen

Breda

Armoured Div

27th Cdn Armd Regt

4th Cdn Armd Div

Roosendaal

6th Cdn Armd R with 4th Lincs 28 Oct

Scheldt

Bergen-op-Zoom

Esschen

Zundert

27 Oct

Alphen

Armoured Div

Krabbendijke

Korteven

25 Oct

16 Oct

Woensdrecht

5th Bde

3 Oct

Baarle Nassau

Rilland

10 Oct

8 Oct

Dorp

104th US Inf Div

Scheldt

Ossendrecht

6 Oct

4th Bde Putte

Calmpthout

Kruisstraat

Wuestwezel

British Corps

30 Sept

1st Polish Armoured Div

Santvliet

1st

Merxplas

26 Sept

4th Cdn Armd Div

Camp de Brasschaet

4 Oct

Brecht

28 Sept

56th Bde

St Leonard

27 Sept

Canal

3 Oct

Oorderen

Cappellen

Lochtenberg

26 Sept

49th (WR) Inf Div with 2nd Cdn Armd Bde from 6 Oct

Turnhout

Eeckeren

Brasschaet

6th Bde
24 Sept

24 Sept

146th Inf Bde

147th Inf Bde

Wilmarsdonck

20 Sept

23 Sept

St Paul

20 Sept

2nd

Merxem

ANTWERP

Cdn Inf Div

22 Sept

21

St Nicolas

Scheldt R

Albert Canal

Meuse-Albert Junction

Herenthals

Canal

C O R P S

Division

49th (WR) Inf Div

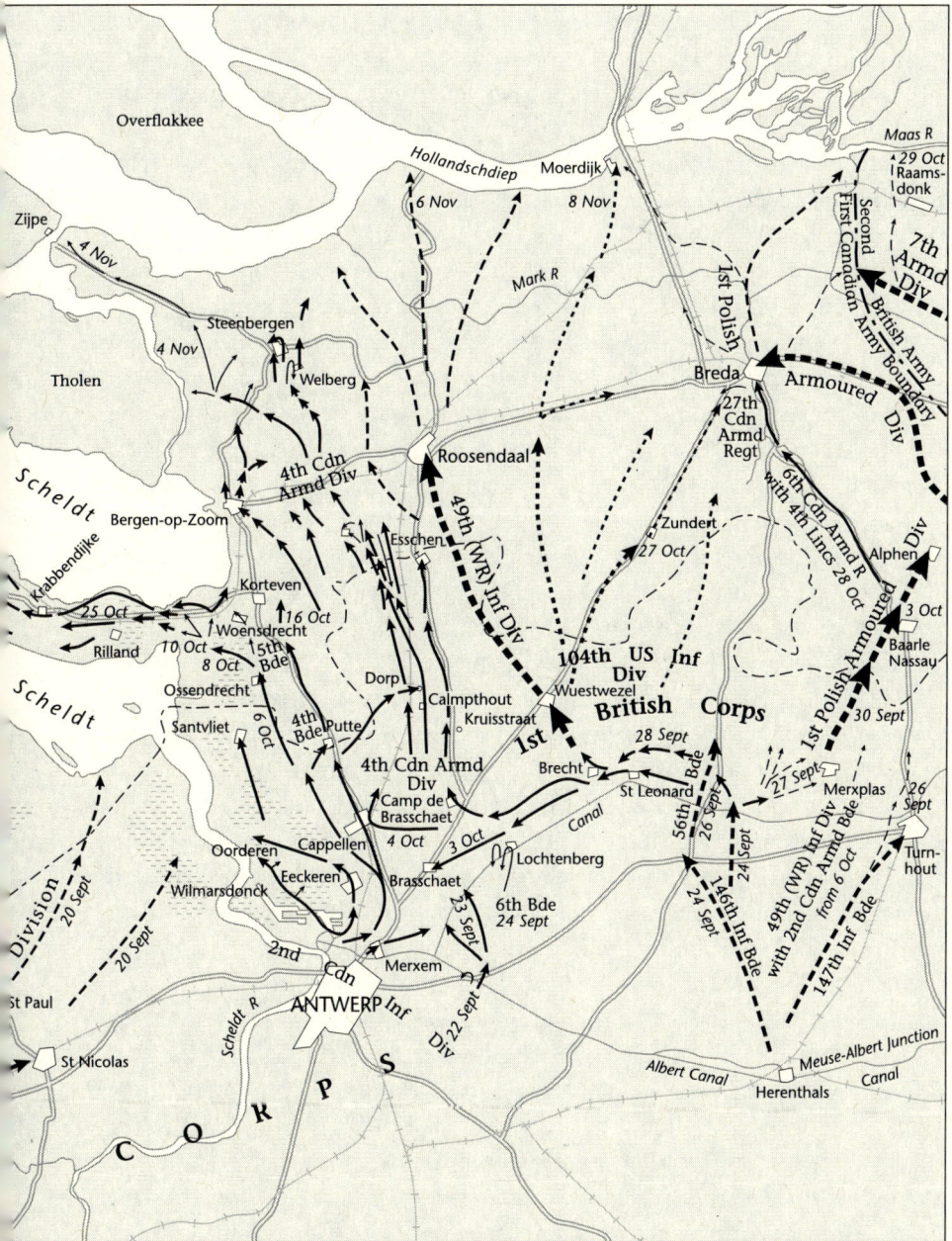

Adapted from Stacey, *The Victory Campaign*, map 8.

causeway, an undertaking that would be, as he put it, "equivalent to an assault landing on a 'one-craft front' on a coast where it was only possible to breach one craft at a single point on which the whole fire power of the defences could be concentrated." To allow for an amphibious assault on west and north Walcheren, Simonds proposed that bombing operations to break the dykes and flood the island should start immediately. Destroying the dykes would accomplish several things: it would provide suitable landing areas for amphibious assault; it would isolate the enemy defenders and their reserves to the limited areas where the island could not be flooded; and the restriction of enemy forces to tightly packed pockets would make them vulnerable to air attack. With characteristic clarity, Simonds saw that the operation had to be conducted in three stages – sealing off the isthmus leading to South Beveland and clearing the Breskens Pocket; "exploiting the land approach along South Beveland as far as practicable"; and, finally, assaulting Walcheren both from South Beveland and from the sea.[200]

Crerar accepted Simonds's recommendations. There was nothing out of the ordinary in that. He trusted Simonds as a commander. Totalize and Tractable had been army operations, but Crerar had essentially allowed Simonds to drive the planning processes for both operations. At a 21 September meeting with Admiral Bertram Ramsay, Commander-in-Chief Allied Naval Expeditionary Forces, and Major-General Francis "Freddie" de Guingand, Chief of Staff 21st Army Group, Crerar more or less parroted Simonds, emphasizing the importance of clearing "the left bank of the West Scheld[t]" and the requirement for seizing the ground north of Antwerp to cut off the South Beveland peninsula.[201] He also suggested that both the flooding of Walcheren and a combined operation against the island be considered. He repeated these points two days later at a much larger planning conference, this one attended by representatives of the Naval Task Force assigned to the operation, 21st Army Group, 84th Group RAF, First Allied Airborne Army, and Simonds. Old tensions between Crerar and Simonds surfaced when the latter stood up to correct and clarify what Crerar had said, although later that day Simonds felt compelled to assure Crerar of his "complete and continued loyalty" despite his "suggestions" in a public forum.[202] Responses from the airborne, naval, and air force representatives to the proposed operation varied. Brigadier-General Stuart Cutler of the First Allied Airborne Army agreed to examine the feasibility of using airborne troops to support the operation, and Captain A.F. Pugsley, Royal Navy, identified the 4th Special Service Brigade as the amphibious landing force should such an assault take place on Walcheren; however, a reluctant Air Vice Marshal R.D. Oxland from the 84th Group "could NOT say if dykes could be breached by h[eav]y bombing." He made no promises, although he agreed to investigate the feasibility of the operation. Crerar's staff studied it too. On 24 September, the Chief Engineer First Canadian Army, Brigadier Geoffrey Walsh, gave his opinion that heavy bombing of the dykes on the seaward side of Walcheren should not be pursued because he did not believe the earthworks could be broken by bombing, and even if they could be breached, the flooding would not be deep enough to permit the manoeuvre of landing craft.[203] Crerar was willing to take Walsh at his word. Not Simonds. When Crerar advised him that, based on Walsh's opinion, he would not seek permission to flood Walcheren, Simonds sent back a note that breaking the dykes "cannot be said to be *impossible* no matter how large the quantity of earth to be shifted by bombs. Operationally, there is nothing to lose and much to gain by an attempt to flood the island."[204] Based on this rationale, he implored Crerar to ignore Walsh's advice and urge the 21st Army Group to press the Allied Expeditionary Air Forces for the use of heavy bombers in the dyke-busting operation. Crerar, who was very ill with dysentery, and very much more conduit than commander at this stage, complied and sent the request as discussed on 26 September. Later that day, on the recommendation of his physician, he handed over command of the army to Simonds and proceeded to England for treatment.

The minute Simonds set foot in First Canadian Army Headquarters, he had an effect on the staff. The idea that someone would present the commander with a ready-made list of tactical options was foreign to him. Staffs were for coordinating actions and implementing plans, not generating courses of action; that was his responsibility. As the army BGS, Brigadier G.E. Beament, remembered: "We gave him the facts and he went away to his quarters and made his own appreciation, called together a meeting of everybody involved and said 'Gentlemen, this is what we are going to do ... everybody gulped a couple of times, disappeared and we got on with it."[205] This stood in sharp contrast to Crerar's conferences, which were more "like tactical exercises at the staff college but with no real conclusions." At another conference with representatives of all the services, Simonds, as acting army commander, forced his ideas through in a way that Crerar never could have done. He made a pitch that the flooding of Walcheren Island should at least be tried because it offered "so many military advantages" if it worked and no drawbacks if it did not.[206] When the RAF representatives seemed to waver, Simonds "fixed them with his eyes" and asserted that a failure to try would cost lives – lives that would be on their conscience.[207] The combination of will, confidence, and guilt worked. The conference adjourned with the resolution that "Bomber Com[man]d will undertake a deliberate attempt to breach the dykes" as soon as permission was received from the Supreme Headquarters Allied Expeditionary Force and the weather permitted. With that, Simonds continued his preparations to clear the Scheldt Estuary.

He still operated under severe restrictions, however. Montgomery's orders of 27 September, even after the failure of Operation Market Garden, continued to assign priority to operations aimed at capturing the Ruhr. They essentially left Simonds with one corps and not much else to complete his assigned tasks. Not only did he have to complete his current operations to open Boulogne and Calais but he also had to clear the Scheldt and drive Crocker's 1st Corps northeast – away from the Scheldt – to conform with the long left flank of Dempsey's Second Army, now exposed after Market Garden.[208] Simonds had planned to have the 1st Polish Armoured Division attack north of Antwerp to cut off South Beveland, but he had to hand the Poles off to Crocker, for the thrust to the northeast. At this point, then, Simonds had 1st Corps with the 1st Polish Armoured and the 49th (West Riding) Divisions set to attack away from the Scheldt and 2nd Canadian Corps with the 4th Canadian Armoured Division holding the line of the Leopold Canal, the 3rd Canadian Infantry Division finishing the capture of Calais and preparing to clear the Breskens Pocket (Operation Switchback), and the 2nd Canadian Infantry Division in Antwerp, poised to attack north, seal off the South Beveland peninsula, *and* drive east to clear the enemy from the peninsula. Opposing all of these operations was the German 67th Corps, deployed with the 711th and 719th Divisions in the area east and northeast of Antwerp, the remnants of the 346th and 344th Infantry Divisions in blocking positions north of Antwerp, the 64th Division defending the Breskens Pocket, and the 70th Division (or most of it) holding Walcheren Island. The 15th Army, to which these formations belonged, was under orders "to hold under all circumstances the Breskens bridgehead and Walcheren Island ... and [to] use whatever resources are available to defend the line Antwerp-Tilburg-s-Hertogenbosche."[209] The enemy's task was made easier by the terrain, which largely favoured the defender. The ground was "completely flat, with a network of minor canals and numerous areas which [were] completely flooded," so most movement was restricted to roads on top of dykes, where the enemy could easily concentrate his firepower.[210] Surely Simonds realized that he did not have enough resources to accomplish all his tasks. There is no evidence that he ever demanded more resources from Montgomery, but, as we have seen, it would have been entirely in character for him to have done so. Unfortunately, it would have been equally in character for Montgomery to have said that opening Antwerp was not as important as capturing the Ruhr, so Simonds would just have to make do with what he had. Whatever the dialogue between the two may have been, Simonds accepted the restrictions, sequenced his operations (since there was too much to do for it all to be done at once), and set himself to crafting well-orchestrated operations.

Again, subordinates' initiative and input did not figure prominently in his planning. Crocker's northeastern thrust had more to do with protecting Dempsey's flank than with assisting the Scheldt operations, so Simonds was content to let his British colleague drive his divisions as he saw fit. This was not at all the case with Foulkes, who, by virtue of seniority over Spry and Foster, had assumed acting command of 2nd Canadian Corps when Simonds took over from Crerar. As we have seen, the concept of operations for clearing the Scheldt was developed by Simonds before he turned over the corps to Foulkes. Not only that, but Simonds had sketched out a plan for eliminating the enemy in the Breskens Pocket – Operation Switchback – which he handed to Foulkes and which Foulkes used when drafting his own directive on 30 September.[211] Because the enemy was so well disposed with all the advantages the terrain had to offer, Simonds still figured he had to attack the pocket from two directions simultaneously. Across the Leopold Canal, one brigade would fight for a bridgehead through which a second brigade would pass to attack north and west. While this was happening, a third brigade would conduct an amphibious assault, from Terneuzen across the Braakman inlet, land in the area of Hoofdplaat, then clear west towards Breskens and Knocke-sur-Mer. Simonds had already arranged for the assistance of ninety-six Landing Vehicles Tracked from the 79th Armoured Division for the amphibious operation, so Foulkes had little choice but to live with the outline plan and pass it on to Spry when he showed up after the Calais task had been completed. Simonds clearly did not trust Foulkes to use his initiative, but he was reassured that Foulkes had the now highly efficient 2nd Canadian Corps staff to assist him, even if most of the staff officers hated him.[212] Foulkes was cold and aloof, but he had none of Simonds's tactical sense or the confidence that came with it. Rodger wrote in his diary that he, the Chief Signals Officer, and the CCRA were all "feeling let down with [Simonds] gone."[213] Still, the corps staff was composed of competent professionals, and they worked extremely hard to ensure the operations' success in spite of Foulkes. There was really not a lot for Foulkes to do.

As Simonds had predicted, the clearance of the West Scheldt north of the Leopold Canal was a major operation, and it took a week to complete. Operation Switchback began with an assault by the 7th Canadian Infantry Brigade across the Leopold Canal south of Aardenburg on 6 October. The enemy was known to have his three infantry regiments forward along the canal with his reserve, the 1st Parachute Training Regiment, further north, near Sluis. Patrols and reconnaissance had reported that the "enemy positions on the far side of the canal were known to be dug in on the reverse side of the canal dyke," where they were difficult to neutralize with small-arms fire, so twenty-seven Wasp flamethrowers pulled up to the friendly bank and lobbed liquid fire across the ninety feet of the canal.[214] Immediately after that dousing, the Canadian Scottish Regiment and the Regina Rifles scrambled across the canal in assault boats. On the other side, they managed to establish very tenuous but separate bridgeheads against fierce opposition, as the enemy responded with mortars and machine gun fire. From their bridgeheads, which were mere metres deep, and from slit trenches that filled with water, the two lead battalions held their positions as the brigade commander, Brigadier J.G. Spragge, committed his third battalion, the Royal Winnipeg Rifles, on the night of 6-7 October. Over the next several days, the enemy counterattacked, and often, even committing the divisional reserve, the 1st Parachute Training Regiment, to try to eliminate the Canadian bridgehead on the Leopold Canal. The 64th Division should have been able to destroy the Canadian bridgehead, and probably would have done so had it not been for the superb artillery support that had been arranged by the 3rd Canadian Infantry Division CRA, Brigadier P.A.S. Todd. The fire plan, which included the support of two AGsRA, incorporated a system of on-call concentrations and stonks on known or suspected enemy positions – no timed barrage, no timed concentrations. "The chief advantage of this system," according to Todd, "is that it will produce quick and effective fire, and ... if not abused it is more economical than the too-liberal barrage."[215] In other words, attacking infantry were no longer bound to the timings of the guns and fewer bullets would fall on unoccupied ground. Now the infantry could call for fire when they needed it, where they needed it. The system was much more responsive than the timing-rigid fire plans of Atlantic and Spring.[216] (A few weeks later, Simonds would select Todd as his CCRA when Matthews left to take over the 2nd Canadian Infantry Division.) With excellent artillery support and the determined fighting of its soldiers, Spragge's brigade held its bridgehead but was unable to expand it.

The real impact of the 7th Canadian Infantry Brigade bridgehead was that it made the complex amphibious operation by 9th Canadian Infantry Brigade relatively simple. By the time Brigadier J.M. Rockingham launched his attack across the Braakman inlet on 9 October, the 64th Division had very little with which to oppose him. The counterattacks on the Leopold Canal bridgehead had chewed up most of the German reserves, and the 9th Canadian Infantry Brigade was able to land against "negligible" opposition east of Hoofdplaat.[217] Surprised by the landing, the Germans responded with mortar fire from Biervliet and artillery fire from Flushing on Walcheren. They also ferried two 70th Division companies from Walcheren as the 64th Division tried to reorganize itself to meet the new 9th Canadian Infantry Brigade threat, but the Canadians pushed steadily inland, capturing Breskens on 10 October and Biervliet on 11 October.[218]

This progress convinced Spry to change the plan for his third brigade. His original intention had been to push the 8th Canadian Infantry Brigade through the Leopold Canal bridgehead, but the painful stalemate there, combined with the good progress of the 9th Canadian Infantry Brigade advance in the north, convinced him to send the 8th Brigade to Hoofdplaat instead, where it landed on 11 and 12 October. This is not to say that the fighting was in any way easy; there were still three more weeks of fighting on difficult ground. The situation improved considerably after 16 October, however, when Montgomery, who had been under pressure from Eisenhower to switch priorities and open Antwerp soon, finally gave up his push for the Ruhr, at least for a while. Two days later, the 157th Brigade from the 52nd (Lowland) Division, which had recently come under Canadian command, relieved the beleaguered 7th Canadian Infantry Brigade in the Leopold Canal bridgehead. This enabled Spry to concentrate the full force of his division to the westward advance in the north, where the enemy had reorganized his defences to cover the only areas still not saturated and suitable for movement – roads. With the assistance of their responsive artillery support, as well as considerable close air support whenever weather permitted, Spry's troops renewed their attacks on 21 October and slogged relentlessly until they finally cleared the Breskens Pocket of enemy on 3 November. In the process, the division netted some 12,707 prisoners and inflicted extremely heavy losses on the 64th Division.[219] But, as might have been expected given the nature of the terrain and the enemy defending it, Canadian casualties were also heavy. By the time the 3rd Canadian Infantry Division had cleared the Breskens Pocket of enemy, it had suffered 2,077 casualties, over 500 of them killed.

Simonds kept a close watch on all operations as they progressed. Crerar had his own small aircraft that he often used for surveying the battlefield and making visits, but Simonds did not like to fly, so he made most of his rounds in a staghound scout car.[220] As was his custom as corps commander, he visited a division or a brigade headquarters almost daily to see for himself what was happening and to give direction as necessary. He was no backslapper, however, and certainly not one to joke with subordinates. Improving morale was not foremost in his thoughts. He wanted to ensure that subordinate commanders were properly implementing his orders and "[keeping] the pressure on."[221] Robert Moncel remembered that Simonds often remarked that a commander "can't believe a CO who says the men are tired. Too often it [was] the commander who [was] tired."[222] Simonds really was dead serious most of the time because he believed war to be a dead serious business. He was not above "tearing a strip" off a brigadier or two who were not performing or driving their formations hard enough. He did not put a lot of effort into winning the hearts of his subordinates or pulling them along as willing followers. He pushed.

He also had to keep a close grip on the fighting to isolate and clear South Beveland, where the fighting was equally tough. Simonds would have preferred to attack north from Antwerp, with the 2nd Canadian Infantry Division focused on cutting the South Beveland isthmus at its base near Woensdrecht and 1st Corps advancing north to Bergen-op-Zoom, Roosendaal, and Breda, but 1st Corps had been directed to the northeast. Simonds was not one to sit still though. Even though he had only the 2nd Canadian Infantry Division for the drive north, he made the gutsy call to launch that division and a regiment of tanks towards Woensdrecht. The enemy resisted stiffly and counterattacked predictably, but the division, now under acting command of Brigadier Holly Keefler, slugged steadily north, reaching Putte on 5 October and Ossendrecht and Santvliet a day later. This ten-kilometre penetration on the right flank of the 15th Army caused tremendous concern in the enemy camp, so much so that the army commander ordered his reserve, "Battle Group Chill," so named after its commander, Lieutenant-General Kurt Chill, to move from the area of Baarle-Nassau, where it had checked the 1st Polish Armoured Division advance, to the area of Woensdrecht.[223] There the battle group counterattacked from the east on 13-14 October, but, according to a German report, "gained very little ground because of fierce enemy resistance."[224] The enemy was so desperate to keep the Canadians off South Beveland that elements of the 70th Division from Walcheren launched a counterattack "3 kilometres west of Woensdrecht" to "re-establish contact with 346th Division elements north of the rail line."[225] Painful fighting continued for days with no decisive result. Finally, on 16 October, the Royal Hamilton Light Infantry and the 10th Canadian Armoured Regiment took Woensdrecht in a carefully planned attack that included the fire support of the entire divisional artillery plus three medium regiments, some of which the commanding officer, Lieutenant-Colonel Denis Whitaker, had fire on his own position to break up an enemy counterattack. The very weary, very worn-down 2nd Canadian Infantry Division finally managed to cut the isthmus on 24 October.

That it was able to do so owed much to Montgomery's reluctant change in priorities on 16 October. Releasing Crocker's corps from its task on the left flank of the Second Army meant that it could be directed north in the way that Simonds would have preferred in the first place. Montgomery's very belated *volte-face* on Antwerp also brought a few additional resources: the 52nd (Lowland) Division, which Simonds assigned to the clearance of South Beveland (Operation Vitality), and the US 104th Infantry (Timberland) Division, which went to Crocker, giving the latter a total four divisions with which to drive towards Breda and Bergen-op-Zoom. Crocker struck northward with all four divisions on 20 October, and the 4th Canadian Armoured Division on his left reached Esschen on 22 October and Bergen-op-Zoom on 27 October. Operation

Suitcase, the code name given to Crocker's advance, eliminated any eastern withdrawal route for the enemy near Woensdrecht, loosened enemy defences at the base of the isthmus, and assisted the 2nd Canadian Infantry Division's cutting of the isthmus, something that probably would not have been possible while the division was facing counterattacks from two directions.

Clearing the rest of the estuary took from 24 October to 3 November. Operation Vitality I took a week of most miserable fighting to push the enemy off South Beveland, over what an after-action report noted was wretched terrain: "It is difficult to imagine a more unsuitable piece of country in which to fight a battle. Movement is restricted to the one main road, and the minor approaches along the dykes SOUTH of the road. Large areas have been flooded ... while the remainder was saturated ground."[226] In such conditions, the exhausted 2nd Canadian Infantry Division began its advance up the spine of the exposed isthmus on 24 October, reaching the Beveland Canal two days later. There they were assisted in breaking the last major defensive line before Walcheren by the 156th Brigade of the 52nd (Lowland) Division, which executed an amphibious assault across the West Scheldt to Hoedekenskerke (Operation Vitality II). The 157th Brigade soon followed into the small bridgehead behind the Beveland Canal. With the enemy's position thus unhinged, both divisions pressed west, pursuing the enemy until they reached the Walcheren Causeway on 30 October. Operation Infatuate, as Simonds had conceived it several weeks earlier, could now commence.

It took another week to secure completely Walcheren Island, but the operation unfolded as Simonds had said it would. The amphibious landings were a tricky business. Landing craft had to proceed through fairly narrow breaches in the dykes and put ashore on fairly narrow fronts. This left the assaulting troops and their landing craft vulnerable to enemy indirect fire. Intelligence estimates indicated that only eleven of twenty-five enemy batteries had been destroyed since the dykes had been breached in early October, leaving a significant number of guns that could spoil the landings.[227] Planners had to coordinate the firepower of aircraft, warships, and artillery to subdue these guns during the amphibious assault. Even with such fire support, an attack would have to be launched from South Beveland to distract the defenders from the two landing points at Westkapelle and Flushing. No one in the 2nd Canadian Infantry Division relished the idea of attacking across a causeway that was 1,100 metres long, 35 metres wide, surrounded by saturated ground, and covered by anti-tank and machine gun fire, but Simonds insisted on an attack from South Beveland and the officers of the 5th Canadian Infantry Brigade, who would lead the attack, agreed that it had to be done. The ground left and right of the causeway was too soggy for vehicle or dismounted movement, yet lacked enough water to support an amphibious assault of some sort, so movement was dangerously restricted to the narrow neck of the causeway. The attacks were gut-wrenching. It took three separate assaults by three separate battalions between 31 October and 2 November to gain a foothold on the Walcheren end of the causeway, but the brigade succeeded in establishing a tiny toehold during a night attack, heavily supported by artillery. While the 5th Canadian Infantry Brigade battered away at the causeway, Simonds and Admiral Ramsay deliberated over whether or not to launch the amphibious assaults, not a simple matter of just giving a go-ahead. The weather forecast was bad and it looked as though the air support for the operation would be suspended. In spite of this uncertainty, on the evening of 31 October, they ordered the amphibious force to sail. The following morning, the assault forces went in successfully at Flushing and Westkapelle. Nine support ships were lost to coastal fire, probably due to reduced air support for the operation, but the assault troops did land safely. By 8 November, the Scheldt Estuary was completely clear of German land forces.

The operations to clear the Scheldt were arguably the First Canadian Army's greatest contribution to the Allied war effort. In unimaginably foul conditions, with too many tasks for the troops available, with shortages of ammunition and supplies, and with an enemy that was both fully cognizant of what the port of Antwerp meant to the Allied war effort and willing to fight for it, the First Canadian Army under Simonds achieved the near-impossible. It captured 41,043 prisoners, destroyed nearly three divisions, and opened the best port facility in northern Europe. Once the Scheldt had been swept for mines and the port was functioning, 19,000 tons of stores passed Antwerp daily, a 70 percent increase over what existing ports had been taking in during September.[228] The Allied supply problems were much closer to being solved, and perhaps this justified the terrible cost – 12,873 killed, wounded, or captured.[229] Simonds understood the importance of Antwerp to the Allies, which is why he pressed his troops so hard and so vigorously. It might have been done more quickly and at less cost but for Montgomery's misjudgment on how difficult the task would be and his unwillingness to assign it a higher priority. Still, Simonds understood his mission and pursued it with a certainty and a cold-bloodedness that few other commanders could match. Indeed, it is difficult to imagine a successful completion to the Scheldt operations without Simonds at the helm of the army.

Montgomery was well pleased with the performance of his Canadian protégé, as he explained in a 2 November letter:

I want to express to you personally and to all commanders and troops in the Canadian Army, my admiration for the way in which you have all carried out the very difficult task given to you ...

The operations were conducted under the most appalling conditions of ground – and water – and the advantage in these respects favoured the enemy. But in spite of great difficulties you slowly and relentlessly wore down the enemy resistance, drove him back and captured great numbers of prisoners ...

I congratulate you personally.[230]

If Montgomery had had his way, Simonds would have remained in command of the First Canadian Army. In early October, just as the Scheldt operations were getting underway, Montgomery spoke with the Canadian Minister of National Defence, hoping to plant some seeds of doubt on the succession of command in the First Canadian Army: "He said Crerar adequate but not a ball of fire. Not in same parish as Simmonds [sic] as Army Commander ... [He] would like to see Crerar back but don't have him come back until he is in shape."[231] Montgomery made the same case to the War Office, asking that Crerar "NOT return until he is able to stand up to the rigours of a winter campaign in a damp and cold climate."[232] Crerar caught wind of Montgomery's scheming, however, and quickly had himself assessed by two specialists, whose reports were communicated back to the War Office. In effect, that was enough to trump arguments about his health and his ability to withstand the strains of a winter campaign, and Crerar returned to the First Canadian Army – but only after Simonds had seen the Scheldt operations through to completion. Whether Simonds was aware of these manoeuvres is unclear. If Charles Foulkes is to be believed, Montgomery spoke freely about Simonds remaining in command of the army,[233] so it is not unlikely that Montgomery would at least have hinted at the possibility during any one of his many meetings with Simonds during September and October. Regardless of whether or not Simonds knew what was happening, Crerar, who was already sensitive to his subordinate's favoured position with Montgomery, must have suspected that Simonds was in on the plot. It would certainly help to explain his shabby treatment of Simonds at war's end.

Simonds must have thought that the shabby treatment began earlier. After having commanded an army in one of the most important Allied operations of the war, and after having been championed by Montgomery, he soon found himself commanding a corps again, and playing second fiddle to Brian Horrocks, to boot. When the First Canadian Army launched Operation Veritable on 8 February 1945, Horrocks's 30th Corps was under its command and leading the Canadian assault during the first phase. Not only did Simonds have to watch while a British corps commander took the lead in the largest battle ever conducted under Canadian command but he also had to hand over his two infantry divisions for it. By the time Simonds entered the battle in earnest on 22 February, he was determined to prove himself, and this adversely affected his performance, much as it had done during the final stages of Operation Atlantic. During the second stage of Operation Blockbuster (27 February to 3 March), he badly battered the 4th Canadian Armoured Division against a very strong enemy defensive position at the Hochwald Gap defile[234] (see Map 15). Historian Terry Copp, after his very thorough analysis of the operation, rightly asked, "What was Simonds thinking?"[235] The first stage of Blockbuster was a classic Simonds battle – carefully planned, well coordinated, and successful. But, in the second stage, he hastily attempted to force an armoured-infantry battle group, based on the Algonquin Regiment and the 29th Armoured Reconnaissance Regiment, through a gap without first clearing the woods on either side of it. It was a bit like Crocker's attempt to punch his armour through the Fondouk gap without dealing sufficiently with the mines to his front and the anti-tank defences to his left and right, in an effort to cut off a German withdrawal route.[236] But Crocker was trying to cut off a German retreat during a rapidly closing window of opportunity. Simonds had no such rush. In Operation Grenade, the US Ninth Army was making excellent progress from the Roer Valley in the south and quickly closing on the Rhine, but perhaps that was the problem – for Simonds anyway. Everyone could see that the days of German forces in the Rhineland were numbered. Simonds wanted to put the final nail in that coffin. He pursued Blockbuster with such zeal that it is difficult to escape the conclusion that he wanted desperately to reach his objectives on the Rhine before the Americans reached theirs – for his reputation and that of his Canadians. His personal and national pride were stung after Infatuate. As important as the Scheldt operations were to feeding, fuelling, and arming the Allied armies, Simonds was not even invited to the ceremony commemorating the opening of the port at Antwerp. In fact, not a single representative of the First Canadian Army participated in the ceremony.[237] How could Simonds not have felt slighted, or compelled to prove his mettle and that of his troops? His piqued pride may have been warranted, but that did not in turn justify his actions before the Hochwald Gap. After a week of very hard fighting, Simonds finally broke through the gap, but it took what was essentially an attack with three divisions up to do it – two to clear the forest north and south, and one to force through the gap. He fought his divisions well through the remaining week of the Rhineland campaign, as indeed he did for the remainder of the war, but the moment before the Hochwald Gap was not his best.

THE HOCHWALD GAP AND the tail end of Atlantic aside, Guy Simonds commanded his corps, and, in the case of the Scheldt, his army, with considerable skill and determination. No commander is perfect and Simonds was no exception, but, on balance, considering how much fighting he did and what he had

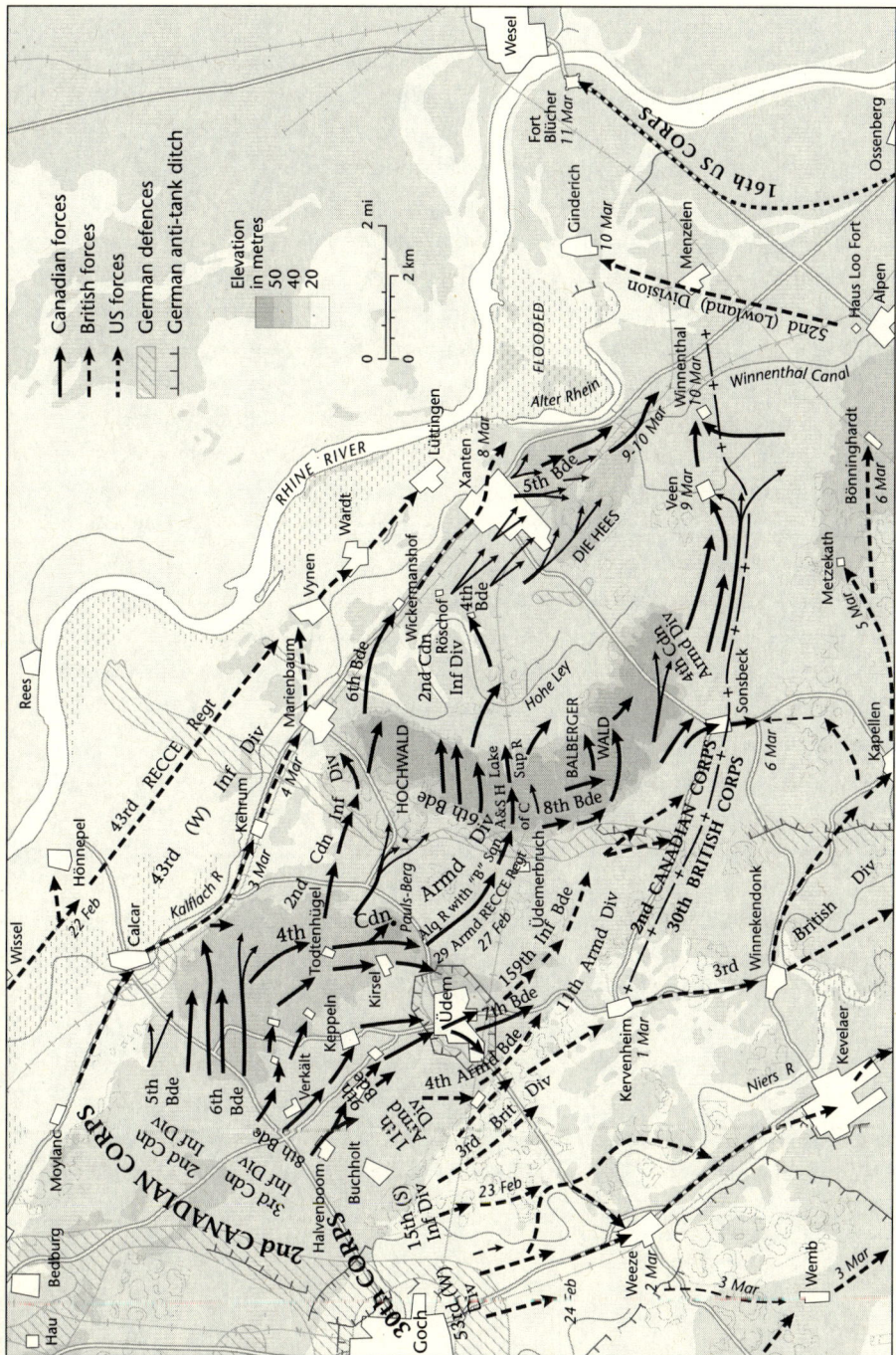

MAP 15  Operation Blockbuster, 22 February–10 March 1945. Adapted from Stacey, *The Victory Campaign*, map 11.

to work with, he did extremely well. Brian Horrocks was correct when he wrote that Simonds was a "first-class commander with a most original brain and full of initiative."[238] Simonds was always ahead of his peers, and often his superiors, in terms of technical skill. His sharp analytical mind served him well, but it was more than that. Like his idol Montgomery, Simonds took the business of war seriously and he strove to build upon his skills at every opportunity. He focused singularly on fighting, which may help explain why he was outfoxed by Foulkes and Crerar for the position of Chief of the General Staff at war's end. (See pages 293-95 below.) In terms of human skills, Simonds understood both what soldiers thought and how to keep them fighting better than has generally been acknowledged in the secondary literature, but a warm personality was not part of his constitution. Elliot Rodger noted that Simonds was "not a man one wanted to go fishing with,"[239] but the staff at 2nd Canadian Corps was genuinely grateful for having had him: "He ... command[s] and we, his staff ... provide the information on which to base his decisions and ... also implement in detail his commands and decisions. A staff officer could hardly ask more of his com[man]d[er]."[240] Most of them anticipated that Simonds would ascend to army command, something they dreaded as "a sad day for us here when he goes for good."[241] The man they served consistently drew good performances from the formations, units, and soldiers under his command. Victories were what soldiers wanted and Simonds gave them these most of the time, not by plying them with praise but by training them thoroughly, giving them well-conceived plans to execute, and driving them hard. He was also sufficiently ruthless – ruthless in the sense that he regularly sacked substandard performers and was willing to accept casualties, heavy casualties even, if it meant achieving an important objective, as was the case in the Scheldt. Simonds knew what he wanted and trusted his own judgment. He had no difficulty confronting peers or superiors if he disagreed with their views, whether it was his classmates at the Royal Military College, "Tommy" Burns over tactics, Montgomery over a training plan, McNaughton over just about anything, Miles Dempsey over operations in Southern Italy, Harry Crerar over operations, or the RAF over dyke bombing in the Scheldt. Simonds had drive and determination in spades, which, given his personality, is what he needed to transform "good ideas and intentions" into the "high morale, battle discipline and fighting efficiency of [his] formations."[242]

# 5

# The Master Bureaucrat: General Charles Foulkes

*Sound and competent, and possessed of drive and determination. I think*
*he had some difficulty at first in finding his feet here, but having got used to*
*the place he has made full value of his time at the Staff College.*

*He thinks for himself, is prepared to express his views and to accept*
*responsibility for them. Very thorough and determined to get to the bottom of*
*a problem: practical and with plenty of common sense. Should make a good*
*commander, though possibly not a very sympathetic one. Is a critic rather*
*than a creator, but has a wide outlook on the world.*

*Average.*

– STAFF COLLEGE FINAL REPORT, CAPTAIN C. FOULKES

HARDWORKING BUT AWKWARD AND unremarkably average: that is not the sort
of Staff College course report one expects to find for a future corps commander,
full general, and Chairman of the Chiefs of Staff Committee. No one at Camberley would have predicted such a rise for Charles Foulkes. It certainly left his
Canadian contemporaries scratching their heads.[1] He had few friends in the
army and even fewer admirers. None of his confidential reports during the
interwar period identified him as anything better than an "above average" talent
in the Permanent Force.[2] During his first three years of war, as a senior staff
officer at brigade, divisional, and army headquarters, all of his commanders
were relieved at some point, a record that does not reflect well on Foulkes as
their key advisor. His control of the 2nd Canadian Infantry Division in July
1944 was so shaky that his corps commander, Guy Simonds, had to be talked
out of firing him.[3] He also drank too much on occasion and had several embarrassing incidents because of it. And yet Foulkes went on to command 1st Canadian Corps, both in Italy and in Northwest Europe during 1944-45, and he
leapt over his former boss, Simonds, to capture the post of Chief of the General
Staff at war's end. Subsequent to that, in 1951 Foulkes rose to the newly created
post of Chairman of the Chiefs of Staff Committee, the highest military appointment in Canada and one that he held until his retirement in 1960. It was
a remarkable rise for someone so unremarkable. Foulkes seemed to defy the
Peter Principle. Indeed, he flipped it on its head: the higher he went, the more
comfortable – and competent – he got. The evidence is clear that Charles Foulkes

was a better politico-military leader than he was a battlefield commander. But how did he avoid getting sacked long enough to make the climb to corps command and beyond? And how did an officer of such limited tactical ability manage to command a corps in a competent, if unspectacular, fashion?

These questions are not simple to answer. No single explanation suffices. Jack Granatstein has suggested that "Foulkes played the army political game as well as any man."[4] That was part of it. "Political," "politician," and "diplomat" are common descriptors used by his contemporaries to sum up their thoughts on Foulkes.[5] Certainly, he was far less abrasive with his superiors than someone like Simonds, for example, and few Canadian officers knew how to use people above them and below them – the weak and the strong – to advance their careers as Charles Foulkes did. Somehow Foulkes hung on to his job as General Staff Officer First Grade (GSO 1) 3rd Canadian Infantry Division when Major-General Basil Price was sacked. He similarly clung to his post as Brigadier General Staff (BGS) First Canadian Army when Lieutenant-General A.G.L. McNaughton lost his appointment in November 1943, even managing to secure command of the 2nd Canadian Infantry Division two months later. And when that division did not perform well in July 1944, he offered up the heads of two battalion commanders and his GSO 1. He was also lucky. As a corps commander, he had two strong divisional commanders – Bert Hoffmeister and Harry Foster – and a highly competent chief of staff in George Kitching. Not lacking in cleverness, Foulkes also made an ally and friend of Harry Crerar, whom many contemporaries believed was a key protector.[6] In all, Foulkes could probably best be described as a master bureaucrat. He was not a man who rose on ability alone. He knew how the army hierarchy functioned. He knew how to sniff out power and influence. And, probably most important, he knew how to make such power and influence work for him when he could get them on his side, and he knew how to defend himself against them when he could not. This chapter traces Charles Foulkes's development as a battlefield commander, paying particular attention to how he rose through the officer ranks and how he fought his corps in Italy and in Northwest Europe.

CHARLES FOULKES REMAINS SOMEWHAT of an enigma because he wanted it that way. He left no memoirs. His papers, which are retained by the Directorate of History and Heritage at National Defence Headquarters in Ottawa, are scant and selective, reflecting a desire to clear his closet of skeletons. The only battles for which he compiled significant lecture notes and comments were Operation Chuckle between the Lamone and Senio Rivers and Operations Cannonshot/ Cleanser in and around Arnhem – all of which went fairly well.[7] He did keep the text of a statement by the Minister of National Defence on Operation Spring, the disastrous assault on Verrières ridge by Foulkes's 2nd Canadian Infantry Division on 25 July 1944, but the statement more or less exonerated the divisional commander of any fault in the debacle.[8] He also retained numerous papers on the surrender of German forces in Holland, which he handled well, and which convey an aura of importance and authority.[9] And, while he may have cleared his own closet of skeletons, he kept the bones of his competitors close. The relief of E.L.M. Burns from command of 1st Canadian Corps is the subject of a fairly extensive file,[10] and there is a dossier on Guy Simonds that includes, among other things, Crerar's voluminous correspondence outlining his concerns that Simonds's "highly-strung temperament" had become strained "beyond its limit of balance."[11] How he got the files on Burns and Simonds is unclear. They may have come from Crerar, or they may simply have been in the files of the Chief of the General Staff (CGS) when he took over that office. However he may have gotten his hands on them, his retention of the files on Simonds and Burns suggests that he had some concern for his competition.

His roots were humble. Born at Stockton-on-Tees, England, on 3 January 1903, Charles Foulkes was one of eight children. He had four brothers and three sisters; one brother apparently had some sort of mental disability.[12] His family emigrated to Canada while Charles was still a schoolboy and settled in London, Ontario. The family lived at 230 Hill Street, a small and modest residence in a lower-middle-class neighbourhood at the time, and Charles completed his secondary schooling at the nearby London Collegiate Institute, a public high school. This must have occurred in 1921 or 1922, but there is an inexplicable gap of two years before he entered the University of Western Ontario in 1924. His personnel file contains no evidence that he ever wrote the entrance examination for the Royal Military College (RMC), so he may simply have chosen to work in order to save for university. In December 1922, Foulkes enlisted as a soldier in the 2nd Battalion Canadian Machine Gun Corps of the Non-Permanent Active Militia (NPAM), quickly qualified as sergeant, and was commissioned as a provisional lieutenant in September 1923. By 1925, he had passed through the Canadian Small Arms School, worked as an instructor at the same school, and been promoted to captain. He never did finish university.[13] In the autumn of 1925, he applied for a commission in the Permanent Force and travelled to RMC for the Long Course, a year of training and instruction designed to prepare non-RMC graduates for employment in the Permanent Force.[14] At the time that he accepted his commission as a twenty-three-year-old lieutenant in "C" Company of the Royal Canadian Regiment in July 1926, he still listed his occupation as "student" and he still lived with his parents.[15]

His Permanent Force career of the 1920s and 1930s followed a fairly typical pattern for a junior infantry officer of that period. He spent a very long time as a platoon commander, from 1926 to 1933. This is a bit misleading, however. Promotion was slow for everyone in the interwar Permanent Force, the primary function of which was to train the NPAM or militia, not to command companies, brigades, or battalions. Indeed, there were no Permanent Force field training exercises between 1929 and 1938, and only a few desultory militia concentrations.[16] An officer with ambition had to grab whatever training opportunities he could, wherever and whenever he could find them. Thus, Foulkes instructed on the Small Arms Course in the summer of 1927 and he attended the first Instructors Course in Machine Gun Carriers at Kingston and Petawawa in 1931. His confidential reports for the period identify a particular strength as an instructor, and he continued to hone his skills in this regard.[17] In the summer of 1932, he passed several small arms courses at Netheravon and Winterbourne Gunner in England. During this stay in the United Kingdom, he met and married Phyllis May Armbrister (née Beck), a thirty-year-old divorcée from California. Not much is known about Mrs. Foulkes except that she came from money, "liked hats," was "elegant," and was hard on Foulkes's aides-de-camp in the postwar years; but Foulkes definitely married up.[18] In September 1934, he left regimental duty to assume the responsibilities of a General Staff Officer Third Grade (GSO 3) at Military District Number 3 in Kingston. Although he continued to instruct on machine guns and various small arms during NPAM summer concentrations, his duties as a GSO 3 mostly involved the organization and administration of such training. Possessed of serious ambition for his army career, Foulkes completed the preparatory course for Staff College, Camberley, in the autumn of 1935 and proceeded to England for two years of staff training in December 1936. Upon successful completion of that training, he returned to Military District Number 2 in Toronto, where he again assumed the duties of a GSO 3. At the outbreak of the Second World War, Foulkes was promoted to the rank of major and appointed as a GSO 2 at Military District Number 1 in his hometown of London. One of only forty-eight staff-trained officers in the Canadian Army,[19] Foulkes soon found himself assigned as Brigade Major of the 3rd Canadian Infantry Brigade, part of the first Canadian contingent to deploy to England in December 1939. He never commanded a company.

He had a definite talent for small-arms instruction, but his confidential reports were still remarkably average, well below those of Simonds and Burns, for example. He wrote the exam for promotion to captain in 1928 and passed all of his subjects – organization and regimental duties in peace, military law, imperial military geography, military history and tactics – but he failed to attain a special certificate (honours pass) in any of them, and in military law, he achieved the absolute minimum passing score.[20] "Good but not brilliant" is the common theme of Foulkes's performance between 1926 and 1939. In the format for confidential reports before 1929, his superiors rated him, on average, a middle-of-the-road "good" in the categories of command and control of subordinates, judgment, and professional ability.[21] In a slightly different format between 1930 and 1936, assessors had to choose between three descriptors for each of twenty-seven different assessment categories. More often than not, they selected the middle option for the key categories of general ability, tactical knowledge, and imagination.[22] By comparison, Simonds and Burns consistently scored top marks in each of these categories.[23] They were thinkers; Foulkes was not. Burns and Simonds had a running debate on army organizations and the mechanization of divisions.[24] Foulkes accepted other people's ideas on tactics and operations holus-bolus, and tried to put them into practice. He did, however, consistently manage to achieve top-end confidential report scores in categories such as reliability, obedience to command and attitude towards superiors, loyalty, tact, and leadership. Overall, Foulkes's performance record of the 1920s and 1930s is consistent with the observations of his wartime and postwar contemporaries, most of whom thought him an average battlefield commander at best, but a skilled bureaucrat and accomplished careerist.[25]

Foulkes was certainly less luminary than functionary. His wartime papers reveal a man who let others do the hard thinking about war, while he worked to put their theories and direction into practice. He retained pieces penned by Simonds, including a "Report on [a] Visit to Eighth Army," which outlined how to run and organize a corps headquarters, a memorandum on "Efficiency in Command," direction on "Operational Policy [in] 2 Cdn Corps," and Simonds's guidance on the highly unorthodox Operation Totalize.[26] He also kept a memorandum entitled "Formation and Procedure in the Tank and Infantry Attack" by Burns and he held on to a November 1942 aide-memoire by Crerar on orders at the corps level.[27] None of his personal Second World War papers show the same level of originality at the tactical and operational levels of war. This consistent character trait can also be traced to the interwar period. His Staff College course report from Camberley pegged his professional ability as "average," identifying him as a "critic rather than a creator."[28] Unlike Simonds, Burns, or Crocker, Foulkes was not recommended as a future Staff College instructor.[29]

Foulkes had a knack for ingratiating himself with his superiors and sometimes it saved him. In June 1939, as a staff officer with Military District Number 2 in Toronto, Captain Foulkes was involved in some capacity with the Royal Visit of Their Majesties King George VI and Queen Elizabeth. At 0300 hours on the morning of 8 June, Foulkes got behind the wheel of a rented automobile and began driving to the army camp at Niagara-on-the-Lake, a distance of approximately twenty kilometres. He had accompanied the Royal couple during their 7 June visit to Niagara Falls and had seen them off that afternoon when they crossed the border into Buffalo, New York, for a week-long visit to the United States. Foulkes claimed that, en route to the army camp, after having travelled less than ten kilometres, he became very "sleepy and fatigued," so he "stopped the motor car and slept for about two hours."[30] Sometime around 0500, he resumed driving, but he soon struck a tree not far from Niagara-on-the-Lake. A witness heard the crash followed by the continuous sounding of a motor car horn, and went to the scene of the accident to find the vehicle on the west side (the wrong side) of the road, and a "dazed" Charles Foulkes trying to disconnect the horn. Foulkes groggily asked the gentleman "where he was," then promptly "fell asleep." The gentleman then drove the young captain to Niagara-on-the-Lake, where Foulkes "directed [him] to a certain place, got out of my car and walked to a tent." A Major Hodson of the Royal Canadian Regiment (RCR) went into Foulkes's tent at 0645 and "found him asleep." An hour later, Hodson reported that Foulkes was still in a "sleepy condition," so he left the tent, found a medical officer, and asked him to attend Foulkes. After an investigation into the incident, Brigadier R.O. Alexander, the District Officer Commanding Military District Number 2, a senior member of the Royal Canadian Regiment and Foulkes's boss at the time, quite incredibly concluded that Foulkes "was not to blame, in that the cause of the accident was excessive fatigue following a long and strenuous period of duty on 7th June."[31] Foulkes was not out of place as a Permanent Force officer who drank too much. That was fairly common. For example, all three of the brigade majors in the 1st Canadian Infantry Division of 1939 had reputations as heavy drinkers – Rod Keller, Chris Vokes, and Foulkes; but Foulkes's drinking habits do differentiate him from the other corps commanders of this study, three of whom drank only moderately while one was an abstainer.[32] An officer such as Foulkes could have risen from major to lieutenant-general in five years only in an army starved for command talent and experience. There simply wasn't much competition. In April 1942, after observing 1st Canadian Corps for nearly four months, Lieutenant-General Bernard Law Montgomery, the commander of South-Eastern Army, noted with some disappointment: "The soldiery in the Canadian Corps are probably the best material in any armies in the Empire. And they are fit and tough. But they are going to be killed in large numbers unless [their] commanders can learn to put them properly into battle."[33] Montgomery was equally hard on British formations but the Canadian command deficit was particularly acute, and explainable. An interwar Permanent Force of a meagre 450 officers could be expected to produce only a limited number of truly able commanders and staff officers. Canada had sent just over 60 officers to Camberley or Quetta for staff training between 1919 and 1939.[34] As of one of the 48 trained staff officers still serving in 1939, Foulkes was certain to rise quickly, particularly as the army expanded into a fighting formation of five divisions and two armoured brigades. Foulkes also benefited from the fact that the infantry corps was underrepresented in the interwar crop of Staff College graduates; only 15 infantry officers (or 23 percent) passed through either Camberley or Quetta between the wars. By contrast, the artillery, the engineers, and the corps of signals had a combined total of 41 Staff College graduates, for a disproportionate 65 percent of the tally – this for an army in which the combined manpower of those three corps accounted for only 22.6 percent of the total manpower.[35] In his immediate peer group, Foulkes was even more exceptional in that he was one of only 6 infantry officers in a group of 30 to gain a "psc" qualification between 1930 and 1939.[36] The roots of the imbalance can be traced to the interwar years and the leadership of Andy McNaughton, Chief of the General Staff (1929-36) and Senior Combatant Officer for the Canadian Forces Overseas (1939-43). As John A. English has argued, McNaughton believed that officers of the technical trades, those with the more scientific minds, were best suited to lead an army of citizen soldiers in war, and he sent potential staff officers and commanders for training in accordance with this abiding belief.[37] After December 1943, his successor in command of the First Canadian Army, Lieutenant-General H.D.G. Crerar, sought to redress the imbalance and actively supported the advancement of infantry officers.[38] Foulkes was infantry. He was staff-trained. And he was young. As long as he did not make too many mistakes, he was sure to be swept up in Crerar's affirmative action plan.

He also had the good fortune to work for a succession of weak leaders who were incapable of recognizing his limitations. One of them was Brigadier C. Basil Price, commander of the 3rd Canadian Infantry Brigade, whom Foulkes served as brigade major at the start of the war. Price was an officer of the NPAM who had joined the army as a soldier and distinguished himself as a major with the Royal Montreal Regiment during the First World War, winning a Distinguished Service Order.[39] He had retired from the militia in 1929 to devote himself full-time to the running of a large Montreal dairy. When war broke out in 1939, the well-heeled and well-connected Westmount resident came out of retirement to secure the appointment of brigade commander in the 1st Canadian Infantry Division. Ten years out of the army business, and with his most recent combat experience over twenty years in the past, it was predictable that Price would rely heavily on his Permanent Force brigade major, who had completed Camberley only a year before. The emphasis of the training program during the first half of 1940 also played to Foulkes's strength as a training coordinator, essentially the same job he had done as a GSO 3 in Militia District headquarters between 1934 and 1936. Between January and March 1940, all the brigades and battalions of the 1st Canadian Infantry Division worked primarily at individual skills –

marksmanship, first aid, gas drills, signals, and the like.[40] Price, who was clearly out of his depth, needed help. Foulkes was by Price's side for the few Tactical Exercises without Troops (TEWTs) conducted by the division headquarters during 1940, and he also planned and supervised all brigade training.[41] He gave lectures on appreciations, orders, the attack, the withdrawal, and fighting in woods.[42] Price gave none. Foulkes followed up the lectures with sand model exercises and TEWTs for officers. There were also a few demonstration exercises for selected companies and battalions from the brigade, but field training exercises involving all the units and subunits were rare because of equipment shortages and the fact that a high proportion of officers were away for individual training courses of their own.[43] The regimen of officer and collective training for 1940 was something of a box-ticking exercise, driven by a belief that all officers and headquarters had to do was understand the principles of the defence, the attack, the withdrawal, whatever – and they would be able to apply them satisfactorily in battle. There was no apparent recognition that repetition and practice had a role in perfecting such collective skills. To be fair, Foulkes was only following the lead set by the divisional commander, Andy McNaughton, and he did do a fairly reasonable job of training, given the circumstances of 1940. Price would have been completely lost without him. But the fact remains that by the time Foulkes was promoted to lieutenant-colonel and posted to 3rd Canadian Infantry Division Headquarters as GSO 1 in September 1940, he had not had much opportunity to exercise his brigade headquarters – as a formation headquarters in the field.[44]

This technical deficiency would not be redressed anytime soon. The appointment to the 3rd Canadian Infantry Division took Foulkes back to Canada, where the new formation was still being assembled under the direction of Major-General Ernest J. Sansom, and back to the role of training coordinator. Like Price, Sansom was a friend of McNaughton, although, as a Permanent Force officer, he had not been out of the army for ten years during the interwar period. As one of few staff-trained senior officers in the Canadian Army, Sansom too had risen quickly, rising from lieutenant-colonel to major-general in three months during the spring and summer of 1940. With Foulkes as his primary staff officer, he completed the job of assembling the 3rd Canadian Infantry Division in Canada before taking command of the 5th Canadian Armoured Division in March 1941. From that appointment, he went on to command 2nd Canadian Corps from January 1943 to January 1944, but was relieved following universal condemnation of his performance during Exercise Spartan and other field training exercises.[45] Foulkes impressed Sansom, doing what he had been doing for years – organizing a progressive training plan, supervising the conduct of low-level training, and sending weekly progress reports to higher head-quarters.[46] His original training directive had anticipated that individual training would be completed by April 1941, section to battalion collective training done by June 1941, and the division "ready for active operations" in July 1941.[47] He later revised the optimistic timetable such that only brigade group field firing exercises would be complete before the division sailed for the United Kingdom in August 1941.[48] Sansom did not see the division through its pre-deployment training. When he left Debert, Nova Scotia, to take command of the 5th Canadian Armoured Division, he was replaced by none other than Basil Price. Within a month of taking command of the 3rd Canadian Infantry Division, the newly promoted Price recommended Foulkes for command of an infantry brigade – even though Foulkes had yet to command a battalion. Price wrote that Foulkes was "an able G[eneral].S[taff]. Officer who thinks quickly, clearly and logically and expresses himself well both orally and on paper. He possesses definite powers of Command and qualities of leadership."[49] Sansom endorsed the recommendation, signing as "Late G.O.C. 3rd Cdn Div."

Price, who barely knew what he was doing with a brigade, struggled with his division. In May 1942, Montgomery correctly assessed that the Canadian training difficulties – and they were many – started with inadequate divisional com-manders like Price: "It is of course quite impossible to make progress ... unless the Divisional Commanders are themselves competent to train their subordin-ates."[50] Montgomery had expressed his concerns about Price as early as February 1942,[51] but by May he had concluded that Price was "a complete amateur," which was true, and "unable to train his Division," which was also true.[52] He pressed the corps commander, Harry Crerar, for Price's dismissal: "I gave it as my opinion on 6 March that Price was unfit to command a Division in the field army. I now do so again, very definitely." Crerar agreed, but it took until September 1942 to find a suitable replacement in Major-General Rod Keller, who, to that point, had been gaining experience commanding the 1st Canadian Infantry Brigade. That Keller, like Foulkes, had been one of the three original brigade majors at the start of the war spoke to the shallowness of the Canadian command pool in 1942.

Foulkes survived Price's demise, and survived it well. In August 1942, he took command of the 3rd Canadian Infantry Brigade in spite of the fact that his only command experience between his platoon-commanding days in 1933 and his appointment to formation command was a fifty-one-day stint as the Acting Commanding Officer of the Regina Rifles between December 1941 and January 1942, another "box-ticking" exercise probably arranged by Harry Crerar.[53] Foulkes had good reports from commanders who really did not know any bet-ter, but they were good enough to get him onto Harry Crerar's watch list for command appointments. Crerar kept a spreadsheet of all the up-and-comers in the corps and Foulkes was high on it. Crerar noted Price's recommendation of June 1942, which identified Lieutenant-Colonel Foulkes as an officer of "exceptional ability [and] sound tactical knowledge."[54] Price also remarked that, "after a short period in com[man]d of a brigade, I consider that he would be qualified to com[man]d a div[ision]." This in itself may not have been enough to secure an appointment to divisional command, but, combined with the appraisal of Major-General H.L.N. Salmon, GOC 1st Canadian Infantry Division (and a member of the Royal Canadian Regiment), it carried more weight with Crerar. Salmon wrote that Foulkes was "particularly good in the organization and supervision of training. Would make a good senior G Staff officer or com[an]d[er]. Recommended for appointment as BGS of a Corps or Army or to com[man]d an Inf[antry] Div[ision]."[55] In fact, Crerar followed Salmon's recommendations to the letter. After commanding the 3rd Canadian Infantry Brigade for a little over seven months, Foulkes proceeded to First Canadian Army Headquarters, where he served as BGS for nine months. Then in January 1944, Foulkes took command of the 2nd Canadian Infantry Division.

On the surface, it appears that Foulkes's climb up the command and staff ladder was a perfect preparation for divisional command – brigade major to GSO 1, to battalion commanding officer, to brigade commander, to BGS of the army – but closer examination of his experience in each of these appointments reveals that he rarely broke out of his role as a coordinator of training. During his tenure as Brigade Major 3rd Canadian Infantry Brigade, training did not progress beyond battalion level. As GSO 1 3rd Canadian Infantry Division, he oversaw the organization and equipment of the new division as well as its deployment to Britain, where low-level training continued until the end of 1941. As the Acting Commanding Officer of the Regina Rifles, Foulkes presided over platoon-level training and attended four brigade TEWTs, but he was absent from his battalion for twenty-one days during his fifty-one-day command.[56] For seven of those twenty-one days, he worked his old job as GSO 1 3rd Canadian Infantry Division during the skeleton exercises Beaver I and II. When he did return to his duties as Price's GSO 1 in February 1942, he did not do well. His division played a defensive role during Exercise Beaver IV (10-13 May), and his commander received scathing criticism from Montgomery.[57] Exercise Tiger (19-30 May 1942) pitted 1st Canadian Corps against the British 12th Corps in an encounter battle and Montgomery assessed that the Canadians had done "splendidly," but the poor performance of the 3rd Canadian Infantry Division cost Price his job.[58] There was one more divisional exercise for the division – Exercise Harold under the British 12th Corps in July 1942 – before training for the remainder of 1942 settled back into a period of individual and low-level training designed to eliminate "deficiencies."[59] Foulkes took command of the 3rd Canadian Infantry Brigade a month later and spent his first five months as a brigade commander doing little more than watching over training that barely rose above battalion level. That changed a bit in March 1943, when his brigade proceeded to Inverary, Scotland, where it underwent training in combined operations.[60] The training itself culminated in Exercise Dalmally, a one-day brigade amphibious assault, but the preceding two weeks, as might have been expected, were spent with familiarizing soldiers with amphibious landing craft, loading and unloading drills, and two battalion amphibious assault exercises, Eagle I and Eagle II. After he left the 3rd Canadian Infantry Brigade for the position of BGS First Canadian Army in April 1943, he settled back into the role of training coordinator – arranging for the training and deployment of the 1st Canadian Infantry Division and the First Canadian Army Tank Brigade to Sicily, overseeing the 1st Canadian Corps Exercise Harlequin in August 1943, assisting with the formation of the 4th Canadian Armoured Division and 2nd Canadian Corps, and dealing with equipment issues. That he had very little opportunity to coordinate the actions of an army on a field training exercise was not his fault. He joined McNaughton's headquarters a month after the last army-level manoeuvres in England, Exercise Spartan, and his army commander had shown, and continued to show, very little inclination to put his headquarters through the paces of practising its own procedures. In fact, according to one senior staff officer, Foulkes did try to get McNaughton to exercise his headquarters more frequently, but the army commander, more interested in issues of national politics and technological development, merely went through the motions.[61] Foulkes's career progression may have benefited from indifferent commanders of limited ability, but it was a double-edged sword. What could he realistically have learned about moving brigades, divisions, corps, and armies, when he spent most of his time supervising the training of soldiers, sections, platoons, companies, and battalions? Who would have given him the guidance he needed to hone his skills? With the likes of Price, Sansom, and McNaughton as supervisors, there was only so much he could learn. It was an entirely imperfect apprenticeship for divisional command, but Foulkes ascended to that position in January 1944.

It should come as no surprise then that Foulkes performed poorly as GOC 2nd Canadian Infantry Division. He had none of the innate intelligence of either Burns or Simonds, and the rapidly expanding Canadian Army of 1939-43 had too many training handicaps to ensure that raw material such as Foulkes developed into capable senior commanders. Foulkes was a survivor, however, accomplished at winning the acceptance of his superiors and deflecting blame when things went wrong. Working for Simonds, the newly-appointed commander of 2nd Canadian Corps, clearly intimidated him. Even before Simonds won his spurs as GOC 1st Canadian Infantry Division in Sicily, his reputation as a brilliant and talented officer was well established in the Canadian Army. On 31 January 1944, Simonds took command of the corps, nearly two weeks after Foulkes had settled into his new appointment. Within a week, the new corps commander had replaced a number of key staff officers in whom he "had not much confidence."[62] Foulkes followed suit with similarly decisive action. On 7 February, he replaced his GSO 1, Lieutenant-Colonel J.S. Lind, with Lieutenant-Colonel G.S. Archibald, and less than a month later he replaced all three of his brigadiers, a cue he took from Simonds.[63] Simonds had inspected the three brigades on 2 February and, more than likely, had given Foulkes his unvarnished opinion of Brigadiers J.E. Sager, J.C. Jefferson, and G.S.N. Gostling.[64] On 19 February, Simonds had also circulated to "All Formation Commanders 2nd Canadian Corps" a letter, "Efficiency in Command," in which he emphasized: "I regard it as a first duty of every commander and commanding officer to see to it that the command of his subordinate formations or units is in fit, competent and energetic hands. In this matter there can be no compromise and I consider a commander or commanding officer who tolerates ineffective subordinates is himself unfitted for the responsibilities of command."[65]

A week later, Sager, Jefferson, and Gostling were out and Brigadiers Sherwood Lett, W.J. Megill, and H.A. Young were in. Lett, a Rhodes Scholar and First World War veteran, had previously commanded the 4th Canadian Infantry Brigade and had been wounded at Dieppe. Young was an RMC graduate who had also previously commanded his brigade in the second half of 1942. Megill, the youngest of the new lot at thirty-seven years of age, was a graduate of the Staff College at Quetta and had been on the 3rd Canadian Infantry Division staff in 1940-41, when Foulkes was the GSO 1. Foulkes went for a combination of youth and experience in replacing his brigadiers, but he was also motivated by a desire to stay off Simonds's hit list. Simonds wanted changes and Foulkes was happy to deliver.

Foulkes did his best to train his division. Following Simonds's lead, he established a progressive training plan designed to prepare his formation for battle. He led a TEWT for staff officers and commanders down to battalion level to practise communications in the field, road movement, and the setting up and tearing down of field headquarters.[66] The war diarist noted that "valuable lessons were learned re continuous functioning of HQ of a div[ision] during and immediately after a move."[67] Foulkes and all the commanders and key staff in his divisional headquarters and brigades attended a 2nd Canadian Corps study week, during which Simonds laid down the methods for executing the tasks likely to be undertaken by his corps during the coming campaign in Northwest Europe – attacks by infantry and armoured divisions, pursuing or "following retiring German Forces," night attacks, clearing towns and villages, and "the forcing and crossing of obstacles."[68] Flowing from this initial training period, Exercise Step (1-3 April) practised the movement and assembly of a division in a bridgehead; a corps signals exercise, Last (13-19 April), drilled commanders and staffs "in op[eration]s immediately following the breakout of a br[idge]-h[ea]d"; Exercises Allez and Hike gave the brigades an opportunity to train in both the attack and the advance; and finally, the ambitious Exercise Kate (23 April to 7 May) challenged each of the division's brigades in "crossing a tidal estuary."[69] Kate was directly related to Operation Axehead, the planned crossing of the Seine and seizure of the French port of Le Havre, and it was hoped that as many lessons as possible could be gleaned from the exercise crossing of the Trent River.[70] The joint report on Kate, although it went out under Foulkes's signature, was principally written by Archibald, who bled a staggering 100 pages' worth of lessons out of the exercise. Foulkes clearly hoped that the excruciatingly detailed "interim report" would be "accepted as a basis for the re-examination of the problem of crossing a tidal river, and the formation of a common doctrine."[71] He was trying hard to impress, but no final report followed. The Overlord training was far from perfect, but for the most part Foulkes was well pleased with what he had done with the 2nd Canadian Infantry Division in the five months before he led it to battle in Normandy: "When I took the Second Division into Northwest Europe it had had four years of hard training. We trained day and night and I thought it was about as perfect a fighting machine as we could get."[72] That was how he felt before July 1944.

What happened in Normandy suggests that perhaps Foulkes and his staff did not get as much as they might have from their extensive period of training. His 1948 statement to the Canadian Infantry Association that "when we bumped into battle experienced German troops we were no match for them" and that "we would not have been successful had it not been for our air and artillery support" suggests that the shortfalls festered at levels lower than his.[73] Canadian military historians John A. English and Terry Copp may have markedly different assessments of the Canadian Army's performance in Normandy, but they both agree that Foulkes intended his statement to deflect blame.[74] His division had problems making decisions, passing information, and coordinating the actions of tanks, infantry, and artillery during Operation Atlantic (18-21 July 1944), problems that owed much to a dysfunctional headquarters and that became even more apparent during Operation Spring (25 July). His divisional headquarters was simply not ready for the intense combat of the Normandy campaign. It had spent too much time coordinating training for subordinate formations and units, and not enough time exercising itself in managing a high-tempo, high-intensity battle. The headquarters that produced a 100-page "interim report" on river crossings, and that expected to have *twenty days* of battle procedure in which to conduct an assault water crossing, was too deliberate and too inflexible for battle with a first-class enemy.[75] Part of the problem stemmed from Archibald, who was a very meticulous staff officer but a slow thinker.[76] Part of it was due to Foulkes, who picked a thorough yet pedestrian GSO 1 because he did not want to make mistakes.[77] During Spring, the 2nd and 3rd Canadian Infantry Divisions had less than forty-eight hours to prepare for an assault against a well-posted enemy on the reverse slopes of Verrières ridge south of Caen, slopes from which they had been thrown back with heavy losses only days earlier, during Atlantic. Foulkes's headquarters was not ready for that pace of operations because it had not trained properly for it.

The story of Operation Spring has been well told and well analyzed by several distinguished historians,[78] but a few issues need emphasis for this study of Foulkes.[79] Simonds, who had little faith in either Foulkes or Keller, controlled the battle tightly, assigning very specific intermediate objectives on Verrières ridge to the 2nd and 3rd Canadian Infantry Divisions before he could send the British 7th and Guards Armoured Divisions over the ridge and on to the final objectives to the south. (See Map 11, page 225.) The first two phases – the capture of the line May-sur-Orne to Verrières and the capture of a second line, Fontenay-le-Marmion to Rocquancourt – would be executed in darkness, the first phase beginning at 0330 hours, the second phase two hours later. But night operations had not been a training priority in the 2nd Canadian Infantry Division, and Foulkes further complicated matters by breaking up and reassembling his brigades. He did it to ensure that the most beaten-up battalions from Atlantic were not part of the initial Spring assault, which sounds reasonable enough, but replacing the Essex Scottish Regiment with Les Fusiliers de Mont-Royal in the 4th Canadian Infantry Brigade and swapping Le Régiment de Maisonneuve for the Queen's Own Cameron Highlanders of Canada in 5th Canadian Infantry Brigade caused problems.[80] Too many battalions were working beside and for organizations they did not know well, or trust. His manner of assigning the tanks also complicated the execution of the tasks. Because the enemy was certain to counterattack with tanks, Simonds had placed the 2nd Canadian Armoured Brigade (less one armoured regiment) under Foulkes's command, but Foulkes did not assign any tanks to the two assaulting brigades until the second phase of the attack, after which time the brigades would have been fully engaged with the enemy. Regrouping and marrying up *after* an attack has commenced was never simple. And when he did assign tanks to the 4th and 5th Canadian Infantry Brigades, he assigned the brigades only a single tank squadron each from the 6th Canadian Armoured Regiment for the second phase, with a third squadron "on call to the first brigade requesting assistance."[81] A muddled plan and poor staff work: none of it boded well for the attack.

Even before the first phase commenced, the two lead brigades had to fight to secure their start lines. On the left, in Brigadier Lett's 4th Canadian Infantry Brigade area, the CO of the Royal Hamilton Light Infantry (RHLI), Lieutenant-Colonel John Rockingham, delayed his assault by forty minutes, called up his reserve companies, and used them to clear the start-line area before stepping off. As a result of this prudent move, the RHLI successfully seized the town of Verrières and held it against strong counterattacks by enemy artillery and tanks. On the right, in Brigadier Megill's 5th Canadian Infantry Brigade sector, things were much worse. The Camerons of Canada had not yet secured St. Martin-de-Fontenay, although this setback was not clear to anyone outside the Cameron ranks. The passage of accurate information was breaking down, so Megill had to go forward, wisely so, to confirm the stalemate with the Camerons' commanding officer. Next, he went to Foulkes and Brigadier H.A. Young, to see whether he could have his Régiment de Maisonneuve battalion back for use in clearing the start line. Foulkes refused and told Megill to have the Camerons finish the job they had started, probably because bringing forward the Maisonneuves would have delayed H-hour. When Megill went back to St. Martin, he told the Calgary Highlanders to conduct their phase 1 assault on May-sur-Orne by skirting the problem at St. Martin to the east. Communications continued to unravel. In a terrible indication of how badly the passage of information had broken down, sometime around 0500 hours, the commanding officer of the Black Watch was killed when he entered what he thought was a secure hamlet of St. Martin.

To his credit, Foulkes did go forward to see for himself what was happening and to give direction as necessary. His Tactical Headquarters was deployed and he sent a number of situation reports back to his divisional Main Headquarters on the progress of the battle. At 0220 hours, he relayed that the situation with the Camerons in St. Martin was "very poor" and that they had only "half" of their objective.[82] At 0350, he reported that the Calgary Highlanders were "17 min[ute]s late crossing MCDUFF," which was the start line.[83] By 0455, he optimistically reported that the Calgary Highlanders were "300 y[ard]s past S[tart] L[ine],"[84] but two hours later, when he learned that one of their companies had started to dig in as a result of intense enemy machine gun and mortar fire, he felt that he had to order them on and he told the Maisonneuves to be on one hour's notice to move in case he had to reinforce the Calgaries.[85] Inexplicably, however, his headquarters reported that May-sur-Orne was secure at 0720, which was really wishful thinking. The location of Foulkes's Tactical Headquarters during this period is impossible to determine, but he was not with Megill at 5th Canadian Infantry Brigade headquarters and it is unlikely that he had ventured forward of Megill, given the confused situation. Wherever he had placed himself, he showed very little appreciation for the battle and how one problem – like the failure to completely secure May-sur-Orne – could have a cascading effect on adjacent units or subsequent phases. And he compounded the confusion by sending incomplete or overly optimistic situation reports back to his headquarters and on to Simonds. Based on reports that the situation in May-sur-Orne and St. Martin was good or improving, and based on reports that the RHLI were secure at Verrières, Simonds ordered his divisions to press on with their phase 2 tasks.[86] This accelerated the deterioration of an already bad situation.

The knock-on effect was that the Black Watch walked into disaster. Major Phillip Griffin, who had to take over the battalion after his commanding officer was killed in St. Martin and the senior company commanders were wounded, found a situation in which the enemy still held both the designated assembly area at St. Martin and his proposed start line in May-sur-Orne. The original plan had been for his battalion to form up in the southern outskirts of a secure May-sur-Orne and assault due east with tank and artillery support towards Fontenay-le-Marmion. But with May-sur-Orne still in enemy hands and some holdout Germans in the "factory" just south of St. Martin, and with his brigade, division, and corps commanders pressing him to get on with the attack, Griffin decided not to enter May-sur-Orne at all. He decided instead to assault directly from the southern outskirts of St. Martin, straight over the exposed ridge, while his supporting tanks entered May-sur-Orne to protect his right flank and an artillery barrage shot him onto the ridge. After the war, Megill stated that he thought Griffin's plan a "dicey proposition," and claimed to have thought about telling the twenty-six-year-old Griffin to secure May-sur-Orne first, then assault Fontenay from a firm base.[87] But the message log from the period shows that Megill was feeling the pressure to press on quickly, and he passed that on to Griffin: "Understand the reason you are being held up is because of 3 M[achine] G[un]s near the burnt out t[an]ks [at May-sur-Orne]. [I] have plastered them. It is essential you get on immediately. Suggest you take them on with your own guns."[88] Griffin "got on" shortly after 0900 hours, but when he did, his troops and tanks were caught in a maelstrom of machine gun, mortar, and anti-tank fire. Six tanks fell to anti-tank fire even before reaching the outskirts of May-sur-Orne, so the enemy machine guns in May-sur-Orne had a sickeningly easy time cutting down the Black Watch soldiers as they advanced up the open ridge. Those who survived the advance up the incline only lasted long enough to collide with a reverse-slope enemy position just beyond the crest. Of the 339 Black Watch officers and other ranks that made the assault on Verrières ridge, 324 were killed, wounded, or captured. Griffin was among the 119 killed.[89] The attack had failed terribly, but, because communications were bad and because neither Foulkes nor Simonds was well positioned to get a good appreciation of the battle, it took until 1145 for reports of problems to reach 2nd Canadian Infantry Division Headquarters. The failure of renewed attacks on May-sur-Orne and Rocquancourt later in the day forced Simonds to call off the offensive.

Simonds was furious about the failures across his corps front. The 3rd Canadian Infantry Division had failed to take Tilly-la-Campagne, and Foulkes's 2nd Canadian Infantry Division had failed to take either Rocquancourt or Fontenay-le-Marmion. Worse, as the battle picture developed, he learned that next to nothing had been secured – not St. Martin, not May-sur-Orne, not even St. André-sur-Orne. At 1610, seven hours after the start of the Black Watch assault, 2nd Canadian Corps still had the battalion listed as "whereabouts unknown."[90] The 2nd Canadian Infantry Division's situational awareness in this battle was very bad, but it was predictable given how little the headquarters had practised itself for fast-paced battles, battles fought in the dark, or battles in which communications were sporadic.

Then there was the problem of Foulkes. Working under the likes of Price, Sansom, and McNaughton, he had been conditioned to act more as training coordinator than training participant. His ambitious streak, combined with his reluctance to place himself in positions in which he could make mistakes, kept him from participating in training. In other words, he was the trainer far more often than he was the trainee. That he picked his GSO 1 more for his thoroughness than for his quickness of mind is a further indication that Foulkes had little appreciation for how battles can change quickly. It is almost as though he denied that there was any "fog" in war. Why Simonds did not adequately address these shortcomings in training is unclear, but he recognized a train-wreck battle when he saw it. At one point, probably sometime after midday, Simonds, exasperated by the 2nd Canadian Infantry Division's string of failures and Foulkes's inability to relay an accurate assessment of how the fight was progressing, turned to his GSO 1, Lieutenant-Colonel Robert Moncel, and said, "I'm going over to relieve the Div[ision] Com[man]d[er]."[91] Moncel, who had been forward to both 2nd Canadian Infantry Division Headquarters and 4th Canadian Brigade Headquarters to assess the situation, claimed to have talked Simonds out of sacking Foulkes in the middle of the battle for fear that things would deteriorate further.[92] Simonds agreed, reluctantly at the time, but when he calmed down, he probably realized that he did not have much choice in the matter.

How did Foulkes keep his job after Operation Spring? George Kitching wrote that Simonds had confided to him on at least three occasions "that he wanted to get rid of Charles Foulkes."[93] Kitching's explanation for Foulkes's survival was that Crerar must have intervened, and this seems entirely plausible. Crerar had earlier ordered Simonds to look into whether or not Keller should be relieved of his command, as both John Crocker and Miles Dempsey had recommended, and it is unlikely that Crerar would have countenanced getting rid of Foulkes before Keller's fate had been decided.[94] Simonds submitted his report on Keller only on 27 July,[95] two days after Spring, and, almost immediately afterwards, started battle procedure for holding operations in support of Operation Bluecoat and Operation Totalize. Foulkes also bought himself some time during his most vulnerable period in July and August 1944. Immediately after Spring, he fired Archibald and brought in Lieutenant-Colonel C.M. Drury, an able gunner who would later go on to become the Commander Royal Artillery (CRA) of the 4th Canadian Armoured Division.[96] Brigadier H.A. Young was also bounced, with the approval of Simonds, from the 6th Canadian Infantry Brigade by the end of August. These were not minor personnel changes, so Simonds had to consider the cost to the overall continuity of command, to say nothing of morale in the 2nd Canadian Infantry Division, when deciding whether or not to fire Foulkes. It is also worth noting that the division's casualties during Atlantic and Spring had also eaten away a number of battalion and company commanders and even forced a change in the command of the 4th Canadian Infantry Brigade. Events following Totalize also effectively precluded any replacement of Foulkes. The only potential replacements – Dan Spry and Harry Foster – would soon be employed elsewhere. Spry took over the 3rd Canadian Infantry Division a week after Keller was wounded on 8 August, and Foster found his way to the 4th Canadian Armoured division on 21 August after Kitching had been relieved as a result of his division's difficulties during both Operation Totalize and Operation Tractable.[97] In the end, Simonds decided to keep Foulkes, but it was not because he had faith in the divisional commander's abilities. It was only the better of two bad options.

Foulkes showed no tremendous improvement as a divisional commander, but it did not appear to hold him back. The 2nd Canadian Infantry Division fought reasonably well during the first phase of Operation Totalize,[98] but Totalize was a Simonds battle and the corps commander did not give the divisional commanders much latitude in terms of timings, objectives, or fire planning.[99]

Foulkes's troops also entered and cleared Falaise during 16-18 August, but his ability to read and anticipate battle remained questionable. In the Forêt de la Londe, Foulkes, whose division by that point was short a staggering 1,820 infantry other ranks, persisted in a series of costly and isolated battalion attacks against a strongly held German position on the west side – the Allied side – of the river near the town of Elbeuf, in spite of the fact that the 3rd Canadian Infantry and 4th Canadian Armoured Divisions had crossed the river two days earlier.[100] In these ill-coordinated attacks, which Foulkes pressed despite the protests of his battalion and brigade commanders, the 4th and 6th Canadian Infantry Brigades suffered 577 casualties that they could not afford, and two of the battalions in the latter brigade panicked during a hasty withdrawal. Foulkes added to the absurdity of a pointless battle by ordering that brigade to hold its defensive positions west of the river at all costs, an order that revealed a stunning lack of battle sense.[101] Why would the German defenders, who were obviously fighting a delaying action on the Allied side of the river, do anything but hold or withdraw? How Foulkes retained his command after the Forêt de la Londe battle is still unclear, but it was probably due to a combination of factors. He did manage to hand Simonds and Crerar another head, that of Brigadier J.E. Ganong, who had commanded the 4th Canadian Infantry Brigade for less than a month. But were the corps and army commanders really satisfied with that alone? Perhaps losing both Ganong and Young within a week had persuaded them to avoid further disruption in the 2nd Canadian Infantry Division chain of command. They certainly would have considered the fact that both the 4th Canadian Armoured and the 3rd Canadian Infantry Divisions had only recently changed commanders. Crerar also weighed the fact that he might eventually have to replace Lieutenant-General E.L.M. Burns as GOC-in-C 1st Canadian Corps in response to complaints by the GOC-in-C Eighth Army and the Commander Allied Armies in Italy. If that happened, Foulkes was one of very few options to replace Burns. The two other obvious choices were Chris Vokes and Bert Hoffmeister, neither of whom was a perfect fit either. Both Crerar and Montgomery had concluded that Chris Vokes had reached his ceiling as a divisional commander,[102] while Bert Hoffmeister, a thirty-seven-year old militia officer then commanding the 5th Canadian Armoured Division, had been commanding a battalion less than a year earlier and was still considered inexperienced. Foulkes had a better chance of being acceptable to the British chain of command in Italy, simply because they knew less of him. Whatever the reason or reasons for Foulkes's not being sacked after the Forêt de la Londe, by the end of August 1944 he was the senior divisional commander in 2nd Canadian Corps, and by November 1944 he was commanding 1st Canadian Corps in Italy. It seems incredible that he got that appointment with such limited technical skill, but the dearth of talented and experienced senior Canadian commanders was such that Foulkes was the best choice available.

His human skills were not great either. He was "unpopular up and down."[103] He got into shouting matches with brigadiers,[104] and some openly questioned his orders. If he tried to secure the loyalty of his subordinates at all, Foulkes usually chose to generate fear rather than affection. He fired enough people that the others got the message that they could be next, and he occasionally embarrassed people in public. While acting commander of 2nd Canadian Corps during the battle of the Scheldt, he made no friends or followers in the corps headquarters. Brigadier Elliot Rodger, the corps chief of staff, remembered that Foulkes once "dressed [him] down ... in front of everyone."[105] Not surprisingly, Rodger had "no respect" for Foulkes and "simply ... blocked out" from memory the period during which Foulkes had been acting corps commander. Foulkes took an unwise tack for a technically deficient commander who truly needed a competent staff in order to be successful, but he was insecure with those who saw through his weaknesses, officers like Rodger and Simonds. Rodger he could berate. Simonds he could not, so he fired subordinates instead. Neither of his two divisional commanders in 1st Canadian Corps had a good word to say about him. Hoffmeister described him as a "vain egotistical man who spent time determining what was good for Chas Foulkes."[106] And Foster allegedly described Foulkes as a "fraud, an incompetent and a nasty man."[107] To say that his people skills were poor would be an understatement. George Kitching could not understand why Foulkes chose to denigrate the Italian theatre to Italian Campaign veterans when he took command of 1st Canadian Corps in November 1944. As Chief of Staff 1st Canadian Corps, Kitching advised Foulkes to say a few complimentary words about the record of the corps and the Eighth Army to a gathering of every officer in the corps between the rank of lieutenant-colonel and major-general:

> For some reason or other, Charles Foulkes took an opposite tack. Instead of praising them he implied that the tactics used by the formations in Italy were a little out of date and would have to change to make use of the new equipment which the divisions in Belgium and Holland were using and which would be made available shortly in Italy. He remarked that we were crossing the same rivers that Caesar had crossed and were using the same equipment as he had.
>
> I watched the faces of his audience as he spoke and it was obvious to me that he had failed to win their enthusiastic support ... there was little interest in the eyes of his audience. He missed a great opportunity.[108]

This was Charles Foulkes at his insecure worst. Any commander coming to a new theatre and a new command would have had concerns. Foulkes had all of them and more. It did not help that, earlier that day, his aircraft had landed at the wrong airfield, where there was no one from 1st Canadian Corps to greet him, and from which he had to hitch a ride with a military policeman to Eighth Army Headquarters.[109] He felt snubbed. He also knew his own limitations as a tactician, but, instead of acknowledging the experience and expertise of his audience, even asking for their assistance, Foulkes adopted an I-know-something-you-don't-know attitude, which failed. Montgomery got away with that sort of thing because he was so highly skilled. Foulkes, whose technical skills were shaky at best, could not. Kitching was right. The new corps commander had missed an excellent opportunity to win over staff officers and commanders who could help compensate for his deficiencies. He won few hearts. Brigadier William Ziegler, CRA 1st Canadian Corps and one of those present for Foulkes's inappropriate speech, was another staff officer who had "no respect" for the corps commander and "never heard a good word about him."[110] Foulkes also had a few displays of drunkenness in Italy, which further eroded his credibility.[111] He did not get off to a good start as a corps commander.

He did improve, however, with the help of some talented subordinates such as George Kitching. Kitching may have had difficulties as a divisional commander but he was an exceptional staff officer.[112] He had been GSO 1 for the 1st Canadian Infantry Division during Operation Husky and the staff officer most responsible for that formation's successful preparation for, and deployment to, Sicily in the summer of 1943.[113] Kitching arrived at 1st Canadian Corps on 10 November and fully assumed his duties four days later, a week before Foulkes's arrival on 20 November.[114] With the acting corps commander, Chris Vokes, Kitching began planning the role of 1st Canadian Corps in a much larger army group effort to capture Bologna (see Map 16). General Alexander's plan called for a northward thrust east of the city by the Eighth Army, which would force the Germans to commit reserves in the immediate area of Bologna and set the conditions for a successful Fifth Army assault straight at Bologna from the south. Eighth Army commander General Sir Richard McCreery issued orders to his corps commanders on 18 November.[115] McCreery wanted the 2nd Polish Corps and 5th Corps to cross the Montone River and secure jumping-off points for 1st Canadian Corps, which would then drive hard "along the axis RUSSI ... LUGO ... MASSA LOMBARDA."[116] Kitching steered the staff planning for Operation Chuckle with skill. At this early planning stage, he saw three possibilities for which there had to be plans – that 5th Corps would fail to gain a crossing over the Montone River; that 5th Corps would be successful in crossing

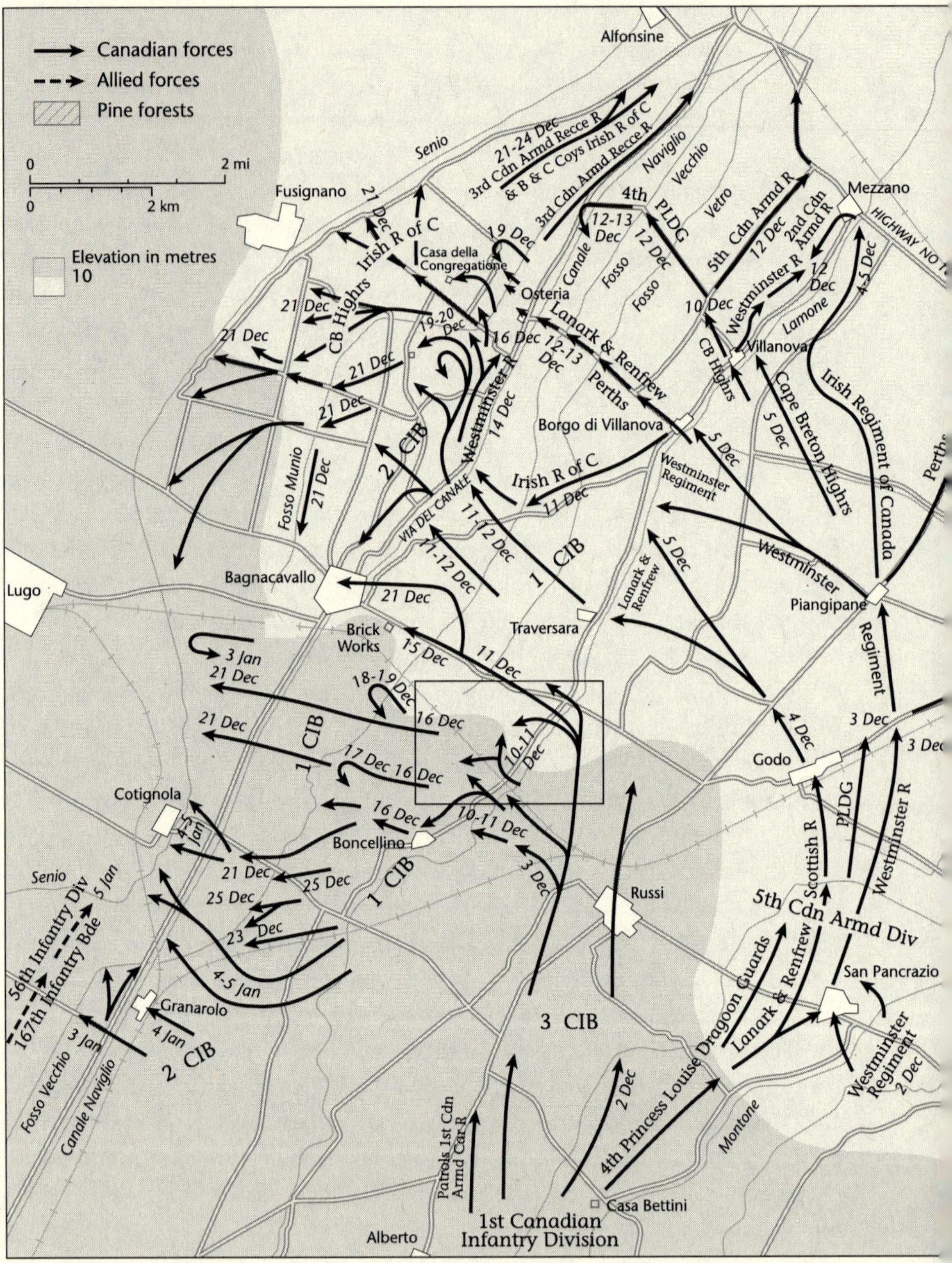

MAP 16    From the Montone to the Senio, 2 December 1944 to 5 January 1945.

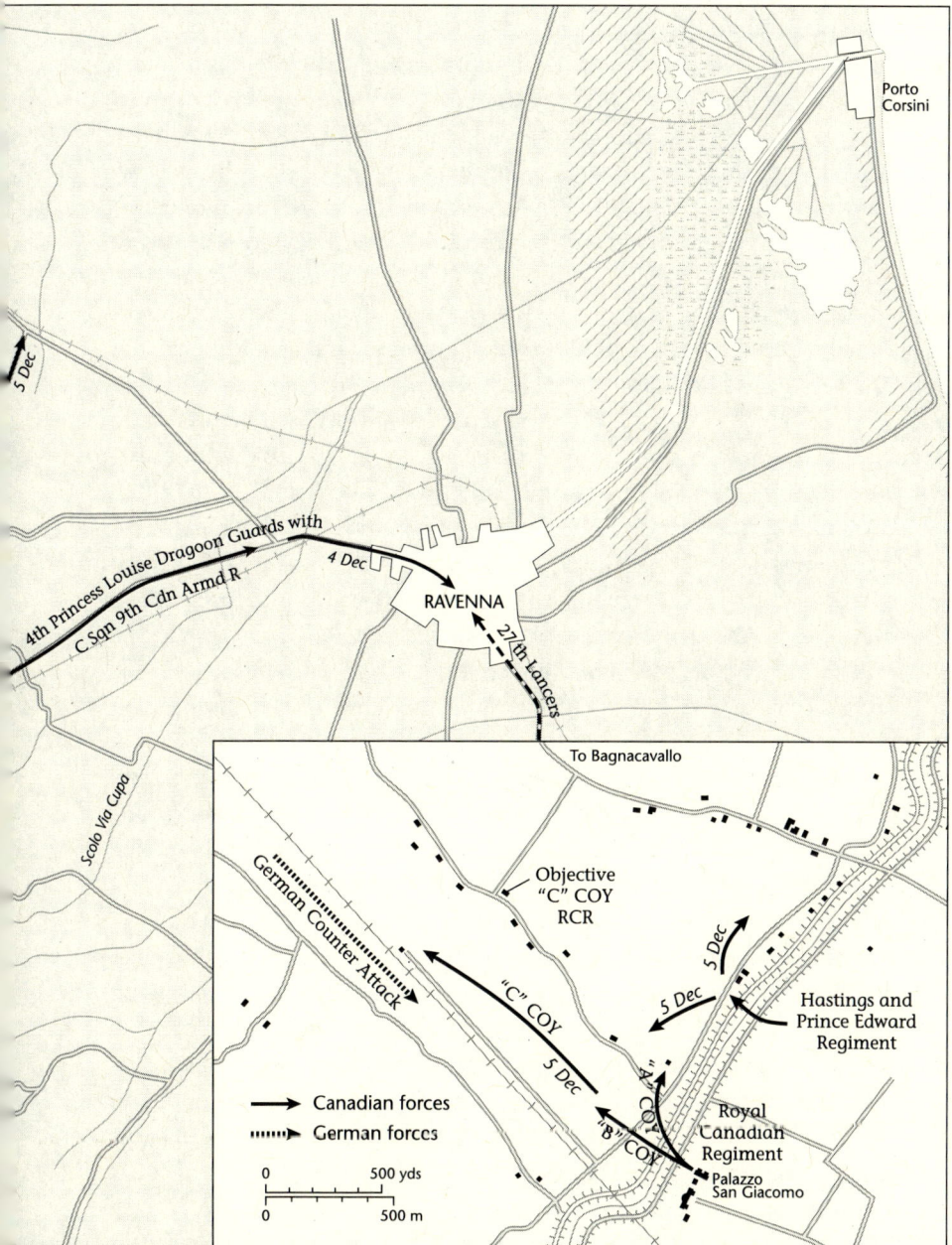

*Source:* Douglas E. Delaney, *The Soldiers' General: Bert Hoffmeister at War* (Vancouver: UBC Press, 2005), 200-1.

the Montone River and forcing the enemy back to the Lamone River; or that flooding would place 5th Corps' operations completely on hold. Later that day, at a planning conference attended by the key corps staff, the Commander, Corps Royal Artillery (CCRA), and the Commander, Corps Royal Engineers (CCRE), Kitching and Vokes passed on the planning parameters. By 20 November, Kitching had received the CCRA's planning notes for the three contingencies and a verbal briefing from the CCRE.[117] With these appreciations in hand and with the assistance of other staff members, Kitching prepared an outline plan, which he presented to Foulkes just before the corps commander's 21 November conference.[118] Foulkes made a few minor ink amendments, but essentially accepted the plan as it had been devised by Kitching – a four-phase operation to advance along the Highway 9 axis towards Massa Lombarda and Argenta, 1st Canadian Infantry Division on the left and 5th Canadian Armoured Division on the right. In phase 1, the Canadians would relieve the 10th Indian Division and cross the Montone River with both divisions. In phase 2, the corps would cross the Lamone River, then capture Bagnacavallo with the 1st Canadian Infantry Division and Ravenna with the 5th Canadian Armoured Division. Phase 3 would see the capture of both Lugo and Cotignola. Finally, in phase 4, the corps would exploit as far as possible towards Argenta. To ensure that the defending Germans would have little opportunity to recover, the outline plan emphasized that the operation would be "continuous day and night," and that brigades and battalions would be "stepped up, but not passed through until [the lead] f[or]m[atio]n or unit [was] completely tired out." On 28 November, Foulkes presented a "Revised Outline Plan," the only change in which was the elimination of the phase 1 task to cross the Montone because the 10th Indian Division had done that on 24 November and was currently cleaning up the start line for the Canadian attack.[119] The timings for the relief of the 10th Indian Division by the 1st Canadian Infantry Division and the start of the attack would hinge on the completion of a tank-supportable bridge across the Montone. The relief-in-place would begin twenty-four hours before the bridge was complete, so that the Canadians would be ready to start their attack at 1800 hours on the day of its completion. This made perfect sense. There was no point in starting the attack until a sturdy bridge ensured that tanks and anti-tank guns could cross the Montone quickly.

The attack from the 10th Indian Division bridgehead on 2 December went well until the 1st Canadian Infantry Division attackers reached the Lamone River. The Canadians struck hard at the boundary between the 356th Infantry Division and the 114th Jaeger Division, two formations belonging to the 73rd Corps.[120] After hard fighting, Russi fell to the 1st Canadian Infantry Division on 3 December, forcing a withdrawal of German delaying forces back and across the Lamone River, and the 5th Canadian Armoured Division seized a crossing of the Montone at San Pancrazio then swept east, to cut off Ravenna and close up to the Lamone River. Brigadier J.D.B. Smith, acting GOC of the 1st Canadian Infantry Division until the arrival of Harry Foster on 9 December, had planned to break out of the bridgehead and seize the initial crossings of the Lamone with the 3rd Canadian Infantry Brigade, then drive to Bagnacavallo with the 2nd Canadian Infantry Brigade, and finally capture Lugo with the 1st Canadian Infantry Brigade. The 3rd Brigade, however, had suffered 106 casualties and it had taken a full forty-eight hours for its battalions to reach the Lamone.[121] Here Smith made a judgment call. Because he was sure that any crossing of the Lamone would trigger a German counterattack, he decided that it would be best to bring up fresh troops from the 1st Canadian Infantry Brigade for the assault across the river, instead of having the 3rd Canadian Infantry Brigade execute the crossing as planned. Unfortunately, bad tactical decisions at the brigade and battalion level exacerbated a difficult transition. Brigadier "Ding" Calder, commander of the 1st Brigade, who had been planning how to attack out of Bagnacavallo and capture Lugo in accordance with Smith's original plan, now prepared to cross the Lamone River, quickly and without the benefit of detailed reconnaissance. His first attempt, with the Hastings and Prince Edward Regiment (H & PER) during the afternoon of 4 December, ran into a hail of machine gun fire from the twenty-five-foot-high flood embankments that lined the forty-foot-wide river. He tried again at 0100 hours the next morning, following the return of evening reconnaissance patrols that had crossed the river. This second attempt on a two-battalion front did not fare much better. The attack – the Royal Canadian Regiment (RCR) left and the H & PER right – took place between the railway line and the Godo-Bagnacavallo road. With the support of four medium artillery regiments, his battalions managed to gain a foothold on the west bank.

Staying there proved to be a problem. Sometime around 0300 hours on 5 December, Kitching advised Foulkes of the RCR bridgehead. Although satisfied with the good news of the crossing, Foulkes rightly worried that the infantry would be vulnerable to German counterattack. Through Kitching, Foulkes directed Smith to "ensure immediately that six-pounder anti-tank guns were rafted or dragged across to give the infantry the necessary support in case of a German counter attack."[122] The situation was worse than Foulkes had thought. The railway embankment was 20-25 feet high and it dominated the pancake flat and open ground around it, but the RCR never gained control of it, even though they had penetrated 1,000 yards beyond the river. Thus they were blind to the well-planned and well-rehearsed counterattack that was coming. The 356th Division hurled the 356th Reconnaissance Battalion, reinforced with assault guns and a company of infantry from the 741st Regiment, at the bridgehead. Enemy assault guns fired through gaps in the embankment while machine guns fired unmolested from its heights. The official historian of the Canadians in the Italian Campaign was unnecessarily kind in accepting that "the obscuring fog prevented effective use of the battalion PIATs."[123] If German machine-gunners could engage their targets, Canadian PIAT anti-tank gunners and machine-gunners should have been able to do the same.[124] The problem was that no one had been tasked with taking and holding the railway embankment, a fatal error in both planning and execution.

Foulkes acted as he normally did when faced with a setback – he fired people – but in this instance he was entirely justified. Smith's decision to replace the 3rd with the 1st Canadian Infantry Brigade for the Lamone crossing had forced Brigadier Calder and Lieutenant-Colonel J.W. Ritchie, the RCR commanding officer, to cobble together an unplanned action in fairly short order. Nevertheless, they showed breathtakingly bad tactical judgment in not realizing the importance of the railway. Attacking on only one side of the embankment was an extremely hazardous undertaking because it more or less surrendered to the enemy the approaches on the west side of the embankment, and the embankment's heights. Calder and, to a lesser extent, Smith should have realized this. Calder made things worse by not ordering the RCR either to observe what might be coming or to engage it with direct or indirect fire.[125] It should also have been obvious to Ritchie, whose patrols had seen the embankment only hours earlier. What should have been a battle for the railway embankment instead became a barrel-shoot for the 356th Reconnaissance Battalion and its supporting arms attachments.[126] More than half of the 205 RCR soldiers who crossed the river were killed, wounded, or captured.[127] The H & PER added another 58 casualties to the total, most of them the result of their own artillery fire when the lead companies mistakenly formed up ahead of their start line. Calder had to go. So did Ritchie. Foulkes later claimed that he "should have also replaced Brigadier Smith,"[128] but Smith's questionable decision to substitute the 3rd with the 1st Canadian Infantry Brigade for the crossing was understandable, especially considering that the predictable German counterattacks meant that the bridgehead battle would likely be fought for a day or two longer than the forty-eight hours that the 3rd Canadian Infantry Brigade had already been fighting. Smith was only an acting GOC and was due to be replaced by Foster in a matter of days, and his battle record as the commander of 5th Canadian Armoured Brigade had also been good as well.[129] Foulkes sent Smith to 1st Canadian Infantry Brigade to replace Calder instead. That was a good decision too because Smith fought the brigade well for the rest of the war.

Foulkes's first instinct after the Lamone setback was to regroup and attempt another crossing as quickly as possible, but the weather forced delays that, ironically, proved beneficial. By midday on 6 December, the 1st Canadian Infantry Division had issued orders for a renewed attack, this time with the 3rd Canadian Infantry brigade "three b[attalio]ns up" astride both the railway embankment and the Godo-Bagnacavallo road.[130] The 5th Canadian Armoured Division planned a silent attack (with no preparatory bombardment) by the 11th Canadian Infantry Brigade at Borgo di Villanova and Villanova, while the 12th Canadian Infantry Brigade on its left and the 5th Canadian Armoured Brigade on its right created distractions with whatever mortars, machine guns, and anti-tank weapons they could muster. Unfortunately, heavy rains threatened the Montone bridges and therefore the ability to reinforce any planned gains over the Lamone. Foulkes postponed the operation by twenty-four hours although he was still anxious to get on with it. He was not alone in believing that an attack was better sooner rather than later, because the rain forecast for the next week or so would only make matters worse. On 7 December, even with a reported eight inches of water on the road near the main Montone crossing site south of Russi, Foulkes, his staff, and his commanders were still willing to attempt the attack.[131] The army commander took a bit longer to reach that conclusion. Concerned that the Canadians could lose the bridges behind them during the attack, McCreery visited Foulkes on the morning of 7 December "to discuss the advisability of staging the attack across the F[osso] LAMONE tonight in view of the probability of continued bad weather."[132] Later that afternoon, he and Foulkes met with the two divisional commanders to get their thoughts. The forecast of "ten more days of intermittent rain" brought a now-or-never haste to the deliberations. All of them, McCreery included, "decided to put in the attack tonight."[133] As it turned out, that decision was short-lived because flooding of the Lamone later that day forced yet another postponement. The on-again, off-again nature of the preparations annoyed the troops, but the time spent waiting was not time wasted. All across the corps front, Canadian patrols reconnoitred bridges and crossing sites, snapped prisoners, conducted small raids, and laid ambushes behind the enemy's front line.[134] By the time they launched across the Lamone on 10 December, the attackers had a very clear picture of where they were going and what they had to do.

The 1st Canadian Corps did well considering that the ground to be crossed presented so many problems. In the seven kilometres that separated the Lamone and Senio Rivers, four dyked waterways, each about eight feet high, cut across flat and fairly drenched farmland. The waterways impeded vehicle movement and the flat, open ground meant that any defender perched on an embankment could observe and shoot would-be attackers at will – at least during daylight. If the Germans decided to stand on any of these water obstacles, nothing short of a deliberate, set-piece attack would push them back. The 10 December attack took place much as it had been planned in the preceding five days and was very successful in the initial stages. The corps achieved complete tactical surprise over the enemy with a silent attack that began at 2130 hours. On the 5th Canadian Armoured Division front, the 11th Canadian Infantry Brigade with the Westminster Regiment under command slipped across the Lamone in assault boats at Villanova and Borgo di Villanova, while the two neighbouring brigades made as much noise as possible. Once across, the Westminsters had to fend off a very determined counterattack by two battalions, one each from the 278th and 98th Infantry Divisions, and at least fifteen tanks. Using their PIATs and supporting artillery, the Westminsters held their little bridgehead at Villanova, allowing the 12th Canadian Infantry Brigade and 5th Canadian Armoured Brigade to push out to the Fosso Vecchio and Highway 16.[135] On the 1st Canadian Infantry Division front, the 3rd Canadian Infantry Brigade with the 48th Highlanders of Canada under command executed a similarly stealthy assault at the site of the 1st Canadian Infantry Brigade failure of 5 December. This time, however, the attackers assaulted both sides of the railway embankment without a preparatory bombardment to announce their arrival, and Foulkes had arranged a diversionary attack by the 43rd Indian Brigade along the Via Emilia to the south, where the Germans had counterattacked with the 90th Panzergrenadier Division on 8 December.[136] All the reconnaissance, staff work, and preparation paid off. The supporting guns began to fire approximately thirty minutes after H-hour and the 1st and 4th Field Companies of engineers managed to raft anti-tank guns to the three assaulting battalions before first light. From this foothold, the Royal 22e Régiment advanced towards the Fosso Vecchio until it met with fire from enemy positions just south of Bagnacavallo. Any approach to the walled and well-fortified town from the south and southwest exposed attackers to observation and fire from Bagnacavallo itself, from the enemy in the dry Canale Naviglio, and from the dominating twenty-five-foot embankments of the Senio.

So instead of taking Bagnacavallo head-on, Foulkes focused on breaking the new line north and east of town, where the enemy had withdrawn across the Canale Naviglio on the morning of 12 December. Things happened quickly. During daylight hours, Foulkes moved around the battlefield a lot, to confer with his divisional commanders and to view the ground for himself. The 1st Canadian Corps Log shows that, for the period 11-12 December, he visited the headquarters of both his divisions three times each. This was fairly typical for Foulkes during Operation Chuckle.[137] From these discussions, and those he had with Kitching and the corps staff in the evenings, he worked out a plan whereby both divisions would attack simultaneously across the Naviglio – the 1st Canadian Infantry Division 1 kilometre northeast of Bagnacavallo and the 5th Canadian Armoured Division between Osteria and the road 1.5 kilometres to the northeast. Unfortunately, this was precisely the area that the German 98th Division was in the process of reinforcing. The Canadian attacks since 2 December had worn down the 73rd Corps to such a precarious state that the 10th Army commander had no choice but to reinforce it. In spite of this, the Canadians still made it across the Canale Naviglio in yet another night assault. Hoffmeister attacked over the Fosso Vecchio with Brigadier J.S. Lind's 12th Canadian Infantry Brigade, and the 4th Princess Louise Dragoon Guards actually made it over the Canale Naviglio, but very determined German counterattacks drove them back to the Fosso Vecchio with 88 casualties, 21 of them fatal. The Lanark and Renfrew Scottish Regiment made it to the east bank of the Vecchio, but no further. Thus, the 5th Canadian Armoured Division attack failed, but in the 1st Canadian Infantry Division sector, the 1st Canadian Infantry Brigade established a crossing two kilometres northwest of Bagnacavallo. Following an artillery bombardment of the Naviglio positions, Brigadier Smith sent the Carleton and York Regiment across, then quickly reinforced their initial success with the H & PER. On hearing that a counterattack by the 190th Panzer Reconnaissance Battalion was imminent, he ordered the two battalions to stop and hold firm while he brought forward the RCR and arranged for air support at first light. When the counterattack came at 0800 hours on 13 December, German tanks and infantry very nearly overran the H & PER and forced the bridgehead back to a small perimeter near the crossing site. The Carleton and Yorks also faced a tank-infantry counterattack, but they held it off with towed anti-tank guns and artillery fire. Shortly after midday, the supporting engineers completed tank crossing sites over the Vecchio and the Naviglio, enabling the British Columbia Dragoons to pour into the beleaguered bridgehead and save it. That evening, Smith used the Loyal Edmonton Regiment, which Major-General Foster had just placed under his command, to attack and expand the bridgehead. Smith's performance during this gruelling contest vindicated Foulkes's decision not to fire him.

Other subordinates came through for Foulkes as well. Hoffmeister, who saw no chance of crossing the Naviglio in his sector without very heavy casualties, thought he might use the bridgehead that Smith had made instead. As the battle to hold the 1st Canadian Infantry Brigade bridgehead raged, he proposed to Foulkes that he send the Westminster Regiment through that bridgehead, provided it held, and have the regiment sweep north along the Naviglio to Osteria.[138] This was an extremely risky manoeuvre, moving parallel to the line of enemy defences, but Foulkes agreed and directed the 5th Canadian Armoured Division to have a "combat g[rou]p ... be prepared to pass through the 1 Cdn Inf Div br[idge]head [and] strike N[orth]W[est]."[139] The Westminsters and a squadron of tanks executed this well-orchestrated manoeuvre on 14 December while Desert Air Force Spitbombers attacked enemy defences on their left flank as they advanced. It worked. At a cost of 4 killed and 16 wounded, the Westminsters took 106 prisoners and so weakened enemy defences around Osteria that the Lanark and Renfrew Scottish were able to cross the Naviglio with very little difficulty.[140] The 4th Princess Louise Dragoon Guards did the same further north.

After this remarkable accomplishment in appalling conditions and against a freshly reinforced enemy, the Canadians found themselves facing yet another well-defended obstacle at the Fosso Munio on the right and the still-strong defences of Bagnacavallo on the left. Figuring that Bagnacavallo was the vital ground of the German line, Foulkes set about trying to capture it. His first attempt – a one-two punch on either side of the city on 16-18 December – failed. A 1st Canadian Infantry Brigade attack between Boncellino and Bagnacavallo faltered when enemy counterattacks drove the RCR and the H & PER back across the Fosso Vecchio, so Foulkes cancelled the second "punch," which was an assault across the Fosso Munio by the 11th Canadian Infantry Brigade. At 1000 hours on the morning of 18 December, he held an orders group attended by both divisional commanders, his CCRA, his Chief Engineer, and two key brigade commanders, Lieutenant-Colonel Pat Bogert of the 2nd Canadian Infantry Brigade and Brigadier Ian Johnston of the 11th Canadian Infantry Brigade.[141] There was a change in plans. The corps would put in a two-division attack centred on Osteria, again in darkness and again without any preparatory bombardment to announce the attack. The assaulting battalions of the 11th Canadian Infantry Brigade pushed over the Munio while the 2nd Canadian Infantry Brigade's battalions advanced across the open ground towards Casa Argelli and Casa Peli. The fight against the 98th Division enemy was difficult – it could hardly have been anything but difficult – but the troops of 1st Canadian Corps succeeded. There were a few close calls as the Canadian engineers struggled to bring forward tanks and anti-tank guns to help the infantry against German counterattacks, but the guns and tanks got to where they were needed. In fact, the breakthrough in the centre of the corps front so threatened the defences around Bagnacavallo that the enemy began to thin out in the south, making the advance of the 1st Canadian Infantry Brigade across the Naviglio a fairly simple affair. By 22 December, the Canadians had reached the Senio across the corps front. This was short of their phase 3 objectives for Operation Chuckle – just short – but, given the conditions of the terrain and the reaction of the enemy, they had done very well to make it that far. And they had succeeded in drawing away from the Bologna sector both the 98th Division and the Field Marshal Keselring Machine Gun Battalion, which was what McCreery wanted. Unfortunately, the US Fifth Army drive on Bologna never materialized, in spite of the fact that the Eighth Army offensive had drawn a total of three divisions away from that city. General Lucian Truscott believed his army to be too short on ammunition to capture Bologna, and Field Marshal Alexander, Supreme Commander Mediterranean since 12 December, agreed to cancel the planned offensive until the spring.[142]

How much of the hard-won 1st Canadian Corps successes during the miserable Battle of the Rivers can be credited to Foulkes? Not much, because not many of the ideas for the offensive originated with him. Brigadier Megill's experience with the 2nd Canadian Infantry Division in Northwest Europe had been that Foulkes "got all his advice from his staff."[143] There was some of that in Operation Chuckle. He more or less accepted the outline plan as it had been drawn up by Kitching and Vokes prior to his arrival, but his faith in Kitching and the 1st Corps staff was well placed. They reacted well to the many adjustments and plan changes during the operation, ensuring that fighting troops, ammunition, bridging equipment, and supplies got to where they were needed when they were needed. Foulkes was also willing to accept advice from subordinate commanders, something he had been loath to do in Normandy. Whereas he had quarrelled with the likes of Megill and Young only months earlier, in Italy he conferred constantly with Hoffmeister and Foster. He accepted Hoffmeister's risky scheme to send the Westminsters through the 1st Canadian Infantry Brigade bridgehead on 14 December, and he agreed to several "silent" attacks, which was something that had been rare in Northwest Europe but common in Italy. His staff and his divisional commanders delivered results. His awkward arrival in Italy aside, Foulkes adjusted fairly well to his new environment and learned as he went. As Kitching remembered, "The more I worked with Charles Foulkes in Italy the more I respected his judgment in tactical matters."[144] How much of that respect was tied to Foulkes's ready acceptance of Kitching's suggestions is unclear, but given how little tactical acumen Foulkes had displayed as a divisional commander, it probably had a lot to do with the upward swing of Kitching's opinion. So although most of the plans or actions in Operation Chuckle did not originate with the corps commander, the successes the Canadians achieved under appalling conditions suggest that he had gotten better at harnessing the talent of those under him.

The pattern continued when 1st Canadian Corps rejoined the First Canadian Army in Northwest Europe. After arriving in Holland, Foulkes had his first conference with Crerar late in the afternoon of 21 February 1945.[145] The army

MAP 17 The western Netherlands, 2-25 April 1945. *Source:* Delaney, *The Soldiers' General*, 208.

commander's planning staff had just completed an appreciation for Operation Anger, an attack out of the Nijmegen bridgehead, the purpose of which was to seize a crossing site over the Neder Rijn at Arnhem and establish a point from which 2nd Canadian Corps could attack Emmerich from behind and thereby secure a crossing of the Rhine (see Map 17). Crerar had intended that 1st Canadian Corps would execute Anger, and he tasked Foulkes with examining the operation in detail. Kitching caught up with Foulkes at the Main Headquarters of First Canadian Army late that evening: "He [Foulkes] had had a session with General Crerar and, after passing on whatever instruction he had received from Harry Crerar, went on a well-deserved five days' leave in England."[146] The appreciation, based on a detailed study of the terrain, the weather, and enemy dispositions was signed on 26 February, so Foulkes really did not have much input to the final product beyond setting the planning parameters and signing it.[147] The assessment was that there were "so many limiting factors ... that quick decisive results could not be expected." Flooding on the northern half of the "Island," the land between the Neder Rijn and the Waal River, would slow any attempt to cross the Neder Rijn, and the Germans' ability to flood the Ijssel River at will precluded any rapid thrust southward towards Emmerich, to say nothing of the Germans' ability to deploy troops to the "Doesburg-Zevenaar switch." Foulkes concluded: "It is therefore my opinion that this operation should be considered only as a subsidiary operation to be undertaken only if conditions of the weather and of the enemy prove advantageous." This was a perfectly sensible recommendation. Kitching wrote that, at this stage, he "continued to be impressed with Charles Foulkes' military decisions. The many plans *we* worked on were all based on sound common sense."[148] His use of the first person plural speaks volumes about how the planning process worked at 1st Canadian Corps, and contrasts with the "I" that Foulkes used in his correspondence with Crerar. Simonds's Chief of Staff could never have used "we" in describing how plans were formulated at 2nd Canadian Corps.[149]

Crerar accepted Foulkes's recommendation to hold Anger in abeyance, but events soon conspired to put a version of it back into play. On 9 March, Montgomery issued his "Orders for the Battle of the Rhine." While the British Second and US Ninth Armies crossed the Rhine, Crerar's task was to hold along the Rhine, the Meuse, and the Waal, and this included the bridgehead on the "Island." Then, as Montgomery's other two armies drove east and northeast into Germany, Crerar was to develop operations to capture Deventer and Zutphen, attack the Ijssel defences from the east, cross the Ijssel to capture Apeldoorn and the high ground between it and Arnhem, and finally bridge the Neder Rijn at Arnhem and open up the important supply route that ran Nijmegen-Arnhem-Zutphen. As far as the army group commander was concerned, the latter task was the most critical because the supply route was critical to sustaining his drive into Germany. The day after Montgomery's conference, Crerar ordered Foulkes to "secure a bridgehead over the NEDER RIJN and capture ARNHEM at the same time 2nd Canadian Corps are developing operations" to "capture APELDOORN and the high ground between that place and ARNHEM."[150] Crerar confirmed this basic scheme of manoeuvre on 24 March and again on 2 April.[151]

Years later, Foulkes implied that the idea for converging and concurrent attacks at Apeldoorn and Arnhem originated with him:

> My plan was ... to put an attack across the Ijssel toward Apeldoorn. I had hoped that that attack would draw all the enemy reserves from Arnhem to the North, and as soon as those reserves had moved it was my hope to then force a crossing of the [Neder Rijn] and secure a bridgehead across the [Neder Rijn] near Arnhem ...
>
> The attack at Apeldoorn was to be done by 1st Canadian Division. Before this attack the 1st Canadian Division was placed under the command of General Simonds, for the commencement of the operation. As there was complete confidence between Simonds and myself I was quite prepared to let Simonds start the attack and I would take over as soon as my communications allowed.[152]

Clearly, Foulkes was not the wellspring of these ideas. In his 10 March and 24 March directives, Crerar assigned the task of capturing the high ground along "the general line APELDOORN-OTTERLO" to 2nd Canadian Corps.[153] He also stated that, during the planning, the 1st Canadian Infantry Division would remain "under command 1 Canadian Corps [only] on arrival [in the battle area] but remaining in Army Reserve pending request for release to 2 Canadian Corps." Crerar intended that Foster's division would go to Simonds for the Ijssel crossing all along. Foulkes had very little say in it, but this was not the first time he had taken credit for an idea that was not his. And the best that might be said about his claim that complete confidence existed between him and Simonds is that it was probably wishful thinking on his part.

The origins of the battle plan notwithstanding, in late March and early April, Foulkes worked with his staff and his subordinate commanders to complete the tasks Crerar had assigned him. His primary task while the assault crossing of the Rhine was underway was to hold his positions on the Waal and on the "Island," which he did on 23-27 March. Then, after the successful Rhine crossing of Operation Plunder, Foulkes issued orders for the next stage. First, he would clean up the southern end of the "Island" with the 49th (West Riding) Division, then he would clear the northern half of the "Island" with the 5th Canadian Armoured and 49th (West Riding) Divisions. This would be followed with a crossing of the Neder Rijn west of Arnhem.[154] On 2-3 April, he executed Operation Destroyer, easily clearing the flooded northern half of the "Island," with the 5th Canadian Armoured Division closing up to the Neder Rijn between Driel and Opheusden, and the 49th (West Riding) Division between Arnhem and Doornenburg. Once closed up to the Neder Rijn, however, Foulkes "found that the Bosch was moving his main reserves toward the left [west] side of

Arnhem ... I felt it was necessary to gain surprise, therefore I decided to change the point of attack from the vicinity of Rhenen on the Rhine [Neder Rijn] to Westervoort on the Ijssel, and to take Arnhem from the right."[155] In this decision, Foulkes leaned heavily on the counsel of his Chief Engineer, Brigadier Colin Campbell: "[He] recommended that we could build a bridge at Nijmegen, push it up the [Neder Rijn] on a barge and swing it into position ... at Westervoort. This would mean if I was successful that I would have a tank bridge across the river within eight hours."[156] The advantages of a rapid bridging operation were obvious: the sooner Foulkes could get tanks across, the better he would be able to defend his bridgehead against counterattack. The eastern attack option also had the advantage of a shorter water obstacle to span: the Ijssel was only 145 feet wide at Westervoort, compared with the 254-foot span of the Neder Rijn west of Arnhem. To enhance the element of surprise, the operation by the 49th (West Riding) Division to capture Arnhem and open the Nijmegen-Arnhem-Zutphen road, a revised version of Operation Anger, would not begin until at least twenty-four hours after 2nd Canadian Corps had launched Operation Cannonshot, the attack by the 1st Canadian Infantry Division across the Ijssel River towards Apeldoorn. Beyond the military requirement to open the Nijmegen-Arnhem-Zutphen road, Montgomery directed that, upon completion of Cannonshot and Anger, the First Canadian Army would clear Western Holland in order to bring relief to starving Dutch civilians.[157] Crerar passed down the task to Foulkes on 7 April and Foulkes adjusted his plans accordingly.[158] On 12 April, he issued a methodical four-phase plan "to clear the Germans out of Western Holland," all the way from Arnhem and Apeldoorn to Amsterdam and Rotterdam, using the 49th (West Riding), 1st Canadian Infantry, and 5th Canadian Armoured Divisions.[159]

But when Montgomery later decided that he needed all available resources east of the Rhine, he restricted operations south of the Zuider Zee (Ijsselmeer) to two divisions, adding that they could advance westward only after they had opened the Nijmegen-Arnhem-Zutphen road, and only if they could do so "on their own resources ... no additional engineer units or transport are available until a later stage."[160] On receiving Crerar's amended orders, which were in line with the army group commander's intentions, Foulkes revised his plan. Considering what he had available and what he knew of what was left of the 361st Volksgrenadier Division on the Ijssel and the 346th Infantry Division along the Neder Rijn, Foulkes scaled back his intention from marching to Amsterdam and Rotterdam "to clear[ing] the enemy from WESTERN HOLLAND between the IJSSEL and the GREBBE LINE."[161] At a conference of his divisional commanders and key staff on 14 April, he issued orders for achieving these more modest objectives: the 1st Canadian Infantry Division would capture Apeldoorn and advance on Voorthuizen; the 49th (West Riding) Division would mop up in Arnhem, open the Nijmegen-Arnhem-Zutphen road, then advance to Ede and Luntern; and the 5th Canadian Armoured Division would burst out of the Arnhem bridgehead and dash to the Zuider Zee (Ijsselmeer) by way of Otterlo, Barneveld, Voorthuizen, and Putten. That the corps adapted so well to the many changes in the plan owes much to Kitching, the corps staff, and the staffs of the divisions, all of whom played a part in ensuring that the artillery had adequate manoeuvre areas, that route management and traffic control were maintained, that liaison with 2nd Canadian Corps was such that operations at Apeldoorn and Arnhem complemented each other, and that specialized equipment such as flails, amphibious craft, and flamethrowers were assigned to the divisions in a manner commensurate with their tasks.[162] Staffs everywhere in the Canadian Army had improved since the spring of 1944. Rolling with similar changes would have been difficult for 1st Canadian Corps during the Liri Valley battles. Both 2nd Canadian Corps and its divisions definitely had their difficulties during Operations Atlantic and Spring in July 1944. But, by the spring of 1945, commanders from brigade to army level could trust their staffs in a way that was not possible a year earlier. Ten months of combat had done much to hone collective skills. It had also done much to weed out the old and the incompetent and replace them with the young and the capable. Certainly, Foulkes could rely on Kitching, whose real calling was as a chief of staff, in a way that he could not have relied on Archibald in the 2nd Canadian Infantry Division.

He also had the benefit of commanders who did not need a whole lot of direction. A day after 2nd Canadian Corps launched Operation Cannonshot and crossed the Ijssel on the evening of 11 April, Major-General S.B. Rawlins, the GOC 49th (West Riding) Division, launched his 56th Brigade across the same river some twenty-four kilometres to the southeast, at Westervoort. Further west, diversionary fire in the area of Driel enhanced the distraction of Cannonshot such that the Operation Anger crossing at Westervoort at 2240 hours met little resistance. The bridge that had been assembled ahead of time near Pannerden and floated upstream to Westervoort paid off as well. By the morning of 13 April, it was in place and Rawlins committed his two remaining brigades (147th and 146th) plus the tanks of the Ontario Regiment to the battle for Arnhem. Action was fast and resistance was slight. The 49th (West Riding) Division secured Arnhem before midday on 14 April, bagging some 601 German prisoners in the process.[163] With the 49th Division making good progress in Arnhem and Velp, and the 1st Canadian Infantry Division, which had reverted to Foulkes's command on 13 April, meeting stiff resistance on the eastern outskirts of Apeldoorn, Foulkes visited Hoffmeister at 5th Canadian Armoured Division Headquarters at 1600 on 13 April.[164] After some discussion of the situation at Arnhem and Apeldoorn, he ordered Hoffmeister "to capture Ede, then go straight through to the Zuider Zee, to cut off the Germans in the area East of the line Ede-Barneveld."[165] At this stage in the war, and with a commander as competent as Hoffmeister, direction did not need to be more detailed than that. In fact, Foulkes's confirmatory written orders on 15 April were less than two pages long, and the tasks assigned to the 5th Canadian Armoured Division took up a mere five lines.[166]

Hoffmeister translated direction into action quickly. While his staff coordinated with the staffs of 1st Canadian Corps and the 49th (West Riding) Division about how his brigades and units would cross the Westervoort bridge and assemble in Arnhem, Hoffmeister figured out how he would reach the Ijsselmeer. Looking at the terrain and considering what he knew of enemy dispositions, he determined that he would have to pivot hard to his left after breaking out of the woods north of Arnhem, a manoeuvre that could leave his right flank vulnerable; so he decided that his first objective would be the high ground north of Arnhem, at Terlet and Deelen, to block any potential counterattack. With his flank secure, he could then tackle in succession the capture of Otterlo, the reduction of Barneveld, the cutting of the Apeldoorn-Amersfoort road, and the dash to the Zuider Zee.[167] To maintain a rapid pace of advance, Hoffmeister also chose to have his 5th Canadian Armoured Brigade, under Brigadier Ian Cumberland, lead the whole way, with the 11th Canadian Infantry Brigade under Ian Johnston mopping up behind. This was a somewhat unorthodox method for the advance, but Foulkes, to his credit, accepted it and let Hoffmeister fight his battle his way. This was really the only way in which the relationship between Hoffmeister and Foulkes could have worked: telling Hoffmeister what had to be achieved, then letting him get on with it. Hoffmeister's attack worked pretty much as planned. His 5th Canadian Armoured Brigade burst out of Arnhem shortly after 0630 hours on 15 April, again without preparatory bombardment, overrunning the surprised soldiers of the 858th Grenadier Regiment at Terlet and Deelen by late morning.[168] By last light, Hoffmeister's tanks had turned hard left and driven to Otterlo and Luntern. By the close of the following day, Cumberland's brigade had isolated the enemy strongpoint at Barneveld and cut the Apeldoorn-Amersfoort road. On 17 April, after handing off the Barneveld strongpoint to the 11th Canadian Infantry Brigade for destruction, Cumberland smashed his tanks through a desperate German anti-tank screen north of Voorthuizen and advanced to Putten. Hoffmeister's troops reached the Ijsselmeer on 18 April, very much to Foulkes's satisfaction: "The action of the 5th [Canadian] Armoured Division was, in my opinion, one of the best actions I have ever seen. The armour went into the attack with all the zeal and zest for which it is known, and the [11th Canadian] Infantry Brigade followed suit, and they destroyed every German in their path and cut them off between the Ijssel and the Zuider Zee."[169] The Charles Foulkes of April 1945 was a less insecure corps commander than the Charles Foulkes who showed up in Italy in November 1944. By the end of the war, he considered capable subordinates such as Hoff-meister more as assets than as threats.

Even Foster, who detested Foulkes, was a usable asset. After forcing a fairly easy crossing of the Ijssel with the 2nd Canadian Infantry Brigade on 11 April, his 1st and 3rd Canadian Infantry Brigades ran into stiff resistance from the 953rd Grenadier Regiment of the of the 361st Volksgrenadier Division. An attempt by the 1st Canadian Infantry Brigade to cross the Apeldoorn Canal in the centre of the city, using a company of the Royal Canadian Regiment and a squadron of 1st Hussars, failed on the evening of 13-14 October. Foster's original plan had been for "1 Cdn Inf Bde to face up to [Apeldoorn] and thus keep the enemy garrison there occupied," then put "3rd Cdn Inf Bde across the canal south of Apeldoorn, thus coming in from the rear."[170] However, the success of the 49th (West Riding) Division in the south led Foster to rethink his plan. Foulkes had ordered him to have the 2nd Canadian Infantry Brigade, then in the process of clearing the bridgehead at Hoven, move south with two battalions, link up with the 49th (West Riding) Division, and establish a crossing further south along the canal, if possible. Thus, while Hoffmeister's tanks rumbled towards Otterlo and Luntern on 15 April, the Loyal Edmonton Regiment and the Princess Patricia's Canadian Light Infantry moved south and made contact with the flanking division at Dieren and Eerbeek, respectively. The engineers bridged the canal, first at Dieren, then later at Veldhuizen. On hearing of these successes, Foster seized the opportunity to bring the rest of the 2nd Canadian Infantry Brigade cross the Apeldoorn Canal at Veldhuizen and advance on Apeldoorn from the south to assist the 3rd Canadian Infantry Brigade with its river-crossing operation. By last light on 16 April, the 2nd Brigade had positioned itself on the west bank of the canal, just south of Apeldoorn. This occurred just as Hoffmeister's tanks were cutting the Apeldoorn-Amersfoort road twenty kilometres to the enemy's rear. These combined actions caused German resistance to crumble. The Apeldoorn garrison withdrew on the evening of 16-17 April, but not before 2,555 of its soldiers and officers became prisoners of the 1st Canadian Infantry Division.[171] The reduction of the Apeldoorn fortress thus complete, Foster gave his troops little respite, ordering them to advance westward and relieve Hoffmeister's troops at Voorthuizen, Barneveld, and Amersfoort. Foster was a competent battlefield commander with a nimble and experienced division under his command. The corps commander had every reason to trust his tactical judgment and his division's ability to get the job done, and Foulkes did.[172] Given his own technical limitations and his inability to inspire, Foulkes, as a corps commander, really did not have any other choice.

In a 1991 interview, Major-General Bruce Matthews, who succeeded Foulkes as GOC 2nd Canadian Infantry Division, made the interesting comment that Foulkes "was a better corps commander than [he was] a div[ision] GOC."[173] Considering how he fought Operation Spring and the Forêt de la Londe battle, and comparing those actions with his performance during Operation Chuckle and the battles for Western Holland, one must concede that Matthews had a point. But how can that have been the case? How does one do better in command of 60,000 to 80,000 troops than when one is in command of 20,000? The answer lies in two key factors: subordinate talent and timing. Foulkes had better subordinate commanders and key staff at corps level than he had at the 2nd Canadian Infantry Division. Collectively, Hoffmeister and Foster were more reliable than Lett, Megill, and Young; and Kitching was head and shoulders above Archibald. Foulkes was also a much more trusting commander at corps than he had ever been at the divisional level. He also had the good fortune to take command of 1st Canadian Corps at a time when it was well experienced and battle-tested. The succession of river battles in Operation Chuckle was grim, but the corps and divisional staffs had learned much since their first battle in May 1944, and this helped them between the Lamone and Senio Rivers. If the 1st Canadian Corps experience in the Liri Valley is any indication, it is difficult to imagine Foulkes doing as well with a green corps staff under Brigadier Nick McCarter.[174] Conversely, he probably would have done better at the 2nd Canadian Infantry Division, with its much-improved November 1944 slate of commanders and staff: Lieutenant-Colonel P.W. Bennet as GSO 1, Brigadier F.N. Cabeldu in command of the 4th Canadian Brigade, Megill in the 5th Brigade, and Brigadier H.F. Keefler in the 6th Brigade. Foulkes was wily enough to survive while the army under him improved. There is nothing new in the revelation that experienced commanders and staffs performed better than green commanders and staffs. But Foulkes survived and gave himself a chance to grow as a commander while many others failed. Kitching and Spry were both sacked. Keller was on his way out when he was wounded. Burns got the boot too, not to mention the long line of British generals fired in the Western Desert as the British Army cut its teeth between 1940 and 1943.[175] There was nothing common about Foulkes's ability to survive.

This same wiliness got him appointed as Chief of the General Staff after the war. In July 1945, the CGS, Lieutenant-General J.C. Murchie, wired Crerar on behalf of McNaughton, then Minister of National Defence, asking for Crerar's opinion regarding the future employment of both Simonds and Foulkes.[176]

Crerar was effusive in his praise of both officers, but he identified Simonds to be "of commander type" and "suitably qualified for any appointment of high military responsibility," while he singled out Foulkes as a "very able intelligent and thoughtful officer ... [with] qualities that make him specifically suitable for very senior staff appointment."[177] The implication that Foulkes was better suited to leading the postwar peacetime army was obvious. Crerar had already expressed his opinion to the Prime Minister that Simonds, although the better battlefield general, "might not be the best man for postwar planning," and this was fairly well known in the senior ranks of the army at the time.[178] Crerar had butted heads with Simonds, who could be uncompromising. He feared that Simonds would do the same with his political masters, provoking little but their enmity in the process. That, Crerar felt, would not bode well for the postwar army. Foulkes, who never butted heads with superiors and who was more like the politicians he would serve, might be better suited to leading the peacetime army. So Foulkes got the post of Chief of the General Staff, not Simonds. There is evidence to suggest that Crerar, who knew well how Ottawa operated, was right. During a postwar visit to Ottawa, Simonds, aggrieved at having been passed over for someone he clearly believed his lesser, coolly "brushed by" then Minister of National Defence Douglas Abbott. An annoyed Abbott later admonished one of Simonds's staff officers: "Tell Gen[eral] Simonds the war is over."[179] Foulkes needed no such reminder. J.W. Pickersgill, who held a number of key public service appointments and Cabinet portfolios between 1937 and 1957, described Foulkes as "a real politician who got as much as he could get by taking the political temperature and not going beyond what the politicians would tolerate."[180] That was Foulkes's real strength.

Foulkes was equally cunning in his dealings with Simonds. Knowing that his former boss could antagonize politicians at a time when the army needed the goodwill of Cabinet, and knowing that Simonds would probably not conceal his contempt for a former underling, Foulkes conspired to keep Simonds out of Canada for as long as possible. In November 1945, he discussed with Abbott several options for Simonds's future employment: creating a largely ceremonial post such as Inspector General in Canada, which Simonds was sure to reject; appointing Simonds to CGS while Foulkes himself took a reduction in rank, which he knew Abbott would never accept; and temporary employment with, or transfer to, the British Army, which is what they pursued.[181] By March 1946, Foulkes had arranged for Simonds to attend the Imperial Defence College, while the British Army reallocated its own general officers, and he also sought a position in which Simonds could be employed on loan.[182] Keeping Simonds away was important, keeping him underemployed equally so. When Montgomery, as Chief of the Imperial General Staff, suggested that Simonds might be given a corps in Southeast Asia, Foulkes told Montgomery, even before discussing the issue with his Minister, "that I did not consider this would be in accordance with the desires of the Canadian government, and that the Canadian Government did not wish to become in any way involved, either directly or indirectly, with the United Kingdom's overseas policy."[183] Foulkes gauged rightly the government's opinion on staying out of imperial conflicts, but it is equally clear that he did not want to countenance anything that would enhance Simonds's reputation. That could have been a problem for him when Simonds eventually did come home. Foulkes's insecurities never fully subsided. He suggested instead that "it would be much more in keeping with Canadian policy if General Simonds could be employed in a training establishment to which personnel of the Canadian Forces were involved."[184] Simonds stayed at the Imperial Defence College, first as a candidate, then as an instructor, until the autumn of 1949, when he returned to Canada as Commandant of the National Defence College in Kingston, Ontario. Given his war record, his experience, and his reputation, Simonds expected better, justifiably so. In January 1950, he confronted Foulkes, asking whether he had been dealt with "in frankness and good faith."[185] Three days later, Foulkes responded that he was "quite surprised and somewhat upset" by the remarks, adding that he could not "accept [the] suggestion that there is any intrigue as far as I am concerned."[186] Among the many items of evidence that he marshalled to prove his innocence in this affair was his November 1945 suggestion to Abbott that he was "prepared to take a voluntary reduction in rank myself to go and command a District and to leave the post of CGS vacant for you." Simonds did eventually become CGS in January 1951, but only after Foulkes had ascended to the newly created post of Chairman of the Chiefs of Staff Committee. The "Master Bureaucrat" had outmanoeuvred the "Master of the Battlefield."[187]

CHARLES FOULKES WAS NOT brilliant. Neither was he a good tactician, although he did improve somewhat with experience, nor an inspiring leader. He was, however, a master at making other people's strengths and weaknesses – sometimes the same person's – work for him. He made himself indispensable to weak commanders like Price and Sansom, and he sacrificed subordinates to strong commanders like Simonds. And he was also clever enough to let Simonds run himself afoul of Crerar and Canadian politicians, while he made sure never to quarrel with anyone who could advance his career. He was a master bureaucrat and careerist. In that respect, for a limited man dealt a limited hand, he played his cards brilliantly.

# Observations and Conclusions

*Commanders must be chosen carefully; in war it is "the man" that matters.*
— GENERAL BERNARD LAW MONTGOMERY

MONTGOMERY WAS ONLY half-right. It is true that few factors influence the outcomes of campaigns more than the capabilities of commanders. As this examination of five British and Canadian generals has demonstrated, battles are often won or lost based on the plans commanders make, the orders they issue, and the influence they exert. But this study has also demonstrated the importance of the system that creates the commander and supports him in his enterprise. A corps is an all-arms formation within a larger army system, including the staff colleges, schools, and training establishments that impart the common doctrine, convey a common lexicon for doing business, train the soldiers, and assemble the staffs that are the tools of the commander's trade. Although Canadian authorities retained the final say on where, when, and how their forces would be committed during the Second World War, the Canadian Army functioned entirely within the British imperial system. Its organizations were based on War Office guidance, its equipment was mostly British in design, and, perhaps most importantly, its commanders and staffs learned the methods and procedures of the Camberley and Quetta curricula. Canadian and British units, formations, commanders, and staff officers were more or less interchangeable, which is why Horrocks and Crocker could work for Canadians, and have Canadians work for them, with relative ease, a few personality difficulties notwithstanding. It is also why twenty British Army officers could serve so seamlessly on the staff of the First Canadian Army in 1945.[1] The Canadian Army, building on a meagre foundation of 450 Permanent Force officers, only 10 percent of whom were staff-trained in 1939, took nearly four years to reach a reasonable level of command-and-staff competence across an army formation of five divisions and two armoured brigades; so "psc"-qualified officers like Burns, Foulkes, and Simonds were critical during this building period.[2] By the end of 1944, however, after four years of churning captains and majors through wartime staff courses, after training and battle-testing commanders and staffs, and after weeding out the weak and the ineffective, the Canadian Army could safely "float" a corps commander as tactically inept as Charles Foulkes. Competent staffs and capable subordinate commanders were the best insurance policy against the odd mistake that the system might spit up.

ALTHOUGH THEY HAD A number of things in common, Brian Horrocks, "Tommy" Burns, John Crocker, Guy Simonds, and Charles Foulkes were five very different men. None came from a particularly privileged background. Horrocks and Simonds were both "army brats" who attended private schools, Crocker was raised by a widow with four other children and was home-schooled, and Foulkes was one of eight siblings who grew up in a lower-middle-class neighbourhood and attended public secondary school. If anyone had anything approaching a posh childhood, it was the Canadian-born Burns, who lived in a ritzy Montreal neighbourhood and attended one of the most exclusive private schools in Canada, although he probably had the least happy childhood of the five. Not surprisingly, different circumstances forged different personalities. Burns, although he never finished college, was a man of academic brilliance and the unfortunate awkwardness that went with it. Simonds, the only benefici- ary of a college education, had some of the same intellectual ability, but he also had willpower that put most, especially Burns, to shame. Crocker had the same attributes of taciturnity, skill, and determination, even if he could not quite match Simonds for ruthlessness. The only one of the lot with unreserved charm was Horrocks, whose ability to read people and to adopt the appropriate posture for any situation complemented solid, if not brilliant, technical skills. Foulkes, unfortunately, was unique in that he had neither charm nor tactical skill, but he survived by dint of his bureaucratic acumen and the help of good subordin- ates and staff.

In spite of their personality differences, they all came to plan and fight their battles with the same basic assumption – it was unwise to move unless you had sufficiently neutralized, or were prepared to neutralize, enemy weapons systems that could do you harm. They may have differed in how they nullified, or at- tempted to nullify, enemy guns or machine guns, but they all worked towards the same aim. Sometimes that meant using overwhelming firepower, as Crocker did when he employed heavy bombers and artillery to pound enemy positions in his attacks on Caen and Le Havre. Horrocks did it too. He integrated the fire of five Army Groups Royal Artillery (AGsRA) and seven divisional artilleries to deliver an average of nine tons of shell onto each of 268 targets during the first twenty-four hours of Operation Veritable.[3] He also used artillery barrages and on-call tactical air forces to pave a way for his armoured spearhead during Operation Market Garden. For the first phase of Totalize, Guy Simonds ar- ranged for 1,020 bombers to strike selected targets with 3,462 tons of ordnance *before* his armoured and infantry columns advanced behind a barrage fired by 360 guns.[4] In Italy, Burns called on the fire of 810 guns to help him breach the formidable Hitler Line, and later Foulkes used the fire of 36 Desert Air Force Spitbombers, two divisional artilleries, and two medium regiments to assist his two assaulting divisions as they made their way across the flat ground between the Montone and Lamone Rivers.[5] Sometimes the corps commanders used supporting attacks to distract the enemy, disperse his firepower and reserves, or simply neutralize those positions that might interfere from the flanks. That was fundamental to Simonds's plan for Operation Infatuate. It was also part of Crocker's plan for the Fondouk battle, although the attacks to clear the flanks failed. Occasionally, attacks took place at night, when the enemy could not effectively engage the attackers. Simonds used darkness *and* firepower to penetrate the enemy defences south of Caen during Operation Totalize. A few days later, in Operation Tractable, he had his gunners fire what amounted to a smoke barrage to mask the attackers from enemy observation and fire. And, at the Gothic Line, Burns improvised and launched his attack in darkness to take advantage of both the reduced visibility and the enemy's disorganized state. Not every operation succeeded, and sometimes even the successful ones had problems, but none of the five corps commanders of this study would ever have questioned the necessity of doing everything possible to neutralize or eliminate whatever might hurt them before or during any attempt at manoeuvre. None was particularly fond of risky moves that could result in high casualties.

How did five different men come to frame tactical problems in the same manner? To begin with, their own experience had burned into their brains how dangerous and costly it could be to advance without subduing enemy firepower. Having lived through the terrifying experience of the Great War, neither Burns, nor Horrocks, nor Crocker had any desire to risk fighting fire with targets. The campaigns in France and North Africa confirmed this line of logic for the latter two. Simonds and Foulkes were too young to have experienced the 1914-18 war, but they both commanded divisions in major actions before handling their corps – Simonds in Sicily and Foulkes in Normandy. Strategic circumstances also imposed a common tactical doctrine on the Canadian and British armies. By the end of 1942, Montgomery had managed to ram "a single interpretation of doctrine" down the throats of both armies.[6] His operational and tactical methods favoured the careful application of firepower, the attrition of enemy infantry, advancing in measured steps, and quickly consolidating gains to meet and defeat German counterattacks – because this was the most sensible way for the Anglo-Canadian armies to fight the *Wehrmacht*.[7] Neither Canada nor Britain had the seemingly bottomless manpower pools of either the Americans or the Soviets, and by the summer of 1944, both the Canadian and British armies faced serious manpower problems, particularly with infantry reinforcements.[8] Full mobilization and land campaigns in three theatres had badly stretched British human resources, making manpower conservation a fundamental principle of British doctrine. In fact, the British Army had to resort to disbanding two divisions in the summer of 1944 to come up with sufficient infantry reinforcements.[9] For the Canadians, the constraints of an all-volunteer force, the spectre of conscription, and the high summer and autumn casualties in both Italy and Northwest Europe imposed a similar manpower pinch.[10] If Canadian and British corps commanders seemed a bit too deliberate in their methods, a little disinclined to take risks, and a trifle disposed to favour firepower as a prerequisite to manoeuvre, they had good reason. They simply could not afford excessive and unnecessary casualties, and the *Wehrmacht* could afford them even less. There were times when strategic imperatives justified high casualties for British and Canadian operations – the opening of Antwerp and the capture of Caen were two such examples – but even on those occasions Crocker and Simonds did everything possible to minimize the human cost.

The influence of the staff colleges on how British and Canadian commanders fought cannot be overstated. Two years of intensive study gave them the tools they needed to tackle the problems of modern war. They learned the capabilities of the various arms and services, they learned how to conduct appreciations for operations from the brigade to corps level, they learned how to organize and use staffs, and they learned how to produce and disseminate orders. They also spent a fair amount of time studying past campaigns and the great commanders of history. With a Directing Staff made up entirely of Great War veterans, the staff colleges would certainly have imparted a certain predilection for carefully planned, firepower-intensive operations, but, by and large, Staff College was more about method and process – how to use all the elements of modern military formations. It was also about learning the common "language" and military method for all the armies of the British Empire. Staff College was what enabled a gunner from Montreal to understand a guardsman from London. They may not have liked each other, and they may even have had opposing ideas of how this or that tactical problem should be solved, but they understood each other, and that was important – arguably more important than the adoption of one particular tactical doctrine or another. Armies simply cannot function if the component parts do not understand each other. That the British Army was able to achieve such a high level of interoperability with the Canadian Army – indeed, with all the Dominion armies – was a major and too-often overlooked accomplishment.

The Camberley and Quetta curricula, even in the abbreviated form of the wartime staff courses, also furnished our corps commanders with the staff officers they needed to control their formations. This took some time to achieve, especially for the two Canadian corps. Staff-trained officers were scarce in 1939 and it took a while to produce enough of them to flesh out the headquarters of fifteen brigades, five divisions, two corps, and an army. The building process was not always steady, because in a rapidly expanding army there were always more staff vacancies than staff officers to fill them. The case of 1st Canadian Corps makes the point. It needed a British Brigadier General Staff (BGS), Miles Dempsey, to help it along in 1940 and 1941, but it really did not achieve any semblance of staff efficiency until Simonds took over as BGS in August 1941. Not that all the improvement was Simonds's doing, although he definitely had a positive effect on the staff function of the corps in the thirteen months that he was there. He benefited from an influx of freshly trained staff officers who had completed either the Canadian Junior War Staff Course or one of the British War Staff Courses. It also helped that his corps commander, Harry Crerar, took the task of training the headquarters seriously, something that Crerar's predecessor, Andy McNaughton, had neglected badly. The expansion of the army meant that command and staff positions in other formations had to be filled, so officers of talent and ability moved frequently, leading to a high turnover rate in the corps staff. Simonds, for example, left in September 1942 to command a brigade. By 1944, however, thanks largely to the steady production of staff officers, a more stable personnel situation existed in the 1st Canadian Corps headquarters. By the time Burns took over as GOC in March, Nick McCarter had been BGS for six months and the rest of his staff had been at their jobs for a while as well. They were reasonably well trained, though not yet battle-tested. That test came during the Liri Valley campaign in the late spring of 1944, when a few, including McCarter, were found wanting and had to be replaced. But replacing them was possible in the summer of 1944 because the army had at its disposal enough staff-trained officers to fill the voids, a situation very different from the staff officer–starved days of 1940-43. The staff changes at 1st Canadian Corps produced positive results too. At the Gothic Line, at the Lamone River, and at Arnhem, the corps staff performed with considerable skill and efficiency. By the time Foulkes took over as GOC in November 1944, the corps and division staffs were well drilled and battle-worn, and the divisions and brigades were in the hands of experienced fighters. It had taken four and a half long years of staff training, TEWTs, exercises, and battle to reach that state.

All corps staffs suffered similar growing pains. The 2nd Canadian Corps staff fumbled a few times in Normandy, but Simonds and N. Elliot Rodger made adjustments that helped it shine at the Scheldt. Crocker introduced the 9th Corps Headquarters to battle in North Africa, and he was ably assisted by G.H.A.

MacMillan as his BGS, but even then there were some missteps at Fondouk. In mid-June 1944, despite a successful amphibious assault at the start of Overlord, Crocker's 1st Corps staff stumbled a bit during its first attempt to coordinate air, naval, and land assets for the attack on Caen. Three months later, however, when Crocker conducted the siege of Le Havre, his staff expertly integrated the fire of bombers, warships, and artillery to smash the enemy's defences and capture the port with negligible Allied casualties. Foulkes and Horrocks had the good fortune never to have fought with green staffs. Foulkes inherited a corps head-quarters that had already worked out its kinks, and Horrocks, despite assuming command of four separate corps, always stepped into a battle-tested headquar-ters. This, of course, presented its own leadership challenges – shaking the "new guy" stigma being a big one – but at least most of the headquarters personnel knew each other and had established how they would do things. Even that was no guarantee of success. Sometimes experienced command-staff teams slipped, as Horrocks and his headquarters did when they tried to cram the 43rd (Wessex) Division through a vehicle-clogged gap during Operation Veritable.

Despite common training, doctrine, and assumptions about how to conduct offensive operations, the five corps commanders of this study were not uniform in how they used their staffs or exercised command. Simonds stands out for his independence in planning. He did not hold any brainstorming sessions, nor did he seek the advice of subordinate commanders or staff when deciding what course of action to take for any particular operation. That was his domain. After reflecting on the object to be achieved and the factors to be considered in achieving it, he formulated a plan then presented a *fait accompli* to subordinate commanders and staff. They would see to the detailed coordination and execu-tion, and Simonds would check to ensure that they did, but the plan, once issued, rarely changed. The other corps commanders were more consensual in their approach. Horrocks and Crocker sought the input of subordinate com-manders and staffs, as Crocker did for Overlord and Horrocks did for Veritable, although Crocker cared less about keeping people happy than did Horrocks, who tried hard to placate difficult subordinates such as Bernard Freyberg. Once Crocker had accepted input and made a plan, he was far less likely than Horrocks to brook any "belly-aching." Burns tended to give broad direction – phases, boundaries, timings, and so on – but allowed his divisional commanders wide latitude in planning their portions as they saw fit, too much at times. At the Hitler Line, Vokes clearly pushed beyond the parameters given him by Burns, and his actions added unnecessarily to the body count in the 2nd Can-adian Infantry Brigade. As a corps commander, Foulkes sought advice, allowed his staff to conduct a good deal of the planning, and interfered as little as possible. Considering his technical shortfalls, and given that he had a superb staff and strong divisional commanders, this was probably the best modus operandi he could have adopted.

How they used the basic infrastructure of their headquarters reveals something of their methods of command. All used the basic Main, Rear, and Tactical division of the corps headquarters, and all used the Main Headquarters to support current operations and planning, while the Rear Headquarters dealt mainly with administration and logistics. But there were fundamental differences in how each handled his Tactical Headquarters. Crocker was the only one for whom the "Tac" was something permanent during operations. His Tactical Headquarters personnel parked at a place from which the commander could view the battle, put up antennae, propped up their map boards, turned on their radios, and manned them until the action ended. Crocker used it as a sort of advanced Main Headquarters, from which he could visit forward formations and units, something he did often, to get a better feel for the battle or to push someone on. Many times, he ventured beyond the headquarters of his brigades, occasionally even beyond those of his battalions. Crocker never lacked for courage. Horrocks was just as willing to hazard forward, but his Tactical Headquarters was smaller and he usually returned to Main Headquarters by last light. Always concerned with the human factor in war, Horrocks also went forward to be seen, to radiate confidence, and to offer encouragement. His troops loved him for that. He believed in being forward to "smell the battlefield," but he believed just as strongly that the locus of control for the corps battle was Main Headquarters. Simonds thought so too. Having watched Horrocks operate in North Africa, he followed the example of using a tiny Tactical Headquarters for daylight visits only and keeping the hub of headquarters activity at Main. He also liked to observe the fighting and gain a better appreciation for the battle, but when he went forward to visit divisions or brigades, it was usually to place his boot on the seat of someone's pants, not to offer encouragement. Burns too kept his Tactical Headquarters small and he liked to conduct his own reconnaissance, often by aircraft, of his area of operations. Unfortunately, his visits forward occasionally caused more harm than good. Quite often, he would show up at a brigade, discuss an operation with the brigadier, and perhaps issue direction, without first notifying the divisional commander. This annoyed the latter no end and did Burns damage in the long run, when the divisional commanders became complicit in the actions that led to his sacking. Foulkes, who also favoured a small non-permanent Tactical Headquarters, was careful not to repeat Burns's mistakes. He went to brigades as well, but he rarely went without the divisional commanders and he never showed up unannounced.

In probing the *who* and the *how* of five British and Canadian corps command-ers at war, this study has highlighted the importance of will for higher command in war. Certainty of purpose in the face of mounting casualties, the willingness to defend one's convictions with superiors, and the strength to excise indolent or errant subordinates: these were key determinants of the success or failure of the commander in battle. No one in this survey had more will than Simonds and no one had less of it than Burns. Their records reveal clearly how different they were as commanders. Over the course of his wartime career, Simonds questioned direction from McNaughton, Montgomery, Dempsey, and Crerar. Burns accepted flawed plans from Oliver Leese, then allowed Leese to lay blame at his feet when the plans went awry. Simonds fired his best friend in Normandy for poor performance and refusal to follow direction. Burns allowed Vokes to show open contempt, fiddle about at the Hitler Line, and muck up plans for a set-piece attack. Simonds had some battlefield failures, but for the most part he succeeded and survived. Burns, although he had success on the battlefield, lost his job. It is worth noting that Simonds also commanded an army during a major operation, the only corps commander in the 21st Army Group to do so. A battle like the one Simonds fought as acting army commander in the Scheldt Estuary demanded strength of will – to deal with his higher headquarters, a reluctant Royal Air Force, the Royal Navy, a determined enemy, and mounting casualties. In the Scheldt, Simonds had what it took to get the miserable job done – no question. Crocker was probably more like Simonds than any of the others in this survey. He too regularly questioned direction from superiors like Percy Hobart, Alan Brooke, and Crerar, and he took action with inadequate subordinates like Rod Keller. He also had similar nerve to Simonds when it came to maintaining his aim in difficult operations. In capturing Caen, despite the high casualties of Operation Charnwood, he showed the same grit that Simonds demonstrated in the Scheldt, albeit in a much shorter operation. That he had some of his nerve knocked out of him after the loss of his son was understandable, and very sad. Horrocks, like Simonds and Crocker, questioned higher direction, as he did with Montgomery at Enfidaville in North Africa or when he politely declined Crerar's fire plan for Veritable, and he was capable of sacking weak subordinates, such as J.M.L. Renton after Alam Halfa, but he lacked the ruthless streak that ran through Simonds and Crocker. He admitted to it openly several times when he confessed to having "too much imagination" to be sufficiently cold-blooded for higher command. His "proper role," he thought, was one of "subaltern general," not army commander, because he be-lieved he did not possess the stomach for high casualties in war.[11] Foulkes, on the other hand, could be callous about friendly casualties and could lop off heads when things went wrong, but he never questioned higher direction. He was too cunning and self-serving for that.

Another observation from this study is that there were few differences attributable to nationality but one: human skill. All three Canadians had poor people skills, whereas the two Britons did not. This assessment of the Canadian corps commanders is entirely in line with Jack Granatstein's survey of Canadian Second World War generals, which found that the great majority of Canadian senior leaders, with very few exceptions, demonstrated an "utter lack of charisma."[12] Why was this so? The British Army suffered no such endemic personality failing among its general officers, and those officers attended the same staff colleges and schools as their Canadian colleagues.[13] Horrocks became an absolute master of human skills, and even Crocker engendered admiration and affection with his modest manner. One might search for an explanation in elements of national character, but, as one Canadian brigadier noted, they conflicted with the reality that Canadian generals, on the whole, were more stuffy than their British counterparts: "We were supposed to be ... less stiff and formal than the British."[14] A more satisfactory explanation may be found in the nature of the interwar armies that reared these commanders. In this respect, the Canadian Permanent Force fell far short of the British and Indian armies, and the problem was not so much that Canada's interwar army was not professional; the problem was that it was not an army. It was a babysitting service for the militia.[15] All of Canada's mobilization plans counted on the Non-Permanent Active Militia to provide the bulk of expeditionary forces, and the first job of Permanent Force officers was to get them ready, not necessarily to fight themselves. So, whereas Horrocks and Crocker spent their interwar years on active service in places like Ireland, India, and Germany, commanding companies or working in Territorial Army units, the Canadians spent nearly all of their time on staffs or planning militia training. As a result, they had very little face time with troops, something that their British counterparts could not have avoided even if they had tried. Burns, for example, did not have a single command appointment between 1916 and 1942, when he assumed command of an armoured brigade. During that twenty-six-year interval, he spent most of his time working on topographical surveys, toiling in Militia District Headquarters, or writing to keep himself occupied. Similarly, Charles Foulkes was a platoon commander without a platoon from 1926 to 1933, during which time he instructed militia trainees in small arms or attended courses himself. He would not command again until a very brief fifty-one-day stint of acting battalion command in late 1941 and early 1942. Even Simonds, who spent a total of seven years with gun batteries during the interwar period, passed most of his time instructing militia gunners, attending courses, or teaching at the Royal Military College of Canada

(RMC). He never commanded a battery before taking the helm of the 1st Field Regiment of Royal Canadian Artillery in July 1940. Given their Permanent Force experiences, and how little time they spent commanding soldiers of their own, is it any wonder that the three Canadians lacked good human skills? They were not in an organization that valued such talents much anyway. In Andy McNaughton's Permanent Force, officers with technical skills were valued most.[16] Reputations were made or lost on technical ability, instructional skills, training plans, and staff duties, not on charisma or performance in the field. Staff colleges could impart technical skills; they could not immediately infuse a candidate with the ability to read soldiers and subordinate officers, learn their likes and dislikes, and take the actions necessary to motivate them. That took time and lots of contact with subordinates, which is something the three Canadians, unfortunately, did not get in the 1920s and 1930s.

WHATEVER CONCLUSIONS MIGHT BE drawn, and whatever criticisms may be levied, the five corps commanders examined in this book did everything their nations asked of them in war, and they succeeded far more often than they failed. They wielded the implements of war as they had been taught to do, and they played no small part in forming and forging those implements to make them battle-ready. Indeed, the wartime expansion of their national armies, the Canadian Army in particular, would not have been possible without "psc"-qualified professionals like them – soldiers who had persevered during the disheartening interwar years, learned as much as they could about their profession, then built the formations and trained the people that brought their armies to victory against a first-class foe. It is impossible to overstate the training and organizational deficit that had to be overcome to grow the armies, build corps, and prepare them for war. In a way, the real story is not the deficiencies in the Canadian and British armies before 1939, but how men like Horrocks, Burns, Crocker, Simonds, and Foulkes overcame them to produce – and fight – the effective corps of "the last great British Imperial army."[17]

# Notes

**Foreword**
1 Douglas E. Delaney, *The Soldiers' General: Bert Hoffmeister at War* (Vancouver: UBC Press, 2005).

**Introduction: Who, How, and the Common Ground**
1 On Burns, see Lieutenant-General E.L.M. Burns, *General Mud: Memoirs of Two World Wars* (Toronto: Clark, Irwin, 1970); and J.L. Granatstein, *The Generals: The Canadian Army's Senior Commanders in the Second World War* (Toronto: Stoddart, 1993), 116-44. On Horrocks, see Sir Brian Horrocks, *A Full Life* (London: Collins, 1960); Sir Brian Horrocks, with Eversley Belfield and Major-General H. Essame, *Corps Commander* (New York: Charles Scribner's Sons, 1977); and Philip Warner, *Horrocks: The General Who Led from the Front* (London: Sphere Books, 1984).
2 Dominick Graham, *The Price of Command: A Biography of General Guy Simonds* (Toronto: Stoddart, 1993); and Terry Copp, *Guy Simonds and the Art of Command* (Kingston, ON: Canadian Defence Academy Press, 2007). Simonds left handwritten draft memoirs, which, unfortunately, only cover the period 1939-40. They are in the possession of his son Charles Simonds, Battersea, ON.
3 On Crocker, see Douglas E. Delaney, "A Quiet Man of Influence: General Sir John Crocker," *Journal of the Society for Army Historical Research* 85 (2007): 185-207. No article or book on the wartime career of Charles Foulkes exists. On his postwar career, see Sean M. Maloney, "General Charles Foulkes: A Primer on How to Be CDS," in *Warrior Chiefs: Perspectives on Senior Canadian Military Leadership,* edited by Lieutenant-Colonel Bernd Horn and Stephen Harris (Toronto: Dundurn, 2001), 219-36. Good operational histories of the Anglo-Canadian armies include John A. English, *The Canadian Army and the Normandy Campaign: A Study of Failure in High Command* (New York: Praeger, 1991); Terry Copp, *Fields of Fire: The Canadians in Normandy* (Toronto: University of Toronto Press, 2003); Terry Copp, *Cinderella Army: The Canadians in Northwest Europe, 1944-1945* (Toronto: University of Toronto Press, 2006); Stephen Ashley Hart, *Montgomery and "Colossal Cracks": The 21st Army Group in Northwest Europe, 1944-45* (Westport, CT: Praeger, 2000); and Brian Reid, *No Holding Back: Operation Totalize, Normandy, August 1944* (Toronto: Robin Brass, 2005).
4 Martin Van Crevald, *Command in War* (Cambridge, MA: Harvard University Press, 1985), 5 (emphasis added).
5 See Douglas E. Delaney, *The Soldiers' General: Bert Hoffmeister at War* (Vancouver: UBC Press, 2005), 4-6.
6 Other useful comparative studies of Second World War generals include J.L. Granatstein, *The Generals: The Canadian Army's Senior Commanders in the Second World War* (Toronto: Stoddart, 1993); John Keegan, ed., *Churchill's Generals* (London: Weidenfeld and Nicolson, 1991); Raymond Callahan, *Churchill and His Generals* (Lawrence: University Press of Kansas, 2007); and Harold R. Winton, *Corps Commanders of the Bulge: Six American Generals and Victory in the Ardennes* (Lawrence: University Press of Kansas, 2007).

7 Simonds and Foulkes were the youngest when they took command of their corps, both 41 years old in 1944. Horrocks and Burns were both 47 when they ascended to corps command in 1942 and 1944, respectively. Crocker was 46 when he received the appointment to corps command in 1942.

8 Richard A. Preston, "The Military Structures of the Old Commonwealth," *International Journal* 17 (Spring 1962): 108.

9 See the extensive correspondence between the India Office and the War Office on the 1938 reorganization of Staff College, Camberley into a Junior Wing at Camberley and a Senior Wing at Minley Manor and how that affected the program at Quetta: British Library (BL), India Office Records (IOR), L/MIL/7/3203. This correspondence includes discussion about vacancies for Indian Army officers at both Camberley and Minley Manor, vacancies for British Services officers at Quetta, and positions reserved for Dominion officers at both colleges. On common entrance examinations, see, as just one example, *Report on the Examination for Admission to Staff Colleges at Camberley and Quetta Held in February-March 1925* (London: His Majesty's Stationery Office, 1925).

10 Quoted in Eric Hutton, "A Scientist General Commands Canada's First Division," *Star Weekly*, December 1939. I am grateful to John Rickard for this reference. In 1939, Major-General McNaughton was GOC 1st Canadian Infantry Division and Senior Combatant Officer Overseas.

11 Quoted in Niall Barr, *Pendulum of War: The Three Battles of Alamein* (London: Jonathan Cape, 2004), 215. Major-General Dorman-Smith was Deputy Chief of Staff Middle East, May-July 1942.

12 See app. 2 to John A. Macdonald, "In Search of Veritable: Training the Canadian Army Staff Officer, 1899-1945" (MA thesis, Royal Military College of Canada, 1992).

13 Brigadier C.N. Barclay, CBE, DSO, psc, "1930," in *The Story of the Staff College 1858-1958*, edited by Lieutenant-Colonel F.W. Young, MBE (Aldershot, UK: Gale and Polden, 1958), 26.

14 On the Junior Division curricula, see Joint Services Command and Staff College (JSCSC), Staff College 1933, Junior Division Years Work, vols. 1 and 2; and Staff College 1937, Junior Division Years Work, vols. 1 and 2.

15 The staff designations "G," "A," and "Q" stand for General Staff, Adjutant General Staff, and Quartermaster General Staff, respectively.

16 Barclay, "1930," 26.

17 JSCSC, Staff College 1933, Junior Division Years Work, vols. 1 and 2; and Staff College 1937, Junior Division Years Work, vols. 1 and 2.

18 The training also prepared students "for the appointment of Brigade Major" and prepared them "to fill 2nd grade [GSO 2] appointments after practical experience": Library and Archives Canada (LAC), RG 24, vol. 9873, War Office letter, 26 September 1939. On the stripped down War Staff Course curriculum, see JSCSC, Senior Officers War Course, SD/INT/A/Q Precis, n.d.

19 Macdonald, "In Search of Veritable," app. 4. The Canadian War Staff Course relocated from Ford Manor to the Royal Military College at Kingston, Ontario, in mid-1941.

20 C.P. Stacey, *Arms, Men and Governments: The War Policies of Canada 1939-1945* (Ottawa: Queen's Printer, 1970), 74-75.

21 See Douglas E. Delaney, "Co-operation in the Anglo-Canadian Armies, 1939-1945," in *Britain, Power and the International System, 1856-1956. Festschrift in Honour of David French,* edited by Keith Neilson and Greg Kennedy (London: Ashgate, 2009); and Alex Danchev and Daniel Todman, eds., *War Diaries, 1939-1945: Field Marshal Lord Alanbrooke* (London: Weidenfeld and Nicolson, 2001), 137 (entry for 31 January 1941).

22  Sir Brian Horrocks with Eversley Belfield and Major-General H. Essame, *Corps Commander* (New York: Charles Scribner's Sons, 1977), xiv.

23  Armoured divisions after 1942 contained one armoured and one infantry brigade, plus a field regiment, a self-propelled gun regiment, an armoured reconnaissance regiment, and other supporting arms and services, for a total of some 12,000-15,000 troops. After the spring of 1944, however, armoured divisions in Italy had an additional infantry brigade. After 1940, infantry divisions had three infantry brigades, three field regiments of artillery, a reconnaissance regiment, and supporting assets, for a troop strength of 18,000-20,000.

24  Corps troops typically consisted of an anti-tank regiment, a survey regiment, an infantry company for headquarters defence and security, casualty clearing stations, workshops for vehicle and weapon repair, and provost assets.

25  Colonel G.W.L. Nicholson, *The Gunners of Canada: The History of the Royal Regiment of Canadian Artillery. Vol. 2: 1919-1967* (Toronto: McClelland and Stewart, 1972), 313, 400.

26  JSCSC, Staff College War Course, 1939-45, Senior Officers War Course, SD/INT/A/Q Precis, SD 4 Staff Duties in a Corps.

27  "Staff duties" refers to those functions associated with the preparation and dissemination of orders.

28  See, for example, how Guy Simonds organized his 2nd Canadian Corps GS branch under his GSO 1. LAC, RG 24, vol. 13711, War Diary HQ 2nd Canadian Corps (GS) (April 1944), "Organization of Staff – Headquarters 2nd Canadian Corps," 16 April 1944.

29  See the chart "Corps HQ" (WE/III/5/5) in John Grodzinski, *Operational Handbook for the First Canadian Army, 1944-1945* (Nepean, ON: The Regimental Historian, 1996), 76.

30  Horrocks et al., *Corps Commander*, 32. In Crocker's 9th Corps (1942-43), the term "Advanced Headquarters" was used instead of "Main Headquarters": The National Archives (TNA), WO 166/6125, War Diary (WD) HQ 9th Corps, HQ 9 Corps Standing Orders, n.d. Horrocks also preferred the term "Commander's Recce [Reconnaissance]" to "Tactical Headquarters" because he thought it "indicate[d] a more temporary function than TAC HQ," but he later started using the term "Tac" as well: TNA, WO 169/8591, WD HQ 10th Corps (GS) (January 1943), Organisation of H.Q.'s, 31 January 1943.

31  In some instances, the DA & QMG remained at Rear Headquarters, in which case he "visited Main at least once a day and placed an administrative state before the corps commander." See LAC, MG 30 E 133, Papers of Lieutenant-General A.G.L. McNaughton, vol. 132, Report on Visit to Eighth Army by Brig G.G. Simonds, 29 April 1943, 5.

32  Ibid.

33  Ibid., 1; and Horrocks et al., *Corps Commander,* 32.

34  English, *The Canadian Army and the Normandy Campaign,* xiii.

### Chapter 1: The Actor

1  *A Bridge Too Far,* directed by Richard Attenborough (Joseph E. Levine Productions, 1977); and Cornelius Ryan, *A Bridge Too Far* (New York: Simon and Schuster, 1974).

2  The Imperial War Museum (IWM) Sound Archives contain interviews in which soldiers and officers of all ranks heap praise on Horrocks. For just a few examples, see Accession No. 21658, Interview with Anthony Bernard Colgan (9th Durham Light Infantry), 25 July 2001; Accession No. 18571, Interview with Mary Haddie Swan (Nursing Sister), 26 October 1998; and Accession No. 13420, reel 2, Interview with Trooper Ronald William Mole, n.d.

3  See, for example, Gregory Blaxland, *The Middlesex Regiment* (London: Leo Cooper, 1977). Blaxland refers to Horrocks's "breezy, bracing, and ubiquitous impact on his men" (104).

4 Major-General Sir Francis de Guingand, *Operation Victory* (London: Hodder and Stoughton, 1947), 142.

5 Sir Brian Horrocks, *A Full Life* (London: Collins, 1960), 123.

6 Ibid., 80, 122, 144.

7 Sir Brian Horrocks, with Eversley Belfield and Major-General H. Essame, *Corps Commander* (New York: Charles Scribner's Sons, 1977), 121 (emphasis in original).

8 Unless otherwise noted, the information on Horrocks's childhood has been gleaned from Horrocks, *A Full Life*, 13-14.

9 Army Personnel Records Section (APRS), Glasgow, Scotland, Personnel File of B.G. Horrocks (Horrocks Pers File), MT 284, Brian Gwynne Horrocks, 23 January 1913.

10 Horrocks, *A Full Life*, 14.

11 See Philip Warner, *Horrocks: The General Who Led from the Front* (London: Sphere Books, 1984), 6-7.

12 Horrocks, *A Full Life*, 15; and APRS, Horrocks Pers File, Record of Service.

13 Warner, *Horrocks*, 12.

14 Horrocks, *A Full Life*, 17.

15 Ibid.

16 A short account of what came to be known as the battle of Armentières can be found in Brigadier-General J.E. Edmonds, *History of the Great War: Military Operations, France and Belgium, 1914*, vol. 2 (London: Macmillan, 1925), 149-52.

17 APRS, Horrocks Pers File, Statement regarding circumstances which led to capture, Capt Brian Gwynne Horrocks, n.d.

18 Horrocks, *A Full Life*, 17-18.

19 Ibid., 25-26.

20 Ibid., 35.

21 Ibid., 21-24.

22 APRS, Horrocks Pers File, Statement regarding circumstances which led to capture.

23 Horrocks, *A Full Life*, 62.

24 Ibid. On the slow rate of promotion in the senior ranks of the British Army, see David French, "'An Extensive Use of Weedkiller': Patterns of Promotion in the Senior Ranks of the British Army, 1919-1939," in *The British General Staff: Reform and Innovation, 1890-1939*, edited by David French and Brian Holden Reid (London: Frank Cass, 2002), 159-74.

25 APRS, Horrocks Pers File, Record of Service.

26 Horrocks, *A Full Life*, 65.

27 On the interwar activities of the 1st and 2nd Battalions of the Middlesex Regiment, see Lieutenant-Commander P.K. Kemp, *The Middlesex Regiment (Duke of Cambridge's Own), 1919-1952* (Aldershot, UK: Gale and Polden, 1956), 1-17.

28 Horrocks, *A Full Life*, 66.

29 Ibid.

30 APRS, Horrocks Pers File, Horrocks to Sir Eric B.B. Speed, 16 December 1947.

31 Ibid., Record of Service. On the 9th Battalion Middlesex Regiment during the period 1919-39, see Kemp, *The Middlesex Regiment*, 23-26.

32 Horrocks, *A Full Life*, 68.

33 Warner, *Horrocks*, 45.

34 Horrocks, *A Full Life*, 280.

35 By 1938, the age limit for British Army officers entering Staff College was thirty-two, and a candidate could sit the exams only twice. British Library (BL), India Office Records (IOR), L/MIL/7/3203, India Army Order, Reorganization of the Training of Officers of the Army in India for Staff Appointments, 1938.

36 Horrocks, *A Full Life*, 67. See the numerous personal accounts of the transforming effect of staff training in F.W. Young, ed., *The Story of the Staff College, 1858-1958* (Aldershot, UK: Gale and Polden, 1958).

37 Horrocks, ibid., 70. See also the personal account of Brigadier C.N. Barclay, CBE, DSO, psc, who attended Camberley one year ahead of Horrocks, in Young, ibid., 25-28.

38 The papers for Horrocks's Junior Division in 1931 and his Senior Division in 1932 do not exist. The complete Senior Division papers for 1933 do exist, however, as do the Junior Division papers for the same year. The curricula for these were very similar to those that guided Horrocks's courses. See Joint Services Command and Staff College (JSCSC), Staff College 1933, Senior Division Years Work, vols. 1 and 2; and Staff College 1933, Junior Division Years Work, vols. 1 and 2.

39 Horrocks's Camberley course report is not in his personnel file at the Army Personnel Records Section, but it may safely be assumed that he did very well on the course. After Camberley, he went on to fill a series of key staff appointments and later returned as a member of the Directing Staff, none of which would have happened without a very strong course report and a rare recommendation that he return as an instructor.

40 APRS, Horrocks Pers File, Record of Service.

41 Horrocks, *A Full Life*, 71.

42 APRS, Horrocks Pers File, Record of Service; and Horrocks to Lindsell, 23 July 1935.

43 On Field Marshal Earl Wavell, see Ronald Lewin, *The Chief* (London: Hutchinson, 1980), and Ian Beckett, "Wavell: Field Marshal Earl Wavell" in *Churchill's Generals*, edited by John Keegan (New York: Weidenfeld and Nicolson, 1991), 70-88.

44 Horrocks, *A Full Life*, 72.

45 Ibid., 78.

46 The National Archives (TNA), WO 167/791, War Diary (WD) 2nd Battalion Middlesex Regiment, 18-19 May 1940. See also Gregory Blaxland, *The Middlesex Regiment (Duke of Cambridge's Own) (57th and 77th Foot)* (London: Leo Cooper, 1977), 115-21; Kemp, *The Middlesex Regiment*, 64-75; and Horrocks, *A Full Life*, 81.

47 Major L.F. Ellis, *The War in France and Flanders, 1939-1940* (London: Her Majesty's Stationery Office, 1953), 193-204. See also Montgomery's brief account of the operation and its difficulties in Viscount Montgomery of Alamein, *The Memoirs of Field-Marshal the Viscount Montgomery of Alamein* (London: Collins, 1958), 61-62.

48 TNA, WO 167/792, WD 2nd Battalion Middlesex Regiment, 27-28 May 1940.

49 Horrocks, *A Full Life*, 83. See also Montgomery of Alamein, *Memoirs*, 61.

50 Horrocks, ibid., 80. See David Fraser, *Alanbrooke* (New York: Atheneum, 1982), 131-71.

51 Horrocks, ibid. See the chapter entitled "Saving the Army" in Arthur Bryant, *The Turn of the Tide* (New York: Doubleday, 1957), 67-122; and Alex Danchev and Daniel Todman, eds., *War Diaries, 1939: Field Marshal Lord Alanbrooke* (London: Weidenfeld and Nicolson, 2001), 68-75.

52 Horrocks, ibid., 82.

53 Ibid.

54 Michael Howard makes this point in his essay, "Leadership in the British Army in the Second World War: Some Personal Observations," in *Leadership and Command: The Anglo-American Experience since 1861*, edited by G.D. Sheffield (London: Brassey's, 1997), 118-19.

55 Horrocks, *A Full Life*, 93.

56 Ibid., 99-100.

57 Ibid., 99.

58 TNA, WO 166/522, WD 44th (Home Counties) Division, July 1941.

59  IWM, Sound Archive, Accession No. 13429, reel 2, Interview with Ronald William Mole (4/7 Royal Dragoon Guards), n.d.

60  Horrocks, *A Full Life,* 101.

61  TNA, WO 166/650, WD 9th Armoured Division, March-August 1942.

62  Horrocks, *A Full Life,* 102.

63  Ibid., 104.

64  Ibid., 107.

65  TNA, WO 221/556, Appreciation by Comd 13 Corps, 1 August 1942. This appreciation has been reproduced as app. A in Niall Barr, *Pendulum of War: The Three Battles of El Alamein* (London: Jonathan Cape, 2004), 415-18.

66  Horrocks, *A Full Life,* 108.

67  Corelli Barnett, *The Desert Generals* (London: Cassel, 2001), 262. He has based his conclusion largely on the claims of Auchinleck and his Chief of Staff, Eric Dorman-Smith (O'Gowan).

68  Ralph Bennett argues that "there is plainly a resemblance" between the two plans, "but the mobile defense in the south was the exact opposite of the static role Montgomery imposed on armor and infantry in the area when battle was joined": *Ultra and the Mediterranean Strategy* (New York: William Morrow, 1989), 142-46.

69  TNA, WO 201/556, Appreciation by Comd 13 Corps, 1 August 1942.

70  TNA, WO 169/4006, WD 13 Corps (August 1942), 13 Corps Operation Order No. 146, 17 August 1942.

71  Niall Barr gives credit to Gott for developing the framework of the defensive battle that took place at Alam Halfa. See Barr, *Pendulum of War,* 189.

72  TNA, WO 169/4006, WD 13 Corps (August 1942), 13 Corps Operation Order No. 145, 14 August 1942.

73  TNA, CAB 106/654, Battle of Alam Halfa: Personal account of battle dictated by Lt-Gen. Sir Brian Horrocks who commanded 13 Corps, n.d., 5.

74  Major-General G.P.B. Roberts, *From the Desert to the Baltic* (London: William Kimber, 1987), 92-93.

75  Horrocks, *A Full Life,* 116.

76  Roberts, *From the Desert to the Baltic,* 94.

77  TNA, CAB 106/654, Battle of Alam Halfa, 8.

78  The two defensive lines that crumbled were the Gazala Line (26 May-17 June) and Mersa Matruh (26-28 June). After the successful defence of the El Alamein Line, 1-3 July, offensive operations Bacon (14-15 July), Splendour (23 July), and Manhood (26-27 July) all failed to achieve their objectives.

79  Barr, *Pendulum of War,* 204; and TNA, WO 201/556, Western Front: Appreciation of the Situation, 2 August 1942.

80  Montgomery of Alamein, *Memoirs,* 100.

81  See the sad photograph "Auchinleck stands beside the desert road at El Daba, 28 June 1942" in Barr, *Pendulum of War,* 244 overleaf.

82  Horrocks, *A Full Life,* 120.

83  Michael Carver, *Out of Step: Memoirs of a Field Marshal* (London: Hutchinson, 1989), 134.

84  TNA WO 169/4006, WD 13th Corps, 13 August 1942.

85  F M de Butts, cited in Horrocks, *A Full Life,* 118. De Butts was the GSO 2 (Intelligence) at 13th Corps Headquarters.

86  Paul Freyberg, *Bernard Freyberg, VC: Soldier of Two Nations* (London: Hodder and Stoughton, 1991), 188, 392.

87 Quoted in Nigel Hamilton, *Monty: The Making of a General* (New York: McGraw-Hill, 1981), 643.
88 Barr, *Pendulum of War*, 213-14.
89 Major-General Sir Howard Kippenberger, *Infantry Brigadier* (London: Oxford University Press, 1949), 180-81.
90 Montgomery of Alamein, *Memoirs*, 104.
91 TNA, WO 169/4006, WD 13th Corps.
92 Carver, *Out of Step*, 135-36.
93 Warner, *Horrocks*, 76.
94 Kippenberger, *Infantry Brigadier*, 206; Ronald Walker, *Alam Halfa and Alamein* (Wellington: New Zealand Historical Publications Branch, 1967), 31.
95 TNA, WO 169/4006, WD 13th Corps (August 1942), Personal Memorandum from Comd 13 Corps, 23 August 1942.
96 Ibid.
97 Ibid., 13 Corps Operation Order No. 147, 27 August 1942.
98 Ibid., 22 August 1942, 28 August 1942.
99 Horrocks, *A Full Life*, 122-23.
100 TNA, CAB 106/654, Battle of Alam Halfa, 10.
101 Carver, *Out of Step*, 137-39.
102 Walker, *Alam Halfa and Alamein*, 100.
103 Major-General I.S.O. Playfair, *The Mediterranean and the Middle East*, vol. 2 (London: Her Majesty's Stationery Office, 1960), 386.
104 TNA, CAB 106/654, Battle of Alam Halfa, 10.
105 Ibid., 9.
106 Roberts, *From the Desert to the Baltic*, 99.
107 Ibid.
108 TNA, CAB 106/654, Battle of Alam Halfa, 9.
109 TNA, WO 169/4007, WD 13th Corps, 1 September 1942; and Roberts, *From the Desert to the Baltic*, 100-2.
110 Horrocks, *A Full Life*, 124.
111 Ibid., 118.
112 TNA, CAB 106/654, Battle of Alam Halfa.
113 Roberts, *From the Desert to the Baltic*, 104-5.
114 TNA, CAB 106/766, Enemy Documents Section, Rommel and the Battle of Alam Halfa, 28 October 1957.
115 Montgomery had originally conceived that this action would be combined with a thrust by the 7th Armoured Division from the south, but the 7th Armoured Division lacked the combat power to provide the second prong of a pincer movement.
116 Freyberg, *Bernard Freyberg*, 392.
117 Freyberg's son has suggested that the idea to use the 132nd Brigade for the assault originated with Horrocks, although he cites no reference. Ibid., 392-93.
118 Playfair, *The Mediterranean and the Middle East*, vol. 2, 389.
119 TNA, CAB 106/654, Battle of Alam Halfa.
120 Playfair, *The Mediterranean and the Middle East*, vol. 3, 391.
121 Ibid., vol. 4, 9-10. By October, Montgomery would have 252 new Shermans and 170 Grants in three armoured divisions, while Rommel would have 218 Mark IIIs and Mark IVs: ibid., vol. 3, 391. Rommel's total does not include 278 Italian medium battle tanks.
122 The Desert Air Force, although evenly matched with the Luftwaffe for fighters, was gaining the upper hand in terms of air superiority, and it had 165 bombers, which pounded armoured concentrations day and night.

123  Playfair, *The Mediterranean and the Middle East,* vol. 3, 391.

124  IWM, Sound Archive, Accession No. 19939, Interview with Alan Lazarus, 12 January 1999. Lazarus was GSO 2 (Intelligence) at 13th Corps Headquarters.

125  Ibid., Accession No. 12022, John Winthrop "Shan" Hackett, n.d.

126  A future Field Marshal and Chief of the Imperial General Staff, Allan Francis "John" Harding, had been BGS to Sir Richard O'Connor during the defeat of the Italian Tenth Army, December 1940-February 1941. Wounded while commanding the 7th Armoured Division in March 1943, he later served as Field Marshal Sir Harold Alexander's Chief of Staff in Italy, and he went on to command 13th Corps from March 1945 to the end of the campaign in the Mediterranean.

127  Horrocks, *A Full Life,* 130.

128  A cavalry officer who had won praise for his command of the 12th Lancers during the withdrawal to Dunkirk in 1940, Lumsden had commanded the 1st Armoured Division in the desert since November 1941 and was twice wounded in battle. His flamboyant cavalry style – white silk scarf and immaculate dress – did not mesh well with Montgomery's approach.

129  Horrocks, *A Full Life,* 142.

130  Ibid.

131  Montgomery of Alamein, *Memoirs,* 141.

132  Ibid. During Operation Lightfoot, Lumsden, as 10th Corps Commander, and Major-General Alec Gatehouse, GOC 10th Armoured Division, both balked at sending their tanks through a minefield corridor until it had been more completely cleared. Montgomery did not approve and ordered them to get on with it. See de Guingand, *Operation Victory,* 199-202.

133  TNA, WO 169/3990, WD 10th Corps, December 1942.

134  Horrocks, *A Full Life,* 150-51. See also de Guingand, *Operation Victory,* 254-63.

135  TNA, WO 169/8591 WD 10th Corps, 25 March 1943.

136  TNA, CAB 106/657, Comments by Lt.Gen. Sir Brian Horrocks on Draft Narrative on 2 New Zealand Division in Tunisia, 14 November 1950. See also Freyberg, *Bernard Freyberg,* 427-28.

137  Horrocks, *A Full Life,* 152.

138  Ibid.

139  The battle of the Tabaga Gap is described in Playfair, *The Mediterranean and the Middle East,* vol. 4, 350-55.

140  TNA WO 169/3990, WD 10th Corps (General Staff; December 1942), Reorganization of H.Q. 10 Corps, 12 December 1942.

141  TNA, WO 169/8591, WD 10th Corps (General Staff; January 1943), Organization of H.Q.s, 31 January 1943.

142  Horrocks also suggested that division headquarters in his corps should be similarly organized, with small Commander's Recce Groups (or "Tacs") built for speed: ibid.

143  IWM, Sound Archive, Accession No. 19956/7, Interview with General Sir Brian Wyldbore-Smith, n.d.; and Accession No. 21658, Interview with Anthony Bernard Colgan, 25 July 2001. Wyldebore-Smith was a GSO 3 on the corps artillery staff. Colgan was a driver in the 9th Durham Light Infantry.

144  Library and Archives Canada (LAC), MG 30 E 133, Papers of Lieutenant-General A.G.L. McNaughton, vol. 132, Report on Visit to Eighth Army by Brig G.G. Simonds, 29 April 1943, 3.

145  Ibid., 10.

146  Horrocks, *A Full Life,* 163.

147 Churchill Archives Centre, Churchill College, Cambridge, Ronald Lewin Papers, RLEW 2/13, Further Comments on Montgomery's Memoirs – by one of the foremost divisional commanders.
148 Horrocks, *A Full Life*, 163.
149 Ibid., 164.
150 Playfair, *The Mediterranean and the Middle East*, vol. 4, 449-57.
151 Horrocks, *A Full Life*, 173-74.
152 APRS, Horrocks Pers File, A. Williams to Mrs. N. Horrocks, 25 August 1943.
153 Horrocks, *A Full Life*, 178.
154 Ibid., 179. Horrocks was a major-general when he visited Montgomery. Having had to relinquish corps command, he also reverted to his substantive rank. APRS, Horrocks Pers File, Jeanne Horrocks (sister) to War Office, acknowledging reversion of rank on her brother's behalf, 9 November 1943.
155 Horrocks et al., *Corps Commander*, 9-10.
156 See, for example, the memoir of Eisenhower's deputy commander, Marshal of the Royal Air Force Lord Tedder, *With Prejudice* (London: Cassell, 1966), 552-85.
157 Horrocks et al., *Corps Commander*, 4.
158 General Sir Harold Pyman, *Call to Arms* (London: Leo Cooper, 1971), 42.
159 Webb was killed later in the war: Horrocks et al., *Corps Commander*, 33.
160 IWM, Papers of Lieutenant-General Gerald Corfield Bucknall, Folder 12, Horrocks to Bucknall, 16 September 1944.
161 Horrocks et al., *Corps Commander*, 34.
162 IWM, Sound Archive, Accession No. 13420, reel 2, Interview with Trooper Ronald William Mole, n.d. There is no doubt that Horrocks related well to the average soldier. See the following for similar testimony: ibid., Accession No. 19939, reel 3, Interview with Alan Lazarus, 12 January 1999; Accession No. 16601/9, Interview with Major A.C.E. Vizard, n.d.; Accession No. 18812, reel 8, Interview with Alexander Charles Barr, 1996; Accession No. 18560/133, Interview with Harry Simpson, 26 October 1998.
163 IWM, Sound Archive, Accession No. 12778/7, Interview with Peter Martin (2nd Battalion Cheshire Regiment), 12 November 1992.
164 Major-General H. Essame, *The 43rd Wessex Division at War 1944-1945* (London: William Clowes and Sons, 1952), 73.
165 IWM, Sound Archive, Accession No. 12778/7, Interview with Peter Martin, 12 November 1992.
166 See TNA, CAB 106/960, Advance of 30 Corps across the R. Seine to Brussels and Antwerp, 30 Corps Operation Order No. 20, SUPERCHARGE II, 28 August 1944; and 30 Corps Operation Order No. 21, SABOT, 2 September 1944.
167 See, for example, Major L.F. Ellis, *Victory in the West. Vol. 2: The Defeat of Germany.* (London: Her Majesty's Stationery Office, 1968), 29-58; Martin Middlebrook, *Arnhem 1944: The Airborne Battle* (London: Viking 1994); and Ryan, *A Bridge Too Far.* A few notable memoir accounts are Horrocks, *A Full Life*, 207-32; Horrocks et al., *Corps Commander*, 92-126; James Gavin, *On to Berlin: Battles of an Airborne Commander, 1943-1946* (New York: Viking, 1978), 144-85; and R.E. Urquhart, *Arnhem* (London: Cassel, 1958). A recent reappraisal that disputes the "total failure" of Operation Market Garden is Lloyd Clark, *Arnhem: Operation Market Garden, September 1944* (Stroud, UK: Sutton, 2002).
168 IWM, Sound Archive, Accession No. 21034/3, Interview with Major-General R.E. Urquhart, n.d.
169 Horrocks et al., *Corps Commander*, 24.

170  Stephen Ashley Hart, *Montgomery and "Colossal Cracks": The 21st Army Group in Northwest Europe, 1944-45* (Westport, CT: Praeger, 2000), 176-78.

171  APRS, Horrocks Pers File, Professor John Morey to Brigadier John Fettes, 22 December 1947.

172  IWM, Montgomery Papers, BLIM 119/47, Montgomery to CIGS, 27 December 1944.

173  Horrocks et al., *Corps Commander,* 161-62.

174  Ibid., 182-83.

175  Horrocks, *A Full Life,* 247.

176  TNA, WO 171/4075, WD HQ 30th Corps (GS Branch; January 1945), Operation "VERITABLE" Planning Intelligence Dossier No. 2, 23 January 1945. See also the overprint maps with detailed enemy positions: ibid. (March 1945), Folio Maps, etc.

177  TNA, CAB 106/991, "Operation VERITABLE" (n.d.), 8.

178  Quoted in C.P. Stacey, *The Victory Campaign: The Operations in Northwest Europe, 1944-1945* (Ottawa: Queen's Printer, 1966), 456.

179  Horrocks, *A Full Life,* 243.

180  TNA, WO 171/346, WD 13th Corps (December 1944), "VERITABLE" Planning Notes No. 4: The Principle of the Operation, 14 December 1944.

181  Horrocks et al., *Corps Commander,* 32.

182  See the 30th Corps War Diaries (December 1944 to February 1945): TNA, WO 171/346, WO 171/4075, WO 171/4076.

183  TNA WO 171/4075, WD 30th Corps (January 1945), Planning Notes No. 26: "VERITABLE," 27 January 1945.

184  The papers for Exercise Evolution match, nearly exactly, the decisions and guidance in 30th Corps Planning Notes No. 26: ibid. See IWM, Papers of Major-General Ronald Frederick King Belcham, Horrocks to Belcham, 7 September 1946; and Exercise "EVOLUTION" Papers.

185  Ibid.

186  IWM, Sound Archive, Accession No. 2977/04, Sir Brian Horrocks interviewed by Peter Batty, n.d.

187  Ibid.

188  Horrocks, *A Full Life,* 247-48.

189  James Alan Roberts, *The Canadian Summer: The Memoirs of James Alan Roberts* (Toronto: University of Toronto Press, 1981), 107-8.

190  TNA, WO 171/4076, WD 30th Corps (February 1945), 30 Corps Operation Instruction No. 47: "VERITABLE," 3 February 1945.

191  TNA, WO 171/4076, WD 30th Corps (February 1945), 30 Corps Operation Instruction No. 46, Operation "VERITABLE": Development of the Battle, 3 February 1945.

192  The definitive work on Harry Crerar is Paul Douglas Dickson, *A Thoroughly Canadian General: General H.D.G. Crerar* (Toronto: University of Toronto Press, 2007).

193  LAC, MG 30 E 157, Papers of General H.D.G. Crerar (Crerar Papers), vol. 16, Address to Senior Officers First Canadian Army, 22 January 1945.

194  On the fire plan for Amiens, see Colonel G.W.L. Nicholson, *Canadian Expeditionary Force, 1914-1919* (Ottawa: Queen's Printer, 1964), 398; and Shane B. Schreiber, *Shock Army of the British Empire: The Canadian Corps in the Last 100 Days of the Great War* (Westport, CT: Praeger, 1997), 43-44.

195  TNA, CAB 106/991, "Operation VERITABLE," 51.

196  Ibid., 54.

197  Ibid., 17.

198  Canadian Military Headquarters Report No. 185, 25, quoted in Terry Copp, *Cinderella Army: The Canadians in Northwest Europe, 1944-1945* (Toronto: University of Toronto Press, 2006), 204.

199  Horrocks, *A Full Life*, 248.

200  *O.K.W. – W.F.St.* situation map *Lage West Stand*. 6.2.45 with additions 7.2.45, cited in Stacey, *Victory Campaign*, 475.

201  Horrocks, *A Full Life*, 248.

202  TNA, CAB 106/991, "Operation VERITABLE," 56.

203  Ibid., 55.

204  TNA, WO 171/4076, WD 30th Corps (February 1945), Operations Log.

205  Horrocks et al., *Corps Commander*, 184; and TNA, WO 171/4076, WD 13th Corps (February 1945), Operations Log, entry 1045 hrs, 8 February 1945.

206  Horrocks, *A Full Life*, 249.

207  Horrocks et al., *Corps Commander*, 184; and TNA, WO 171/4076 WD 13th Corps (February 1945), Operations Log, entry 1235 hrs, 8 February 1945.

208  LAC, Crerar Papers, War Diary, 8 February 1945.

209  Hans-Martin Stimpel, *Die Deutsche Fallschirmtruppe, 1942-1945: Einsatz auf Kriegsschauplatzen im Osten und Westen* (Hamburg: Verlag E.S. Mittler und Sohn, 2001), 352; and Kamen Nvenkin, *Fire Brigades: The Panzer Divisions, 1943-1945* (Winnipeg: J.J. Fedorowicz, 2008), 595.

210  TNA, CAB 106/991, "Operation VERITABLE," 21.

211  TNA, WD 171/4194, WD 15th (Scottish) Division, 8 February 1945.

212  TNA, CAB 106/991, "Operation VERITABLE," 22.

213  TNA, WD 171/4194, WD 15th (Scottish) Division (February 1945), 15 (S) Div O.O. No. 8, 4 February 1945.

214  TNA, WD 171/4194, WD 15th (Scottish) Division (February 1945), Operations Log, 9 February 1945, Serial 155.

215  Ibid., Serial 159.

216  Horrocks, *A Full Life*, 250.

217  Essame, *43rd Wessex Division at War* (London: William Clowes and Sons, 1952), 206.

218  Horrocks et al., *Corps Commander*, 187.

219  The breakdown for the vehicles by units is: 214th Infantry Brigade Group, 470; 43rd (Wessex) Division Tac and 8th Armoured Brigade, 60; and 129th Infantry Brigade Group, 520. See TNA, WO 171/476, WD 30th Corps (February 1945), Planning Notes No. 37, "VERITABLE": Movement Forward During the Battle, 7 February 1945.

220  It did not exactly work out that way. In the end, the 43rd Reconnaissance Regiment held fast while the 130th Brigade remained near Nijmegen.

221  TNA, CAB 106/991, "Operation VERITABLE," 22.

222  Ellis, *Victory in the West*, vol. 2, 263-64.

223  Horrocks, *A Full Life*, 250.

224  Stacey, *Victory Campaign*, 478.

225  Horrocks et al., *Corps Commander*, 187.

226  TNA, CAB 106/991, "Operation VERITABLE," 22. These were the 116th Panzer, 15th Panzer, 190th Infantry, 84th Infantry, 80th Infantry, 2nd Parachute, 6th Parachute, 7th Parachute, and 8th Parachute Divisions.

227  Philip Warner makes the analogy to Passchendaele in *Horrocks*, 124.

228  At this point, 2nd Canadian Corps consisted of the 2nd Canadian, 3rd Canadian, 4th Canadian Armoured, and 11th British Armoured Divisions.

229  Horrocks et al., *Corps Commander*, 187.

230  Horrocks, *A Full Life,* 251-52.
231  Ibid., 187-88.
232  Essame, *43rd Wessex Division,* 79.
233  IWM, Sound Archive, Accession No. 16812, Interview with Alexander Charles Barr, n.d.
234  Horrocks, *A Full Life,* 264-65.
235  Ibid., 266.
236  APRS, Horrocks Pers File, Horrocks to Sir Eric B.B. Speed, 16 December 1947; Horrocks to the Under Secretary of State for War, 14 January 1948; and E.B.B. Speed to Lieutenant-General Sir Brian Horrocks, 12 February 1948.
237  APRS, Horrocks Pers File, Record of Service; and Lambert to Horrocks, 6 November 1948.
238  Montgomery of Alamein, *Memoirs,* 105.

### Chapter 2: Wit in Want of Will

 1  J.L. Granatstein, *The Generals: The Canadian Army's Senior Commanders in the Second World War* (Toronto: Stoddart, 1993), 116-44.
 2  National Defence Headquarters (NDHQ), Directorate of History and Heritage (DHH), J.L. Granatstein's *The Generals* Interviews (Granatstein Interviews), Interviews with W.H. Pope, 3 April 1991, Uxbridge, ON (W.H. "Harry" Pope was aide-de-camp to Burns in 1944); Major-General Desmond B. Smith, 14 September 1991, London, UK (Smith was BGS to Burns, June-October 1944); and Major-General M.P. Bogert, 8 September 1991, Donnington, UK (Bogert was acting commander, 3rd Canadian Infantry Brigade, in September and October 1944).
 3  Imperial War Museum (IWM), Papers of General Sir Oliver Leese (Leese Papers), Box 2, Leese to Kennedy, 8 June 1944.
 4  NDHQ, DHH, Papers of General Charles Foulkes (Foulkes Papers), 73/1223, Series 6, Box 225, Documents Related to Replacement of Lt-Gen E.L.M. Burns GOC 1 Cdn Corps, McCreery to Alexander, 24 October 1944.
 5  Library and Archives Canada (LAC), Papers of General H.D.G. Crerar (Crerar Papers), vol. 4, Montague to Murchie and Stuart, 4 November 1944, cited in Granatstein, *The Generals,* 143.
 6  LAC, Personnel Records Unit (PRU), Personnel File of Eedson Louis Millard Burns (Burns Pers File), Extract of Baptism, Eedson Louis Millard Burns, 4 March 1914.
 7  LAC, MG 31 G 6, Papers of Lieutenant-General E.L.M. Burns (Burns Papers), vol. 8, Personal Report Cards 1906, 1910-13.
 8  LAC, PRU, Burns Pers File, Chief of the General Staff to Mr. E.L.M. Burns, 13 July 1914.
 9  Royal Military College of Canada (RMC), Registrar's Files, E.L.M. Burns File, Report, 23 June 1915.
10  Arlington B. Conway [Burns], "In Praise of War," *The American Mercury* 11 (August 1927): 387.
11  As a wartime exigency, cadets were offered commissions in the Canadian Permanent Force or the British Army as they became available. See Richard Arthur Preston, *Canada's RMC: A History of the Royal Military College* (Toronto: University of Toronto Press, 1969), 213-15.
12  LAC, PRU, Burns Pers File, Statement of Service and Qualifications, 11 February 1936.
13  Conway, "In Praise of War," 387.
14  Lieutenant-General E.L.M. Burns, *General Mud: Memoirs of Two World Wars* (Toronto: Clark, Irwin, 1970), 4.
15  LAC, RG 9, Accession No. 92-93/166, E.L.M. Burns File, Casualty Form Active Service, E.L.M. Burns.

16  Burns, *General Mud,* 53.

17  Ibid., 4.

18  Ibid., 46. Burns's account of the battle of Vimy can be found at ibid., 42-49.

19  Ibid., 62.

20  Ibid., 79.

21  Conway, "In Praise of War," 385.

22  Ibid., 386-87.

23  LAC, PRU, Burns Pers File, Annual Confidential Report for 1919, 15 December 1919.

24  Ibid., Completion Report, School of Military Engineering Chatham, Captain E.L.M. Burns, 2 December 1921.

25  Ibid., Annual Confidential Report, Captain E.L.M. Burns, 24 January 1924.

26  Ibid., Final Report: Staff College Camberley and Quetta, Major E.L.M. Burns, 18 December 1929.

27  Ibid., Confidential Reports for 1923-26, 1930-38.

28  Ibid., Confidential Report, E.L.M. Burns, 1926.

29  LAC, MG 30 D52, Papers of Madge Macbeth, vol. 2, Burns to Macbeth, 15 June 1924.

30  Madge Macbeth and A.B. Conway, *The Great Fright: Onesiphore, Our Neighbour* (Montreal: Louis Carrier, 1929).

31  LAC, PRU, Burns Pers File, McNaughton to Adjutant-General, 2 December 1932.

32  See, for example, Captain E.L.M. Burns, "The Mechanization of Cavalry," *Canadian Defence Quarterly* 1, no. 3 (April 1924): 3-7; Arlington B. Conway, "The Training of the Soldier," *The American Mercury* 2 (June 1924): 210-14; E.L.M. Burns, "The Defense in Modern War," *The American Mercury* 7 (February 1926): 202-5; E.L.M. Burns, "The Mind of the General," *The American Mercury* 13 (February 1928): 184-89; E.L.M. Burns, "The Study of War," *The American Mercury* 21 (October 1930): 193-95; Arlington B. Conway, "Tanks," *The American Mercury* 27 (September 1932): 58-65; Major E.L.M. Burns, "Protection of Rearward Services and Headquarters in Modern War," *Canadian Defence Quarterly* 10, no. 3 (April 1933): 295-313; Major E.L.M. Burns, "A Step towards Modernization," *Canadian Defence Quarterly* 12, no. 3 (April 1935): 298-305; Arlington B. Conway, "Wings over Japan," *The American Mercury* 35 (August 1935): 429-32; Arlington B. Conway, "Artillery in the Next War," *The American Mercury* 40 (March 1937): 338-44; Lieutenant-Colonel E.L.M. Burns, "The Theory of Military Organization," *Canadian Defence Quarterly,* 14, no. 3 (April 1937): 326-31; Lieutenant-Colonel E.L.M. Burns, "A Division that Can Attack," *Canadian Defence Quarterly* 15, no. 3 (April 1938): 282-98; and Lieutenant-Colonel E.L.M. Burns, "Where Do the Tanks Belong?" *Canadian Defence Quarterly* 16, no. 1 (October 1938): 28-31.

33  On Burns's interwar writings and theorizing, see Lieutenant-Colonel Bernd Horn and Michel Wyczynski, "E.L.M. Burns: Canada's Intellectual General," in *Warrior Chiefs: Perspectives on Canadian Military Leaders,* edited by Lieutenant-Colonel Bernd Horn and Stephen Harris (Toronto: Dundurn, 2001), 143-63.

34  Burns continued to draw on Fuller's work throughout the interwar period. In his 1935 *Canadian Defence Quarterly* article entitled "A Step towards Modernization," he cites extensively from Fuller's *Notes on Field Service Regulations,* vol. 3.

35  Burns, *General Mud,* 60.

36  The best analysis of Canadian Corps actions in the Hundred Days is Shane B. Schreiber, *Shock Army of the British Empire: The Canadian Corps in the Last 100 Days of the Great War* (Westport, CT: Praeger, 1997).

37  See Burns, *General Mud,* 60-61.

38  Burns, "The Mechanization of Cavalry," 5.

39  Ibid., 6. For his views on tanks and their possibilities, see Conway, "Tanks."

40  Burns, "The Mechanization of Cavalry," 3.
41  Ibid., 7.
42  Burns, "A Step towards Modernization," 298-99. Burns had discussed Fuller's idea of enemy "motor guerrillas" as a threat to rearward services in his 1932 prize-winning essay, "Protection of Rearward Services in Modern War," 305. See also Major-General J.F.C. Fuller, *Lectures on FSR III* (London: Sifton Praed, 1932), 62-69.
43  Burns, "A Step towards Modernization," 298-99, 305.
44  On the Kirke Committee and the resulting doctrinal and organizational changes for the British Army, see David French, *Raising Churchill's Army: The British Army and the War against Germany, 1919-1945* (London: Oxford University Press, 2000), 30-38.
45  Burns, "A Division that Can Attack," 283.
46  Ibid., 291.
47  Burns, "Where Do the Tanks Belong?" 30.
48  Captain G.G. Simonds, "An Army that Can Attack – A Division that Can Defend," *Canadian Defence Quarterly* 15, no. 4 (July 1938): 416.
49  Ibid., 417.
50  Burns, "Where Do the Tanks Belong?" 28.
51  French, *Raising Churchill's Army,* 41.
52  Niall Barr, *Pendulum of War: The Three Battles of Alamein* (London: Jonathan Cape, 2004), 186-87.
53  Not many people predicted the problem for all-arms cooperation in the same way. One of them was Major-General Alan Brooke, GOC Mobile Division, 1937-38. See Liddell Hart Centre for Military Archives (LHCMA), Papers of Field Marshal Lord Alanbrooke (Alanbrooke Papers), 5/2/14, Armour (1st Mobile Division 1937-38). See also pages 127-28 in Chapter 3.
54  Conway, "The Training of the Soldier," 210.
55  Ibid., 212.
56  Ibid., 211.
57  Ibid., 213.
58  Burns, "The Mind of the General," 187.
59  Ibid., 185.
60  Ibid.
61  Ibid., 189.
62  Ibid.
63  LAC, PRU, Burns Pers File, "Education or Inspiration?" (unpublished article, n.d.) by Major and Brevet Lieutenant-Colonel E.L.M. Burns.
64  Burns, *General Mud,* 9.
65  LAC, PRU, Burns Pers File, Record of Service, Major-General Eedson Louis Millard Burns, 14 June 1946.
66  Ibid., "Education or Inspiration?"
67  Ibid., Confidential Report, 30 November 1933.
68  Ibid., Confidential Report, 31 December 1935; Confidential Report, 19 December 1936.
69  Burns, *General Mud,* 99.
70  LAC, Crerar Papers, vol. 1, Crerar to Minister of National Defence J.L. Ralston, 17 June 1940. See also Paul Douglas Dickson, *A Thoroughly Canadian General: A Biography of General H.D.G. Crerar* (Toronto: University of Toronto Press, 2007), 122-27.
71  Crerar had originally been recalled to Canada to become Vice Chief of the General Staff (VCGS), but shortly after his arrival he ascended to the post of CGS. I am grateful to Jack Granatstein for bringing this point to my attention.

72  LAC, Crerar Papers, vol. 1, Crerar to McNaughton, 9 September 1940. See also Paul Dickson, "The Politics of Army Expansion: General H.D.G. Crerar and the Creation of First Canadian Army, 1941," *Journal of Military History* 60, no. 2 (April 1996): 271-98. See also C.P. Stacey, *Six Years of War: The Canadian Army in Canada, Britain and the Pacific* (Ottawa: Queen's Printer, 1966), 87-93.

73  LAC, PRU, Burns Pers File, Copy of intercepted letter to [name blacked out], 1700 MacGregor Street, Montreal, Canada, 22 July 1941.

74  Ibid., Postal & Telegraph Censorship Submission No. M.I. 12/Sub/.1., 28 July 1941.

75  Ibid.

76  Ibid., Copy of intercepted letter to [name blacked out], 1700 MacGregor Street, Montreal, Canada, 22 July 1941.

77  Ibid., Crerar to Minister, 25 August 1941.

78  Ibid., McNaughton to Pownall, 6 August 1941.

79  Ibid., Ralston to CGS, 27 August 1941.

80  Ibid., Crerar to Ralston, 25 August 1941.

81  NDHQ, DHH, Granatstein Interviews, Interviews with Major-General Roger Rowley, 23 May 1991, Ottawa; and Major-General J. Desmond B. Smith, 14 September 1991, London, UK.

82  George Kitching certainly thought that Burns had "blotted his copybook" with the British chain of command. See NDHQ, DHH, Granatstein Interviews, Interview with Major-General George Kitching, 25 February 1992, Victoria.

83  Alex Danchev and Daniel Todman, eds., *War Diaries, 1939-1945: Field Marshal Lord Alanbrooke* (London: Weidenfeld and Nicolson, 2001), 164 (entry for 15 June 1941).

84  LAC, Burns Papers, vol. 12, Scrapbook, telegram, McNaughton to Stuart, 17 January 1942.

85  Burns, *General Mud*, 110.

86  These issues completely preoccupied Burns between August 1941 and February 1942. See LAC, Burns Papers, vol. 1, Personal War Diary (PWD), 30 August 1941-15 February 1942.

87  LAC, RG 24, vol. 14050, War Diary (WD) 4th Canadian Armoured Brigade, Exercise GOPHER II: Attack on an Infantry Formation, 3 May 1942.

88  Ibid. (August 1942), Exercise SHOCK, 6 August 1942.

89  Ibid. (August-September 1942), Exercise BELCHER, 19 August 1942; Exercise RINGER, 27 August 1942; and Exercise ROLL, 15 September 1942.

90  Burns, *General Mud*, 110-11. On the promulgation of British Army doctrine, or lack of it, see Timothy Harrison Place, *Military Training in the British Army, 1940-1944: From Dunkirk to D-Day* (London: Frank Cass, 2000), 8-17; and French, *Raising Churchill's Army*, 12-47.

91  LAC, RG 24, vol. 14050, WD 4th Canadian Armoured Brigade, "Tank vs Tank Tactics," 7 August 1942.

92  Ibid. (November 1942-February 1943). For example, Exercise Rampant (November 1942) was a field training exercise, whereas Exercises Rival (November 1942) and Gremlin (December 1942) were wireless exercises and Exercise Well (November 1942) was a Tactical Exercise without Troops (TEWT).

93  Stacey, *Six Years of War*, 252.

94  Burns, *General Mud*, 114-17.

95  Ibid., 115.

96  Ibid., 116.

97  LAC, RG 24, vol. 13749, WD 2nd Canadian Infantry Division (June 1943), Tr[ainin]g of the NCO, 2 June 1943.

98  Ibid., Clothing – Other Ranks, 3 June 1943.

99 Ibid., Organization of Small Arms Tr[ainin]g, 22 June 1943.

100 Ibid. (July 1943), 20 July 1943. Montgomery had harped on this point after his inspections of Canadian brigades and units in February 1942. See LAC, Crerar Papers, vol. 2, Lieutenant-General B.L. Montgomery, "Some General Notes on What to Look for When Visiting a Unit," 6 March 1942.

101 Two companies of the Essex Scottish had "broken," causing the battalion to become "disorganized" on 19 July. See C.P. Stacey, *The Victory Campaign: Operation in Northwest Europe, 1944-1945* (Ottawa: Queen's Printer, 1966), 175. And the Camerons panicked, resulting in a "disorderly retreat" during the Forêt de la Londe battle on 25 August. See Terry Copp, *Cinderella Army: The Canadians in Northwest Europe* (Toronto: University of Toronto Press, 2006), 31.

102 LAC, Crerar Papers, vol. 4, Deserter Reported by Cdn Sec 2 Ech 21 A Group, Period 1 Sep 44-20 Jan 45, dated 26 January 1945.

103 NDHQ, DHH, Granatstein Interviews, Interview with John W.H. Bassett, 5 June 1991, Toronto.

104 LAC, RG 24, vol. 13749, WD 2nd Canadian Infantry Division (June-August 1943).

105 Ibid., T[an]k and Inf[antry] Exercise "HAMMER," 13 July 1943; OUTBURST: Exercise Instruction 10 June 1943.

106 Ibid. (July 1943), T[an]k & Inf[antry] Attack: 4 Cdn Inf Bde Operation Order No. 1, 4 July 1943.

107 Ibid. (August 1943), Lessons Exercise PICKAXE.

108 Ibid. (September 1943), 2 C[ana]d[ia]n Div[ision] Tr[ainin]g Instr[uction] No. 16.

109 LAC, Crerar Papers, vol. 8, Crerar to the Minister (Ralston), 29 November 1943.

110 Lieutenant-Colonel G.W.L. Nicholson, *The Canadians in Italy, 1943-1945* (Ottawa: Queen's Printer, 1966), 380.

111 LAC, RG 24, vol. 13796, WD 5th Canadian Armoured Division (January-February 1944).

112 Ibid., 11 February 1944.

113 NDHQ, DHH, Granatstein Interviews, Interview with Major-General George Kitching, 25 February 1992, Victoria.

114 LAC, RG 24, vol. 13796, WD 5th Canadian Armoured Division, 16 February 1944.

115 LAC, Crerar Papers, vol. 8, Letter, Crerar to Stuart, 22 January 1944; and Message, Stuart from Crerar, 28 [February 1944], 1330.

116 LAC, Burns Papers, PWD, 12 March 1944.

117 The Commander of the Allied Armies in Italy, General Sir Harold Alexander, did not like the addition of either a Canadian corps headquarters or an armoured division. In October 1943, he wrote the CIGS: "We already have as much armour in the Mediterranean as we can usefully employ in Italy ... I do not want another Corps Headquarters at this stage": The National Archives (TNA), WO 214/55, Papers of Field Marshal Earl Alexander of Tunis (Alexander Papers), Alexander to Brooke, 16 October 1943.

118 LAC, Burns Papers, PWD, Staff Study 1 Cdn Corps: "The Break through Operation," 22 March 1944.

119 Ibid., 1 Canadian Corps Training Instruction No. 3: Drill for Tank Infantry Co-operation – Sq[uadro]n and Co[mpan]y Basis, 26 March 1944.

120 On 5th Canadian Armoured Division training before the Liri Valley operation, see Douglas E. Delaney, *The Soldiers' General: Bert Hoffmeister at War* (Vancouver: UBC Press, 2005), 126-29.

121 LAC, Burns Papers, PWD, Planning Notes: Operation "HONKER," Skeleton Appreciation by GOC 1 Cdn Corps, 11 April 1944.

122 Ibid.

123  LAC, RG 24, vol. 13686, WD GS 1st Canadian Corps, 1 Cdn Corps Study Period, 5 May 1944.
124  LAC, RG 24, vol. 10779, McCarter to Nicholson, 3 April 1951.
125  LAC, PRU, Personnel File of George Arnold McCarter, Record of Service.
126  LAC, Burns Papers, PWD, August 1944.
127  TNA, WO 216/168, Alexander Papers, Leese to Kennedy, 16 April 1944.
128  LAC, Burns Papers, PWD, 3 May 1944; and NDHQ, DHH, Granatstein Interviews, Interview with Major-General C.B. Ware, 24 February 1992, Victoria.
129  NDHQ, DHH, Granatstein Interviews, Interview with General Bert Hoffmeister, 2 March 1992, Vancouver.
130  LAC, Burns Papers, PWD, 27 March 1944.
131  Ibid. (March 1944), Notes for Talk to Brigs on Necessity for Economy of Manpower, 11 May 1944.
132  As an example, Desmond Smith, who later served for a time as Burns's BGS, also recalled that the corps commander would turn to him when he wanted to prod his divisional commanders, instead of addressing them himself: NDHQ, DHH, Granatstein Interviews, Interview with Major-General J. Desmond B. Smith, 14 September 1991, London, UK. See also ibid., Interview with W.H. Pope, 3 April 1991, Uxbridge, ON.
133  Quoted in Nicholson, *Canadians in Italy*, 399.
134  LAC, Burns Papers, PWD, 19 May 1944.
135  LAC, RG 24, vol. 13686, WD GS 1st Canadian Corps (May 1944), 1 Cdn Corps Operation Instr No. 8, 15 May 1944.
136  LAC, Burns Papers, PWD, Burns to Vokes, 16 May 1944.
137  LAC, RG 24, vol. 10779, 1 Cdn. Inf. Div. in the Liri Valley Battle, 15-28 May 1944, by GOC 1 Cdn. Inf. Div., 29 May 1944, 2.
138  LAC, Burns Papers, PWD, Burns to Vokes, 16 May 1944.
139  LAC, RG 24, vol. 10779, 1 Cdn. Inf. Div. in the Liri Valley Battle, 2.
140  Nicholson, *Canadians in Italy*, 408.
141  LAC, RG 24, vol. 10779, 1 Cdn. Inf. Div. in the Liri Valley Battle.
142  Ibid., The Liri Valley Battle, 1 Cdn Corps, 15 May-4 June 1944, Trace of Enemy Dispositions in the Adolph Hitler (DORA) Line Opposite 1 Cdn Div at 0900 hrs 22 May 1944.
143  National Archives and Records Administration (NARA), T78, Roll 623, frame 314. *OKH – Gen. Insp. der Pz.Tr./Abt. Org. Fuhrervertrag am 5.2.1944 abends.*
144  LAC, Burns Papers, PWD, Notes on the Fortifications of the "ADOLPH HITLER" Line, 17 June 1944.
145  LAC, RG 24, vol. 13686, WD "G" 1 Cdn Corps, 1 Canadian Corps Operation Order No. 1, 22 May 1944.
146  LAC, Burns Papers, PWD, Burns to Vokes, 16 May 1944.
147  See the account of the 20 May meeting between Vokes and Burns in Mark Zuehlke, *The Liri Valley: Canada's World War II Breakthrough to Rome* (Toronto: Stoddart, 2001), 232-33.
148  RMC, Papers of Major-General Chris Vokes (Vokes Papers).
149  LAC, Burns Papers, PWD, Burns to Vokes, 20 May 1944.
150  LAC, RG 24, vol. 10779, 1 Cdn. Inf. Div. in the Liri Valley Battle, 4.
151  LAC, Burns Papers, PWD, Burns to Vokes, 20 May 44.
152  I am grateful to my former student and artillery officer, Second-Lieutenant Stephen Paish, for his research on the fire planning for Operation Chesterfield: OCdt Stephen Paish, "The Marriage of Flexibility and Concentration: Canadian Fire-Planning Experiences in the Italian Campaign" (unpublished paper, MSE 426, Royal Military College of Canada, 2008).
153  NDHQ, DHH, 142.2013(D1), Report by CCRA 1 Cdn Corps on Operations of Canadian Artillery in Italy, May-June 1944, 17.

154 LAC, RG 24, vol. 10779, 1 Cdn. Inf. Div. in the Liri Valley Battle, 15-28 May 1944, Artillery 1 Cdn. Inf. Div. in the Liri Valley Battle – CRA 1 Cdn. Inf. Div., 29 May 1944; and LAC, RG 24, vol. 14435, WD 3rd Field Regiment RCA, 22 May 1944.

155 Burns, *General Mud,* 148.

156 Burns made these points in *General Mud,* 148.

157 G.R. Stevens, *A City Goes to War* (Brampton, ON: Charters Publishing, 1964), 293.

158 NDHQ, DHH, Report by CCRA 1 Cdn Corps.

159 G.R. Stevens, *Princess Patricia's Canadian Light Infantry, 1919-1957* (Montreal: Southam, 1960), 163.

160 Nicholson, *Canadians in Italy,* 419.

161 Ibid., 423.

162 LAC, RG 24, vol. 13686, WD G Staff 1st Cdn Corps, G Log, 23 May 1944, 230948, Serial 782.

163 NDHQ, DHH, Report by CCRA 1 Cdn Corps.

164 Ibid.

165 LAC, RG 24, vol. 10779, Burns, "The Set-Piece Attack: Lessons from the Breakthrough of the HITLER LINE," 6 July 1944.

166 Ibid., McCarter to Nicholson, 3 April 1951.

167 TNA, WO 170/498 WD 78th Division (G Staff) (May 1944), Main 78 Div, date-time group 230050B May 44.

168 LAC, RG 24, vol. 10779, Burns, "The Set-Piece Attack."

169 Burns, *General Mud,* 151.

170 LAC, Burns Papers, PWD, 23 May 1944.

171 LAC, RG 24, vol. 13796, 5th Canadian Armoured Division (G Staff), 19 May 1944; LAC, Burns Papers, PWD, 19 May 1944.

172 LAC, RG 24, vol. 13796, WD 5th Canadian Armoured Division (G Staff) (June 1944), app. 23, 5 Cdn Armd Div Report on Ops, 23-31 May 1944.

173 See Delaney, *The Soldiers' General,* 139-42.

174 LAC RG 24, vol. 13796, WD 5th Canadian Armoured Division (G Staff) (June 1944), app. 23, 5 Cdn Armd Div Report on Ops, 23-31 May 1944; app. D, The Crossing of the Melfa and the Securing of a Bridgehead by 5 Cdn Armd Bde, signed by J.D.B. Smith, 4 June 1944.

175 For the action at the Melfa River, Major Jack Mahony received the Victoria Cross and Lieutenant E.J. Perkins, the Strathcona scout troop leader, won a Distinguished Service Order.

176 LAC, Burns Papers, PWD, 24 May 1944.

177 LAC, RG 24, vol. 13686, WD G 1st Cdn Corps, GS Log, Serials 984, 902, 931.

178 LAC, RG 24, vol. 10779, McCarter to Nicholson, 3 April 1951.

179 LAC, Burns Papers, PWD, 24 May 1944.

180 LAC, RG 24, vol. 13796, WD 5 Cdn Armd Div (G Staff) (May 1944), SITREP, 25 [May] 1200B.

181 IWM, Leese Papers, Box 1, Draft Memoir, ch. 12, 8.

182 LAC, Burns Papers, PWD, 24 May 1944.

183 Leese had commanded 30th Corps from September 1942 to January 1944, when he took over as Eighth Army commander from Montgomery. Kirkman had been Brigadier Royal Artillery of the Eighth Army during the battle of El Alamein in October-November 1942, and he had served as Brigadier RA of the 18th Army Group in Tunisia. Evelegh had commanded the 78th Division while it served with the First Army in Tunisia.

184 LAC, RG 24, vol. 13796, WD 5th Canadian Armoured Division (G Staff) (June 1944), app. 23, 5 Cdn Armd Div Report on Ops, 23-31 May 1944.

185  Slow battle procedure also delayed the advance of the 11th Canadian Infantry Brigade. See Delaney, *The Soldiers' General,* 146-48.

186  Nicholson, *Canadians in Italy,* 436.

187  Hans-Martin Stimpel, *Die Deutsche Fallschirmtruppe, 1942-1945: Einsatz auf dem Kriegs-schauplatzen im Suden* (Hamburg: Verlag E.S. Mittler und Sohn, 1998), 391.

188  War Diary, *Tenth (German) Army,* app. 1032, 15 May 1944, cited in Nicholson, *Canadians in Italy,* 436.

189  Burns, *General Mud,* 159.

190  LAC, RG 24, vol. 13686, WD "G" 1st Cdn Corps (May 1944), Operation Instr No. 15, 31 May 1944.

191  Nicholson, *Canadians in Italy,* 449-50.

192  LAC, Burns Papers, PWD, 5 June 1944.

193  Burns, *General Mud,* 162.

194  LAC, Burns Papers, PWD, 5 June 1944.

195  Burns, *General Mud,* 163.

196  LAC, Crerar Papers, vol. 7, Burns to Crerar, 7 June 1944.

197  Ibid.

198  LAC, Burns Papers, Burns to Chief of Staff CMHQ, 11 June 1944.

199  LAC, RG 24, vol. 13687, WD GS 1 Cdn Corps, Notes on Conference held by GOC 1 Cdn Corps with GOsC 1 Cdn Inf Div and 5 Cdn Armd Div, 9 June 1944.

200  Ibid., app. 48, Memorandum on Training Conference Held at 1 Cdn Corps 0900 hrs 16 June 1944 (dated 17 June 1944).

201  Ibid., 5 June 1944; and app. 17.

202  Burns, *General Mud,* 168.

203  LAC, RG 24, vol. 13687, WD GS 1 Cdn Corps, 18 June 1944.

204  Ibid., "The Set-Piece Attack: Lessons from the HITLER Line," 6 July 1944; and "The Pursuit from the Melfa to Anagni," 18 July 1944.

205  Ibid.

206  IWM, Leese Papers, Box 4, Leese to Kennedy, 8 June 1944.

207  TNA, Alexander Papers, Alexander to CIGS (Brooke), 29 Jun 1944; copy in DHH, Papers of General Charles Foulkes, 73/1223, Box 225.

208  LAC, Crerar Papers, vol. 3, Memorandum to C of S CMHQ re GOC-in-C AAI Message to CIGS Concerning Comd 1 Cdn Corps, 2 July 1944.

209  The report also recommended a remedy based on the railway block system proposed by Burns's headquarters. LAC, RG 24, vol. 13691, WD GS 1 Cdn Corps, Report on the Factors which slowed up the Eighth Army's Advance in the Liri Valley from D Day to the Capture of Anagni, n.d. See also IWM, Leese Papers, Box 4, Leese to Montgomery, 11 June 1944, 3.

210  IWM, Leese Papers, Box 2, Leese to his wife, 26 May 1944.

211  Ibid., Box 4, Leese to Major-General J.N. Kennedy, 26 May 1944.

212  Ibid., Box 2, Leese to his wife, 4 June 1944.

213  NDHQ, DHH, Granatstein Interviews, Telephone conversation with John W.H. Bassett, 20 May 1991.

214  NDHQ, DHH, Foulkes Papers, 73/1223, Box 225, Notes by Lt-Gen K. Stuart Regarding his Trip to Italy, 21 July 1944. Walsh's successor as the Eighth Army Chief of Staff, Harry Floyd, also suggested that someone on the 1st Canadian Corps Staff "had been disloyal to General Burns," although Floyd did not provide any names. See George Kitching, *Mud and Green Fields: The Memoirs of Major-General George Kitching* (St. Catharines, ON: Vanwell, 1993), 215.

215  NDHQ, DHH, Foulkes Papers, ibid.

216 Ibid.
217 Ibid., Leese to Stuart, 14 July 1944.
218 IWM, Leese Papers, Box 4, Leese to Kennedy, 25 July 1944.
219 TNA, Alexander Papers, Brooke to Alexander, 22 July 1944.
220 See, for example, 5th Canadian Armoured Division exercises Frame-up and Canyon: LAC, RG 24, vol. 13796, WD 5th Canadian Armoured Division (G Staff), 23-24 July 1944 and 9 August 1944.
221 LAC, RG 24, vol. 13687, WD GS 1 Cdn Corps, 8 June 1944.
222 Ibid., 20 June 1944; app. 57. See also 20 July 1944 and app. 26.
223 Ibid., 1 July 1944; app. 1.
224 Ibid., 10 July 1944; apps. 15 and 26.
225 For a discussion of 5th Canadian Armoured Division training during the period June-August 1944, see Delaney, *The Soldiers' General,* 154-66.
226 NDHQ, DHH, Foulkes Papers, 73/1223, Box 225, Notes by Lt-Gen K. Stuart Regarding his Trip to Italy.
227 IWM, Leese Papers, Box 4, Leese to Kennedy, 8 June 1944; and Nicholson, *Canadians in Italy,* 479-80.
228 LAC, Burns Papers, PWD, 2 July 1944.
229 LAC, RG 24, vol. 13796, WD 5th Cdn Armd Div (G Staff), 16-17 August 1944.
230 LAC, Burns Papers, PWD, 20 July 1944.
231 Ibid., Notes on the Method of planning for an Op[eration] to Break Through the "GOTHIC" Line, 23 July 1944.
232 Burns, *General Mud,* 172.
233 LAC, Burns Papers, PWD, 1 August 1944.
234 IWM, Leese Papers, Box 1, Draft Memoir, ch. 14, 1.
235 Ibid., 2.
236 Ibid., Box 4, Leese to Kennedy, 25 July 1944. See also William J. McAndrew, "Eighth Army at the GOTHIC Line: The Dog-Fight," *Journal of the Royal United Services Institute* (June 1986): 55-62.
237 LAC, Burns Papers, PWD, 4-8 August 1944.
238 LAC, RG 24, vol. 10431, Extracts for WD-GS 8th Army Sept 44, Notes on the Army Commanders [sic] Meeting 10th August [sic], 10 August 1944.
239 LAC, RG 24, vol. 13691, WD "G Staff" 1st Canadian Corps, The GOTHIC Line Battle and the Advance to the F. Ronco – 1 Cdn Corps – 2 August to 28 October 1944 (hereafter 1st Canadian Corps GOTHIC Line Report), app. A, 1 Cdn Corps Operation Instruction no. 23, 23 August 1944.
240 See Delaney, *The Soldiers' General,* 172.
241 NDHQ, DHH, Granatstein Interviews, Interview with General Bert Hoffmeister, 2 March 1992, Vancouver.
242 RMC, William J. McAndrew Collection, Letter, Hoffmeister to McAndrew, 30 July 1986.
243 LAC, RG 24, vol. 13691, WD "G Staff" 1st Canadian Corps, 1st Canadian Corps GOTHIC Line Report, app. A.
244 LAC, Burns Papers, PWD, 22 August 1944; and LAC, RG 24, vol. 13796, WD "G Staff" 5th Cdn Armd Div, 22 August 1944.
245 Nicholson, *Canadians in Italy,* 499.
246 NARA, T312, Roll 99, 10 AOK, Ia, *Kriegstagebuch Nr. 8, Italy, 14 June-20 September 1944. Anlagen z.KTB 7 und 8, Abtlg. Ia, Chefsachen,* entries for 26-30 August 1944. See also Nicholson, *Canadians in Italy,* 512-13.
247 LAC, Burns Papers, PWD, 27 August 1944.

248   LAC, RG 24, vol. 13729, WD 1st Canadian Infantry Division (G Staff), Message Log, 27 August 1944, Serial 15124.

249   RMC, McAndrew Collection, General B.M. Hoffmeister, Interview by B. Greenhous and W. McAndrew, 1980, 94.

250   NARA, T312, Roll 99, *10 AOK, Ia, Kriegstagebuch Nr. 8, Italy* (entry for 29 August 1944).

251   LAC, Burns Papers, PWD, 30 August 1944.

252   Burns, *General Mud,* 185.

253   See the first-hand account of this action in Stanley Scislowski, *Not All of Us Were Brave* (Toronto: Dundurn, 1997), 255-56.

254   See Nicholson, *Canadians in Italy,* 516; and Steven, *Princess Patricia's Canadian Light Infantry,* 185.

255   LAC, Burns Papers, PWD, 31 August 1944.

256   McAndrew, "Eighth Army at the GOTHIC Line," 60.

257   LAC, Burns Papers, PWD, Leese to Burns, 9 September 1944.

258   Burns, *General Mud,* 189.

259   See LAC, Burns Papers, PWD (September-October 1944).

260   NDHQ, DHH, Granatstein Interviews, Interview with General Bert Hoffmeister, 2 March 1992, Vancouver. This meeting likely took place on 29 September 1944. See LAC, Burns Papers, PWD, 29 September 1944.

261   NDHQ, DHH, Granatstein Interviews, Interview with General Bert Hoffmeister, 2 March 1992, Vancouver; and LAC, Burns Papers, PWD, 8 October 1944.

262   See LAC, Burns Papers, PWD, 9 October 1944.

263   LAC, Crerar Papers, vol. 4, W126 Montague from Weeks, 03 [November 1944] 1442 [hours].

264   NDHQ, DHH, Granatstein Interviews, Interview with General Bert Hoffmeister, 2 March 1992, Vancouver.

265   See NDHQ, DHH, Granatstein Interviews, Interviews with Major-General Desmond B. Smith, 14 September 1991, London, UK; and Major-General M.P. Bogert, 8 September 1991, Donnington, UK; and LAC, MG 31 G 21, Papers of M.H.S. Penhale, vol. 1, Vokes to Penhale, 2 November 1944.

266   NDHQ, DHH, Foulkes Papers, 73/1223, Series 6, Box 225, McCreery to Alexander, 24 October 1944.

267   Ibid., Burns to Crerar, 12 November 1944.

268   LAC, Penhale Papers, vol. 1, Vokes to Penhale, 2 November 1944.

269   LAC, Crerar Papers, vol. 4, W126 Montague from Weeks, 03 [November 1944] 1442 [hours].

270   NDHQ, DHH, Foulkes Papers, 73/1223, Series 6, Box 225, Burns to Crerar, 12 November 1944.

271   Major-General E.L.M. Burns, *Manpower in the Canadian Army, 1939-1945* (Toronto: Clarke, Irwin, 1956).

272   Eedson Louis Millard Burns, *Between Arab and Israeli* (Toronto: Clarke, Irwin, 1962).

273   Lieutenant-General E.L.M. Burns, *Megamurder* (New York: Pantheon Books, 1966).

274   E.L.M. Burns, *A Seat at the Table: The Struggle for Disarmament* (Toronto: Clarke, Irwin, 1972).

275   E.L.M. Burns, *Defence in the Nuclear Age: An Introduction for Canadians* (Toronto: Clarke, Irwin, 1972).

**Chapter 3: The Quiet Gentleman**

Portions of this chapter have appeared in Douglas E. Delaney, "A Quiet Man of Influence: General Sir John Crocker," *Journal of the Society for Army Historical Research* 85, no. 343 (2007): 185-207.

1   Major L.F. Ellis, *Victory in the West, Vol. 1: The Battle of Normandy* (London: Her Majesty's Stationery Office, 1962), 171.
2   Imperial War Museum (IWM), Papers of Field Marshal the Viscount Montgomery of Alamein (BLM), BLM 187/3, Montgomery to Crocker, 8 October 1948. Sir Basil Liddell Hart, "Obituary: Gen. Sir John Crocker," *The Times*, 11 March 1963; and Kenneth Macksey, *The Tank Pioneers* (London: Jane's, 1981), 218.
3   General Sir Harold E. Pyman, *Call to Arms* (London: Leo Cooper, 1971), 61.
4   Papers of General Sir John T. Crocker (Crocker Papers), Annual Confidential Report – 1935, 11 October 1935. These papers are in the possession of John Bingham, Crocker's grandson. I am most grateful to Mr. Bingham for very generously allowing me to quote from his grandfather's collection.
5   Army Personnel Records Section (APRS), Glasgow, Personnel File of John Tredinnick Crocker (Crocker Pers File), Birth Certificate; Form M.T. 315b, 20 November 1918.
6   Macksey, *Tank Pioneers*, 178.
7   Pyman, *Call to Arms*, 61.
8   APRS, Crocker Pers File, Attestation Papers, J.T. Crocker, 25 November 1915.
9   Crocker Papers, Distinguished Service Order Citation, L.G. 27 July 1918.
10  Michael Carver, *Out of Step: Memoirs of a Field Marshal* (London: Hutchinson, 1989), 32.
11  APRS, Crocker Pers File, Crocker to The Secretary War Office, 29 June 1923; and Record of Service.
12  J.T. Crocker, "Tanks in India," *Royal Tanks Corps Journal* 7, no. 75 (July 1925): 93-97.
13  Ibid., 96-97.
14  Liddell Hart Centre for Military Archives (LHCMA), LH 9/28/40, "General Sir John Crocker," n.d.
15  Crocker Papers, Copy of Annual Confidential Report – 1927/28, n.d.
16  Crocker Papers, Extract from Final Report – Staff College, n.d.
17  Sir Percy Hobart was, by the mid-1930s, Britain's foremost serving authority on armour and mechanization, having commanded tank battalions in the experimental period of the 1920s and 1930s.
18  LHCMA, LH 11/1943/64, Notes on "Talk with J.C. (morning) 10th October 1943."
19  Ibid.
20  Tank Museum (Bovington), Tank Brigade Files, 1934-36, Instructions for Assembly (Conference at Perham Down Camp May 24th 1934) and 1st Tank Brigade "B" Echelon Exercises – 24/26th May 1934.
21  Cited in Macksey, *Tank Pioneers*, 179.
22  Crocker Papers, Annual Confidential Report 1936, n.d.
23  Carver, *Out of Step*, 32.
24  APRS, Crocker Pers File, Record of Service.
25  Crocker Papers, Copy of Confidential Report 1937, 10 November 1937.
26  Ibid., Copy of Confidential Reports 1930-39.
27  Ibid., Copy of Confidential Reports 1938, 1939.
28  Field Marshal Lord Carver, *The Apostles of Mobility: The Theory and Practice of Armoured Warfare* (London: Weidenfeld and Nicolson, 1979), 52-53; J.P. Harris, *Men, Ideas and Tanks: British Military Thought and Armoured Forces, 1903-1939* (Manchester: Manchester University Press, 1995), 289-90; and Kenneth Macksey, *Armoured Crusader: A Biography of Major-General Sir Percy Hobart* (London: Hutchinson, 1967), esp. 133-54, 178-95.
29  See LHCMA, Papers of Field Marshal Lord Alanbrooke (Alanbrooke Papers), 5/2/14, Armour (1st Mobile Division 1937-38).
30  Ibid., 6/5/2, Brooke to Wavell, 16 January 1938.
31  Ibid., 5/2/14, Armour (1st Mobile Division 1937-38).

32  Crocker was not the only officer to catch Brooke's eye during his tenure as Director of Military Training or as GOC Mobile Division. He also advanced the careers of Richard McCreery, Charles Norrie, M.G.H Barker, and W.H.E. "Strafer" Gott. See David French, "Colonel Blimp and the British Army: British Divisional Commanders in the War against Germany, 1939-1945," *English Historical Review* 3 (1996): 1194.

33  The National Archives (TNA), WO 64/421, War Diary (WD), 3rd Armoured Brigade (May 1940), 1st Armoured Division Operation Order No. 2, 25 May 1940.

34  Crocker had only two tank battalions because one of them, 3rd Battalion Royal Tank Regiment (3 RTR), had been sent to Calais: L.F. Ellis, *The War in France and Flanders, 1939-1940* (London: Her Majesty's Stationery Office, 1953), 153.

35  TNA, WO 64/421, WD 3rd Armoured Brigade (May 1940), 3rd Armoured Brigade Operation Order No. 1 (issued verbally), 26 May 1940; see also the scathing comments on French inaction in Summary of Events and Information, 27 May 1940.

36  Macksey, *Tank Pioneers*, 183. See also Major L.F. Ellis, *The War in France and Flanders* (London: Her Majesty's Stationery Office, 1954), 301.

37  TNA, WO 166/823, WD 6th Armoured Division (October 1940), 6th Armoured Division: Training Instruction No. 1 – Individual Training, October 1940.

38  Ibid.

39  For a good discussion on the doctrine officers would have studied, see Timothy Harrison Place, *Military Training in the British Army, 1940-1944: From Dunkirk to D-day* (London: Frank Cass, 2000), 95-111.

40  TNA, WO 166/823, WD 6th Armoured Division (June 1941), Recce [Reconnaissance], n.d.

41  Because the threat of invasion was still alive, training had to be integrated into operational tasks. See, for example, the movement exercise in ibid. (January 1941), 6 Armd Div, Operation Order No. 1, 22 January 1941.

42  TNA, WO 166/6125, WD 9th Corps (December 1942), HQ 9 Corps Standing Orders, 7 December 1942.

43  For Exercise Robin, see ibid. (November 1942), Exercise ROBIN, Move to Assembly Area, 29 October 1942 (1 page); Order No. 1, 2 November 1942 (4 pages plus overlay); 9 Corps O.O. No. 2, 3 November 1942 (2 pages), 9 Corps O.O. No. 3, 4 November 1942 (2 pages). For the Tunisian Campaign, see TNA, WO 175/97, WD 9th Corps (March-May 1943). See Operational Order No.1, 5 April 1943 (1 page); Operational Order No. 2, 6 April 1943 (3 pages); Operational Order No. 3, 8 April 1943 (1 page plus overlay); Operational Order No. 5, 12 April 1943 (1 page); Operational Order No. 7, 15 April 1943 (1 page plus move matrix); Operational Order No. 8, 19 April 1943 (4 pages plus overlay).

44  LHCMA, LH 9/28/40. Liddell Hart to Crocker, 29 December 1942. The draft article "The Problem of Quickening Manoeuvre" can be found at LH 11/1942/104.

45  See TNA, CAB 120/52. First convened under the chairmanship of Prime Minister Winston Churchill in May 1941, the "Tank Parliament" included, among others, the CIGS, the Vice-CIGS, the C-in-C Home Forces, the commanders of all the armoured divisions in the army, the Minister of Supply, and representatives from the various directorates within the Ministry of Supply. Its purpose was to consider tank and anti-tank issues, including technology, production, and supply.

46  LHCMA, LH 11/1942/104, "The Problem of Quickening Manoeuvre: The Potential Value of a 'Five-Finger' Organization," 1.

47  Ibid., 4.

48  LHCMA, LH 9/28/40, Crocker to Liddell Hart, 2 February 1943. The armoured division organization, for example, changed five times between May 1939 and March 1944. See the diagrams in Place, *Military Training in the British Army*, 98-100.

49 LHCMA, LH 11/1943/3, "Too Much Top Hamper?" 11 February 1943.

50 See LHCMA, LH 9/28/40, Liddell Hart to Crocker, 11 June 1943; and LH 10/1943/9, "Is Our Soldiery Carrying Too Much Top Hamper?" *Daily Mail,* 11 February 1943.

51 See TNA, WO 175/97, WD 9th Corps (General Staff) (April 1943), HQ 9 Corps Wireless Diagram (effective from 1200 hrs 6 Apr 43); and 9 Corps Comd's Outline Narrative of Operations, 8-12 April 1943.

52 On MacMillan, see Nick Smart, *Biographical Dictionary of British Generals of the Second World War* (Barnsley, South Yorkshire, UK: Pen and Sword, 2005), 203-4.

53 TNA, WO 166/6125, WD HQ 9th Corps (December 1942), HQ 9 Corps Standing Orders, n.d.

54 LHCMA, LH 9/28/40, Crocker to Liddell Hart, 18 June 1943.

55 See TNA, WO 175/97, WD 9th Corps (General Staff) (April 1943), 9 Corps Operation Order No. 2, 6 April 1943.

56 Ibid.; Crocker Papers, MacMillan to Crocker, 4 September 1950.

57 Crocker Papers, MacMillan to Crocker, 4 September 1950. On Ryder's postwar recollections, see Rick Atkinson, *An Army at Dawn: The War in North Africa, 1942-1943* (New York: Henry Holt, 2002), 471-72.

58 TNA, WO 175/146, WD 6th Armoured Division, 8 April 1943.

59 TNA, WO 175/97, WD 9th Corps (General Staff) (April 1943), 9 Corps Comd's Outline Narrative of Operations, 8-12 April 1943.

60 Crocker Papers, MacMillan to Crocker, 4 September 1950.

61 Major-General I.S.O. Playfair, *The Mediterranean and the Middle East,* vol. 4 (London: Her Majesty's Stationery Office, 1966), 382.

62 Dwight D. Eisenhower, *Crusade in Europe* (London: William Heinemann, 1948), 168; Macksey, *Tank Pioneers,* 188-89; and Atkinson, *An Army at Dawn,* 477. I should point out that I too was guilty of perpetuating this distorted view of events. See Delaney, "A Quiet Man of Influence," 195-96. I have revised my views based on Crocker's correspondence with Eisenhower, documents provided me by John Bingham.

63 Crocker Papers, Crocker to Eisenhower, 16 January 1949.

64 Quoted in Atkinson, *An Army at Dawn,* 477.

65 Crocker Papers, Crocker to Eisenhower, 16 January 1949.

66 Ibid.

67 Eisenhower, *Crusade in Europe,* 168.

68 Crocker Papers, Crocker to Eisenhower, 16 January 1949.

69 LHCMA, LH9/28/40, Crocker to Liddell Hart, 18 June 1943.

70 Ibid.

71 LHCMA, Alanbrooke Papers 6/2/17, Alexander to Brooke, 19 May 1943.

72 Brooke had earmarked Crocker for corps command as early as October 1941, when as C-in-C Home Forces, he recommended that Crocker should succeed Lieutenant-General Sir Beresford Wilcox in command of 1st Corps: LHCMA, Alanbrooke Papers 6/5/7, Forecast of Possible Changes, Armies, Oct 23/41.

73 For an analysis of Montgomery's attempts to bring in his own people before D-day, see David French, "Invading Europe: The British Army and Its Preparations for the Normandy Campaign, 1942-1944," *Diplomacy and Statecraft* 14, no. 2 (2003): 285-86.

74 LHCMA, LH 9/28/40, Crocker to Liddell Hart, 1 May 1944.

75 Ibid.

76 TNA, WO 166/10371, WD 1st Corps (August 1943), Instruction for Exercise CONTACT II, n.d.

77 Ibid. (September 1943), Standing Orders for Organization and Move of Main Headquarters, September 1943.

78  Ibid. (August 1943), Exercise EUCLID, n.d.
79  Ibid. (September 1943), Report on Discussion Held by Comd 1 Corps, 6 September 1943.
80  C.P. Stacey, *The Victory Campaign: The Campaign in Northwest Europe, 1944-1945* (Ottawa: Queen's Printer, 1966), 12, 36; and TNA, WO 166/10371, WD 1st Corps (October 1943).
81  TNA, WO 166/10371, WD 1st Corps (September 1943), Report on Discussion Held by Comd 1 Corps, 6 September 1943.
82  Ibid. (October 1943), EXERCISE BRIDGEHEAD, Exercise Instructions.
83  On the training before D-day, see French, "Invading Europe: The British Army and Its Preparations for the Normandy Campaign," 271-94; and Stacey, *Victory Campaign*, 34-36.
84  See Ellis, *Victory in the West*, vol. 1, 149-92; Stacey, *Victory Campaign*, 90-120; and Terry Copp, *Fields of Fire* (Toronto: University of Toronto Press, 2003), 33-58.
85  TNA, WO 171/258, WD 1st Corps (June 1944), 1 Corps Operational Order, 5 May 1944.
86  Stacey, *Victory Campaign*, 102-10.
87  Ellis, *Victory in the West*, vol. 1, 228-30.
88  Ibid., 248-49.
89  Von Runstedt and Rommel disagreed on how best to defend against an Allied invasion. Von Runstedt wanted to wait until the Allied forces had penetrated beyond the range of naval guns, then mass armoured forces for a massive counterattack to destroy the bridge-head. Rommel, who believed that Allied air power would make it impossible to mass sufficient armoured forces, favoured a more decentralized approach, advocating the early release of armoured forces for the destruction of the Allied invaders while they were still on the beaches. But the piecemeal counterattacks by the 12th SS Panzer Division and 21st Panzer Division on 6-10 June, although they halted the Allied advance in the eastern bridgehead, failed to destroy the lodgement.
90  If the assaults by 30th Corps and 1st Corps had succeeded, Montgomery had hoped to drop the 1st Airborne Division between the two thrusts to close the pincer. See Ellis, *Victory in the West*, vol. 1, 248-50.
91  Hitler relieved von Rundstedt on 2 July, replacing him with Field Marshal Gunther von Kluge.
92  Horst Boog, Detelef Vogel, and Gerhard Krebs, *Germany and the Second World War: The Strategic Air War in Europe and the War in the West and East Asia, 1943-1944/5*, translated and edited by Derry Cook Radmore (Oxford: Oxford University Press, 2005), 599; Stacey, *Victory Campaign*, 151.
93  National Archives and Records Administration (NARA), T311, Roll 28, *Heeresgruppe D. Anlagen z. KTB, Befeble, Meldungen*, 1-10 July 1944.
94  Viscount Montgomery of Alamein, *Normandy to the Baltic* (London: Hutchinson, 1947), 72-73.
95  The two men most responsible for the idea were Air Commodore E.J. Kingston-McCloughry, Leigh-Mallory's Head of Operational Plans and Deputy Chief of Operations, and Professor Solly Zuckerman, a scientific advisor to the AEAF. See Air Vice Marshal E.J. Kingston-McCloughry, *The Direction of War* (New York: Frederick A. Praeger, 1958), 142-46; Solly Zuckerman, *From Apes to Warlords* (London: Harper and Row, 1978), 266-67; and Carlo D'Este, *Decision in Normandy: The Unwritten Story of Montgomery and the Normandy Campaign* (London: Collins, 1983), 226-27.
96  TNA, WO 285/9, WD of General Sir Miles Dempsey (Dempsey Diary), 14 June 1944.
97  Ibid.
98  TNA, WO 171/258, WD 1st Corps, 14 June 1944.
99  LHCMA, Papers of Chester Wilmot (Wilmot Papers), LH15/15/159, Crocker to Wilmot, 10 May 1947.

100 Ibid.; Lord Tedder, *With Prejudice* (London: Cassel, 1966), 552-53.
101 On Leigh-Mallory's difficult relationship with fellow "Air Chiefs" such as Tedder, Arthur "Mary" Coningham, and the American Carl Spaatz, see D'Este, *Decision in Normandy*, 215-18.
102 Kingston-McCloughry, *Direction of War*, 146-47.
103 Stacey, *Victory Campaign*, 157.
104 Major-General Sir Francis de Guingand, *Operation Victory* (London: Hodder and Stoughton, 1947), 402.
105 Ibid. De Guingand was Montgomery's Chief of Staff, first in the Eighth Army (1942-43), then in the 21st Army Group (1944-45).
106 On 24 June, after consulting with division commanders, Crocker's staff prepared a one-page brief, "NOTES FOR CORPS COMD ON AIR SUPPORT REF VISIT OF AOC 83 GROUP," which called for, among other things, closer coordination between air and ground force staffs and more medium bomber support on difficult targets. It did not, however, mention *heavy* bomber support. TNA, WO 171/258, WD 1st Corps (June 1944).
107 Library and Archives Canada (LAC), MG 30 E 157, Papers of General H.D.G. Crerar (Crerar Papers), vol. 3, Crocker to Dempsey, 5 July 1944.
108 Copp, *Fields of Fire*, 98.
109 For accounts of Operation Windsor, see Stacey, *Victory Campaign*, 153-57; Copp, *Fields of Fire*, 98-101; and Reginald H. Roy, *1944: The Canadians in Normandy* (Ottawa: Canadian War Museum, 1984), 45-50. For a highly critical account, see John A. English, *The Canadian Army and the Normandy Campaign: A Study of Failure in High Command* (New York: Praeger, 1991), 214-17.
110 LAC, RG 24, vol. 14140, WD 8th Canadian Infantry Brigade (July 1944), OP "WINDSOR," 8 Cdn Inf Bde OO No. 14, 3 July 1944.
111 Hubert Meyer, *The 12th SS: The History of the Hitler Youth Panzer Division*, vol. 1 (Mechanicsburg, PA: Stackpole Books, 1994), 456-59.
112 Stacey, *Victory Campaign*, 155.
113 LAC, RG 24, vol. 10673, Enemy Tactics (Lessons of War No. 1). See also Copp, *Fields of Fire*, 101.
114 LAC, RG 24, vol. 14140, WD 8th Canadian Infantry Brigade, OP WINDSOR, 8 Cdn Inf Bde O.O. No. 14, 3 July 1944.
115 Enemy mortars were very difficult to detect, even when they were firing, and therefore hard to target. See the operational research findings in "Report No. 11, The Location of Enemy Mortars," in *Montgomery's Scientists: Operational Research in Northwest Europe*, edited by Terry Copp (Waterloo, ON: Laurier Centre for Military Strategic and Disarmament Studies, 2000), 431-40. "Stonk" was the term given to a short and concentrated artillery bombardment.
116 Statement by Oberscharfuhrer Erwin Wohlgemuth, cited in H. Meyer, *12th SS*, 463.
117 LAC, RG 24, vol. 10925, 8 CDN INF BDE, "BARRAGE IN THE ATTACK," 3 August 1944.
118 Excellent discussions of Anglo-Canadian battle doctrine, its evolution, and its impact can be found in David French, *Raising Churchill's Arm: The British Army and the War against Germany* (London: Oxford University Press, 2000), 240-73; and English, "The Imprint of Doctrine," in *The Canadian Army and the Normandy Campaign*, 159-80.
119 National Defence Headquarters (NDHQ), Directorate of History and Heritage (DHH), J.L. Granatstein's *The Generals* Interviews (Granatstein Interviews), Interview with Lieutenant-Colonel Don Mingay, 6 June 1991, Creemore, ON.
120 Ibid.
121 Historian Terry Copp's research into censorship reports, which surveyed the letters of Canadian soldiers during the summer of 1944, found no such sign of "general

despondency." The reports are contained in LAC, RG 24, vol. 10784. See Copp, *Fields of Fire,* 119-21.

122   *NDHQ,* DHH, Granatstein Interviews, Interview with Lieutenant-Colonel Don Mingay, 6 June 1991, Creemore, ON. See also interviews with Colonel Ernest A. Coté, 19 July 1991, Ottawa; Brigadier P.A.S. Todd, 8 May 1991, Ancaster, ON; and Lieutenant-Colonel Peter Bennett [Brigade Major, 7th Canadian Brigade], 6 September 1991, London, UK.

123   Ibid., Interviews with Brigadier P.A.S. Todd, 8 May 1991, Ancaster, ON; and Lieutenant-Colonel Don Mingay, 6 June 1991, Creemore, ON.

124   LAC, Crerar Papers, vol. 3, Extract, Montgomery to Crerar, 8 July 1944.

125   Ibid., Memorandum, 14 July 1944.

126   Ibid., Simonds to Dempsey, 27 July 1944.

127   Ibid.

128   LAC, Crerar Papers, vol. 3, Crocker to Dempsey, 5 July 1944.

129   Nigel Hamilton, *Monty: Master of the Battlefield, 1942-1944* (London: Hamish Hamilton, 1983), 715.

130   "Report No. 5, Heavy Bombing in Support of Operation CHARNWOOD (No. 2 Operational Research Section)," in Copp, *Montgomery's Scientists,* 71-77; Zuckerman, *From Apes to Warlords,* 272.

131   The Operation Order for Charnwood, dated 5 July, clearly shows that 1st Corps had asked for "h[eav]y and med[ium] conc[entration]s – COLOMBELLES FACTORY as near H-Hour as possible": TNA, WO 171/258, WD 1st Corps (July 1944), Operation CHARNWOOD, 1 Corps OO No. 3, 5 July 1944. The 1st Corps operations log, however, records that the Second Army advised 1st Corps by phone message at 1815 that 450 bombers would attack the northern outskirts of Caen at 2150: ibid., GS Log and Summary of Events, 7 July 1944, Serial 805.

132   TNA, WO 171/258, WD 1st Corps, 4 July 1944. Significantly, because Operation Windsor was still underway, neither Keller nor his GSO 1 attended for the 3rd Canadian Infantry Division. In their place, a GSO 2 with the rank of major attended Crocker's conference.

133   Examples in which the Germans were able to concentrate troops and firepower to stop narrow-front attacks include the 152nd Brigade attack at St. Honorine (11-12 June), the 2nd Canadian Armoured Brigade attack on Le Mesnil-Patry (11 June), the 3rd Division attack on La Bijude (27-28 June), and the 8th Canadian Infantry Brigade attack on Carpiquet (4 July).

134   Terry Copp discusses how the lessons of narrow frontages had been learned by everyone from the officers of the 8th Canadian Infantry Brigade to Montgomery: Copp, *Fields of Fire,* 101.

135   TNA, WO 171/258, Operation CHARNWOOD, 1 Corps OO No. 3, 5 July 1944.

136   Some of the bombs dropped on 7 July had their fuses set for a six-hour delay, such that they would explode just before H-hour: Zuckerman, *From Apes to Warlords,* 273.

137   See the marginal tally of guns at LAC, RG 24, vol. 10790, Operation CHARNWOOD, 5 July 1944.

138   On the disposition of enemy forces around Caen, see H. Meyer, *12th SS,* 473-74 and map, 444-45. There are also good maps and discussion of the enemy layout at Caen in Simon Trew and Stephen Badsey, *Battle for Caen* (Gloucestershire: Sutton, 2004), 33-35, 128. See also NARA, T311, Roll 28, Frame 7034325, Deployment of *16 Luftwaffe Field Division* as of 0700 5 July 1944.

139   As an example, see the air photographs with overprints on the positions at Galmanche and La Bijude: Laurier Centre for Military Strategic and Disarmament Studies, Box 309, air photos 4177 and 4180, 5 July 1944.

140   Cited in H. Meyer, *12th SS,* vol. 1, 472.

141 Copp, *Fields of Fire,* 86-87.
142 H. Meyer, *12th SS,* vol. 1, 472.
143 TNA, WO 171/258, WD 1st Corps, GS Log and Summary of Events, 7 July 1944, Serial 760.
144 Ibid., Serial 761.
145 "Report No. 5, Heavy Bombing in Support of Operation CHARNWOOD," in Copp, *Montgomery's Scientists,* 75.
146 Ibid.
147 The exception to the phases-on-order method of progression was phase 5, the seizure of bridgeheads over the Orne: "Comds 3 Br and 59 Inf Divs will launch Phase V at their own discretion," TNA, WO 171/258, Operation CHARNWOOD, 1 Corps OO No. 3, 5 July 1944.
148 Ibid.; TNA, WO 171/258 WD 1st Corps, 8 July 1944.
149 Ibid., GS Log and Summary of Events, 8 July 1944, Serial 852.
150 Ibid., Serials 851 and 854.
151 TNA, WO, 171/571, WD 59th (Staffordshire) Division, 8 July 1944. For the operation, Major-General L.O. Lyne, GOC 59th (Staffordshire) Division, placed 2/6th South Staffordshire Regiment, from the 177th Brigade, under command of the 197th Brigade. See ibid., Operation CHARNWOOD, 59th Inf Div O.O. No. 1, 6 July 1944.
152 TNA, WO 171/28, WD 1st Corps (July 1944), GS Log and Summary of Events, 8 July 1944, Serial 867.
153 Kurt Meyer, *Grenadiers: The Story of Waffen SS General "Panzer" Meyer* (Mechanicsburg, PA: Stackpole Books, 2005), 260.
154 TNA, WO 171/28, WD 1st Corps (July 1944), GS Log and Summary of Events, 8 July 1944, Serial 911. At the same time, Crocker arranged to have the 34th Tank Brigade placed under 1st Corps command in order to reconstitute a reserve.
155 Stacey, *Victory Campaign,* 161.
156 TNA, WO 171/28, WD 1st Corps (July 1944), GS Log and Summary of Events, 8 July 1944, Serial 873. In the 1st Corps Log, the attack on the high ground was erroneously recorded as being assigned to 59th (Staffordshire) Division.
157 Ibid., Serial 882.
158 Ibid., Serial 909.
159 K. Meyer, *Grenadiers,* 262; H. Meyer, *12th SS,* vol. 1, 486-87.
160 Copp, *Fields of Fire,* 104; H. Meyer, ibid., 489-90.
161 TNA, WO 171/28, WD 1st Corps (July 1944), GS Log and Summary of Events, 8 July 1944, Serial 954.
162 Ibid., Serial 970.
163 Ibid., Serial 972.
164 Ibid., Serial 995.
165 Ibid., Serial 994.
166 K. Meyer, *Grenadiers,* 264-65; Stacey, *Victory Campaign,* 161.
167 H. Meyer, *12th SS,* vol. 1, 490-92.
168 K. Meyer, *Grenadiers,* 265.
169 TNA, WO 171/28, WD 1st Corps (July 1944), GS Log and Summary of Events, 8 July 1944, 9 July 1944, Serial 14.
170 LAC, RG 24, vol. 13766, WD 3rd Canadian Infantry Division July 1944), 3rd Canadian O.O. No. 4 Operation CHARNWOOD, 6 July 1944.
171 Ellis, *Victory in the West,* vol. 1, 316.
172 Zuckerman, *From Apes to Warlords;* see also D'Este's criticism of the bombing in *Decision in Normandy,* 315-16.
173 K. Meyer, *Grenadiers,* 262.

174   Crocker's corps fought one major action between the end of Charnwood and 23 July – an attack from Escoville to Troarn-Emieville to protect the left flank of 8th Corps during Operation Goodwood. See Ellis, *Victory in the West,* vol. 1, 343.

175   LAC, Crerar Papers, vol. 2, Memorandum on Conference with C-in-C 21 Army Group held at Tac HQ 21 Army Group at 2100 hrs, 20 July 1944.

176   Ibid., vol. 8, Correspondence General Crocker, Crerar to GOC 1 Corps, 22 July 1944.

177   This is the suggestion in J.L. Granatstein, *The Generals: The Canadian Army's Senior Commanders in the Second World War* (Toronto: Stoddart, 1993), 111; and English, *The Canadian Army and the Normandy Campaign,* 191.

178   LAC, Crerar Papers, vol. 8, Crocker to Crerar, 24 July 1944.

179   Crerar had only the limited experience of commanding 1st Canadian Corps for two months of static operation in Italy, January-March 1944.

180   LAC, Crerar Papers, vol. 3, Crerar to C of S CMHQ, 2 July 1944.

181   Ibid., vol. 8, Crerar to Stuart, 16 May 1944.

182   Ibid., vol. 3, Crerar to Stuart, 10 July 1944. He expressed the same doubts about Crocker's judgment to Simonds: "It is possible that Crocker's handling of Keller has not brought out the best in the latter": ibid., Crerar to Simonds, 10 July 1944.

183   TNA, WO 171/258, WD 1st Corps, 14 November 1944.

184   LAC, Crerar papers, vol. 8, Crerar to Montgomery, 24 July 1944.

185   LHCMA, Alanbrooke Papers, 41/1, Montgomery to Brooke, 26 July 1944.

186   LAC, Crerar Papers, vol. 8, Montgomery to Crerar, 26 July 1944.

187   Ibid., vol. 2, Operations RAWLINSON and BYNG, 27 July 1944. See also the other planning documents in the same file, 1-0-7, RAWLINSON and BYNG.

188   Ibid., AVAILABILTY OF FIRE S[U]P[PORT] AND SPECIAL EQ[UI]P[MEN]T, 26 July 1944.

189   LAC, RG 24, vol. 13607, WD First Canadian Army, G (Plans), Operation AXEHEAD, Briefing Notes by Chief of Staff First Cdn Army, 26 May 1944.

190   Not much has been written about the siege of Le Havre. See L.F. Ellis, *Victory in the West. Vol. 2: The Defeat of Germany* (London: Her Majesty's Stationery Office, 1968), 13-16; and Stacey, *Victory Campaign,* 331-36. A short account of the 51st (Highland) Division's battle at Le Havre can be found in J.B. Salmond, *The History of the 51st Highland Division, 1939-1945* (London: William Blackwood and Sons, 1953), 177-78. The commanding officer of the 1st Gordon Highlanders has published a very interesting personal diary, which includes his perspective on the battle. See Martin Lindsay, *So Few Got Through* (London: Collins, 1946), 79-86.

191   See, for example, the maps of the Le Havre area (with enemy dispositions) at WO 171/500, WD 49th (West Riding) Division (September 1944), or the air photographs at the Laurier Centre for Military Strategic and Disarmament Studies, Box 0081. See also NARA, T311, Roll 28, Frame 7034088, *Heeresgruppe D. Kampframeisung die Festung,* Le Havre, 8 February 1944.

192   LAC, RG 24, vol. 10789, Operation ASTONIA, 10-12 September 1944. This document can also be found at TNA, CAB 106/958, OPERATION ASTONIA, 10-12 September 1944, 2. See the air photograph with the detailed disposition of enemy defences at Fontaine le Mallet at TNA, WO 171/675, WD 152nd Brigade (September 1944).

193   LAC, RG 24, vol. 13607, WD First Canadian Army G (Plans), NOTES ON CONFERENCE AT TAC 1 BRIT CORPS 1430 B HRS, 3 SEP 44, OP "ASTONIA."

194   LAC, RG 24, vol. 10789, Operation ASTONIA, 10-12 September 1944, 2.

195   See LAC, RG 24, vol. 13607, WD First Canadian Army G (Plans), NOTES ON CONFERENCE AT TAC 1 BRIT CORPS 1430 B HRS, 3 SEP 44, OP "ASTONIA."

196   Ibid.

197  TNA, WO 171/259, WD 1st Corps (September 1944), 5 September 1944.

198  Ibid., OPERATION ASTONIA, 1 CORPS OPERATION INSTRUCTION No. 14, 6 September 1944.

199  Stacey, *Victory Campaign,* 331-36. See also Ellis, *Victory in the West,* vol. 2, 13-16; and LAC, RG 24, vol. 10789, Operation ASTONIA, 10-12 September 1944.

200  For a civilian perspective on the bombings, see Andrew Knapp, "The Destruction and Liberation of Le Havre in Modern Memory," *War in History* 14, no. 4 (2007): 476-98; and Lindsey Dodd and Andrew Knapp, "'How Many Frenchmen Did You Kill?' British Bombing Policy towards France, 1940-1945," *French History* 22, no. 4 (December 2008): 469-92.

201  LAC, RG 24, vol. 10789, Operation ASTONIA, 10-12 September 1944, 14.

202  "Report No. 14, Heavy Bombing in Support of the Army," in Copp, *Montgomery's Scientists,* 106. This report was based on operational research following operations Charnwood, Goodwood, Bluecoat, and Totalize.

203  LAC, RG 24, vol. 10789, Operation ASTONIA, 10-12 September 1944, 14-15. In fact, the lanes were never completely clear: "Throughout the night and the following day both tracked and wheeled vehicles continued to strike mines" (16).

204  Ibid., 16. The engineer vehicles were AVsRE (Armoured Vehicle Royal Engineers).

205  TNA, WO 171/650, WD 56th Brigade (September 1944), Operation ASTONIA, 56th Inf Bde O.O. No. 2, 9 September 1944.

206  LAC, RG 24, vol. 10789, Operation ASTONIA, 10-12 September 1944, 16.

207  See TNA, WO 171/650, WD 56th Brigade (September 1944), 11 September 1944; and WO 171/667, WD 147th Brigade (September 1944), 11 September 1944.

208  TNA, WO 171/675, WD 152nd Brigade, 11 September 1944.

209  LAC, RG 24, vol. 10789, Operation ASTONIA, 10-12 September 1944, 18.

210  Ibid., 19.

211  TNA, WO 171/678, WD 153rd Brigade, 11 September 1944.

212  LAC, RG 24, vol. 10789, Operation ASTONIA, 10-12 September 1944, 23; TNA, WO 171/675, WD 152nd Brigade, 11 September 1944.

213  TNA, WO 171/664, WD 146th Brigade, 11 September 1944.

214  LAC, RG 24, vol. 10789, Operation ASTONIA, 10-12 September 1944, 24.

215  The total number of casualties for 1st Corps on 10-12 September was 388: Stacey, *Victory Campaign,* 336.

216  LAC, RG 24, vol. 10789, Operation ASTONIA, 10-12 September 1944, 26.

217  Stacey, *Victory Campaign,* 388.

218  Ibid., 390-91.

219  LHCMA, Papers of General Sir Richard O'Connor (O'Connor Papers), 5/4/49, Crocker to O'Connor, 2 October 1944.

220  TNA, WO 171/260, WD 1st Corps (November 1944). The war diary shows that Crocker and his aide-de-camp were "temporarily away" during 14-21 November 1944.

221  LAC, Crerar Papers, vol. 8, file 6-10-9, MGA 176, FOR LT GEN CROCKER FROM LT GEN CRERAR, 21 October 1944; Crocker Papers, Montgomery to Crocker, 18 February 1945.

222  Crocker Papers, John Crocker to George Crocker, 6 December 1944.

223  IWM, BLM 119/73, Message, Montgomery to CIGS, 18 February 1945.

224  Ibid., 15 February 1945.

225  Stephen Ashley Hart, "The Forgotten Liberator. The 1939-1945 Military Career of General Sir Andrew Thorne," *Journal of the Society for Army Historical Research* 79 (2001): 240-41.

226  Montgomery removed Bucknall from command of 30th Corps in August 1944. He posted O'Connor to India in November 1944.

227  TNA, WO 216/257, Montgomery to Crocker, 30 April 1948.

228  Ibid., Report by Committee on Army Training Pamphlets, 28 May 1948.
229  Ibid., Montgomery to Crocker, 4 September 1948.
230  Ibid., Crocker to Montgomery, 13 September 1948.
231  *The Conduct of War* was superseded by *High Command* (London: War Office, 1961).
232  *The Armoured Division in Battle* (London: Her Majesty's Stationery Office, 1952) does not deviate doctrinally from the 21st Army Group publication *The Armoured Division in Battle* (Holland: 21st Army Group, 1944).
233  Alun Gwynne Jones, "Training and Doctrine in the British Army since 1945," in *The Theory and Practice of War*, edited by Michael Howard (London: Cassel, 1965), 316.
234  The area of British Army tactical doctrine in the post-1945 period has been left largely unplowed by military historians. Most analysis has been at the policy level. See, for example, Colin McInnes, *Hot War, Cold War: The British Army's Way in Warfare* (London: Brassey's, 1996), 3-25; and David French, *The British Way in Warfare, 1688-2000* (London: Unwin Hyman, 1990), 212-24.
235  On Dempsey, see Nigel Hamilton, *Monty: The Field Marshal, 1944-1976* (London: Hamish Hamilton, 1986), 725, 728. On Horrocks, see Sir Brian Horrocks, *A Full Life* (London: Collins, 1960), 284-85.
236  Hamilton, ibid., 725-26.
237  IWM, BLM 187/3, Montgomery to Crocker, 8 October 1948.
238  Ibid., BLM 187/4, Crocker to Montgomery, 9 October 1948.
239  Carver, *Out of Step*, 32.
240  Crocker Papers, Hobart to Crocker, 30 August 1953.
241  Ibid., John Cross to Crocker, 14 June 1945.

**Chapter 4: Wit with Will to Spare**

  1  See, for example, John A. English, *The Canadian Army and the Normandy Campaign: A Study of Failure in High Command* (New York: Praeger, 1991), 307; J.L. Granatstein, *The Generals: The Canadian Army's Senior Commanders in the Second World War* (Toronto: Stoddart, 1993), 146; Dominick Graham, *The Price of Command: A Biography of General Guy Simonds* (Toronto: Stoddart, 1993), 281-86; Terry Copp, *Fields of Fire: The Canadians in Normandy* (Toronto: University of Toronto Press, 2003), 261; and Brian Reid, *No Holding Back: Operation Totalize, Normandy, August 1944* (Toronto: Robin Brass, 2005), 26. On contemporaries who admired Simonds, see Lieutenant-General Sir Richard O'Connor's letters to Lieutenant-General Sir Miles Dempsey and General Sir Bernard L. Montgomery, both dated 24 August 1944, Liddell Hart Centre for Military Archives (LHCMA), Papers of Lieutenant-General Sir Richard O'Connor. See also National Defence Headquarters (NDHQ), Directorate of History and Heritage (DHH), J.L. Granatstein's *The Generals* Interviews (Granatstein Interviews), Interviews with General N. Elliot Rodger, 21 May 1991, Ottawa; and General Robert Moncel, 6 October 1991, Mahone Bay, NS.
  2  Ibid., Interviews with General Bert Hoffmeister, 2 March 1992, Vancouver; Brigadier H.P. Bell-Irving, 4 March 1992, Vancouver; Major-General W.J. Megill, 18 January 1992, Kingston, ON.
  3  Quoted in Granatstein, *The Generals*, 159; and Lieutenant-Colonel Roman Jarymowycz, "General Guy Simonds: The Commander as Tragic Hero," in *Warrior Chiefs: Perspectives on Senior Canadian Military Leaders*, edited by Lieutenant-Colonel Bernd Horn and Stephen Harris (Toronto: Dundurn, 2001), 108.
  4  NDHQ, DHH, Granatstein Interviews, Interviews with Lieutenant-Colonel Don Mingay [GSO 1 3rd Canadian Infantry Division], 6 June 1991, Creemore, ON; and Brigadier George Pangman [GSO 1 Plans First Canadian Army], 23 April 1991, Cambridge, ON.

5 Ibid., Interview with General A. Bruce Matthews [CRA 1st Canadian Infantry Division, CCRA 2nd Canadian Corps, GOC 2nd Canadian Infantry Division], 25 April 1991, Toronto.

6 Imperial War Museum (IWM), Papers of Lieutenant-Colonel Trumbull Warren, Montgomery to Warren, 1 January 1969.

7 On the early life of Simonds, see Graham, *Price of Command,* 9-16; and Granatstein, *The Generals,* 146-49.

8 *Times Colonist,* n.d., in Papers of Lieutenant-General Guy Simonds (Simonds Papers). This private collection remains in the possession of Colonel (Retired) Charles Simonds (son of G.G. Simonds), Battersea, ON. I am grateful to Colonel Simonds for permission to quote from his father's papers. I am also grateful to J.L. Granatstein, who has shared his notes from the collection.

9 Graham, *Price of Command,* 12.

10 Ibid., 13.

11 LAC, Personnel Records Unit (PRU), Personnel File of Guy Granville Simonds (Simonds Pers File), "RMC Entrance Examinations, 1921," 16 July 1921. Brigadier Churchill Mann (Chief of Staff First Canadian Army, 1944-45) placed 29th; Major-General Chris Vokes (GOC 1st Canadian Infantry Division 1943-44 and GOC 4th Canadian Armoured Division 1944-45) ranked 39th; and Brigadier E.C. "Johnny" Plow (Brigadier Royal Artillery First Canadian Army) was 56th in the order of merit on entrance to RMC in 1921.

12 Ibid., Marks Obtained and Standing at Final Examinations, 1925, n.d.

13 See NDHQ, DHH, Granatstein Interviews, Interviews with General Geoffrey Walsh, 24 May 1991, Ottawa; and Colonel Robert Raymont, 23 May 1991, Ottawa.

14 Royal Military College of Canada (RMC), Student File, Cadet Guy Granville Simonds, Medical Examination of Candidates, Guy Simonds.

15 LAC, Simonds Pers File, Macdonnell to Secretary Dept. National Defence (Militia Services), 3 February 1925.

16 Simonds Papers, Memoirs Box, Draft Memoir, 4.

17 Ibid., 14.

18 Ibid., 10.

19 Ibid., 13.

20 Ibid., 13-14.

21 *RMC Review* (1925): 27.

22 Ibid., 34.

23 LAC, Simonds Pers File, Confidential Reports for 1926, 1927, and 1929.

24 Graham, *Price of Command,* 38.

25 Ibid., 46. See also the extracts from Simonds's letters to Mona Anderson, ibid., app. 2, 297-99.

26 NDHQ, DHH, Granatstein Interviews, Interview with General W.A.B. Anderson, 21 May 1991, Ottawa.

27 See, for example, ibid., Interviews with Brigadier P.A.S. Todd, 8 May 1991, Ancaster, ON; and Mrs. F.F. Worthington, 23 May 1991, Ottawa.

28 LAC, Simonds Pers File, Confidential Reports, 1932-36.

29 Simonds Papers, Draft Memoir, ch. 6, quoted in Granatstein, *The Generals,* 151.

30 LAC, Simonds Pers File, Staff College Camberley, Final Report (Captain G.G. Simonds), 3 December 1937.

31 Ibid., Confidential Report, 8 December 1938.

32 See Lieutenant-Colonel E.L.M. Burns, "A Division that Can Attack," *Canadian Defence Quarterly* 15, no. 3 (April 1938): 282-98; and Captain G.G. Simonds, "An Army that Can

Attack – A Division that Can Defend," *Canadian Defence Quarterly* 15, no. 4 (July 1938): 413-17.

33  LAC, Simonds Pers File, Confidential Report, Capt. G.G. Simonds, R.C.A., 27 March 1935.

34  Wanting to avoid high casualties and anything else that might precipitate another conscription crisis like the one that had badly divided the country during 1917-18, the Liberal government of William Lyon Mackenzie King opted at first for a small army component, preferring to concentrate instead on the British Commonwealth Air Training Plan, shipping, and the production of armaments and supplies.

35  See app. 2 to John A. Macdonald, "In Search of Veritable: Training the Canadian Army Staff Officer, 1899-1945" (MA thesis, Royal Military College of Canada, 1992), 271-72.

36  Ibid., 275.

37  LAC, RG 24, vol. 13721, War Diary (WD) 1st Canadian Division (December 1939), 1 Canadian Division Training Instruction No. 1, 26 December 1939. Simonds signed this document for the GSO 1, Lieutenant-Colonel G.R. Turner.

38  Ibid., app. G.

39  A review of divisional and brigade war diaries for the period January-May 1940 reveals that a combination of TEWTs and lectures managed to deal, however briefly, with the defence, road movement, the attack, patrols, the withdrawal, and fighting in wooded areas. See LAC, RG 24, vol. 13721, WD 1st Canadian Division (January-May 1940); and LAC, RG 24, vol. 14082, WD 3rd Canadian Infantry Brigade (January-May 1940).

40  On the training difficulties facing the Canadian army in the United Kingdom during 1940-43, see J.N. Rickard, *The Politics of Command: Lieutenant-General A.G.L. McNaughton and the Canadian Army, 1939-1943* (Toronto: University of Toronto Press, 2010), 89-167.

41  In 1942, Lieutenant-General Montgomery described Pearkes as being "unable to appreciate the essentials of a military problem ... a gallant soldier without a doubt; but he has no brains": LAC, MG 30 E 157, Papers of General H.D.G. Crerar (Crerar Papers), vol. 2, BEAVER III Notes on Commanders, 25 April 1942.

42  Quoted in Rickard, *Politics of Command,* 89.

43  Simonds to Trumbull Warren, 1969, quoted in Graham, *Price of Command,* 59.

44  Quoted in J.N. Rickard, "McNaughton's Dagger: The Raising, Training and Employment of the Canadian Army, 1939-1943" (PhD dissertation, University of New Brunswick, 2006), 150.

45  See NDHQ, DHH, Granatstein Interviews, Interviews with General N. Elliot Rodger, 21 May 1991, Ottawa; Major-General J. Desmond B. Smith, 14 September 1991, London, UK; and Major-General M.P. Bogert, 8 September 1991, Donnington, UK.

46  Ibid., Interview with Major-General J. Desmond B. Smith, 14 September 1991.

47  LAC, RG 24, vol. 13721, WD 1st Canadian Division (January 1940), Memorandum of a Meeting Held at Headquarters 1st Canadian Division 1500 Hours, 4 January 1940.

48  NDHQ, DHH, Granatstein Interviews, Interview with Major-General M.P. Bogert, 8 September 1991, Donnington, UK. Bogert was GSO 3 Operations under Simonds. He later went on to command the West Nova Scotia Regiment and the 2nd Canadian Infantry Brigade in Italy.

49  Ibid., Interview with General W.A.B. Anderson, 21 May 1991, Ottawa.

50  Ibid., Interview with Major-General R.P. Rothschild, 24 May 1991, Ottawa.

51  Designated 7th British Corps until 25 December 1940.

52  LAC, RG 24, vol. 9873, War Office letter, 26 September 1939.

53  Ibid., War Office letter, 15 January 1940. See also Macdonald, "In Search of Veritable," 97-104.

54  NDHQ, DHH, Granatstein Interviews, Interview with Colonel Ernest A. Coté, 19 July 1991, Ottawa.

55 Macdonald, "In Search of Veritable," 125. Lieutenant-Colonel John A. Macdonald was a member of the Directing Staff and the Canadian Land Forces Command and Staff College during the 1990s.
56 A journalist and newspaper owner in civilian life, Victor Odlum fought with the Royal Canadian Regiment in South Africa (1900) and served in the 7th Battalion of the Canadian Expeditionary Force during the First World War. Wounded three times, he rose quickly to take command of the 11th Canadian Infantry Brigade, which he led from July 1916 until the end of the war.
57 See, for example, LAC, RG 24, vol. 13745, WD 2nd Canadian Infantry Division (May 1941), Memorandum Approach March of a Division in G.H.Q. Reserve, 10 pp.
58 LAC, MG 30 E 300, Papers of Major-General Victor Odlum, vol. 26, Odlum to McNaughton, 12 August 1941.
59 For a scathing indictment of McNaughton as both a trainer and a commander, see English, *The Canadian Army and the Normandy Campaign*, 77-80, 310-11. For an account sympathetic to McNaughton as a trainer, see Rickard, *Politics of Command*, 81-167.
60 Alex Danchev and Daniel Todman, eds., *War Diaries, 1939-1945: Field Marshal Lord Alanbrooke* (London: Weidenfeld and Nicolson, 2001), 164 (entry for 15 June 1941).
61 LAC, RG 24, vol. 13682, WD 1st Canadian Corps (August 1941).
62 Ibid. (1944), Canadian Corps Operation Instruction No. 24: Road Moves.
63 Simonds Papers, BGS to Army Commander, 12 December 1941.
64 The other corps in the Southeastern Army was 12th Corps.
65 On the Montgomery-Crerar relationship, see Douglas E. Delaney, "When Harry Met Monty: Canadian National Politics and the Crerar-Montgomery Relationship," *The Canadian Way of War: Serving the National Interest*, edited by Bernd Horn (Toronto: Dundurn, 2006), 213-34.
66 LAC, Crerar Papers, vol. 2, Montgomery to Crerar, 30 May 1942. On improvements in 1st Canadian Corps' training and performance, see also C.P. Stacey, *Six Years of War: The Army in Canada, Britain and the Pacific* (Ottawa: Queen's Printer, 1966), 238-47. See also Montgomery's comments at the end of Exercise Tiger: IWM, Papers of Field Marshal the Viscount Montgomery of Alamein (Montgomery Papers), BLM 26/1, S.E. Army Exercise "TIGER," Final Conference – 4 June 1942: Remarks of Army Commander, 4 June 1942.
67 Danchev and Todman, *Alanbrooke War Diaries*, 388 (entry for 7 March 1943).
68 Stacey, *Six Years of War*, 408-10.
69 LAC, MG 30 E 133, Papers of Lieutenant-General A.G.L. McNaughton (McNaughton Papers), vol. 248, McNaughton to Simonds et al., 13 September 1942, quoted in Granatstein, *The Generals*, 155.
70 Stacey, *Six Years of War*, 243-48.
71 NDHQ, DHH, Granatstein Interviews, Interview with Brigadier G.E. Beament, 24 May 1991, Old Chelsea, QC.
72 For a good account of Spartan, see J.N. Rickard, "The Test of Command: McNaughton and Exercise 'Spartan,' 4-12 March 1943," *Canadian Military History* 8 (summer 1999): 22-38.
73 Danchev and Todman, *Alanbrooke War Diaries*, 388 (entry for 7 March 1943).
74 Guy Simonds to Trumbull Warren, 1969, quoted in Graham, *Price of Command*, 59.
75 LAC, Simonds Pers File, Record of Service.
76 LAC, McNaughton Papers, vol. 132, Simonds to GOC-in-C First Cdn Army, 29 April 1943.
77 Major-General I.S.O. Playfair, *The Mediterranean and the Middle East*, vol. 4 (London: Her Majesty's Stationery Office, 1966), 362-76.
78 Simonds, "An Army that Can Attack," 416-17.

79  LAC, McNaughton Papers, Report on Visit to Eighth Army by Brig G.G. Simonds, 29 April 1943, 11.

80  Ibid., 4.

81  Before assuming command of the 1st Canadian Infantry Division, Simonds had been at the helm of the 2nd Canadian Infantry Division for barely two weeks.

82  On the strategic planning for Operation Husky, see Brigadier C.J.C. Molony, *The Mediterranean and the Middle East*, vol. 5 (London: Her Majesty's Stationery Office, 1973), 1-34; Carlo D'Este, *Bitter Victory: The Battle for Sicily, July-August 1943* (Glasgow: Collins, 1988), 71-178; and Lieutenant-Colonel G.W.L. Nicholson, *The Canadians in Italy, 1943-1945* (Ottawa: Queen's Printer, 1966), 1-26.

83  George Kitching, *Mud and Green Fields: The Memoirs of Major-General George Kitching* (St. Catharines, ON: Vanwell, 1993), 142.

84  LAC, RG 24, vol. 10797, Personal Diary – Brig. N.E. Rodger, Chief of Staff, 2 Cdn Corps (see 26-27 September 1944).

85  LAC, RG 24, vol. 13725, WD 1st Canadian Infantry Division (May-June 1943), "WETSHOD," 4 May 1943; and Exercise "STYMIE," 29 May 1943.

86  Ibid. (May 1943), Note to All Comds and COs 1 Cdn Div, 15 May 1943.

87  Howard Graham, *Citizen and Soldier: The Memoirs of Lieutenant-General Howard Graham* (Toronto: McClelland and Stewart, 1987), 157-63.

88  See William J. McAndrew, "Fire or Movement? Canadian Tactical Doctrine, Sicily – 1943," *Military Affairs* 51 (July 1987): 140-45.

89  See Douglas E. Delaney, *The Soldiers' General: Bert Hoffmeister at War* (Vancouver: UBC Press, 2005), 66-69.

90  D[irectorate of] Hist[ory], AHQ Report No. 14, "Exercise Report," 15 Panzer Grenadier Division, 4 September 1943, quoted in McAndrew, "Fire or Movement?" 144.

91  LAC, Crerar Papers, vol. 7, Montgomery to Crerar, 25 August 1943; and Montgomery to Crerar, 23 July 1943.

92  Simonds Papers, Simonds to Dempsey, 22 September 1943. This letter is reprinted in Terry Copp, *Guy Simonds and the Art of Command* (Kingston, ON: Canadian Defence Academy Press, 2007), 4-6.

93  Dempsey to Simonds, 22 September 1943, quoted in Graham, *Price of Command*, 103.

94  See, for example, Dempsey's comments on Simonds's Operational Policy Directive (dated 17 February 1944). Dempsey stated most cordially that he was "very glad to see you and I left Italy with exactly the same views. I really have no comments to make on the paper because I agree with everything you say": LAC, RG 24, vol. 10799, GOC 2 Cdn Corps Comds' Policy Letters, Dempsey to Simonds, 27 February 1944.

95  See LAC, Crerar Papers, vol. 8, Simonds to Crerar, 15 December 1943.

96  Ibid. On the "caravan incident," see Paul Douglas Dickson, *A Thoroughly Canadian General: A Biography of General H.D.G. Crerar* (Toronto: University of Toronto Press, 2007), 227-30.

97  LAC, Crerar Papers, vol. 8, Crerar to Simonds, 10 December 1943.

98  Ibid., vol. 7, Montgomery to Crerar, 21 December 1943.

99  On 16 October 1943, the Commander-in-Chief 15th Army Group, General Sir Harold Alexander, wrote to the CIGS: "We already have as much armour in the Mediterranean as we can usefully employ in Italy ... I do not want another Corps Headquarters at this stage": The National Archives (TNA), WO 214/55, Papers of Field Marshal Earl Alexander of Tunis (Alexander Papers), Alexander to Brooke, 16 October 1943.

100  LAC, Crerar Papers, vol. 8, Crerar to Simonds, 8 December 1943.

101  Ibid., Crerar to Simonds, 10 December 1943; Crerar to Montgomery 17 December 1943; and Crerar to Stuart, 13 January 1944.

102 Ibid., vol. 7, Montgomery to Crerar, 21 December 1943.

103 Ibid., vol. 8, Simonds to Crerar, 2 January 1944.

104 After observing Sansom as a corps commander in Exercise Spartan, C-in-C Home Forces General Sir Bernard Paget stated that 2nd Canadian Corps was "slow and deliberate and hampered by tactical and administrative mistakes": LAC, RG 24, vol. 10414, Extracts from Copy No. 20 of Exercise SPARTAN, Report of Chief Umpire, 22 March 1943. In notes that he had prepared for the Minister of National Defence, the Canadian Chief of the General Staff, Lieutenant-General Ken Stuart, acknowledged the criticism of Sansom's Spartan performance, adding also that Sansom was "inclined to enjoy life and is most popular at entertainments ... His commanders complained that orders were received, or continuously changed, at the last minute ... Not temperate enough for an officer of such high rank and went too high before experiencing the handling of large formations in action": LAC, MG 27, III, B 11, Papers of Colonel J.L. Ralston (Ralston Papers), vol. 54, Notes on Officers in Canadian Army Overseas. In spite of universal condemnation of Sansom, McNaughton refused to relieve the fledgling corps commander, insisting instead that Sansom be given a second chance: LAC, McNaughton Papers, vol. 249, Memorandum of Conversation General McNaughton and General Sir Alan Brooke, CIGS, War Office at 1530 hrs, 5 April 1943.

105 NDHQ, DHH, Granatstein Interviews, Interview with General S.F. Clark, 24 February 1992, Victoria.

106 Ibid., Interview with General Robert Moncel, 6 October 1991, Mahone Bay, NS.

107 LAC, Ralston Papers, Notes on Officers in Canadian Army Overseas.

108 LAC, RG 24, vol. 9873, Junior War Course No. 4, Staff College Camberley, Final Report on Major N.E. Rodger, R.C.E., Cdn, 21 December 1940.

109 LAC, Crerar Papers, vol. 8, Simonds to Crerar, 15 December 1943.

110 See LAC, RG 24, vol. 13711, WD 2nd Cdn Corps (G Staff) (March 1944), Weekly Progress Report to Canada, 4 March 1944.

111 LAC, RG 24, vol. 10799, GOC 2 Cdn Corps Comds' Policy Letters, Efficiency of Command, 19 February 1944. This directive in reproduced in full in Copp, *Guy Simonds and the Art of Command*, 17-24.

112 LAC, Crerar Papers, vol. 8, Simonds to Crerar, 2 January 1944.

113 LAC, RG 24, vol. 10799, GOC 2 Cdn Corps Comds' Policy Letters, Operational Policy – 2 Cdn Corps, 17 February 1944.

114 Ibid., GOC 2 Cdn Corps Comds' Policy Letters, Montgomery to Simonds, 23 February 1944; and Dempsey to Simonds, 27 February 1944.

115 LAC, RG 24, vol. 13711, WD 2nd Cdn Corps (G Staff) (February 1944), 2nd Cdn Corps Study period 13-18 March, 16 February 1944; and 2nd Cdn Corps Study Period Gen[eral] Instr[uction]s, 25 February 1944.

116 Ibid., 2nd Cdn Corps Study period 13-18 March, 16 February 1944.

117 LAC, RG 24, vol. 13711, WD 2nd Cdn Corps (G Staff) (February 1944), 18 March 1944

118 Ibid. (March 1944), Calendar of Events 2 Cdn Corps, 16 March 1944.

119 Ibid. (April 1944), 1-7 April 1944.

120 Ibid., 6 April 1944. Based on some lessons learned during the initial headquarters exercises, Simonds wrote and distributed a directive entitled "Organization of Staff – Headquarters 2nd Canadian Corps," which formalized the position of the chief of staff, who had the "duty of coordinating the work of the [commander's] staff," thereby allowing the commander "to devote his attention to the broader aspects of operations." In the instruction, Simonds also included a detailed line diagram of the "G" staff, noting positions and function of each down to third-grade (captain) level: ibid. (April 1944), Organization of Staff – Headquarters 2nd Canadian Corps.

121  Ibid., 2nd Corps Exercise LAST, Gen[eral] Exercise Instructions, n.d.

122  Ibid., 15 April 1944.

123  C.P. Stacey, *The Victory Campaign: The Operations in Northwest Europe, 1944-1945* (Ottawa: Queen's Printer, 1966), 40; and Angelo N. Caravaggio, "Commanding the Green Centre Line in Normandy: A Case Study of Division Command in the Second World War" (PhD dissertation, Wilfrid Laurier University, 2009), ch. 3.

124  LAC, RG 24, vol. 13711, WD 2nd Cdn Corps, 20 April 1944.

125  Ibid., 29 April 1944.

126  Ibid., 4 May 1944.

127  NDHQ, DHH, Granatstein Interviews, Interview with General Robert Moncel, 6 October 1991, Mahone Bay, NS.

128  LAC, RG 24, vol. 13711, WD 2nd Cdn Corps, 8 July 1944.

129  Ibid., 28 June 1944. See also ibid., Draft Policy – Tactical Handling of Troops, reprinted in Copp, *Guy Simonds and the Art of Command,* 37-41.

130  TNA, WO 285/9, Papers of General Sir Miles Dempsey (Dempsey Papers), War Diary of General Sir Miles Dempsey, The First 100 Days, Jul 44.

131  TNA, WO 285/2, WD 21st Army Group, M-510, The General Situation, 10 July 1944.

132  Quoted in Carlo D'Este, *Decision in Normandy: The Unwritten Story of Montgomery and the Allied Campaign* (London: Collins, 1983), 355.

133  TNA, CAB 106/959, The "GOODWOOD" MEETING, 18-21 July 1944; TNA, WO 285/2, WD 21st Army Group, Notes on Second Army Operations 16-18 July; Stacey, *Victory Campaign,* 169.

134  LAC, RG 24, vol. 13711, WD 2nd Cdn Corps, 2nd Cdn Corps Operation Instruction No. 2, 16 July 1944.

135  LAC, Crerar Papers, vol. 3, Crocker to Dempsey, 5 July 1944; Crerar to Simonds, 10 July 1944.

136  Ibid., Memorandum, 14 July 1944. Simonds's address to the senior officers of 3rd Canadian Infantry Division on 16 July suggests that he was addressing the "fatigue and nervousness" that Crocker had noted in Keller, and which he thought was reflected in the state of the division. Simonds welcomed them to 2nd Canadian Corps and told them that he was proud of their achievements since D-day, but he also spoke about the importance of imbuing troops with the offensive spirit: "The drive must always come from the top ... one has only to mingle with the troops themselves to find that the Offensive Spirit is always present with the Canadian soldier, and it should not be destroyed by a Commander who is tired ... [the commander] must keep finding a way to break through the enemy. It is fatal to stop. He must never sit down": "General Officer Commanding 2nd Canadian Corps to Officers of 3rd Canadian Infantry Division and 2nd Canadian Armoured Brigade, at the Chateau near Cairon ... on 16 July 1944," in Copp, *Guy Simonds and the Art of Command,* 43.

137  LAC, RG 24, vol. 13712, WD 2nd Cdn Corps (July 1944), 2 Canadian Corps Operation Instruction Number 2 Operation ATLANTIC, 16 July 1944.

138  "Draft Policy – Tactical Handling of Troops," in Copp, *Guy Simonds and the Art of Command,* 37-41.

139  Colonel G.W.L. Nicholson, *The Gunners of Canada: The History of the Royal Regiment of Canadian Artillery. Vol. 2: 1919-1967* (Toronto: McClelland and Stewart, 1972), 295.

140  LAC, RG 24, vol. 10797, Notes from 2 Cdn Corps Operations Log: ATLANTIC, 18 Jul 1944, 1020. See also Copp, *Fields of Fire,* 139.

141  LAC, RG 24, vol. 13711, WD 2nd Cdn Inf Div (G Staff), 18 July 1944.

142  Ibid., Ops Log, 19 July 1944, Serial 1355.

143  Copp, *Fields of Fire,* 137, 144; and Major L.F. Ellis, *Victory in the West. Vol. 1: The Battle of Normandy* (London: Her Majesty's Stationery Office, 1962), 340-48.

144  LAC, RG 24, vol. 13750, WD 2nd Cdn Inf Div (G Staff), Ops Log, 19 July 1944, Serial 1355. See also Serial 1374, ibid., in which Foulkes and Brigadier H.A. Young discuss the 6th Canadian Infantry Brigade attack for "to-morrow night [20 July]."

145  Copp, *Fields of Fire,* 147.

146  LAC, RG 24, vol. 13711, WD 2nd Cdn Corps, 7 July 1944.

147  Nicholson, *Gunners of Canada,* 297.

148  Stacey, *Victory Campaign,* 176.

149  On Operation Spring, see also pages 267-71 in Chapter 5.

150  LAC, RG 24, vol. 13712, WD 2nd Cdn Corps (G Staff)(July 1944), 2 Cdn Corps Operation Instruction Number Three: Operation "SPRING," 24 July 1944.

151  Gregory Liedtke, "Canadian Offensive Operations in Normandy Revisited," *Canadian Military Journal* 8, no. 2 (Summer 2007): 62.

152  LAC, RG 24, vol. 13766, WD 3rd Cdn Inf Div (G Staff) (July 1944), 3rd Cdn Inf Div O.O. No. 6, 23 July 1944.

153  LAC, RG 24, vol. 13712, WD 2nd Cdn Corps (G Staff) (July 1944), 21st Army Group Intelligence Summary, No. 149, 25 July 1944. Intelligence sources did not know that the 2nd SS Panzer Division had recently moved into the area.

154  Copp, *Fields of Fire,* 182.

155  LAC, RG 24, vol. 10798, GOC's Activities (entries for 25 July 1944).

156  Stacey, *Victory Campaign,* 193.

157  LAC, RG 24, vol. 13711, WD 2nd Cdn Corps (G Staff), 30-31 July 1944.

158  Robert Moncel, Simonds's GSO 1 during Spring, claims that he talked Simonds out of firing Foulkes during the battle: NDHQ, DHH, Granatstein Interviews, Interview with General Robert Moncel, 6 October 1991, Mahone Bay, NS. On the decision to retain Keller for the sake of 3rd Canadian Infantry Division morale, see LAC, Crerar Papers, vol. 3, Simonds to Dempsey, 27 July 1944.

159  NDHQ, DHH, Granatstein Interviews, Interview with General A. Bruce Matthews, 25 April 1991, Toronto; and General N. Elliot Rodger, 21 May 1991, Toronto.

160  LAC, RG 24, vol. 13712, WD 2nd Cdn Corps (G Staff), "Leadership and the Fighting Spirit," 29 July 1944.

161  See, for example, Simonds's comments on Spring at LAC, RG 24, vol. 12745, Operation "SPRING," 31 January 1946.

162  Reid, *No Holding Back.* Other informed discussions will be found in Copp, *Fields of Fire,* 186-213; English, *The Canadian Army and the Normandy Campaign,* 263-88; Stacey, *Victory Campaign,* 207-31; and Jody Perrun, "Best-Laid Plans: Guy Simonds and Operation TOTALIZE, 7-10 August 1944," *Journal of Military History* 67, no. 1 (January 2003): 137-73.

163  LAC, RG 24, vol. 13712, WD 2nd Cdn Corps, 29 July 1944.

164  N. Elliot Rodger, quoted in Graham, *Price of Command,* 148.

165  NDHQ, DHH, Granatstein Interviews, Interview with General N. Elliot Rodger, 21 May 1991, Ottawa.

166  TNA, CAB 106/1047, British Army of the Rhine, Battlefield Tour Operation TOTALIZE, September 1947, 9. By the time the Totalize attack took place, the 1st SS Panzer Division had been replaced by the 89th Infantry Division and a large proportion of the 9th SS Panzer Division had been withdrawn and replaced by 272nd Infantry Division troops. See LAC, RG 24, vol. 13712, WD 2nd Cdn Corps (G Staff), Corps Intelligence Summary, 6 August 1944.

167 The first round of bombings would be done with High Explosive (HE) bombs, with some cratering accepted on the flanks of the corridor. During the second round of bombing, however, the attack would be executed with fragmentation bombs, so as not to crater the main axis astride the Caen-Falaise highway. See LAC, RG 24, vol. 13712, WD 2nd Cdn Corps (G Staff), Op TOTALIZE – Air Programme, 6 August 1944.

168 NDHQ, DHH, Papers of General Charles Foulkes (Foulkes Papers), 72/1223, Simonds to Foulkes, 2 August 1944.

169 Nicholson, *Gunners of Canada*, 313.

170 Simonds had originally conceived the operation in three phases, but opted for a two-phase operation based on enemy redeployments during the first week of August. On the evolution of the plan, see Reid, *No Holding Back*, 61-103. When Simonds learned that the 1st SS Panzer Division had been relieved by the 89th Infantry Division on 4-5 August, he anticipated that the former would redeploy to the second-line defences near Bretteville-sur-Laize. This assumption informed his decision to retain the second round of heavy bombing for phase 2 of Totalize.

171 Nicholson, *Gunners of Canada*, 312-13.

172 See Reid, *No Holding Back*, 117-33.

173 No. 2 Operational Research Section, "Report No. 8, RAF Heavy Bombing on the Night of 7/8 August 1944," in *Montgomery's Scientists: Operational Research in Northwest Europe*, edited by Terry Copp (Waterloo, ON: Laurier Centre for Military Strategic and Disarmament Studies, 2000), 96.

174 Quoted in Stacey, *Victory Campaign*, 247.

175 Liedtke, "Canadian Offensive Operations in Normandy Revisited," 65. See also Niklas Zetterling, *Normandy 1944: German Military Organization, Combat Power and Operational Effectiveness* (Winnipeg: J.J. Fedorowicz, 2000), 178, 361.

176 For first-hand German accounts of their reaction to Totalize, see Kurt Meyer, *Grenadiers: The Story of Waffen SS General Kurt "Panzer" Meyer* (Mechanicsburg, PA: Stackpole Books, 2005), 275-90; and Hubert Meyer, *The 12th SS: The History of the Hitler Youth Panzer Division*, vol. 2 (Mechanicsburg, PA: Stackpole Books, 2005), 17-50.

177 Quoted in Graham, *Price of Command*, 153-54.

178 See English's criticism of Halpenny Force in *The Canadian Army and the Normandy Campaign*, 278-79.

179 On the tragic actions of the combined British Columbia Regiment and Algonquin Regiment battle group – Worthington Force – see Reid, *No Holding Back*, 301-23.

180 On Operation Tractable, see Copp, *Fields of Fire*, 236-51; English, *The Canadian Army and the Normandy Campaign*, 293-99; Stacey, *Victory Campaign*, 207-31.

181 Stacey, *Victory Campaign*, 243.

182 Simonds wrote: "After a successful operation, I consider that a change in command [of the 3rd Canadian Infantry Division] could be made": LAC, Crerar Papers, vol. 8, Simonds to Dempsey, 27 July 1944.

183 Spry was young but a very experienced commander. He had commanded the Royal Canadian Regiment in Southern Italy, and the 1st Canadian Infantry Brigade at the Moro River and in the Liri Valley.

184 Kitching, *Mud and Green Fields*, 195.

185 See Reid, *No Holding Back*, 301-2, n. 4.

186 LAC, RG 24, vol. 13789, WD 4th Cdn Armoured Division (G Staff), 16-17 August 1944, quoted in Copp, *Fields of Fire*, 236.

187 Kitching, *Mud and Green Fields*, 204-5.

188 LAC, RG 24, vol. 10799, "Essential Qualities in the Leader," 19 February 1944.

189 The best account of these siege operations will be found in Terry Copp, *Cinderella Army: The Canadians in Northwest Europe, 1944-1945* (Toronto: University of Toronto Press, 2006), 59-83.
190 Norman R. Denny, "Seduction in Combat: Losing Sight of Logistics after D-Day" (MA thesis, US Army Command and General Staff College, 2003), 6, 45. See also Roland Ruppenthal, *Logistical Support of the Armies,* vol. 2 (Washington, DC: US Government Printing Office, 1959), 105.
191 LAC, RG 24, vol. 10469, Antwerp and Ghent, 215/PORTS/1 (Q Mov) Clearance from Port of Antwerp, 16 October 1944.
192 Ruppenthal, *Logistical Support of the Armies,* 45-48; and Denny, "Seduction in Combat," 8-9.
193 LAC, Crerar Papers, vol. 8, Montgomery to Crerar, 13 September 1944.
194 Ibid., 21st Army Group Directive, M 525, 14 September 1944.
195 Viscount Montgomery of Alamein, *The Memoirs of Field-Marshal the Viscount Montgomery of Alamein* (London: Collins, 1958), 297.
196 LAC, RG 24, vol. 13607, WD Plans Section First Canadian Army, 8 September 1944. See also ibid., 603/FUTURE/2, The Walcheren Operation, 10 September 1944.
197 See Dickson, *A Thoroughly Canadian General,* 337-54.
198 LAC, RG 24, vol. 13607, WD Plans Section First Canadian Army, 603/FUTURE/2, Operation Infatuate: An Appreciation by the Plans Section, Headquarters First Canadian Army, 19 September 1944. This document is reproduced in full in Copp, *Guy Simonds and the Art of Command,* 112-22. LAC, RG 24, vol. 10799, Simonds to Crerar, 21 September 1944. This document is also reproduced in *Guy Simonds and the Art of Command,* 122-25.
199 On the enemy dispositions and strengths in the Scheldt, see National Archives and Records Administration (NARA), T311, Roll 3, *Heeresgruppe B, Op. Befehle 2, Ia H.Gr.B,* 1-30 September 1944.
200 See the after-action report in LAC, Crerar Papers, vol. 8, Clearance of the Scheldt Estuary: Oct-Nov 1944, 2.
201 LAC, RG 24, vol. 13607, WD Plans Section First Canadian Army (September 1944), C of S 1-1-8, OP INFATUATE, Notes of Conference – 1400 hrs, 21 September 1944, n.d.
202 LAC, Crerar Papers, vol. 7, Simonds to Crerar, 23 September 1944; and LAC, RG 24, vol. 13608, WD Plans Section First Canadian Army (September 1944), 603/FUTURE/2, Conference Operation INFATUATE 1430A hrs, 23 September 1944, n.d.
203 LAC, RG 24, vol. 13608, WD Plans Section First Canadian Army (September 1944), COS/FUTURE/2, Flooding of Walcheren, 25 September 1944.
204 LAC, RG 24, vol. 10798, Operations Log Notes, 2 Cdn Corps, 25 September 1944.
205 Quoted in Dickson, *A Thoroughly Canadian General,* 354-55. See also NDHQ, DHH, Granatstein Interviews, Interview with Brigadier G.E. Beament, 24 May 1991, Old Chelsea, QC.
206 LAC, RG 24, vol. 13608, WD Plans Section First Canadian Army (September 1944), C of S 1-1-2, Operation Infatuate Conference – 29 Sep 44, 30 September 1944.
207 NDHQ, DHH, Granatstein Interviews, Interview with Brigadier G.E. Beament, 24 May 1991, Old Chelsea, QC.
208 Stacey, *Victory Campaign,* 379.
209 NARA, T311, Roll 4, Orders from OB West to 15th Army, 4 October 1944.
210 LAC, Crerar Papers, vol. 8, Clearance of the Scheldt Estuary: Oct-Nov 1944, 4.
211 In a covering letter to his outline plan for Operation Switchback, Charles Foulkes wrote: "This operation was planned from the preliminary instructions issued by Lieut-Gen Simonds before he left for Army and it is not my desire to make any drastic changes in

the work which has already been undertaken": LAC, RG 24, vol. 10809, GOC 10, Operation "SWITCHBACK," 30 September 1944.

212 NDHQ, DHH, Granatstein Interviews, Interview with General S.F. Clark, 24 February 1992, Victoria; and General N. Elliot Rodger, 21 May 1991, Ottawa.
213 LAC, RG 24, vol. 10798, Rodger Diary, 28 September 1944.
214 LAC, Crerar Papers, vol. 8, Clearance of the Scheldt Estuary: Oct-Nov 1944, 5.
215 "Artillery in Operation Switchback, Account by Brigadier P.A.S. Todd," reproduced in Copp, *Cinderella Army,* 304-7.
216 According to Todd, the system had been perfected at Boulogne and Calais a month earlier: ibid., 305.
217 LAC, Crerar Papers, vol. 8, Clearance of the Scheldt Estuary: Oct-Nov 1944, 6.
218 Stacey, *Victory Campaign,* 397.
219 Ibid., 400.
220 NDHQ, DHH, Granatstein Interviews, Telephone interview with Giles Perodeau, 24 March 1992, Sidney, BC. Perodeau was Crerar's aide-de-camp from August 1944 to March 1945. He spent the battle of the Scheldt with Simonds.
221 Ibid., Interview with General A. Bruce Matthews, 25 April 1991, Toronto.
222 Ibid., Interview with General Robert Moncel, 6 October 1991, Mahone Bay, NS.
223 NARA, T311, Roll 4, Report of Army Group B to OB West, 10 October 1944.
224 Ibid., 13 October 1944.
225 Ibid.
226 LAC, Crerar Papers, vol. 8, Clearance of the Scheldt Estuary: Oct-Nov 1944, 9.
227 Ibid., 17.
228 Denny, "Seduction in Combat," 55. Denny points out that a number of port clearance problems prevented Antwerp from reaching its full capacity of 100,000 tons per day – a bridge blocked on the Albert Canal prevented barges from leaving the port; a lack of storage depots meant that many supplies had to be temporarily stored in the port; and a lack of rail cars slowed down the movement of supplies from the port.
229 Stacey, *Victory Campaign,* 424.
230 Quoted in ibid., 425.
231 Quoted in Dickson, *A Thoroughly Canadian General,* 358.
232 IWM, Montgomery Papers, BLM 115/64, Montgomery to Brooke, 18 October 1944.
233 Dickson, *A Thoroughly Canadian General,* 358.
234 On Operation Blockbuster, see TNA, CAB 106/99, Operation VERITABLE Clearing the Area Between the R. Maas and the R. Rhine 8 Feb-10 Mar 45, 115-38; Copp, *Cinderella Army,* 225-45; and Stacey, *Victory Campaign,* 491-526.
235 Copp, *Cinderella Army,* 236.
236 See pages 133-35 above.
237 Stacey, *Victory Campaign,* 423-24.
238 Brian Horrocks, *A Full Life* (London: Collins, 1960), 254.
239 NDHQ, DHH, Granatstein Interviews, Interview with General N. Elliot Rodger, 21 May 1991, Ottawa.
240 LAC, RG 24, vol. 10798, Rodger Diary, 22 February 1944.
241 Ibid., 28 September 1944.
242 LAC, RG 24, vol. 10799, "Essential Qualities in the Leader," 19 February 1944.

**Chapter 5: The Master Bureaucrat**
1 National Defence Headquarters (NDHQ), Directorate of History and Heritage (DHH), J.L. Granatstein's *The Generals* Interviews (Granatstein Interviews), Interviews with Brigadier G.E. Beament, 24 May 1991, Old Chelsea, QC; Brigadier-General Denis Whitaker,

19 March 1991, Toronto; Major-General W.J. Megill, 18 January 1992, Kingston, ON; General A. Bruce Matthews, 25 April 1991, Toronto; and Major-General N. Elliot Rodger, 21 May 1991, Ottawa.

2 Library and Archives Canada (LAC), Personnel Records Unit (PRU), Personnel File, Charles Foulkes (Foulkes Pers File). Foulkes's personnel file contains confidential reports for the years 1926-27 and 1929-39. It also includes his course report from the British Army Staff College at Camberley (1938).

3 NDHQ, DHH, Granatstein Interviews, Interview with General Robert Moncel, 6 October 1991, Mahone Bay, NS; George Kitching, *Mud and Green Fields: The Memoirs of Major-General George Kitching* (St. Catharines, ON: Vanwell, 1993), 189.

4 J.L. Granatstein, *The Generals: The Canadian Army's Senior Commanders in the Second World War* (Toronto: Stoddart, 1993), 176.

5 NDHQ, DHH, Granatstein Interviews, Interviews with J.W. Pickersgill, 21 May 1991, Ottawa; General Geoffrey Walsh, 24 May 1991, Ottawa; General N. Elliot Rodger, 21 May 1991, Ottawa; Brigadier-General Denis Whitaker, 19 March 1991, Toronto; and Colonel Robert Raymont, 23 May 1991, Ottawa.

6 Ibid., Interviews with General S.F. Clark, 24 February 1992, Victoria; Major-General J. Desmond B. Smith, 14 September 1991, London, UK; and J.W. Pickersgill, 21 May 1991, Ottawa.

7 NDHQ, DHH, Papers of General Charles Foulkes (Foulkes Papers), 72/1223, Series 6, Box 123, Final Operations 1st Canadian Corps in Italy: Operation "Chuckle"; and Operations in Northwest Holland.

8 Ibid., 72/1223, Series 6, Box 122, File 30015, "Black Watch 1944."

9 Ibid., Box 123, Surrender of German Armed Forces.

10 Ibid., Box 225, Documents Related to Replacement of Lt-Gen E.L.M. Burns GOC 1 Cdn Corps.

11 Ibid., Box 123, File 301, Memorandum by GOC 1 Cdn Corps on contents of letter dated 15 Dec 43 from Maj-Gen Simonds Comd 5 Cdn Armd Div, 21 December 1943.

12 LAC, PRU, Foulkes Pers File, Medical Examination of Candidates for Commission in the Permanent Force or for admission to the Royal Military College of Canada, 23 July 1926. The claim that Foulkes had one "retarded" brother came from an interview with Major-General M.P. Bogert: *NDHQ, DHH,* Granatstein Interviews, Interview with Major-General M.P. Bogert, 8 September 1991, Donnington, UK.

13 In "General Charles Foulkes: A Primer on How to Be CDS," Sean M. Maloney incorrectly states that Foulkes "was a University of Western Ontario graduate with an LLD." Foulkes never graduated from the University of Western Ontario, and the LLD was awarded *honoris causa* in June 1947. Sean M. Maloney, "General Charles Foulkes: A Primer on How to Be CDS," in *Warrior Chiefs: Perspectives on Senior Canadian Military Leadership,* edited by Lieutenant-Colonel Bernd Horn and Stephen Harris (Toronto: Dundurn, 2001), 221.

14 "Lt. Gen. Charles Foulkes, CBE, DSO," *Canadian Army Training Memorandum,* no. 49 (April 1945), 12-14.

15 LAC, PRU, Foulkes Pers File, Medical History of an Invalid (Former trade or occupation); and Active Militia of Canada, Recommendation for Appointment (Residence and Post Office address IN FULL).

16 See Stephen Harris, *Canadian Brass: The Making of a Professional Army, 1860-1939* (Toronto: University of Toronto Press, 1988), 196-99.

17 LAC, PRU, Foulkes Pers File, Confidential Reports for 1929, 1930, 1931, and 1933.

18 NDHQ, DHH, Granatstein Interviews, Interviews with Colonel Robert Raymont, 23 May 1991, Ottawa; and Major-General C.B. Ware, 24 February 1992, Victoria.

19   See app. 2 to John A. Macdonald, "In Search of Veritable: Training the Canadian Army Staff Officer, 1899-1945" (MA thesis, Royal Military College of Canada, 1992).

20   LAC, PRU, Foulkes Pers File, MFA 75, 500-3-27, H.Q. 1772-39-475 (Lieutenant C. Foulkes), 19 January 1928.

21   Ibid., Confidential Reports for 1926-29.

22   Ibid., Confidential Reports for 1930-36.

23   LAC, PRU, Personnel File of Guy Granville Simonds (Simonds Pers File) (see Confidential Reports); Personnel File of Eedson Louis Millard Burns (Burns Pers File) (see Confidential Reports).

24   See Major Jamie W. Hammond, "The Pen before the Sword: Thinking about Mechanization between the Wars," *Canadian Military Journal* (Summer 2000): 93-102; Captain E.L.M. Burns, "The Mechanization of Cavalry," *Canadian Defence Quarterly* 1, no. 3 (April 1924): 3-7; Lieutenant-Colonel E.L.M. Burns, "A Division that Can Attack," *Canadian Defence Quarterly* 15, no. 3 (April 1938): 282-98; Captain G.G. Simonds, "An Army that Can Attack – A Division that Can Defend," *Canadian Defence Quarterly* 15, no. 4 (July 1938): 413-17; Lieutenant-Colonel E.L.M. Burns, "Where Do the Tanks Belong?" *Canadian Defence Quarterly* 16, no. 1 (October 1938): 28-31; and Captain G.G. Simonds, "What Price Assault without Support?" *Canadian Defence Quarterly* 16, no. 2 (January 1939): 147.

25   NDHQ, DHH, Granatstein Interviews, Interviews with Brigadier G.E. Beament, 24 May 1991, Old Chelsea, QC; Brigadier-General R.T. Bennett, 22 May 1991, Ottawa; General Robert Moncel, 6 October 1991, Mahone Bay, NS; General A. Bruce Matthews, 25 April 1991, Toronto; Major-General W.J. Megill, 18 January 1992, Kingston, ON; J.W. Pickersgill, 21 May 1991, Ottawa; Brigadier Beverly Matthews, 16 October 1991, Toronto; and General N. Elliot Rodger, 21 May 1991, Ottawa.

26   NDHQ, DHH, Foulkes Papers, Report on Visit to Eighth Army: Major-General G.G. Simonds, 10 June 1943; 1-8/Ops Operational Policy – 2 Cdn Corps, 17 February 1944; 58-1/SD Efficiency in Command, 19 February 1944; GOC 8-3, Simonds to Foulkes [Outline Plan Operation TOTALIZE], 2 August 1944.

27   Ibid., 2DS(G)/4-4-4 GS 2 Cdn Div, Formation and Procedure in the Tank and Infantry Attack, 9 August 1943; GOC 1-1-3 Adv H.Q. 1 Cdn Corps, Aide Memoire for Orders Corps Level, 27 November 1942.

28   LAC, PRU, Foulkes Pers File, Staff College Final Report, Senior Wing (Captain C. Foulkes), 20 December 1938.

29   Ibid., Simonds Pers File, Staff College Camberley Final Report (Captain G.G. Simonds), 3 December 1937.

30   Ibid., Foulkes Pers File, Case History Sheet, Proceedings of a Court of Inquiry assembled at Niagara-on-the-Lake, Ont on the 30th Day of June 1939.

31   Ibid.

32   Crocker was the abstainer of the crowd. See NDHQ, DHH, Granatstein Interviews, Interview with Major-General George Kitching, 25 February 1992, Victoria.

33   LAC, MG 30 E 157, Papers of General H.D.G. Crerar (Crerar Papers), vol. 2, Exercise "CONQUEROR," 16 April 1942.

34   Macdonald, "In Search of Veritable," app. 3, 272-76.

35   Major-General E.L.M. Burns, *Manpower in the Canadian Army, 1939-1945* (Toronto: Clark, Irwin, 1956), 17. Burns's statistics are based on manpower strengths for the Canadian Army in Italy, Northwest Europe, the United Kingdom, and Canada in November 1944.

36   Macdonald, "In Search of Veritable," 272.

37   John A. English, *The Canadian Army and the Normandy Campaign: A Study of Failure in High Command* (New York: Praeger, 1991), 41-47.

38  On Crerar's efforts to redress the imbalance between infantry officers and senior staff and command appointments, see Paul Douglas Dickson, *A Thoroughly Canadian General: A Biography of General H.D.G. Crerar* (Toronto: University of Toronto Press, 2007), 254-55. Bert Hoffmeister was a prewar NPAM captain with the Seaforth Highlanders of Canada who rose to command the 5th Canadian Armoured Division (March 1944 to June 1945): Douglas E. Delaney, *The Soldiers' General: Bert Hoffmeister at War* (Vancouver: UBC Press, 2005).

39  Royal Montreal Regiment Library, "Chronological Summary of Military Service: Major-General C.B. Price, C.B., D.S.O., D.C.M., V.D., C.D., 15 February 1988.

40  LAC, RG 24, vol. 13721, War Diary (WD) 1st Canadian Division (G Staff), Training Instruction No. 1, 26 December 1939.

41  Ibid., vol. 14082, WD 3rd Canadian Infantry Brigade (January-March 1940). Foulkes attended 1st Canadian Infantry Division TEWTs with his brigadier on 29 January and 16 May 1940.

42  Ibid. See entries for 29 February, 25 March, 1 May, and 13 May 1940.

43  Ibid. The War Diary entry for 11 March shows that the "B.M. [Foulkes] and the Brigade Umpire ... proceeded to Burford, Oxfordshire, to prepare Brigade TEWT," not Price. A weekly progress report dated 19 March 1940 echoed a common complaint: "In most units at least three to four officers are away continuously on courses, which leaves the commanding officer with twelve to fourteen officers for training purposes."

44  One rare example was the "Inter-Brigade Exercise" supervised by the 1st Canadian Infantry Division on 17 July 1940. See ibid. (July 1940), Inter-Brigade Exercise, 17 Jul 40, 14 July 1940.

45  On Sansom's career, see Granatstein, *The Generals*, 44-52.

46  LAC, RG 2, vol. 13759, WD Headquarters 3rd Canadian Division (G Staff) (October 1940-April 1941).

47  Ibid. (October 1940), Memorandum on Training 3 Cdn Division at Debert and Sussex Camps, 1940-41, 23 October 1940.

48  Ibid., Headquarters 3 Cdn Division, Third Canadian Division Training Instruction No. 2, 7 May 1941.

49  LAC, PRU, Foulkes Pers File, Nominations for Selected Lists Commands and Staffs (Charles Foulkes), 16 April 1941.

50  LAC, Crerar Papers, vol. 2, Notes on BEAVER IV, 13 May 1942.

51  Ibid., Notes on Inf Bdes of Canadian Corps – No. 2, 24 February 1942.

52  Ibid., Notes on Comd 3 Div, 13 May 1942.

53  LAC, PRU, Foulkes Pers File, Statement of Service, Charles Foulkes; and LAC, RG 24, vol. 15195, WD Regina Rifles (December 1941-January 1942).

54  LAC, Crerar Papers, vol. 5, Recommendations for Promotion Officers, 1 Cdn Corps (GOC 6-1-1).

55  Ibid.

56  LAC, RG 24, vol. 15195, WD Regina Rifles (December 1941-January 1942).

57  LAC, Crerar Papers, vol. 2, Notes on BEAVER IV, 13 May 1942.

58  Ibid., Montgomery to Crerar, 30 May 1942. George Pangman, who was an umpire with Price's headquarters during Exercise Tiger, remembered that Price "didn't do well" and was singled out for his "ineptitude": NDHQ, DHH, Granatstein Interviews, Interview with Brigadier George Pangman, 23 April 1991, Cambridge, ON.

59  C.P. Stacey, *Six Years of War: The Canadian Army in Canada, Britain and the Pacific* (Ottawa: Queen's Printer, 1966), 245.

60  LAC, RG 24, vol. 14161, 1-21 March 1943. For a description of the training at Inveraray, see Delaney, *The Soldiers' General*, 46-48.

61  NDHQ, DHH, Granatstein Interviews, Interview with Brigadier G.E. Beament, 24 May 1991, Old Chelsea, QC.

62  NDHQ, DHH, Granatstein Interviews, Interview with General S.F. Clark, 24 February 1992, Victoria, BC.

63  LAC, RG 24, vol. 13750, WD 2nd Canadian Infantry Division (February 1944). See also Terry Copp, *Fields of Fire: The Canadians in Normandy* (Toronto: University of Toronto Press, 2003), 140-41.

64  Jefferson was not a problem. Simonds simply moved him from the 6th Canadian Infantry Brigade to the 10th Canadian Infantry Brigade in the 4th Canadian Armoured Division.

65  NDHQ, DHH, Foulkes Papers, 58-1/SD, Efficiency in Command, 19 February 1944. This is the only underlined passage in Simonds's letter.

66  LAC, RG 24, vol. 13750, WD 2nd Canadian Infantry Division (G Staff) (February 1944), HQ 2 Cdn Div Exercise "PLOT," 29 February 1944.

67  LAC, RG 24, vol. 13750, WD 2nd Canadian Infantry Division (G Staff), 7 March 1944.

68  Ibid. (February 1944), 2 Cdn Corps Study Period 11-18 Mar 44, 24 February 1944.

69  LAC, RG 24, vol. 13750, WD 2nd Canadian Infantry Division (G Staff), KATE: Tr[ainin]g in Crossing of a Tidal Estuary, Joint Report by GOC 2nd Cdn Inf Div and C[hief] E[ngineer] 2 Cdn Corps 2D5 (GM-1-0-2).

70  See the planning documents for Operation Axehead at LAC, RG 24, vol. 13607, WD First Canadian Army (G Plans), Operation AXEHEAD Appreciation and Outline Plan, 12 April 1944; and Operation AXEHEAD Appreciation and Outline Plan, 8 May 1944.

71  LAC, RG 24, vol. 13750, WD 2nd Canadian Infantry Division (G Staff), Cover letter signed by Charles Foulkes, 10 May 1944. KATE: Tr[ainin]g in Crossing of a Tidal Estuary, Joint Report by GOC 2nd Cdn Inf Div and C[hief] E[ngineer] 2 Cdn Corps 2D5 (GM-1-0-2).

72  Stacey, *Six Years of War,* 253.

73  Stacey used this quotation in two separate volumes of the official history. See Stacey, *Six Years of War,* 253; and C.P. Stacey, *The Victory Campaign: The Operations in Northwest Europe, 1944-1945* (Ottawa: Queen's Printer, 1966), 276.

74  Copp, *Fields of Fire,* 6; English, *The Canadian Army and the Normandy Campaign,* 250.

75  LAC, RG 24, vol. 13750, WD 2nd Canadian Infantry Division (G Staff), KATE: Tr[ainin]g in Crossing of a Tidal Estuary, Joint Report by GOC 2nd Cdn Inf Div and C[hief] E[ngineer] 2 Cdn Corps 2D5 (GM-1-0-2). See the table at Annex F, Outline Planning and Action Schedule for Assault Crossing of a Tidal Estuary.

76  This was the opinion of Brigadier G.E. Beament, who was Colonel GS at the First Canadian Army during that period: NDHQ, DHH, Granatstein Interviews, Interview with Brigadier G.E. Beament, 24 May 1991, Old Chelsea, QC.

77  Lieutenant-General Robert Moncel, who was a GSO 1 staff officer at 2nd Canadian Corps Headquarters during Operation Spring, thought Foulkes had a "poor staff" at the 2nd Canadian Infantry Division because he "attracted poor officers": NDHQ, DHH, Granatstein Interviews, Interview with General Robert Moncel, 6 October 1991, Mahone Bay, NS.

78  The best accounts are Stacey, *Victory Campaign,* 186-96; English, *The Canadian Army and the Normandy campaign,* 241-51; and Copp, *Fields of Fire,* 157-83.

79  See also pages 224-27 above.

80  The 6th Canadian Infantry Brigade remained in reserve with the three most under-strength battalions.

81  LAC, RG 24, vol. 13750, WD 2nd Canadian Infantry Division (July 1944), 2 Cdn Div OO No. 1, 24 July 1944.

82  LAC, RG 24, vol. 13750, WD 2nd Canadian Infantry Division (G Staff), Ops Log Main HQ 2 Cdn Inf Div, 25 July 1944, Serial 2163.

83   Ibid., Serial 2172.
84   Ibid., Serial 2186.
85   Ibid., Serial 2204.
86   LAC, RG 24, vol. 13711, WD 2nd Canadian Corps, Ops Log, 25 July 1944, Serials 22 and 24; and Copp, *Fields of Fire*, 172.
87   Copp, *Fields of Fire*, 175.
88   LAC, RG 24, vol. 13750, WD 2nd Canadian Infantry Division (G Staff), Ops Log Main HQ 2 Cdn Inf Div, 25 July 1944, Serial 2222.
89   NDHQ, DHH, Foulkes Papers, 73/1223, Series 6, Box 122, File 3095, Attack by R.H.C., 25 Jul 44, dated 8 February 1946.
90   LAC, RG 24, vol. 13750, WD 2nd Canadian Infantry Division (G Staff), Ops Log Main HQ 2 Cdn Inf Div, 25 July 1944, Serial 2306.
91   NDHQ, DHH, Granatstein Interviews, Interview with General Robert Moncel, 6 October 1991, Mahone Bay, NS.
92   The 2nd Canadian Infantry Division Operations Log records that "GSO 1 Corps (Moncel) has just gone fwd to 4 Bde" at 1145: LAC, RG 24, vol. 13750, WD 2nd Canadian Infantry Division (G Staff), Ops Log Main HQ 2 Cdn Inf Div, 25 July 1944, Serial 2268.
93   Kitching, *Mud and Green Fields*, 189.
94   LAC, Crerar Papers, vol. 3, Crerar to Simonds, 10 July 1944.
95   Ibid., Simonds, to Dempsey, 27 July 1944.
96   Drury replaced Archibald as GSO 1 2nd Canadian Infantry Division on 28 July 1944. He assumed the post of CRA 4th Canadian Armoured Division, as a brigadier, on 10 November 1944.
97   Harry Foster had to that point been commanding the 7th Canadian Infantry Brigade in the 3rd Canadian Infantry Division. Spry had to be brought in from Italy, where he had most recently been commanding the newly formed 12th Canadian Infantry Brigade.
98   Copp, *Fields of Fire*, 261.
99   On Totalize, see pages 228-33 above.
100  For good accounts of the Forêt de la Londe battle, see Stacey, *Victory Campaign*, 287-94; and Terry Copp, *Cinderella Army: The Canadians in Northwest Europe, 1944-1945* (Toronto: University of Toronto Press, 2006), 29-35.
101  Terry Copp rightly used the word "absurd" to describe Foulkes's order: *Cinderella Army*, 31.
102  See LAC, Crerar Papers, vol. 8, Crerar to Stuart, 12 February 1944; and vol. 7, Montgomery to Crerar, 21 December 1943.
103  NDHQ, DHH, Granatstein Interviews, Interview with General A. Bruce Matthews, 25 April 1991, Toronto.
104  Copp, *Fields of Fire*, 182.
105  NDHQ, DHH, Granatstein Interviews, Interview with General N. Elliot Rodger, 21 May 1991, Ottawa.
106  Ibid., Interview with General Bert Hoffmeister, 2 March 1992, Vancouver.
107  This was the recollection of Tony Foster, Major-General Harry Foster's son, who also said that Foulkes was "the only senior officer of whom Gen. Foster spoke ill": ibid., Interview with Tony Foster, 2 October 1991, Halifax.
108  Kitching, *Mud and Green Fields*, 214.
109  Ibid., 211-13.
110  NDHQ, DHH, Granatstein Interviews, Interview with Brigadier William Ziegler, 23 October 1991, Edmonton.
111  Ibid., Interviews with Colonel J. Allan ("Ding") Calder, 4 May 1992, Montreal; Major-General George Kitching, 25 February 1992, Victoria; and Brigadier William Ziegler, 23 October 1991, Edmonton.

112   On Kitching's difficulties as a divisional commander, see pages 236-38 above.

113   See, for example, the appreciation and orders produced under Kitching as GSO 1: LAC, RG 24, vol. 13725, Appreciation by Comd 1 Cdn Div at Norfolk House, 27 April 1943; and vol. 13726, 1 Canadian Division Operation Order No. 1, 7 June 1943.

114   LAC, RG 24, vol. 13688, WD 1st Canadian Corps Headquarters (G Branch) (November 1944).

115   General Sir William Jackson, *The Mediterranean and the Middle East,* vol. 6, pt. 3 (Uckfield, East Sussex, UK: The Naval and Military Press, 2004), 48-49.

116   LAC, RG 24, vol. 13688, WD 1st Canadian Corps Headquarters (G Branch) (November 1944), Exercise "CHUCKLE" Notes on Corps Comd's Conference, 18 November 1944.

117   NDHQ, DHH, Foulkes Papers, 72/1223, Series 6, Box 123, Final Operations 1 Cdn Corps Italy, "Operation Chuckle," Operation CHUCKLE RCA 1 Cdn Corps Planning Notes No. 1, 20 November 1944; and Appreciation of the Engr Situation Confronting 1 Cdn Corps by Chief Engineer, 24 November 1944.

118   Ibid., Final Operations 1 Cdn Corps Italy, "Operation Chuckle," OP "CHUCKLE" – OUT-LINE PLAN, 21 November 1944.

119   Ibid., Final Operations 1 Cdn Corps Italy, "Operation Chuckle," Exercise "CHUCKLE" – Revised Outline Plan, 27 November 1944; and LAC, RG 24, vol. 13688, 1st Canadian Corps Headquarters (G Branch) (November 1944), Notes on Corps Comd's Co-ord Conference held at "A" Mess HQ 1 Cdn Corps At 281130A hrs.

120   Jackson, *The Mediterranean and the Middle East,* 116-20.

121   Lieutenant-Colonel G.W.L. Nicholson, *The Canadians in Italy, 1943-1945* (Ottawa: Queen's Printer, 1966), 616.

122   Kitching, *Mud and Green Fields,* 214.

123   Nicholson, *The Canadians in Italy,* 618.

124   Projector, Infantry, Anti-tank (PIAT).

125   In a 1992 interview, Calder speculated that his sacking had to do with Foulkes's being embarrassed about a drunken incident at Calder's headquarters, but this was obviously not the case: NDHQ, DHH, Granatstein Interviews, Interview with Colonel J. Allan ("Ding") Calder, 4 May 1992, Montreal.

126   The regimental history of the Royal Canadian Regiment is very frank about individual failings during this battle. See G.R. Stevens, *The Royal Canadian Regiment. Vol. 2: 1933-1966* (London, ON: London Printing and Lithographing, 1967), 171-78.

127   Nicholson, *The Canadians in Italy,* 618.

128   Kitching, *Mud and Green Fields,* 215.

129   See Delaney, *The Soldiers' General,* 140-48.

130   LAC, RG 24, vol. 13689, WD 1st Canadian Corps Headquarters (G Branch), HQ 1 Cdn Corps GS Branch Log, 6 December 1944, 1315 hours, Serial 158.

131   Ibid., HQ 1 Cdn Corps GS Branch Log, 7 December 1944, 1030 hours, Serial 514.

132   Ibid., 7 December 1944.

133   Ibid.

134   Ibid., 1 Cdn Corps Last Light Sitreps, 6-10 December 1944.

135   Nicholson, *The Canadians in Italy,* 626.

136   Foulkes had first arranged the diversionary attack on 7 December: LAC, RG 24, vol. 13689, WD 1st Canadian Corps Headquarters (G Branch), HQ 1 Cdn Corps GS Branch Log, 7 December 1944, 1550 hours, Serial 533.

137   Ibid., 7 December 1944, Serials 846, 915, 949, 954, and 956.

138   LAC, RG 24, vol. 13798, WD 5th Canadian Armoured Division (G Staff), 13 December 1944.

139   LAC, RG 24, vol. 13689, WD 1st Canadian Corps Headquarters (G Branch), Intentions 1 Cdn Corps night 13/14 Dec and day 14 Dec, 140040A Dec 44.

140 Nicholson, *The Canadians in Italy,* 631.

141 LAC, RG 24, vol. 13689, WD 1st Canadian Corps Headquarters (G Branch), HQ 1 Cdn Corps GS Branch Log, 18 December 1944, Serial 648.

142 When General Sir Henry Maitland Wilson left the Mediterranean to head the British Joint Staff Mission in Washington, Alexander took over as Supreme Commander Mediterranean, Clark became C-in-C Allied Armies in Italy, and Truscott assumed command of the US Fifth Army.

143 NDHQ, DHH, Granatstein Interviews, Interview with Major-General W.J. Megill, 18 January 1992, Kingston, ON.

144 Kitching, *Mud and Green Fields,* 215.

145 LAC, Crerar Papers, vol. 16, War Diary February 1945.

146 Kitching, *Mud and Green Fields,* 223.

147 LAC, RG 24, vol. 13690, WD 1st Canadian Corps Headquarters (G Branch), Outline Appreciation by G.O.C. 1st Cdn Corps, 26 February 1945.

148 Kitching, *Mud and Green Fields,* 225 (emphasis added).

149 NDHQ, DHH, Granatstein Interviews, Interview with General N. Elliot Rodger, 21 May 1991, Ottawa.

150 LAC, Crerar Papers, vol. 16, GOC-in-C 1-0-4/1 Main First Cdn Army, 10 March 1945.

151 Ibid., 24 March 1945 and 2 April 1945.

152 NDHQ, DHH, Foulkes Papers, 72/1223, Series 6, Box 123, "The Last Canadian Battle and the Surrender of Germany," n.d., 3.

153 LAC, Crerar Papers, vol. 16, GOC-in-C 1-0-4/1 Main First Cdn Army, 10 March 1945 and 24 March 1945.

154 LAC, RG 24, vol. 13690, WD 1st Canadian Corps Headquarters (G Branch), Directive to Divisional Commanders, 27 March 1945, G.O.C. 1st Corps file GOC 1-0.

155 NDHQ, DHH, Foulkes Papers, "The Last Canadian Battle," n.d., 5.

156 Ibid.

157 On the origins of the operation to relieve Dutch civilians, see Stacey, *Victory Campaign,* 568-70.

158 LAC, Crerar Papers, vol. 16, GOC-in-C 1-0-4/1 Main First Cdn Army, 7 April 1945.

159 LAC, RG 24, vol. 13690, WD 1st Canadian Corps Headquarters (G Branch), Op on completion of 'ANGER' and 'CANNONSHOT,' Main HQ 1 Cdn Corps, 12 April 1945.

160 LAC, Crerar Papers, vol. 16, Notes on Commander-in-Chief's Conference with Commander First Canadian Army at Grave on 12 April 1945.

161 LAC, RG 24, vol. 13690, WD 1st Canadian Corps Headquarters (G Branch), GOC 1-0 Main 1 Cdn Corps, 15 April 1945.

162 See, for example, the minutes of the 9 April Chief of Staff's Conference attended by CCRA, GSO 1 1st Canadian Corps, GSO 1 49th (West Riding) Division, GSO 1 5th Canadian Armoured Division, Staff Officer Royal Signals (Wireless), Staff Officer Royal Signals (Lines), GSO 3 (Intelligence), GSO 2 (Ops), Staff Officer Royal Engineers, the Deputy Adjutant and Quartermaster General, and others. LAC, RG 24, vol. 13690, WD 1st Canadian Corps Headquarters (G Branch) (April 1944), app. 28, Minutes of Chief of Staff's Conference Held 9 Apr 45 – Main HQ 1 Cdn Corps.

163 Stacey, *Victory Campaign,* 571.

164 LAC, RG 24, vol. 13798, WD 5th Canadian Armoured Division (G Staff), 13 April 1945.

165 NDHQ, DHH, Foulkes Papers, "The Last Canadian Battle," n.d., 6.

166 LAC, RG 24, vol. 13690, WD 1st Canadian Corps Headquarters (G Branch), GOC 1-0 Main 1 Cdn Corps, 15 April 1945.

167 LAC, RG 24, vol. 13798, WD 5th Canadian Armoured Division (G Staff) (April 1945), app. 21, OP CLEANSER, Notes of GOC "O" Gp held 141200 hours, 14 April 1945.

168   LAC, RG 24, vol. 10941, File 245C5.013 (D3), 5th Cdn Armd Div History of Ops in NWE, Part II, 2. See also ibid., Ops Log 5th Cdn Armd Div, 16 April 1945, Serial 729.
169   NDHQ, DHH, Foulkes Papers, "The Last Canadian Battle," n.d., 7.
170   "Comments on Operation 'Cannonshot' by Major General H.W. Foster," given to Historical Off 1st Cdn Inf. Div., 5 June 1945. Quoted in Stacey, *Victory Campaign,* 575.
171   Stacey, *Victory Campaign,* 576.
172   This was certainly the opinion of Brigadier M.P. Bogert, who commanded the 2nd Canadian Infantry Brigade and who thought Foster a "very good GOC": NDHQ, DHH, Granatstein Interviews, Interview with Major-General M.P. Bogert, 8 September 1991, Donnington, UK.
173   Ibid., Interview with General A. Bruce Matthews, 25 April 1991, Toronto.
174   See pp. 80-106 above.
175   In a little over three years of campaigning in the Western Desert, Archibald Wavell, Claude Auchinleck, Alan Cunningham, and Neil Ritchie all lost army commands; Noel de la P. Beresford-Pierse, Alfred R. Godwin-Austen, Charles Willoughby M. Norrie, William H. Ramsden, and Herbert Lumsden were all fired from corps command; and Michael O'Moore Creagh, Frank Messervy, Alexander Gatehouse, and James M.L. Renton all lost command of their divisions.
176   NDHQ, DHH, Foulkes Papers, CGS 342, Crerar from Murchie, 3 July 1945.
177   Ibid., COS 641, Murchie from Crerar, 051753B July 45.
178   Cited in Dickson, *A Thoroughly Canadian General,* 433. See also NDHQ, DHH, Granatstein Interviews, Interviews with General Geoffrey Walsh, 24 May 1991, Ottawa; General N. Elliot Rodger, 21 May 1991, Ottawa; and Major-General J. Desmond Smith, 14 September 1991, London, UK.
179   NDHQ, DHH, Granatstein Interviews, Interview with Colonel Robert Raymont, 23 May 1991, Ottawa.
180   Ibid., Interview with J.W. Pickersgill, 21 May 1991, Ottawa.
181   NDHQ, DHH, Foulkes Papers, CGS 505, Murchie from Foulkes, 2 November 1945.
182   Ibid., COS 1044, Foulkes from Murchie, 051325 Mar 46.
183   Ibid., Memorandum to the Minister: Future Employment – Lt-Gen G.G. Simonds, CB, CBE, DSO, 21 August 1946.
184   Ibid.
185   Ibid., Letter, Simonds to Foulkes, 24 January 1950.
186   Ibid., Letter, Foulkes to Simonds, 27 January 1950.
187   "Master of the Battlefield" was the subtitle of Jack Granatstein's chapter on Simonds. See Granatstein, *The Generals,* 145-78.

**Observations and Conclusions**

1   See app. 3 to John A. Macdonald, "In Search of Veritable: Training the Canadian Army Staff Officer, 1899-1945" (MA thesis, Royal Military College of Canada, 1992), 258-64.
2   Ibid., 275-76.
3   The National Archives (TNA), CAB 106/991, Operation VERITABLE: Clearing the Area Between the R. Maas and the R. Rhine, 8 February-10 March 1945, 51; and C.P. Stacey, *The Victory Campaign: The Operations in Northwest Europe, 1944-1945* (Ottawa: Queen's Printer, 1966), 467.
4   Stacey, ibid., 218.
5   Lieutenant-Colonel G.W.L. Nicholson, *The Canadians in Italy, 1943-1945* (Ottawa: Queen's Printer, 1966), 418; and Colonel G.W.L. Nicholson, *The Gunners of Canada: The History of the Royal Regiment of Canadian Artillery. Vol. 2: 1919-1967* (Toronto: McClelland and Stewart, 1972), 249.

6  David French, *Raising Churchill's Army: The British Army and the War against Germany, 1919-1945* (London: Oxford University Press, 2000), 281. On casualty conservation in particular, see Stephen Ashley Hart, *Montgomery and "Colossal Cracks": The 21st Army Group in Northwest Europe, 1944-1945* (Westport, CT: Praeger, 2000), 49-77.

7  Shelford Bidwell and Dominick Graham, *Firepower: The British Army Weapons and Theories of War* (Barnsley, South Yorkshire, UK: Pen and Sword, 2004), 282-97.

8  See, for example, Stacey, *Victory Campaign,* 284-85; and Major L.F. Ellis, *Victory in the West. Vol. 1: The Battle of Normandy* (London: Her Majesty's Stationery Office, 1962), 492.

9  The two divisions were the 59th (Staffordshire) and the 50th (Northumbrian). See Ellis, *Victory in the West,* vol. 1, 453; and Major L.F. Ellis, *Victory in the West. Vol. 2: The Defeat of Germany* (London: Her Majesty's Stationery Office, 1968), 158-59.

10  The Canadian government, particularly the Prime Minister, desperately wanted to avoid conscription as a means of replacing Canadian casualties. Conscription in 1917 had led to outrage among French Canadians and riots in the province of Quebec, and the results of an April 1942 plebiscite on compulsory military service had shown that Canada was still completely divided on the issue, with 83 percent of English Canadians in favour and 72.9 percent of Quebecers opposed. J.L. Granatstein and J.M. Hitsman, *Broken Promises: A History of Conscription in Canada* (Toronto: Oxford University Press, 1977), 171, 185-244.

11  Imperial War Museum (IWM), Sound Archive, Accession No. 2977/04, Sir Brian Horrocks interviewed by Peter Batty, n.d.; and Sir Brian Horrocks with Eversley Belfield and Major-General H. Essame, *Corps Commander* (New York: Charles Scribner's Sons, 1977), 184.

12  J.L. Granatstein, *The Generals: The Canadian Army's Senior Commanders in the Second World War* (Toronto: Stoddart, 1993), 265-66.

13  See, for example, John Keegan, ed., *Churchill's Generals* (London: Weidenfeld and Nicolson, 1991). See also Nick Smart, *Biographical Dictionary of British Generals of the Second World War* (Barnsley, South Yorkshire, UK: Pen and Sword, 2005).

14  John Alan Roberts, *The Canadian Summer: The Memoirs of John Alan Roberts* (Toronto: University of Toronto Press, 1981), 108.

15  See Stephen J. Harris, *Canadian Brass: The Making of a Professional Army, 1860-1939* (Toronto: University of Toronto Press, 1988), 141-209.

16  John A. English, *The Canadian Army and the Normandy Campaign: A Study of Failure in High Command* (New York: Praeger, 1991), 41-47.

17  Ibid., xiii.

# Bibliography

**Primary Sources**

ARCHIVES – CANADA

National Defence Headquarters (NDHQ), Directorate of History and Heritage (DHH)
    J.L. Granatstein's *The Generals* Interviews
    Papers of General Charles Foulkes
    Kardex Files
Library and Archives Canada (LAC)
    Personnel Records Unit (PRU)
        Personnel Files
    Department of National Defence Records (RG 24 Series)
        War Diaries (1939-45)
        Army Historical Section Files
    Papers of Lieutenant-General E.L.M. Burns (MG 31 G 6)
    Papers of General H.D.G. Crerar (MG 30 E 157)
    Papers of Lieutenant-General A.G.L. McNaughton (MG 30 E 133)
    Papers of Madge Macbeth (MG 30 D52)
    Papers of Major-General Victor Odlum (MG 30 E 300)
    Papers of M.H.S. Penhale (MG 31 G 21)
    Papers of Colonel J.L. Ralston (MG 27, III, B 11)
Royal Military College of Canada
    William J. McAndrew Collection
    Registrar's Files
    Student Files

ARCHIVES – UNITED KINGDOM

Army Personnel Records Section (APRS), Glasgow
    Personnel Files
British Library
    India Office Records (IOR)
The National Archives (TNA), Kew
    War Office (WO) Files
        Directorate of Military Intelligence and Operations (WO 106)
        Home Forces (WO 166)
        British Expeditionary Force (WO 167)
        Middle East Forces (WO 169)
        Central Mediterranean Forces (WO 170)
        North-West Europe (WO 171)
        British North Africa Forces (WO 175)

Papers of Field Marshal Earl Alexander of Tunis (WO 214)
Papers of General Sir Miles Dempsey (WO 285)
Cabinet Files
Official Histories (CAB 106, CAB 120)
Churchill College, Cambridge
Ronald Lewin Papers
Imperial War Museum (IWM), London
Department of Documents
Papers of Major-General Ronald Frederick King Belcham
Papers of Major-General R. Briggs
Papers of Lieutenant-General Gerard Corfield Bucknall
Papers of Field Marshal Baron Ironside of Archangel
Papers of General Sir Oliver Leese
Papers of Field Marshal the Viscount Montgomery of Alamein
Papers of Lieutenant-Colonel Trumbull Warren
Department of Sound Records (Sound Archives)
Joint Services Command and Staff College, Shrivenham
Staff Course Files
War Staff Course Files
Liddell Hart Centre for Military Archives (LHCMA), King's College, London
Papers of Field Marshal Lord Alanbrooke
Papers of Lieutenant-General Charles W. Allfrey
Papers of General Sir Miles C. Dempsey
Papers of Sir Basil Liddell Hart
Papers of General Sir Richard O'Connor
Papers of Chester Wilmot

ARCHIVES – UNITED STATES

The National Archives and Records Administration (NARA), Washington, DC
*Wehrmacht War Diaries, 1939-45*

PRIVATE COLLECTIONS

Papers of Lieutenant-General Guy Simonds (Battersea, ON)
Papers of General Sir John T. Crocker (Wincanton, Somerset, UK)

PUBLISHED OFFICIAL DOCUMENTS

*The Armoured Division in Battle.* Holland: 21st Army Group, December 1944.
*Conduct of War.* London: War Office, 15 February 1950.
*Field Service Pocket Book. Part I: Pamphlet No. 4 Appreciations, Orders, Messages, and Intercommunication.* London: War Office, 1943.
*Field Service Regulations. Vol. II: Operations – General.* Ottawa: King's Printer, 1939.
*Operations. Military Training Pamphlet No. 23. Part I: General Principles, Fighting Troops and Their Characteristics – 1942.* Ottawa: King's Printer, 1942.
*Operations. Military Training Pamphlet No. 23. Part II: Appreciations, Orders, Intercommunications and Movements – 1939.* Ottawa: King's Printer, 1941.
*Operations. Military Training Pamphlet No. 23. Part VIII: River Crossings – 1940.* Ottawa: King's Printer, 1941.

*Report on the Examination for Admission to Staff Colleges at Camberley and Quetta Held in February-March 1925.* London: His Majesty's Stationery Office, 1925.

MEMOIRS, COLLECTED LETTERS, PUBLISHED DIARIES

Burns, Lieutenant-General E.L.M. *General Mud: Memoirs of Two World Wars.* Toronto: Clark Unwin, 1970.

Carver, Michael. *Out of Step: Memoirs of a Field Marshal.* London: Hutchinson, 1989.

Danchev, Alex, and Daniel Todman, eds. *War Diaries 1939-1945: Field Marshal Lord Alanbrooke.* London: Weidenfeld and Nicolson, 2001.

De Guingand, Major-General Sir Francis. *Operation Victory.* London: Hodder and Stoughton, 1947.

Eisenhower, Dwight D. *Crusade in Europe.* London: William Heinemann, 1948.

Gavin, James. *On to Berlin: Battles of an Airborne Commander, 1943-1946.* New York: Viking, 1978.

Graham, Lieutenant-General Howard. *Citizen and Soldier.* Toronto: McClelland and Stewart, 1987.

Horrocks, Sir Brian. *A Full Life.* London: Collins, 1960.

Horrocks, Sir Brian, with Eversley Belfield and Major-General H. Essame. *Corps Commander.* New York: Charles Scribner's Sons, 1977.

Kingston-McCloughry, Air Vice Marshal E.J. *The Direction of War.* New York: Frederick A. Praeger, 1958.

Kitching, George. *Mud and Green Fields: The Memoirs of Major-General George Kitching.* St. Catharines, ON: Vanwell, 1993.

Meyer, Hubert. *The 12th SS: The History of the Hitler Youth Panzer Division,* vol. 1. Mechanicsburg, PA: Stackpole Books, 1994.

–. *The 12th SS: The History of the Hitler Youth Panzer Division,* vol. 2. Mechanicsburg, PA: Stackpole Books, 2005.

Meyer, Kurt. *Grenadiers: The Story of Waffen SS General "Panzer" Meyer.* Mechanicsburg, PA: Stackpole Books, 2005.

Montgomery of Alamein, Field Marshal the Viscount. *Memoirs.* London: Collins, 1958.

–. *Normandy to the Baltic.* London: Hutchinson, 1947.

–. *The Path to Leadership.* London: Fontana Books, 1963.

Pope, Lieutenant-General Maurice A. *Soldiers and Politicians.* Toronto: University of Toronto Press, 1962.

Pyman, General Sir Harold. *Call to Arms.* London: Leo Cooper, 1971.

Roberts, Major-General G.P.B. *From the Desert to the Baltic.* London: William Kimber, 1987.

Roberts, James Alan. *The Canadian Summer: The Memoirs of James Alan Roberts.* Toronto: University of Toronto Press, 1981.

Urquhart, Robert E. *Arnhem.* London: Cassel, 1958.

Vokes, Major-General Chris, with John P. Maclean. *My Story.* Ottawa: Gallery Books, 1985.

Zuckerman, Solly. *From Apes to Warlords.* London: Harper and Row, 1978.

**Secondary Works**

Atkinson, Rick. *An Army at Dawn: The War in North Africa, 1942-1943.* New York: Henry Holt, 2002.

Badsey, Stephen. *Battle for Caen.* Gloucestershire, UK: Sutton, 2004.

Barnett, Corelli. *The Desert Generals.* London: Cassel, 2001.

Barr, Niall. *Pendulum of War: The Three Battles of Alamein.* London: Jonathan Cape, 2004.

Bennet, Ralph. *Ultra and the Mediterranean Strategy.* New York: William Morrow, 1989.

Bidwell, Brigadier S., and D. Graham. *Firepower: British Amy Weapons and Theories of War, 1904-1945.* London: Allen and Unwin, 1982.

–. *Tug of War: The Battle for Italy 1943-1945.* London: Hodder and Stoughton, 1986.

Blaxland, Gregory. *The Middlesex Regiment.* London: Leo Cooper, 1977.

Blumenson, Martin, and James L. Stokesbury. *Masters of the Art of Command.* Boston: Houghton Mifflin, 1975.

Boog, Horst, et al. *Germany and the Second World War: The Strategic Air War in Europe and the War in the West and East Asia, 1943-1944/5.* Translation editor, Derry Cook Radmore. Oxford: Oxford University Press, 2005.

Burns, Eedson Louis Millard. *Between Arab and Israeli.* Toronto: Clarke, Irwin, 1962.

–. *Defence in the Nuclear Age: An Introduction for Canadians.* Toronto: Clarke, Irwin, 1972.

–. *Manpower in the Canadian Army.* Toronto: Clark, Irwin, 1956.

–. *A Seat at the Table: The Struggle for Disarmament.* Toronto: Clarke, Irwin, 1972.

Burns, Lieutenant-General E.L.M. *Megamurder.* New York: Pantheon Books, 1966.

Callahan, Raymond. *Churchill and His Generals.* Lawrence: University Press of Kansas, 2007.

Carver, Field Marshal Lord. *The Apostles of Mobility: The Theory and Practice of Armoured Warfare.* London: Weidenfeld and Nicolson, 1979.

Clark, Lloyd. *Arnhem: Operation Market Garden, September 1944.* Stroud, UK: Sutton, 2002.

Copp, Terry. *Cinderella Army: The Canadians in Northwest Europe, 1944-1945.* Toronto: University of Toronto Press, 2006.

–. *Fields of Fire: The Canadians in Normandy.* Toronto: University of Toronto Press, 2003.

–. *Guy Simonds and the Art of Command.* Kingston, ON: Canadian Defence Academy Press, 2007.

–, ed. *Montgomery's Scientists: Operational Research in Northwest Europe.* Waterloo, ON: Laurier Centre for Military Strategic and Disarmament Studies, 2000.

Copp, Terry, and William J. McAndrew. *Battle Exhaustion: Soldiers and Psychiatrists in the Canadian Army, 1939-1945.* Montreal and Kingston: McGill-Queen's University Press, 1990.

Delaney, Douglas E. "A Quiet Man of Influence: General Sir John Crocker." *Journal of the Society for Army Historical Research* 85, no. 343 (2007): 185-207.

–. *The Soldiers' General: Bert Hoffmeister at War.* Vancouver: UBC Press, 2005.

–. "When Harry Met Monty: Canadian National Politics and the Crerar-Montgomery Relationship." In *The Canadian Way of War: Serving the National Interest,* edited by Bernd Horn, 213-34. Toronto: Dundurn, 2006.

Denny, Norman R. "Seduction in Combat: Losing Sight of Logistics after D-Day." MA thesis, US Army Command and General Staff College, 2003.

D'Este, Carlo. *Bitter Victory: The Battle for Sicily, 1943.* London: Collins, 1988.

–. *Decision in Normandy: The Unwritten Story of Montgomery and the Normandy Campaign.* London: Collins, 1983.

–. *Patton: A Genius for War.* New York: HarperCollins, 1995.

Dickson, Paul. "The Limits of Professionalism: General H.D.G. Crerar and the Canadian Army, 1914-1944." PhD dissertation, University of Guelph, 1993.

–. "The Politics of Army Expansion: General H.D.G. Crerar and the Creation of First Canadian Army, 1941." *Journal of Military History* 60, no. 2 (April 1996): 271-98.

–. *A Thoroughly Canadian General: General H.D.G. Crerar.* Toronto: University of Toronto Press, 2007.

Dodd, Lindsey, and Andrew Knapp. "'How Many Frenchmen Did You Kill?' British Bombing Policy Towards France, 1940-1945." *French History* 22, no. 4 (December 2008): 469-92.

Edmonds, Brigadier-General J.E. *History of the Great War: Military Operations, France and Belgium, 1914,* vol. 2. London: Macmillan, 1925.

Ellis, L.F. *Victory in the West. Vol. 1: The Battle of Normandy.* London: Her Majesty's Stationery Office, 1962.

–. *Victory in the West. Vol. 2: The Defeat of Germany.* London: Her Majesty's Stationery Office, 1968.

–. *The War in France and Flanders, 1939-1940.* London: Her Majesty's Stationery Office, 1953.

English, John A. *On Infantry.* New York: Praeger, 1984.

–. *The Canadian Army and the Normandy Campaign: A Study of Failure in High Command.* New York: Praeger, 1991.

Essame, Major-General H. *The 43rd Wessex Division at War.* London: William Clowes and Sons, 1952.

Fraser, Donald. *Alanbrooke.* New York: Atheneum, 1982.

–. *And We Shall Shock Them: The British Army and the Second World War.* London: Hodder and Stoughton, 1983.

French, David. *The British Way in Warfare, 1688-2000.* London: Unwin Hyman, 1990.

–. "Colonel Blimp and the British Army: British Divisional Commanders in the War against Germany." *English Historical Review* 3 (1996): 1182-1201.

–. "Discipline and the Death Penalty in the British Army in the Second World War." *Journal of Contemporary History* 33 (1998): 531-45.

–. "Invading Europe: The British Army and Its Preparations for the Normandy Campaign, 1942-1944." *Diplomacy and Statecraft* 14, no. 2 (2003): 271-94.

–. *Raising Churchill's Army: The British Army and the War against Germany, 1919-1945.* Oxford: Oxford University Press, 2000.

French, David, and Brian Holden Reid, eds. *The British General Staff: Reform and Innovation, 1890-1939.* London: Frank Cass, 2002.

Freyberg, Paul. *Bernard Freyberg, VC: Soldier of Two Nations.* London: Hodder and Stoughton, 1991.

Graham, Dominick. *The Price of Command: A Biography of General Guy Simonds.* Toronto: Stoddart, 1993.

Granatstein, J.L. *Canada's Army: Waging War and Keeping the Peace.* Toronto: University of Toronto Press, 2002.

–. *The Generals: The Canadian Army's Senior Commanders in the Second World War.* Toronto: Stoddart, 1993.

Granatstein, J.L., and J.M. Hitsman. *Broken Promises: A History of Conscription in Canada.* Toronto: Oxford University Press, 1977.

Grodzinski, John. *Operational Handbook for the First Canadian Army, 1944-1945.* Nepean, ON: The Regimental Historian, 1996.

Hamilton, Nigel. *Monty: Master of the Battlefield, 1942-1944.* London: Hamish Hamilton, 1983.

–. *Monty: The Field Marshal, 1944-1976.* London: Hamish Hamilton, 1986.

–. *Monty: The Making of a General, 1887-1942.* New York: McGraw-Hill, 1981.

Harris, J.P. *Men, Ideas and Tanks: British Military Thought and Armoured Forces, 1903-1939.* Manchester: Manchester University Press, 1995.

Harris, Stephen J. *Canadian Brass: The Making of a Professional Army, 1860-1939.* Toronto: University of Toronto Press, 1988.

Hart, Stephen Ashley. "The Forgotten Liberator: The 1939-1945 Military Career of General Sir Andrew Thorne." *Journal of the Society for Army Historical Research* 79 (2001): 233-49.

–. *Montgomery and "Colossal Cracks": The 21st Army Group in Northwest Europe, 1944-45.* Westport, CT: Praeger, 2000.

Hayes, Geoffrey W. "The Development of the Canadian Army Officer Corps, 1939-1945." PhD dissertation, University of Western Ontario, 1992.

Horn, Bernd, and Stephen Harris, eds. *Generalship and the Art of the Admiral: Perspectives on Canadian Senior Military Leadership.* St. Catharines, ON: Vanwell, 2001.

–. *Warrior Chiefs: Perspectives on Senior Canadian Military Leaders.* Toronto: Dundurn, 2001.

Howard, Michael, ed. *The Theory and Practice of War.* London: Cassel, 1965.

Hutchinson, W.E.J. "Test of a Corps Commander: Lieutenant General Guy Granville Simonds, Normandy – 1944." MA thesis, University of Victoria, 1982.

Jackson, General Sir William. *The Mediterranean and the Middle East,* vol. 6, pt. 3. Uckfield, East Sussex: The Naval and Military Press, 2004.

Jackson, W.F. *Alexander of Tunis as Military Commander.* London: Batsford, 1971.

Jarymowycz, Roman. *Tank Tactics from Normandy to Lorraine.* Boulder, CO: Lynne Rienner, 2001.

Keegan, John, ed. *Churchill's Generals.* London: Weidenfeld and Nicolson, 1991.

Kemp, Lieutenant-Commander P.K. *The Middlesex Regiment (Duke of Cambridge's Own), 1919-1952.* Aldershot, UK: Gale and Polden, 1956.

Knapp, Andrew. "The Destruction and Liberation of Le Havre in Modern Memory." *War in History* 14, no. 4 (2007): 476-98.

Lamb, Richard. *Montgomery in Europe, 1943-1945: Success or Failure?* London: Buchan and Enright, 1983.

Lewin, Ronald. *The Chief: Field Marshal Lord Wavell: Commander-in-Chief and Viceroy, 1939-1945.* London: Hutchinson, 1980.

–. *Montgomery as Military Commander.* London: Batsford, 1971.

Liedtke, Gregory. "Canadian Offensive Operations in Normandy Revisited." *Canadian Military Journal,* 8, no. 2 (Summer 2007): 60-68.

Macbeth, Madge, and A.B. Conway. *The Great Fright: Onesiphore, Our Neighbour.* Montreal: Louis Carrier, 1929.

Macdonald, John A. "In Search of Veritable: Training the Canadian Army Staff Officer, 1899-1945." MA thesis, Royal Military College of Canada, 1992.

Macksey, Kenneth. *Armoured Crusader: A Biography of Major-General Sir Percy Hobart.* London: Hutchinson, 1967.

–. *The Tank Pioneers.* London: Jane's, 1981.

Mansergh, Nicholas. *A Survey of British and Commonwealth Affairs: Problems of Wartime Co-operation and Post-War Change, 1939-1952.* London: Oxford University Press, 1958.

McAndrew, William J. "Eighth Army at the GOTHIC Line: The Dog-Fight." *Journal of the Royal United Services Institute* 131 (June 1986): 55-62.

–. "Fire or Movement? Canadian Tactical Doctrine, Sicily – 1943." *Military Affairs* 51 (July 1987): 140-45.

McInnes, Colin. *Hot War, Cold War: The British Army's Way in Warfare.* London: Brassey's, 1996.

Middlebrook, Martin. *Arnhem 1944: The Airborne Battle.* London: Viking, 1994.

Milner, Marc. "Reflections on the State of Canadian Army History in the Two World Wars." *Acadiensis* 2 (Spring 1989): 135-50.

Molony, Brigadier C.J.C. *The Mediterranean and the Middle East,* vols. 5-6. London: Her Majesty's Stationery Office, 1973, 1984, 1987.

Nicholson, G.W.L. *Canadian Expeditionary Force, 1914-1919.* Ottawa: Queen's Printer, 1964.

–. *The Canadians in Italy, 1943-1945.* Ottawa: Queen's Printer, 1966.

–. *The Gunners of Canada: The History of the Royal Regiment of Canadian Artillery. Vol. 2: 1919-1967.* Toronto: McClelland and Stewart, 1972.

Place, Timothy Harrison. *Military Training in the British Army, 1940-1944: From Dunkirk to D-Day.* London: Frank Cass, 2000.

Playfair, Major-General I.S.O. *The Mediterranean and the Middle East,* vols. 3-4. London: Her Majesty's Stationery Office, 1960, 1966.

Preston, Richard A. "The Military Structures of the Old Commonwealth." *International Journal* 17, no. 2 (Spring 1962): 98-121.

Reid, Brian A. *No Holding Back: Operation Totalize, Normandy, August 1944.* Toronto: Robin Brass, 2005.

Rickard, J.N. "McNaughton's Dagger: The Raising, Training and Employment of the Canadian Army, 1939-1943." PhD dissertation, University of New Brunswick, 2006.

Roy, Reginald H. *1944: The Canadians in Normandy.* Ottawa: Canadian War Museum, 1984.

Ruppenthal, Roland. *Logistical Support of the Armies,* vol. 2. Washington, DC: US Government Printing Office, 1959.

Ryan, Cornelius. *A Bridge Too Far.* New York: Simon and Schuster, 1974.

Salmond, J.B. *The History of the 51st Highland Division, 1939-1945.* London: William Blackwood and Sons, 1953.

Schreiber, Shane B. *Shock Army of the British Empire: The Canadian Corps in the Last 100 Days of the Great War.* Westport, CT: Praeger, 1997.

Smart, Nick. *Biographical Dictionary of British Generals of the Second World War.* Barnsley, South Yorkshire, UK: Pen and Sword, 2005.

Stacey, C.P. *Arms, Men and Governments: The War Policies of Canada, 1939-1945.* Ottawa: Queen's Printer, 1970.

–. "Canadian Leaders of the Second World War." *Canadian Historical Review* 66 (March 1985): 43-50.

–. *Six Years of War.* Ottawa: Queen's Printer, 1956.

–. *The Victory Campaign.* Ottawa: Queen's Printer, 1960.

Stevens, G.R. *A City Goes to War: A History of the Loyal Edmonton Regiment.* Brampton, ON: Charters, 1964.

–. *Princess Patricia's Canadian Light Infantry, 1919-1957,* vol. 3. Montreal: Southam, 1960.

–. *The Royal Canadian Regiment. Vol. 2: 1933-1966.* London, ON: London Printing and Lithographing, 1967.

Stimpel, Hans-Martin. *Die Deutsche Fallschirmtruppe, 1942-1945: Einsatz auf dem Kriegsschauplatzen im Suden.* Hamburg: Verlag E.S. Mittler und Sohn, 1998.

–. *Die Deutsche Fallschirmtruppe, 1942-1945: Einsatz auf Kriegsschauplatzen im Osten und Westen.* Hamburg: Verlag E.S. Mittler und Sohn, 2001.

Swettenham, John. *McNaughton,* 3 vols. Toronto: Ryerson Press, 1969.

Tedder, Lord. *With Prejudice.* London: Cassell, 1966.

Thompson, Reginald William. *Montgomery, the Field Marshal: A Critical Study of the Generalship of Field Marshal the Viscount Montgomery of Alamein, K.G., and the Campaign in North-West Europe, 1944/45.* London: Allen and Unwin, 1969.

Van Crevald, M. *Command in War.* Cambridge, MA: Harvard University Press, 1985.

Walker, Ronald. *Alam Halfa and Alamein.* Wellington: New Zealand Historical Publications Branch, 1967.

Warner, Philip. *Horrocks: The General Who Led from the Front.* London: Hamish Hamilton, 1984.

Whitaker, Denis, and Shelagh Whitaker. *Tug of War: The Canadian Victory that Opened Antwerp.* Toronto: Stoddart, 1984.

Winton, Harold R. *Corps Commanders of the Bulge: Six American Generals and Victory in the Ardennes.* Lawrence: University Press of Kansas, 2007.

Young, Lieutenant-Colonel F.W., ed. *The Story of the Staff College, 1858-1958.* Aldershot, UK: Gale and Polden, 1958.

Zetterling, Niklas. *Normandy 1944: German Military Organization, Combat Power and Organizational Effectiveness.* Winnipeg: J.J. Fedorowicz, 2000.

Zuehlke, Mark. *The Liri Valley: Canada's World War II Breakthrough to Rome.* Toronto: Stoddart, 2001.

# Index

*Notes:* "(f)" after a page reference denotes a figure; "(m)," a map; "(p)," a photograph. Most army units are listed in first section with numeric designations; however, some armies' names are written out, such as First Canadian Army; Eighth Army (British); US Fifth Army. "BGS" stands for Brigadier, General Staff; "GSO" for General Staff Officer; "RCHA" for Royal Canadian Horse Artillery; "RMC" for Royal Military College, Sandhurst

Bennet, P.W., 293

Black Watch (Royal Highland Regiment) of Canada: decimation in Operation Spring, 225(m), 226, 227, 269, 270-71; in Operation Atlantic/Goodwood, 220-21(m), 224; in Operation Total-ize, 230(m)

Blackader, Ken, 144-45, 146, 219. *See also* 8th Canadian Infantry Brigade

Blaskowitz, Johannes, 51-52, 54

Bogert, Pat, 187(p), 284

Booth, B.L., 212, 236

*A Bridge Too Far,* 10

British Army: human skills compared with Canadian commanders', 304-5; manpower shortages in 1944, 299. *See also* Commonwealth armies; First Army (British); Second Army (British)

British Army Staff College, Camberley: Canadian officers at, 4, 196, 260-61; Foulkes's training at, 258, 259; Horrocks's preparations for entrance exams, 15-16; Horrocks's success at, 16; learning of military "language," 3, 200, 296; shortening of courses during Second World War, 5, 199; Simonds's training at, 195; training of staff officers, 299-300. *See also* military training

British Columbia Dragoons, 96-97, 98, 100, 383. *See also* 9th Canadian Armoured Regiment

Brooke, Alan: commander of Mobile Division (*later* 1st Armoured Division), 127-28; concerns re Burns as head of 1st Canadian Corps, 105; in favour of all-arms cooperation, 127-28; high opinion of Crocker, 138, 329n72; Horrocks's admiration for his preservation of order and morale, 18-19; impressed by Simonds's abilities, 203; knowledge of Burns's indiscretions and demotion, 73; opinion of McNaughton's competence, 205; role of Leese in Burns's investigation, 107

Bryant, Arthur, 18

Bucknall, "Jerry," 38, 141, 159, 168-69

Bullen-Smith, Charles, 147-48

Burns, E.L.M.

awards: Companion to the Order of Canada, 121; Distinguished Service Order after Gothic Line battle, 117; Military Cross, 61; Officer to the Order of the British Empire, 63; Pearson Medal of Peace, 121; winner of Bertram Stewart Prize Essay Competition, 64; winner of essay competition of *Canadian Defence Quarterly,* 64

as commander: article on morale in *American Mercury,* 67-68; Burns's discussions with lower-level commanders without divisional commanders present, 118, 302; confidence in own ability, 108; difficulty holding people to account, 59, 78, 79, 80, 102; difficulty imposing will on subordinates, 59, 303; fault-finding and nitpicking, 79-80, 84; firepower used to neutralize enemy, 297-98; HQ organization and use, 302; inability to communicate well orally, 69; inability to inspire, 60, 78, 79, 113, 120; inability to show he cared for his troops, 80; indirect and insufficiently ruthless, 60, 80, 84, 322n132; opinion of morale, 68; others' confidence in Burns, 71, 73, 105, 106, 118, 120; planning methods, 301; subordinates able to question or ignore his orders, 59

early life, 60, 297

education: 17th Hussars (militia unit), 60; Imperial Defence College, 63; Indian Army Staff College at Quetta, 4, 63; Lower Canada College, 60; Royal Military College of Canada, 60; School of Military Engineering (Chatham, UK), 62

in First World War, 60-62; in 3rd Canadian Infantry Division, 61-62; in 4th Canadian Infantry Division as signals officer, 60; in 9th Canadian Infantry Brigade, 61-62; in 11th Canadian Infantry Brigade as signals officer, 61; commission with Royal

STUDIES IN CANADIAN MILITARY HISTORY

Canadian War Museum / Musée canadien de la guerre

John Griffith Armstrong, *The Halifax Explosion and the Royal Canadian Navy: Inquiry and Intrigue*

Andrew Richter, *Avoiding Armageddon: Canadian Military Strategy and Nuclear Weapons, 1950-63*

William Johnston, *A War of Patrols: Canadian Army Operations in Korea*

Julian Gwyn, *Frigates and Foremasts: The North American Squadron in Nova Scotia Waters, 1745-1815*

Jeffrey A. Keshen, *Saints, Sinners, and Soldiers: Canada's Second World War*

Desmond Morton, *Fight or Pay: Soldiers' Families in the Great War*

Douglas E. Delaney, *The Soldiers' General: Bert Hoffmeister at War*

Michael Whitby, ed., *Commanding Canadians: The Second World War Diaries of A.F.C. Layard*

Martin Auger, *Prisoners of the Home Front: German POWs and "Enemy Aliens" in Southern Quebec, 1940-46*

Tim Cook, *Clio's Warriors: Canadian Historians and the Writing of the World Wars*

Serge Marc Durflinger, *Fighting from Home: The Second World War in Verdun, Quebec*

Richard O. Mayne, *Betrayed: Scandal, Politics, and Canadian Naval Leadership*

P. Whitney Lackenbauer, *Battle Grounds: The Canadian Military and Aboriginal Lands*

Cynthia Toman, *An Officer and a Lady: Canadian Military Nursing and the Second World War*

Michael Petrou, *Renegades: Canadians in the Spanish Civil War*

Amy J. Shaw, *Crisis of Conscience: Conscientious Objection in Canada during the First World War*

Serge Marc Durflinger, *Veterans with a Vision: Canada's War Blinded in Peace and War*

James G. Fergusson, *Canada and Ballistic Missile Defence, 1954-2009: Déjà Vu All Over Again*

Benjamin Isitt, *From Victoria to Vladivostok: Canada's Siberian Expedition, 1917-19*

James Wood, *Militia Myths: Ideas of the Canadian Citizen Soldier, 1896-1921*

Timothy Balzer, *The Information Front: The Canadian Army and News Management during the Second World War*

Andrew B. Godefroy, *Defence and Discovery: Canada's Military Space Program, 1945-74*